JOHN KEATS: SELECTED LETTERS

JOHN KEATS was born in October 1795, the son of the manager of a livery stables in Moorfields, London. His father died in 1804 and his mother, of tuberculosis, in 1810. By then he had received a good education at John Clarke's Academy in Enfield. In 1811 he was apprenticed to a surgeon, completing his professional training at Guy's Hospital in 1816, but continued his duties as a dresser there until spring 1817. His earliest surviving letters date from the summer of 1816, as he was deciding to abandon his medical career for poetry – a courageous decision, based as much on a challenge to himself as on any actual achievement.

Keats's genius was quickly perceived and encouraged by his brothers and teacher Charles Cowden Clarke. In October 1816 he met Leigh Hunt, whose *Examiner* had already published Keats's first poem. Only five months later *Poems* (1817) appeared. Despite the high hopes of the Hunt circle, it was a failure. By the time *Endymion* was published in 1818 Keats's name had been identified with Hunt's 'Cockney School', and the Tory *Blackwood's Magazine* delivered a violent attack on Keats as a lower-class vulgarian with no right to aspire to 'Poetry'.

Keats's letters are now seen as a literary achievement in their own right. They make clear the extraordinary speed with which he matured, intellectually, emotionally and artistically. Late in 1818 he began work on the powerful epic fragment *Hyperion* and met Fanny Brawne. In 1819 he wrote 'The Eve of St Agnes', 'La Belle Dame sans Merci', the major odes, 'Lamia' and the visionary *The Fall of Hyperion*. Keats was already unwell in 1820 when preparing his final volume for the press; by the time *Lamia, Isabella, The Eve of St Agnes, and Other Poems* appeared in July he was desperately ill with tuberculosis. He travelled to Italy in September, where he wrote his last letters to his friend Charles Brown and sent his fiancée Fanny Brawne his last 'Good bye'. He died in Rome in 1821. At his request his gravestone reads 'Here lies One Whose Name was writ in Water.'

His poetic reputation began to be established in the mid-nineteenth century, but was not fully recognized until the twentieth century.

JOHN BARNARD is Emeritus Professor of English Literature at the University of Leeds. His edition of *John Keats: The Complete Poems*, first published by Penguin in 1973, is now in its third edition. His book *John Keats* appeared in 1987. He has written extensively on seventeenth-century literature and its publishing history, the second-generation Romantics, and co-edited *The Cambridge History of the Book in Britain, Volume IV 1557–1695* (2002). From 1975 to 2010 he was General Editor of Longman Annotated English Poets.

JOHN KEATS

Selected Letters

Edited by

JOHN BARNARD

PENGUIN BOOKS

For Hermione

PENGUIN CLASSICS

Published by the Penguin Group
Penguin Books Ltd, 80 Strand, London WC2R 0RL, England
Penguin Group (USA) Inc., 375 Hudson Street, New York, New York 10014, USA
Penguin Group (Canada), 90 Eglinton Avenue East, Suite 700, Toronto, Ontario, Canada M4P 2Y3
(a division of Pearson Penguin Canada Inc.)
Penguin Ireland, 25 St Stephen's Green, Dublin 2, Ireland (a division of Penguin Books Ltd)
Penguin Group (Australia), 707 Collins Street, Melbourne, Victoria 3008, Australia
(a division of Pearson Australia Group Pty Ltd)
Penguin Books India Pvt Ltd, 11 Community Centre, Panchsheel Park, New Delhi – 110 017, India
Penguin Group (NZ), 67 Apollo Drive, Rosedale, Auckland 0632, New Zealand
(a division of Pearson New Zealand Ltd)
Penguin Books (South Africa) (Pty) Ltd, Block D, Rosebank Office Park,
181 Jan Smuts Avenue, Parktown North, Gauteng 2193, South Africa

Penguin Books Ltd, Registered Offices: 80 Strand, London WC2R 0RL, England

www.penguin.com

This edition first published in Great Britain by Penguin Classics 2014
009

Set in 10.25/12.25 pt PostScript Adobe Sabon
Typeset by Jouve (UK), Milton Keynes
Printed in Great Britain by Clays Ltd, Elcograf S.p.A.

ISBN: 978-0-141-19279-6

www.greenpenguin.co.uk

Penguin Books is committed to a sustainable
future for our business, our readers and our planet.
This book is made from Forest Stewardship
Council™ certified paper.

Contents

SELECTED LETTERS

August 1816 to March 1817
Commitment to Poetry

April to November 1817
Drafting *Endymion*

December 1818 to 27 June 1819
Wentworth Place

28 June to 8 October 1819
Shanklin and Winchester

List of Illustrations

Introduction

In a period of great letter-writing, Keats's letters are outstanding. They begin in late summer 1816, as he approached his twenty-first birthday, and were written over the next four years. His letters give the fullest and most poignant record we have of Keats's ambitions and hopes as a poet, his life as a literary man about town, his close relationship with his brothers and young sister, and, later, his passionate, jealous and frustrated love for Fanny Brawne.

His tragically early death from the family disease, tuberculosis, in Rome on 23 February 1821, aged twenty-five, was followed only six months later by the publication of P. B. Shelley's elegy *Adonais*. This depicts Keats's cruelly compressed career as a prototype of the young Romantic genius, unrecognized and cut off in his prime by the vituperatively partisan attacks of *Blackwood's Magazine*'s Tory reviewers. It is a sentimental misconception, but one which still has popular force.

The letters, the closest we have to an autobiographical account of Keats's development as a poet and a man, tell a very different story, that of an intensely sociable person, going to the theatre or to William Hazlitt's lectures, visiting galleries, the British Museum and exhibitions, playing cards late into the night or enjoying parties, 'claret feasts' and musical evenings, staying with his friends Benjamin Bailey in Oxford and James Rice in the Isle of Wight, travelling with Charles Brown through the Highlands, dining with friends and acquaintances like the Dilkes and his publishers, or attending B. R. Haydon's 'immortal dinner'. Keats himself confessed he 'could not live without the love of my friends'. He was almost always in company. For the larger part of the time covered by these letters Keats shared lodgings, first with his brothers in the City of London before they moved to 1 Well Walk in Hampstead, and later with Charles Brown at Wentworth Place, or he stayed with other friends.

More than most letters, Keats's seem to echo his conversation – volatile and impetuous, eagerly buttonholing his audience, moving like quicksilver from recording his everyday life to profound reflections on the nature of poetry or the imagination and back again to quotidian reality. They are a literary achievement in their own right, equal to the poems. Letters freed Keats from his anxieties about the expectations of the reading public, which, following the hostile reception of *Poems* (1817), dogged the writing of his poems. Addressed to his close friends or family, these letters allowed him to relax, entertain, experiment, memorialize, speculate, pun and make jokes. In his letters he could indulge his talent for light verse in the nonsense poems and extemporary verses he wrote for his sister and male friends. He could escape from the solitary pressures of composition, secure in his knowledge of his audience's interest and support. Where his published poetry – or (his word) 'Poesy' – rarely admits the colloquial or everyday, his letters are full of the language of day-to-day life in Regency England. They deploy an extraordinary range of linguistic and tonal registers, ranging from slang, wordplay and bawdy puns to his speculative explorations of the 'holiness of the Heart's affections' or life as a 'vale of Soul-making'. They are full of different voices and texts – reports of conversations by or stories about people he knew, quotations from other writers, or sometimes long passages copied out from Shakespeare, Burton or Hazlitt. These are mixed in with copies of his own poems or drafts of work in progress, along with references to other letters he has written or failed to write, or ones he has received. The variety of voices and texts jostling for place alongside one another is a key source of the letters' animated vitality. They are written fluently and with minimal revision, which makes their eloquence and intelligence all the more remarkable.

Very few of the letters written to Keats survive. The intertextual nature of Keats's own letters makes this is a very material loss. For example, the full force of Keats's speculations on 'the poetical Character' is best understood in the light of Richard Woodhouse's letter which prompted them.[1] In other cases, like Keats's letter to J. H. Reynolds about his 'Robin Hood' poem, it is possible to reconstruct the essentials of the exchange. Those letters that do exist show his friends' generous and sympathetic understanding of the nature of his pre-eminence.[2]

Most of Keats's extant letters were preserved by his family, by Fanny Brawne, and by the group of friends (all men) he met in autumn 1816 or 1817, when he gave up medicine for poetry. The latter group includes several who became his most important correspondents. His brother George seems to have introduced Keats to William Haslam, through whom he met the young artist Joseph Severn when he was first at Guy's Hospital in 1815. But it was Cowden Clarke's introduction of Keats to Leigh Hunt at his Hampstead home which established the most important of Keats's other male friendships and future correspondents. Hunt's artistic and literary circle included William Hazlitt, Charles Lamb, the painter B. R. Haydon, all like Hunt a generation older. Keats quickly realized the danger of being seen as 'Hunt's elevé' (*sic*). There is only a single letter, self-consciously literary, to Hunt, written in May 1817, and a brief apologetic note from the summer of 1820. And although Keats remained part of Hunt's literary circle, the only member with whom he had a sustained correspondence was Haydon. But Hunt also introduced Keats to J. H. Reynolds, only a year older than Keats and already a published poet and journalist. Reynolds, in turn, introduced Keats to his own group of friends – Benjamin Bailey, James Rice, Charles Dilke, and his own publishers, John Taylor and James Hessey, whose lawyer and literary adviser was Richard Woodhouse. Keats probably met another friend of Reynolds, Charles Brown, while visiting Dilke. Apart from the correspondence with his brothers, it was to these men that Keats was to write his most significant and revealing letters.

The people Keats met through Hunt and Reynolds were mostly older men in their thirties, with established careers in the arts or publishing, or were professional men with strong literary interests. It is striking that all of them, whether older or his contemporaries, immediately recognized Keats's unusual intelligence and passionate commitment to poetry. And it was the confident and consistent belief of his friends and brothers in his genius which gave Keats the freedom in these letters to pursue his 'speculations' on the nature of poetry and human nature or about politics and history.

Keats clearly had a gift for friendship. Fanny Brawne thought him 'the last person to exert himself to gain people's friendship', yet, as she told his sister immediately after he had left for Italy, 'I cannot tell you . . . how much he is liked', adding 'I am certain he has some spell that attaches them to him.'[3] The nature of that 'spell' is clear from his letters, which always seek to reach out across space and time to their recipients. 'I wish I knew always the humour my friends would be in at opening a letter of mine, to suit it to them nearly as possible.'

Keats always writes with a particular reader in mind. To Haydon he writes with excited vulnerability about their shared artistic ambitions and desire for fame; to his teenaged sister as a protective elder brother; to his brothers and later to George and his wife in America, as a young man about town, but also confiding in them his hopes and fears and his developing thoughts on the nature of poetry; to J. H. Reynolds he writes to amuse him when convalescing or as a fellow poet. Keats wanted his readers to imagine when he was writing and from where, linking them into his circle by giving them news of other friends, family members or correspondents, as well as of his own doings. Keats's multi-voiced letters are one side of an ongoing conversation between writer and readers.

The improvisatory nature of the letters enables Keats to move quickly from reporting the everyday to his most challenging reflections on the nature of poetry, and then, 'content with half knowledge', to turn back to his latest news or 'town talk'. Yet the letters' playfulness – one idea striking off another – is part of a performance, one meant to amuse as well as engage his readers. The vividness with which he describes himself sitting in Wentworth Place late in the evening of 12 March 1819 writing to George and Georgiana in America is in part a strategy to overcome, imaginatively, the chronological and geographical distance which separates them:

> [. . .] the candles are burnt down and I am using the wax taper—which has a long snuff on it—the fire is at its last click—I am sitting with my back to it with one foot rather askew upon the rug and the other with the heel a little elevated from the carpet—I am writing this on the Maid's tragedy which I have read since tea with Great pleasure—Besides this volume of Beaumont & Fletcher—there are on the tabl[e] two volumes of chaucer and a new work of Tom Moores call'd 'Tom Cribb's memorial to Congress—nothing in it—These are trifles—but I require nothing so much of you as that you will give me a like description of yourselves, however it may be when you are writing to me—[. . .] God bless you—I whisper good night in your ears and you will dream of me—

This tender and moving message is at the same time a portrait of the poet as a young man. On this occasion Keats paints a relaxed domestic picture of the writer's life, but elsewhere he reports on his London literary life, copies samples of work in progress, gives his opinions of other writers, past and present, or discusses his hopes or otherwise of financial success. Keats's depiction of his life as an author offered reassurance to George and Georgiana. Given his own and their parlous financial situations and his anxieties about their new life in America, it was essential that his journal letters should convince them of his continuing progress as a writer, and of his hopes of success. But more generally, Keats's self-representation of himself as a writer in his letters, whether to family, friends or publishers, was a matter of both self-exploration and self-validation. Or, as Keats said of Adam's dream, 'he awoke and found it truth'. The letters present Keats as how he wished to be seen and as what he hoped to become.

There is, in consequence, a risk of seeing only the most generous and optimistic side of Keats, remarkable for his 'mature masculinity', as in Lionel Trilling's influential essay 'The Poet as Hero: Keats in his Letters'.[4] That is the self-image Keats projected to his brother and sister-in-law, as they struggled to make their way in America. In fact, Keats was subject to extreme swings of emotion. As he admitted to Haydon, he suffered from 'a horrid Morbidity of Temperament', recurrent periods of self-doubt alternating with bouts of intense excitement. One such bout is his six hour 'rhodomontade' (*sic*) on Sunday, 12 September 1819, which held Woodhouse riveted between breakfast and catching his coach for Bath at three o'clock that afternoon.[5] Similarly, in his attitude to sexuality, Keats could be notably sane ('who shall say between Man and Woman which is the most delighted?'), but he could also be disconcertingly unbalanced. His annotation of Robert Burton's account of sexual desire in the *Anatomy of Melancholy* (1621) reads: 'Here is the old plague spot: the pestilence, the raw scrofula [. . .] nothing disgraces me in my own eyes as much as being one of a race of eyes, nose and mouth beings [. . .] who all from Plato to Wesley have always mingled goatish, winnyish, lustful love with the abstract adoration of the deity.' And that polarized attitude is evident in the poetry, and makes its way into his most painful and private letters to Fanny Brawne.

There are significant differences between the letters which Keats wrote knowing that they would be circulated among family or friends, and those meant only for their recipient. His letters exist on a continuum running from the semi-public to the intensely personal. Family letters were shared or read aloud. The letters Keats sent to his brother Tom in Hampstead recording his northern walk were circulated among their friends, a way of ensuring that they kept in touch with his invalid brother – 'Let any of my friends see my letters,' he told Tom. He was 'Content that probably three or four pair of eyes whose owners I am rather partial to will run over these lines'. Or, knowing that Reynolds and Woodhouse were to meet in Bath, Keats wrote to each separately, hoping that his 'brace of letters' would add to their 'pleasant time together', and expecting them to 'interread' one another's letters. As he told Woodhouse, 'I am still writing to Reynolds as well as yourself—As I say to George I am writing to you but at your Wife.' In return he demanded that 'you two must write me a letter apiece'. Letters of this kind are a mode of sociability *in absentia*. But unlike the promiscuity of print, where the author has no control over circulation, the letter-writer is in control of their immediate readership. Thus, the mutually admiring and self-exciting letters between himself and Haydon, known only because the painter preserved them in his diary, were certainly not intended for others. Similarly, the letters Keats wrote to Reynolds, setting a distance between their poetry and that of Leigh Hunt, were not meant for a wider readership. Nor was Keats's advice to his sister on how best to handle the unkindness of the Abbey family and their dislike of Keats meant to reach the eyes of their guardian. The most intensely private of all Keats's letters are those to Fanny Brawne, which remained completely unknown until their highly controversial publication in 1878. The emotions of some of those written after his haemorrhage in February 1820, like the two desperately unhappy letters he wrote to Charles Brown from Italy on 30 September and 1 November, are so nakedly unmediated that reading them feels perilously close to prurient intrusiveness.

Recent readings of Keats have stressed the extent to which his poetry responds directly and indirectly to contemporary politics. His letters follow closely the political issues of his day, largely seen through the prism of Leigh Hunt's *Examiner*. Keats's views are consistently progressive, and when in autumn 1819 he briefly considered turning to journalism for a living, he told Dilke that he hoped 'to put a Mite of help to the Liberal side of the Question before I die'. Yet when Keats discusses the nature of truth in poetry or in art his focus is on timeless aesthetic value: 'What the imagination seizes as Beauty must be truth—whether it existed before or not.' Or, again, 'I never can feel certain of any truth but from a clear perception of its Beauty.' From 'Sleep and Poetry' onwards Keats hoped to write poetry which would merit 'posterity's award', something 'richer far' than immediate popularity. His scorn for the contemporary reading public sprang from his pursuit of the 'end and aim of Poesy', the 'vast idea' which 'ever rolls . . . before me'. Keats never escapes from the dilemma posed implicitly in 'Ode to a

Nightingale' and explicitly in *The Fall of Hyperion*. Was he a mere 'dreamer' in a world 'full of Misery and Heartbreak' or a true poet, 'a sage, / A humanist, physician to all men', who 'pours out a balm upon the world'? Keats's assertion to his brother George, 'I think I shall be among the English Poets after my death,' voices his hopes of joining the pantheon of Elizabethan poets enjoying the 'double immortality' described in the ode 'Bards of Passion and of Mirth' (p. 292–3) – where they are imagined to have attained permanent fame in 'Elysium' while still partaking in an earthly life through the continued reading of their poetry.

Such high aspirations carry the risk of failure, as Keats knew. Hence he was never convinced that any of his poems were more than promissory. As he wrote to Fanny Brawne in February 1820, 'If I had had time I would have made myself remember'd.' The letters reveal that Keats's extraordinary self-belief went side by side with self-doubt. On the one hand, he could write to his publisher 'I would sooner fail than not be among the greatest' or assert 'The only thing that can ever affect me personally for more than one short passing day, is any doubt about my powers for poetry.' But these moments were offset by an often disabling awareness of the overweening nature of his ambitions – 'the Cliff of Poesy Towers above me' – and the fear that his 'mad ambition' outran his abilities. Hence his conviction that 'There is no greater Sin after the 7 deadly than to flatter oneself into an idea of being a great Poet.' In consequence, he said, 'my greatest elevations of soul leave me every time more humbled'. On occasion he even went so far as to question the claims of poetry: 'I am sometimes so very sceptical as to think Poetry itself a mere Jack a lanthern to amuse whoever may chance to be struck with its brilliance.'

Keats's combination of ambition, humility and scepticism informs the exploratory and provisional nature of his 'speculations' on 'Negative Capability' or his reaction to seeing Benjamin West's painting *Death on a Pale Horse* ('the excellence of every Art is its intensity, capable of making all disagreeables evaporate, from their being in close relationship with Beauty & Truth'). Keats's identification of his own work with that of the 'camelion [*sic*] Poet', who, in opposition to Wordsworth's 'egotistical sublime', lives 'in gusto, be it foul or fair, high or low, rich or poor, mean or elevated' and takes 'as much delight in conceiving an Iago as an Imogen', identifies an essential difference between them. It is characteristic of the letters that these profound insights – to be much analysed by later critics – are dropped into the middle of details of his everyday life, and are never returned to again or developed systematically. Although, taken together, his ideas about poetry do describe a poetics and contain lasting insights into the nature of tragedy, they remain provisional, brilliant aperçus inviting further development. As Keats, half-jokingly, told Bailey, 'Now my dear fellow I must once for all tell you I have not one Idea of the truth of any of my speculations—I shall never be a Reasoner because I care not to be in the right.'

As this account suggests, different readers, or the same reader at different times, come to Keats's letters with differing expectations – for his ideas on poetry and the imagination, for their distinctive vitality, for what they tell us of his life and poetry, for his letters to Fanny Brawne, for their picture of Regency England, or as a literary achievement in themselves. Yet for Keats the letters constantly return to the question of whether or not his poetic ambitions, his hopes for fame, are justified. The letters are a self-representation of the young man as aspirant poet striving to earn a place with his predecessors, sometimes supremely confident, but often doubting himself.

Keats's letters reached out towards his absent readers, both family and friends, imagining them as present, sharing his own concerns and interests. For later readers the letters invite us to participate retrospectively in that interchange and to reanimate Keats's presence and voice. It is an interchange which assumes, flatteringly, that we, as much as the letters' original readers, fully share Keats's emotional intelligence and agility of mind.

NOTES

1 See pp. 260–61 below for extracts from Woodhouse's letter of 21 October 1818.

2 Hyder E. Rollins's 1958 edition (see The Letters and Their Texts) includes most of the known letters sent to Keats. Rollins's *The Keats Circle* (1965) adds letters about Keats by his family, friends and publishers.

3 *Letters of Fanny Brawne to Fanny Keats 1820–1824*, ed. Fred Edgcumbe (London: Oxford University Press, 1936), pp. 2–3.

4 See *The Opposing Self: Nine Essays in Criticism* (New York: Viking Press, 1955), pp. 3–49, reprinted from his Introduction to *The Selected Letters of John Keats* (New York: Farrar, Straus and Young, 1951).

5 See Woodhouse's letter to John Taylor (19, 20 September 1819) in Hyder E. Rollins's *The Letters of John Keats 1814–1821* (1958), II, pp. 162–5.

The Letters and Their Texts

The translation of Keats's manuscript letters into print destroys significant features of their physical presence. Because the form his letters take is in an important part determined by these material facts, a brief account of the writing and sending of letters in Keats's day may be helpful.

In London letters could be sent by messenger. This was the most expensive and quickest method. Keats's first draft of 'On First Looking into Chapman's Homer', composed in his Southwark lodgings after leaving Cowden Clarke 'at day-spring', was immediately sent off by messenger and reached Clarke's breakfast table in Clerkenwell by ten o'clock as 'a letter with no other enclosure than his famous sonnet'.[1] Alternatively, there was the postal service, which cost one penny in central London and two pence in outer London for same-day delivery. From outside the capital postage was determined by the distance from London. Writing from Shanklin on the Isle of Wight to Fanny Brawne in Hampstead, London, on 8 July 1819, Keats had to pay nine pence, though, usually, it was the recipient who paid the postage. Letters were charged by the sheet and, before the introduction of envelopes, a single sheet letter was folded so that one of the top and bottom flaps formed the outer cover for the address, leaving two inner blanks (the 'doublings'). Since paper, like postage, was expensive it was polite in private letters to use all the available space, including the 'doublings'. Hence Keats's apology to Reynolds 'for not filling up the whole sheet' and the reason why the last two or three sentences in the letters are often no more than fillers. To save expense, double use could be made of the sheet by 'crossing' the letter, as when Keats added a sample from 'Lamia' to his letter to Taylor of 5 September 1819 (Illustration 6). For his 'Scotch letters' Keats used a much larger sheet than usual – each page was about 37 × 21 cm – which meant he could cram in twice as many words, write extemporary poems in columns and, on one occasion, add a small sketch of Loch Lomond in the letter to Tom begun on 17 July 1818.

Sending letters to America was altogether more problematic. The service was expensive, slow and erratic. Keats's first letter to George and Georgiana was taken by Haslam to the London stockbrokers Capper and Hazlewood in Throgmorton Street, where it was put in the Boston postbag to await the next ship bound for Philadelphia in six weeks' time. The long letter he sent on 12 November 1819, destined for Kentucky, had in three months only got as far as Edgartown, Massachusetts. As letters were sent as small (presumably waterproof) packets Keats's journal letters take up as many sheets as necessary, and he could enclose, in addition to his own news and work in progress, copies of the *Examiner* and letters from other family and friends.

Some of Keats's letters have contributions by others, for example Bailey's additions to the 'doublings' of his letter of 21 September 1817. These are normally omitted here, but there is one very unusual joint letter which has always been printed as two letters. It is, significantly, an embarrassed business letter to Keats's publisher John Taylor. On 23 August 1819 Keats and Brown sent Taylor a single sheet letter in which Keats first asks for a loan, Brown then offers surety and Keats adds a postscript. The letter is evidently a single document and is printed as such here.

This selection is based where possible on a fresh examination, mainly in digital form, of Keats's autograph letters. The large majority of these are in the Harvard Keats Collection, digital facsimiles of which were made freely available online, beginning in 2010.[2] Otherwise the texts are based on the letters held by institutions in England, New York and Los Angeles, on digital images kindly provided by their owners in the United States, or on the small number of facsimiles or transcripts of letters otherwise unavailable.

Most of Keats's letters are known through his autograph manuscripts (their source is noted at the head of each letter, for instance '[Harvard MS]'). But a sizeable number, including some of his most important letters, are now known only through transcripts. To alert the reader to the transcripts' differing textual status, they are noted as such, together with the date of copying. The transcriptions follow Keats's manuscripts with varying degrees of accuracy. Thus John Jeffrey's transcripts ('[Jeffrey transcript (1845)]'), made from manuscripts in the possession of his wife, George Keats's widow, for use in Richard Monckton Milnes's edition of 1848, are cavalier. Apart from altering accidentals and changing Keats's 'and' into ampersands, he misread Keats's handwriting and freely omitted sentences or even pages with no indication that he had done so. On the other hand, the transcripts made by Richard Woodhouse (1819–21?) are extremely dependable, while those of H. B. Forman (1883) are, apart from minor normalization, similarly accurate.

The standard and most fully documented edition of Keats's complete letters is Hyder E. Rollins's two-volume *The Letters of John Keats 1814–1821* (Cambridge, MA: Harvard University Press, 1958). Since its publication only two new letters have come to light, of which the most important is that to George and Tom Keats of 30 January 1818, now in private hands. The second (not included here) is Keats's note on money matters to William Haslam, dated 2 November 1819.[3] The original of the letter to J. H. Reynolds of 17 April 1818, known previously through Woodhouse's transcript (misdated 10 April), was donated to Harvard University in 1970; and in 1995 Harvard was also given the final leaf of Keats's journal letter to George and Georgiana Keats (14 February–5 May 1819), until then known only through Jeffrey's inadequate transcript (see pp. 301 n., 364 n., 366–7 below). Keats's letter to his brothers of 15 April 1817, for which Rollins followed H. B. Forman's transcript, is now at Princeton University. Finally, Keats's letter to Fanny Brawne of 1(?) March 1820, which was in private hands, came onto the market in 2011 and is now in the collection of Keats House (London Metropolitan Archives).

Rollins's edition records addresses and postmarks, which are omitted here. These confirm, modify or determine the dates of letters, though some can be dated only from internal evidence. The dates of others – the most problematic of which are those Keats wrote to Fanny Brawne after his haemorrhage on 3 February 1820 – can only be conjectural. Rollins's datings are followed here unless otherwise stated.[4] The texts of his edition are notably accurate, though he occasionally fails to mark new paragraphs in the letters.[5] The rare substantive disagreements with Rollins's readings are explained in the notes. Keats's characteristic lower-case 'k' is virtually indistinguishable from his upper-case 'K' and its interpretation often depends upon context; and his 's' and 'S' present similar though lesser difficulties. Keats frequently runs 'to be' together as 'tobe' (here regularized).

Grant F. Scott's *Selected Letters of John Keats* (Cambridge, MA: Harvard University Press, 2002) aims at a 'principled modernization' of Keats's spelling and punctuation on the grounds that it is impossible to replicate handwritten letters in print. Moreover, since then it is has become possible for the general reader to see high-quality reproductions of a large number of the letters. A selection of Keats's manuscripts can be found in Stephen Hebron's *John Keats: A Poet and His Manuscripts* (London: British Library, 2009), and images of the manuscripts and transcripts of his letters and poems in the Harvard Keats Collection are now available online.

Although the physical immediacy of an individual's handwriting and characteristic scribal habits cannot be fully translated into print, this edition, like those of Rollins and Robert Gittings, retains Keats's characteristic spelling, punctuation, capitalization and, usually, his paragraphing. It does so as a reminder that these are manuscript letters, not carefully worked prose. The inconsistencies in his spelling, punctuation and capitalization take us close to Keats's act of writing, and his misspellings ('purplue', 'rediculous') can be imaginatively creative.

Even more importantly, the syntax of his letters is closer to speech than considered prose. This is most apparent in Keats's frequent use of dashes, whose grammatical function is characteristically indeterminate. His choice in this matter is deliberate – in the verse epistles sent to his brother and to Cowden Clarke or when making fair copies of work in progress for Bailey, Taylor and Woodhouse he punctuates normally as if for print. The same is true of his draft review of Reynolds's spoof, *Peter Bell*, for publication in the *Examiner* (pp. 348–9). Changing Keats's dashes into commas, full stop, semi-colons or colons would be counter-productive. In any case, his dashes (represented here as a printed '—') are short and resemble a hyphen. As a result they are not always easy to distinguish from his full stops. In addition, Keats occasionally makes use of a long dash '———', and these are so recorded. Imposing formal punctuation on Keats's prose would destroy its mobility and spontaneity, and obscure the flexible movement of his mind.

Keats usually wrote his letters fluently and in a clear hand with very little if any revision. However, a few may have been fair copies from a draft. His letter of 27 October 1818 to Richard Woodhouse, who had been shocked by Keats's threat to abandon poetry, is so carefully and evenly written that it appears to be a fair copy (though Keats uses dashes for punctuation in the same way that he does elsewhere). Another candidate for a 'fair copy' is the letter he wrote on 16 August 1820 in reply to Shelley's generous offer that he 'take up' residence with him and his family in Pisa. On the other hand, the extremely legible letter Keats sent to his sister from Oxford on 10 September 1817 was not a copy, but written with particular care for a fourteen-year-old girl.

NOTE ON THIS EDITION

This selection differs from previous editions in two ways. First, an explanatory narrative in italics has been added where it seems helpful. This is because some important events in Keats's life either go unmentioned or are only referred to in passing in the letters. The explanatory narrative is fullest for the early years. Before Keats's twentieth year there are no letters at all, and in the dramatic seven-month period between August 1816 and March 1817 – during which he came of age, decided to abandon medicine for poetry and self-published his first volume – Keats wrote very few letters and most of these are brief notes. For their significance to be understood they need to be placed in context.

Secondly, longer letters written over a period of time during which Keats wrote other letters have been divided into chronological sections. Although he wrote most of his letters in a single sitting, some of his most important letters were written over a period of days or even months, notably the four 'journal letters' sent to George and Georgiana Keats in America. Beginning with Buxton Forman's edition of 1883 these have traditionally been placed at the date on which they were completed. For instance, the letter to George and Georgiana, which Keats began on 14 February 1819 but did not finish until three months later on 5 May, is normally preceded by the ten other letters he wrote between those dates. This has its own logic, observing as it does the point at which the letter was completed and ready for the post. But other letters written over several days are placed according to the date on which they were begun. In the case of the overlapping letters Keats wrote to differing correspondents during his northern walking tour, arranging them by the day on which they were begun makes it very difficult to follow the progress of Keats's journey. The traditional practice of printing each of his longer letters as independent units obscures the chronological sequence of Keats's life and his chameleon-like ability to suit his letters to different correspondents. My selection, therefore, breaks up these longer letters according to the days on which individual sections were written and intersperses them with the letters Keats wrote to other people in between.

To the extent that Keats, writing to the moment, used these longer letters to define his ideas and his sense of himself, they are self-discovering and self-creative. They are therefore all the more revealing when read in the sequence in which they were written. However, Keats's letters were always written with particular readers in mind, who read them as completed documents. So, at the end of each section of the letters divided in this way, page references are given to the date on which Keats took up the letter again. The reader can either follow the actual sequence in which Keats wrote his letters and parts of letters or choose to read those letters written over a period of time as single documents.

The following conventions are used in this edition. Editorial additions and comments or corrections of Keats's spelling where confusion might be possible are indicated by square brackets [ ]. Words or letters inserted to fill gaps in the manuscript are enclosed in angle brackets < >. Where the beginning or end of a letter is missing asterisks are given ***. Keats's underlinings are printed as such; where printed transcripts give italicized words or phrases it is assumed these represent the original's underlining.

Keats does not always close quotation or speech marks, and he uses double and single quotes inconsistently: these have been left as Keats wrote them. Where Keats places the £ sign over the sum in question this has been normalized to '£150'. Dashes or stops under superior letters or numbers are omitted.

Interesting cancelled readings are either crossed out (~~thus~~) or given in the notes. Significant interlinear readings are placed between diagonal slashes (//) or reported in the notes. The erasures and interlineations in Keats's drafts or fair copies of poems have been more fully noted than elsewhere. In the letters composed over a period of time Keats occasionally marked a change in the day and date by starting a new line. For clarity, this practice has been adopted throughout, where necessary adding this information in square brackets.

In addition, obvious errors in the transcripts by Jeffrey and others are silently corrected – for instance, James Freeman Clarke's 'Kydal' for 'Rydal' (to Tom Keats , 25–27 June 1818) and Jeffrey's 'the Tun' for 'the Sun' Inn (to Tom Keats, 29 June, 1, 2 July 1818). Woodhouse's correction of the mistakes in his clerk's transcripts are not recorded and when transcripts include the address to which the letter was sent these have been omitted.

NOTES

1 Charles and Mary Cowden Clarke, *Recollections of Writers* (London: Sampson Low & Co., 1878), pp. 128–30.

2 Harvard Keats Collection, http://hcl.harvard.edu/libraries/houghton/collections/modern/keats.cfm. The digitization programme also includes the Collection's holdings of the transcripts made by Richard Woodhouse (1788–1834) and John Jeffrey (1817–81), discussed above.

3 Rollins was able to print only two sentences from sales catalogues. The text is printed by Grant F. Scott, *Selected Letters of John Keats* (Cambridge, MA: Harvard University Press, 2002), p. 393.

4 The most important alteration is that to Keats's long letter to Fanny Brawne of late May/early June 1820, which Rollins dates 5(?) July. Gittings, for different reasons, also favours the earlier date.

5 Thus, in his letter to George and Georgiana Keats of 14–31 October 1818, when Keats describes the Reynolds sisters' reactions to Jane Cox ('Charmian'), he starts a new line, 'They call her a flirt to me', clearly set off from the conclusion of the preceding sentence, 'They think I dont admire her because I did not stare at her—' (p. 248). Or, in the journal letter to George and Georgiana Keats (16 December 1818–4 January 1819), Keats clearly meant his comic conversation piece of the Hunt circle to be set out as a scene from a play (p. 279).

Abbreviations

1820	John Keats, *Lamia, Isabella, The Eve of St Agnes, and Other Poems* (London: Taylor and Hessey, 1820)
1848	*Life, Letters, and Literary Remains of John Keats*, ed. Richard Monckton Milnes, 2 vols (London: Edward Moxon, 1848)
1925	Amy Lowell, *John Keats*, 2 vols (Boston, New York: Houghton Mifflin Co., 1925)
Crutcher	Lawrence M. Crutcher, *George Keats of Kentucky: A Life* (Lexington, KY: University Press of Kentucky, 2012)
Gigante	Denise Gigante, *The Keats Brothers: The Life of John and George* (Cambridge, MA: Belknap Press of Harvard University Press, 2011)
Gittings	*Letters of John Keats: A New Selection*, ed. Robert Gittings (Oxford: Oxford University Press, 1970)
Gittings, *John Keats*	Robert Gittings, *John Keats* (1968; Harmondsworth: Penguin, 1979)
Hazlitt, *Works*	William Hazlitt, *The Works of William Hazlitt*, ed. P. P. Howe, 21 vols (London: J. M. Dent & Sons, 1930–4)
HBF (1883)	*The Poetical Works and Other Writings of John Keats*, ed. Harry Buxton Forman, 4 vols (London: Reeves & Turner, 1883)

KC	*The Keats Circle: Letters and Papers 1816–1879*, ed. Hyder E. Rollins, 2nd ed., 2 vols (Cambridge, MA: Harvard University Press, 1965)
K–SJ	*Keats–Shelley Journal* (Chapel Hill, NC: Keats–Shelley Association of America, University of North Carolina)
L	*The Letters of John Keats 1814–1821*, ed. Hyder E. Rollins, 2 vols (Cambridge, MA: Harvard University Press, 1958)
MBF	*Letters of John Keats*, ed. Maurice Buxton Forman, 4th edn (Oxford: Oxford University Press, 1952)
Mee	*John Keats: Selected Letters*, ed. Robert Gittings, rev. Jon Mee (Oxford: Oxford University Press, 2002)
OED	*Oxford English Dictionary* (Oxford: Oxford University Press)
Recollections	Charles and Mary Cowden Clarke, *Recollections of Writers* (London: Sampson Low & Co., 1878)
Roe	Nicholas Roe, *John Keats: A New Life* (New Haven, CT and London: Yale University Press, 2012)
Rollins	Editorial notes in *L* above.
Stillinger	*Complete Poems: John Keats*, ed. Jack Stillinger (Cambridge, MA: Belknap Press, 1978)
Texts	Jack Stillinger, *The Texts of Keats's Poems* (Cambridge, MA: Harvard University Press, 1974)
Walker	Carol Kyros Walker, *Walking North with Keats* (New Haven, CT and London: Yale University Press, 1992)

References to Shakespeare are to *Complete Works of Shakespeare*, ed. Peter Alexander (London: Collins, 1951; 1981). Digitized images of Keats's holograph letters and poems and related materials can be found at the Harvard Keats Collection (http://hcl.harvard.edu/libraries/houghton/collections/modern/keats.cfm).

SELECTED LETTERS

John Keats was born on 31 October 1795 in Moorfields, London, where his father was manager of the livery stables at the Swan and Hoop Inn. Its lease was owned by his grandfather John Jennings, a prosperous London businessman, who retired to Ponders End, Enfield, in 1802. In 1803 Keats's parents sent him with his younger brother George (b. 1796) to board at a small academy run by John Clarke at Enfield. Keats's time there until 1810 or 1811 provided him with a sound education based on Enlightenment values, and encouraged a tolerant attitude in religion, an interest in the arts and liberal political beliefs. Keats's was a relatively well-to-do family with professional ambitions.

But the year after starting school, when Keats was only eight, his father was killed in a riding accident. Shortly afterwards his mother remarried unwisely. From 1805 the four Keats children, effectively orphans, lived briefly with their grandparents in Enfield, before their grandmother Alice Jennings moved the family to Edmonton in 1806, following the death of her husband. Their mother returned, probably in 1809, only to die of tuberculosis, nursed by Keats, early in 1810. Keats, the oldest child, remained deeply attached to his brothers George and Tom and his young sister Fanny.

The children's grandmother attempted to secure their future by settling money from her husband's estate on them, appointing Richard Abbey, a London tea merchant, as their trustee and guardian. Keats inherited £1,500, much of which was spent on his medical education, leaving enough for him to believe he could live independently. But he died in debt, unaware that a further £800 of his inheritance was held in the Court of Chancery.

His mother's illness changed Keats from a boisterous schoolboy into a prize-winning student. In his final years at Enfield he devoured the books in its library and worked on a prose translation of Virgil's Aeneid. *After leaving school Keats was apprenticed to Thomas Hammond, a surgeon in Edmonton, in 1810. Keats pursued his medical training seriously. In October 1815 he enrolled at Guy's, a hospital at the forefront of medical science, to fulfil the newly instituted course requirements and examinations needed to qualify as an apothecary (the forerunner of a general practitioner). Keats passed these exams successfully at Apothecaries' Hall on 25 July 1816. He was one of the few students chosen to become a surgeon's dresser, a twelve-month post which he began on 3 March 1816.*

*Keats had already begun to write poetry. His earliest known poem, the 'Imitation of Spenser', dates from 1814 when he was nineteen. Charles Cowden Clarke later said that Keats's five years apprenticeship was 'the most placid period of his painful life' (*Recollections, *p. 125). Clarke, the son of Keats's headmaster, a teacher at his school and eight years older than Keats, continued to see his former pupil in their spare time during the years when Keats lived at Edmonton as Hammond's apprentice. As Robert Gittings says, 'The real and major influence on Keats's life during the years from fourteen to nineteen was Charles Cowden Clarke' (*John Keats, *p. 62). Clarke introduced the schoolboy to poetry and music, and Keats probably first began to read the* Examiner *while at school. This was a weekly liberal journal edited by the poet Leigh Hunt, to which the Clarke household subscribed. Clarke was a friend of Hunt, whom he met in 1813, visiting him in Horsemonger Jail, where Hunt was imprisoned for libelling the Prince Regent. Keats did not meet Hunt himself until later, but he shared Clarke's enthusiasm for his politics and his poetry. This enthusiasm was later to damn him in the eyes of Tory reviewers.*

During his medical training Keats went on writing occasional poetry. In the summer before he started at Guy's on 1 October 1815 he was briefly a member of the coterie surrounding the would-be poet George Felton Mathew (1795–?). During the autumn session at Guy's in 1815 Keats wrote the sonnet 'O Solitude! if I must with thee dwell', which appeared in the Examiner *six months later on 5 May 1816, signed 'J. K.' This was his first published poem. In November 1815 Keats also wrote a verse epistle from the hospital, a reply to Mathew's 'To a Poetical Friend'. Thereafter the demands made by his education at Guy's, and from March 1816 his duties at the hospital, kept Keats fully occupied.*

August 1816 to March 1817
Commitment to Poetry

These eight months were the most decisive period in Keats's life. They must also have been the busiest and most demanding. In August he was a newly qualified medical practitioner. By the following March he was a newly published poet, surrounded by a group of admirers, and had given up medicine for poetry. During these months of frenetic activity Keats's few extant letters from October onwards are brief and hastily written, often in a state of high excitement. Compared with his subsequent career, this period is very sketchily documented by his letters.

It started quietly enough with Keats and his brother Tom taking a few weeks' holiday in late August and early September in Margate, then a popular seaside resort for Londoners. There he composed two substantial poems, one to his brother George, the other to Cowden Clarke, tentatively setting out his poetic ambitions. These two verse epistles (a form favoured by Hunt) are the earliest of Keats's extant letters known to have been posted to their recipients. Both announce his commitment to poetry and his patriotism, both describe natural scenes and both assume that his recipients share his admiration for Hunt. The epistle to Clarke is given here as the more confident poem, and because it describes and pays tribute to Clarke's influence on the young Keats. The note of nostalgia reflects the fact that Clarke, too, had left Enfield following his father's retirement, and was living with his sister and brother-in-law in Clerkenwell.

To C. C. Clarke
September 1816

[Huntington MS]

Margate—Sept. 1816—

To Mr C. C. Clarke—[1]

Oft have you seen a Swan superbly frowning,
And, with proud breast, his own white shadow crowning:
He slants his Neck beneath the waters bright,
So silently, it seems a beam of light
Shot from the Galaxy; anon he sports—
With outspread Wings, the Naiad Zephyr courts,
Or ruffles all the surface of the Lake,
In striving, from its crystal face, to take
Some diamond Waterdrops, and them to treasure
In milky Nest, and sip them off at leisure.
But, not a moment, can he there insure them;
Nor, to such downy rest, can he allure them:
For down they rush, as though they would be free,
And drop, like time into Eternity.
  Just like that Bird, am I, in loss of time,
Whene'er I venture on the Stream of Rhyme;
With shattered Boat, Oar snapt, and canvass rent,
I slowly sail, scarce knowing my intent;
Still scooping up the Water with my fingers;
In which, a trembling diamond never lingers.
  By this, Friend Charles! you may, full plainly, see
Why I have never pen'd a Line to thee:
Because my thoughts were never free, and clear,

1 *To Mr C. C. Clarke*: Keats made substantive changes in the version published in *Poems* (1817).

And little fit to please a classic Ear:
Because my Wine was of too poor a savour
For one, whose Palate gladdens in the flavour
Of sparkling Helicon[1]—Small good it were,
To take him to a desert, rude, and bare,
Who, had on Baiæ's shore, reclin'd at ease,
While Tasso's Page was floating in a Breeze
That gave soft Music from Armida's Bowers,[2]
Mingled with fragrance from her rarest flowers:
Small good, to One[3] who had, by Mulla's Stream,[4]
Fondled the Maidens with the Breasts of Cream:[5]
Who had beheld Belphœbe in a Brook,
And lovely Una in a leafy Nook,
And Archimago leaning o'er his Book:[6]
Who had, of all that's sweet, tasted, and seen,
From silv'ry ripple, up to Beauty's Queen;
From the sequester'd haunts of gay Titania,[7]
To the blue dwelling of Divine Urania.
One, who, of late, had ta'en sweet forest walks
With him who elegantly chats, and talks—
The wrong'd Libertas[8]—who hath told you Stories
Of laurel Chaplets, and Apollo's glories;

1 *sparkling Helicon*: A compressed metaphor. Helicon, a Greek mountain, believed to be the home of the Muses, had two springs, Hippocrene and Aganippe, the sources of poetic inspiration.
2 *Armida's Bowers*: Armida, the heroine of *Gerusalemme Liberata* (1580–1) by the Italian Renaissance poet Torquato Tasso (1544–95), whose final home was in the Bay of Naples ('Baiæ's shore').
3 *to One*: The poet Edmund Spenser (*c.* 1552–99).
4 *Mulla's Stream*: Mulla is the stream near Spenser's home in Kilcoman, Ireland.
5 *Maidens . . . Breasts of Cream*: This line resembles Spenser's *Epithalamion* (1595), l. 175, 'Her brest like to a bowle of creame uncrudded'.
6 *Belphœbe . . . Una . . . Archimago . . . his Book*: Belphoebe and Una are the heroines of Spenser's *The Faerie Queene* (1590–6), I and II, where the enchanter Archimago represents false religion and hypocrisy.
7 *Titania*: Queen of the fairies in *A Midsummer Night's Dream* (1595/6) by William Shakespeare (1564–1616). In the next line 'Divine Urania' is the muse of astronomy invoked by John Milton (1608–74) in *Paradise Lost* (1667), VII.
8 *wrong'd Libertas*: i.e., Leigh Hunt: 'wrong'd' because of his imprisonment and named 'Libertas' by Keats for his defence of liberal values in the *Examiner*.

Of Troops chivalrous prancing through a City;
And tearful Ladies, made for Love and Pity:[1]
With many else which I have never known.
Thus have I thought; & days, on days have flown
Slowly, or rapidly—unwilling still,
For you to try my dull unlearned quill.
Nor should I now, but that I've known you long;
That you first taught me all the sweets of song:
The grand, the sweet, the Terse, the free, the Fine;
What swell'd with Pathos, and what right divine;
Spenserian vowels, that elope with ease,
And float along like Birds o'er summer Seas;
Miltonian Storms, and more, Miltonian tenderness;
Michael in Arms, and more, meek Eve's fair slenderness.[2]
Who read for me the Sonnet, swelling loudly
Up to its Climax, and then dying proudly?
Who found for me the Grandeur of the Ode,
Growing, like Atlas,[3] stronger from its load?
Who let me taste that more than cordial dram,
The sharp, the rapier pointed Epigram?
Show'd me that Epic was of all the King,
Round, vast, and spanning all, like Saturn's Ring?[4]
You too, upheld the Veil from Clios[5] beauty,
And pointed out the Patriots stern duty;
The Might of Álfred, and the shaft of Tell,

1 *told you Stories . . . Love and Pity*: Clarke evidently told Keats of his conversations with Hunt while walking on Hampstead Heath. The 'Stories' of 'Troops chivalrous' and 'tearful Ladies' refer to Hunt's *The Story of Rimini* (1816).

2 *Miltonian Storms . . . slenderness*: See *Paradise Lost*, IV–VI and VII.

3 *Atlas*: One of the Titans in the war against the Olympians, condemned by the victorious Zeus to hold up the heavens on his shoulders; also a range of mountains in North Africa.

4 *Saturn's Ring*: First observed by Galileo (1564–1642), but the observations of the astronomer William Herschel (1738–1822) had stimulated fresh interest in 1789, reflected in Bonnycastle's *Introduction to Astronomy* (1807 edn), one of Keats's school prizes.

5 *Clios*: Clio, the muse of history.

The Hand of Brutus,[1] that so grandly fell
Upon a Tyrant's Head.—Ah! had I never seen,
Or known your kindness, what might I have been?
What my Enjoyments in my youthful Years,
Bereft of all that now my Life endears?
And can I e'er these Benefits forget?
And can I e'er repay the friendly debt?
No doubly no—Yet, should these Rhymings please,
I shall roll on the Grass with two fold ease:
For I have long time been my fancy feeding
With Hopes, that you would one day think the reading
Of my rough Verses not an hour mispent:—
Should I e'er hear it what a rich content!
  Some Weeks have pass'd since last I saw the Spires
In lucent Thames reflected:[2]—warm desires
To see the Sun o'er peep the eastern dimness,
And morning Shadows stretching into slimness
Across the lawny Fields, or pebbly water;
To mark the time, as they grow broad, and shorter;
To feel the Air, that plays about the Hills,
And sips its freshness from the little rills;
To see high, golden Corn wave in the light,
When Cynthia smiles upon a Summer's Night,
And ~~play~~ /'peers/[3] among the Cloudlets jet, and white;
As though she were reclining on a bed
Of bean blossoms, in heaven freshly shed.
No sooner had I steppd into these Pleasures,
Than I began to think of Verse, and Measures:
The Air that floated by me, seem'd to say,
"Write! thou wilt never have a better day".

1 *Alfred . . . Tell . . . Brutus*: Three patriot heroes: Alfred the Great (849–99), first king of the Anglo-Saxons, who concluded peace with the Danes and was noted for his learning; William Tell, the legendary liberator of Switzerland; and Marcus Brutus (85–42 BC), who helped assassinate Julius Caesar when he declared himself dictator of Rome.

2 *Some Weeks . . . reflected*: i.e., since he was working in London at Guy's Hospital.

3 i.e., 'appears'.

And so I did.—When many Lines I'd written,
Though, with their grace, I was not over smitten;
Yet, as my hand was in, I thought I'd better
Trust to my feelings, and write you a Letter.
Such an Attempt required an inspiration
Of a peculiar sort;—a consummation.
Which, had I felt, these scribblings might have beene
Verses, from which the Soul would never wean.
But many days have pass'd, since last my heart
Was warm'd luxuriously, by divine Mozart;[1]
By Arne[2] delighted, or by Handel madden'd,
Or by the Songs of Erin[3] pierc'd, and sadden'd:
What time, you were before the Musick sitting,
And the rich Notes, to each Sensation fitting.
Since I have walked with you through shady Lanes,
That freshly terminate in open Plains;
And revel'd in a Chat, that ceased not,
When at night fall among your Books we got;
No, nor when Supper came, nor after that
Nor when, reluctantly, I took my Hat;
No, nor till cordially you shook my Hand
Mid way between our homes:—your accents bland
Still sounded in my Ears, when I no more
Could hear your footsteps touch the grav'ly floor.
Sometimes I lost them, and then found again;
You chang'd the footpath for the grassy plain.
In these still moments, I have wished you joys
That well you know to honor—"Life's very toys
With him," said I, "will take a pleasant charm,
It cannot be, that ought will work him harm"
These thoughts now come o'er me with all their might:
Again I shake your hand:—Friend Charles good Night!

1 *divine Mozart*: Keats recalls listening to Clarke playing the piano ('the Musick') at Enfield Academy. Mozart (1756–91) was a favourite composer in the Hunt circle.

2 *Arne*: Thomas Arne (1710–78) was a prolific composer.

3 *Songs of Erin*: A reference to the highly successful *Irish Melodies* (1808–34) by Thomas Moore (1779–1852).

*Keats left Margate and returned to London in early or mid-September to take up the last six months of his full-time post as dresser to William Lucas at Guy's. He moved into lodgings in Dean Street, close to the hospital, living on his own, 'house-keeper, and solitary' (*Recollections*, p. 128). Keats's medical responsibilities were heavy. In addition to his normal weekday duties, he was required to spend one in every five weeks in the hospital as resident house surgeon. He wrote to Clarke as soon as the 'busy time' – the beginning of the new teaching year at Guy's – had finished. Clarke had promised to introduce Keats to Leigh Hunt. Keats was to take with him examples of his poetry.*

To C. C. Clarke
9 October 1816

[Historical Society of Pennsylvania MS]

[8 Dean Street, Borough, London]
Wednesday Octr 9th—

My dear Sir,

The busy time has just gone by, and I can now devote any time you may mention to the pleasure of seeing Mr Hunt—'t will be an Era in my existence—I am anxious too to see the Author of the Sonnet to the Sun,[1] for it is no mean gratification to become acquainted with Men who in their admiration of Poetry do not jumble together Shakspeare and Darwin[2]—I have coppied out a sheet or two of Verses which I composed some time ago, and find so much to blame in them that the best

1 *the Sonnet to the Sun*: Not by Clarke, as is usually thought, but the 'Sonnet on Sunset' by Charles Ollier (1788–1859), dated August 1813, which Keats had seen in Clarke's Commonplace Book (Brotherton Collection, University of Leeds). Ollier and his brother James were to publish Keats's first book.

2 *Darwin*: Erasmus Darwin (1731–1802), physician, philosopher and poet, published *The Loves of the Plants* (1789), later known as Part II of *The Botanic Garden* (1791).

/worst/ part will go into the fire—those to G. Mathew[1] I will suffer to meet the eye of Mr H. notwithstanding that the Muse is so frequently mentioned. I here sinned in the face of Heaven even while remembring what, I think, Horace says, "never presume to make a God appear but for an Action worthy of a God.[2] From a few Words of yours when last I saw you, I have no doubt but that you have something in your Portfolio[3] which I should by rights see—I will put you in Mind of it—Although the Borough is a beastly place in dirt, turnings and windings; yet No 8 Dean Street is not difficult to find; and if you would run the Gauntlet over London Bridge, take the first turning to the left and then the first to the right and moreover knock at my door which is nearly opposite a Meeting,[4] you would do one a Charity which as St Paul saith is the father of all the Virtues[5]—At all events let me hear from you soon—I say at all events not excepting the Gout in your fingers—

Your's Sincerely
John Keats—

Cowden Clarke took Keats to meet Leigh Hunt at his home in the Vale of Health, Hampstead, on Saturday, 19 October (Roe, p. 102). It was Hunt's birthday and in addition to Clarke and Keats, the painter Benjamin Robert Haydon was a guest. On this long-awaited 'red-letter day' Keats not only impressed Hunt with his poetry but, according to Clarke, 'was suddenly made a familiar of the household'. This was most likely when Clarke was lent a copy of the 1616 folio edition of Chapman's Homer. The following week Clarke introduced Keats to the translation at his lodgings in Clerkenwell, an experience which prompted Keats to write 'On First Looking into Chapman's Homer'. This,

1 *those to G. Mathew*: Keats may mean his epistle 'To George Felton Mathew', as well as other poems.

2 *never presume . . . worthy of a God*: Keats quotes the Earl of Roscommon's translation *Horace: Of the Art of Poetry* ([1680] 1709 edn), p. 9, which has 'a Business' for 'an Action'.

3 *Portfolio*: Either Clarke's Commonplace Book or a lost companion volume.

4 *Meeting*: A Baptist chapel.

5 *Charity . . . Virtues*: I Corinthians 13:13.

*in Hunt’s words, ‘completely announced a new poet taking possession’. Clarke recalled that although Keats left ‘at day-spring, yet he contrived that I should receive the poem from a distance of, may be, two miles by ten o’clock’ (*Recollections, *p. 130).*

To C. C. Clarke

(sent by messenger)

26(?) October 1816[1]

[Harvard MS]

[8 Dean Street, Borough, London]

On the first looking into Chapman’s Homer

Much have I travell’d in the Realms of Gold,
And many goodly States, and Kingdoms seen;
Round many Western islands have I been,
Which Bards in fealty to Apollo hold—
Oft of one wide expanse had I been told,
Which ~~low~~ /deep/ brow’d Homer ruled as his Demesne;
Yet could I never judge what Men could mean,[2]
Till I heard Chapman speak out loud, and bold.
Then felt I like some Watcher of the Skies
When a new Planet swims into his Ken,
Or like stout Cortez,[3] when with wond’ring eyes
He star’d at the Pacific, and all his Men

1 This sonnet is usually dated ‘October 1816’, the date given when it was printed in the *Examiner* (1 December 1816). But Clarke introduced Keats to Hunt on 19 October and Keats’s duties at Guy’s Hospital meant that he could not meet Clarke again until the next weekend, beginning Friday, 25 October (Roe, pp. 102, 108).
2 *Yet . . . mean*: In *Poems* (1817) Keats changed this line to read ‘Yet never did I breathe its pure serene.’ The alteration places Keats within Homer’s world. Clarke said Keats made the change because the original was ‘bald, and too simply wondering’ (*Recollections*, p. 230).
3 *Cortez*: The Spanish conquistadore Hernando Cortez (1485–1547); but as Tennyson pointed out, ‘History requires here *Balbóa*’: the Spanish explorer Vasco de Balboa (1475–1519) founded a colony in Darien.

Look'd at each other with a wild surmise—
Silent upon a Peak in Darien—

On 31 October Keats had his twenty-first birthday. Coming of age meant that he attained his financial freedom. He was free, if he chose, to set up in medical practice, but he must also have been thinking of the possibility of a poetic career. That morning he wrote to Clarke confirming a joint meeting at Haydon's studio.

To C. C. Clarke

31 October 1816

[Berg MS]

[Thursday, 8 Dean Street, Borough, London]

My daintie Davie,[1]

I will be as punctual as the Bee to the Clover—Very glad am I at the thoughts of seeing so soon this glorious Haydon and all his Creation.[2] I pray thee let me know when you go to Ollier's and where he resides—this I forgot to ask you—and tell me also when you will help me waste a sullen day—God 'ield you[3]—

J— K—

Between this letter and the next Keats left 8 Dean Street and moved across the river into lodgings at 76 Cheapside with George and Tom. This was the first time the brothers had lived together since childhood. On 19 November Keats spent the evening at Haydon's studio, where the artist made the profile

1 *daintie Davie*: The phrase is from the poem 'To Davie Second Epistle', l. 44, by Robert Burns (1759–96).

2 *Haydon and all his Creation*: On Sunday, 3 November Keats and Clarke made a breakfast visit to Haydon's studio, where he was working on his huge canvas *Christ's Entry into Jerusalem*. Keats jokingly refers to Joseph Haydn's *The Creation* (1799), which had its London premiere in 1800.

3 *God 'ield you*: See *Hamlet*, IV. v. 41.

sketch now in the National Portrait Gallery. The two men's mutual excitement is echoed in the sonnet Keats sent Haydon the following day (in which the three 'Great Spirits' are William Wordsworth (1770–1850), Hunt and Haydon himself).

To B. R. Haydon
20 November 1816

[Harvard MS]

[76 Cheapside, London]
[Wednesday] Nov[r] 20th

My dear Sir—

Last Evening wrought me up, and I cannot forbear sending you the following— Your's unfeignedly John Keats—

Great Spirits now on Earth are sojourning
He of the Cloud, the Cataract the Lake
Who on Helvellyn's summit wide awake
Catches his freshness from Archangel's wing
He of the Rose, the Violet, the Spring
The social Smile, the Chain for freedom's sake:
And lo!—whose stedfastness would never take
A Meaner Sound than Raphael's Whispering.
And other Spirits are there standing apart
Upon the Forehead of the Age to come;
These, These will give the World another heart
And other pulses—hear ye not the hum
Of mighty Workings in a distant Mart?
Listen awhile ye Nations and be dumb.!

Nov[r] 20—

Removed to 76. Cheapside

Haydon replied by return, promising to send the sonnet to Wordsworth. Keats's description of Haydon's letter as 'a stimulus to exertion' indicates that he was by now committed to poetry. The suggestion by Haydon that the phrase 'in a distant Mart' *in the penultimate line might be omitted was immediately adopted by Keats, who wrote, 'My feelings entirely fall in with yours' in regard to the Elipsis and I glory in it.' He enclosed a revised copy for Haydon to forward (*L, I*, pp. 118–19). But Haydon pasted this into his diary and delayed a month before sending Wordsworth a copy.*

On 1 December Leigh Hunt's article 'Young Poets' appeared in the Examiner. *This named P. B. Shelley (1792–1822), J. H. Reynolds and Keats as representatives of 'the new school of poetry', and printed Keats's 'On First Looking into Chapman's Homer'. Later that month Keats commissioned the Ollier brothers, who were setting up in business, to publish the volume of poems he was putting together.*

To C. C. Clarke
17 December 1816

[Harvard MS]

[76 Cheapside, London]
Tuesday—

My dear Charles,

You may now look at Minerva's Ægis[1] with impunity, seeing that my awful Visage[2] did not turn you into a John Doree[3] you have accordingly a legetimate title to a Copy—I will use my interest to procure it for you. I'll tell you what—I met Reynolds at Haydon's a few mornings since—he promised to be with me this evening and Yesterday I had the same promise from Seve[r]n and I must put you in Mind that on last All hallowmas' day[4] you gave you[r] word that you would spend this Evening with

1 *Minerva's Ægis*: The shield ('Ægis') of Minerva, goddess of wisdom and war, was decorated with a Gorgon's head: those who saw it were turned to stone.
2 *awful Visage*: Haydon's recent life mask of Keats.
3 *John Doree*: A John Dory is an ugly but edible deep-sea fish.
4 *All hallowmas' day*: All Saints' Day, 1 November.

me—so no putting off. I have done little to Endymion[1] lately—I hope to finish it in one more attack—I believe you [know] I went to Richards's[2]—it was so whoreson a Night that I stopped there all the next day—His Remembrances to you—(Ext[ract] from the common place Book of my Mind—Mem[orandum]—Wednesday—Hampstead—call in Warner Street—a Sketch of Mr Hunt[3]—I will ever consider you my sincere and affectionate friend—you will not doubt that I am your's.—

God bless you—

John Keats—

The party which met that evening, 17 December, made up of Cowden Clarke, Joseph Severn, Reynolds and Keats's brothers, may have been the occasion on which Keats announced his intention of publishing Poems *(1817) and abandoning medicine (Roe, pp. 131–2). Throughout December Keats was bringing together early poems and writing new material, including 'I stood tip-toe upon a little hill', whose working title was 'Endymion'. The following day Keats visited Hunt. This was probably when Shelley advised Keats against publishing his 'first-blights', but by 31 December 1816 or shortly thereafter Keats sent the copy for* Poems *(1817) to his printer Charles Richards.*

During the next two months Keats wrote several more sonnets and socialized actively, dining with Horace Smith (1779–1849), Haydon, Hunt and Shelley in January 1817, and meeting Reynolds, Hunt, the Shelleys and others in the course of February. In the meantime, he had to fulfil his duties at Guy's. Two of his sonnets, 'To Kosciusko' and 'After dark vapours have oppressed our plains', were printed by Hunt in the Examiner *on 16 and 23 February; and on Monday, 3 March 1817 Keats, Clarke and Reynolds met at Haydon's to celebrate the*

1 *Endymion*: i.e., 'I stood tip-toe upon a little hill': the autograph copy has 'Dec. eve 16' at the end.

2 *Richards's*: Thomas Richards, brother of Charles, the printer of Keats's *Poems* (1817).

3 *Sketch of Mr Hunt*: Keats evidently meant to call in on Clarke at Warner Street the following day before going on to see Hunt. The 'Sketch' is unidentified.

completion of Keats's term as a dresser and the announcement in that day's Morning Chronicle *of the forthcoming publication of* Poems *(1817) 'on Monday next'. Hunt continued his support by publishing the two sonnets addressed to Haydon on their visit to the Elgin Marbles in the* Examiner *on Sunday, 9 March, only a week after their composition. On the same day Reynolds published a generous preview of the volume in the* Champion, *including the two sonnets to Haydon, and predicted that Keats would 'lay his name in the lap of immortality'. Keats thanked him that evening.*

To J. H. Reynolds
9 March 1817

[Woodhouse transcript (1821?)]

[76 Cheapside, London]
Sunday Evening

My Dear Reynolds,

Your kindness affects me so sensibly that I can merely put down a few mono-sentences—Your Criticism only makes me extremely anxious that I sho^{d} not deceive you.

It's the finest thing by God—as Hazlitt wo^{d} say However I hope I may not deceive you—There are some acquaintances of mine[1] who will scratch their Beards and although I have, I hope, some Charity, I wish their Nails may be long—I will be ready at the time you mention in all Happiness—

There is a report that a young lady of 16 has written the new Tragedy[2] God bless her—I will know her by Hook or by Crook in less than a Week—My Brother's & my Remembrances to your kind Sisters Your's most sincerely

John Keats

1 *acquaintances of mine*: Most likely the Richard Abbeys, the Keats' guardians.
2 *new Tragedy*: Rollins notes that the new tragedy at Drury Lane was in fact *Manuel* by Charles Maturin (1782–1824).

Poems *(1817) was published the following day, Monday, 10 March (as previously announced in the* Morning Chronicle *on 3 and 7 March).*[1] *But interest proved short-lived. Charles Cowden Clarke later recalled, 'The first volume of Keats's minor muse was launched amid the cheers and fond anticipations of his circle . . . Alas! the book might have emerged in Timbuctoo with far stronger chance of fame and approbation . . . The whole community, as if by compact, seemed determined to know nothing about it. The word had been passed that its author was a Radical; and in those days of "Bible-Crown-and-Constitution" supremacy, he might have had better chance of success had he been an Anti-Jacobin' (*Recollections, *p. 140). Sales were slow and the Ollier brothers quickly turned against Keats. But by the end of March or early April Keats had been taken on instead by Reynolds's publishers John Taylor and James Hessey. By then Keats had determined to write a four-book 'Poetic Romance' entitled* Endymion.

To J. H. Reynolds
17 March 1817

[Woodhouse transcript (1821?)]

[76 Cheapside, London]
[Monday]

My dear Reynolds,

My Brothers are anxious that I sho^{d} go by myself into the country—they have always been extremely fond of me; and now that Haydon has pointed out how necessary it is that I sho^{d} be alone to improve myself, they give up the temporary pleasure of living with me continually for a great good which I hope will follow—So I shall soon be out of Town—You must soon bring all your present troubles to a close, and so must I; but we must,

1 See 'The Publication Date of Keats's Poems (1817)', *Keats–Shelley Review*, 28.2 (2014), pp. 83–5.

like the Fox, prepare for a fresh swarm of flies.[1] Banish money—Banish sofas—Banish Wine—Banish Music—But right Jack Health—honest Jack Health, true Jack Health—banish health and banish all the world.[2] I must ~~then~~   myself   ~~if~~ I[3] come this Evening I shall horribly commit myself elsewhere. So I will send my excuses to them & Mrs Dilk by my Brothers

Y^{r} sincere friend John Keats

1 *Fox . . . flies*: In Aesop's fable the Hedgehog offers to rid the Fox of a swarm of horseflies, but the Fox refuses his help on the grounds that others will only take their place.

2 *Banish . . . world*: Adapted from *1 Henry IV*, II. iv. 455–63.

3 ~~*then*~~   *myself*   ~~*if*~~ *I*: The spaces indicate 'a part of the letter torn' (Woodhouse). The sense must be that Keats needs to look after himself: if he visited Reynolds he would be obliged to keep other commitments (Rollins).

April to November 1817
Drafting *Endymion*

By 25 March Keats and his brothers had moved from Cheapside to 1 Well Walk, Hampstead, in rooms rented from Benjamin Bentley, a postman. It was to be Keats's base for the next twenty months. On 12 or 13 April Keats sent a brief note to Taylor and Hessey thanking them for their 'kindness', saying that he was about to 'steal out of town'. The following Monday night, 14 April, Keats left for the Isle of Wight, where he planned to begin his new poem, working eight hours a day.

To George and Tom Keats
15 April 1817

[Princeton MS]

[Southampton]
Tuesday Morn—

My dear Brothers,

I am safe at Southampton—after having ridden three stages outside and the rest in for it began to be very cold. I did not know the Names of any of the Towns I passed through—all I can tell you is that sometimes I saw dusty Hedges sometimes Ponds—then nothing—then a little Wood with trees look you like Launce's Sister "as white as a Lilly and as small as a Wand[1]—then came houses which died away into a few straggling Barns then came hedge trees aforesaid again. As the Lamp

1 *as white . . . a Wand*: See *The Two Gentlemen of Verona*, II. iii. 22 ff.

light crept along the following things were discovered. "long heath brown furze"[1]—Hurdles here and there half a Mile—Park palings when the Windows of a House were always discovered by reflection—One Nymph of Fountain N.B. Stone—lopped Trees—Cow ruminating—ditto Donkey—Man and Woman going gingerly along—William seeing his Sisters over the Heath—John waiting with a Lanthe[r]n for his Mistress—Barber's Pole—Docter's Shop—However after having had my fill of these I popped my Head out just as it began to Dawn—N.B. this tuesday Morn saw the Sun rise—of which I shall say nothing at present—I felt rather lonely this Morning at breakfast so I went and unbox'd a Shakspeare—"There's my Comfort"[2]—I went immediately after Breakfast to the Southampton Water where I enquired for the Boat to the Isle of Wight as I intend seeing that place before I settle—it will go at 3 so shall I after having taken a Chop—I know nothing of this place but that it is long—tolerably broad—has bye streets—two or three Churches—a very respectable old Gate with two Lions to guard it—the Men and Women do not materially differ from those I have been in the Habit of seeing—I forgot to say that from dawn till half past six I went through a most delightful Country—some open Down but for the most part thickly wooded. What surprised me most was an immense quantity of blooming Furze on each side the road cutting a most rural dash—The Southampton Water when I saw it just now was no better than a low Water Water which did no more than answer my expectations—it will have mended its Manners by 3—From the W[h]arf are seen the shores on each side stretching to the isle of Wight. You Haydon, Reynolds &c., have been pushing each other out of my Brain by turns—I have conned over every Head in Haydon's Picture[3]—you must warn them not

1 *long . . . furze*: See *The Tempest*, I. i. 70.
2 *There's my Comfort*: See *The Tempest*, II. ii. 42, 53. The 'Shakspeare' which Keats 'unbox'd' is his newly purchased, seven-volume compact edition of *The Dramatic Works of William Shakspeare* (1814), which he annotated intensively in the coming weeks. It is now at Harvard (Keats *EC8 K2262 Zz814s).
3 *Haydon's Picture*: Haydon included portraits of Keats, William Wordsworth (1770–1850), Charles Lamb (1775–1834) and William Hazlitt (1778–1830)

to be afraid should my Ghost visit them on Wednesday—tell Haydon to Kiss his Hand at Betty over the Way for me yea and to spy at her for me—I hope one of you will be competent to take part in a Trio while I am away—you need only ag[g]ravate your voices a little and mind not to speak Cues and all[1]—when you have said Rum-ti-ti— you must not be rum any more or else another will take up the ti-ti alone and then he might be taken God shield us, for little better than a Titmouse—By the by talking of Titmouse Remember me particularly to all my Friends—give my Love to the Miss Reynoldses and to Fanny who I hope you will soon see. Write to me soon about them all—and you George particularly how you get on with Wilkinson's plan[2]—What could I have done without my Plaid? I don't feel inclined to write any more at present for I feel rather muzzy—you must be content with this fac simile of the rough plan of Aunt Dinah's Counterpane.[3]

Your most affectionate Brother
John Keats—

Reynolds shall hear from me soon—

---

in *Christ's Entry into Jerusalem*. The painting was not completed until 1820 and is now in St Mary's Seminary, Ohio.

1 *ag[g]ravate . . . Cues and all*: Bottom says he will 'aggravate' his voice in *A Midsummer Night's Dream*, I. ii. 73, and Peter Quince tells off Flute for speaking his cues, III. i. 88–91.

2 *Wilkinson's plan*: After leaving Abbey's employment abruptly (see below, p. 575), George worked briefly with a linendraper at 62 Bread Street, off Cheapside, before entering into a business scheme with Wilkinson, for which Keats lent him £40 or £50 (Gittings, *John Keats*, pp. 200–201). This was probably the lawyer Charles Wilkinson, to whom Keats had given a presentation copy of *Poems* (1817) (*L*, I, p. 129). The project came to nothing.

3 *Aunt Dinah's Counterpane*: Perhaps a reference to Aunt Dinah in Laurence Sterne's *Tristram Shandy* (1759–67).

To J. H. Reynolds
17, 18 April 1817

[Woodhouse transcript (1821?)]

[Mrs Cook's, New Village]
Carisbrooke [Thursday] April 17th

My dear Reynolds,

Ever since I wrote to my Brothers from Southampton I have been in a taking, and at this moment I am about to become settled. for I have unpacked my books, put them into a snug corner—pinned up Haydon—Mary Queen [of] Scotts, and Milton with his daughters in a row. In the passage I found a head of Shakspeare which I had not before seen—It is most likely the same that George spoke so well of; for I like it extremely—Well—this head I have hung over my Books, just above the three in a row, having first discarded a french Ambassador—Now this alone is a good morning's work—Yesterday I went to Shanklin, which occasioned a great debate in my mind whether I should live there or at Carisbrooke. Shanklin is a most beautiful place—sloping wood and meadow ground reaches round the Chine, which is a cleft between the Cliffs of the depth of nearly 300 feet at least. This cleft is filled with trees & bushes in the narrow part; and as it widens becomes bare, if it were not for primroses on one side, which spread to the very verge of the Sea, and some fishermen's huts on the other, perched midway in the Ballustrades of beautiful green Hedges along their steps down to the sands.—But the sea, Jack, the sea—the little waterfall—then the white cliff—then St Catherine's Hill[1]—"the sheep in the meadows, the cows in the corn."— Then, why are you at Carisbrooke? say you—Because, in the first place, I shod be at twice the Expense, and three times the inconvenience—next that from here I can see your continent—from a little hill close by, the whole north Angle of the Isle of Wight, with the water between

1 *St Catherine's Hill*: Some six miles west of Ventnor, nearly 778 feet high.

us. In the 3^d place, I see Carisbrooke Castle from my window, and have found several delightful wood-alleys, and copses, and quick freshes[1]—As for Primroses—the Island ought to be called Primrose Island: that is, if the nation of Cowslips agree thereto, of which there are diverse Clans just beginning to lift up their heads and if an how the Rain holds whereby that is Birds eyes[2] abate—another reason of my fixing is that I am more in reach of the places around me—I intend to walk over the island east—West—North South—I have not seen many specimens of Ruins—I dont think however I shall ever see one to surpass Carisbrooke Castle. The trench is o'ergrown with the smoothest turf, and the walls with ivy—The Keep within side is one Bower of ivy—a Colony of Jackdaws have been there many years—I dare say I have seen many a descendant of some old cawer who peeped through the Bars at Charles the first, when he was there in Confinement.[3] On the road from Cowes to Newport I saw some extensive Barracks[4] which disgusted me extremely with Government for placing such a Nest of Debauchery in so beautiful a place—I asked a man on the Coach about this—and he said that the people had been spoiled—In the room where I slept at Newport I found this on the Window "O Isle spoilt by the Milatary"—I must in honesty however confess that I did not feel very sorry at the idea of the Women being a little profligate—The Wind is in a sulky fit, and I feel that it would be no bad thing to be the favorite of some Fairy, who would give one the power of seeing how our Friends got on, at a Distance—I should like, of all Loves, a sketch of you and Tom and George in ink which Haydon will do if you tell him how I want them—From want of regular rest, I have been rather narvus—and the passage in Lear—"Do you not hear the Sea?"[5]—has haunted me intensely.

1 *quick freshes*: A stream of fresh water; see *The Tempest*, III. ii. 64.
2 *Birds eyes*: 'Bird's eye, or germander speedwell, closes its petals in cloudy weather' (Gittings).
3 *Charles . . . Confinement*: Charles I (1600–49) was imprisoned there by the Parliamentary forces in 1647–48.
4 *Barracks*: Albany Barracks. Keats shared the liberals' dislike of standing armies.
5 *Do you not hear the Sea?*: Edgar's words to his blinded father in *King Lear*, IV. vi. 4.

On the Sea.[1]

~~O Sea~~ It keeps eternal Whisperings around
Desolate shores, and with its mighty swell
Gluts twice ten thousand Caverns; till the spell
Of Hecate leaves them their old shadowy sound.
often 'tis in such gentle temper found
That scarcely will the very smallest shell
Be moved for days from whence it sometime fell
When last the winds of Heaven were unbound.
O ye who have your eyeballs vext and tir'd
Feast them upon the wideness of the Sea
O ye whose Ears are dinned with uproar rude
Or fed too much with cloying melody—
Sit ye near some old Cavern's Mouth and brood
Until ye start as if the Sea Nymphs quired—

[Friday] April 18th

Will you have the goodness to do this? Borrow a Botanical Dictionary—turn to the words Laurel and Prunus show the explanations to your sisters and Mrs Dilk and without more ado let them send me the Cups Basket and Books they trifled and put off and off while I was in Town—ask them what they can say for themselves—ask Mrs Dilk wherefore she does so distress me—Let me know how Jane has her health—the Weather is unfavorable for her—Tell George and Tom to write.—I'll tell you what—On the 23rd was Shakespeare born—now If I should receive a Letter from you and another from my Brothers on that day 'twould be a parlous good thing—Whenever you write say a Word or two on some Passage in Shakespeare that may have come rather new to you; which must be continually happening, notwithstand^{g} that we read the same Play forty times—for instance, the following, from the Tempest,[2] never struck me so forcibly as at present,

1 *On the Sea*: Published in the *Champion* (17 August 1817), probably at Reynolds's instigation.
2 *from the Tempest*: I. ii. 326–8, 50.

"Urchins
Shall, for that vast of Night that they may work,
All exercise on thee—"

How can I help bringing to your mind the Line—

In the dark backward and abysm of time—

I find that I cannot exist without poetry—without eternal poetry—half the day will not do—the whole of it—I began with a little, but habit has made me a Leviathan[1]—I had become all in a Tremble from not having written any thing of late—the Sonnet over leaf did me some good. I slept the better last night for it—this Morning, however, I am nearly as bad again—Just now I opened Spencer, and the first Lines I saw were these.—

"The noble Heart that harbors vertuous thought,
And is with Child of glorious great intent,
Can never rest, until it forth have brought
Th' eternal Brood of Glory excellent—"[2]

Let me know particularly about Haydon; ask him to write to me about Hunt, if it be only ten lines—I hope all is well—I shall forthwith begin my Endymion,[3] which I hope I shall have got some way into by the time you come,[4] when we will read our verses in a delightful place I have set my heart upon near the Castle—Give my Love to your Sisters severally—To George and Tom—Remember me to Rice M[r] & M[rs] Dilk and all we know.—

Your sincere Friend
John Keats.

Direct J. Keats M[rs] Cook's new Village
Carisbrooke

1 *Leviathan*: The biblical sea monster.
2 *The noble Heart . . . Glory excellent*: *The Faerie Queene*, I. v. 1, describing the Red Cross Knight.
3 *Endymion*: How much Keats wrote in the rest of the week is unclear, but he certainly drafted the poem's induction and may have completed the 'Hymn to Pan' (*Endymion*, I, 247–306).
4 *by the time you come*: Reynolds did not visit Keats.

After only a week or so at Carisbrooke, Keats, suffering from over-exertion, decided to move to Margate, where he was joined by Tom. They arrived soon after 24 April. Once settled, he wrote to Hunt, who was staying with the Shelleys at Marlow.

To Leigh Hunt
10 May 1817

[British Library MS]

Margate [Saturday,] May 10th—

My dear Hunt,

The little Gentleman that sometimes lurks in a gossips bowl ought to have come in very likeness of a coasted crab[1] and choaked me outright for not having answered your Letter ere this—however you must not suppose that I was in Town to receive it; no, it followed me to the isle of Wight and I got it just as I was going to pack up for Margate, for reasons which you anon shall hear. On arriving at this treeless affair I wrote to my Brother George to request C. C. C. to do the thing you wot of respecting Rimini;[2] and George tells me he has undertaken it with great Pleasure; so I hope there has been an understanding between you for many Proofs—C. C. C. is well acquainted with Bensley. Now why did you not send the key of your Cupboard which I know was full of Papers? We would have lock'd them all in a trunk together with those you told me to destroy; which indeed I did not do for fear of demolishing Receipts. There not b[e]ing a more unpleasant thing in the world (saving a thousand and one others) than to pay a Bill twice. Mind you—Old Wood's[3] a very Varmant—sharded in Covetousness—And now

1 *a coasted crab*: Because he was staying by the sea in Margate, Keats wrote 'coasted' for 'roasted' in Puck's self-description in *A Midsummer Night's Dream*, II. ii. 47–50.

2 *Rimini*: The second edition of Hunt's *The Story of Rimini* (1817), printed by Thomas Bensley. There was confusion over who was to read the proofs in Hunt's absence in Marlow: Clarke did so.

3 *Old Wood's*: 'Probably a bailiff' (Gittings).

I am upon a horrid subject—what a horrid one you were upon last Sunday and well you handled it. The last Examiner was [a] Battering Ram against Christianity—Blasphemy—Tertullian—Erasmus—S[r] Philip Sidney.[1] And then the dreadful Petzelians and their expiation by Blood[2]—and do Christians shudder at the same thing in a Newspaper which the[y] attribute to their God in its most aggravated form? What is to be the end of this?—I must mention Hazlitt's Southey—O that he had left out the grey hairs![3]—Or that they had been in any other Paper not concluding with such a Thunderclap—that sentence about making a Page of the feelings of a whole life appears to me like a Whale's back in the Sea of Prose.[4] I ought to have said a word on Shakespeare's Christianity—there are two, which I have not looked over with you, touching the thing: the one for, the other against: That in favor is in Measure for Measure Act 2. S. 2 Isab. Alas! Alas!

> Why all the Souls that were, were forfeit once
> And he that might the vantage best have took,
> Found out the Remedy—[5]

1 *The last Examiner . . . Sidney*: Hunt's leader 'To the English People. Letter VII' in the *Examiner* (4 May) attacked religious intolerance, with references to Tertullian (b. *c.* 150), Erasmus (*c.* 1467–1536) and Sir Philip Sidney (1554–86), among others (pp. 273–5).
2 *Petzelians . . . by Blood*: The same issue reprints a report from Vienna (16 April) that 'Petzel, a Priest of Branau' and eighty-six of his followers have been arrested for practising community of property and human sacrifice (pp. 276–7, 282).
3 *Hazlitt's Southey . . . grey hairs*: Hazlitt wrote an anonymous review of Robert Southey's *Letter to William Smith, Esq. M. P.* (1817) in the same issue of the *Examiner*, referring mockingly to Southey's 'few contemptible grey hairs' (p. 284).
4 *making a Page . . . Sea of Prose*: Hazlitt attacked Southey's turncoat politics, and said, 'Why should not one make a sentence of a page long, out of the feelings of one's whole life?' (*Examiner*, 4 May 1817, p. 287.)
5 *Why all the Souls . . . the Remedy*: Haydon's report of his fierce dispute about Christianity with Hunt and the poet P. B. Shelley (1792–1822), while at dinner with Horace Smith on 20 January 1817, concludes by quoting these lines; see *The Diary of Benjamin Robert Haydon*, ed. W. B. Pope (Cambridge, MA: Harvard University Press, 1960–63), I, pp. 80–87 (at p. 87).

That against is in Twelfth Night. Act 3. S 2. Maria—for there is no Christian, that means to be saved by believing rightly, can ever believe such impossible Passages of grossness!' Before I come to the Nymphs[1] I must get through all disagreeables—I went to the Isle of Wight—thought so much about Poetry so long together that I could not get to sleep at night[2]—and moreover, I know not how it was, I could not get wholesome food—By this means in a Week or so I became not over capable in my upper Stories, and set off pell mell for Margate, at least 150 Miles—because forsooth I fancied that I should like my old Lodging here, and could contrive to do without Trees. Another thing I was too much in Solitude, and consequently was obliged to be in continual burning of thought as an only resource. However Tom is with me at present and we are very comfortable. We intend though to get among some Trees. How have you got on among them? How are the Nymphs?[3] I suppose they have led you a fine dance—Where are you now—In Judea, Cappadocia, or the Parts of Lybia about Cyrene,[4] Strangers from "Heaven, Hues and Prototypes[5]—I wager you have given given several new turns to the old saying "Now the Maid was fair and pleasant to look on"[6] as well as mad[e] a little variation in "once upon a time" perhaps too you have rather varied "thus endeth

1 *Nymphs*: Hunt's poem 'The Nymphs', to which Keats returns below.
2 *I could not get to sleep at night*: He had been 'narvus' (see above, p. 25).
3 *Nymphs*: Hunt was completing 'The Nymphs', published in *Foliage* (1818), while staying with the Shelleys in Marlow. The poem celebrates the cult of Pan and the natural religion of the ancient pastoral world (as does *Endymion*, which Keats was composing at the same time). Keats, who had seen a draft of at least Part 1, writes jokingly about Hunt's pursuit of his poetic nymphs ('Maids').
4 The MS has a full stop, but a comma must be intended, as editors have recognized. Keats parodies Acts 2:9–10, where a multitude of believers from 'Judaea, and Cappadocia . . . in the parts of Libya about Cyrene, and strangers of Rome, Jews and proselytes' gathered in Jerusalem and were inspired by the Holy Ghost to speak in tongues.
5 *Heaven, Hues and Prototypes*: 'Hues' here has the obsolete sense of 'Form, shape, figure' (*OED* 1a) and is a near-synonym for 'Prototypes'. Compare *Endymion*, IV, 1–3, and *The Faerie Queene*, I. i. 46 and I. ii. 40.
6 *Now the Maid . . . look on*: See Genesis 24:16, 'the damsel was very fair to look upon, a virgin', describing Rebecca as she is about to make Isaac welcome.

the first Lesson" I hope you have made a Horse shoe business[1] of—"unsuperfluous lift" "faint Bowers" and fibrous roots. I vow that I have been down in the Mouth lately at this Work.[2] These last two day however I have felt more confident—I have asked myself so often why I should be a Poet more than other Men,—seeing how great a thing it is,—how great things are to be gained by it—What a thing to be in the Mouth of Fame—that at last the Idea has grown so monstrously beyond my seeming Power of attainment that the other day I nearly consented with myself to drop into a Phaeton[3]—yet 't is a disgrace to fail even in a huge attempt, and at this moment I drive the thought from me. I began my Poem[4] about a Fortnight since and have done some every day except travelling ones—Perhaps I may have done a good deal for the time but it appears such a Pin's Point to me that I will not coppy any out—When I consider that so many of these Pin points go to form a Bodkin point (God send I end not my Life with a bare Bodkin,[5] in its modern sense[6]) and that it requ[i]res a thousand bodkins to make a Spear bright enough to throw any light to posterity—I see that nothing but continual uphill Journeying? Now is there any thing more unpleasant (it may come among the thousand and one) than to be so journeying

1 *a Horse shoe business*: 'Horse shoe' here carries the slang meaning of 'the female pudend', and 'business' that of 'sexual intercourse' (Eric Partridge, *A Dictionary of Slang and Unconventional English*, 5th edn (London: Routledge & Kegan Paul, 1961)). Keats urges Hunt to make explicit the eroticism of a scene in which a 'young poet' is unwittingly 'enticed' by a 'bevy' of water nymphs to swim with them ('The Nymphs', I, 194–229). Keats picks out innocent phrases (I, 229, 257 and 197), which, quoted out of context, carry sexual meanings. Thus 'Bowers' is slang for a woman, and 'roots' (in place of Hunt's innocent 'mould') is slang for penis. In this context Hunt's 'unsuperfluous lift', used by Hunt to describe a swan's wings, becomes another possible double entendre.
2 *Work*: Keats's own 'Work' on *Endymion*.
3 *Phaeton*: A light carriage with four large wheels, fast and dangerous, its name derived from the Greek *phaeton* ('shining'): hence, Keats also invokes Phaethon, the son of Apollo, whose rashness, when allowed to drive the chariot of the sun, threatened a universal conflagration. Both allusions emphasize the rashness of Keats's ambitions.
4 *my Poem*: *Endymion*.
5 *a bare Bodkin*: See *Hamlet*, III. i. 76. 'Bodkin' here means a dagger or stiletto.
6 *in its modern sense*: Written interlineally as an afterthought.

and miss the Goal at last—But I intend to whistle[1] all these cogitations into the Sea where I hope they will breed Storms violent enough to block up all exit from Russia. Does Shelley go on telling strange Stories of the Death of kings?[2] Tell him there are stran<ge> Stories of the death of Poets—some have died before they were conceived "how do you make that out Master Vellum"[3] Does Mrs S—[4] cut Bread and Butter as neatly as ever? Tell her to procure some fatal Scissars and cut the th[r]ead of Life of all to be disappointed Poets. Does Mrs Hunt tear linen half as straight as ever? Tell her to tear from the book of Life all blank Leaves. Remember me to them all—to Miss Kent[5] and the little ones all[6]—

Your sincere friend

John Keats alias Junkets[7]—

You shall know where we move—

That evening Keats replied to a letter from Haydon which warned him against giving 'way to any forebodings', because 'they are nothing more than the over anxieties of a great Spirit

1 *whistle*: Sailors superstitiously believe that whistling can bring up a wind.

2 *Shelley ... Death of kings*: Hunt recalled that when he and Shelley were travelling 'in the Hampstead stage' Shelley took a dislike to an old lady, whom he discomfited by crying out to Hunt, 'For Heaven's sake! let us sit upon the ground / And tell sad stories of the death of kings', lines from *Richard II*, III. ii. 155–6 (*Autobiography of Leigh Hunt*, ed. R. Ingpen (London: Constable, 1903), II, p. 38).

3 *how do you . . . Master Vellum*: The Butler praises the verbal dexterity of the Steward in these words in *The Drummer, Or The Haunted House* (1715), IV. i, by Joseph Addison (1672–1719).

4 *Mrs S—*: Mary Wollstonecraft Shelley (1797–1851), the author of *Frankenstein, or the Modern Prometheus* (1818) and the wife of P. B. Shelley. The 'fatal Scissars' refers to Atropos, one of the Fates, whose shears cut off the life of those about to die.

5 *Miss Kent*: Elizabeth Kent, sister of Mrs Leigh Hunt.

6 *the little ones all*: Thornton (1810), John (1812), Mary Florimel Leigh (1814) and Swinburne (1816), Hunt's children.

7 *Junkets*: On 1 July 1817 Hunt wrote to Clarke, 'What has become of Junkets I know not. I suppose Queen Mab has eaten him' (*Recollections*, p. 194). The play on Keats's name alludes to the supposed fondness of the fairy Queen Mab for junkets (see Milton's 'L'Allegro', l. 102).

stretched beyond its strength, and then relapsing for a time to languid inefficiency'. Haydon advised Keats not to 'despair' and to beware of Leigh Hunt's 'self delusions' (L, I, *p. 135).*

To B. R. Haydon
10, 11 May 1817

[Harvard MS]

Margate Saturday Eve

My dear Haydon,

Let Fame, which all hunt after in their Lives,
Live register'd upon our brazen tombs,
And so grace us in the disgrace of death:
When spite of cormorant devouring time
The endeavour of this present breath may buy
That Honor which shall bate his Scythe's keen edge
And make us heirs of all eternity.[1]

To think that I have no right to couple myself with you in this speech would be death to me so I have e'en written it—and I pray God that our brazen Tombs be nigh neighbors. It cannot be long first the endeavor of this present breath will soon be over—and yet it is as well to breathe freely during our sojourn—it is as well if you have not been teased with that Money affair—that bill-pestilence.[2] However I must think that difficulties nerve the Spirit of a Man—they make our Prime Objects a Refuge as well as a Passion. The Trumpet of Fame is as a tower of Strength the ambitious bloweth it and is safe—I suppose by your telling me not to give way to forebodings George has mentioned to you what I have lately said in my Letters to him[3]—truth is I have been in such a state of Mind as to read over my Lines

1 *Let Fame ... all eternity*: *Love's Labour's Lost*, I. i. 1–7, slightly misquoted.
2 *bill-pestilence*: Haydon was chronically short of money.
3 *my Letters to him*: These 'Letters' to George are not known.

and hate them. I am "one that gathers Samphire dreadful trade"[1] the Cliff of Poesy Towers above me—yet when, Tom who meets with some of Pope's Homer in Plutarch's Lives reads some of those to me they seem like Mice to mine. I read and write about eight hours a day. There is an old saying well begun is half done"—'t is a bad one. I would use instead—Not begun at all 'till half done" so according to that I have not begun my Poem and consequently (a priori) can say nothing about it. Thank God! I do begin arduously where I leave off, notwithstanding occasional depressions: and I hope for the support of a High Power while I clime this little eminence and especially in my Years of more momentous Labor. I remember your saying that you had notions of a good Genius presiding over you—I have of late had the same thought. for things which [I] do half at Random are afterwards confirmed by my judgment in a dozen features of Propriety—Is it too daring to Fancy Shakspeare this Presider? When in the Isle of Wight I met with a Shakspeare in the Passage of the House at which I lodged—it comes nearer to my idea of him than any I have seen—I was but there a Week yet the old Woman made me take it with me though I went off in a hurry—Do you not think this is ominous of good? I am glad you say every Man of great Views is at times tormented as I am—Sunday Aft. [11 May] This Morning I received a letter from George by which it appears that Money Troubles are to follow us up for some time to come perhaps for always[2]—these vexations are a great hindrance to one—they are not like Envy and detraction stimulants to further exertion as being immediately relative and reflected on at the same time with the prime object—but rather like a nettle leaf or two in your bed. So now I revoke my Promise of finishing my Poem by the Autumn

1 *one that . . . dreadful trade*: *King Lear*, IV. vi. 15.

2 *Money Troubles . . . perhaps for always*: This is an early sign of the money troubles which were to beset Keats. The immediate cause was probably George's report of the total commercial failure of *Poems* (1817) and Ollier's outraged response to George's unwise letter laying the blame at his door (Roe, pp. 166–7). But Keats was also anxious about the £40 or £50 lent to George for 'Wilkinson's plan' (see above, p. 23), and about the problems over their inheritance.

which I should have done had I gone on as I have done—but I cannot write while my spirit is fevered in a contrary direction and I am now sure of having plenty of it this Summer—At this moment I am in no enviable Situation—I feel that I am not in a Mood to write any to day; and it appears that the loss of it is the beginning of all sorts of irregularities. I am extremely glad that a time must come when every thing will leave not a wrack behind.[1] You tell me never to despair—I wish it was as easy for me to observe the saying—truth is I have a horrid Morbidity of Temperament which has shown itself at intervals—it is I have no doubt the greatest Enemy and stumbling block I have to fear—I may even say that it is likely to be the cause of my disappointment. How ever every ill has its share of good—this very bane would at any time enable me to look with an obstinate eye on the Devil Himself—ay to be as proud of being the lowest of the human race as Alfred[2] could be in being of the highest. I feel confident I should have been a rebel Angel had the opportunity been mine. I am very sure that you do love me as your own Brother—I have seen it in your continual anxiety for me—and I assure you that your wellfare and fame is and will be a chief pleasure to me all my Life. I know no one but you who can be fully sensible of the turmoil and anxiety, the sacrifice of all what is called comfort the readiness to Measure time by what is done and to die in 6 hours could plans be brought to conclusions.—the looking upon the Sun the Moon the Stars, the Earth and its contents as materials to form greater things—that is to say ethereal things———but here I am talking like a Madman[3]—greater things that [*for* than] our Creator himself made!! I wrote to Hunt yesterday—scar[c]ely know what I said in it—I could not talk about Poetry in the way I should have liked for I was not in humor with either his or mine.[4] His self delusions are very lamentable they have inticed

1 *leave not a wrack behind*: *The Tempest*, IV. i. 156.

2 *Alfred*: Alfred the Great (849–99).

3 *Madman*: This word comes at the end of the line: a dash has been added to indicate the syntactical break.

4 *his or mine*: See his comments on Hunt's 'The Nymphs' and *Endymion* (pp. 30–31 and n above).

him into a Situation which I should be less eager after than that of a galley Slave—what you observe thereon is very true must be in time.[1] Perhaps it is a self delusion to say so—but I think I could not be dece[i]ved in the Manner that Hunt is—may I die tomorrow if I am to be. There is no greater Sin after the 7 deadly than to flatter oneself into an idea of being a great Poet—or one of those beings who are privileged to wear out their Lives in the pursuit of Honor—how comfortable a feel it is that such a Crime must bring its heavy Penalty? That if one can be a Self deluder accounts will be balanced? I am glad you are hard at Work—'t will now soon be done—I long to see Wordsworth's as well as to have mine in:[2] but I would rather not show my face in Town till the end of the Year—if that will be time enough—if not I shall be disappointed if you do not write for me even when you think best—I never quite despair and I read Shakspeare—indeed I shall I think never read any other Book much—Now this might lead me into a long Confab but I desist. I am very near Agreeing with Hazlit that Shakspeare is enough for us—By the by what a tremendous Southean Article his last was—I wish he had left out "grey hairs"[3] It was very gratifying to meet your remarks of the Manuscript[4]—I was reading Anthony and Cleopat[ra] when I got the Paper and there are several Passages applicable to the events you commentate. You say that he arrived by degrees, and not by any single Struggle to the Height of his ambition—and that his Life had been as common in particulars as other Mens—Shakspeare makes Enobarb say—Where's Antony Eros—He's walking in the garden—thus: <u>and spurns the rush that lies</u> before him,

1 *what you observe ... in time*: In his letter Haydon had said that the immorality of Hunt's private life would destroy his reputation and the causes he supported.

2 *Wordsworth's ... mine in*: Haydon told Keats he had 'rubbed in Wordsworth's [portrait]' in his *Christ's Entry into Jerusalem* and might include Keats's 'head' (which he did).

3 *grey hairs*: See above, p. 29.

4 *your remarks ... Manuscript*: Haydon's review, signed 'B. H. R.', in the *Examiner* (4 May), pp. 275–6, of *Bonaparte: Manuscrit venu de St. Hélène* (London, 1817), really written by M. J. G. Lullin de Châteauvieux.

cries fool, Lepidus! In the same scene we find: "let determined things to destiny hold unbewailed their way".[1] Dolabella says of Antony's Messenger

"An argument that he is pluck'd when hither
He sends so poor a pinion of his wing"—Then again,
Eno—"I see Men's Judgments are
A parcel of their fortunes; and things outward
Do draw the inward quality after them,
To suffer all alike"[2]—The following applies well to Bertram[3]

"Yet he that can endure
To follow with allegience a fallen Lord,
Does conquer him that did his Master conquer,
And earns a place i' the story"

But how differently does Buonap bear his fate from Anthony!

'T is good too that the Duke of Wellington has a good Word or so in the Examiner[4] A Man ought to have the Fame he deserves—and I begin to think that detracting from him as well as from Wordsworth is the same thing. I wish he had a little more taste—and did not in that respect "deal in Lieutenantry"[5] You should have heard from me before this—but in the first place I did not like to do so before I had got a little way in the 1st Book and in the next as G. told me you were going to write I delayed till I had hea[r]d from you—Give my Respects the next time you write to the North[6] and also to John Hunt[7]—Remember

1 *Where's Antony . . . their way*: *Antony and Cleopatra*, III. v. 15–17 and III. vi. 84–5.

2 *An argument . . . all alike*: *Antony and Cleopatra*, III. xii. 3–4; III. xiii. 31–4, 43–6. Enobarbus stood by Antony in defeat.

3 *Bertram*: Comte Henri-Gatien Bertrand (1773–1844), French general and aide-de-camp to Napoleon (1769–1821), who accompanied his defeated leader in exile on Elba and then on St Helena.

4 *Duke of Wellington . . . Examiner*: Haydon noted that Wellington was not mentioned in the book under review.

5 *deal in Lieutenantry*: *Antony and Cleopatra*, III. xi. 39.

6 *to the North*: To Wordsworth.

7 *John Hunt*: Hunt's brother John (1775–1848), co-proprietor and printer of the *Examiner*.

me to Reynolds and tell him to write, Ay, and when you sent Westward tell your Sister that I mentioned her in this—So now in the Name of Shakespeare Raphael and all our Saints I commend you to the care of heaven!

Your everlasting friend
John Keats—

To Taylor and Hessey
16 May 1817

[Harvard MS]

Margate [Friday] May 16—

My dear Sirs,

I am extremely indebted to you for your liberality in the Shape of manufactu[r]ed rag value £20 and shall immediately proceed to destroy some of the Minor Heads of that spr[i]ng-headed Hydra[1] the Dun—To conquer which the knight need have no Sword. Shield Cuirass Cuisses Herbadgeon spear Casque, Greves, Pauldrons Spurs Chevron or any other scaly commodity: but he need only take the Bank Note of Faith and Cash of Salvation,[2] and set out against the Monster invoking the aid of no Archimago[3] or Urganda[4]—and finger me the Paper light as the Sybils Leaves in Virgil[5] whereat the Fiend skulks off with his tail between his Legs. Touch him with this enchanted Paper and he whips you his head away as fast as a Snail's Horn—but then the horrid Propensity he has to put it up again has discouraged many very valliant Knights—He is such a never ending still beginning sort of a Body—like my Landlady of the Bell—I should conjecture that the very Spright

1 *spr[i]ng-headed Hydra*: *The Faerie Queene*, II. xii. 23.
2 *Bank Note . . . Salvation*: Echoing Ephesians 6:15–16.
3 *Archimago*: The enchanter in *The Faerie Queene*, I–II.
4 *Urganda*: The enchantress in the fifteenth-century Spanish romance *Amadis of Gaul*.
5 *Virgil*: See his *Aeneid*, III. 445–52. Apollo's priestess, the Sibyl at Cumae, wrote her prophecies on leaves which were scattered to the winds.

that the "g[r]een sour ringlets makes [w]hereof the Ewe not bites"[1] had manufactured it of the dew fallen on said sour ringlets—I think I could make a nice little Alegorical Poem called "the Dun" Where we wold have the Castle of Carelessness—the Draw Bridge of Credit—Sir Novelty Fashion'[s][2] expedition against the City of Taylors—&c &c———I went day by day at my Poem for a Month at the end of which time the other day I found my Brain so overwrought that I had neither Rhyme nor reason in it—so was obliged to give up for a few days—I hope soon to be able to resume my Work—I have endeavoured to do so once or twice but to no Purpose—instead of Poetry I have a swimming in my head—And feel all the effects of a Mental Debauch—lowness of Spirits—anxiety to go on without the Power to do so which does not at all tend to my ultimate Progression—However tomorrow I will begin my next Month—This evening I go to Cantrerbury—having got tired of Margate—I was not right in my head when I came—At Cant^y^ I hope the Remembrance of Chaucer will set me forward like a Billiard-Ball—I am gald [*for* glad] to hear of M^r^ T[aylor]'s health and of the Wellfare of the In-town-Stayers" and think Reynolds will like his trip—I have some idea of seeing the Continent some time in the summer—

In repeating how sensible I am of your kindness I remain

Your Obedient Servt and Friend

John Keats—

I shall be very happy to hear any little intelligence in the literary or friendly way when you have time to scribble—

Messrs Taylor and Hessey.—

After leaving Margate, Keats stayed for few days in Canterbury before moving to Bo Peep near Hastings at the end of May. There he first met Mrs Isabella Jones (see p. 256–8, 308 below for their later encounters). By 10 June Keats was back living at

1 *g[r]een . . . bites*: *The Tempest*, V. i. 36–7.

2 *Sir Novelty Fashion*: A character in the comedy *Love's Last Shift* (1696) by Colley Cibber (1671–1757).

Well Walk with his brothers. He was again short of money, from then on a recurrent feature of his life.

To Taylor and Hessey
10 June 1817

[Harvard MS]

[Well Walk, Hampstead]
Tuesday Morn—

My dear Sirs,

I must endeavour to lose my Maidenhead with respect to money Matters as soon as possible—and I will to—so here goes—A Couple of Duns[1] that I thought would be silent till the beginning, at least, of next Month (when I am certain to be on my legs for certain sure) have opened upon me with a cry most "untunable" never did you hear such un "gallant chiding"[2]

Now you must know I am not desolate but have thank God 25 good Notes in my fob—but then you know I laid them by to write with and would stand at Bay a fortnight ere they should grab me—In a Month's time I must pay—but it would relieve my Mind if I owed you instead of these Pelican duns.[3]

I am affraid you will say I have "wound about with circumstance"[4] when I should have asked plainly—However as I said I am a little maidenish or so—and I feel my virginity come strong upon me—the while I request the loan of a £20 and a £10—which if you would enclose to me I would acknowledge and save myself a hot forehead—I am sure you are confident in my responsibility—and in the sense [of] squareness that is always in me—

Your obliged friend
John Keats—

1 *Duns*: Debt collectors or importunate creditors.
2 *untunable . . . gallant chiding*: *A Midsummer Night's Dream*, IV. i. 121, which has 'tuneable', 112.
3 *these Pelican duns*: *King Lear*, III. 4. 74, 'Those pelican daughters'.
4 *wound . . . circumstance*: *The Merchant of Venice*, I. i. 154.

After this letter to his publishers there is a gap in Keats's correspondence. Apart from a brief note to Haydon no letters written between mid-June and the end of August are now known.

During the summer Keats spent time with Reynolds's family at their home in Little Britain, becoming friendly with his two elder sisters, Jane (1791–1846) and Marianne (1797–1874). There, too, he saw more of Benjamin Bailey, who was courting Marianne Reynolds. In the meantime George Felton Mathew published a grudging review of Poems *(1817) in the May issue of the* European Magazine. *Hunt's largely positive review was spread over three issues of the* Examiner *(1 June, 6 and 13 July), and 'On the Sea', which Keats had sent Reynolds from Carisbrooke, appeared in the* Champion *on 17 July. Keats completed the second book of* Endymion *in August and read passages from it to Cowden Clarke and Severn 'one Sunday' that month. Bailey, who was reading for holy orders, invited Keats to stay with him in Magdalen Hall, Oxford, while George and Tom were in Paris. Keats caught the coach to Oxford on 3 September. He stayed with Bailey for the rest of the month and, in a remarkable burst of creativity, drafted the whole of the third book of* Endymion. *But he began his visit by writing a lighthearted letter to Reynolds's sisters, who had gone for a seaside holiday at Littlehampton in Sussex, and sending Reynolds a parody of Wordsworth.*

To Jane and Marianne Reynolds
4 September 1817

[Harvard MS]

[Thursday, Magdalen Hall,] Oxf—

My dear friends,

You are I am glad to hear comfortable at Hampton where I hope you will receive the Biscuts we ate the other night at Little Brittain. I hope you found them good. There you are among Sands Stocks Stones Pebbles Beaches Cliffs Rocks Deeps Shallows Weeds Ships Boats (at a distance) Carrots—turnips Sun

Moon and Stars and all those sort of things—here am I among Colleges, Halls Stalls plenty of Trees thank God—plenty of Water thank heaven—plenty of Books thank the Muses—plenty of Snuff—thank Sir Walter Raleigh—plenty of Sagars,[1] ditto—plenty of flat Country—thank Tellus's[2] rol[l]ing pin. I'm on the Sofa—Buonopa[r]te is on the Snuff Box—but you are by the <sea> side—argal[3] you bathe—you walk—you say how beautiful—find out resemb<lan>ces between waves and Camels—rocks and dancing Masters—fireshovels and telescopes—Dolphins and Madonas—which word by the way I must acquaint you was derived from the Syriac and came down in a way which neither of you I am sorry to say are at all capaple of comprehending: but as a time may come when by your occasional converse with me you may arrive at "something like prophetic strain"[4] I will unbar the Gates of my Pride and let my Condecension stalk forth like a Ghost at the Circus—The Word Madon a my dear Ladies or—the Word—Mad-o-na—So I say! I am not mad—Howsumever When that aged Tamer Kewthon[5] sold a Certain Camel Called Peter to the Overseer of the Babel Skyworks, he thus spake, adjusting his Cravat round the tip of his Chin—My dear Ten Storyupinair—this here Beast though I say it as shouldn't say't not only has the Power of subsisting 40 day and 40 Nights without fire and Candle but he can sing—here I have in my Pocket a Certificate from Signor Nicolini[6] of the King's Theatre a Certificate to this effect xxxxxxxx I have had dinner since I left that effect upon you and feel to heavy in mentibus to display all the Profundity of the Polyglon—so you had better

1 *Sagars*: A common spelling of 'cigars' at the time.
2 *Tellus*: The Titan god of the earth.
3 *argal*: A perversion of *ergo* ('therefore'), as used by the Clown in *Hamlet*, V. i. 12.
4 *something . . . strain*: Milton's 'Il Penseroso', l. 174.
5 *Tamer Kewthon*: Apparently an invented name, like the following story of the camel, St Peter and the Tower of Babel, based on an engraving of the last in Henry Southwell's *Universal Family Bible* (1773), a copy of which Keats owned.
6 *Signor Nicolini*: Nicolo Grimaldi (1673–1732), Italian mezzo-soprano castrato, stage name Nicolini, who sang title roles in Handel's operas on the London stage.

each of you take a glass of cherry branday and drink to the health of Archimedes who was of so benign a disposition that the [*for* he] never would [leave] Syracuse in his Life so kept himself out of all knight errant[r]y—this I know to be a fact for it is written in the 45 Book of Winkine's treatise on Garden rollers that he trod on a fishwoman's toe in Liverpool and never begged her pardon—Now the long and the short is this—that is by comparison. for a long day may be a short year—a long Pole may <be a very stupid fel>low as a Man[1]—But let us refresh ourself from this dept[h] of thinking and turn to some innocent Jocularity—the Bow cannot always be bent nor the gun always loaded if you ever let it off and the Life of Man is like a great Mountain—his breath is like a Shrewsbury Cake—he comes into the world like a Shoeblack and goes out of it like a Cobler—he eats like a Chimneysweeper, drinks like a Gingerbread Baker and breaths like Achilles—So it being that we are such sublunary creatures let us endeavour to correct all our bad Spelling all our most delightful Abominations and let us wish health to Marian and Jane whoever they be and wherever—Your's truly

John Keats—

To J. H. Reynolds
Fragment, 4(?) September 1817

[Woodhouse transcript (1818)][2]

[Thursday, Magdalen Hall]

Lines—
Rhymed in a Letter to J. H. R. from Oxford.

1 *a long Pole ... a Man*: Possibly an allusion to William Pole-Tylney-Long-Wellesley (1788–1857), 4th Earl of Mornington (MBF).

2 Text from Woodhouse's 'Commonplace book of poems' (W[2]). Normally dated 'September', but 4(?) September inferred here because Keats's reference to 'plenty of trees' appears in both this parody of Wordsworth and his letter to the Reynolds sisters.

"Wordsworth sometimes, though in a fine way, gives us sentences in the Style of School exercises—for Instance

The lake doth glitter
Small birds twitter &c.[1]

Now I think this is an excellent method of giving a very clear description of an interesting place such as Oxford is—

// The Gothic looks solemn,—
The plain Doric column
Supports an old Bishop & crosier;
The mouldering arch,
Shaded o'er by a larch,
Lives next door to Wilson the hosier

Vicè—that is, by turns—
O'er pale visages mourns
The black-tassel trencher, or common-hat:
The Chauntry boy sings,
The steeple bell rings,
And as for the Chancellor—dominat.

There are plenty of trees,
And plenty of ease,
And plenty of fat deer for parsons;
And when it is venison,
Short is the benison,—
Then each on a leg or thigh fastens.

// J.K.

---

1 *The lake . . . twitter &c*: Wordsworth's 'Written in March, While Resting on the Bridge at the Foot of Brother's Water', ll. 3–4.

hope you will see early in the next year—Perhaps you might like to know what I am writing about—I will tell you—

Many Years ago there was a young handsome Shepherd who fed his flocks on a Mountain's Side called Latmus—he was a very contemplative sort of a Person and lived solitry among the trees and Plains little thinking—that such a beautiful Creature as the Moon was growing mad in Love with him—However so it was; and when he was asleep on the Grass, she used to come down from heaven and admire him excessively from [*for* for] a long time; and at last could not refrain from carying him away in her arms to the top of that high Mountain Latmus while he was a dreaming—but I dare say [you] have read this and all the other beautiful Tales which have come down from the ancient times of that beautiful Greece. If you have not let me know and I will tell you more at large of others quite as delightful—

This Oxford I have no doubt is the finest City in the world—it is full of old Gothic buildings—Spires—towers—Quadrangles—Cloisters Groves &[c] and is surrounded with more Clear streams than ever I saw together—I take a Walk by the Side of one of them every Evening and thank God, we have not had a drop of rain these many days—I had a long and interesting Letter from George, cross lines by a short one from Tom yesterday dated Paris—They both send their loves to you—Like most Englishmen they feel a mighty preference for every thing English—the french Meadows the trees the People the Towns the Churches, the Books the every thing—although they may be in themselves good; yet when put in comparison with our green Island they all vanish like Swallows in October. They have seen Cathedrals Manuscripts. Fountains, Pictures, Tragedy Comedy,—with other things you may by chance meet with in this Country such a[s] Washerwomen, Lamplighters, Turnpikemen Fish kettles, Dancing Masters, kettle drums, Sentry Boxes, Rocking Horses &c and, now they have taken them over a set of boxing gloves—I have written to George and requested him, as you wish I shou<ld,> to write to you. I have been writing very hard lately even till an utter incapacity came on, and I feel it now about my head: so you must not mind a little out of the way sayings—though bye the bye where [*for* were] my brain as clear as a bell I think I should have a little propensity thereto. I shall stop here till I have finished the 3rd Book of my Story; which I hope will be accomplish'd in at most three Weeks from to day—about which time you shall see me. How do you like Miss Taylor's essays in Rhyme—I just look'd into the Book and it appeared to me suitable to you—especially since I remember your liking for those pleasant little things the Original Poems[1]—the essays are the more mature production of the same hand. While I was speaking about france it occured to me to speak a few Words on their Language—it is perhaps the poorest one ever spoken since the jabbering in the Tower of Ba<bel> and when you come to know that the real use and greatness of a Tongue is to be referred to its Literature—you will be astonished to find how very inferior it is to our native Speech—I wish the Italian would supersede french in every School throughout the Country for that is full of real Poetry and Romance of a kind more fitted for the Pleasure of Ladies than perhaps our own—It seems that the only end to be gained in acquiring french—is the immense accomplishment of speaking it—it is none at all—a most lamentable mistake indeed—Italian indeed would sound most musically from Lips which had b[e] gan to pronounce it as early as french is cramme'd down our Mouths, as if we were young Jack daws at the mercy of an overfeeding Schoolboy.

Now Fanny you must write soon—and write all you think about, never mind what—only let me have a good deal of your writing—You need not so it all at once—be two or three or four day about it, and let it be a diary of your little life. You will preserve all my Letters and I will secure yours—and thus in the course of time we shall each of us have a good Bundle—which, hereafter, when things may have strangely altered and god knows what happened, we may read over together and look

1 *Miss Taylor's essays in Rhyme . . . the Original Poems*: Jane Taylor's *Essays in Rhyme, or Morals and Manners* (1816) and Jane and Ann Taylor's *Original Poems for Infant Minds* (1804, etc.), both Taylor and Hessey publications by 1817.

with pleasure on times past—that now are to come—Give my respects to the Ladies—and so my dear Fanny I am ever

Your most affectionate Brother

John.

If you direct—Post Office Oxford—your Letter will be brought to me—

To J. H. Reynolds

21 September 1817

[Woodhouse transcript (1821?)]

[Magdalen Hall]
Oxford Sunday Morn

My dear Reynolds.

So you are determined to be my mortal foe—draw a Sword at me, and I will forgive—Put a Bullet in my Brain, and I will shake it out as a dewdrop from the Lion's Mane;[1]—put me on a Gridiron, and I will fry with great complancency—but, oh horror! to come upon me in the shape of a Dun! Send me Bills! as I say to my Taylor send me Bills and I'll never employ you more—However, needs must when the devil drives: and for fear of "before and behind Mr Honeycomb"[2] I'll proceed—I have not time to elucidate the forms and shapes of the grass and trees; for, rot it! I forgot to bring my mathematical case with me; which unfortunately contained my triangular Prism so that the hues of the grass cannot be dissected for you—

For these last five or six days, we have had regularly a Boat on the Isis, and explored all the streams about, which are more in number than your eye lashes. We sometimes skim into a Bed of rushes, and there become naturalized riverfolks,—there is

1 *as a dewdrop . . . Lion's Mane*: *Troilus and Cressida*, III. iii. 224–5.

2 *before . . . Honeycomb*: The Bailiff's catchphrase when dunning the excessively generous Will Honeywood in *The Good Natur'd Man* (1768), III, by Oliver Goldsmith (?1730–74). Will Honeycomb was a character in the *Spectator*.

one particularly nice nest which we have christened "Reynolds's Cove"—in which we have read Wordsworth and talked as may be. I think I see you and Hunt meeting in the Pit.—What a very pleasant fellow he is, if he would give up the sovereignty of a Room pro bono—What Evenings we might pass with him, could we have him from M[rs] H— Failings I am always rather rejoiced to find in a Man than sorry for; they bring us to a Level—He has them,—but then his makes-up are very good. He agrees with the Northe[r]n Poet in this, "He is not one of those who much delight to season their fireside with personal talk"[1]—I must confess however having a little itch that way. and at this present I have a few neighbourly remarks to make—The world, and especially our England, has within the last thirty year's been vexed and teased by a set of Devils, whom I detest so much that I almost hunger after an acherontic promotion to a Torturer, purposely for their accommodation; These Devils are a set of Women, who having taken a snack or Luncheon of Literary scraps, set themselves up for towers of Babel in Languages Sapphos in Poetry—Euclids in Geometry—and everything in nothing. Among such the Name of Montague has been preeminent.[2] The thing has made a very uncomfortable impression on me.—I had longed for some real feminine Modesty in these things, and was therefore gladdened in the extreme on opening the other day one of Bayley's Books—a Book of Poetry written by one beautiful M[rs] Philips, a friend of Jeremy Taylor's, and called "the matchless Orinda"[3]—You must have heard of her, and most likely read her Poetry—I wish you have

1 *He is not . . . personal talk*: Wordsworth's 'Personal Talk', ll. 1–2, 'I am not One who much or oft delight / To season my fireside with personal talk.'

2 *a set of Women . . . Montague has been preeminent*: Keats's more than half-serious outburst against this 'set of Women' is indicative of his conventional ideas of femininity. Elizabeth Montagu (1720–1800), author and literary patron, was a prominent member of the late eighteenth-century group of intellectual women, mockingly known as 'Blue Stockings'.

3 *Bayley's Books . . . M[rs] Philips . . . the matchless Orinda*: Katherine Philips (1631–64), a royalist poet known as the 'Matchless Orinda'. Bailey's edition must have been *Poems by the Incomparable Mrs. K. P.* (1664), an octavo (see *The Collected Works of Katherine Philips*, ed. Patrick Thomas (Stump Cross: Stump Cross Books, 1990–93), I, p. 359).

5

Inspired with a flame divine
  I scorn to court a stay;
For from that noble soul of thine
  I ne'er can be away.
But I shall weep when thou dost grieve
Nor can I die whilst thou dost live

6

By my own temper I shall guess
  At thy felicity,
And only like my happiness
  Because it pleaseth thee.
Our hearts at any time will tell
If thou, or I be sick or well.

—7—

All honour sure I must pretend,
  All that is good or great;
She that would be Rosania's friend,
  Must be at least compleat,[1]
If I have any Bravery,
'Tis cause I have so much of thee

8

Thy Leiger Soul in me shall lie,
  And all thy thoughts reveal;
Then back again with mine shall flie
  And thence to me shall steal.
Thus still to one another tend;
Such is the sacred name of friend.

1 *compleat*: (Woodhouse's note) 'A compleat friend—this Line sounded very oddly to me at first.'

9–

Thus our twin souls in one shall grow,
  And teach the world new Love,
Redeem the age and sex, and show
  A Flame Fate dares not move:
And courting death to be our friend,
Our Lives together too shall end

10

A Dew shall dwell upon our Tomb
  of such a Quality
That fighting Armies thither come
  Shall reconciled be
We'll ask no epitaph but say
Orinda and Rosannia.

In other of her Poems there is a most delicate fancy of the Fletcher Kind—which we will con over together: So Haydon is in Town—I had a letter from him yesterday[1]—We will contrive as the Winter comes on—but that [is] neither here nor there. Have you heard from Rice? Has Martin[2] met with the Cumberland Beggar or been wondering at the old Leech gatherer? Has he a turn for fossils? that is, is he capable of sinking up to his Middle in a Morass?—I have longed to peep in and see him at supper after some tolerable fatigue. How is Hazlitt? We were reading his Table[3] last night—I know he thinks himself not estimated by ten People in the world—I wishe he knew he is—I am getting on famous with my third Book—have written 800 lines thereof, and hope to finish it next week—Bailey likes what I have done very much—Believe me, my Dear Reynolds, one of my chief layings-up is the pleasure I shall have in showing it to

1 *a letter from him yesterday*: See Keats's answer, 28 September 1817.
2 *Martin*: John Martin (1791–1855), a partner in Rodwell and Martin, the booksellers and publishers, 46 New Bond Street, London. A friend of Reynolds and publisher of his early work, Martin published editions by Charles Dilke. After retiring he became a noted bibliographer.
3 *Table*: Hazlitt's and Hunt's two-volume *Round Table* (1817).

you; I may now say, in a few days—I have heard twice from my Brothers, they are going on very well, and send their Remembrances to you. We expected to have had notices from little Hampton this Morning—we must wait till Tuesday. I am glad of their Days with the Dilks.[1] You are I know very much teased in that precious London, and want all the rest possible; so shall be content with as brief a scrall—a word or two—till there comes a pat hour.—

Send us a few of your Stanzas to read in "Reynolds's cove" Give my Love and respects to your Mother and remember me kindly to all at home. Yours faithfully

John Keats

I have left the doublings[2] for Bailey who is going to say that he will write to you to Morrow.

*Bailey's additions on the 'doubling' testify to the swiftness with which Keats could compose. He reported that 'last night' (Saturday) Keats had written a forty-line passage 'on death' (*Endymion*, III, 766–806) which 'beats all he has written' (*KC*, I, 6–7). Keats completed Book III on 26 September. The next day he took up a request from Haydon, which was to involve him until the following February. Haydon had been impressed by the work of a young painter, Charles Cripps (b. 1796), when visiting Oxford the previous month. He asked Keats to track down Cripps and to judge whether he had 'ambition' and 'power' and if he wished 'to be great' as a painter. If so, Haydon would train him for a year, provided Keats's friends, including Bailey and Keats, would support him to live in London (*L, I, p. 161). Cripps joined Haydon's other pupils in his studio later that autumn. But over the next few months Keats found himself acting as an intermediary first between Haydon and Bailey, and*

1 *their Days with the Dilks*: The Reynolds sisters left Littlehampton for a visit to Bedhampton, staying with John Snook, the husband of Charles Dilke's sister, when Dilke and his family were also there.

2 *doublings*: The two flaps leaving blank space for more writing, when folding a letter for the post.

then between the painter and Cripps, while at the same time trying to drum up financial support for the latter (see below, pp. 66, 87 and 110). Keats's attempt at artistic patronage demonstrates his assumption (one shared by his acquaintances at this time) that he had private means.

To B. R. Haydon

28 September 1817

[Harvard MS]

[Magdalen Hall]
Oxford [Sunday] Septr 28th—

My dear Haydon,

I read your last[1] to the young Man whose Name is Crips. He seemed more than ever anxious to avail himself of your offer. I think I told you we asked him to ascertain his Means. He does not possess the Philosophers stone—nor Fortunatus' purse,[2] nor Gyges' ring[3]—but at Bailey's suggestion, whom I assure you is a very capital fellow, we have stummed up[4] a kind of contrivance whereby he will be enabled to do himself the benifits you will lay in his Path—I have a great Idea that he will be a tolerable neat brush. 'T is perhaps the finest thing that will befal him this many a year: for he is just of an age to get grounded in bad habits from which you will pluck him. He brought a Copy of Mary Queen of Scotts. it appears to me that he has coppied the bad style of the painting as well as couloured the eyebals yellow like the original. He has also the fault that you pointed out to

1 *your last*: Haydon's letter of 17 September asking Keats to approach Charles Cripps (on whom see headnote above). It reached Keats on Saturday, 20 September (*L*, I, p. 161).

2 *Fortunatus' purse*: Fortunatus was a legendary medieval hero with an inexhaustible purse.

3 *Gyges' ring*: A Lydian king, Gyges was famous for his prodigious wealth and magic ring of invisibility.

4 *stummed up*: 'To set going, work up' (*OED*, noting 'The use may be due to some misapprehension').

me in Hazlitt[1]—on the constringing[2] and diffusing of substance. However I really believe that he will take fire at the sight of your Picture—and set about things. If he can get ready in time to return to Town with me which will be in a few days—I will bring [him] to you. You will be glad to hear that within these last three weeks I have written 1000 lines—which are the third Book of my Poem. My Ideas with respect to it I assure you are very low—and I would write the subject thoroughly again. but I am tired of it and think the time would be better spent in writing a new Romance which I have in my eye for next summer—Rome was not built in a Day. and all the good I expect from my employment this summer is the fruit of Experience which I hope to gather in my next Poem. Bailey's kindest wishes and my vow of being

Yours eternally.
John Keats—

On Thursday, 2 October Keats and Bailey visited Shakespeare's birthplace and the church at Stratford-upon-Avon. The following Sunday he rejoined his brothers in Hampstead.

To Benjamin Bailey
8 October 1817

[Harvard MS]

[Well Walk]
Hamps[t]ead Oct[r] Wednesday

My dear Bailey,

After a tolerable journey I went from Coach to Coach to as far as Hampstead where I found my Brothers—the next Morning finding myself tolerably well I went to Lambs Conduit

1 *fault . . . in Hazlitt*: Hazlitt had hoped to be a painter. His portrait of Charles Lamb is in the National Portrait Gallery, London.
2 *constringing*: A medical word (like 'diffusing'), it means 'causing constriction' (James Alleyne, *New English Dispensatory* (1733 edn), p. 591).

Street[1] and delivered your Parcel—Jane and Marianne were greatly improved Marianne especially she has no unhealthy plumpness in the face—but she comes me healthy and angular to the Chin—I did not see John I was extrem<e>ly sorry to hear that poor Rice after having had capital Health During his tour, was very ill. I dare say you have heard from him. From No 19 I went to Hunt's and Haydon's who live now neighbours.[2] Shelley was there—I know nothing about any thing in this part of the world—every Body seems at Loggerheads. There's Hunt infatuated—theres Haydon's Picture in statu quo. There's Hunt walks up and down his painting room criticising every head most unmercifully—There's Horace Smith[3] tired of Hunt. The web of our Life is of mingled Yarn"[4] Haydon having removed entirely from Marlborough street Crips[5] must direct his Letter to Lisson Grove North Paddington. Yesterday Morning while I was at Brown's in came Reynolds—he was pretty bobbish we had a pleasant day—but he would walk home at night that cursed cold distance. Mrs Bentley's children[6] are making a horrid row—whereby I regret I cannot be transported to your Room to write to you. I am quite disgusted with literary Men and will never know another except Wordsworth—no not even Byron—Here is an instance of the friendships of such—Haydon and Hunt have known each other many years—now they live pour ainsi dire jealous Neighbours. Haydon says to me Keats dont show your Lines to Hunt on any account or he will have done half for you—so it appears Hunt wishes it to be thought. When he met Reynolds in the Theatre John told him that I was getting on to the completion of 4000 Lines. Ah! says Hunt, had it not been for me they would have been 7000! If he

1 *Lambs Conduit Street*: The Reynolds family lived at 19 Lamb's Conduit Street, Little Britain, London.
2 *Hunt's and Haydon's . . . neighbours*: Hunt had moved to 22 Lisson Grove, North Paddington, London.
3 *Horace Smith*: (1779–1849), writer and humorist, and friend of Hunt.
4 *The web . . . mingled Yarn*: *All's Well That Ends Well*, IV. iii. 67–8.
5 *Crips*: Cripps was as yet in Oxford.
6 *Mrs Bentley's children*: The wife and children of Benjamin Bentley, from whom the brothers rented their rooms in Well Walk, Hampstead.

will say this to Reynolds what would he to other People? Haydon received a Letter a little while back on this subject from some Lady—which contains a caution to me through him on this subject—Now is not all this a most paultry thing to think about? You may see the whole of the case by the following extract from a Letter I wrote to George in the Spring[1] "As to "what you say about my being a Poet, I can retu[r]n no answer "but by saying that the high Idea I have of poetical fame makes "me think I see it towering to high above me. At any rate I have "no right to talk until Endymion is finished—it will be a test, a "trial of my Powers of Imagination and chiefly of my invention "which is a rare thing indeed—by which I must make 4000 "Lines of one bare circumstance and fill them with Poetry; and "when I consider that this is a great task, and that when done it "will take me but a dozen paces towards the Temple of Fame— "it makes me say—God forbid that I should be without such a "task! I have heard Hunt say and [I] may be asked—why "endeavour after a long Poem? To which I should answer—Do "not the Lovers of Poetry like to have a little Region to wander "in where they may pick and choose, and in which the images "are so numerous that many are forgotten and found new in a "second Reading: which may be food for a Week's stroll in the "Summer? Do not they like this better than what they can read "through before Mrs Williams comes down stairs? a Morning "work at most. Besides a long Poem is a test of Invention which "I take to be the Polar Star of Poetry, as Fancy is the Sails, and "Imagination the Rudder. Did our great Poets ever write short "Pieces? I mean in the shape of Tales—This same invention "seems i<n>ndeed of late Years to have been forgotten as a "Poetical excellence<—>But enough of this, I put on no Laurels "till I shall have finished Endymion, and I hope Apollo is <not>

1 *I wrote to George in the Spring*: This letter is unknown. This is the one extensive occasion on which Keats uses double quotes down the left-hand margin to indicate that he is copying out another text, a nineteenth-century print convention. Here it emphasizes the importance of this passage to Keats.

"angered at my having made a Mockery at him at Hunt's"[1] You see Bailey how independant my writing has been—Hunts dissuasion was of no avail—I refused to visit Shelley, that I might have my own unfetterd scope—and after all I shall have the Reputation of Hunt's elevé—His corrections and amputations will by the knowing ones be trased in the Poem—This is to be sure the vexation of a day—nor would I say so many Words about it to any but those whom I know to have my wellfare and Reputation at Heart—Haydon promised to give directions for those Casts[2] and you may expect to see them soon—with as many Letters You will soon hear the dinning of Bells—never mind you and Gleg[3] will defy the foul fiend[4]—But do not sacrifice your heal[t]h to Books do take it kindly and not so voraciously. I am certain if you are your own Physician your stomach will resume its proper strength and then what great Benefits will follow. My Sister wrote a Letter to me which I think must be at y[e] post office Ax Will[5] to see. My Brothers kindest remembrances to you—we are going to dine at Brown's where I have some hopes of meeting Reynolds. The little Mercury I have taken has corrected the Poison[6] and improved my Health—though I feel from my employment that I shall never be again secure in Robustness—would that you were as well as

your sincere friend & brother

John Keats

The Dilks are expected to day—

1 *made a Mockery . . . at Hunt's*: Recalling the occasion recorded in the sonnets 'On Receiving a Laurel Crown from Leigh Hunt' and 'To the Ladies who Saw Me Crowned', which led Keats to write his apologetic 'Ode to Apollo' ('God of the golden bow').

2 *Casts*: Presumably of his life mask of Keats.

3 *Gleg*: Bailey's room-mate George Robert Gleig (1796–1888), fellow student at Magdalen Hall, Oxford, the son of the Scottish Episcopal Bishop of Brechin, and later Bailey's brother-in-law (see below, p. 310 and n). Keats often spells as 'Gleg'.

4 *foul fiend*: *King Lear*, III. iv. 96.

5 *Ax Will*: 'Slang expression, possibly referring to a college servant' (Gittings).

6 *Mercury . . . the Poison*: Keats's use of mercury was the recommended treatment for gonorrhoea, which he may have contracted in Oxford (see Gittings, *John Keats*, pp. 234–7, 642–9; also below, pp. 59, 238). Keats's final comment may indicate that Bailey was suffering from the same complaint.

To Benjamin Bailey
28, 29–30 October 1817

[Harvard MS]

[Well Walk, Hampstead,
Tuesday, 28 October]

My dear Bailey,

So you have got a Curacy! good—but I suppose you will be obliged to stop among your Oxford favorites during term-time—never mind. When do you p[r]each your first sermon tell me—for I shall propose to the two R s[1] to hear it so dont look into any of the old corner oaken pews for fear of being put out by us—Poor Johnny Martin cant be there He is ill—I suspect—but that's neither here nor there—all I can say I wish him as well through it as I am like to be. For this fortnight I have been confined at Hampstead[2]—Saturday evening was my first day in town—when I went to Rices as we intend to do every Saturday till we know not when—Rice had some business at Highgate yesterday—so he came over to me and I detained him for the first time of I hope 24860 times. We hit upon an old Gent.[3] we had known some few years ago and had a veray pleausante daye, In this World there is no quiet nothing but teasing and snubbing and vexation—my Brother Tom look'd very unwell yesterday and I am for shipping him off to Lisbon. perpaps I ship there with him. I have not seen M[rs] Reynolds since I left you—wherefore my conscience smites me—I think of seeing her tomorrow have you any Message? I hope Gleg came soon after I left.

1 *the two R s*: James Rice and J. H. Reynolds. But Bailey did not get this curacy (see below, p. 64).

2 *Hampstead*: If the illness Keats was treating with mercury 'confined' him to the house, he was unable to leave Well Walk from at least 8 to 25 September. He also suspected that their bookseller friend John Martin was suffering from the same ailment.

3 *an old Gent*: Chaucer (Gittings).

I dont suppose I've w[r]itten as many Lines as you have read Volumes or at least Chapters since I saw you. However, I am in a fair way now to come to a conclusion in at least three Weeks when I assure you I shall be glad to dismount for a Month or two—although I'll keep as tight a reign as possible till then nor suffer myself to sleep. I will copy for you the opening of the 4 Book—in which you will see from the Manner I had not an opportunity of mentioning any Poets, for fear of spoiling the effect of the passage by particularising them!

Muse of my Native Land, Loftiest Muse!
O First born of the Mountains, by the hues
Of Heaven on the spiritual air begot—
Long didst thou sit alone in northern grot
While yet our England was a wolfish den;
Before our forests heard the talk of Men;
Before the first of Druids was a child.—
Long didst thou sit amid our regions wild
Wrapt in a deep, prophetic Solitude.
There came a hebrew voice of solemn Mood
Yet wast thou patient: then sang forth the Nine
Apollo's Garland; yet didst thou divine
Such homebred Glory, that they cry'd in vain
"Come hither Sister of the Island." Plain
Spake fair Ausonia, and once more she spake
A higher Summons—still didst thou betake
Thee to thy /darling/[1] hopes. O thou hast won
A full accomplishment—the thing is done
Which undone these our latter days had risen
On barren Souls. O Muse thou knowst what prison
Of flesh and bone curbs and confines and frets
Our Spirits Wings: despondency besets
Our Pillows and the fresh tomorrow morn
Seems to give <forth> its light in very scorn
Of our dull uni<nspired> snail paced lives.

1 *darling*: 'darling' inserted interlineally in place of 'self and to thy' crossed out. The published version has 'native' for 'darling' (*Endymion*, IV, 17).

Long have I said "how happy he who shrive<s>
To thee"—but then I thought on Poets gone
And could not pray—nor can I now—so on
I move to the end in Humbleness of Heart. —

[Wednesday night and Thursday morning, 29–30 October][1]
Thus far had I written when I received your last which made me at the sight of the direction caper for despair—but for one thing I am glad that I have been neglectful—and that is, therefrom I have received a proof of your utmost kindness which at this present I feel very much—and I wish I had a heart always open to such sensations—but there is no altering a Man's nature and mine must be radically wrong for it will lie dormant a whole Month—This leads me to suppose that there are no Men thouroughly wicked—so as never to be self spiritualized into a kind of sublime Misery—but alas! 't is but for an Hour—he is the only Man "who has kept watch on Man's Mortality"[2] who has philantrophy enough to overcome the disposition [to] an indolent enjoyment of intellect—who is brave enough to volunteer for uncomfortable hours.[x]

[[x]You must forgive although I have only written 300 Lines—they would have been five but I have been obliged to go to town. yesterday I called at Lambs—St[3] Jane look'd very flush when I first went in but was much better before I left.][4]
You remember in Hazlit's essay on commonplace people—He says they read the Edinburgh and Quarterly and think as they do" Now with respect to Wordsworth's Gipseys I think he is

1 Keats began to cross this letter after completing the next paragraph on this page (f. 2[r], 'Thus far . . . uncomfortable hours'). The sequence of the passages in the rest of the letter is clear enough, but not their timing. Writing to Jane Reynolds (31 October) Keats said a letter from Bailey was waiting 'at home the other night' and he 'finished my Letter to him immediately' (*L*, I, p. 176). Keats called on the Reynoldses on 29 October ('Yesterday'), hence he began writing to Bailey at night on 29 October, and completed it in 'the early hours' of 30 October (Gittings, p. 401).

2 *who has . . . Mortality*: Wordsworth's 'Ode: Intimations of Immortality', l. 201.

3 *Lambs—St*: 19 Lamb's Conduit Street, the Reynoldses' family home.

4 *You must . . . I left*: An afterthought, added on same page (f. 2[r]).

right and yet I think Hazlitt is right[er][1] and yet I think Wordsworth is rightest. Wordsworth had not been idle he had not been without his task—nor had they Gipseys—they in the visible world had been as picturesque an object as he in the invisible. The Smoke of their fire—their attitudes—their Voices were all in harmony with the Evenings—It is a bold thing to say and I would not say it in print—but it seems to me that if Wordsworth had though[t] a little deeper at that Moment he would not have written the Poem at all—I should judge it to have been written in one of the most comfortable Moods of his Life—it is a kind of sketchy intellectual Landscape—not a search after Truth—nor is it fair to attack him on such a subject—for it is with the Critic as with the poet had Hazlitt thought a little deeper and been in a good temper he would never have spied an imaginary fault there. The Sunday before last I asked Haydon to dine with me. when I thought of settling all Matters with him in regard to Crips and let you know about it—now although I engaged him a Fortnight before—he sent illness as an excuse—he will never come—I have not been well enough to stand the chance of a Wet night, and so have not seen him nor been able to expurgatorize those Masks[2] for you—but I will not spaek: your speakers are never dooers—then Reynolds—every time I see him and mention you he puts his hand to his head and looks like a son of Niobe's—but he'll write soon. Rome you know was not built in a day—I shall be able, by a little perseverence to read your Letters off hand. I am affraid your health will suffer from over study before your examination—I think you might regulate the thing according to your own Pleasure—and I would too—They[3] were talking of your being up at Christmas—will it be before you have passed? There is nothing my dear Bailey I should rejoice at more that

1 *Wordsworth's Gipseys . . . right[er]*: Keats argues for a more sympathetic reading of Wordsworth's 'Gipsies' (1807) than Hazlitt's in 'On Manner', *Round Table* (1817), I, pp. 120–22.

2 *expurgatorize those Masks*: i.e., to get copies of Keats's life mask.

3 *They*: The Reynoldses.

[*for* than] to see you comfortable with a little Pæòna[1] Wife—an affectionate Wife I have a sort of confidence would do you a great happiness May that be one of the many blessings I wish you—Let me be but [t]he 1/10 of one to you and I shall think it great—My Brother Georges kindest wishes to you. My dear Bailey I am

your affectionate friend.
John Keats

I should not like to be Pages in your way when in a tolerable hungry mood—you have no Mercy—your teeth are the Rock tarpeian[2] down which you capsise Epic Poems like Mad—I would not for 40 shillings be Coleridge's Lays[3] in your way. I hope you will soon get through this abominable writing in in the schools—and be able to keep the terms with more comfort in the hope of retu[r]ning to a comfortable and quiet home out of the way of all Hopkinses[4] and black beetles[5]—When you are settled I will come and take a peep at your Church—your house—try whether I shall have grow[n] two [*for* too] lusty for my chair—by the fire side—and take a peep at my cordials Bower[6]—A Question is the best beacon towards a little Speculation. You ask me after my health and spirits—This Question ratifies in my Mind what I have said above—Health and Spirits can only belong unalloyed to the selfish Man—the Man who thinks much of his fellows can never be in Spirits—when I am not suffering for vicious beastliness I am the greater part of [t]he week in spirits.

1 *Pæòna*: Peona, Endymion's sister in Keats's poem.
2 *the Rock tarpeian*: The Tarpeian Rock on the Capitoline Hill, from which traitors in ancient Rome were cast to their death.
3 *Coleridge's Lays*: *Lay Sermons* (1816, 1817) by Samuel Taylor Coleridge (1772–1834).
4 *Hopkinses*: H. J. Hopkins was a contemporary of Bailey's at Magdalen Hall (Gittings).
5 *black beetles*: Probably refers to Oxford officials in their black gowns.
6 *my chair . . . cordials Bower*: An extended sexual joke. In Regency slang 'chair' meant the male sex, 'cordials' semen and 'Bower' a woman (Gittings). Rollins reads 'cardials'.

Shortly before Keats wrote the next letter, the first of the notorious articles 'On the Cockney School of Poetry' had appeared in the October issue of Blackwood's (Edinburgh) Magazine, *signed 'Z.'. This politically motivated attack pilloried Hunt's 'moral depravity', 'jacobinical' politics, ignorant vulgarity and pretensions to gentility, taking particular issue with his coterie of 'New Poets'. Although it was centred on Hunt, Keats had every reason to believe he was next in line to be abused. The identity of its author, John Gibson Lockhart (1794–1854), was kept secret until some years later. The Tory publisher William Blackwood (1776–1834) had newly set up the magazine in April 1817 as a rival to Archibald Constable's Whig* Edinburgh Review *(1802–1929). Blackwood took over the editorship himself with the October issue.*

Keats's outrage at the Blackwood's *review fuelled his attack on the Bishop of Lincoln, who he believed was responsible for Bailey's failure to gain the curacy he had expected.*

To Benjamin Bailey
3 November 1817

[Harvard MS]

[Well Walk]
Monday—Hampstead

My dear Bailey,

Before I received your Letter I had heard of your disappointment[1]—an unlook'd for piece of villainy. I am glad to hear there was an hindrance to your speaking your Mind to the Bishop: for all may go straight yet—as to being ordained—but the disgust consequent cannot pass away in a hurry—it must be shocking to find in a sacred Profession such barefaced oppression and impertinence—The Stations and Grandeurs of the World have taken it into their heads that they cannot commit themselves

1 *your disappointment*: Bailey's hopes for a curacy in the diocese of Lincoln had been dashed. He was not ordained until 19 July 1818 in the diocese of Carlisle, where he took up a curacy.

towards and [*for* an] inferior in rank—but is not the impertinence from one above to one below more wretchedly mean than from the low to the high? There is something so nauseous in self-willed yawning impudence in the shape of conscience—it sinks the Bishop of Lincoln into a smashed frog putrifying: that a rebel against common decency should escape the Pillory! That a mitre should cover a Man guilty of the most coxcombical, tyranical and indolent impertinence! I repeat this word for the offence appears to me most especially impertinent—and a very serious return would be the Rod—Yet doth he sit in his Palace. Such is this World—and we live—you have surely [been] in a continual struggle against the suffocation of accidents—we must bear (and my Spleen is mad at the thought thereof) the Proud Mans Contumely[1]—O for a recourse somewhat human independant of the great Consolations of Religion and undepraved Sensations. of the Beautiful. the poetical in all things—O for a Remedy against such wrongs within the pale of the World! Should not those things be pure enjoymen<t> should they stand the chance of being contaminated by being called in as antagonists to Bishops? Would not earthly thing[s] do? By Heavens my dear Bailey, I know you have a spice of what I mean—you can set me and have set it in all the rubs that may befal me you have I know a sort of Pride which would kick the Devil on the Jaw Bone and make him drunk with the kick—There is nothing so balmy to a soul imbittered as yours must be, as Pride—When we look at the Heavens we cannot be proud—but shall stocks and stones be impertinent and say it does not become us to kick them? At this Moment I take your hand let us walk up yon Mountain of common sense now if our Pride be vainglorious such a support woud fail—yet you feel firm footing—now look beneath at that parcel of knaves and fools. Many a Mitre is moving among them. I cannot express how I despise the Man who would wrong or be impertinent to you—The thought that we are mortal makes us groan. I will speak of something else or my Spleen will get higher and higher—and I am not a bearer of the two egded Sword. I hope you will recieve an answer from Haydon soon—if not Pride! Pride! Pride!

1 *the Proud Mans Contumely*: *Hamlet*, III. i. 71.

I have received no more subscription[1]—but shall soon have a full health Liberty and leisure to give a good part of my time to him—I will certainly be in time for him—We have promised him one year let that have elapsed and then do as we think proper. If I did not know how impossible it is, I should say 'do not at this time of disappointments disturb yourself about others'[2] There has been a flaming attack upon Hunt in the Endinburgh Magazine—I never read any thing so virulent—accusing him of the greatest Crimes—dep[r]eciating his Wife his Poetry—his Habits—his company, his Conversation—These Philipics are to come out in Numbers—calld 'the Cockney School of Poetry' There has been but one Number published—that on Hunt to which they have prefixed a Motto from one Cornelius Webb[3] Poetaster—who unfortunately was of our Party occasionally at Hampstead and took it into his head to write the following—something about—"we'll talk on Wordsworth Byron—a theme we never tire on and so forth till he comes to Hunt and Keats. In the Motto they have put Hunt and Keats in large Letters[4]—I have no doubt that the second Number was intended for me: but have hopes of its non appearance from the following advertisement in last Sunday's Examiner. "To Z. The writer of the Article signed Z in Blackwood's Ed[i]nburgh magazine for October 1817 is invited to send his address to the printer of the Examiner, in order that Justice may be executed of the proper person"[5] I dont mind the thing much—but if he should go to such lenghts with me as he has done with Hunt I mu[s]t infalibly call him to an account[6]—if

1 *subscription*: Towards the scheme to pay for Cripps's expenses while studying with Haydon.

2 An inked line running across the page here is by Bailey, who noted on the cover: 'Respecting Hunts' Conduct & Keats.'

3 *Webb*: Cornelius Webb(e) (1789–1858), poet and essayist, a member of the Hunt circle, was modestly successful.

4 *In the Motto . . . large Letters*: The 'Motto' from Webb's (lost) poem read: 'Our talk shall be (a theme we never tire on) / Of Chaucer, Spenser, Shakespeare, Milton, Byron, / (Our England's Dante)—Wordsworth—HUNT, and KEATS, / The Muses' son of promise; and of what feats / He yet may do.'

5 *To Z . . . proper person*: *Examiner* (2 November 1817), p. 693. Hunt attempted to identify 'Z' with no success.

6 *call him to an account*: i.e., challenge the author to a duel.

he be a human being and appears in Squares and Theatres where we might possibly meet—I dont relish his abuse
Yesterday[1] Rice and I were at Reynolds—John was to be articled[2] tom[or]row I suppose by this time it is done. Jane was much better—At one time or other I will do you a Pleasure and the Poets a little Justice—but it ought to be in a Poem of greater moment than Endymion—I will do it some day—I have seen two Letters of a little Story[3] Reynolds is writing—I wish he would keep at it—Here is the song[4] I enclosed to Jane if you can make it out in this cross wise writing.

O Sorrow
Why dost borrow
The natural hue of health from vermil Lips?
To give maiden blushes
To the white Rose bushes
Or ist thy dewy hand the daisy tips?

O Sorrow
Why dost borrow
The Lustrous Passion from an orbed eye?
To give the glow worm Light?
Or on a moonless night
To tinge on syren shores the salt sea spry?

O Sorrow
Why dost borrow
The tender ditties from a mourning tongue?
To give at Evening pale
Unto the Nightingal
That thou mayest listen the cold dews among?

1 *Yesterday*: Keats starts 'crossing' his letter with this sentence. This part of the letter 'may well have been' continued on 4 November (Rollins).
2 *articled*: At James Rice's suggestion, Reynolds became articled to the lawyer Francis Fladgate (1773–1821). Rice paid the £110 fee.
3 *a little Story*: 'The Fancy', published in 1820.
4 *the song*: Keats had included the first five stanzas from the 'song' (*Endymion*, IV, 146–81) in his letter to Jane Reynolds of 31 October (*L*, I, pp. 176–7). The two drafts vary from one another and the published version.

O Sorrow
Why dost borrow
Heart's lightness from the Merriment of May?
A Lover would not tread
A Cowslip on the head
Though he should dance from eve to peep of day;
Nor any drooping flower
Held sacred to thy bower
Wherever he may sport himself and play.

To Sorrow
I bade <good morrow,>
And thought to leave her far away behind
But cheerly, cheerly,
She loves me dearly—
She is to me so constant, and so kind—
I would deceive her
And so leave her
But ah! she is too constant and too kind.

O that I had Orpheus lute—and was able to cha[r]m away all your Griefs and Cares—but all my power is a Mite—amid all you[r] troubles I shall ever be—

your sincere and affectionate friend
John Keats

My brothers remembrances to you
Give my respects to Gleig and Whitehead[1]

On 21 November Keats left Hampstead for Burford Bridge, near Dorking, Surrey, where he hoped to complete Endymion. *Keats's lodgings, the Fox and Hounds, were at the foot of Box Hill, then as now a noted beauty spot.*

1 *Whitehead*: Joseph Charles Frederick Whitehead (1784–1825), a student at Magdalen Hall, Oxford, also studying for the Church.

To Benjamin Bailey
22 November 1817

[Harvard MS]

[Saturday, Burford Bridge, Surrey]

My dear Bailey,

I will get over the first part of this (unsaid) Letter as soon as possible for it relates to the affair of poor Crips—To a Man of your nature, such a letter of Haydon's must have been extremely cutting[1]—What occasions the greater part of the World's Quarrels? simply this, two Minds meet and do not understand each other time enough to p[r]aevent any shock or surprise at the conduct of either party—As soon as I had known Haydon three days I had got enough of his character not to have been surp[r] ised at such a Letter as he has hurt you with. Nor when I knew it was it a principle with me to drop his acquaintance although with you it would have been an imperious feeling. I wish you knew all that I think about Genius and the Heart— and yet I think you are thoroughly acquainted with my innermost breast in that respect or you could not have known me even thus long and still hold me worthy to be your dear friend. In passing however I must say of one thing that has pressed upon me lately and encreased my Humility and capability of submission and that is this truth—Men of Genius are great as certain ethereal Chemicals operating on the Mass of neutral intellect—by [*for* but] they have not any individuality, any determined Character. I would call the top and head of those who have a proper self Men of Power[2]—

—But I am running my head into a Subject which I am certain I could not do justice to under five years S[t]udy and 3 vols

1 *such a letter . . . extremely cutting*: Haydon had evidently written peremptorily to Bailey, probably because he had failed to contribute towards the expenses enabling Charles Cripps to study with him in London (see above, p. 54).
2 *Men of Genius . . . Men of Power*: The distinction between 'Men of Genius' and 'Men of Power', and the former's lack of 'individuality', develops into Keats's idea of Negative Capability a month later (see below, p. 79).

octavo—and moreover long to be talking about the Imagination—so my dear Bailey do not think of this unpleasant affair if possible—do not—I defy any ha[r]m to come of it—I defy—I'll shall write to Crips this Week and reque[s]t him to tell me all his goings on from time to time by Letter whererever I may be—it will all go on well—so dont because you have suddenly discover'd a Coldness in Haydon suffer yourself to be teased. Do not my dear fellow. O I wish I was as certain of the end of all your troubles as that of your momentary start about the authenticity of the Imagination. I am certain of nothing but of the holiness of the Heart's affections and the truth of Imagination—What the imagination seizes as Beauty must be truth[1]—whether it existed before or not—for I have the same Idea of all our Passions as of Love they are all in their sublime, creative of essential Beauty—In a Word, you may know my favorite Speculation by my first Book and the little song I sent in my last[2]—which is a representation from the fancy of the probable mode of operating in these Matters—The Imagination may be compared to Adam's dream—he awoke and found it truth.[3] I am the more zealous in this affair, because I have never yet been able to perceive how any thing can be known for truth by consequitive reasoning—and yet it must be—Can it be that even the greatest Philosopher ever arrived at his goal without putting aside numerous objections—However it may be, O for a Life of Sensations rather than of Thoughts! It is 'a Vision in the form of Youth' a Shadow of reality to come—and this consideration has further conv[i]nced me for it has come as auxiliary to another favorite Speculation of mine, that we shall enjoy ourselves here after by having what we called happiness on Earth repeated in a finer tone and so repeated—And yet such a fate can only befall those who delight in Sensation rather than hunger as you do after Truth—Adam's dream will do here and seems to be a conviction that Imagin-

1 *Beauty must be truth*: Compare the concluding couplet of 'Ode on a Grecian Urn'.

2 *I sent in my last*: See his previous letter to Bailey.

3 *Adam's dream . . . truth*: *Paradise Lost*, VIII, 309–11, 452–90.

ation and its empyreal reflection is the same as human Life and its Spiritual repetition. But as I was saying—the simple imaginative Mind may have its rewards in the repeti[ti]on of its own silent Working coming continually on the spirit with a fine Suddenness—to compare great things with small—have you never by being Surprised with an old Melody—in a delicious place—by a delicious voice, fe[l]t over again your very Speculations and Surmises at the time it first operated on your Soul—do you not remember forming to you[r]self the singer's face more beautiful that [*for* than] it was possible and yet with the elevation of the Moment you did not think so—even then you were mounted on the Wings of Imagination so high—that the Prototype must be here after—that delicious face you will see—What a time! I am continually running away from the subject—sure this cannot be exactly the case with a complex Mind—one that is imaginative and at the same time careful of its fruits—who would exist partly on Sensation partly on thought—to whom it is necessary that years should bring the philosophic Mind—such an one I consider your's and therefore it is necessary to your eternal Happiness that you not only ~~have~~ /drink/ this old Wine of Heaven which I shall call the redigestion of our most ethereal Musings on Earth; but also increase in knowledge and know all things. I am glad to hear you are in a fair Way for Easter—you will soon get through your unpleasant reading and then!—but the world is full of troubles and I have not much reason to think myself pesterd with many—I think Jane or Marianne has a better opinion of me than I deserve—for really and truly I do not think my Brothers illness connected with mine—you know more of the real Cause than they do—nor have I any chance of being rack'd as you have been[1]—you perhaps at one time thought there was such a thing as Worldly Happiness to be arrived at, at certain periods of time marked

1 *Jane or Marianne . . . as you have been*: Reynolds's sisters Jane and Marianne feared Keats might be suffering from the same illness as his brother Tom: tuberculosis. Bailey knew that Keats was taking mercury for gonorrhoea (see above, p. 58 and n). The troubles which 'rack'd' Bailey may have been caused by his love life or his loss of a curacy.

out—you have of necessity from your disposition been thus led away—I scarcely remember counting upon any Happiness—I look not for it if it be not in the present hour—nothing startles me beyond the Moment. The setting sun will always set me to rights—or if a Sparrow come before my Window I take part in its existence and pick about the Gravel. The first thing that strikes me on hea[r]ing a Misfortune having befalled another is this. 'Well it cannot be helped.—he will have the pleasure of trying the resourses of his spirit, and I beg now my dear Bailey that hereafter should you observe any thing cold in me not to but [*for* put] it to the account of heartlessness but abstraction— for I assure you I sometimes feel not the influence of a Passion or Affection during a whole week—and so long this sometimes continues I begin to suspect myself and the genuiness of my feelings at other times—thinking them a few barren Tragedy-tears—My Brother Tom is much improved—he is going to Devonshire—whither I shall follow him—at present I am just arrived at Dorking to change the Scene—change the Air and give me a spur to wind up my Poem, of which there are wanting 500 Lines.[1] I should have been here a day sooner but the Reynoldses persuaded me to spop [*for* stop] in Town to meet your friend Christie[2]—There were Rice and Martin—we talked about Ghosts—I will have some talk with Taylor and let you know—when please God I come down a[t] Christmas—I will find that Examiner if possible. My best regards to Gleig—My Brothers to you and M[rs] Bentley[3]

Your affectionate friend
John Keats—

1 *to wind up my Poem . . . 500 Lines*: Keats did so. Woodhouse recorded that Keats wrote 'Burford Bridge, Nov. 28, 1817' at the end of the (lost) draft of *Endymion*.

2 *Christie*: J. H. Christie (d. 1876) later fought a duel on 16 February 1821 with John Scott, then editor of the *London Magazine*, over Lockhart's attack on Keats in *Blackwood's Review*. Scott died on 27 February: Christie was acquitted of his murder.

3 *M[rs] Bentley*: The brothers' landlady in Well Walk, the postman's wife.

I want to say much more to you—a few hints will set me going
Direct Burford Bridge near dorking[1]

To J. H. Reynolds
22 November 1817

[Woodhouse transcript (1821?)]

Saturday [evening, Burford Bridge, Surrey]

My Dear Reynolds,

There are two things which tease me here—one of them is Crips—and the other that I cannot go with Tom into Devonshire—however I hope to do my duty to myself in a week or so; and then Ill try what I can do for my neighbour—now is not this virtuous? on returning to Town—Ill damn all Idleness—indeed, in superabundance of employment, I must not be content to run here and there on little two penny errands—but turn Rakehell i e go a making[2] or Bailey will think me just as great a Promise keeper as he thinks you—for my self I do not,—and do not remember above one Complaint against you for matter o' that—Bailey writes so abominable a hand, to give his Letter a fair reading requires a little time; so I had not seen when I saw you last, his invitation to Oxford at Christmas—I'll go with you[3]—You know how poorly Rice was—I do not think it was all corporeal—bodily pain was not used to keep him silent. Ill tell you what; he was hurt at what your Sisters said about his joking with your Mother he was, soothly to sain[4]—It will all blow over. God knows, my Dear Reynolds, I should not talk any sorrow to you—you must have enough vexations—so I won't any more. If ever I start a rueful subject in a Letter to you—blow me! Why dont you—Now I was a going to ask a very silly

1 *I want to say . . . near dorking*: Written on the final blank leaf.
2 *a making*: 'Mating, matchmaking' (*OED*, a single example from Dekker, 1608). Woodhouse suggests Keats meant to write 'a masking'.
3 *I'll go with you*: They did not go.
4 *soothly to sain*: i.e., 'truth to say'.

Question neither you nor any body else could answer, under a folio, or at least a Pamphlet—you shall judge—Why dont you, as I do, look unconcerned at what may be called more particularly Heart-vexations? They never surprize me—lord! a man should have the fine point of his soul taken off to become fit for this world—I like this place very much—There is Hill & Dale and a little River—I went up Box hill this Evening after the Moon—you a' seen the Moon—came down—and wrote some lines. Whenever I am separated from you, and not engaged in a continued Poem—every Letter shall bring you a lyric—but I am too anxious for you to enjoy the whole, to send you a particle. One of the three Books I have with me is Shakespear's Poems: I neer found so many beauties in the sonnets—they seem to be full of fine things said unintentionally—in the intensity of working out conceits—Is this to be borne? Hark ye!

> When lofty trees I see barren of leaves
> Which erst from heat did canopy the herd,
> And Summer's green all girded up in sheaves,
> Borne on the bier with white and bristly beard.[1]

He has left nothing to say about nothing or any thing: for look at Snails, you know what he says about Snails, you know where he talks about "cockled snails"[2]—well, in one of these sonnets, he says—the chap slips into—no! I lie! this is in the Venus and Adonis: the Simile brought it to my Mind.

> Audi—As the snail, whose tender horns being hit,
> Shrinks back into his shelly cave with pain,
> And there all smothered up in shade doth sit,
> Long after fearing to put forth again:
> So at his bloody view her eyes are fled,
> Into the deep dark Cabins of her head.[3]

1 *When lofty trees . . . bristly beard*: Shakespeare's Sonnet 12, ll. 5–8.
2 *cockled snails*: *Love's Labour's Lost*, IV. iii. 334, 'the tender horns of cockled snails'.
3 *As the snail . . . her head*: Shakespeare's *Venus and Adonis*, ll. 1033–8.

He overwhelms a genuine Lover of Poesy with all manner of abuse, talking about—

"a poets rage
And stretched metre of an antique song—"

Which by the by will be a capital Motto for my Poem[1]—wont it?—He speaks too of "Time's antique pen"—and "aprils first born flowers"—and "deaths eternal cold"—By the Whim King! I'll give you a Stanza, because it is not material in connection and when I wrote it I wanted you to——give your vote, pro or con.—

Christalline Brother of the Belt of Heaven,
Aquarius! to whom King Jove ha'th given
Two liquid pulse streams! s'tead of feather'd wings—
Two fan like fountains—thine illuminings
For Dian play:
Dissolve the frozen purity of air;
Let thy white shoulders silvery and bare
Show cold through watery pinions: make more bright
The Star-Queen's Crescent on her marriage night:
Haste Haste away!—[2]

Now I hope I shall not fall off in the winding up, as the Woman said to the—[rounce][3]—I mean up and down. I see there is an advertizement in the chronicle to Poets—he is so overloaded with poems on the late Princess.—I suppose you do not lack—send me a few[4]—lend me thy hand to laugh a little—send me a

1 *a poets rage . . . Motto for my Poem*: Shakespeare's Sonnet 17, ll. 11–12, and quoted on the title page of *Endymion*.
2 *Christalline Brother . . . Haste away!*: *Endymion*, IV, 581–90
3 *[rounce]*: Conjectural: the transcript leaves this word blank: there is an illegible pencilled suggestion. A 'rounce' is the handle in a printing press for winding the carriage in and out (Mee).
4 *overloaded . . . a few*: Princess Charlotte, the daughter of the Prince Regent, died on 6 November. The advertisement in the *Morning Chronicle* refusing to consider any more elegies appeared on 20 November. Keats assumes that Reynolds, the poetry editor of the *Champion*, had received similar effusions.

little pullet sperm, a few finch eggs[1]—and remember me to each of our Card playing Club[2]—when you die you will all be turned into Dice, and be put in pawn with the Devil—for Cards they crumple up like any King—I mean John in the stage play what pertains Prince Arthur[3]—I rest

Your affectionate friend
John Keats

Give my love to both houses—hinc atque illinc.[4]

1 *lend me thy hand to laugh a little . . . pullet sperm . . . finch eggs*: All quotations from Shakespeare: *1 Henry IV*, II. iv. 2–3, *The Merry Wives of Windsor*, III. v. 27–8, *Troilus and Cressida*, V. i. 33.
2 *our Card playing Club*: The Saturday gathering at Rice's (pp. 82, 86 below).
3 *crumple up . . . Prince Arthur*: *King John*, V. vii. 31, 'all my bowels crumble up to dust'.
4 *hinc atque illinc*: Virgil's *Georgics*, III, 257, 'in this place and that'.

December 1817 to June 1818
London and Teignmouth

Keats completed the first draft of Endymion *at Burford Bridge on Friday, 28 November. He returned to Hampstead about a week later. On Sunday, 14 December, after his brothers had left to stay in Teignmouth for the sake of Tom's health, Keats dined with Haydon. For the next two months, Keats, alone at Well Walk, spent much of his time in London, renewing his friendships and meeting new people, going to the theatre and art exhibitions, and revising* Endymion *for the press.*

On 15 December Keats saw the celebrated actor Edmund Kean (1787–1833) play Richard III at Drury Lane. Three nights later he saw Kean again as Luke Traffic in Sir J. B. Burge's Riches: Or, the Wife and Brother *(1810) so that he could write a review for the* Champion *on Reynolds's behalf.*

To George and Tom Keats
21, 27(?) December 1817

[Jeffrey transcript (1845)][1]

[Well Walk]
Hampstead Sunday

My dear Brothers

I must crave your pardon for not having written ere

1 Jeffrey mistakenly gives the date as '22 December 1818'. The issue of the *Champion* in which Keats's 'critique' of Kean appeared came out on Sunday, 21 December.

this & &[1] I saw Kean return to the public in Richard III, & finely he did it, & at the request of Reynolds I went to criticise his Luke in Riches—the critique is in todays champion, which I send you with the Examiner in which you will find very proper lamentation on the obsoletion of christmas Gambols & pastimes: but it was mixed up with so much egotism of that drivelling nature that pleasure is entirely lost.[2] Hone the publisher's trial, you must find very amusing; & as Englishmen very encouraging[3]—his <u>Not Guilty</u> is a thing, which not to have been, would have dulled still more Liberty's Emblazoning—Lord Ellenborough has been paid in his own coin—Wooler & Hone[4] have done us an essential service—I have had two very pleasant evenings with Dilke yesterday & today; & am at this moment just come from him & feel in the humour to go on with this, began in the morning, & from which he came to fetch me. I spent Friday evening with Wells[5] & went the next morning to see <u>Death on the Pale horse</u>.[6] It is a wonderful picture, when West's Age is considered; But there is nothing to be intense upon; no women one feels mad to kiss; no face swelling into reality. the excellence of every Art is its intensity, capable of making all disagreeables evaporate, from their being in close relationship with Beauty & Truth—Examine King Lear & you will find this examplified throughout; but in this picture we have unpleasantness without any momentous depth of speculation

1 *& &*: Indicates an omission in Jeffrey's transcript of anything from a few words to whole pages.

2 *lamentation ... lost*: Hunt's essay 'Christmas and Other Old National Merry-Makings Considered', *Examiner* (21 (and 28) December 1817).

3 *Hone ... encouraging*: William Hone (1780–1842), political writer and journalist, successfully defended himself against a charge of blasphemous libel in 1817: his third trial, with its 'not guilty' verdict, was reported in the same issue of the *Examiner* (21 December) that Keats sent to his brothers.

4 *Lord Ellenborough ... Wooler & Hone*: Lord Ellenborough (1750–1818), who presided at Hone's trial, had earlier sentenced Leigh Hunt to prison. Thomas Wooler (1786–1853) was, like Hone, a radical journalist.

5 *Wells*: Charles Jeremiah Wells (1800–79), lawyer and minor poet, with whom Keats was friendly until discovering the cruel joke he played on Tom with the 'Amena' letters (see below, p. 338, 345–6).

6 *<u>Death on the Pale horse</u>*: By Benjamin West (1738–1820), historical painter. Keats saw the painting at Somerset House on Saturday, 20 December.

excited, in which to bury its repulsiveness—The picture is larger than Christ rejected—I dined with Haydon the sunday after you left, & had a very pleasant day, I dined too (for I have been out too much lately) with Horace Smith & met his two Brothers[1] with Hill & Kingston & one Du Bois,[2] they only served to convince me, how superior humour is to wit in respect to enjoyment—These men say things which make one start, without making one feel, they are all alike; their manners are alike; they all know fashionables; they have a mannerism in their very eating & drinking, in their mere handling a Decanter—They talked of Kean & his low company—Would I were with that company instead of yours said I to myself! I know such like acquaintance will never do for me & yet I am going to Reynolds, on wednesday—[3]

[Saturday, 27 (?) December 1817] Browne & Dilke walked with me & back from the Christmas pantomime. I had not a dispute but a disquisition with Dilke, on various subjects; several things dovetailed in my mind, & at once it struck me, what quality went to form a Man of Achievement especially in Literature & which Shakespeare posessed so enormously—I mean Negative Capability,[4] that is when man is capable of being in uncertainties, Mysteries, doubts, without any irritable reaching after fact & reason—Coleridge, for instance, would let go by a fine isolated verisimilitude[5] caught from the Penetralium of mystery, from being incapable of remaining content with half knowledge. This pursued through Volumes would perhaps take

1 *his two Brothers*: Smith's elder brother James (1775–1839), writer and humorist, and Leonard Smith (1778–1837).

2 *Hill & Kingston . . . Du Bois*: All men loosely connected with the Hunt circle and part of literary London. For John Kingston, see below, p. 80.

3 Jeffrey omitted something here. The next sentence was written after Keats saw the Christmas pantomime *Harlequin's Vision*, on 26 December at Drury Lane (and reviewed in the *Champion*, 4 January 1818).

4 *Negative Capability*: This famous phrase grows from Keats's idea that 'Men of Genius' are distinguished from 'Men of Power' by their lack of 'any individuality' (p. 69 above).

5 *isolated verisimilitude*: Jeffrey has 'insolated verisimilature'. Keats's phrase means something like 'striking metaphor', 'sudden perception of likeness or connection'.

us no further than this, that with a great Poet the sense of Beauty overcomes every other consideration, or rather obliterates all consideration.

Shelley's poem is out & there are words about its being objected to, as much as Queen Mab was.[1] Poor Shelley I think he has his Quota of good qualities, in sooth la!! Write soon to your most sincere friend & affectionate Brother

John

The first letter Keats wrote in 1818 to his brothers is confusing because it is not narrated sequentially. The main events are as follows. After finishing the previous letter to his brothers on Saturday, 27 December 1817, Keats spent the evening with the 'Club' at Rice's, where he was 'initiated' into Regency slang. The following day, he was one of the guests at Haydon's 'immortal dinner' given in front of his huge canvas, Christ's Entry into Jerusalem. *Haydon brought together Wordsworth, Charles Lamb (1775–1834), the painter John Landseer (1769–1852), various other friends, and Keats, who was the youngest person there. The arrival of John Kingston, Deputy Comptroller of the Stamp Office, Wordsworth's official employer as Distributor of Stamps in Westmorland, led Lamb, ignorant of who Kingston was, to quiz him mercilessly. Keats's letter gives the only independent account of this incident.*

Over the Christmas period Keats found time to pick up theatrical gossip, call on the Hunts, dine with William Haslam, and see his sister Fanny twice. On 1 or 2 January 1818 he saw John Dillon's 'new tragedy' Retribution *at Covent Garden, which he was reviewing for the* Champion *together with the Christmas pantomime he had seen earlier. On Saturday, 3 January he*

1 *objected to . . . as Queen Mab was*: Keats had heard about the objections to the incest theme of *Laon and Cythna*, published by the Olliers that December, which was withdrawn, drastically revised and issued as *The Revolt of Islam* (1818). Shelley had *Queen Mab*, which advocated republicanism, free love, atheism and vegetarianism, privately printed and circulated in 1813. His authorship of the poem was the decisive evidence against him in his very public legal battle for custody of his children in August 1817.

called on Wordsworth, who was preparing to meet Kingston again. Keats spent the evening with Rice and the 'Club'. This time they met at the house of George Reddell, a sword-cutler, at 236 Piccadilly, to play cards, dance with the ladies and drink. On Sunday Charles Wells (c. 1800–79) and Severn dined with Keats at Well Walk, staying until ten at night.

To George and Tom Keats
5 January 1818

[Pforzheimer MS][1]

Featherstone Buildgs [London] Monday

My dear Brothers,

I ought to have written before and you should have had a long Letter last week; but I undertook the Champion for Reynolds who is at Exeter. I wrote two articles, one on the Drury Lane Pantomime, the other on the Covent Garden New Tragedy, which they have not put in.[2] The one they have inserrted is so badly punc[t]uated that, you perceive, I am determined never to write more without some care in that particular. Wells tells me, that you are licking your Chops Tom, in expectation of my Book coming out; I am sorry to say I have not begun my corrections yet: tomorrow I set out. I called on Sawrey[3] this morning. He did not seem to be at all out at any thing I said and the enquiries I made with regard to your spitting of Blood: and moreover desired me to ask you to send him a correct accou[n]t of all your sensations and symptoms concerning the

1 Facsimile and transcript, *Shelley and his Circle*, ed. Donald H. Reiman (Cambridge, MA: Harvard University Press, 1973), V, pp. 428–36. Keats is writing in the morning from Charles Wells's home in Featherstone Buildings, Holborn.
2 *they have not put in*: Keats was mistaken, as his postscript acknowledges. Both reviews appeared in the *Champion* on Sunday, 4 January.
3 *Sawrey*: Solomon Sawrey (1765–1825), surgeon and the brothers' doctor, who subsequently treated Keats. He was an expert on venereal diseases, on which he had published.

Palpitation and the spitting and the Cough—if you have any. Your last Letter gave me at [*for* a] great Pleasure for I think the Invalid is in a better spirit there along the Edge[1]—and as for George I must immediately, now I think of it, correct a little misconception of a part of my last Letter. The Miss Reynolds have never said one word against me about you,[2] or by any means endeavoured to lessen you in my estimation. That is not what I refered to: but the manner and thoughts which I knew they internally had towards you—time will show. Wells and Severn dined with me yesterday: we had a very pleasant day—I pitched upon another bottle of claret—Port—we enjoyed ourselves very much were all very witty and full of Rhyme—we played a Concert[3] from 4 o'clock till 10—drank your Healths the Hunts and N. B. Severn Peter Pindars.[4] I said on that day the only good thing I was ever guilty of—we were talking about Stephens and the 1[s] Gallery. I said I wondered that careful Folks would go there for although it was but a Shilling still you had to pay through the Nose. I saw the Peachey family[5] in a Box at Drury one Night. I have got such a curious[6]—or rather I had such, now I am in my own hand. I have had a great deal of pleasant time with Rice lately, and am getting initiated into a little Cant—they call dr[i]nking deep dying scarlet, and when you breathe in your wartering they bid you cry hem and play it off[7]—they call good Wine a pretty tipple, and call getting a Child knocking out an apple, stopping as at a Tave[r]n they call hanging out—Where do you sup? is where do you hang out? This day I promised to dine with Wordsworth and the Weather

1 *along the Edge*: Presumably the brothers were staying on the hills overlooking Teignmouth.

2 *never said . . . about you*: Keats means to say that the Reynolds sisters had not spoken to him against George.

3 *Concert*: By imitating various musical instruments.

4 *Severn Peter Pindars*: Peter Pindar is the pseudonym of the satirist John Wolcot (1738–1819), with a punning reference to Severn.

5 *the Peachey family*: Richard Peachey and Son were ironmongers in Hanover Street. For James Peachey, see below, p. 274 n.

6 *such a curious*: Referring to a bad quill, which he changes at this point.

7 *they call dr[i]nking . . . play it off*: Keats is here quoting from Prince Hal in *1 Henry IV*, II. iv. 19–21.

is so bad that I am undecided for he lives at Mortimer street I had an invitation to meet him at Kingstons[1]—but not liking that place I sent my excuse—What I think of doing to day is to dine in Mortimer Street (wordsth) and sup here in Feathers^{ne} Buildg^{s} as Mr Wells has invited me—On Saturday I called on Wordsworth before he went to Kingston's and was surp[r]ised to find him with a stiff Collar. I saw his Spouse and I think his Daughter—I forget whether I had written my last before my Sunday Evening at Haydon's—no I did n<o>t or I should have told you Tom of a y<oung> Man you met at Paris at Scott's of the n<ame of> Richer[2] I think—he is going to Fezan in Africa there to proceed if possible like Mungo Park—he was very polite to me and enquired very particularly after you—then there was Wordsworth, Lamb, Monkhouse,[3] Landseer, Kingston and your humble Sarvant. Lamb got tipsey and blew up Kingston—proceeding so far as to take the Candle across the Room hold it to his face and show us wh-a-at-sor^{t}-fello he-waas I astonished Kingston at supper with a pertinacity in favour of drinking—keeping my two glasses at work in a knowing way—I have seen Fanny twice lately—she enquired particularly af[t]er you and wants a Co-partnership Letter from you—she has been unwell but is improving—I think she will be quick—Mrs Abbey was saying the Keatses were ever indolent—that they would ever be so and that it was born in them—Well whispered fanny to me

If it is born with us how can we help it—

She seems very anxious for a Letter—I asked her what I should get for her, she said a Medal of the Princess.[4] I called on Haslam—we dined very snugly together—he sent me a Hare

1 *Kingstons*: John Kingston (see headnote).

2 *Richer*: Joseph Ritchie (*c.* 1788–1819), surgeon, died in Murzuk, capital of Fezzan, on the northern edge of the Sahara Desert, before reaching Timbuctoo.

3 *Monkhouse*: Thomas Monkhouse (1783–1825), a merchant, cousin of Wordsworth's wife and her sister Mary Hutchinson. For the other men mentioned, see headnote.

4 *Medal of the Princess*: Commemorative medals were struck to mark Princess Charlotte's death on 6 November 1817.

last Week which I sent to M[rs] Dilk. Brown is not come back—I and Dilk are getting capital Friends—he is going to take the Champion[1]—he has sent his farce to Consent Garden—I met Bob Harris in the Slips at Covent Garden—we had a good deal of curious chat—he came out with his old humble Opinion—The Covent Garden Pantonine is a very nice one—but they have a middling Harlequin, a bad Pantaloon, a worse Clown and a shocking Columbine who is one of the Miss Dennets. I suppose you will see my Critique on the new Tragedy in the next Weeks Champion—It is a shocking bad one. I have not seen Hunt, he was out when I called—M[rs] Hunt looks as well as ever I saw her after her Confinement—There is an article in the sennight Examiner—on Godwin's Mandeville signed E. K. I think it Miss Kents[2]—I will send it. There are fine Subscriptions going on for Hone.[3] You ask me what degrees there are between Scotts Novels and those of Smollet—They appear to me to be quite distinct in every particular—more especially in their Aim—Scott endeavours to th[r]ow so interesting and ramantic a colouring into common and low Characters as to give them a touch of the Sublime—Smollet on the contrary pulls down and levels what with other Men would continue Romance. The Grand parts of Scott are willing [*for* within] the reach of more Minds that [*for* than] the finest humours in Humphrey Climker—I forget whether that fine thing of the Sargeant is Fielding's or Smollets but it gives me more pleasure that [*for* than] the whole Novel of the Antiquary[4]—you must remember what I mean. Some one says to the Sargeant "thats a non sequiter," "if you come to that" replies the Sargeant "you're another."[5] I see by Wells Letter, M[r] Abbey does not overstock you with Money—you must insist—I have not seen Loveless

1 *Champion*: Dilke had agreed to act as the *Champion*'s drama critic. His 'farce' is not known.

2 *I think it Miss Kents*: The review of Godwin's novel in the *Examiner* (28 December 1817) was actually by Shelley, using his pseudonym 'Elfin Knight'.

3 *Hone*: See above, p. 78.

4 *the Antiquary*: (1816), a novel by Walter Scott (1771–1832).

5 *if you . . . you're another*: In fact, *Tom Jones* (1749), IX. vi, by Henry Fielding (1707–54).

yet—but expect it on Wednesday—I am affraid it is gone. Severn tells me he has an order for some drawings for the Emperor of Russia I was at a dance at Redhall's[1] and passed a pl[e]asant time enough—drank deep and won 10.6 at cutting for Half Guinies there was a younger Brother of the Squibs[2] made him self very conspicuous after the Ladies had retired from the supper table by giving Mater Omnium[3]—Mr Redhall said he did not understand any thing but plain english—whereat Rice egged the young fool on to say the World [*for* Word] plainly out. After which there was an enquirey about the derivation of the Word C—t when while two parsons and Grammarians were setting together and settling the matter Wm Squibs interrupting them said a very good thing—'Gentlemen says he I have always understood it to be a Root and not a Derivitive.' On proceeding to the Pot in the Cupboard it soon became full on which / the Court door was opened/ Frank Floodgate[4] bawls out, Hoollo! Here's an opposition pot—Ay, says Rice in one you have a Yard for your pot, and in the other a pot for your Yard—Bailey was there and seemed to enjoy the Evening Rice said he cared less about the hour than any one and the p[r]oof is his dancing—he cares not for time, dancing as if he was deaf. Old Redall not being used to give parties had no idea of the Quantity of wine that would be drank and he actually put in readiness on t<he> kitchen Stairs 8 dozen[5]—E[v]ery one enquires after you—an<d every> one desires their remembrances to you You must get well Tom and then I shall feel 'Whole and general as the casing Air.'[6] Give me as many Letters as you like and write

1 *Redhall's*: Identified by Gittings as George Reddell, a sword cutler living at 236 Piccadilly (*John Keats*, pp. 268–9). For Keats's fuller description of Reddell, see p. 278 below.

2 *Squibs*: Probably George Squibbs, younger brother of Frank and William Squibbs, childhood friends of Reynolds. Their father George was an auctioneer.

3 *Mater Omnium*: 'Mother of all', apparently a slang word for the female pudenda.

4 *Frank Floodgate*: Frank Fladgate, the son of Francis Fladgate, the lawyer to whom Reynolds had recently been articled (see above, p. 67).

5 *8 dozen*: Keats was so struck by this incident that he repeated it a year later (p. 278 below).

6 *Whole . . . Air*: *Macbeth*, III. iv. 23.

to Sawrey soon—I received a short Letter from Bailey about Crips and one from Haydon ditto—Haydon thinks he improves very much[1] Here a happy twelveth days to you and may we pass the next together—Mrs Wells desires [remembrances] particularly to Tom and her respects to George—and I desire no better than to be ever your most affectionate

Brother John—

I had not opened the Champion before—I find both my articles in it—

On Saturday morning, 10 January 1818, Keats wrote to his publisher John Taylor, saying 'I have been racketing too much, & do not feel over well', and promised to give him the revised version of the first book of Endymion *'in four days' (*L, I, pp. *201–2).*

To B. R. Haydon

10 January 1818

[Harvard MS]

[Well Walk, Hampstead]
Saturday Morn—

My dear Haydon,

I should have seen you ere this, but on account of my sister being in Town: so that when I have sometimes made ten paces towards you, Fanny has called me into the City; and the Xmas Holiday[s] are your only time to see Sisters, that is if they are so situated as mine. I will be with you early next week—to night it should be, but we have a sort of a Club every Saturday

1 *Haydon . . . very much*: By 31 December 1817 Cripps had been in Haydon's studio long enough for the painter to say, 'I think he will shine also', that is, prove an 'honor to the Country' as would his pupil William Bewick (*The Diary of Benjamin Robert Haydon*, ed. W. B. Pope, 5 vols (Cambridge, MA: Harvard University Press, 1960), II, p. 177).

evening—to morrow—but I have on that day an insuperable engagement—Crips has been down to me, and appears sensible that a binding[1] to you would be of the greatest advantage to him—if such a thing be done it cannot be before £150 or £200 are secured in subscriptions to him—I will write to Bailey about it, give a Copy of the Subscribers names to every one I know who is likely to get a £5 for him. I will leave a Copy at Taylor and Hesseys, Rodwell and Martin[2] and will ask Kingston and Cº to cash up. Your friendship fo<r> me is now getting into its teens—and I feel the past. Also eve[r]y day older I get—the greater is my idea of your atchievements in Art: and I am convinced that there are three things to rejoice at in this Age—The Excursion Your Pictures, and Hazlitt's depth of Taste.

Your's affectionately
John Keats

To George and Tom Keats
13, 19 January 1818

[Jeffrey transcript (1845)]

[Well Walk]
Tuesday Hampstead 1818

My dear Brothers

I am certain I think of having a letter tomorrow morning for I expected one so much this morning, having been in town two days, at the end of which my expectations began to get up a little, I found two on the table, one from Bailey & one from Haydon, I am quite perplexed in a world of doubts & fancies—there is nothing stable in the world—uproar's your only musick, I do not mean to include Bailey in this & so I dismiss him from

1 *binding*: If by 'binding' Keats means that Cripps wanted to become one of Haydon's paying pupils, the usual fee was 200 guineas for three years' instruction (*L*, I, pp. 161n). It appears that to raise this extra sum Keats would have had to return to his original subscribers and others a second time. Whether he was successful is unclear. Haydon never mentions Cripps again.
2 *Rodwell and Martin*: Booksellers and publishers (see above, p. 52 n).

this, with all the oprobrium he deserves, that is in so many words, he is one of the noblest men alive at the present day. In a note to Haydon about a week ago, (which I wrote with a full sense of what he had done, and how he had never manifested any little mean drawback in his value of me) I said if there were three things superior in the modern world, they were "the Excursion." "Haydon's pictures" & "Hazlitts depth of Taste" So I do believe—Not thus speaking with any poor vanity that works of genius were the first things in this world. No! for that sort of probity & disinterestedness which such men as Bailey possess, does hold & grasp the tip top of any spiritual honours, that can be paid to any thing in this world—And moreover having this feeling at this present come over me in its full force, I sat down to write to you with a grateful heart, in that I had not a Brother, who did not feel & credit me, for a deeper feeling & devotion for his uprightness, than for any marks of genius however splendid I was speaking about doubts & fancies—I Mean there has been a quarrel of a severe nature between Haydon & Reynolds & another ("the Devil rides upon a fiddle stick"[1]) between Hunt & Haydon—the first grew from the sunday on which Haydon invited some friends to meet Wordsworth.[2] Reynolds never went, & never sent any Notice about it, this offended Haydon more than it ought to have done—he wrote a very sharp & high note to Reynolds & then another in palliation—but which Reynolds feels as an aggravation of the first—Considering all things—Haydon's frequent neglect of his Appointments &c. his notes were bad enough to put Reynolds on the right side of the question but then Reynolds has no powers of sufferance; no idea of having the thing against him; so he answered Haydon in one of the most cutting letters I ever read; exposing to himself all his own weaknesses, & going on to an excess, which whether it is just or no, is what I would fain have unsaid, the fact is they are both in the right & both in the wrong.

The quarrel with Hunt I understand thus far. Mrs H. was in

1 *the Devil . . . fiddle stick*: *1 Henry IV*, II. iv. 470–1.
2 *the sunday . . . meet Wordsworth*: i.e., the 'immortal dinner' of 28 December 1817.

the habit of borrowing silver of Haydon, the last time she did so, Haydon asked her to return it at a certain time—She did not—Haydon sent for it; Hunt went to expostulate on the indelicacy &c. they got to words & parted for ever—All I hope is at some time to bring them all together again—Lawk! Molly there's been such doings—Yesterday evening I made an appointment with Wells, to go to a private theatre & it being in the neighbourhood of Drury Lane, & thinking we might be fatigued with sitting the whole evening in one dirty hole; I got the Drury Lane ticket & therewith we divided the evening with a Spice of Richard III[1]—

[Monday, 19 January 1818] Good Lord,! I began this letter nearly a week ago, what have I been doing since—I have been—I mean not sending last sunday's paper[2] to you I believe because it was not near me—for I cannot find it, & my conscience presses heavy on me for not sending it; You would have had one last thursday but I was called away, & have been about somewhere ever since. Where. What. well I rejoice almost that I have not heard from you, because no news is good news.—I cannot for the world recollect why I was called away, all I know is, that there has been a dance at Dilke's & another at the London Coffee House; to both of which I went. But I must tell you in another letter the circumstances thereof—for though a week should have passed since I wrote on the other side it quite appalls me—I can only write in scraps & patches, Brown is returned from Hampshire[3]—Haydon has returned an answer[4] in the same style—they are all dreadfully irritated against each other. On sunday[5] I saw Hunt & dined with Haydon, met Hazlitt & Bewick[6] there; & took Haslam with me—forgot to

1 *Drury Lane ticket . . . Richard III*: Keats gives a fuller account of this evening (12 January) below, p. 99. The 'ticket' was no doubt Brown's lifetime admission ticket to Drury Lane.

2 *last sunday's paper*: The *Examiner*.

3 *Hampshire*: Jeffrey has 'Hampstead', but Brown had been staying in Bedhampton.

4 *an answer*: To Reynolds presumably.

5 *sunday*: 18 January.

6 *Bewick*: William Bewick (1795–1866), painter and friend of Hazlitt.

speak about Crips though I broke my engagement to Haslams on purpose—Mem. Haslam came to meet me, found me at Breakfast, had the goodness to go with me my way—I have just finished the revision of my first book, & shall take it to Taylor's tomorrow[1]—intend to persevere—Do not let me see many days pass without hearing from you

Your most affectionate Brother

John—

Keats wrote three letters and most of a fourth on the morning of Friday, 23 January. He had given his publisher the revised first book of Endymion *three days earlier. Taylor proposed publishing Keats's poem in a de luxe quarto if Haydon would provide a 'Drawing' as a frontispiece. Keats approached Haydon, who thought a portrait of Keats would be more appropriate. Keats's letters to the two men mediate in favour of the painter's proposal. In the event* Endymion *was published in octavo with no illustrations.*

To B. R. Haydon
23 January 1818

[British Library MS]

[Well Walk, Hampstead]
Friday 23rd—

My dear Haydon,

I have a complete fellow-feeling with you in this business—so much so that it would be as well to wait for a choice out of Hyperion—when that Poem is done there will be a wide range for you—in Endymion I think you may have many bits of the deep and sentimental cast—the nature of Hyperion will lead me to treat it in a more naked and grecian Manner—and

1 *tomorrow*: Almost a week later than he had promised Taylor on 10 January (p. 86 above).

the march of passion and endeavour will be undeviating—and one great contrast between them will be—that the Hero of the written tale[1] being mortal is led on, like Buonaparte, by circumstance; whereas the Apollo in Hyperion being a fore-seeing God will shape his actions like one. But I am counting &c.[2]

Your proposal pleases me—and, believe me, I would not have my Head in the shop windows[3] from any hand but yours—no by Apelles![4]

I will write Taylor and you shall hear from me

Your's ever John Keats—

To John Taylor
23 January 1818

[Facsimile (1924)][5]

[Well Walk, Hampstead]
Friday 23rd

My dear Taylor,

I have spoken to Haydon about the Drawing—he would do it with all his Art and Heart too if so I will it—however he has written thus to me—but I must tell you first, he intends painting a finished picture from the Poem[6]—thus he writes

"When I do any thing for your poem, it must be effectual—an honor to both of us—to hurry up a sketch for the season

1 *the written tale*: i.e., *Endymion.*

2 *I am counting &c*: Keats was indeed counting his chickens too soon: *Endymion* announces that Keats will praise 'Thy lute-voic'd brother [Apollo] . . . ere long' (IV. 774), but Keats did not begin *Hyperion* until late 1818.

3 *my Head . . . windows*: i.e, the windows of the London printsellers: Keats saw a portrait of Kotzebue's murderer in 'Colnaghi's window' in September 1819 (p. 425 below).

4 *Apelles*: A celebrated painter in classical Greece.

5 Anderson Galleries, *Catalogue of the William Arnold Harris Collections of Manuscripts, Books & Autograph Letters* [New York], 11–12 November 1924, no. 507.

6 *painting . . . the Poem*: Haydon never did so.

won't do. I think an engraving from your head, from a Chalk drawing of mine—done with all my might—to which I would put my name, would answer Taylor's Idea more than the other indeed I am sure of it—this I will do & this will be effectual and as I have not done it for any other human being—it will have an effect"

What think you of this? Let me hear—I shall have my second book in readiness forthwith—

Your's most sincerely
John Keats—

If Reynolds calls tell him three lines would be acceptable for I am squat[1] at Hampstead

To Benjamin Bailey
23 January 1818

[Harvard MS]

[Well Walk, Hampstead]
Friday Jany 23rd

My dear Bailey,

Twelve days have pass'd since your last reached me—what has gone through the myriads of human Minds since the 12th we talk of the immense number of Books, the Volumes ranged thousands by thousands—but perhaps more goes through the human intelligence in 12 days than ever was written. How has that unfortunate Family[2] lived through the twelve? One saying of your's I shall never forget—you may not recollect it—it being perhaps said when you were looking on the surface and seeming of Humanity alone, without a thought of the past or the future—or the deeps of good and evil—you were at the moment estranged from speculation and I think you have arguments

1 *squat*: 'Sitting close to the ground', as a hare or other animal (*OED*).
2 *that unfortunate Family*: Bailey noted: '"The unfortunate family" mentioned was most kindly treated by poor Keats.'

ready for the Man who would utter it to you—this is a formidable preface for a simple thing—merely you said; "Why should Woman suffer?" Aye. Why should she? 'By heavens I'd coin my very Soul and drop my Blood for Drachmas."![1] These things are, and he who feels how incompetent the most skyey Knight errantry its [*for* is] to heal this bruised fairness is like a sensitive leaf on the hot hand of thought. Your tearing, my dear friend, a spiritless and gloomy Letter up to rewrite to me is what I shall never forget—it was to me a real thing. Things have happen'd lately of great Perplexity—You must have heard of them—Reynolds and Haydon retorting and recrimminating—and parting for ever—the same thing has happened between Haydon and Hunt—It is unfortunate—Men should bear with each other—there lives not the Man who may not be cut up, aye hashed to pieces on his weakest side. The best of Men have but a portion of good in them—a kind of spiritual yeast in their frames which creates the ferment of existence—by which a Man is propell'd to act and strive and buffet with Circumstance. The sure way Bailey, is first to know a Man's faults, and then be passive, if after that he insensibly draws you towards him then you have no Power to break the link. Before I felt interested in either Reynolds or Haydon—I was well read in their faults yet knowing them I have been cementing gradually with both—I have an affection for them both for reasons almost opposite—and to both must I of necessity cling—supported always by the hope that when a little time—a few years shall have tried me more fully in their esteem I may be able to bring them together—the time must come because they have both hearts—and they will recollect the best parts of each other when this gust is overblown. I had a Message from you through a Letter to Jane[2] I think about Cripps—there can be no idea of binding till a sufficient sum is sure for him—and even then the thing should be maturely consider'd by all his helpers. I shall try my luck upon as many fat-purses as I can meet with—Cripps is improving

1 *By heavens . . . for Drachmas*: *Julius Caesar*, IV. iii. 72–3, substituting 'Soul' for 'heart'.

2 *Jane*: Jane Reynolds.

very fast—I have the greater hopes of him because he is so slow in devellopment—a Man of great executing Powers at 20—with a look and a speech almost stupid is sure to do something. I have just look'd th[r]ough the second side of your Letter—I feel a great content at it.

I was at Hunt's the other day,[1] and he surprised me with a real authenticated Lock of Milton's Hair. I know you would like what I wrote thereon—so here it is—as they say of a Sheep in a Nursery Book

On Seeing a Lock of Milton's Hair—[2]
Ode.

Chief of organic Numbers!
Old scholar of the spheres!
Thy spirit never slumbers,
But rolls about our ears
For ever and for ever.
O, what a mad endeavour
Worketh he
Who, to thy sacred and ennobled hearse,
Would offer a burnt sacrifice of verse
And Melody!

How heavenward thou soundedst
Live Temple of sweet noise;
And discord unconfoundedst:
Giving delight new joys,
And Pleasure nobler pinions—
O where are thy Dominions!
Lend thine ear
To a young delian[3] oath—aye, by thy soul,
By all that from thy mortal Lips did roll;
And by the kernel of thine earthly Love,

1 *the other day*: Wednesday, 21 January.
2 *On Seeing . . . Hair*: First published in 1838. On the complicated history of this text, see *Texts*.
3 *delian*: i.e., as from the island of Delos, birthplace of Apollo, god of poetry.

Beauty, in things on earth and things above,
When every childish fashion
Has vanish'd from my rhyme
Will I grey-gone in passion,
Give to an after-time
Hymning and harmony
Of thee, and of thy Works and of thy Life:
But vain is now the burning and the strife—
Pangs are in vain—until I grow high-rife
With Old Philosophy
And mad with glimpses at futurity!
For many years my offerings must be hush'd:
When I do speak I'll think upon this hour,
Because I feel my forehead hot and flush'<d,>
Even at the simplest vassal of thy Po<wer—>
A Lock of thy bright hair!
Sudden it came,
And I was startled when I heard thy name
Coupled so unaware—
Yet, at the moment, temperate was my blood:
Methought I had beheld it from the flood.

Jany 21st

This I did at Hunt's at his request—perhaps I should have done something better alone and at home—I have sent my first book to the Press—and this afternoon shall begin preparing the second—my visit to you[1] will be a great spur to quicken the Proceeding—I have not had your Sermon[2] returned—I long to make it the subject of a Letter to you—What do they say at Oxford? I trust you and Gleig pass much fine time together. Remember me to him and Whitehead. My brother Tom is getting stronger

1 *my visit to you*: Keats failed to make the visit.
2 *your Sermon*: Bailey's Oxford sermon was published anonymously by Taylor and Hessey in November or December 1817 as *Athanasia: A Discourse inscribed to the Memory of Princess Charlotte Augusta*. Keats had evidently lent out his copy to Wordsworth, who three months later still had not returned it (p. 124 below).

but his Spitting of blood continues—I sat down to read King Lear yesterday, and felt the greatness of the thing up to the writing of a Sonnet preparatory thereto—in my next you shall have it There were some miserable reports of Rice's health—I went and lo! Master Jemmy had been to the play the night before and was out at the time—he always comes on his Legs like a Cat—I have seen a good deal of Wordsworth. Hazlitt is lectu[r]ing on Poetry[1] at the Surry institution—I shall be there next Tuesday.

Your most affectionate Friend
John Keats—

To George and Tom Keats
23, 24 January 1818

[Jeffrey transcript (1845)]

[Well Walk, Hampstead]
Friday 23[d] January 1818

My dear Brothers.

I was thinking of what hindered me from writing so long, for I have many things to say to you & know not where to begin. It shall be upon a thing most interesting to you my Poem. Well! I have given the 1st book to Taylor; he seemed more than satisfied with it, & to my surprise proposed publishing it in Quarto if Haydon would make a drawing of some event therein, for a Frontispeice. I called on Haydon, he said he would do anything I liked, but said he would rather paint a finished picture, from it, which he seems eager to do; this in a year or two will be a glorious thing for us; & it will be, for Haydon is struck with the 1st Book. I left Haydon & the next day received a letter from him, proposing to make, as he says, with all his might, a finished chalk sketch of my head, to be engraved in the first style & put

1 *Hazlitt . . . on Poetry*: Hazlitt's lectures, published as *Lectures on the English Poets* (1818), were given at the Surrey Institution between 13 January and 3 March.

at the head of my Poem, saying at the same time he had never done the thing for any human being, & that it must have considerable effect as he will put the name to it—I begin to day to copy my 2nd Book "thus far into the bowels of the Land"[1]—You shall hear whether it will be Quarto or non Quarto, picture or non Picture. Leigh Hunt I showed my 1st Book to, he allows it not much merit as a whole; says it is unnatural & made ten objections to it in the mere skimming over. He says the conversation is unnatural & too high-flown for the Brother & Sister. Says it should be simple forgetting do ye mind, that they are both overshadowed by a Supernatural Power, & of force could not speak like Franchesca[2] in the Rimini. He must first prove that Caliban's poetry is unnatural,—This with me completely overturns his objections—the fact is he & Shelley are hurt & perhaps justly, at my not having showed them the affair officiously & from several hints I have had they appear much disposed to dissect & anatomize, any trip or slip I may have made.—But whose afraid Ay! Tom! demme if I am.[3] I went last tuesday, an hour too late, to Hazlitt's Lecture on poetry, got there just as they were coming out, when all these pounced upon me. Hazlitt, John Hunt & son, Wells, Bewick, all the Landseers, Bob Harris, Cox[4] of the Borrough Aye & more; the Landseers enquired after you particularly—I know not whether Wordsworth has left town—But sunday I dined with Hazlitt & Haydon, also that I took Haslam with me—I dined with Brown lately. Dilke having taken the Champion, Theatricals[5] was obliged to be in Town. Fanny has returned to Walthamstow—Mr Abbey appeared very glum, the last time I went [to] see her,

1 *thus far ... the Land*: *Richard III*, V. ii. 3, the future Henry VII's words shortly before joining battle at Bosworth Field.

2 *Franchesca*: The heroine Francesca in Hunt's *The Story of Rimini* (1816).

3 *whose afraid ... I am*: Keats quotes from Horace Smith's unpublished anti-Methodist satire *Nehemiah Muggs*: 'Pooh! Nonsense! damme! Who's afraid?' See also below, pp. 111, 113–14.

4 *Cox*: Jeffrey has 'Rox' (identified by Rollins as one of the Rokes brothers, undertakers in the Borough), a mistake for Cox, a medical bookseller near Keats's lodgings (Gittings).

5 *Champion, Theatricals*: Dilke agreed to take over reviewing plays for the *Champion* from Reynolds.

& said in an indirect way, that I had no business there—Rice has been ill, but has been mending much lately—I think a little change has taken place in my intellect lately—I cannot bear to be uninterested or unemployed, I, who for so long a time, have been addicted to passiveness—Nothing is finer for the purposes of great productions, than a very gradual ripening of the intellectual powers—As an instance of this—observe—I sat down yesterday to read King Lear once again the thing appeared to demand the prologue of a Sonnet, I wrote it & began to read—(I know you would like to see it)

"On sitting down to King Lear once Again"[1]
O golden tongued Romance with serene Lute!
Fair plumed syren! Queen! of[2] far away!
Leave melodizing on this wintry day,
Shut up thine olden volume & be mute.
Adieu! for once again the fierce dispute,
Betwixt Hell torment & impassioned Clay
Must I burn through; once more [humbly] assay
The bitter sweet of this Shakespeareian fruit
Cheif Poet! & ye clouds of Albion.
Begettors of our deep eternal theme,
When I am through the old oak forest gone
Let me not wander in a barren dream
But when I am consumed with the Fire
Give me new Pheonix-wings to fly at my desire

So you see I am getting at it, with a sort of determination & strength, though verily I do not feel it at this moment—this is my fourth letter this morning & I feel rather tired & my head rather swimming—so I will leave it open till tomorrow's post.—[late evening, Saturday, 24 January 1818] I am in the habit of taking my papers to Dilkes & copying there; so I chat &

1 *On sitting . . . Again*: Keats made a fair copy of this sonnet and of 'On Seeing a Lock of Milton's Hair' in his copy of the 1808 facsimile of Shakespeare's First Folio. Neither poem was published until 1838. Keats's fair copy of the sonnet has 'damnation' for 'Hell torment' in l. 6.

2 *of*: Jeffrey has 'if' in error.

proceed at the same time. I have been there at my work this evening, & the walk over the Heath takes off all sleep, so I will even proceed with you—I left off short in my last, just as I began an account of a private theatrical[1]—Well it was of the lowest order, all greasy & oily, insomuch that if they had lived in olden times, when signs were hung over the doors; the only appropriate one for that oily place would have been—a guttered Candle—they played John Bull The Review. & it was to conclude with Bombastes Furioso[2]—I saw from a Box the 1st Act of John Bull, then I went to Drury [Lane] & did not return till it was over; when by Wells' interest we got behind the scenes. there was not a yard wide all the way round for the actors, scene shifters & interlopers to move in; for 'Nota Bene' the Green Room was under the stage & there was I threatened over & over again to be turned out by the oily scene shifters—there did I hear a little painted Trollop own, very candidly, that she had failed in Mary, with a "damned if she'd play a serious part again, as long as she lived," & at the same time she was habited as the Quaker in the Review—there was a quarrel & a fat good natured looking girl in soldiers Clothes wished she had only been a man for Tom's sake[3]—One fellow began a song but an unlucky finger-point from the Gallery sent him off like a shot, One chap was dressed to kill for the King in Bombastes. & he stood at the edge of the scene in the very sweat of anxiety to show himself, but Alas the thing was not played. the sweetest morsel of the night moreover was, that the musicians began pegging & fagging away at an overture—never did you see faces more in earnest, three times did they play it over,

1 *I began . . . private theatrical*: On 13 January, p. 89 above. Wells and Keats spent the evening by beginning at the 'private theatrical', left after Act I of the first of three plays to see Kean in *Richard III* at Drury Lane, and returned to see the final play, which was not performed.
2 *John Bull The Review . . . Bombastes Furioso*: George Colman's popular *John Bull* (1803) and his musical farce *The Review* (1801) were meant to be followed by W. B. Rhodes's burlesque opera *Bombastes Furioso* (1810).
3 *painted Trollop . . . Tom's sake*: The first actress had played the part of Mary Thornberry in *John Bull* and was now dressed for her part as the Quaker girl in *The Review*; the second, dressed for her part in *The Review*, is interested in the actor playing Tom Shuffleton in *John Bull*.

dropping all kinds of correctness & still did not the curtain draw up—Well then they went into a country-dance then into a region they well knew, into their old boonsome Pothouse.[1] & then to see how pompous o' the sudden they turned; how they looked about, & chatted; how they did not care a Damn; was a great treat—I hope I have not tired you by this filling up of the dash in my last,[2]—Constable the Bookseller has offered Reynolds ten guineas a sheet to write for his magazine. it is an Edinburgh one which, Blackwoods started up in opposition to. Hunt said he was nearly sure that the 'Cockney School' was written by Scott,[3] so you are right Tom!—There are no more little bits of news I can remember at present I remain

My dear Brothers Your very affectionate Brother

John

To John Taylor

30 January 1818

[Morgan MS]

[Well Walk, Hampstead]

My dear Taylor, Friday

These Lines as they now stand, about Happiness have rung in my ears like a 'chime a mending'.[4] see here,

Behold

Wherein Lies happiness Pœona? fold—

This appears to me the very contrary of blessed. I hope this will appear to you more eligible.

1 *Pothouse*: Public house.

2 *filling up of the dash in my last*: See p. 89 ('I have been –') above.

3 *Edinburgh one . . . written by Scott*: For the rivalry between Constable's well-established *Edinburgh Review*, to which Reynolds did contribute, and *Blackwood's Magazine*, and for J. G. Lockhart, the true author of the 'Cockney School' attacks, see above, p. 64.

4 *chime a mending*: Keats quotes Ulysses' description of Patroclus' mocking imitations of his fellow Greeks in *Troilus and Cressida*, I. iii. 159.

Wherein lies Happiness? In that which becks
Our ready Minds to fellowship divine;
A fellowship with essence, till we shine
Full alchymized and free of space. Behold
The clear Religion of heaven—fold &c—

You must indulge me by putting this in[1] for setting aside the badness of the other, such a preface is necessary to the Subject. The whole thing must I think have appeared to you, who are a consequitive Man, as a thing almost of mere words—but I assure you that when I wrote it, it was a regular stepping of the Imagination towards a Truth.[2] My having written that ~~Passage~~ /Argument/ will perhaps be of the greatest Service to me of any thing I ever did—It set before me at once the gradations of Happiness even like a kind of Pleasure Thermometer—and is my first Step towards the chief Attempt in the Drama—the playing of different Natures with Joy and Sorrow.

Do me this favor and believe Me, Your sincere friend
John Keats

I hope your next Work[3] will be of a more general Interest—I s[u]ppose you cogitate a little about it now and then.

1 *putting this in*: As requested, Taylor copied this revision of *Endymion*, I, 777–81 into Keats's revised Fair Copy of Book I (Morgan Library).
2 *when I wrote . . . a Truth*: The long passage in *Endymion*, I, 777–842, which concludes by claiming there would be no natural world of generation unless 'human souls did . . . kiss and greet'. Benjamin Bailey was shocked by Keats's 'inclination to that abominable principle of *Shelley's*—that *Sensual Love* is the principle of things' (*KC*, I, 34–5).
3 *your next Work*: The second edition of Taylor's *The Identity of Junius with a Distinguished Living Character Established* (1818).

To George and Tom Keats
30 January 1818

[Private New York Collection MS][1]

[Friday, Well Walk]
Hampstead—

My dear Brothers,

You shall have the Papers.[2] I lent the last to Dilke and he has not returned it—or rather I have been in Town two days gelding the first Book [of *Endymion*] which is I think going to the Press today. It will not be in Quarto, nor shall I have my head therein. Taylor on looking attentively through it has changed his Mind. I have got five pounds but then I owe th<e>m Brown and have been delaying these two or three days to give it him, I must owe him still. Perhaps this will do till Haslam sends you some. £10 to Mrs Bentley £10 to Crip[p]s and the £5 to Brown nearly swallowed up the Balance Mr A[bbey] gave me.[3] I understand about Mr Fry and will speak to Mr A[bbey] about it. I am convinced now that my Poem will not sell. hope, they say, so I will wait about three Months before I make my determination—either to get some employment at Home or abroad or to retire to a very cheap way of living in the Country—Haydon will take my Likeness all the same—but I think he will keep it—however we can get it engraved—Horace Twiss[4] dined the other day with Horace Smith—now Horace Twiss has an affectation of repeating extempore verses—which however he writes at home. After dinner Horace

1 The transcript by Dearing Lewis, 'A Keats Letter Rediscovered', *Keats–Shelley Journal*, 47 (1998), pp. 14–18, varies in some details.

2 *the Papers*: Keats habitually forwarded his copies of the *Examiner* to his brothers.

3 *£10 . . . gave me*: These new details show Keats's concern about his own and his brothers' finances. Mr Fry appears to have joined Abbey as second guardian of the Keats children on the death of Sandell in May 1816. By 1819, if not sooner, he was living in Holland (see below, pp. 414 n., 471).

4 *Horace Twiss*: (1787–1849), lawyer, politician and later MP. As a young man known for his squibs and jeux d'esprit in the newspapers.

T. was to recite some verses and before he did he went aside to pretend to make on the spot verses composed before hand. While H. T was out of the Room H. S. wrote the following and handed it about, when H. Twiss had done his spouting.

'What precious extempore verses are Twiss's
Which he makes ere he waters, and vows as he pisses,
'T would puzzle the Sages of greece to unriddle
Which flows out the fastest his verse or his piddle,
And 'twould pose them as much to know whether or not
His Piss or his Poems go quickest to Pot!

I wrote the following which has pleased Reynolds and Dilke beyond any thing I ever did. I was thinking of Ben Jonson, Beaumont and Fletcher and the rest who used to meet at the Mermaid in days of yore and to finish did this.

Souls of Poets dead and gone[1]
What Elysium have ye known,
Happy field, or mossy cavern
Fairer than the Mermaid Tavern?
   Have ye tippled drink more fine
Than mine host's canary wine;
Or are fruits of Paradise
Richer than those dainty pies
Of venison. Oh! generous food!
Dress'd as though bold Robin Hood
Would, with his Maid Marian,
Sup and bouze from Horn and Can.
   I have heard that on a day
Mine Host's sign board flew away,
Nobody knew whither till
An Astrologer's old Quill
To a Sheepskin gave the story:
Says he saw ye in your glory
Underneath a new old sign

1 *Souls ... gone*: Keats published this poem with alterations as 'Lines on the Mermaid Tavern' in *1820*. The text here is closest to the Fair Copy at Harvard.

Sipping beverage divine,
And pledging with contented smack
The Mermaid in the Zodiac!
Souls of Poets dead and gone
Are the Winds a sweeter home,
Richer is uncellar'd Cavern
Than the merr<y> mermaid Tavern?

May the £5 do and this please you—trust to the Spring and farewell my dear Tom and Geo<rg>e[1]

Your affectionate Brother
John——

To J. H. Reynolds
31 January 1818

[Woodhouse transcript (1821?)]

[Well Walk]
My Dear Reynolds Hampstead Saturday

I have parcelld out this day for Letter Writing—more resolved thereon because your Letter will come as a refreshment and will have (sic parvis &c)[2] the same effect as a Kiss in certain situations where people become over-generous. I have read this first sentence over, and think it savours rather; however an inward innocence is like a nested dove; or as the old song says.

1

O blush not so, O blush not so[3]
or I shall think ye knowing;
And if ye smile, the blushing while
Then Maidenheads are going.

1 *and farewell . . . Geo<rg>e*: The last sentence is written vertically in the margin.
2 *sic parvis &c*: *sic parvis componere magna solebam* ('I have only measured great by small'), Virgil's *Eclogues*, I, 24.
3 O *blush not so*, O *blush not so*: First published 1883.

2

There's a blush for want, and a blush for shan't
And a blush for having done it,
There's a blush for thought, and blush for naught
And a blush for just begun it.

3

O sigh not so, O sigh not so
For it sounds of Eve's sweet Pipin
By those loosen'd hips, you have tasted the pips
And fought in an amorous nipping.

4

Will ye play once more, at nice cut core
For it only will last our youth out,
And we have the prime, of the Kissing time
We have not one sweet tooth out.

—5—

There's a sigh for yes, and a sigh for no,
And a sigh for "I can't bear it"—
O what can be done, shall we stay or run
O cut the sweet apple and share it?

Now I purposed to write to you a serious poetical Letter—but I find that a maxim I met with the other day is a just one "on cause mieux quand on ne dit pas causons"[1] I was hindered however from my first intention by a mere muslin Handkerchief very neatly pinned—but "Hence vain deluding &c"[2] Yet I cannot write in prose, It is a sun-shiny day and I cannot so here goes,

Hence Burgundy, Claret & Port[3]
Away with old Hock and Madeira
Too couthly ye are for my sport
There's a Beverage brighter and clearer

1 *on cause . . . pas causons*: 'You talk better when you don't say "Let's talk".'
2 *Hence vain deluding &c*: Milton's 'Il Penseroso', l. 1.
3 *Hence Burgundy, Claret & Port*: First published in *1848*.

Instead of a pitiful rummer
My Wine overbrims a whole Summer
My bowl is the sky
And I drink at my eye
Till I feel in the brain
A delphian[1] pain—
The[n] follow my Caius[2] then follow
On the Green of the Hill
We will drink our fill
Of golden sunshine
Till our brains intertwine
With the glory and grace of Apollo!

God of the Meridian[3]
And of the East and West
To thee my soul is flown
And my body is earthward press'd—
It is an awful mission
A terrible division
And leaves a gulph austere
To be filled with worldly fear—
Aye, when the Soul is fled
To high above our head
Affrighted do we gaze
After its airy maze—
As doth a Mother wild
When her young infant child
Is in an eagle's claws—
And is not this the cause
of Madness? God of Song
Thou bearest me along
Through sights I scarce can bear
O let me, let me share

1 *delphian*: From Apollo's oracle at Delphi.
2 *Caius*: Reynolds's pseudonym when writing for the *Yellow Dwarf*.
3 *God of the Meridian*: First published *1848*.

With the hot Lyre and thee
The staid Philosophy.
Temper my lonely hours
And let me see thy bowr's
More unalarm'd!—

My Dear Reynolds, you must forgive me all this ranting—but the fact is I cannot write sense this Morning—however you shall have some—I will copy my last Sonnet.

When I have fears that I may cease to be[1]
 Before my pen has glean'd my teeming brain,
Before high piled Books in charactery[2]
 Hold like full garners the full ripen'd grain—
When I behold upon the night's starr'd face
 Huge cloudy symbols of a high romance
And feel that I may never live to trace
 Their shadows with the magic hand of Chance:
And when I feel, fair creature of an hour,
 That I shall never look upon thee more
Never have relish in the fairy power
 Of unreflecting Love: then on the Shore
 Of the wide world I stand alone and think
 Till Love and Fame to Nothingness do sink.—

I must take a turn, and then write to Teignmouth—Remember me to all, not excepting yourself.

Your sincere friend,
John Keats.

To J. H. Reynolds
3 February 1818

[Woodhouse transcript (1821?)]

1 *When I have fears that I may cease to be*: First published in *1848*.
2 *charactery*: 'Expression of thought by symbols or characters' (*OED*). Rare, but used by Shakespeare.

[Well Walk]
Hampstead Tuesday.

My dear Reynolds,

I thank you for your dish of Filberts[1]—Would I could get a basket of them by way of desert every day for the sum of two pence—Would we were a sort of ethereal Pigs, & turn'd loose to feed upon spiritual Mast & Acorns—which would be merely being a squirrel & feed [*for* feeding] upon filberts. for what is a Squirrel but an airy pig, or a filbert but a sort of archangelical acorn. About the nuts being worth cracking, all I can say is that where there are a throng of delightful Images ready drawn simplicity is the only thing. the first is the best on account of the first line, and the "arrow—foil'd of its antler'd food"—and moreover (and this is the only word or two I find fault with, the more because I have had so much reason to shun it as a quicksand) the last has "tender and true"[2]—We must cut this, and not be rattlesnaked into any more of the like—It may be said that we ought to read our Contemporaries. that Wordsworth &c should have their due from us. but for the sake of a few fine imaginative or domestic passages, are we to be bullied into a certain Philosophy engendered in the whims of an Egotist[3]—Every Man has his speculations, but every man does not brood and peacock over them till he makes a false coinage and deceives himself—Many a man can travel to the very bourne of Heaven, and yet want confidence to put down his own halfseeing. Sancho will invent a Journey heavenward as well as any body. We hate poetry that has a palpable design upon us—and if we do not agree, seems to put its hand in its breeches pockets.

1 *dish of Filberts*: These are, as Woodhouse notes, '2 Sonnets on Robin Hood sent by R[eynolds] by the [twopenny] post.' Keats calls them 'Filberts' (hazelnuts) because Reynolds had described the lines of W. L. Bowles's sonnets as 'fourteen nutshells'. Reynolds subsequently published both sonnets in the *Yellow Dwarf* (21 February 1818) and his *Garden of Florence* (1821).

2 *tender and true*: Reynolds emended l. 8 of his second sonnet to read 'young as the dew'.

3 *Egotist*: Keats echoes Hazlitt's criticism of Wordsworth's *The Excursion* in which 'intellectual egotism swallows up every thing' (*Examiner*, 21 August–2 October 1814, p. 542). See his later ideas on the 'egotistical sublime' (p. 262 below).

Poetry should be great & unobtrusive, a thing which enters into one's soul, and does not startle it or amaze it with itself but with its subject.—How beautiful are the retired flowers! how would they lose their beauty were they to throng into the highway crying out, "admire me I am a violet! dote upon me I am a primrose! Modern poets differ from the Elizabethans in this. Each of the moderns like an Elector of Hanover governs his petty state, & knows how many straws are swept daily from the Causeways in all his dominions & has a continual itching that all the Housewives should have their coppers well scoured: the antients were Emperors of vast Provinces, they had only heard of the remote ones and scarcely cared to visit them.—I will cut all this—I will have no more of Wordsworth or Hunt in particular—Why should we be of the tribe of Manasseh, when we can wander with Esau?[1] why should we kick against the Pricks, when we can walk on Roses? Why should we be owls, when we can be Eagles? Why be teased with "nice Eyed wagtails" when we have in sight "the Cherub Contemplation"?[2]—Why with Wordsworths "Matthew with a bough of wilding in his hand" when we can have Jacques "under an oak &c"[3]—The secret of the Bough of Wilding will run through your head faster than I can write it—Old Matthew spoke to him some years ago on some nothing, & because he happens in an Evening Walk to imagine the figure of the old man—he must stamp it down in black & white, and it is henceforth sacred—I don't mean to deny Wordsworth's grandeur & Hunt's merit, but I mean to say we need not be teazed with grandeur & merit—when we can have them uncontaminated & unobtrusive. Let us have the old Poets, and Robin Hood Your letter and its sonnets gave

1 *Manasseh . . . Esau*: The tribe of Manasseh contributed to the defeat of the Midianites (Judges 7:23), but Keats is probably also thinking of the tyrannical seventh-century king of Judah. Esau, a hunter like Robin Hood, killed 'venison' for his father.

2 *the Cherub Contemplation*: Keats compares Leigh Hunt's image of 'nice Eyed wagtails' ('The Nymphs', *Foliage* (1818), p. xxxiii) with Milton's 'Il Penseroso', l. 54.

3 *Wordsworths . . . oak &c*: Wordsworth's 'The Two April Mornings', ll. 59–60, is set against Shakespeare's *As You Like It*, II. i. 31–63.

me more pleasure than will the 4th Book of Childe Harold[1] & the whole of any body's life and opinions. In return for your Dish of filberts, I have gathered a few Catkins, I hope they'll look pretty.

To J. H. R. In answer to his Robin Hood Sonnets.

"No those days are gone away &c"— See Coll: p 58.[2]

I hope you will like them they are at least written in the Spirit of Outlawry.—Here are the Mermaid lines

"Souls of poets dead and gone &c"— ib. p 61.[3]

I will call on you at 4 tomorrow, and we will trudge together for it is not the thing to be a stranger in the Land of Harpisicols.[4] I hope also to bring you my 2d book—In the hope that these Scribblings will be some amusement for you this Evening—I remain copying on the Hill

Yr sincere friend and Coscribbler
John Keats.

Keats finished copying Book II of Endymion *by 5 February, but needed a further day 'to overlook it' and still had a 'very particular employ in the affair of Cripps'* (L, I, *p.* 226). *The following week he attended Hazlitt's lecture at the Surrey Institution on Tuesday, 10 February, and dined at Hunt's with Shelley and others the next evening.*

1 *4th Book of Childe Harold*: Canto IV of Byron's *Childe Harold's Pilgrimage* was published the following April.
2 *See Coll: p 58*: Woodhouse refers to the transcript of Keats's poem in his 'Commonplace book of poems' (W2), Harvard Keats MS 3.2, ff. 58–60. Keats later printed the poem with revisions in *1820*. In reply to Reynolds, Keats insists that the age of Robin Hood's 'outlawry' and pre-capitalist pastoral world is gone. Further see, John Barnard, 'Keats's "Robin Hood", John Hamilton Reynolds, and the "Old Poets"', *Proceedings of the British Academy*, 75 (1989), pp. 181–200.
3 *ib. p 61*: Keats here copied out 'Lines on the Mermaid Tavern', sent earlier to his brothers (pp. 103–4 above). Woodhouse's reference is again to his own transcript (ibid., f. 61).
4 *Harpisicols*: i.e., harpsichords, a reference to the musical evenings at the house of Vincent Novello (see below, p. 273).

To George and Tom Keats
14(?) February 1818

[Jeffrey transcript 1845]

[Well Walk]
My dear Brothers Hampstead Saturday Night

When once a man delays a letter beyond the proper time, he delays it longer for one or two reasons; first because he must begin in a very commonplace style, that is to say, with an excuse; & secondly things & circumstances become so jumbled in his mind, that he knows not what, or what not, he has said in his last—I shall visit you as soon as I have copied my poem all out, I am now much beforehand with the printer, they have done none yet, & I am half afraid they will let half the season by before the printing, I am determined they shall not trouble me when I have copied it all.—Horace Smith has lent me his manuscript called "Nehemiah Muggs, an exposure of the Methodists" perhaps I may send you a few extracts—Hazlitts last Lecture was on Thomson, Cowper & Crabbe, he praised Cowper & Thompson but he gave Crabbe an unmerciful licking—I think Hunts article of Fazio—no it was not, but I saw Fazio the first night,[1] it hung rather heavily on me—I am in the high way of being introduced to a squad of people, Peter Pindar, Mrs Opie. Mrs Scott[2]—Mr Robinson[3] a great friend of Coleridges called on me—Richards tell[s] me that my Poems are known in the west country & that he saw a very clever copy of verses, headed with a Motto from my Sonnet to George—Honors rush so thickly upon me that I shall not be able to bear up against them. What think you, am I to be crowned in the

1 *I saw Fazio the first night*: Henry Hart Milman's *Fazio* premiered at Covent Garden on 5 February.
2 *Peter Pindar*: pseudonym of the satirist John Wolcot (1738–1819) (see below, p. 493). *Mrs Opie*: Amelia Alderson Opie (1769–1853), novelist and poet. *Mrs Scott*: Caroline Colnaghi, the wife of John Scott.
3 *Robinson*: The diarist Henry Crabb Robinson (1775–1867).

Capitol,[1] am I to be made a Mandarin—No! I am to be invited, M[rs] Hunt tells me, to a party at Ollier's to keep Shakespeares birthday Shakespeare would stare to see me there—The Wednesday before last Shelley, Hunt & I wrote each a Sonnet on the River Nile,[2] some day you shall read them all. I saw a sheet of Endymion & have all reason to suppose they will soon get it done.[3] there shall be nothing wanting on my part. I have been writing at intervals many songs & Sonnets, & I long to be at Teignmouth, to read them over to you: however I think I had better wait till this Book is off my mind; it will not be long first,

Reynolds has been writing two very capital articles in the Yellow Dwarf on popular Preachers[4]—All the talk here is about D[r] Croft the Duke of Devon &c[5] Your most affectionate Brother

John.

1 *crowned in the Capitol*: Compare Keats's reference to a 'petrarchal coronation' (pp. 158–9 below).

2 *Shelley, Hunt . . . River Nile*: Sonnet competitions were common in the Hunt circle. Hunt published 'The Nile', written on 4 February, in *Foliage* (1818). Keats's 'To The Nile' was not published until 1838 and was printed again in *1848*. Shelley's sonnet was 'Month after month the gather'd rains descend' and not 'Ozymandias'. It was not published until 1876.

3 *I saw a sheet . . . get it done*: This shows, as Rollins notes, that Jeffrey made omissions from Keats's letter, which was written on more than one day. At its start Keats says the printers have done nothing, but here he has seen a sheet and expects printing to be completed 'soon'.

4 *articles . . . on popular Preachers*: Two of Reynolds's satirical articles on evangelical priests, entitled 'Pulpit Oratory' and signed 'Caius', had appeared in the *Yellow Dwarf* on 7 and 14 February 1818. The third and last came out on 28 February.

5 *D[r] Croft the Duke of Devon &c*: Sir Richard Croft (1762–1818), physician of Princess Charlotte, bore the blame for her death following childbirth on 6 November 1817. His suicide on 12 February 1818 was reported in the *Examiner* (Sunday, 15 February). This issue also repeated the scandal that Croft had connived at an exchange of infants in the Duke of Devonshire's family, indicating that Keats completed his letter after reading it.

(The following Extracts from Horace Smith's Manuscript[1] are on a loose sheet enclosed in the previous letter of date Hampstead. February 16th[2]—)

—Poem. Nehemiah Muggs—An Exposure of the Methodists—

Muggs had long wished to be a father
And told his wish without succeeding
At length Rose brought him two together
And there I think she show'd her breeding

Behold them in the Holy place
With others all agog for Grace
Where a perspiring preacher vexes
Sundry old women of both sexes

Thumping as though his zeal were pushing
To make a convert of the cushion

But in their hurry to proceed
Each reached the door at the same minute
Where as the[y] scuffled for the lead
Both struggling stuck together in it

Shouting rampant amorous hymns
Under pretext of singing Psalms

He shudder'd & withdrew his eye
Perk'd up his head some inches higher
Drew his chair nearer to the fire
And hummed as if he would have said
Pooh! Nonsense! damme! who's afraid
Or sought by bustling up his frame
To make his courage do the same
Thus would some blushing trembling Elves

1 *Horace Smith's Manuscript*: The complete MS is in Essex County Record Office (Gittings). Part of it was printed in the *London Magazine* (March–June 1821).
2 *February 16th*: Jeffrey's date, '16 February 1819', is mistaken. Keats heard Hazlitt's lecture attacking Crabbe on Tuesday, 10 February 1818, and wrote this letter the following Saturday.

Conceal their terrors from themselves
By their own cheering wax the bolder
And pat themselves upon the shoulder

A Saint's a sort of human Mill
That labours when the body's still
And gathers grist with inward groans
And creaking melancholy moans
By waving heavenward o'er his head
His arms & working them for bread

Is it that addled brains perchance
When the skull's dark with ignorance
Like rotten eggs surveyed at night
Emit a temporary light?
Or is that a heated brain
When it is rubbed against the grain,
Like a Cat's back though black as charcoal
Will in the gloom appear to sparkle

New Missions sent
To make the Antipodes relent
Turn the Anthropophagetic race
To sucking lambs & babes of grace
Or tempt the hairy Hebrew rogues
To cut their beards & Synagogues

This grave advertisement was seen
"Wanted a serious Shopman, who
To Gospel principles is true
Whose voice for Hymns is not too gruff
Who can grind brick dust, mix up snuff
And has an undisputed Nack in
Fearing the Lord & making Blacking

(The above in all probability is published but they are copied to show John Keats Choice in the selection of Extracts)

To J. H. Reynolds
19 February 1818

[Princeton MS]

[Thursday, Well Walk, Hampstead]

My dear Reynolds,

I have an idea that a Man might pass a very pleasant life in this manner—let him on any certain day read a certain Page of full Poesy or distilled Prose and let him wander with it, and muse upon it, and reflect from it, and bring home to it, and prophesy upon it, and dream upon it—untill it becomes stale—but when will it do so? Never—When Man has arrived at a certain ripeness in intellect any one grand and spiritual passage serves him as a starting post towards all "the two and thirty Pallaces"[1] How happy is such a "voyage of conception,' what delicious diligent Indolence! A doze upon a Sofa does not hinder it, and a nap upon Clover engenders ethereal finger-pointings—the prattle of a child gives it wings, and the converse of middle age a strength to beat them—a strain of musick conducts to 'an odd angle of the Isle' and when the leaves whisper it puts a 'girdle round the earth.[2] Nor will this sparing touch of noble Books be any irreverance to their Writers—for perhaps the honors paid by Man to Man are trifles in comparison to the Benefit done by great Works to the 'Spirit and pulse of good'[3] by their mere passive existence.[4]

Memory should not be called Knowledge—Many have original Minds who do not think it—they are led away by

1 *two and thirty Pallaces*: The Chinese Empire was reported to contain thirty-two palaces: see, for example, Charles Middleton's *A New and Complete System of Geography* (1778–9 edn), I, p. 28.

2 *an odd angle of the Isle . . . girdle round the earth*: *The Tempest*, I. ii. 223; *A Midsummer Night's Dream*, II. i. 175.

3 *Spirit and pulse of good*: Wordsworth's 'The Old Cumberland Beggar', l. 77.

4 *passive existence*: This sentence ends at the bottom of the letter's first page, and is followed by a substantial space, indicating that a new paragraph starts on the next page.

Custom—Now it appears to me that almost any Man may like the Spider spin from his own inwards his own airy Citadel—the points of leaves and twigs on which the Spider begins her work are few and she fills the Air with a beautiful circuiting: man should be content with as few points to tip with the fine Webb of his Soul and weave a tapestry empyrean—full of Symbols for his spiritual eye, of softness for his spiritual touch, of space for his wandering of distinctness for his Luxury—But the Minds of Mortals are so different and bent on such diverse Journeys that it may at first appear impossible for any common taste and fellowship to exist between two or three under these suppositions—It is however quite the contrary—Minds would leave each other in contrary directions, traverse each other in Numberless points, and all [at] last greet each other at the Journeys end—A old Man and a child would talk together and the old Man be led on his Path, and the child left thinking—Man should not dispute or assert but whisper results to his neighbour, and thus by every germ of Spirit sucking the Sap from mould ethereal every human might become great, and Humanity instead of being a wide heath of Furse and Briars with here and there a remote Oak or Pine, would become a grand democracy of Forest Trees. It has been an old Comparison for our urging on—the Bee hive—however it seems to me that we should rather be the flower than the Bee—for it is a false notion that more is gained by receiving than giving[1]—no the receiver and the giver are equal in their benefits—The f[l]ower I doubt not receives a fair guerdon from the Bee—its leaves blush deeper in the next spring—and who shall say between Man and Woman which is the most delighted? Now it is more noble to sit like Jove that [*for* than] to fly like Mercury—let us not therefore go hurrying about and collecting honey-bee like, buzzing here and there impatiently from a knowledge of what is to be arrived at: but let us open our leaves like a flower and be passive and receptive—budding patiently under the eye of Apollo and taking hints from eve[r]y noble insect that favors us

1 *more is gained ... than giving*: 'It is more blessed to give than to receive' (Acts 20:35).

with a visit—sap will be given us for Meat and dew for drink—I was led into these thoughts, my dear Reynolds, by the beauty of the morning operating on a sense of Idleness—I have not read any Books—the Morning said I was right—I had no Idea but of the Morning and the Thrush said I was right—seeming to say—

'O thou whose face hath felt the Winter's wind;[1]
  Whose eye has seen the Snow clouds hung in Mist
And the black-elm tops 'mong the freezing Stars
To thee the Spring will be a harvest-time—
O thou whose only book has been the light
Of /supreme/ darkness which thou feddest on
Night after night, when Phœbus was away
To thee the Spring shall be a tripple morn—
O fret not after Knowledge—I have none
And yet my song comes native with the warmth
O fret not after Knowledge—I have none
And yet the Evening listens—He who saddens
At thought of Idleness cannot be idle,
And he's awake who thinks himself asleep.'

Now I am sensible all this is a mere sophistication, however it may neighbour to any truths, to excuse my own indolence—so I will not deceive myself that Man should be equal with jove—but think himself very well off as a sort of scullion-Mercury[2] or even a humble Bee—it is not [*for* no] matter whether I am right or wrong either one way or another, if there is sufficient to lift a little time from your Shoulders.

Your affectionate friend
John Keats—

1 *O thou whose face hath felt the Winter's wind*: First published in *1848*. Stillinger says it is not known whether this is a draft or fair copy (*Texts*, p. 176): the interlineation in l. 6 suggests it is a fair copy.
2 *scullion*: A kitchen-worker. *Mercury*: The messenger of the Gods.

To George and Tom Keats
21 February 1818

[Harvard MS]

[Well Walk]
Hampstead Saturday—

My dear Brothers,

I am extremely sorry to have given you so much uneasiness by not writing: however you know good news is no news or vice versa—I do not like to write a short Letter to you—or you would have had one long before—The Weather although boisterous to day has been very much milder—and I think Devonshire is no[t] the last place to receive a temperate change—The occasion of my writing to day is the enclosed Letter by the Post Mark from Miss Wylie[1]—does she expect you in town George? I have been abominably id[l]e since you left—but have just turned over a new leaf—and used as a marker a Letter of excuse to an invitation from Horace Smith. I received a Letter from Haydon the other day in which he says, his essays on the elgin Marbles are being translated into italian—the which he superintends. I did not mention that I had seen the British Gallery—there are some nice things by Stark and Bathsheba by Wilkie which is condemned[2]—I could not bear Leslie's Uriel[3]—Reynolds has been very ill for some time—confined to the house—and had Leeches applied to the chest—When I

1 *Miss Wylie*: Georgiana Augusta Wylie (1801/2–79), George's future wife. Although this is the first mention of her in his letters, Keats's sonnet 'To G. A. W', published in *Poems* (1817), had been written at George's request more than a year earlier in December 1816.

2 *British Gallery . . . condemned*: The British Institution (1805–67) admitted connoisseurs to its membership, not artists, and held regular public exhibitions in its Pall Mall gallery. James Stark (1794–1859) exhibited there (1814–18), winning the £50 prize in 1818. *Bathsheba* by the Scottish painter David Wilkie (1785–1841) attracted both negative and positive responses.

3 *Leslie's Uriel*: *Uriel in the Sun* by the American artist Washington Allston (1779–1843) and not his pupil Charles Leslie (1794–1859).

saw him on Wednesday he was much the same—and he is in the worst place in the world for amendment—among the strife of womens tongues in a hot and parch'd room—I wish he would move to Butler's for a short time. The Thrushes and Blackbirds have been singing me into an idea that it was spring, and almost that Leaves were on the trees—so that black clouds and boisterous winds seem to have muster'd and collected to full Divan[1] for the purpose of convincing me to the contrary—I have not been to Edmonton all this While, and there is not a day but Le Mesurier's image reproaches me for it—and I suppose the Haughton's[2] think us dead—I will shortly go and set matters right thereabouts Taylor says my Poem shall be out in a Month. I think he'll be out before it[3]—The Thrushes are singing now—af it [*for* as if] they would speak to the Winds because their big brother Jack, the spring was'nt far off—I am reading Voltaire and Gibbon, although I wrote to Reynolds the other day to prove reading of no use—I have not seen Hunt since. I am a good deal with Dilke and Brown—we are very thick—they are very kind to me—they are well—I don't think I could stop in Hampstead but for their neighbourhood. I hear Hazlitt's Lectures regularly—his last was on Grey Collins, Young &c and he gave a very f<ine> piece of discriminating criticism on Swift, Vo<ltaire> And Rabelais—I was very disappointed at his treatment of Chatterton—I generally meet with many I know there. Lord Byron's 4th Canto is expected out—and I heard somewhere that Walter Scott has a new Poem in readiness[4]—I am sorry that Wordsworth has left a bad impression wherever he visited in Town—by his egotism, Vanity and bigotry—yet he is a great Poet if not a Philosopher. I have not yet read Shelly's Poem[5]—I don't suppose you have it at

1 *Divan*: An Oriental (especially Turkish) council of state, hence, in general, a council.

2 *Haughton's*: Possibly the family of Moses Haughton (1773–1849), miniature painter and engraver.

3 *he'll be out before it*: Probably refers to the publication of Taylor's own book (see above, p. 101.)

4 *a new Poem in readiness*: Scott published his novel *Heart of Midlothian* in June 1818.

5 *Shelly's Poem*: *The Revolt of Islam*, see above, p. 80 n.

the Teignmouth Libraries—These double Letters must come rather heavy—I hope you have a moderate portion of Cash—but dont fret at all if you have not—Lord I intend to play at cut and run as well as Falstaff—that is to say before he got so lusty—I have not time to chequer work this Letter for I should like to be sure of the 4 o Clock Post—So I remain praying for your hea[l]th; my dear Brothers, your affectionate Brother—

John—

To John Taylor
27 February 1818

[Morgan Library MS]

[Well Walk]
Hampstead [Friday] 27 Feby—

My dear Taylor,

Your alteration strikes me as being a great improvement—the page looks much better. And now I will attend to the Punctuations you speak of—the comma should be at soberly, and in the other passage the comma should follow quiet, .[1] I am extremely indebted to you for this attention and also for your after admonitions—It is a sorry thing for me that any one should have to overcome Prejudices in reading my Verses—that affects me more than any hypercriticism on any particular Passage. In Endymion I have most likely but moved into the Go-cart from the leading strings. In Poetry I have a few Axioms, and you will see how far I am from their Centre. 1st I think Poetry should surprise by a fine excess and not by Singularity—it should strike the Reader as a wording of his own highest thoughts, and appear almost a Remembrance—2nd Its touches of Beauty should never be half way therby making the reader breathless instead of content: the rise, the progress, the setting of imagery should like the Sun come natural natural too him—shine over him and set soberly although in magnificence leaving him in the

1 *comma should . . . follow quiet*: *Endymion*, I, 149, 247.

Luxury of twilight—but it is easier to think what Poetry should be than to write it—and this leads me on to another axiom. That if Poetry comes not as naturally as the Leaves to a tree it had better not come at all. However it may be with me I cannot help looking into new countries with 'O for a Muse of fire to ascend!'[1]—If Endymion serves me as a Pioneer perhaps I ought to be content. I have great reason to be content, for thank God I can read and perhaps understand Shakspeare to his depths, and I have I am sure many friends, who, if I fail, will attribute any change in my Life and Temper to Humbleness rather than to Pride—to a cowering under the Wings of great Poets rather than to a Bitterness that I am not appreciated. I am anxious to get Endymion printed that I may forget it and proceed. I have coppied the 3rd Book and have begun the 4th. On running my Eye over the Proofs—I saw one Mistake I will notice it presently and also any others if there be any—There should be no comma in 'the raft branch down sweeping from a tall Ash top'[2]—I have besides made one or two alteration<s> and also altered the 13 Line Page 32 to make sense of it as you will see. I will take care the Printer shall not trip up my Heels—There should be no dash after Dryope in the Line 'Dryope's lone lulling of her Child.[3] Remember me to Percy Street.[4]

Your sincere and oblig^{d} friend
John Keats—

P. S. You shall have a sho[r]t Preface in good time—

Keats left London on Wednesday, 4 March, to take care of Tom in Teignmouth, and to relieve George. There was a violent storm as he travelled overnight 'on the outside of the coach' to Exeter, and the rainy weather continued for much of March. Before leaving Well Walk, Keats had completed the fair copy of the third book of Endymion, *which George delivered to his publishers on Saturday, 7 March, or the following Monday. Tom's*

1 *O for . . . to ascend*: *Henry V*, Prologue, I. i (slightly misquoted).
2 *the raft . . . Ash top*: *Endymion*, I, 334–5.
3 *Dryope's . . . Child*: *Endymion*, I, 495.
4 *Percy Street*: See below, p. 161 n.

health meant that Keats had to remain in Teignmouth with his brother for the next two months. They lodged at 20 Strand, near the port, with Mrs Jeffery and her two daughters (for whom see below, pp. 369, 574), and returned to London in early May.

*Keats had written 'the first stanzas' of 'Isabella' while still in Hampstead (*L*, I, pp. 274, 283). He finished the poem in Teignmouth during the final stages of preparing* Endymion *for publication.*

His first known letter from Teignmouth replies to one from Benjamin Bailey asking why he had not kept a long-standing promise to make a return visit to Oxford.

To Benjamin Bailey
13 March 1818

[Harvard MS]

My dear Bailey, Teignmouth Friday

When a poor devil is drowning, it is said he comes thrice to the surface, ere he makes his final sink if however, even at the third rise, he can manage to catch hold of a piece of weed or rock, he stands a fair chance,—as I hope I do now, of being saved. I have sunk twice our Correspondence, have risen twice and been too idle, or something worse, to extricate myself—I have sunk the third time and just now risen again at this two of the Clock P.M. and saved myself from utter perdition—by beginning this, all drench'd as I am and fresh from the Water—and I would rather endure the present inconvenience of a Wet Jacket, than you should keep a laced one in store for me. Why did I not stop at Oxford in my Way?—How can you ask such a Question? Why did I not promise to do so? Did I not in a Letter to you make a promise to do so? Then how can you be so unreasonable as to ask me why I did not? This is the thing—(for I have been rubbing up my invention; trying several sleights—I first polish'd a cold, felt it in my fingers tried it on the table, but could not pocket it: I tried Chilblains, Rheumatism, Gout, tight Boots, nothing of that sort would do, so this is, as I was going to say, the thing.—I had a Letter from Tom saying how much better he had got, and thinking he had better stop—I went down to prevent his coming up—Will not this do? Turn it which way you like—it is selvaged all round—I have used it these last three days to keep out the abominable Devonshire Weather—by the by you may say what you will of devonshire: the thuth [*for* truth] is, it is a splashy, rainy, misty snowy, foggy, haily floody, muddy, slipshod County—the hills are very beautiful, when you get a sight of 'em—the Primroses are out, but then you are in—the Cliffs are of a fine deep Colour, but then the Clouds are continually vieing with them—The Women like your London People in a sort of negative way—because the native men are the poorest creatures in England—because Government never have thought it worth while to send a recruiting party among them. When I think of Wordswo[r]th's Sonnet 'Vanguard of Liberty! ye Men of Kent!'[1] the degenerated race about me are Pulvis Ipecac. Simplex[2] a strong dose—Were I a Corsair I'd make a descent on the South Coast of Devon, if I did not run the chance of having Cowardice imputed to me: as for the Men they'd run away into the methodist meeting houses, and the Women would be glad of it—Had England been a large devonshire we should not have won the Battle of Waterloo—There are knotted oaks—there are lusty rivulets there are Meadows such as are not—there are vallies of femminine Climate—but there are no thews and Sinews—Moor's Almanack[3] is here a curiosity—A[r]ms Neck and shoulders may at least be seen there, and The Ladies read it as some out of way romance—Such a quelling Power have these thoughts over me, that I fancy the very Air of a deteriorating quality—I fancy the flowers, all precocious, have an Acrasian[4] spell about them—I feel able to beat off the devonshire waves

1 *Vanguard . . . Kent*: The opening line of Wordsworth's sonnet 'To the Men of Kent. October, 1803' (1807), a patriotic call to arms.

2 *Pulvis . . . Simplex*: An emetic or purgative prepared from ipecacuanha, a South American plant.

3 *Moor's Almanack*: See below, p. 488 n.

4 *Acrasian*: Spenser's enchantress, embodying the destructive side of sexual passion, in the Bower of Bliss, *The Faerie Queene*, II. v. 27; xii. 69–87.

like soap froth—I think it well for the honor of Brittain that Julius Cæsar did not first land in this County—A Devonshirer standing on his native hills is not a distinct object—he does not show against the light—a wolf or two would dispossess him. I like, I love England, I like its strong Men—Give me a "long brown plain" for my Morning[1] so I may meet with some of Edmond Iron side's descendants—Give me a barren mould so I may meet with some shadowing of Alfred in the shape of a Gipsey, a Huntsman or as Shepherd. Scenery is fine—but human nature is finer—The Sward is richer for the tread of a real, nervous, english foot—the eagles nest is finer for the Mountaineer has look'd into it—Are these facts or prejudices? Whatever they are, for them I shall never be able to relish entirely any devonshire scenery—Homer is very fine, Achilles is fine, Diomed is fine, Shakspeare is fine, Hamlet is fine, Lear is fine, but dwindled englishmen are not fine—Where too the Women are so passable, and have such english names, such as Ophelia, Cordelia &—that they should have such Paramours or rather Imparamours—As for them I cannot, in thought help wishing as did the cruel Emperour,[2] that they had but one head and I might cut it off to deliver them from any horrible Courtesy they may do their undeserving Countrymen—I wonder I meet with no born Monsters—O Devonshire, last night I thought the Moon had dwindled in heaven—I have never had your Sermon[3] from Wordsworth but Mrs Dilke lent it me—You know my ideas about Religion—I do not think myself more in the right than other people and that nothing in this world is proveable. I wish I could enter into all your feelings on the subject merely for one short 10 Minutes and give you a Page or two to your liking. I am sometimes so very sceptical as to think Poetry itself a mere Jack a lanthern to amuse whoever may chance to be struck with its brilliance—As Tradesmen say every thing is worth what it will fetch, so probably every mental pursuit takes its reality and worth from the ardour of the

1 *Morning*: Woodhouse suggests that Keats meant to write 'Money'.
2 *the cruel Emperour*: The Roman Emperor Caligula (AD 12–41).
3 *your Sermon*: See above, p. 95.

pursuer—being in itself a nothing—Ethereal thing[s] may at least be thus real, divided under three heads—Things real—things semireal—and no things—Things real—such as existences of Sun Moon & Stars and passages of Shakspeare—Things semireal such as Love, the Clouds &c which require a greeting of the Spirit to make them wholly exist—and Nothings which are made Great and dignified by an ardent pursuit—Which by the by stamps the burgundy mark on the bottles of our Minds, insomuch as they are able to "consec[r]ate whate'er they look upon"[1] I have written a Sonnet here of a somewhat collateral nature—so don't imagine it an a propos des bottes.[2]

Four Seasons fill the Measure of the year;[3]
  Four Seasons are there in the mind of Man.
He hath his lusty spring when fancy clear
  Takes in all beauty with an easy span:
He hath his Summer, when luxuriously
  He chews the honied cud of fair spring thoughts,
Till, in his Soul dissolv'd they come to be
  Part of himself. He hath his Autumn ports
And Havens of repose, when his tired wings
  Are folded up, and he content to look
On Mists in idleness: to let fair things
  Pass by unheeded as a threshold brook.
    He hath his Winter too of pale Misfeature,
    Or else he would forget his mortal nature.

Aye this may be carried—but what am I talking of—it is an old maxim of mine and of course must be well known that eve[r]y point of thought is the centre of an intellectual world—the two uppermost thoughts in a Man's mind are the two poles of his World he revolves on them and every thing is southward or

1 consec[r]ate . . . upon: Echoes Shelley's 'Hymn to Intellectual Beauty', 'Spirit of BEAUTY, that doth consecrate / With thine own hues all thou dost shine upon' (ll. 13–14), published in the *Examiner* (19 January 1817).
2 *a propos des bottes*: i.e., the sonnet is not on another subject.
3 *Four Seasons . . . the year*: First printed in Leigh Hunt's *Literary Pocket-Book* (1818 for 1819), with substantive alterations, which may be Hunt's (see *Texts*). Not included in *1820*.

northward to him through their means—We take but three steps from feathers to iron. Now my dear fellow I must once for all tell you I have not one Idea of the truth of any of my speculations—I shall never be a Reasoner because I care not to be in the right, when retired from bickering and in a proper philosophical temper—So you must not stare if in any future letter I endeavour to prove that Appollo as he had a cat gut string to his Lyre used a cats' paw as a Pecten[1]—and further from said Pecten's reiterated and continual teasing came the term Hen peck'd. My Brother Tom desires to be remember'd to you—he has just this moment had a spitting of blood poor fellow—Remember me to Greig [*for* Gleig] and Whitehed—

Your affectionate friend
John Keats—

To J. H. Reynolds
14 March 1818

[Woodhouse transcript (1821?)]

Teignmouth Saturday

Dear Reynolds,

I escaped being blown over & blown under & trees and house[s] being toppled on me.[2]—I have since hearing of Brown's accident had an aversion to a dose of parapet. and being also a lover of antiquities I would sooner have a harmless piece of herculaneum sent me quietly as a present, than ever so modern a chimney pot tumbled onto my head—Being agog to see some Devonshire, I would have taken a walk the first day, but the rain wo^d^ not let me; and the second, but the rain wo^d^ not let

1 *Pecten*: A possible play on 'plectrum' and Latin *pecten*, a comb or the pubis (Mee).

2 *I escaped . . . toppled on me*: Newspaper accounts of the violent storm on the night of 4–5 March, when Keats travelled to the West Country, reported 'houses unroofed – stacks of chimnies and walls blown down – trees, innumerable, rooted up – and property of various descriptions destroyed' (*Trewman's Exeter Flying Post*, 12 March 1818).

me; and the third; but the rain forbade it—Ditto 4 ditto 5—ditto—So I made up my Mind to stop in doors, and catch a sight flying between the showers; and behold I saw a pretty valley—pretty cliffs, pretty Brooks, pretty Meadows, pretty trees, both standing as they were created, and blown down as they are uncreated—The green is beautiful, as they say, and pity it is that it is amphibious—mais! but alas! the flowers here wait as naturally for the rain twice a day as the Muscles do for the Tide.—so we look upon a brook in these parts as you look upon a dash in your Country—there must be something to support this, aye fog, hail, snow rain—Mist—blanketing up three parts of the year—This devonshire is like Lydia Languish,[1] very entertaining when at smiles, but cursedly subject to sympathetic moisture. You have the sensation of walking under one great Lamplighter: and you cant go on the other side of the ladder to keep your frock clean, and cosset your superstition. Buy a girdle—put a pebble in your Mouth—loosen your Braces—for I am going among Scenery whence I intend to tip you the Damosel Radcliffe[2]—I'll cavern you, and grotto you, and waterfall you, and wood you, and water you, and immense-rock you, and tremendous sound you, and solitude you. Ill make a lodgment on your glacis by a row of Pines, and storm your covered way with bramble Bushes. Ill have at you with hip and haw small-shot, and cannonade you with Shingles[3]—Ill be witty upon salt fish, and impede your cavalry with clotted cream. But ah Coward! to talk at this rate to a sick man, or I hope to one that was sick—for I hope by this that you stand on your right foot.—If you are not—that's all,—I intend to cut all sick people if they do not make up their minds to cut sickness—a fellow to whom I have a complete aversion, and who strange to say is harboured and countenanced in several houses where I visit—he is sitting now quite impudent between me and

1 *Lydia Languish*: The sentimental heroine of *The Rivals* (1775) by Richard Brinsley Sheridan (1751–1816).

2 *Damosel Radcliffe*: Keats goes on to parody stock elements in the Gothic novels of Ann Radcliffe (1764–1823).

3 *hip and haw ... Shingles*: The military references parody Uncle Toby's monomania in Sterne's *Tristram Shandy* (1759–67).

Tom—He insults me at poor Jem Rice's—and you have seated him before now between us at the Theatre—where I thought he look'd with a longing eye at poor Kean. I shall say, once for all, to my friends generally and severally, cut that fellow, or I cut you—I went to the Theatre here the other night, which I forgot to tell George, and got insulted, which I ought to remember to forget to tell any Body; for I did not fight, and as yet have had no redress—"Lie thou there, sweetheart!"[1] I wrote to Bailey yesterday, obliged to speak in a high way, and a damme who's affraid.—for I had owed him so long; however, he shall see I will be better in future. Is he in Town yet? I have directed to Oxford as the better chance. I have copied my fourth Book, and shall write the preface soon. I wish it was all done; for I want to forget it and make my mind free for something new—Atkins the Coachman, Bartlet the Surgeon, Simmons the Barber, and the Girls over at the Bonnet shop say we shall now have a Month of seasonable Weather. warm, witty, and full of invention[2]—Write to me and tell me you are well or thereabouts, or by the holy Beaucœur,—which I suppose is the virgin Mary, or the repented Magdalen, (beautiful name, that Magdalen) Ill take to my Wings and fly away to any where but old or Nova Scotia—I wish I had a little innocent bit of Metaphysic in my head, to criss-cross this letter: but you know a favorite tune is hardest to be remembered when one wants it most and you, I know, have long ere this taken it for granted that I never have any speculations without assoc[i]ating you in them, where they are of a pleasant nature and you know enough to [*for* of] me to tell the places where I haunt most, so that if you think for five minutes after having read this you will find it a long letter and see written in the Air above you,

Your most affectionate friend
John Keats.

Remember me to all. Tom's remembrances to you.

1 *Lie thou there, sweetheart*: Pistol's address to his sword as he lays it down after an argument in 2 *Henry IV*, II. iv. 173.
2 *witty . . . invention*: *Twelfth Night*, III. ii. 40–41.

On 13 or 14 March Keats wrote to his brother in London to tell him of the recurrence of Tom's 'spitting of blood'. George's prompt reply of 18 March began by expressing his shock: 'who could have imagined such a change?' He went on to warn Keats that 'the printer's are in immediate want of the Fourth book [of Endymion*] and the preface', and enclosed a bill for £20. Keats was clearly short of ready money, since George hoped the bill would reach him 'before you are quite aground'. The brothers' finances were increasingly confused. George told Keats that now he was back in London he was sorting out their affairs:'I am about paying your's as well as Tom's bills, of which I shall keep regular accounts and for the sake of justice and a future proper understanding I intend calculating the probable amount Tom and I are indebted to you, something of this kind must be done, or at the end of two or three years we shall be all at sixes and sevens' (*L*, I, pp. 247–8). In fact, neither George (who had decided to marry and emigrate) or Keats had a 'proper understanding' of their inheritance. Unfortunately for Keats, the true nature of their financial situation would not be untangled until after his death. When, only three months later, George and his new wife departed for America, Keats was left chronically short of money for the remainder of his life.*

The immediate effect of George's letter was to prompt Keats's completion of his work on Endymion *and its preface. He sent these off apologetically to Taylor and Hessey on the following Saturday, expecting them to reach London on Monday, 23 March (*L*, I, p. 253).*

To James Rice
24 March 1818

[Harvard MS]

Teignmouth Tuesday,

My dear Rice,

Being in the midst of your favorite Devon, I should not by rights, pen one word but it should contain a vast portion of

Wit, Wisdom, and learning—for I have heard that Milton ere he wrote his Answer to Salmasius came into these parts, and for on [*for* one] whole Month, rolled himself, for three whole hours in a certain meadow hard by us—where the mark of his nose at equidistances is still shown. The exhibitor of said Meadow further saith that after these rollings, not a nettle sprang up in all the seven acres for seven years and that from said time a new sort of plant was made from the white thorn, of a thornless nature very much used by the Bucks of the present day to rap their Boots withall—This accou[n]t made me very naturally suppose that the nettles and thorns etherealized by the Scholars rotatory motion and garner'd in his head, thence flew after a <n>ew fermentation against the luckless Salmasius and accasioned his well known and unhappy end.[1] What a happy thing it would be if we could settle our thoughts, make our minds up on any matter in five Minutes and remain content—that is to build a sort of mental Cottage of feelings quiet and pleasant—to have a sort of Philosophical Back Garden, and cheerful holiday-keeping front one—but Alas! this never can be: for as the material Cottager knows there are such places as france and Italy and the Andes and the Burning Mountains—so the spiritual Cottager has knowledge of the terra semi incognita of things unearthly; and cannot for his Life, keep in the check rein—Or I should stop here quiet and comfortable in my theory of Nettles. You will see however I am obliged to run wild, being attracted by the Loadstone Concatenation. No sooner had I settle[d] the notty point of Salmasius that [*for* than] the Devil put this whim into my head in the likeness of one of Pythagora's questionings 'Did Milton do more good or ha[r]m to the world? He wrote let me info[r]m you (for I have it from a friend, who had it of —) he wrote Lycidas, Comus, Paradise Lost and other Poems, with much delectable prose—he was moreover an active friend to Man all his Life and has been since his death. Very good—but my dear fellow I

1 *the luckless ... unhappy end*: Claudius Salmasius (1588–1653) defended Charles I and attacked the regicides in his *Defensio Regia pro Carolo I* (1649), but was forcefully rebutted by Milton's *Pro Populo Anglicano Defensio* (1651).

must let you know that as there is ever the same quantity of matter constituting this habitable globe—as the ocean notwithstanding the enormous changes and revolutions taking place in some or other of its demesnes—notwithstanding Waterspouts whirlpools and mighty Rivers emptying themselves into it, it still is made up of the same bulk—nor ever varies the number of its Atoms—And as a certain bulk of Water was instituted at the Creation—so very likely a certain portion of intellect was spun forth into the thin Air for the Brains of Man to prey upon it—You will see my drift without any unnecessary parenthesis. That which is contained in the Pacific and [*for* can't] lie in the Caspian—that which was in Miltons head could not find Room in Charles the seconds—he like a Moon attracted Intellect to its flow—it has not ebbd yet—but has left the shore pebble all bare—I mean all Bucks Authors of Hengist and Castlereaghs of the present day[1]—who without Miltons gormandizing might have been all wise Men—Now for as much as—I was very peedisposed to a Country I had heard you speak so highly of, I took particular notice of every thing during my journey and have bought some folio asses skin for Memorandums—I have seen eve[r]y thing but the wind—and that they say becomes visible by taking a dose of Acorns or sleeping on[e] night in a hog trough with your tail to the Sow Sow west. Some of the little Barmaids look'd at me as if I knew Jem Rice—but when I took <a glass of> Brandy they were quite convinced. One asked whether <you pres>er<v>ed a secret she gave you on the nail—another how m[an]y buttons of your Coat were buttoned in general—I <told> her it used to be four—but since you had become acqu<ain>ted with one Martin you had reduced it to three and had been turning this third one in your Mind—and would do so with finger and thumb only you had taken to snuff—I have met with a Brace or twain of little Long

1 *has left the shore ... present day*: i.e., Milton's intellectual achievement leaves nothing over for minor authors like the dramatist Charles Bucke (1781–1846) and the anonymous writer of the melodrama *Hengist* (1816), or for a Tory politician like Lord Castlereagh (1769–1822), despised by the liberal press.

heads—not a kit[1] o' the german—all in the neatest little dresses, and avoiding all the pudd[l]es—but very fond of peppermint drops, laming ducks, and seeing little Girls affairs. Well I cant tell! I hope you are showing poor Reynolds the way to get well—send me a good account of him and if I can I'll send you one of Tom—Oh! for a day and all well! I went yesterday to dawlish fair—

Over the hill and over the dale,[2]
And over the bourn to Dawlish—
Where Gingerbread Wives have a scanty sale
And gingerbred nuts are smallish—

Rantipole Betty she ran down a hill
And ki[c]k'ed up her pettic[o]ats fairly
Says I I'll be Jack if you will be Gill—
So she sat on the Grass debonnairly—

Here's somebody coming, here's somebody coming!
  Says I 't is the Wind at a parley
So without any fuss any hawing and humming
  She lay on the grass debonnai[r]ly—

Here's somebody here and here's somebody <u>there!</u>
  Say's I hold your tongue you young Gipsey.
So she held her tongue and lay plump and fair
  And dead as a venus tipsy—

O who would'nt hie to Dawlish fair
  O who would'nt stop in a Meadow
O [who] would not rumple the daisies there
  And make the wild fern for a bed do—

Tom's Remembrances and mine to all—

Your sincere friend
John Keats

1 *kit*: Rollins reads as 'bit'. 'Kit' is 'slang for male sex, and the whole passage is clearly another piece of sexual joking', implying that Rice had left several bastards behind while in Devon (Gittings).
2 *Over the hill . . . the dale*: Stanza 1 first printed in *1848*, and the whole poem in 1925.

To J. H. Reynolds
25 March 1818

[Woodhouse transcripts][1]

[Teignmouth, Wednesday]

Dear Reynolds, as last night I lay in bed,[2]
There came before my eyes that wonted thread
Of Shapes, and Shadows and Remembrances,
That every other minute vex and please:
Things all disjointed come from North and south,
Two witch's eyes above a cherub's mouth,
Voltaire with casque and shield and Habergeon,
And Alexander with his night-cap on—
Old Socrates a tying his cravat;
And Hazlitt playing with Miss Edgeworth's cat;
And Junius Brutus pretty well so, so,[3]
Making the best of 's way towards Soho.
  Few there are who escape these visitings—
P'erhaps one or two, whose lives have pat[i]ent wings;
And through whose curtains peeps no hellish nose,
No wild boar tushes, no mermaid's toes:
But flowers bursting out with lusty pride;
And young Æolian harps personified,
Some, Titian colours touch'd into real life.—
The sacrifice goes on; the pontif knife

1 Transcript of poem from Woodhouse's 'Commonplace book of poems' (W[2]), Harvard Keats MS 3.2, ff. 65–68. Transcript of prose letter from Woodhouse transcript (1821?).

2 *Dear Reynolds . . . in bed*: First published in *1848* (without the last four lines).

3 *Junius Brutus . . . so, so*: Shakespearian actor Junius Brutus Booth (1796–1852) made his debut at Covent Garden in 1816, but in early 1818 was drinking excessively through frustration ('so so' is slang for 'tipsy').

Gloams[1] in the sun, the milk-white heifer lows,
The pipes go shrilly, the libation flows:[2]
A white sail shews above the green-head cliff
Moves round the point, and throws her anchor stiff.
The Mariners join hymn with those on land.—
You know the Enchanted Castle[3] it doth stand
Upon a Rock on the Border of a Lake
Nested in Trees, which all do seem to shake
From some old Magic like ~~the witch's~~ /Urganda's[4]/ sword.
O Phœbus that I had thy sacred word
To shew this Castle in fair dreaming wise
Unto my friend, while sick and ill he lies.
  You know it well enough, where it doth seem
A mossy place, a Merlin's Hall, a dream.
You know the clear lake, and the little Isles,
The Mountains blue, and cold near neighbour rills—
All which elsewhere are but half animate
Here do they look alive to love and hate;
To smiles and frowns; they seem a lifted mound
Above some giant, pulsing underground.
  Part of the building was a chosen See
Built by a banish'd santon[5] of Chaldee:[6]
The other part two thousand years from him
Was built by Cuthbert de Saint Aldebrim;
Then there's a little wing, far from the sun,

1 *Gloams*: Woodhouse notes '<u>so</u>' in the margin. There is no need to emend to 'Gleams'.

2 *The sacrifice . . . libation flows*: This description of a classical sacrifice foreshadows 'Ode on a Grecian Urn', stanza 4.

3 *the Enchanted Castle*: Claude Lorrain's painting of that name is now in the National Gallery, London. Keats and his circle knew it through the engraving (1782) by François Vivarès and William Woollett.

4 *Urganda*: The enchantress in the fifteenth-century Spanish romance *Amadis of Gaul*.

5 *santon*: An Islamic monk or hermit.

6 *Chaldee*: (Woodhouse's note) 'Here the following line is written and erased. "Poor Man he left the Terrace Walls of Ur."'

Built by a Lapland Witch[1] turn'd maudlin nun—
And many other juts of aged stone
Founded with many a mason-devil's groan.
  The doors all look as if they oped themselves,
The windows as if latch'd by fays & elves—
And from them comes a silver flash of light
As from the Westward of a summer's night;
Or like a beauteous woman's large blue eyes
Gone mad through olden songs and Poesies—
  See what is coming from the distance dim!
A golden galley all in silken trim!
Three rows of oars are lightening moment-whiles
Into the verdurous bosoms of those Isles.
Towards the Shade under the Castle Wall
It comes in silence—now tis hidden all.
The clarion sounds; and from a postern grate
An echo of sweet music doth create
A fear in the poor herdsman who doth bring
His beasts to trouble the enchanted spring:
He tells of the sweet music and the spot
To all his friends, and they believe him not.
  O that our dreamings all of sleep or wake
Would all their colours from the sunset take:
From something of material sublime,
Rather than shadow our own Soul's daytime
In the dark void of Night. For in the world
We jostle—but my flag is not unfurl'd
On the Admiral staff[2]—and to philosophize
I dare not yet!—Oh never will the prize,
High reason, and the lore of good and ill
Be my award. Things cannot to the will
Be settled, but they tease us out of thought.

1 *Lapland Witch*: See *Paradise Lost*, II, 664–5, 'Lured with the smell of infant blood, to dance / With Lapland witches.'

2 *my flag . . . Admiral staff*: i.e., Keats is not yet mature: the image is of Alcibiades raising a flag over his galley to show he is admiral (Plutarch's *Lives*, tr. North (1676 edn), p. 178).

Or is that Imagination brought
Beyond its proper bound, yet still confined,—
Lost in a sort of Purgatory blind,
Cannot refer to any standard law
Of either earth or heaven?—It is a flaw
In happiness to see beyond our bourn—
It forces us in Summer skies to mourn:
It spoils the singing of the Nightingale.
  Dear Reynolds. I have a mysterious tale
And cannot speak it. The first page I read
Upon a Lampit[1] rock of green sea weed
Among the breakers—'Twas a quiet Eve;
The rocks were silent—the wide sea did weave
An untumultuous fringe of silver foam
Along the flat brown sand. I was at home,
And should have been most happy—but I saw
Too far into the sea; where every maw
The greater on the less feeds evermore:—
But I saw too distinct into the core
Of an eternal fierce destruction,
And so from Happiness I far was gone.
Still am I sick of it: and though to day
I've gathered young spring-leaves, and flowers gay
Of Periwinkle and wild strawberry,
Still do I that most fierce destruction see,
The shark at savage prey—the hawk at pounce,
The gentle Robin, like a pard or ounce,[2]
Ravening a worm—Away ye horrid moods,
Moods of one's mind! You know I hate them well,
You know I'd sooner be a clapping bell
To some Kamschatkan missionary church,
Than with these horrid moods be left in lurch—
Do you get health—and Tom the same—I'll dance,

1 *Lampit*: Variant spelling of 'limpet'.
2 *pard or ounce*: i.e., leopard or ocelet.

And from detested moods in new Romance[1]
Take refuge—Of bad lines a Centaine dose
Is sure enough—and so "here follows prose."[2]—

My Dear Reynolds.

In hopes of cheering you through a Minute or two I was determined nill he will he to send you some lines so you will excuse the unconnected subject, and careless verse—You know, I am sure, Claude's Enchanted Castle and I wish you may be pleased with my remembrance of it—The Rain is Come on again—I think with me Devonshire stands a very poor chance, I shall damn it up hill and down dale, if it keeps up to the average of 6 fine days in three weeks. Let me have better news of you.

Your affectionate friend
John Keats.

Toms Rememb[s] to you. Rem[r]
us to all—

To B. R. Haydon
8 April 1818

[Harvard MS]

[Teignmouth] Wednesday—

My dear Haydon,

I am glad you were pleased with my nonsense[3] and if it so happen that the humour takes me when I have set down to prose to you I will not gainsay it. I should be (god forgive me) ready to swear because I cannot make use of you[r] assistance in going

1 *new Romance*: i.e., 'Isabella; or, The Pot of Basil', which Keats had returned to writing.

2 *here follows prose*: *Twelfth Night*, II. v. 128–9.

3 *pleased with my nonsense*: Much of this letter replies to Haydon's of 25 March 1818 (*L*, I, pp. 257–9), which begins by praising the light verse ('For there's Bishop's teign') Keats had sent him (*L*, I, pp. 249–50).

through Devon[1] if I was not in my own Mind determined to visit it thoroughly at some more favorable time of the year. But now Tom (who is getting greatly better) is anxious to be in Town therefore I put off my threading the County. I purpose within a Month to put my knapsack at my back and make a pedestrian tour through the North of England, and part of Scotland[2]—to make a sort of Prologue to the Life I intend to pursue—that is to write, to study and to see all Europe at the lowest expence. I will clamber through the Clouds and exist. I will get such an accumulation of stupendous recollolections that as I walk through the suburbs of London I may not see them—I will stand upon Mont Blanc and remember this coming Summer when I intend to straddle ben Lomond—with my Soul!—galligaskins[3] are out of the Question—I am nearer myself to hear your Christ[4] is being tinted into immortality—Believe me Haydon your picture is a part of myself—I have ever been too sensible of the labyrinthian path to eminence in Art (judging from Poetry) ever to think I understood the emphasis of Painting. The innumberable compositions and decompositions which take place between the intellect and its thousand materials before it arrives at that trembling delicate and snail-horn perception of Beauty—I know not you[r] many havens of intenseness—nor ever can know them—but for this I hope no[ugh]t you atchieve is lost upon me: for when a Schoolboy the abstract Idea I had of an heroic painting—was what I cannot describe I saw it somewhat sideways large prominent round and colour'd with magnificence—somewhat like the feel I have of Anthony and Cleopatra. Or of Alcibiades, leaning on his Crimson Couch in his Galley, his broad shoulders imperceptibly heaving with the Sea—That [*for* What] passage in Shakspeare is finer than this

1 *you[r] . . . Devon*: Haydon's married sister Harriet lived in Devon and he had suggested Keats visit his own friends there.
2 *tour . . . Scotland*: The first mention of Keats's northern tour with Charles Brown, who he had known since summer 1817.
3 *galligaskins*: Wide hose or breeches in the sixteenth and seventeenth centuries, later a ludicrous term for wide breeches.
4 *your Christ*: Haydon was still painting his *Christ's Entry into Jerusalem.*

'See how the surly Warwick mans the Wall'[1]

I like your consignment of Corneille—that's the humor of it—They shall be called your Posthumous Works.[2] I don't understand you[r] bit of Italian.[3] I hope she will awake from her dream and flourish fair—my respects to her—The Hedges by this time are begin[n]ing to leaf—Cats are becoming more vociferous—young Ladies that wear Watches are always looking at them—Women about forty five think the Season very back ward—Lady's Mares have but half an allowance of food—It rains here again, has been doing so for three days—however as I told you I'll take a trial in June July or August next year—

I am affraid Wordsworth went rather huff'd out of Town—I am sorry for it. he cannot expect his fireside Divan[4] to be infallible he cannot expect but that every Man of worth is as proud as himself. O that he had not fit with a Warrener[5] that is din'd at Kingston's. I shall be in town in about a fortnight and then we will have a day or so now and then before I set out on my northern expedition—we will have no more abominable Rows—for they leave one is [*for* in] a fearful silence having settled the Methodists let us be rational—not upon compulsion—no if it will out let it—but I will not play the Basoon any more delibe[r]ately—Remember me to Hazlitt, and Bewick[6]—

Your affectionate friend
John Keats—

1 *See how . . . the Wall*: *3 Henry VI*, V. i. 17.
2 *your consignment of Corneille . . . Posthumous Works*: In his letter Haydon rejected the seventeenth-century French dramatist – 'I hate Corneille, a heartless tirade maker' – in favour of Homer, Dante, Ariosto, Tasso and Shakespeare.
3 *you[r] bit of Italian*: Haydon had praised the black eyes of Mrs Scott, wife of John Scott and an admirer of Keats.
4 *Divan*: Oriental council of state, esp. in Turkey, where it was presided over by the Sultan or Grand Vizier.
5 *fit with a Warrener*: Keats echoes *The Merry Wives of Windsor*, I. iv. 25, 'he hath fought with a warrener [gamekeeper]', mocking Wordsworth's subservience to Kingston (see below, p. 80).
6 *Bewick*: William Bewick (1795–1866), a portrait and history painter, a pupil of Haydon's from 1815 to 1818.

To J. H. Reynolds
9 April 1818

[Woodhouse transcript (1821?)]

My Dear Reynolds, [Teignmouth] Th[y] Morn[g]

Since you all agree that the thing[1] is bad, it must be so—though I am not aware that there is any thing like Hunt in it, (and if there is, it is my natural way, and I have something in common with Hunt) look it over again and examine into the motives, the seeds from which any one sentence sprung—I have not the slightest feel of humility towards the Public—or to any thing in existence,—but the eternal Being, the Principle of Beauty,—and the Memory of great Men—When I am writing for myself for the mere sake of the Moment's enjoyment, perhaps nature has its course with me—but a Preface is written to the Public; a thing I cannot help looking upon as an Enemy, and which I cannot address without feelings of Hostility—If I write a Preface in a supple or subdued style, it will not be in character with me as a public speaker—I wo[d] be subdued before my friends, and thank them for subduing me—but among Multitudes of Men—I have no feel of stooping, I hate the idea of humility to them—

I never wrote one single Line of Poetry with the least Shadow of public thought.

Forgive me for vexing you and making a Trojan Horse of such a Trifle, both with respect to the matter in Question, and myself—but it eases me to tell you—I could not live without the love of my friends—I would jump down Ætna for any great Public good[2]—but I hate a Mawkish Popularity.—I cannot be subdued before them—My glory would be to daunt and dazzle

1 *the thing*: Keats's original preface to *Endymion*: its apologetic tone was objected to by Reynolds and his publishers.

2 *jump down . . . Public good*: The pre-Socratic philosopher Empedocles (*c.* 490–430 BC) is supposed to have thrown himself into the crater of Mount Etna to prove himself immortal.

the thousand jabberers about Pictures and Books—I see swarms of Porcupines with their Quills erect "like lime-twigs set to catch my Winged Book"[1] and I would fright 'em away with a torch—You will say my preface is not much of a Torch. It would have been too insulting "to begin from Jove" and I could not set a golden head upon a thing of clay[2]—if there is any fault in the preface it is not affectation: but an undersong of disrespect to the Public.—if I write another preface. it must be done without a thought of those people—I will think about it. If it should not reach you in four—or five days—tell Taylor to publish it without a preface, and let the dedication simply stand "inscribed to the memory of Thomas Chatterton." I had resolved last night to write to you this morning—I wish it had been about something else—something to greet you towards the close of your long illness—I have had one or two intimations of your going to Hampstead for a space; and I regret to see your confounded Rheumatism keeps you in Little Brittain where I am sure the air is too confined—Devonshire continues rainy. As the drops beat against the window, they give me the same sensation as a quart of cold water offered to revive a half drowned devil—No feel of the clouds dropping fatness; but as if the roots of the Earth were rotten cold and drench'd—I have not been able to go to Kents' Cave at Babbicun[3]—however on one very beautiful day I had a fine Clamber over the rocks all along as far as that place: I shall be in Town in about Ten days.—We go by way of Bath on purpose to call on Bailey.[4] I hope soon to be writing to you about the things of the north,

1 *like lime-twigs . . . Winged Book*: *2 Henry VI*, III. iii. 16, which has 'winged soul'.

2 *begin from Jove . . . thing of clay*: i.e., Keats's Preface could not have made high claims ('from Jove') on behalf of *Endymion*, 'a thing of clay'. His references are to the opening line of Robert Herrick's 'Evensong' in *Hesperides* (1648) and Nebuchadnezzar's dream of an image with head of gold and feet of clay in Daniel 2:31–3.

3 *Kents' Cave at Babbicun*: Kents Cavern, Babbacombe, Torquay, an extensive cave system used by prehistoric man, which Keats later visited (see below, p. 442). Declared a Scheduled Historic Monument in 1957.

4 *We go . . . on Bailey*: They did not leave until 4 or 5 May, and did not visit Bailey.

purposing to wayfare all over those parts. I have settled my accoutrements in my own mind, and will go to gorge wonders: However we'll have some days together before I set out—

I have many reasons for going wonder-ways: to make my winter chair free from spleen—to enlarge my vision—to escape disquisitions on Poetry and Kingston Criticism.—to promote digestion and economise shoe leather—I'll have leather buttons and belt; and if Brown holds his mind, over the Hills we go.—If my Books will help me to it,—thus will I take all Europe in turn, and see the Kingdoms of the Earth and the glory of them—Tom is getting better he hopes you may meet him at the top o' the hill—My Love to your nurses.[1] I am ever

Your affectionate Friend,
John Keats.

To J. H. Reynolds
17 April 1818

[Harvard MS]

[Teignmouth] Friday—

My dear Reynolds,

I am anxious you should find this Preface tolerable—if there is an affectation in it, 'tis natural to me. Do let the Printer's Devil cook it—and let me be 'as the casing air.'[2]

You are too good in this Matter—were I in your state I am certain I should have no thought but of discontent and illness—I might tho' be taught patience. I had an idea of giving no Preface however don't you think this had <bett>er go?—O, let it, one should not be too <afra>id—of committing faults.

The Climate here weighs us d<own> completely. Tom is quite low spirited. <It is> impossible to live in a country which is continually under hatches—Who would live in the Region of Mists, Game Laws, indemnity Bills &c when there is such a

1 *your nurses*: Reynolds's sisters.
2 *as the casing air*: *Macbeth*, III. iv. 23.

place as Italy? It is said this England from its Clime produces a Spleen able to engender the finest Sentiment—and covers the whole face of the Isle with green[1]—so it ought, I'm sure. I should still like the Dedication simply as I said in my last.

I wanted to send you a few Songs written in your favorite Devon——it cannot be—Rain! Rain! Rain! I am going this morning to take a fac simile of a Letter of Nelson's, very much to his honor—you will be greatly pleased when you see it—in about a Week. What a spite it is one cannot get out the like way I went yesterday I found a lane bank'd on each side with store of Primroses—while the earlier bushes are beginning to leaf—

I shall hear a good Account of you soon—

Your Affectionate friend
John Keats

My Love to all and remember me to Taylor—

To John Taylor
24 April 1818

[Morgan MS]

Teignmouth Friday

My dear Taylor,

I think I Did very wrong to leave you all the trouble of Endymion[2]—but I could not help it then—another time I shall be more bent to all sort of troubles and disagreeables—Young Men for some time have an idea that such a thing as happiness is to be had and therefore are extremely impatient under any unpleasant restraining—in time however, of such stuff is the world about them, they know better and instead of striving from Uneasiness greet it as an habitual sensation, a pannier which is to weigh upon them through life.

1 *green*: A play on the name of Matthew Green (1696–1737), author of *The Spleen* (1737).
2 *to leave . . . Endymion*: Keats, sent an advance copy of *Endymion*, apologizes to Taylor for leaving him the proof-reading of Books III and IV.

And in proportion to my disgust at the task is my sense of your kindness & anxiety—the book[1] pleased me much—it is very free from faults; and although there are one or two words I should wish replaced, I see in many places an improvement greatly to the purpose—

I think those speeches which are related—those parts where the speaker repeats a speech—such as Glaucus' repetition of Circe's words, should have inverted commas to every line—In this there is a little confusion. If we divide the speeches into identical and related: and to the former put merely one inverted comma at the beginning and another at the end; and to the latter inverted commas before every line, the book will be better understood at the first glance. Look at pages 126 and 127 you will find in the 3 line the beginning of a related speech marked thus "Ah! art awake—while at the same time in the next page the continuation of the identical speech is mark'd in the same manner "Young Man of Latmos[2]—You will find on the other side[3] all the parts which should have inverted commas to every line—

I was purposing to travel over the north this Summer—there is but one thing to prevent me—I know nothing I have read nothing and I mean to follow Solomon's directions of 'get Wisdom—get understanding'[4]—I find cavalier days are gone by. I find that I can have no enjoyment in the World but continual drinking of Knowledge—I find there is no worthy pursuit but the idea of doing some good for the world—some do it with their society—some with their wit—some with their benevolence—some with a sort of power of conferring pleasure and good humour on all they meet and in a thousand ways all equally dutiful to the command of Great Nature—there is but one way for me—the road lies th[r]ough application study and thought. I will pursue it and to that end purpose retiring for

1 *the book*: The advance copy.

2 *Ah! art awake . . . Young Man of Latmos*: i.e., *Endymion*, III, 429, 449.

3 *on the other side*: Keats wrote an errata list in the blank space beneath his signature and on the 'doublings' (a belated making up). Taylor included only four in the printed errata slip.

4 *get Wisdom . . . understanding*: Proverbs 4:5.

some years. I have been hovering for some time between an exquisite sense of the luxurious and a love for Philosophy—were I calculated for the former I should be glad—but as I am not I shall turn all my soul to the latter. My Brother Tom is getting better and I hope I shall see both him and Reynolds well before I retire from the World. I shall see you soon and have some talk about what Books I shall take with me—

Your very sincere friend
John Keats

Remember me to Hessey—Woodhouse and Percy Street[1]

To J. H. Reynolds
27 April 1818

[Woodhouse transcript (1821?)]

Teignmouth Monday

My dear Reynolds.

It is an awful while since you have heard from me—I hope I may not be punished, when I see you well, and so anxious as you always are for me, with the remembrance of my so seldom writing when you were so horribly confined—the most unhappy hours in our lives are those in which we recollect times past to our own blushing—If we are immortal that must be the Hell—If I must be immortal, I hope it will be after having taken a little of "that watery labyrinth"[2] in order to forget some of my schoolboy days & others since those.

I Have heard from George at different times how slowly you were recovering. it is a tedious thing—but all Medical Men will tell you how far a very gradual amendment is preferable; you will be strong after this, never fear.—We are here still envel-oppd in clouds—I lay awake last night—listening to the Rain with a sense of being drown'd and rotted like a grain of wheat—There is a continual courtesy between the Heavens and the

1 *Percy Street*: See below, p. 161 n.
2 *that watery labyrinth*: The waters of Lethe in *Paradise Lost*, II, 584.

Earth.—the heavens rain down their unwelcomeness, and the Earth sends it up again to be returned to morrow. Tom has taken a fancy to a Physician here, Dr Turton,[1] and I think is getting better—therefore I shall perhaps remain here some Months.—I have written to George for some Books—shall learn Greek, and very likely Italian—and in other ways prepare myself to ask Hazlitt in about a years time the best metaphysical road I can take.—For although I take poetry to be Chief, there is something else wanting to one who passes his life among Books and thoughts on Books—I long to feast upon old Homer as we have upon Shakespeare. and as I have lately upon Milton.—if you understood Greek, and would read me passages, now and then, explaining their meaning, 't would be, from its mistiness, perhaps a greater luxury than reading the thing one's self.—I shall be happy when I can do the same for you.—I have written for my folio Shakespeare, in which there is the first few stanzas of my "Pot of Basil":[2] I have the rest here finish'd, and will copy the whole out fair shortly—and George will bring it to you—The Compliment is paid by us to Boccace, whether we publish or no:[3] so there is content in this world—mine is short—you must be deliberate about yours: you must not think of it till many months after you are quite well:—then put your passion to it,—and I shall be bound up with you in the shadows of mind, as we are in our matters of human life—Perhaps a Stanza or two will not be too foreign to your Sickness.

1 *Dr Turton*: Dr William Turton (1762–1835), conchologist and scientific author, briefly practised in Teignmouth.

2 *Pot of Basil*: Keats drafted the beginning of 'Isabella; or, The Pot of Basil' before he left Hampstead on 4 March 1818, but mistakenly thought he had done so in his facsimile edition of the First Folio (1808), now in Keats House. For Reynolds's reaction to the completed poem, which he did not see until October, see below, p. 242.

3 *Boccace . . . or no*: Keats's and Reynolds's plan to publish a joint volume of poems based on Boccaccio came to nothing. Reynolds printed two 'Stories' from the Italian poet in *The Garden of Florence* (1821).

'Were they unhappy then? It cannot be:
  Too many tears &c &c——   } 2 Stanzas[1]
——
But for the general award of love &c

———

She wept alone for Pleasures &c &c   1 Stanza—

The 5th line ran thus "What might have been too plainly did she see."[2]—

———

I heard from Rice this morning—very witty—and have just written to Bailey—Don't you think I am brushing up in the letter way? and being in for it,—you shall hear again from me very shortly:—if you will promise not to put hand to paper for me until you can do it with a tolerable ease of health—except it be a line or two—Give my Love to your Mother and Sisters Remember me to the Butlers[3]—not forgetting Sarah

Your affectionate friend
John Keats

To J. H. Reynolds
3 May 1818

[Woodhouse transcript (1821?)]

Teignmouth [Sunday] May 3d

My dear Reynolds.

What I complain of is that I have been in so uneasy a state of Mind as not to be fit to write to an invalid. I cannot write to

1 2 *Stanzas*: Keats here copied out stanzas 12, 13 and 30 of 'Isabella; or, The Pot of Basil'.
2 *What might . . . she see*: Woodhouse's note records Keats's draft version of line 5 in stanza 30: the line as printed reads 'His image in the dusk she seem'd to see.'
3 *the Butlers*: Reynolds was convalescing with Charles Butler's family in Spencer Place, Kennington, London.

any length under a dis-guised feeling. I should have loaded you with an addition of gloom, which I am sure you do not want. I am now thank God in a humour to give you a good groats worth—for Tom, after a Night without a Wink of sleep, and overburdened with fever, has got up after a refreshing day sleep and is better than he has been for a long time; and you I trust have been again round the Common without any effect but refreshment.—As to the Matter I hope I can say with Sir Andrew "I have matter enough in my head"[1] in your favor And now, in the second place, for I reckon that I have finished my Imprimis, I am glad you blow up the weather—all through your letter there is a leaning towards a climate-curse, and you know what a delicate satisfaction there is in having a vexation anathematized: one would think there has been growing up for these last four thousand years, a grandchild Scion of the old forbidden tree, and that some modern Eve had just violated it; and that there was come with double charge, "Notus and Afer black with thunderous clouds from Sierra-leona"[2]—I shall breathe worsted stockings sooner than I thought for.[3] Tom wants to be in Town—we will have some such days upon the heath like that of last summer and why not with the same book: or what say you to a black Letter Chaucer printed in 1596:[4] aye I've got one huzza! I shall have it bounden gothique a nice sombre binding—it will go a little way to unmodernize. And also I see no reason, because I have been away this last month, why I should not have a peep at your Spencerian[5]—notwithstanding you speak of your office, in my thought a little too early, for I do not see why a Mind like yours is not capable of harbouring and digesting the whole Mystery of Law as easily as Parson

1 *I have matter enough in my head*: Keats recalls not Sir Andrew Aguecheek in *Twelfth Night* but Slender in *The Merry Wives of Windsor*, I. i. 111–12.
2 *Notus and Afer . . . Sierra-leona*: *Paradise Lost*, X, 702–3.
3 *I shall breathe . . . thought for*: That is, the smell of childrens' stockings in the household of the postman Benjamin Bentley in Well Walk.
4 *a black . . . in 1596*: Keats's copy, its whereabouts unknown, must have been Thomas Speght's 1598 edition.
5 *your Spencerian*: Reynolds's 'Romance of Youth', published in *The Garden of Florence* (1821).

Hugh does Pepins—which did not hinder him from his poetic Canary[1]—Were I to study physic or rather Medicine again,—I feel it would not make the least difference in my Poetry; when the Mind is in its infancy a Bias is in reality a Bias, but when we have acquired more strength, a Bias becomes no Bias. Every department of knowledge we see excellent and calculated towards a great whole. I am so convinced of this, that I am glad at not having given away my medical Books, which I shall again look over to keep alive the little I know thitherwards; and moreover intend through you and Rice to become a sort of Pip-civilian.[2] An extensive knowledge is needful to thinking people—it takes away the heat and fever; and helps, by widening speculation, to ease the Burden of the Mystery:[3] a thing I begin to understand a little, and which weighed upon you in the most gloomy and true sentence in your Letter. The difference of high Sensations with and without knowledge appears to me this—in the latter case we are falling continually ten thousand fathoms deep and being blown up again without wings and with all [the] horror of a bare shoulderd Creature—in the former case, our shoulders are fledge, and we go thro' the same air and space without fear. This is running one's rigs[4] on the score of abstracted benefit—when we come to human Life and affections it is impossible how a parallel of breast and head can be drawn—(you will forgive me for thus privately treading out [of] my depth and take it for treading as schoolboys tread the water)—it is impossible to know how far knowledge will console us for the death of a friend and the ill "that flesh is heir to[5]—With respect to the affections and Poetry you must know by a sympathy my thoughts that way; and I dare say these few

1 *Parson Hugh . . . poetic Canary*: Sir Hugh Evans in *The Merry Wives of Windsor*, I. ii. 11–12. Keats argues that Reynolds's new profession in the law need not prevent him from writing.

2 *Pip-civilian*: i.e., a 'pipsqueak' of a 'civilian' (practitioner of Roman law).

3 *the Burden of the Mystery*: Wordsworth's 'Lines Written a few miles above Tintern Abbey' (1798), l. 38.

4 *running one's rigs*: Playing tricks or pranks.

5 *that flesh is heir to*: *Hamlet*, III. i. 63.

lines will be but a ratification: I wrote them on May-day—and intend to finish the ode all in good time.—

Mother of Hermes! and still youthful Maia![1]
    May I sing to thee
As thou wast hymned on the shores of Baiæ?
    Or may I woo thee
In earlier Sicilian? or thy smiles
Seek as they once were sought, in Grecian isles,
By Bards who died content in pleasant sward,
Leaving great verse unto a little clan?
O give me their old vigour, and unheard,
Save of the quiet Primrose, and the span
    Of Heaven, and few ears
Rounded by thee, my song should die away
    Content as theirs
Rich in the simple worship of a day.—

You may be anxious to know for fact to what sentence in your Letter I allude. You say "I fear there is little chance of any thing else in this life." You seem by that to have been going through with a more painful and acute zest the same labyrinth that I have—I have come to the same conclusion thus far. My Branchings out therefrom have been numerous: one of them is the consideration of Wordsworth's genius and as a help, in the manner of gold being the meridian Line of worldly wealth,—how he differs from Milton.—And here I have nothing but surmises, from an uncertainty whether Miltons apparently less anxiety for Humanity proceeds from his seeing further or no than Wordsworth: And whether Wordsworth has in truth epic passion, and martyrs himself to the human heart, the main region of his song[2]—In regard to his genius alone—we find what he says true as far as we have experienced and we can

1 *Mother ... Maia!*: First published in *1848*. Keats seems not to have completed this 'ode', of which Woodhouse's transcripts are the sole record.
2 *main region of his song*: In the Preface to *The Excursion* (1814), p. xii, Wordsworth had quoted from his unpublished *The Recluse*, ll. 40–41: 'the Mind of Man, / The main region of my Song.'

judge no further but by larger experience—for axioms in philosophy are not axioms until they are proved upon our pulses: We read fine——things but never feel them to thee full until we have gone the same steps as the Author.—I know this is not plain; you will know exactly my meaning when I say, that now I shall relish Hamlet more than I ever have done—Or, better—You are sensible no man can set down Venery as a bestial or joyless thing until he is sick of it and therefore all philosophizing on it would be mere wording. Until we are sick, we understand not;—in fine, as Byron says, "Knowledge is Sorrow";[1] and I go on to say that "Sorrow is Wisdom"—and further for aught we can know for certainty! "Wisdom is folly"—So you see how I have run away from Wordsworth, and Milton; and shall still run away from what was in my head, to observe, that some kind of letters are good squares others handsome ovals, and others some orbicular, others spheroid—and why should there not be another species with two rough edges like a Rat-trap? I hope you will find all my long letters of that species, and all will be well; for by merely touching the spring delicately and etherially, the rough edged will fly immediately into a proper compactness, and thus you may make a good wholesome loaf, with your own leven in it, of my fragments—If you cannot find this said Rat-trap sufficiently tractable—alas for me, it being an impossibility in grain for my ink to stain otherwise: If I scribble long letters I must play my vagaries. I must be too heavy, or too light, for whole pages—I must be quaint and free of Tropes and figures—I must play my draughts as I please, and for my advantage and your erudition, crown a white with a black, or a black with a white, and move into black or white, far and near as I please—I must go from Hazlitt to Patmore,[2] and make Wordsworth and Coleman[3] play at leap-frog—or keep one of them down a whole half holiday

1 *Knowledge is Sorrow*: Byron's *Manfred* (1817), I. i. 10, 'Sorrow is knowledge'.
2 *Patmore*: Peter George Patmore (1786–1855), author and friend of Hazlitt and Lamb.
3 *Coleman*: George Colman the younger (1762–1836), a popular dramatist.

at fly the garter[1]—"From Gray to Gay, from Little to Shakespeare"[2]—Also as a long cause requires two or more sittings of the Court, so a long letter will require two or more sittings of the Breech wherefore I shall resume after dinner.—

Have you not seen a Gull, an orc, a Sea Mew, or any thing to bring this Line to a proper length, and also fill up this clear part; that like the Gull I may dip[3]—I hope, not out of sight—and also, like a Gull, I hope to be lucky in a good sized fish—This crossing a letter is not without its association—for chequer work leads us naturally to a Milkmaid, a Milkmaid to Hogarth Hogarth to Shakespeare, Shakespear to Hazlitt—Hazlitt to Shakespeare and thus by merely pulling an apron string we set a pretty peal of Chimes at work—Let them chime on a while, with your patience,—I will return to Wordsworth—whether or no he has an extended vision or a circumscribed grandeur—whether he is an eagle in his nest, or on the wing—And to be more explicit and to show you how tall I stand by the giant, I will put down a simile of human life as far as I now perceive it; that is, to the point to which I say we both have arrived at—' Well—I compare human life to a large Mansion of Many Apartments, two of which I can only describe, the doors of the rest being as yet shut upon me—The first we step into we call the infant or thoughtless Chamber, in which we remain as long as we do not think—We remain there a long while, and notwithstanding the doors of the second Chamber remain wide open, showing a bright appearance, we care not to hasten to it; but are at length imperceptibly impelled by the awakening of the thinking principle—within us—we no sooner get in to this second Chamber, which I shall call the Chamber of Maiden-Thought, than we become intoxicated with the light and the atmosphere, we see nothing but pleasant wonders, and think of delaying there for ever in delight: However among the effects this breathing is father of is that

1 *fly the garter*: A playground game in which players leap from one side of a 'garter' (a line of stones) over the back of another.

2 *From Gray . . . Shakespeare*: Parodying the *Essay on Man* (1733–4), IV, 380, by Alexander Pope (1688–1744); 'Thomas Little' being the pseudonym of Thomas Moore (1779–1852).

3 Woodhouse notes that Keats begins to cross his letter at this point.

tremendous one of sharpening one's vision into the heart and nature of Man—of convincing ones nerves that the World is full of Misery and Heartbreak, Pain, Sickness and oppression—whereby This Chamber of Maiden Thought becomes gradually darken'd and at the same time on all sides of it many doors are set open—but all dark—all leading to dark passages—We see not the ballance of good and evil. We are in a Mist—We are now in that state—We feel the "burden of the Mystery," To this point was Wordsworth come, as far as I can conceive when he wrote 'Tintern Abbey' and it seems to me that his Genius is explorative of those dark Passages. Now if we live, and go on thinking, we too shall explore them. he is a Genius and superior to us, in so far as he can, more than we, make discoveries, and shed a light in them—Here I must think Wordsworth is deeper than Milton—though I think it has depended more upon the general and gregarious advance of intellect, than individual greatness of Mind[1]—From the Paradise Lost and the other Works of Milton, I hope it is not too presuming, even between ourselves to say, his Philosophy, human and divine, may be tolerably understood by one not much advanced in years, In his time englishmen were just emancipated from a great superstition—and Men had got hold of certain points and resting places in reasoning which were too newly born to be doubted, and too much opposed by the Mass of Europe not to be thought etherial and authentically divine—who could gainsay his ideas on virtue, vice, and Chastity in Comus, just at the time of the dismissal of Cod-pieces and a hundred other disgraces? who would not rest satisfied with his hintings at good and evil in the Paradise Lost, when just free from the inquisition and burning in Smithfield?[2] The Reformation produced such immediate and great benefits, that Protestantism was considered under the immediate eye of heaven, and its own remaining Dogmas and superstitions, then,

1 *advance of intellect . . . of Mind*: Here, and in his comments below on the 'grand march of the intellect', Keats accepts a belief in the historical progress of human development. This is integral to *Hyperion*, but his second version of the story, *The Fall of Hyperion*, is sceptical and tragic.

2 *Smithfield*: The first victim of the Marian persecution, John Rogers (b. 1500) was burnt at Smithfield, 4 February 1555.

as it were, regenerated, constituted those resting places and seeming sure points of Reasoning—from that I have mentioned, Milton, whatever he may have thought in the sequel, appears to have been content with these by his writings—He did not think into the human heart, as Wordsworth has done—Yet Milton as a Philosop[h]er, had sure as great powers as Wordsworth—What is then to be inferr'd? O many things—It proves there is really a grand march of intellect—, It proves that a mighty providence subdues the mightiest Minds to the service of the time being, whether it be in human Knowledge or Religion—I have often pitied a Tutor who has to hear "Nom^e: Musa"[1]—so often dinn'd into his ears—I hope you may not have the same pain in this scribbling—I may have read these things before, but I never had even a thus dim perception of them; and moreover I like to say my lesson to one who will endure my tediousness for my own sake—After all there is certainly something real in the World—Moore's present to Hazlitt is real[2]—I like that Moore, and am glad I saw him at the Theatre just before I left Town.. Tom has spit a leetle blood this afternoon, and that is rather a damper—but I know—the truth is there is something real in the World Your third Chamber of Life shall be a lucky and gentle one—stored with the wine of love—and the Bread of Friendship—When you see George if he should not have recēd a letter from me tell him he will find one at home most likely—tell Bailey I hope soon to see him—Remember me to all The leaves have been out here, for mOny a day——I have written to George for the first Stanzas of my Isabel—I shall have them soon and will copy the whole out for you.

Your affectionate friend
John Keats.

Taylor and Hessey advertised Endymion *in the* Morning Chronicle *on Monday, 4 and 11 May as 'Published this Day'. Keats*

1 *Nom^e: Musa*: i.e., pupils declining Latin cases ('Nominative, "Musa". . .', etc.).

2 *Moore's . . . is real*: Peter Moore (1753–1828), Whig politician and reformist, and a trustee of the Drury Lane Theatre. The nature of his 'present' is unknown.

*and his brother left Teignmouth on 4 or 5 May, travelling via Bridport, where Tom suffered a violent haemorrhage, which delayed their journey. They were back in Hampstead before Monday, 11 May, when Keats dined at Haydon's. It is unclear whether or not George had told his brothers before their arrival in London of his intention to marry Georgiana Wylie and emigrate to America. Certainly Keats was depressed at the prospect of their departure and his brother had acted with considerable haste. George returned to London from Teignmouth at the beginning of March, having attained his majority on 28 February 1818. He had swiftly gained Mrs Wylie's consent to her daughter's marriage and set about obtaining his inheritance. In the newsy letter to his brothers of 18 March (*L, *II, pp. 247–8) George said he was sorting out their finances, but gave no indication of his own more radical plan of investing in Morris Birkbeck's 'prairie' settlement at Wanborough, Illinois.*

*On 17 May Tom Keats reported the imminent changes in the three brothers' lives: 'George embarks for America', and John, who had been 'very much engaged with his Friends', expected his 'Northern Expedition' with Charles Brown to take 'four months', covering 'two thousand miles mostly on Foot'. Tom himself hoped to travel to Italy (*L, *I, pp. 285–6).*

To Benjamin Bailey
21, 25 May 1818

[Harvard MS]

My dear Bailey, Hampstead Thursday [21 May]—

I should have answered your letter on the moment—if I could have said yes to your invitation.[1] What hinders me is insuperable; I will tell it at a little length. You know my Brother

1 *your invitation*: Keats had been unable visit Bailey in Oxford on his way to Teignmouth in March (see above, p. 122). Keats here replies to another invitation from Bailey written on or before 20 May (*KC*, I, 27).

George has been out of employ for some time. it has weighed very much upon him, and driven him to scheme and turn over things in his Mind. the result has been his resolution to emigrate to the back settlements of America, become farmer and work with his own hands after purchacing 1400 hundred Acres of the American Government.[1] This for many reasons has met with my entire consent—and the chief one is this—he is of too independant and liberal a Mind to get on in trade in this Country—in which a generous Ma<n> with a scanty recourse [*for* resource] must be ruined. I would sooner he should till the ground than bow to a Customer—there is no choice with him; he could not bring himself to the latter—I would not consent to his going alone—no; but that objection is done away with—he will marry before he sets sail a young Lady he has known some years—of a nature liberal and highspirited enough to follow him to the Banks of the Mississipi.[2] He will set off in a month or six weeks, and you will see how I should wish to pass that time with him—and then I must set out on a journey of my own—Brown and I are going on a pedestrian tour through the north of England and Scotland as far a[s] John o Grots. I have this morning such a Lethargy that I cannot write—the reason of my delaying is oftentimes from this feeling—I wait for a proper temper—Now you ask for an immediate answer I do not like to wait even till tomorrow—However I am now so depressed I have not an Idea to put to paper—my hand feels like lead—and yet it is and [*for* an] unpleasant numbness it does not take away the pain of existence—I don't know what to write—Monday [25 May]—You see how I have delayed—and even now I have but a confused idea of what I should be

1 *purchacing . . . Government*: Morris Birkbeck (1764–1825) described how he had bought 1,440 acres for his 'intended settlement' in his *Notes on a Journey . . . to the Territory of Illinois* (1818). Birkbeck's book persuaded a first band of emigrants to set out in March that year. Part of the attraction of his scheme for George was its promise of freedom from England's social and commercial constrictions. George misunderstood Birkbeck's over-optimistic plans, something he began to realize even before leaving England (*L*, II, pp. 294–5). He settled instead in Henderson, Kentucky (see below, p. 270 n.).

2 *Banks of the Mississipi*: Birkbeck's settlement was actually on the Ohio river.

about my intellect must be in a degen[er]ating state—it must be for when I should be writing about god knows what I am troubling you with Moods of my own Mind or rather body—for Mind there is none. I am in that temper that if I were under Water I would scarcely kick to come to the top—I know very well 't is all nonsense. In a short time I hope I shall be in a temper to fell [*for* feel] sensibly your mention of my Book[1]—in vain have I waited till Monday to have any interest in that or in any thing else. I feel no spur at my Brothers going to America and am almost stony-hearted about his wedding. All this will blow over—all I am sorry for is having to write to you in such a time—but I cannot force my letters in a hot bed—I could not feel comfortable in making sentences for you—I am your debtor—I must ever remain so—nor do I wish to be clear of my rational debt—There is a comfort in throwing oneself on the charity of ones friends—'t is like the albatros sleeping on its wings—I will be to you wine in the cellar and the more modestly or rather indolently I retire into the backward Bin, the more falerne[2] will I be at the drinking. There is one thing I must mention. My Brother talks of sailing in a fortnight if so I will most probably be with you a week[3] before I set out for Scotland. The middle of your first page should be suffic[i]ent to rouse me—what I said is true and I have dreamt of your mention of it and m<y> not a[n]swering it has weighed on me since—If I com<e,> I will bring your Letter and hear more fully your sentiments on one or two points. I will call about the Lectures at Taylors and at Little Britain tomorrow—Yesterday I dined with Hazlitt; Barnes,[4] and Wilkie at Haydon's. The topic was the Duke of Wellington very amusingly pro and con'd. Reynolds has been getting much better; and Rice may begin to crow for he got a little so so at a Party of his and was none the

1 *your mention of my Book*: For Keats's less than grateful response to Bailey's publication of his views on *Endymion* see his next letter to him.

2 *the more falerne*: i.e., the more like Falernian wine, the legendary white wine of the Romans.

3 *with you a week*: In the event, Keats did not go to Oxford.

4 *Barnes*: Thomas Barnes (1785–1841), essayist and friend of Hunt and his circle; from 1817 he was editor of *The Times*.

worse for it the next morning. I hope I shall soon see you for we must have many new thoughts and feelings to analize, and to discover whether a little more knowledge has not made us more ignorant—

Your's affectionately John Keats—

George and Georgiana Wylie were married at St Margaret's, Westminster, on Thursday, 28 May 1818. The following Friday George cashed in the stock left him by his grandmother. This realized over £1,600, of which he promptly deposited £500 in Keats's account to cover his own debts, leaving the balance to his brothers.

To Benjamin Bailey
10 June 1818

[Harvard MS]

My dear Bailey [Wednesday] London—

I have been very much gratified and very much hurt by your Letters in the Oxford Paper:[1] because independant of that unlawful and mortal feeling of pleasure at praise, there is a glory in enthusia[s]m; and because the world is malignant enough to chuckle at the most honorable Simplicity. Yes on my Soul my dear Bailey you are too simple for the World—and that Idea makes me sick of it—How is it that by extreme opposites we have as it were got discont[ent]ed nerves—you have all your Life (I think so) believed every Body—I have suspected every Body—and although you have been so deceived you make a simple appeal—the world has something else to do, and I am glad of it—were it in my choice I would reject a petrarchal

1 *your Letters in the Oxford Paper*: Bailey's two letters on *Endymion*, signed 'N.Y.', were printed in the *Oxford University and City Herald, and Midland County Chronicle* (30 May and 6 June 1818). Bailey was trying to persuade Taylor to publish a book of his essays, including his 'account' of Keats, but with no success (*KC*, I, 25–7).

coronation[1]—on accou[n]t of my dying day, and because women have Cancers. I should not by rights speak in this tone to you—for it is an incendiary spirit that would do so. Yet I am not old enough or magnanimous enough to anihilate self—and it would perhaps be paying you an ill compliment. I was in hopes some little time back to be able to releive your dullness by my spirits—to point out things in the world worth your enjoyment—and now I am never alone without rejoicing that there is such a thing as death—without placing my ultimate in the glory of dying for a great human purpose Perphaps if my affairs were in a different state I should not have written the above—you shall judge—I have two Brothers one is driven by the 'burden of Society' to America the other, with an exquisite love of Life, is in a lingering state—My Love for my Brothers from the early loss of our parents and even for earlier Misfortunes has grown into a affection 'passing the Love of Women'[2]—I have been ill temper'd with them, I have vex'd them—but the thought of them has always stifled the impression that any woman might otherwise have made upon me—I have a Sister[3] too and may not follow them, either to America or to the Grave—Life must be undergone, and I certainly derive a consolation from the thought of writing one or two more Poems before it ceases—I have heard some hints of your retiring to scotland—I should like to know your feeling on it—it seems rather remote—perhaps Gleg will have a duty near you. I am not certain whether I shall be able to go my Journey on account of my Brother Tom and a little indisposition of my own[4]—If I do not you shall see me soon—if no on my return—or I'll quarter myself upon you in Scotland next Winter. I had know[n] my sister in Law some time before she was my Sister and was very fond of her. I like her better and better—she is the most disinterrested woman I ever knew—that is to say she goes

1 *petrarchal coronation*: Petrarch (1304–74), Italian poet, was crowned Poet Laureate in Rome on 8 April 1341.
2 *passing the Love of Women*: 2 Samuel 1:26.
3 *Sister*: His sister-in-law Georgiana.
4 *indisposition of my own*: On 6 June Keats told Severn 'The Doctor says I mustn't go out' (*L*, I, pp. 291).

beyond degree in it—To see an entirely disinterrested Girl quite happy is the most pleasant and extraordinary thing in the world—it depends upon a thousand Circumstances—on my word 'tis extraordinary. Women must want Imagination and they may thank God for it—and so m[a]y we that a delicate being can feel happy without any sense of crime. It puzzles me and I have no sort of Logic to comfort me—I shall think it over. I am not at home and your letter being there I cannot look it over to answer any particular—only I must say I felt that passage of Dante—if I take any book with me it shall be those minute volumes of carey[1] for they will go into the aptest corner. Reynolds is getting I may say robust—his illness has been of service to him—like eny one just recovered he is high-spirited. I hear also good accounts of Rice—With respect to domestic Literature—the Endinburgh Magasine in another blow up against Hunt calls me 'the amiable Mister Keats' and I have more than a Laurel from the Quarterly Reviewers for they have <u>smothered</u> me in 'Foliage'[2] I want to read you my 'Pot of Basil' if you go to scotland I should much like to read it there to you among the Snows of next Winter. My Brothers' remembrances to you.

Your affectionate friend
John Keats—

1 *carey*: H. F. Cary's translation of Dante's *Divine Comedy* (1814) was reissued by Taylor and Hessey in 1818. Keats took the three volumes on his Northern tour and gave them to Fanny Brawne when he left for Italy.

2 *the amiable Mister Keats . . . Foliage*: In his 'Letter from Z. to Leigh Hunt' J. G. Lockhart describes Keats as an 'amiable but infatuated bardling, Mister John Keats' (*Blackwood's Magazine*, May 1818). Hunt's *Foliage* (1818) was attacked in the *Quarterly Review* (January 1818).

To John Taylor
21 June 1818

[Harvard MS]

[Well Walk, Hampstead]

My dear Taylor, Sunday Evening

I am sorry I have not had time to call and wish you health till my return—Really I have been hard run these three last days. However Au revoir! God keep us all well.—I start tomorrow morning. My Brother Tom will I am affraid be lonely—I can scarcely ask the loan of Books for him—since I still keep those you lent me a year ago—if I am overweening you will be I know will be indulgent—Therefore when he shall write do send him some you think will be most amusing—he will be careful in returning them. Let him have one of my Books bound. I am ashamed to catalogue these Messages there is but one more which ought to go for nothing as there is a Lady concernd I promised Mrs Reynolds one of my Books bound. As I cannot write in it let the opposite[1] be pasted in prythee Remember me to Percy Street—Tell Hilton[2] that one gratification on my return will bee to find him engaged in a History Piece to his content—and Tell Dewint I shall become a disputant on the Landscape—bow for me very genteelly to M^rs^ D[3] or she will not admit your diploma. Remember me to Hessey saying I hope he will Carey his point[4]—I would not forget Woodhouse. Adieu Your sincere friend

John O'Grots

Mrs Reynolds with J. K's repects

1 *opposite*: Tom's presentation copy of *Endymion* has been lost, but Mrs Reynolds's is at Harvard. Taylor did not, as asked, cut out Keats's inscription from this letter: Mrs Reynolds's copy has 'Mrs Reynolds from her friend J. K.'

2 *Hilton*: William Hilton (1786–1839), a history painter and friend of Taylor, Keats, Lamb and John Clare, painted the posthumous portrait of Keats now in the National Portrait Gallery, London. He and the landscape painter Peter DeWint (1784–1849) lived at 10 Percy Street, Rathbone Place, London.

3 *M^rs^ D*: i.e., Mrs Dilke.

4 *Carey his point*: Presumably referring to Taylor and Hessey's negotiations with H. F. Cary over his translation of Dante.

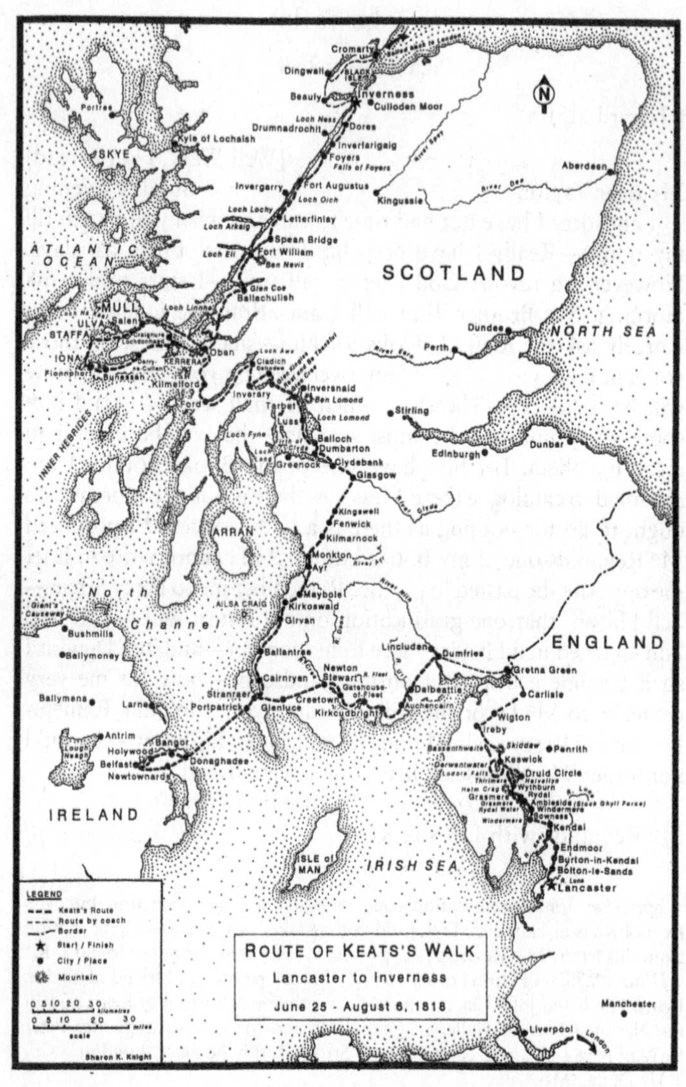

1. *Keats's Northern Walk, 25 June–6 August 1818*

25 June to 6 August 1818
'Scotch Letters'

Keats and Brown shared a coach with George and his new wife, leaving London early on Monday, 22 June. They reached Liverpool late the following afternoon. That evening Keats said goodbye to the newly married couple before they embarked for America. First thing next day he and Brown took the coach to Lancaster, where they stayed the night. Their walk began the next morning on Thursday, 25 June. After being delayed by rain and finding the inn at Burton-in-Kendal was full, they continued until they found rooms at Endmoor.

The two men had intended to walk to John O'Groats, but Keats's illness meant that he had to return early on his own, leaving Cromarty for London on 8 August. Brown computed that by then they had walked 642 miles (L, I, p. 361) in just over six weeks.

As Keats's first 'Scotch Letter' makes clear, the two men's usual pattern was to leave shortly after dawn at 4 or 5 a.m. and walk five or more miles before breakfast, after which Keats might begin or continue a letter. They would then walk, weather permitting, until 'dinner' that afternoon, sometimes staying on overnight at the same place or finding lodgings further on. Keats therefore had the opportunity to continue his correspondence in either the afternoon or evening. Unless there are lost letters, the seven-day gap in Keats's letters between 26 July and 3 August was probably caused by the 'violent cold' he had caught on Mull (L, I, p. 362).

Details of the two men's itinerary draws on Nelson S. Bushnell's A Walk after John Keats *(New York: Farrar & Rinehart, 1936). A detailed account of Carol Kyros Walker's journey in*

Keats's footsteps, accompanied by photographs and the texts of his 'Scotch Letters', is given in her Walking North with Keats *(New Haven: Yale University Press, 1992).*

*Keats meant these letters to be read by his family and friends. They were at once a record of his journey and a way of maintaining contact. Those addressed to Tom (the majority) tried to ensure that their friends and family kept in touch with his seriously ill brother, and from the start these were meant to be sent on to – or copied out for – George and Georgiana in America. All the extant holograph originals are written on much larger sheets of paper than Keats normally used. This allowed him to cram in more information per sheet, but writing them, often over several days, must have been even more difficult than would otherwise have been the case (see below Keats's account of Brown trying to write in a smoky cottage in Mull, pp. 214–15). Brown also made a record of their 'Northern walk' in his 'Journal'. Although neither seems to have had publication in mind, Brown many years later had part of his 'Journal' printed as 'Walks in the North, During the Summer of 1818', but only up to 9 July, when they stopped at Ballantrae (*L, I*, pp. 421–2).*

To Tom Keats

25–27 June 1818

[Transcript (1836)][1]

[Mrs Black's inn, Endmoor]

Here beginneth my journal, this Thursday, the 25th day of June, Anno Domini 1818. This morning we arose at 4, and set off in a Scotch mist; put up once under a tree, and in fine, have walked wet and dry to this place, called in the vulgar tongue Endmoor, 17 miles; we have not been incommoded by our knapsacks; they serve capitally, and we shall go on very well.

1 Text from *Western Messenger* [Louisville, Kentucky], 1 (1836), pp. 724–77, to whose editor, James Freeman Clarke, George Keats had loaned the lost original.

[Friday afternoon, White Lion Inn, Bowness] June 26—I merely put pro forma, for there is no such thing as time and space, which by the way came forcibly upon me on seeing for the first hour the Lake and Mountains of Winander[1]—I cannot describe them—they surpass my expectation—beautiful water—shores and islands green to the marge—mountains all round up to the clouds. We set out from Endmoor this morning, breakfasted at Kendal with a soldier who had been in all the wars for the last seventeen years—then we have walked to Bowne's[2] to dinner—said Bowne's situated on the Lake where we have just dined, and I am writing at this present. I took an oar to one of the islands to take up some trout for dinner, which they keep in porous boxes. I enquired of the waiter for Wordsworth—he said he knew him, and that he had been here a few days ago, canvassing for the Lowthers. What think you of that—Wordsworth versus Brougham!![3] Sad—sad—sad—and yet the family has been his friend always. What can we say? We are now about seven miles from Rydale,[4] and expect to see him to-morrow. You shall hear all about our visit.

There are many disfigurements to this Lake—not in the way of land or water. No; the two views we have had of it are of the most noble tenderness—they can never fade away—they make one forget the divisions of life; age, youth, poverty and riches; and refine one's sensual vision into a sort of north star which can never cease to be open lidded and stedfast over the wonders of the great Power. The disfigurement I mean is the miasma of London. I do suppose it contaminated with bucks and soldiers, and women of fashion—and hat-band ignorance. The border inhabitants are quite out of keeping with the romance about them, from a continual intercourse with London rank

1 *Winander*: Winandermere was the earlier name for Windermere.

2 *Bowne's*: Bowness.

3 *Wordsworth versus Brougham*: Wordsworth, to Keats's disgust, supported the Tory William Lowther, son of his patron Lord Lowther, in the 1818 election against Henry Brougham, the reformist Whig candidate, supported by Hunt's *Examiner*. Brougham was defeated.

4 *Rydale*: i.e., Rydal, between Windermere and Grasmere, where Wordworth had his house, Rydal Mount.

and fashion. But why should I grumble? They let me have a prime glass of soda water[1]—O they are as good as their neighbors. But Lord Wordsworth, instead of being in retirement, has himself and his house full in the thick of fashionable visitors quite convenient to be pointed at all the summer long. When we had gone about half this morning, we began to get among the hills and to see the mountains grow up before us—the other half brought us to Wynandermere, 14 miles to dinner. The weather is capital for the views, but is now rather misty, and we are in doubt whether to walk to Ambleside to tea—it is five miles along the borders of the Lake. Loughrigg will swell up before us all the way—I have an amazing partiality for mountains in the clouds. There is nothing in Devon like this, and Brown says there is nothing in Wales to be compared to it. I must tell you, that in going through Cheshire and Lancashire, I saw the Welsh mountains at a distance. We have passed two castles, Lancaster and Kendal.

[Saturday, after breakfast, Salutation Inn, Ambleside] 27th—We walked here to Ambleside yesterday along the border of Windandermere all beautiful with wooded shores and Islands—our road was a winding lane, wooded on each side, and green overhead, full of Foxgloves—every now and then a glimpse of the Lake, and all the while Kirkstone and other large hills nestled together in a sort of grey black mist. Ambleside is at the northern extremity of the Lake. We arose this morning at six, because we call it a day of rest, having to call on Wordsworth who lives only two miles hence—before breakfast we went to see the Ambleside water fall. The morning beautiful—the walk easy[2] among the hills. We, I may say, fortunately, missed the direct path, and after wandering a little, found it out by the noise—for, mark you, it is buried in trees, in the bottom of the valley—the stream itself is interesting throughout with "mazy

1 *soda water*: Invented by Joseph Priestley in 1767 and a fashionable commercial product from at least the 1780s.
2 *easy*: Rendered as 'early' in Clarke's transcript, an obvious misreading.

error over pendant shades."[1] Milton meant a smooth river—this is buffeting all the way on a rocky bed ever various—but the waterfall itself, which I came suddenly upon, gave me a pleasant twinge. First we stood a little below the head about half way down the first fall, buried deep in trees, and saw it streaming down two more descents to the depth of near fifty feet—then we went on a jut of rock nearly level with the second fall-head, where the first fall was above us, and the third below our feet still—at the same time we saw that the water was divided by a sort of cataract island on whose other side burst out a glorious stream—then the thunder and the freshness. At the same time different falls have as different characters; the first darting down the slate-rock like an arrow; the second spreading out like a fan—the third dashed into a mist—and the one on the other side of the rock a sort of mixture of all these. We afterwards moved away a space, and saw nearly the whole more mild, streaming silverly through the trees. What astonishes me more than any thing is the tone, the coloring, the slate, the stone, the moss, the rock-weed; or, if I may say so, the intellect, the countenance of such places. The space, the magnitude of mountains and waterfalls are well imagined before one sees them; but this countenance or intellectual tone must surpass every imagination and defy any remembrance. I shall learn poetry here and shall henceforth write more than ever, for the abstract endeavor of being able to add a mite to that mass of beauty which is harvested from these grand materials, by the finest spirits, and put into etherial existence for the relish of one's fellows. I cannot think with Hazlitt that these scenes make man appear little.[2] I never forgot my stature so completely—I live in the eye; and my imagination, surpassed, is at rest—We shall see another waterfall near Rydal to which we

1 *mazy . . . shades*: *Paradise Lost*, IV, 239, part of Milton's description of the 'river large' running through Eden.

2 *with Hazlitt . . . appear little*: Reviewing Wordsworth's *The Excursion*, Hazlitt commented, 'The immensity of their mountains makes the human form seem little and insignificant' (*Examiner*, 21 August–2 October 1814, p. 638).

shall proceed after having put these letters in the post office. I long to be at Carlisle, as I expect there a letter from George and one from you. Let any of my friends see my letters—they may not be interested in descriptions—descriptions are bad at all times—I did not intend to give you any; but how can I help it? I am anxious you should taste a little of our pleasure; it may not be an unpleasant thing, as you have not the fatigue. I am well in health. Direct henceforth to Port Patrick till the 12th July. Content that probably three or four pair of eyes whose owners I am rather partial to will run over these lines I remain; and moreover that I am your affectionate brother John.

To George and Georgiana Keats

27, 28 June 1818[1]

[Harvard MS]

[Nag's Head, Wythburn, Saturday evening]
My dear George, Foot of Helvellyn June 27

We have passed from Lancaster to Burton from Burton to En[d]moor, from En[d]moor to Kendal from Kendal to Bownes on turning down to which place there burst upon us the most beautiful and rich view of Winander mere and the surrounding Mountains—we dined at Bownes on Trout which I took an oar to fetch from some Box preserves close on one of the little green Islands. After dinner we walked to Ambleside down a beautiful shady Lane along the Borders of the Lake with ample opportunity for Glimpses all the way—We slept at Ambleside not above two Miles from Rydal the Residence of Wordsworth We arose not very early on account of having marked this for a day of rest—Before breakfast we visited the first waterfall I ever saw and certainly small as it is it surpassed my expectation, in what I

1 Keats posted the letter from Keswick to 'M[r] George Keats / Crown Inn / Liverpool', from where it was sent on to 'Mess[rs] Frampton & Son / Leadenhall Street / London', where Tom Keats collected it. Although Tom endorsed the letter 'To be sent to George', he did not forward it (see below, p. 425).

have mentioned in my letter to Tom, in its tone and intellect its light shade slaty Rock, Moss and Rock weed—but you will see finer ones I will not describe by comparison a teapot spout—We ate a Monstrous Breakfast on our return (which by the way I do every morning) and after it proceeded to Wordsworths He was not at home nor was any Member of his family—I was much disappointed. I wrote a note for him and stuck it up over what I knew must be Miss Wordsworth's[1] Portrait and set forth again & we visited two Waterfalls in the neighbourhood, and then went along by Rydal Water and Grasmere through its beautiful Vale—and then through a defile in the Mountains into Cumberland[2] and So to the foot of Helvellyn whose summit is out of sight four Miles off rise above rise—I have seen Kirkstone, Loughrigg and Silver How—and discovered without a hint "that ancient woman seated on Helm Craig."[3] This is the summary of what I have written to Tom and dispatched from Ambleside—I have had a great confidence in your being well able to support the fatigue of your Journey since I have felt how much new Objects contribute to keep off a sense of Ennui and fatigue 14 Miles here is not so much as the 4 from Hampstead to London. You will have an enexhaustible astonishment; with that and such a Companion you will be cheered on from day to day—I hope you will not have sail'd before this Letter reaches you—yet I do not know for I will have my Series to Tom coppied and sent to you by the first Packet you have from England.[4] God send you both as good Health as I have now. Ha! my dear sister George, I wish I knew what humour you were in that I might accomodate myself to any one of your Amiabilities—Shall it be a Sonnet or a Pun or an Acrostic, a Riddle or a Ballad—'perhaps it may turn out a Sang, and perhaps turn out a Sermon'[5] I'll write you on my

1 *Miss Wordsworth*: Wordsworth's sister Dorothy (1771–1855).

2 *into Cumberland*: They crossed the boundary between Westmorland and Cumberland, separate counties until they were merged into Cumbria in 1974.

3 *that ancient . . . Helm Craig*: Wordsworth's 'Poems on the Naming of Places II: To Joanna', l. 56.

4 *I will have . . . from England*: For the 'coppies' and 'Scotch letters' Keats actually sent the George Keatses see below, pp. 256, 425–6.

5 *perhaps it may . . . a Sermon*: Burns's 'Epistle to a Young Friend', ll. 7–8.

word the first and most likely the last I ever shall do, because it has strucke me—what shall it be about?

Give me your patience Sister while I frame[1]
Enitials ve[r]se-wise of your golden name:
Or sue the fair Apollo and he will
Rouse from his Slumber heavy and instill
Great Love in me for thee and Poesy—
Imagine not that greatest Mastery
And kingdom over all the realms of verse
Nears more to heaven in aught than when we nurse
And surety give to[2] Love and Brotherhood.—

Anthropopagi in Othello's Mood,[3]
Ulysses stormed, and his enchanted Belt[4]
~~By the sweet Muse are never never felt~~
Glow with the Muse but they are never felt
Unbosom'd so, and so eternal made,
Such selfsame insence in their Laurel shade
To all the regent sisters of the Nine[5]
As this poor offering to thee Sister mine.

Kind Sister! aye this third name says you are
Enhanced has it been the Lord knows where.
Ah! may it taste to you like good old wine—
Take you to real happiness and give
Sons and daughters and a Home like honied hive.

1 *Give me . . . I frame*: Keats's acrostic on his sister-in-law's name was drafted directly into his letter. When copying the poem out again later for the George Keatses he said he would not have done so 'If I thought it would ever be seen by any but yourselves' (see below, p. 426). Nevertheless, in doing so Keats made substantive alterations.
2 *And surety give to*: Interlineal replacement for 'In its vast safety'.
3 *Anthropopagi . . . Mood*: Alludes to *Othello*, I. iii. 142–4, 'the cannibals that each other eat, / The Anthropophagi [eaters of men]'.
4 *Ulysses . . . Belt*: Appears to be a reference to Homer's *Odyssey*, V, 346–7, where Ulysses, threatened by storm, is saved by a magic veil given him by Leucothea.
5 *the Nine*: The nine Muses.

[Oak Inn, Keswick, Sunday morning] June 28th I have slept and walked eight miles to Breakfast at Keswick on derwent water—We could not mount Helvellyn for the mist so gave it up with hopes of Skiddaw which we shall try tomorrow if it be fine—to day we shall walk round Derwent water, and in our Way see the Falls of Low-dore—The Approach to derwent water is rich and magnificent beyond any means of conception—the Mountains all round sublime and graceful and rich in colour—Woods and wooded Islands here and there—at the same time in the distance among Mountains of another aspect we see Bassenthwaite—I <shall> drop like a Hawk on the Post Office at Carlisle <to ask for> some Letters from you and Tom—

Sweet sweet is the greeting of eyes,[1]
And sweet is the voice in its greeting,
When Adieux have grown old and goodbyes
Fade away where old time is retreating—

Warm the nerve of a welcoming hand
And earnest a kiss on the Brow,
When we meet over sea and o'er Land
Where furrows are new to the Plough.

This is all < . . . > in the m< . . . > please a< . . . > Letters as possi<bly . . . >[2] We will before many Years are over have written as many folio volumes which as a Matter of self-defence to one whom you understand intends to be immortal in the best points and let all his Sins and peccadillos die away—I mean to say that the Booksellers with [*for* will] rather decline printing ten folio volumes of Correspondence printed as close as the Apostles creed in a Watch paper[3]—I have been looking out my dear Georgy for a joke or a Pun for you—there is none but the Names of romantic Misses on the Inn window Panes. You will of course have given me directions brother George where to direct on the other side of the Water. I have not had time to

1 *Sweet sweet . . . eyes*: First published in 1925.
2 Letter torn.
3 *Watch paper*: Small decorative pieces of paper inside a watch cover, with printed images or text.

write to Henry[1]—for I have a journal to keep for Tom nearly enough to employ all my leisure—I am a day behind hand with him—I scarcely know how I shall manage Fanny and two or three others I have promised—We expect to be in Scotland in at most three days so you must if this should catch you before you set sail give me a line to Port-Patrick—

God bless you my dear Brother and Sister.

John—

To Tom Keats
29 June, 1, 2 July 1818

[Jeffrey transcript (1845)]

[Monday] Keswick[2]—June 29th 1818.

My dear Tom

I cannot make my Journal as distinct & actual as I could wish, from having been engaged in writing to George. & therefore I must tell you without circumstance that we proceeded from Ambleside to Rydal, saw the Waterfalls there, & called on Wordsworth, who was not at home. nor was any one of his family. I wrote a note & left it on the Mantlepiece. Thence on we came to the foot of Helvellyn, where we slept, but could not ascend it for the mist. I must mention that from Rydal we passed Thirlswater, & a fine pass in the Mountains from Helvellyn we came to Keswick on Derwent Water. The approach to Derwent Water surpassed Winandermere—it is richly wooded & shut in with rich-toned Mountains. From Helvellyn to Keswick was eight miles to Breakfast, After which we took a complete circuit of the Lake going about ten miles, & seeing on our way the Fall of Low-dore. I had an easy climb among the streams, about the fragments of Rocks & should have got I think to the summit, but unfortunately I was damped by

1 *Henry*: Henry Wylie, Keats's new brother-in-law.

2 *Keswick*: In fact, Keats had left Keswick and was writing from Ireby after climbing Skiddaw.

slipping one leg into a squashy hole. There is no great body of water, but the accompaniment is delightful; for it ooses out from a cleft in perpendicular Rocks, all fledged with Ash & other beautiful trees. It is a strange thing how they got there. At the south end of the Lake, the Mountains of Burrowdale, are perhaps as fine as any thing we have seen—On our return from this circuit, we ordered dinner, & set forth about a mile & a half on the Penrith road, to see the Druid temple.[1] We had a fag up hill, rather too near dinner time, which was rendered void, by the gratification of seeing those aged stones, on a gentle rise in the midst of Mountains, which at that time darkened all round, except at the fresh opening of the vale of St. John. We went to bed rather fatigued, but not so much so as to hinder us from getting up this morning,[2] to mount Skiddaw It promised all along to be fair, & we had fagged & tugged nearly to the top, when at halfpast six there came a mist upon us & shut out the view; we did not however lose anything by it, we were high enough without mist, to see the coast of Scotland; the Irish sea; the hills beyond Lancaster; & nearly all the large ones of Cumberland & Westmoreland, particularly Helvellyn & Scawfell: It grew colder & colder as we ascended, & we were glad at about three parts of the way to taste a little rum which the Guide brought with him, mixed, mind ye with mountain water, I took two glasses going & one returning—It is about six miles from where I am writing to the top. so we have walked ten miles before Breakfast today. We went up with two others, very good sort of fellows, All felt on arising into the cold air, that same elevation, which a cold bath gives one—I felt as if I were going to a Tournament. Wordsworth's house is situated just on the rise of the foot of mount Rydall, his parlor window looks directly down Winandermere; I do not think I told you how fine the vale of Grassmere is, & how I discovered "the ancient

1 *the Druid temple*: The prehistoric Castlerigg Stone Circle, formerly thought to be a Druid place of worship. Keats's description of 'a dismal cirque / Of Druid stones, upon a forlorn moor' in *Hyperion*, II, 34–5, probably draws on a memory of this visit.

2 *getting up this morning*: At 4 a.m., as usual.

woman seated on Helm Crag."—We shall proceed immediately to Carlisle, intending to enter Scotland on the 1st of July via ——

The next day Keats and Brown walked to Carlisle, where they stopped the night.

[Wednesday morning] July 1st—We are this morning at Carlisle—After Skiddow, we walked to Ireby the oldest market town in Cumberland—where we were greatly amused by a country dancing school, holden at the Sun, it was indeed "no cotillon fresh from France."[1] No they kickit & jumpit with mettle extraordinary, & whiskit, & fleckit, & toe'd it, & go'd it, & twirld it, & wheel'd it, & stampt it, & sweated it, tattooing the floor like mad; The differenc[e] between our country dances & these scotch figures, is about the same as leisurely stirring a cup o' Tea & beating up a batter pudding. I was extremely gratified to think, that if I had pleasures they knew nothing of. they had also some into which I could not possibly enter I hope I shall not return without having got the Highland fling, there was as fine a row of boys & girls as you ever saw, some beautiful faces, & one exquisite mouth. I never felt so near the glory of Patriotism, the glory of making by any means a country happier. This is what I like better than scenery. I fear our continued moving from place to place, will prevent our becoming learned in village affairs; we are mere creatures of Rivers, Lakes, & mountains. Our yesterday's journey was from Ireby to Wigton, & from Wigton to Carlisle—The Cathedral does not appear very fine; The Castle is very Ancient, & of Brick The City is very various, old white washed narrow streets; broad red brick ones more modern—I will tell you anon, whether the inside of the Cathedral is worth looking at. It is built of a sandy red stone or Brick. We have now walked 114 miles & are merely a little tired in the thighs, & a little blistered; We shall ride 38 miles to Dumfries, when we shall linger a while, about Nithsdale & Galloway, I have written two

1 *no cotillion ... France*: Burns's 'Tam o' Shanter', l. 116.

letters to Liverpool. I found a letter from sister George.[1] very delightful indeed. I shall preserve it in the bottom of my knapsack for you.
[Dumfries, Scotland, Wednesday evening, 1 July]

—On visiting the Tomb of Burns—[2]

The Town, the churchyard, & the setting sun,
The Clouds, the trees, the rounded hills all seem
Though beautiful, Cold—strange—as in a dream,
I dreamed long ago, now new begun
The shortlived, paly summer is but won
From winters ague, for one hours gleam;
Through saphire warm, their stars do never beam,
All is cold Beauty; pain is never done
For who has mind to relish Minos-wise,[3]
The real of Beauty, free from that dead hue
Fickly[4] imagination & sick pride
[5]wan upon it! Burns! With honor due
I have oft honoured thee. Great shadow; hide
Thy face, I sin against thy native skies.

You will see by this sonnet that I am at Dumfries, we have dined in Scotland. Burn's tomb is in the Churchyard corner, not very much to my taste, though on a scale, large enough to show they wanted to honour him[6]—M[rs] Burns lives in this place,

1 *two letters . . . a letter from sister George*: Only one holograph of Keats's 'Scotch Letters' to George and Georgiana Keats is known, and that did not reach them (see above, p. 168, and below, p. 425): the letter from Georgiana, sent from Liverpool before the couple sailed, is also lost.
2 *On visiting . . . Burns*: First published in *1848*.
3 *Minos-wise*: The legendary King Minos was believed by the Greeks to be one of the final judges of the spirits of the dead, because of his wisdom as a law-giver and judge when alive.
4 *Fickly*: *OED* records 'fickly' (1300–1721) as 'now rare'. See J. C. Maxwell, *K–SJ*, 4 (1955), p. 78, for its use in *King Lear*.
5 (Jeffrey's note) 'An illegible word occurs here—' R. M. Milnes's conjecture ('Cast') in *1848* has not been bettered.
6 *Burn's tomb . . . honour him*: The newly completed Grecian-style mausoleum in St Michael's Churchyard, erected by public subscription, to which the Prince Regent contributed, and to where Burns's remains had been moved in

most likely we shall see her tomorrow—This Sonnet I have written in a strange mood, half asleep. I know not how it is, the Clouds, the sky, the Houses, all seem anti[1] Grecian & anti Charlemagnish[2]—I will endeavour to get rid of my prejudices, & tell you fairly about the Scotch—

[Dumfries, Thursday morning] July 2nd In Devonshire they say "Well where be yee going." Here it is, "How is it all wi yoursel"—A man on the Coach said the horses took a Hellish heap o' drivin—the same fellow pointed out Burn's tomb with a deal of life, "There de ye see it, amang the trees; white, wi a roond tap." The first well dressed Scotchman we had any conversation with, to our surprise confessed himself a Deist.[3] The careful manner of his delivering his opinions, not before he had received several encouraging hints from us, was very amusing—Yesterday was an immense Horse fair at Dumfries, so that we met numbers of men & women on the road, the women nearly all barefoot, with their shoes & clean stockings in hand, ready to put on & look smart in the Towns. There are plenty of wretched Cottages, where smoke has no outlet but by the door—We have now begun upon whiskey, called here whuskey very smart stuff it is—Mixed like our liquors with sugar & water tis called toddy, very pretty drink, & much praised by Burns.[4]

1815. Burns had spent the last years of his life in Dumfries as an exciseman, and his wife Jean Armour continued to live there until her death in 1834. Keats's admiration for Burns was twofold: Burns was an example of a Romantic poet who died tragically young, and his republican sympathies allied him with the liberal cause.

1 *anti*: Jeffrey has 'ante' (*bis*).

2 *Charlemagnish*: Charlemagne (742–814), king of the Franks, famous for his court's learning, and the subject of an Old French chanson de geste. Keats evidently associated him with the Greeks and the cult of the South.

3 *Deist*: Deists draw their belief from natural reason and not revelation (unlike Christians).

4 As Rollins notes, 'Nobody can tell how much Jeffrey omits here.'

To Fanny Keats
2, 3, 5 July 1818

[Morgan MS]

My dear Fanny, [Thursday morning] Dumfries July 2nd

I intended to have written to you from Kirkudbright the town I shall be in tomorrow—but I will write now bec[a]use my knapsack has worn out my coat in the Seams, my coat has gone to the Taylors and I have but one Coat to my back in these parts. I must tell you how I went to Liverpool with George and our new Sister and the Gentleman my fellow traveller through the Summer and Autumn—We had a tolerable journey to Liverpool—which I left the next morning before George was up for Lancaster—Then we set off from Lancaster on foot with our knapsacks on, and have walked a Little zig zag through the mountains and Lakes of Cumberland and Westmoreland—We came from Carlisle yesterday to this place—We are employed in going up Mountains, looking at Strange towns prying into old ruins and eating very hearty breakfasts. Here we are full in the Midst of broad Scotch 'How is it a' wi yoursel'—the Girls are walking about bare footed and in the worst cottages the Smoke finds its way out of the door—I shall come home full of news for you and for fear I should choak you by too great a dose at once I must make you used to it by a letter or two—We have been taken for travelling Jewellers, Razor sellers and Spectacle venders because friend Brown wears a pair—The first place we stopped at with our knapsacks contained one Richard Bradshaw a notorious tippler—He stood in the shape of a ℥[1] and ballanced himself as well as he could saying with his nose right in Mr Brown's face 'Do— - yo u sell Spect—ta—cles?' Mr Abbey says we are Don Quixotes—tell him we are more generally taken for Pedlars—All I hope is that we may not be taken for excisemen[2] in this whiskey country—We are generally up

1 ℥: The sign for an apothecary's or fluid ounce.
2 *excisemen*: Formerly government officials whose function was to collect excise tax on goods and spirits and to prevent smuggling, hence their unpopularity.

about 5 walking before breakfast and we complete our 20 Miles before dinner—Yesterday we visited Burns's Tomb and this morning the fine Ruins of Lincluden[1]—

Keats broke off here to leave for Dalbeattie, where the two men stayed overnight. Next morning they walked eight miles before stopping for breakfast on their way to Kirkcudbright.

[Auchencairn, Friday morning, 3 July] I had done thus far when my coat came back fortified at all points—so as to lose no time we set forth again through Galloway—all very pleasant and pretty with no fatigue when one is used to it—We are in the midst of Meg Merrilies' country[2] of whom I suppose you have heard—

Old Meg she was a Gypsey[3]
  And liv'd upon the Moors
Her bed it was the brown heath turf
  And her house was out of doors

Her apples were swart blackberries
  Her currants pods o' broom
Her wine was dew o' the wild white rose
  Her book a churchyard tomb

Her Brothers were the craggy hills
  Her Sisters larchen trees—
Alone ~~wht~~ with her great family
  She liv'd as she did please—

1 *Ruins of Lincluden*: Lincluden Collegiate Church, just north of Dumfries.

2 *Meg Merrilies' country*: Keats had not read Scott's *Guy Mannering* (1815) in which Meg Merrilies appears. However, Brown told him about Scott's character as they walked, although Keats probably knew of her through reviews, stage versions or paintings: he depicts her here as a 'Romantic Gypsey' (see Claire Lamont, *English*, 36 (1987), pp. 137–45).

3 *Old Meg . . . Gypsey*: First published in 1838 (*Texts*).

No breakfast has she many a ~~day~~/morn/
  No dinner many a noon
And 'stead of supper she would stare
  Full hard against the Moon—

But every morn of woodbine fresh
  She made her garlanding
And every night the dark glen Yew
  She wove and she would sing—

And ~~sometimes~~ with her fingers old and brown
  She plaited Mats o' Rushes
And gave them to the Cottagers
  She met among the Bushes—

Old Meg was brave as Margaret Queen
  And tall as Amazon:
An old red blanket cloak she wore;
  A chip hat[1] had she on—
God rest her aged bones somewhere
  She died full long agone!

If you like these sort of Ballads I will now and then scribble one for you—if I send any to Tom I'll tell him to send them to you—

(continued that evening, p. 181 below)

1 *chip hat*: Hat made of thin strips of wood.

To Tom Keats
3, 5, 7, 9 July 1818[1]

[Harvard MS]

My dear Tom, [Friday morning,] Auchencairn July 3[rd]

I have not been able to keep up my journal completely on accou[n]t of other letters to George[2] and one which I am writing to Fanny from which I have turned to loose no time whilst Brown is coppying a song about Meg Merrilies[3] which I have just written for her—We are now in Meg Merrilies county and have this morning passed through some parts exactly suited to her—Kirkudbright County is very beautiful, very wild, with craggy hills somewhat in the westmoreland fashion—we have come down from Dumfries to the Sea coast part of it—The song I mention you would have from Dilke:[4] but perhaps you would like it here—

[copies out 'the song' from the previous letter with minor variants]

Now I will return to Fanny—it rains. I may have time to go on here presently.

(*Keats was not able to continue this letter until 5 July, p. 185 below*)

1 Tom endorsed this letter: 'Received 13 July | Answered —"—"— | No 3 from John.'

2 *other letters to George*: Only one is now known, that of 27, 28 June.

3 *Brown . . . Meg Merrilies*: Brown used his copy (now lost) when he printed the poem in 1838 (see *Texts*).

4 *from Dilke*: Keats and Brown intended to send these mock ballads to Charles Dilke in the hopes of taking him in (see below, p. 191).

To Fanny Keats

(continued)

3, 5 July 1818

[Kirkcudbright, Friday evening, 3 July] I have so many interruptions that I cannot manage to fill a Letter in one day—since I scribbled the Song we have walked through a beautiful Country to Kirkudbright—at which place I will write you a song about myself—

There was a naughty Boy[1]
A naughty boy was he
He would not stop at home
He could not quiet be—
He took
In his knapsack
A Book
Full of vowels
And a shirt
With some towels—
A slight cap
For night cap—
A hair brush
Comb ditto
New Stockings
For old ones
Would split O!
This knapsack
Was tight at 's back
He revetted[2] close
And followed his Nose
To the North
To the North

1 *There was a naughty Boy*: First published in HBF (1883).
2 *revetted*: As in 'reveting' or facing an embankment, etc., with masonry or other material.

And follow'd his nose
To the North—

There was a naughty boy
And a naughty boy was he
For nothing would he do
But scribble poetry—
He took
An inkstand
In his hand
And a Pen
Big as ten
In the other
And away
In a Pother
He ran
To the mountains
And fountains
And ghostes
And Postes
And witches
And ditches
And wrote
In his coat
When the weather
Was ~~warm~~ cool
Fear of gout
And without
When the w[e]ather
Was ~~cool~~/warm/—
Och the cha[r]m
When we choose
To follow ones nose
To the north
To the north
To follow one's nose to the north!

There was a naughty boy
And a naughty boy we [*for* was] he

He kept little fishes
In washing tubs three
In spite
Of the might
Of the Maid
Nor affraid
Of his Granny-good—
He often would
Hurly burly
Get up early
And go
By hook or crook
To the brook
And bring home
Miller's thumb[1]
Tittle bat[2]
Not over fat
Minnows small
As the stall
Of a glove
Not above
The size
Of a nice
Little Baby's
Little finger—
O he made
'T was his trade
Of Fish a pretty kettle
A kettle—A kettle
Of Fish a pretty kettle
A kettle!

There was a naughty Boy
And a naughty Boy was he
He ran away to Scotland

1 *Miller's thumb*: A small fish otherwise called a Bullhead, now a threatened species in England.
2 *Tittle bat*: A child's word for 'stickleback', a fish.

The people there to see—
There he found
That the ground
Was as hard
That a yard
Was as long,
That a song
Was as merry,
That a cherry
Was as red—
That lead
Was as weighty
That fourscore
Was as eighty
That a door
Was as wooden
As in england—
So he stood in
His shoes
And he wonderd
He wonderd
He stood in his
Shoes and he wonder'd—

My dear Fanny I am ashamed of writing you such stuff, nor would I if it were not for being tired after my days walking, and ready to tumble int<o bed> so fatigued that when I am asleep you might sew my nose to my great toe and trundle me round the town like a Hoop without waking me—Then I get so hungry—a Ham goes but a very little way and fowls are like Larks to me—A Batch of Bread I make no more ado with than a sheet of parliament;[1] and I can eat a Bull's head as easily as I used to do Bull's eyes[2]—I take a whole string of Pork Sausages down as easily as a Pen'orth of Lady's fingers[3]—Oh dear I must soon be contented with an acre or two of oaten cake

1 *a sheet of parliament*: A thin, flat cake.
2 *Bulls-eyes*: Peppermint boiled sweets.
3 *Lady's fingers*: Sponge fingers.

a hogshead[1] of Milk and a Cloaths basket of Eggs morning noon and night when I get among the Highlanders—Before we see them we shall pass into Ireland and have a chat with the Paddies,[2] and look at the Giant's Cause-way[3] which you must have heard of—I have not time to tell you particularly for I have to send a Journal to Tom of whom you shall hear all particulars or from me when I return—

[Newton Stewart, Sunday morning, 5 July 1818] Since I began this we have walked sixty miles to newton stewart at which place I put in this Letter—to ~~day~~/night/ we sleep at Glenluce—tomorrow at Portpatrick and the next day we shall cross in the passage boat to Ireland—I hope Miss Abbey has quite recovered—Present my Respects to her and to Mr And Mrs Abbey—God bless you—

Your affectionate Brother John—

Do write me a Letter directed to Inverness. Scotland—

To Tom Keats

(continued)

5, 7, 9 July 1818

[Newton Stewart, Sunday morning] July 5—You see I have missed a day from fanny's Letter. Yesterday was passed in Kircudbright—the Country is very rich—very fine—with a little of Devon—I am now writing at Newton Stuart six Miles into Wigton—Our Landlady of yesterday said very few Southrens passed these ways—The children jabber away as in a foreign Language—The barefooted Girls look very much in keeping—I mean with the Scenery about them—Brown praises

1 *hogshead*: A unit of capacity, esp. for alcohol (52.5 gallons for wine); a large cask for transporting wine or spirits.

2 *Paddies*: A colloquial name for Irishmen ('Paddy' for Patrick). *OED*'s first occurrence is from 1714.

3 *Giant's Cause-way*: A geological outcrop in County Antrim of vertical basalt columns, the tops of which form stepping stones. Declared a World Heritage Site in 1986.

their cleanliness and appearance of comfort—the neatness of their cottages &c It may be—they are very squat among trees and fern and heaths and broom, on levels slopes and heights—They are very pleasant because they are very primitive—but I wish they were as snug as those up the Devonshire vallies—We are lodged and entertained in great varieties—we dined yesterday on dirty bacon dirtier eggs and dirtiest Potatoes with a slice of Salmon—we breakfast this morning in a nice carpeted Room with Sofa hair bottomed chairs and green-baized mehogany—A spring by the road side is always welcome—we drink water for dinner diluted with a Gill[1] of wiskey.

The next day Keats and Brown took the packet boat from Portpatrick to the Irish port of Donaghadee. The twenty-one mile crossing is the shortest in the United Kingdom. They lodged at an inn in Donaghadee, from where Keats continued his letter.

July 7th Yesterday Morning we set out from Glenluce going some distance round to see some Ruins[2]—they were scarcely worth the while—we went on towards Stranrawier in a burning sun and had gone about six Miles when the Mail overtook us—we got up—were at Portpatrick in a jiffy, and I am writing now in little Ireland—The dialect on the neighbouring shores of Scotland and Ireland is much the same—yet I can perceive a great difference in the nations from the Chambermaid at this nate Inn kept by Mr Kelly—She is fair, kind and ready to laugh, because she is out of the horrible dominion of the Scotch kirk—A Scotch Girl stands in terrible awe of the Elders—poor little Susannas[3]—They will scarcely laugh—they are greatly to be pitied and the kirk is greatly to be damn'd. These kirkman have done scotland good (Query?) they have made Men, Women,

1 *Gill*: An old measure, a quarter of a pint.
2 *Ruins*: Of Glenluce Abbey (founded *c.* 1190) by the Water of Luce.
3 *Elders . . . Susannas*: In the apocryphal thirteenth chapter of the Book of Daniel, the Elders spy on Susanna bathing naked and accost her; she rejects their advances, so they falsely accuse her of adultery.

Old Men Young Men old Women, young women boys, girls and infants all careful—so that they are formed into regular Phalanges[1] of savers and gainers—such a thrifty army cannot fail to enrich their Country and give it a greater appearance of comfort than that of their poor irish neighbours—These kirkmen have done Scotland harm—they have banished puns and laughing and kissing (except in cases where the very danger and crime must make it very fine and gustful. I shall make a full stop at kissing for after that there should be a better parent-thesis: and go on to remind you of the fate of Burns. Poor unfortunate fellow—his disposition was southern—how sad it is when a luxurious imagination is obliged in self defence to deaden its delicacy in vulgarity, and riot in thing[s] attainable that it may not have leisure to go mad after thing[s] which are not. No Man in such matters will be content with the experience of others—It is true that out of suffrance there is no greatness, no dignity; that in the most abstracted Pleasure there is no lasting happiness: yet who would not like to discover over again that Cleopatra was a Gipsey, Helen a Rogue and Ruth a deep one? I have not sufficient reasoning faculty to settle the doctrine of thrift—as it is consistent with the dignity of human Society—with the happiness of Cottagers—All I can do is by plump contrasts—Were the fingers made to squeeze a guinea or a white hand? Were the Lips made to hold a pen or a kiss? Yet in Cities Man is shut out from his fellows if he is poor, the Cottager must be dirty and very wretched if she be not thrifty—The present state of society demands this and this convinces me that the world is very young and in a verry ignorant state—We live in a barbarous age. I would sooner be a wild deer than a Girl under the dominion of the kirk, and I would sooner be a wild hog than be the occasion of a Poor Creatures pennance before those execrable elders—It is not so far to the Giant's Cause way as we supposed—we thought it 70 and hear it is only 48 Miles—so we shall leave one of our knapsacks here at Donoghadee, take our immediate wants and be back in a

1 *Phalanges*: A variant spelling of 'phalanxes', a Greek formation for foot soldiers presenting long spears from behind a wall of overlapping shields.

week—when we shall proceed to the County of Ayr. In the Packet Yesterday we heard some Ballads from two old Men—one was a romance which seemed very poor—then there was the Battle of the Boyne[1]—then Robin Huid as they call him—'Before the king you shall go, go, go, before the king you shall go.'[2] There were no letters for me at Port Patrick so I am behind hand with you I dare say in news from George. Direct to Glasgow till the 17th of this month.

[Ballantrae, Thursday evening, July] 9th We stopped very little in Ireland and that you may not have leisere to marvel at our speedy return to Portpatrick I will tell you that is it as dear living in Ireland as at the Hummums[3]—thrice the expence of Scotland—it would have cost us £15 before our return—Moreover we found those 48 Miles to be irish ones which reach to 70 english—So having walked to Belfast one day and back to Donoghadee the next we left Ireland with a fair breeze—We slept last night at Port patrick where I was gratified by a letter from you. On our walk in Ireland we had too much opportunity to see the worse than nakedness, the rags, the dirt and misery of the poor common Irish—A Scotch cottage, though in that some times the Smoke has no exit but at the door, is a pallace to an irish one—We could observe that impetiosity in Man <and b>oy and Woman—We had the pleasure of finding our way through a Peat-Bog—three miles long at least—dreary, black, dank, flat and spongy: here and there were poor dirty creatures and a few strong men cutting or carting peat. We heard on passing into Belfast through a most wretched suburb that most disgusting of all noises worse than the Bag pipe, the laugh of a Monkey, the chatter of women solus the scream of Macaw—I mean the sound of the Shuttle[4]—What

1 *Battle of the Boyne*: An Orange ballad on William III's bloody defeat of James II and the Jacobites in 1690.

2 *Before the king . . . you shall go*: Lines from the ballad 'Robin Hood and the Bishop of Hereford' (Child ballad 144).

3 *Hummums*: An expensive hotel near Covent Garden, formerly a bagnio ('hammam' in Arabic, hence its name).

4 *Shuttle*: By 1800 the cotton industry employed 27,000 people in and around Belfast, and by 1811 there were fifteen steam-driven mills and a further

a tremendous difficulty is the improvement of the condition of such people—I cannot conceive how a mind 'with child' of Philantrophy could gra[s]p at possibility[1]—with me it is absolute despair. At a miserable house of entertainment half way between Donaghadee and Bellfast were two Men Sitting at Whiskey one a Laborer and the other I took to be a drunken Weaver—The Laborer took me for a Frenchman and the other hinted at Bounty Money[2] saying he was ready to take it—On calling for the Letters at Port patrick the man snapp'd out 'what Regiment?' On our return from Bellfast we met a Sadan[3]—the Duchess of Dunghill—It is no laughing matter tho—Imagine the worst dog kennel you ever saw placed upon two poles from a mouldy fencing—In such a wretched thing sat a squalid old Woman squat like an ape half starved from a scarcity of Buiscuit in its passage from Madagascar to the cape,—with a pipe in her mouth and looking out with a round-eyed skinny lidded, inanity—with a sort of horizontal idiotic movement of her head—squab and lean she sat and puff'd out the smoke while two ragged tattered Girls carried her along—What a thing would be a history of her Life and sensations. I shall endeavour when I know more and have though[t] a little more, to give you my ideas of the difference between the scotch and irish—The two Irishmen I mentioned were speaking of their treatment in England when the Weaver said—'Ah you were a civil Man but I was a drinker' Remember me to all—I

---

eighteen powered by horses, hand or water, supplying yarn for the home industry of weaving. The cotton trade suffered in the depression following the Napoleonic Wars, and in autumn 1818 the weavers of Belfast had gone on strike, as had those in Manchester (see E. E. R. Green, *Ulster Journal of Archeology*, 3rd ser., 7 (1944), pp. 30–41).

1 *with child . . . possibility*: The phrase 'with child' is from Spenser's *The Faerie Queene*, I. v. 1, 'The noble hart, that harbours virtuous thought, / And is with childe of glorious intent.' Keats cannot conceive how such an idealist could possibly hope for ('grasp at') the 'possibility' of any improvement in the factory workers' conditions.

2 *hinted at Bounty Money*: Keats was mistaken for a military or naval recruiter seeking men to enlist: those who did so were given government 'Bounty Money'.

3 *Sadan*: i.e., a sedan chair, in which the passenger is carried by two people.

intend writing to Haslam—but dont tell him for fear I should delay—We left a notice at Portpatrick that our Letters should be thence forwarded to Glasgow—Our quick return from Ireland will occasion our passing Glasgow sooner than we thought—so till further notice you must direct to Inverness

Your most affectionate Brother John—

Remember me to the Bentleys

To Tom Keats

10, 11, 13, 14 July 1818[1]

[British Library MS]

[Ballantrae, Friday morning]

Ah! ken ye what I met the day[2]
Out oure the Mountains
A coming down by craggis grey
An mossie fountains
A goud hair'd Marie yeve I pray
Ane minute's guessing—
For that I met upon the way
Is past expressing—
As I stood where a rocky brig
A torrent crosses
I spied upon a misty rig
A troup o Horses—
And as they trotted down the glen
I sped to meet them
To see if I might know the Men
To stop and greet them.
First Willie on his sleek mare came
At canting gallop
His long hair rustled like a flame

1 Tom endorsed this letter: 'Rec^{d} July 17th | Ans^{d} —D^{o}—D^{o}.'

2 *Ah! ken . . . the day*: First published in HBF (1883).

On board a shallop—
Then came his brother Rab and then
Young Peggy's Mither
And Peggy too—adown the glen
They went togither—
I saw her wrappit in her hood
Fra wind and raining—
~~There was a blush upon her~~
Her cheek was flush wi timid blood
Twixt growth and waning—
She turn'd her dazed head full oft
For thence her Brithers
Came riding with her Bridegroom soft
An mony ithers.
Young Tam came up an eyed me quick
With reddened cheek
Braw Tam was daffed like a chick
He coud na speak—
Ah Marie they are all 'gane hame
Through blustring weather
An every heart is ~~light on~~ /full/ on flame
An light as feather
Ah! Marie they are all gone hame
Fra happy wedding,
Whilst I—Ah is it not a shame?
Sad tears am shedding—

—— —— —— —— ——

My dear Tom, Belantree[1] July 10

The reason for my writing these lines was that Brown wanted to impose a galloway song upon dilke—but it wont do[2]—The subject I got from meeting a wedding just as we came down into this place—Where I am affraid we shall be emprisoned awhile by the weather—Yesterday we came 27 Miles from

1 *Belantree*: Keats's spelling for Ballantrae 'probably reflects' the local pronunciation (Walker).
2 *it wont do*: That is, the song will not fool Charles Dilke (see above, p. 180).

Stranraer—enterd Ayrshire a little beyond Cairn, and had our path th[r]ough a delightful Country. I shall endeavour that you may follow our steps in this walk—it would be uninteresting in a Book of Travels—it can not be interest<ing> but by my having gone through it—When we left Cairn our Road lay half way up the sides of a green mountainous shore, full of Clefts of verdure and eternally varying—sometimes up sometimes down, and over little Bridges going across green chasms of moss rock and trees—winding about every where. After two or three Miles of this we turned suddenly into a magnificent glen[1] finely wooded in Parts—seven Miles long—with a Mountain Stream winding down the Midst—full of cottages in the most happy Situations—the sides of the Hills coverd with sheep—the effect of cattle lowing I never had so finely—At the end we had a gradual ascent and got among the tops of the Mountains whence In a little time I descried in the Sea Ailsa Rock 940 feet hight[2]—it was 15 Miles distant and seemed close upon us—The effect of ailsa with the peculiar perspective of the Sea in connection with the ground we stood on, and the misty rain falling gave me a complete Idea of a deluge—Ailsa struck me very suddenly—really I was a little alarmed—

[King's Arms, Girvan, that evening] Thus far had I written before we set out this morning—Now we are at Girvan 13 Miles north of Belantree—Our Walk has been along a more grand shore to day than yesterday—Ailsa beside us all the way—From the heights we could see quite at home Cantire[3] and the large Mountains of ~~Arran~~ Annan[4] one of the Hebrides—We are in comfortable Quarters. The Rain we feared held up

1 *glen*: Glen App.

2 *Sea Ailsa . . . feet hight*: Ailsa Craig is well over 1,000 feet. Keats's underestimate probably comes from his guidebook.

3 *Cantire*: Kintyre, the southern peninsula of Argyll.

4 *Annan*: Actually, as Keats first thought, it is Arran, in the Firth of Clyde: it is not one of the Hebrides.

bravely and it has been 'fu fine this day"[1]—<To>morrow we sh<all be> at Ayr—

To Ailsa Rock—

Hearken thou craggy ocean pyramid,
Give answer by thy voice the Sea fowls screams!
When were thy shoulders mantled in huge Streams?
When from the Sun was thy broad forehead hid?
How long ist since the mighty Power bid
Thee heave to airy sleep from fathom dreams—
Sleep in the Lap of Thunder or Sunbeams,
Or when grey clouds are thy cold Coverlid—
Thou answerest not for thou art dead asleep
Thy Life ~~has been~~ ~~will be~~ /is but/ two dead eternities
The last in Air, the former in the deep—
First with the Whales, last with the eglle [*for* eagle] skies—
Drown'd wast thou till an Earthquake made thee steep—
Another cannot wake thy giant Size!

This is the only Sonnet of any worth I have of late written[2]—I hope you will like it.
[Kirkoswald, Saturday morning] 'T is now the 11th of July and we have come 8 Miles to Breakfast to to Kirkoswald—I hope the next Kirk will be Kirk-Alloway—I have nothing of consequence to say now concerning our Journey—so I will speak as far as I can judge on the irish and Scotch—I know nothing of the higher Classes. Yet I have a persuasion that there the Irish are victorious—As to the 'profanum vulgus'[3] I must incline to the scotch—They never laugh—but they are always com-

1 *fu fine this day*: Echoes the refrain in Burns's 'The Holy Friar'.
2 *the only Sonnet . . . late written*: The only poem written during his Northern walk which Keats thought worthy of publication. It was printed anonymously in Leigh Hunt's *Literary Pocket-Book* (1818 for 1819). Stillinger believes the text here is probably a fair copy (*Texts*).
3 *profanum vulgus*: The common people.

paritively neat and clean—Their constitutions[1] are not so remote and puzzling as the irish—The Scotchman will never give a decision on any point—he will never commit himself in a sentence which may be refer[r]ed to as a meridian[2] in his notions of things—so that you do not know him—and yet you may come in nigher neighbourhood to him than to the irishman who commits himself in so many places that it dazes your head—A Scotchman's motive is more easily discovered than an irishman's. A Scotchman will go wisely about to deceive you, an irishman cunningly—An Irishman would bluster out of any discovery to his disadvantage—~~An Irishman~~ /Scotchman/ would retire perhaps without much desire of revenge—An Irishman likes to be thought a gallous[3] fellow—A scotchman is contented with himself—It seems to me that they are both sensible of the Character they hold in England and act accordingly to Englishmen—Thus the Scotchman will become over grave and over decent and the Irishman over-impetuous. I like a Scotchman best because he is less of a bore—I like the Irishman best because he ought to be more comfortable—The Scotchman has made up his Mind within himself in a sort of snail shell wisdom—The Irishman is full of strong headed instinct—The Scotchman is farther in Humanity that the Irishman—there his [*for* he] will stick perhaps when the Irishman shall be refined beyond him—for the former thinks he cannot be improved the latter would grasp at it for ever, place but the good plain before him.

[Saturday afternoon, 11 July] Maybole—Since breakfast we have come only four Miles to dinner, not merely, for we have examined in the <way> t<wo> Ruins, one of them very fine called Crossragual Abbey. there is a winding Staircase to the top of a little Watch Tower.

(continued 13 July, p. 199 below)

1 *constitutions*: Temperaments.

2 *meridian*: Reference point (astronomy, geography).

3 *gallous*: i.e., 'gallows', an intensive, meaning 'excellent, fine' (slang).

To J. H. Reynolds
11, 13 July 1818

[Woodhouse transcript (1821?)]

[Saturday afternoon] Maybole July 11.

My Dear Reynolds.

I'll not run over the Ground we have passed. that would be merely as bad as telling a dream—unless perhaps I do it in the manner of the Laputan printing press[1]—that is I put down Mountains, Rivers, Lakes, dells, glens, Rocks, and Clouds, With beautiful enchanting, gothic picturesque fine, delightful, enchancting, Grand, sublime—a few Blisters &c—and now you have our journey thus far: where I begin a letter to you because I am approaching Burns's Cottage very fast—We have made continual enquiries from the time we saw his Tomb at Dumfries—his name of course is known all about—his great reputation among the plodding people is "that he wrote a good MONY sensible things"—One of the pleasantest means of annulling self is approaching such a shrine as the Cottage of Burns—we need not think of his misery—that is all gone—bad luck to it—I shall look upon it hereafter with unmixed pleasure as I do upon my Stratford on Avon day with Bailey[2]—I shall fill this sheet for you in the Bardies Country, going no further than this till I get into the Town of Ayr which will be a 9 miles' walk to Tea—

Continued two days later: the two men having visited Ayr, were now on their way to Glasgow. Keats took the opportunity to resume his letter when they were held up by heavy rain.

1 *the Laputan printing press*: In Jonathan Swift's *Gulliver's Travels* (1726), III, chapter 5, the Laputan Academy, a satire on the Royal Society, features the invention of a hand-driven engine which arbitrarily puts together 'broken sentences' to create 'a compleat Body of all Arts and Sciences'.

2 *my Stratford . . . with Bailey*: Keats and Bailey had visited Shakespeare's birthplace on 2 October 1817 and signed the visitors book at Holy Trinity Church. Keats was 'struck' by 'the simple statue there' (*KC*, II, 271).

[Kingswells, Monday morning, 13 July] We were talking on different and indifferent things, when on a sudden we turned a corner upon the immediate County of Air—the Sight was as rich as possible—I had no Conception that the native place of Burns was so beautiful—the Idea I had was more desolate, his rigs of Barley[1] seemed always to me but a few strips of Green on a cold hill—O prejudice! it was rich as Devon—I endeavour'd to drink in the Prospect, that I might spin it out to you as the silkworm makes silk from Mulbery leaves—I cannot recollect it—Besides all the Beauty, there were the Mountains of Annan [*for* Arran] Isle, black and huge over the Sea—We came down upon every thing suddenly—there were in our way, the 'bonny Doon,'[2] with the Brig that Tam O' Shanter cross'ed—Kirk Alloway, Burns's Cottage and then the Brigs of Ayr—First we stood upon the Bridge across the Doon; surrounded by every Phantasy of Green in tree, Meadow, and Hill,—the Stream of the Doon, as a Farmer told us, is covered with trees from head to foot—you know those beautiful heaths so fresh against the weather of a summers evening—there was one stretching along behind the trees. I wish I knew always the humour my friends would be in at opening a letter of mine, to suit it to them nearly as possible I could always find an eggshell for Melancholy[3]—and as for Merriment a Witty humour will turn any thing to Account—my head is sometimes in such a whirl in considering the million likings and antipathies of our Moments—that I can get into no settled strain in my Letters—My Wig! Burns and sentimentality coming across you and frank Floodgate in the office—O scenery that thou shouldst be crush'd between two Puns[4]—As for them I venture the rascalliest in the Scotch

1 *rigs of Barley*: The refrain, 'Amang the rigs wi' Annie', etc., from Burns's 'It was upon a Lammas night'.

2 *bonny Doon*: Referring to Burn's 'The Bank o' Doon'.

3 *an eggshell for Melancholy*: Compare Jacques in *As You Like It*, II. v. 11–12, 'I can suck melancholy out of a song, as a weasel sucks eggs.'

4 *Burns . . . Floodgate . . . two Puns*: Keats is punning on Fladgate's name and that of Burns (= streams). Reynolds shared an office with Frank Fladgate (1799–1892) having been articled to his father, the lawyer Francis Fladgate (see above, p. 67).

Region—I hope Brown does not put them punctually in his Journal—If he does I must sit on the cutty-stool[1] all next winter. We Went to Kirk allow'y "a Prophet is no Prophet in his own Country"[2]—We went to the Cottage and took some Whiskey—I wrote a sonnet for the mere sake of writing some lines under the roof—they are so bad I cannot transcribe them[3]—The Man at the Cottage was a great Bore with his Anecdotes—I hate the rascal—his Life consists in fuz, fuzzy, fuzziest—He drinks glasses five for the Quarter and twelve for the hour,[4]—he is a mahogany faced old Jackass who knew Burns—He ought to be kicked for having spoken to him. He calls himself "a curious old Bitch"[5]—but he is a flat old Dog—I sho[d] like to employ Caliph Vatheck to kick him[6]—O the flummery of a birth place! Cant! Cant! Cant! It is enough to give a spirit the guts-ache—Many a true word they say is spoken in jest—this may be because his gab hindered my sublimity.—The flat dog made me write a flat sonnet—My dear Reynolds—I cannot write about scenery and visitings—Fancy is indeed less than a present palpable reality, but it is greater than remembrance—you would lift your eyes from Homer only to see close before you the real Isle of Tenedos.[7]—you would rather read Homer afterwards than remember yourself—One song of Burns's is of more worth to you than all I could think for a whole year in his native country—His Misery is a dead weight upon the nimbleness of one's quill—I tried to forget it—to drink Toddy without

1 *cutty-stool*: Formerly a stool of repentance in a Scottish kirk for offenders against chastity.
2 *no Prophet . . . own Country*: Mark 6:4.
3 *so bad . . . transcribe them*: 'This mortal body of a thousand days', preserved in Brown's lost transcript (*Texts*).
4 *five . . . the hour*: Parodies Coleridge's 'Christabel' (1816), l. 10, 'Four for the quarters, and twelve for the hour'.
5 *curious old Bitch*: James Humphrey, a Mauchline mason, is mocked for his ignorance as a 'bleth'ran bitch' in Burns's 'On a Noisy Polemic'.
6 *employ . . . kick him*: See *Vathek* (1786) by William Beckford (1759–1844) in which Caliph Vathek orders his eunuch to kick from his presence a group of protesting *santons* (eastern holy men).
7 *Isle of Tenedos*: A small island in the Aegean Sea; in Homer's *Odyssey* the supposed home of Poseidon.

any Care—to write a merry Sonnet—it wont do—he talked with Bitches—he drank with Blackguards, he was miserable—We can see horribly clear in the works of such a man his whole life, as if we were God's spies.[1]—What were his addresses to Jean in the latter part of his life[2]—I should not speak so to you—yet why not—you are not in the same case—you are in the right path, and you shall not be deceived—I have spoken to you against Marriage, but it was general—the Prospect in those matters has been to me so blank, that I have not been unwilling to die—I would not now, for I have inducements to Life—I must see my little Nephews in America,[3] and I must see you marry your lovely Wife—My sensations are sometimes deadened for weeks together—but believe me I have more than once yearne'd for the time of your happiness to come, as much as I could for myself after the lips of Juliet.—From the tenor of my occasional rhodomontade in chitchat, you might have been deceived concerning me in these points—upon my soul, I have been getting more and more close to you every day, ever since I knew you, and now one of the first pleasures I look to is your happy Marriage[4]—the more, since I have felt the pleasure of loving a sister in Law. I did not think it is possible to become so much attached in so short a time—Things like these, and they are real, have made me resolve to have a care of my health—you must be as careful—The rain has stoppd us to day at the end of a dozen Miles, yet we hope to see Loch-Lomond the day after to Morrow;—I will piddle out my information, as Rice says, next Winter at any time when a substitute is wanted for Vingt-un. We bear the fatigue very well.—20 Miles a day in general—A cloud came over us in getting up Skiddaw—I hope to be more lucky in Ben Lomond—and more lucky still in Ben

1 *as if . . . God's spies*: One of the roles the Fool imagines for the powerless, imprisoned Lear in *King Lear*, V. iii. 17.

2 *his addresses . . . his life*: Burns belatedly married Jean Armour in 1788, but notoriously continued to be unfaithful.

3 *Nephews in America*: The George Keatses's first child was a daughter (b. 1819): John, their first son, was born in 1827.

4 *your happy Marriage*: Reynolds's marriage to Eliza Drewe was not to take place until 31 August 1822.

Nevis—what I think you wo[d] enjoy is poking about Ruins—sometimes Abbeys, sometimes Castle. The short stay we made in Ireland has left few remembrances—but an old woman in a dog-kennel Sedan with a pipe in her Mouth, is what I can never forget—I wish I may be able to give you an idea of her—Remember me to your Mother and Sisters, and tell your Mother how I hope she will pardon me for having a scrap of paper pasted in the Book sent to her.[1] I was driven on all sides and had not time to call on Taylor—So Bailey is coming to Cumberland[2]—well, if you'll let me know where at Inverness, I [will] call on my return and pass a little time with him—I am glad 'tis not Scotland—Tell my friends I do all I can for them, that is drink their healths in Toddy—Perhaps I may have some lines by and by to send you fresh on your own Letter—Tom has a few to shew you.

your affectionate friend
John Keats

To Tom Keats

(continued)

13, 14 July 1818

[Monday morning] July 13. Kingswells—I have been writing to Reynolds—therefore any particulars since Kirkoswald have escaped me—from said kirk we went to Maybole to dinner—then we set forward to Burnes's town Ayr—the Approach to it is extremely fine—quite outwent my expectation richly meadowed, wooded, heathed and rivuleted—with a grand Sea view terminated by black Mountains of the isle of Annan [*for* Arran]. As soon as I saw them so nearly I said to myself 'How is it they did not beckon Burns to some grand attempt at Epic'—The bonny Doon is the sweetest river I ever saw overhung with fine

1 *the Book sent to her*: The presentation copy of *Endymion* that Keats had asked Taylor to send Mrs Reynolds on 21 June (see above, p. 161).
2 *Bailey . . . Cumberland*: Bailey was ordained and given a curacy near Carlisle some time before 29 August that summer.

trees as far as we could see—we stood some time on the Brig across it, over which Tam o' Shanter fled—we took a pinch of snuff on the key stone—Then we proceeded to 'auld Kirk Alloway'—As we were looking at it a Farmer pointed out the spots where Mungo's Mither hang'd hersel' and 'drunken Charlie brake's neck's bane'[1]—Then we proceeded to the Cottage he was born in—there was a board to that effect by the door Side—it had the same effect as the same sort of memorial at Stradford on Avon—We drank some Toddy to Burns's Memory with an old Man who knew Burns—damn him—and damn his Anecdotes—he was a great bore—it was impossible for a Southren to understand above 5 words in a hundred—There was something good in his description of Burns's melancholy the last time he saw him. I was determined to write a sonnet in the Cottage—I did—but it is so bad I cannot venture it here[2]—Next we walked into Ayr Town and before we went to Tea, saw the new Brig and the Auld Brig and wallace tower[3]—Yesterday we dinned [*for* dined] with a Traveller—We were talking about Kean[4]—He said he had seen him at Glasgow 'in Othello in the Jew, I me an er, er, er, the Jew in Shylock' He got bother'd completely in vague ideas of the Jew in Othello, Shylock in the Jew, Shylock in Othello, Othello in Shylock, the Jew in Othello &c &c &c he left himself in a mess at last—Still satisfied with himself he went to the Window and gave an abortive whistle of some tune or other—it might have been Handel. There is no end to these Mistakes—he'll go and tell people how he has seen 'Malvolio in the Countess' 'Twehth [*for* Twelfth] night in 'Midsummer nights dream—Bottom in much ado about

1 *Tam o' Shanter . . . neck's bane*: All references to Burns's 'Tam o' Shanter' (1791), ll. 32, 96, 92.

2 *sonnet . . . here*: See above, p. 197

3 *Auld Brig and wallace tower*: The old Baronial tower (replaced in 1834 by the present Wallace Tower) in High Street, and mentioned in Burns's 'The Brigs of Ayr'.

4 *Kean*: The actor Edmund Kean (1787/90–1833), famous for his naturalism. Keats had reviewed Kean's performance as Richard III (see above, pp. 77–8).

Nothing—Viola in Barrymore[1]—Antony in Cleopatra—Falstaff in the mouse Trap.[2]—
[Glasgow, Tuesday morning] July 14 We enterd Glasgow last Evening under the most oppressive Stare a body could feel—When we had crossed the Bridge Brown look'd back and said its whole pop<ulation> had turned to wonder at us—we came on till a drunken Man came up to me—I put him off with my Arm—he returned all up in Arms saying aloud that, 'he had seen all foreigners bu-u-u t he never saw the like 'o me—I was obliged to mention the word Officer and Police before he would desist—The City of Glasgow I take to be a very fine one—I was astonished to hear it was twice the size of Edinburgh—It is built of Stone and has a much more solid appearance than London—We shall see the Cathedra<l> this morning—they have devilled it into a 'High Kirk—I want very much to know the name of the Ship George is g<one> in—also what port he will land in—I know nothing about it—I hope you are leading a quiet Life and gradually improving—Make a long Lounge of the whole Summer—by the time the Leaves fall I shall be near you with plenty of confab—there are a thousand things I cannot write—Take care of yourself—I mean in not being vexed or bothered at any thing—God bless you!

John—

To Tom Keats
17, 18, 20, 21 July 1818

[Keats House MS]

[Cairndow Inn, Friday morning]

My dear Tom — Cairn-something July 17th

Here's Brown going on so that I cannot bring to Mind how the two last days have vanished—for example he says 'The

1 *Barrymore*: William Barrymore (1759–1830), an actor whose real name was Blewit.
2 *the mouse Trap*: i.e., *Hamlet*.

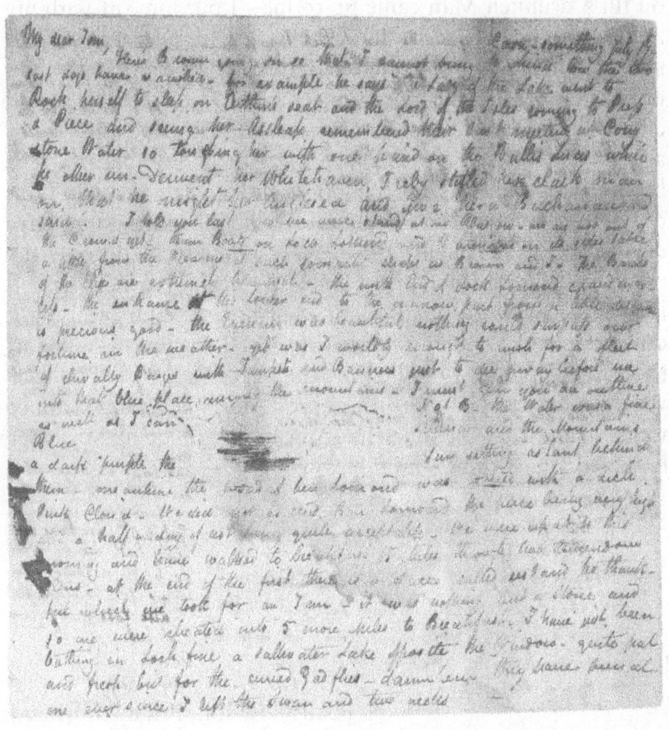

2. *Sketch of Loch Lomond in letter to Tom Keats, 17 July 1818 (detail)*

Lady of the Lake went to Rock herself to sleep on Arthur's seat and the Lord of the Isles coming to Press a Piece and seeing her Assleap remembered their last meeting at Cony[1] stone Water so touching her with one hand on the Vallis Lucis[2] while he un-Derwent her Whitehaven, Ireby stifled her clack man on, that he might her Anglesea and give her a Buchanan and said.' I told you last how we were stared at in Glasgow—we are not out of the Crowd yet—Steam Boats on Loch Lomond[3] and Barouches on its sides take a little from the Pleasure of such romantic chaps as Brown and I—The Banks of the Clyde are extremely beautiful—the north End of Loch Lomond grand in excess—the entrance at the lower end to the narrow part from a little distance is precious good—the Evening was beautiful nothing could surpass our fortune in the weather—yet was I worldly enough to wish for a fleet of chivalry Barges with Trumpets and Banners just to die away before me into that blue place among the mountains—I must give you an outline as well as I can [*Keats gives small sketch of the Loch*][4] Not[a] B[ene]—the Water was a fine Blue silverd and the Mountains a dark purple the Sun setting aslant behind them—meantime the head of ben Lomond was covered with a rich Pink Cloud—We did not ascend Ben Lomond—the price being very high and a half a day of rest being quite acceptable—We were up at 4 this morning and have walked to breakfast 15 Miles through two t[r]emendous Glens—at the end of the first there is a place called rest and be thankful which we took for an Inn—it was nothing

1 *Cony*: Most editors misread as 'Corry', but Gittings notes the obvious sexual meaning in keeping with the rest of Brown's punning sentence, and glosses the other puns (*John Keats*, Appendix 4).

2 *Vallis Lucis*: 'Valley of Light' is another name for Glenluce, where they spent the night of 6 July.

3 *Steam Boats on Loch Lomond*: The wooden paddle steamer *Marion* began taking tourists round Loch Lomond the summer Keats and Brown were there. It was withdrawn in 1827.

4 See Illustration 2.

but a Stone[1] and so we were cheated into 5 more Miles to Breakfast—I have just been bathing in Loch fine a saltwater Lake opposite the Window—quite pat and fresh but for the cursed Gad flies—damn 'em they have been at me ever since I left the Swan and two necks[2]—

All gentle folks who owe a grudge[3]
  To any living thing
Open your ears and stay your t[r]udge
  Whilst I in dudgeon sing—

The gad fly he hath stung me sore
  O may he ne'er sting you!
But we have many a horrid bore
  He may sting black and blue.

Has any here an old grey Mare
  With three Legs all her store
O put it to her Buttocks bare
  And Straight she'll run on four

Has any here a Lawyer suit
  Of 17, 43
Take Lawyer's nose and put it to 't
  And you the end will see

Is there a Man in Parliament
  Dum founder'd in his speech
O let his neighbour make a rent
  And put one in his breech

1 *Stone*: A stone seat bearing the inscription 'Rest and be thankful', a stopping point marking the pass between Glen Croe and Glen Kinglas on the military road built by General Wade as part of his pacification of the Highlands (1725–37); see Walker's extensive note and illustration no. 80.

2 *the Swan and two necks*: The coaching inn from which Keats and Brown had left London.

3 *All gentle . . . grudge*: First published in HBF (1883).

O Lowther[1] how much better thou
  Hadst figur'd to'ther day
When to the folks thou madst a bow
  And hadst no more to say

If lucky gad fly had but ta'en
  His seat upon thine A—e
And put thee to a little pain
  To save thee from a worse.

Better than Southey it had been
  Better than M^r D—[2]
Better than Wordsworth too I ween
  Better than M^r V—[3]

Forgive me pray good people all
  For deviating so
In spirit sure I had a call—
  And now I on will go—

Has any here a daughter fair
  Too fond of reading novels
Too apt to fall in love with care
  And charming Mister Lovels[4]

O put a gadfly to that thing
  She keeps so white and pert
I mean the finger for the ring
  And it will breed a Wert—

Has any here a pious spouse
  Who seven times a day
Scolds as King David pray'd;[5] to chouse[6]
  And have her holy way—

1 *Lowther*: See above, p. 165 and n.
2 *M^r D—*: Robert Saunders Dundas (1771–1851), 2nd Viscount Melville.
3 *M^r V—*: Nicholas Vansittart (1766–1851), 1st Baron Bexley, Chancellor of the Exchequer.
4 *Mister Lovels*: Lovel, the hero of Scott's *The Antiquary* (1816).
5 *seven times . . . pray'd*: See Psalms 119:164.
6 *to chouse*: To dupe, cheat or swindle.

O let a Gadfly's litt[l]e sting
　Persuade her sacred tongue
That noises are a common thing
　But that her bell has rung

And as this is the summum bo
　Num of all conquering
I leave withouten wordes mo'
　The Gadfly's little sting

(continued 18 July, p. 209 below)

To Benjamin Bailey

18, 22 July 1818

[Harvard MS]

My dear Bailey, [Saturday morning] Inverary July 18th

The only day I have had a chance of seeing you when you were last in London I took every advantage of—some devil led you out of the way—Now I have written to Reynolds to tell me where you will be in Cumberland—so that I cannot miss you—and when I see you the first thing I shall do will be to read that about Milton and Ceres and Proserpine—for though I am not going after you to John o' Grotts it will be but poetical to say so.[1] And here Bailey I will say a few words written in a sane and sober Mind, a very scarce thing with me, for they may her<eaf>ter save you a great deal of trouble about me, which you do not deserve, and for which I ought to be ba[s]tinadoed. I carry all matters to an extreme—so that when I have any little

1 *Milton . . . say so*: A mock comparison between Keats's attempts to meet Bailey and Ceres's search for her daughter Proserpine, abducted by Dis, the god of the underworld, a myth recounted by Milton in *Paradise Lost*, IV, 268–72. The thought of Proserpine prompts him to a consideration of his attitudes to women and earlier exchanges with Bailey, such as his letter of 10 June.

vexation it grows in five Minutes into a theme for Sophocles—then and in that temper if I write to any friend I have so little selfpossession that I give him matter for grieving at the very time perhaps when I am laughing at a Pun. Your last Letter made me blush for the pain I had given you—I know my own disposition so well that I am certain of writing many times hereafter in the same strain to you—now you know how far to believe in them—you must allow for imagination—I know I shall not be able to help it. I am sorry you are grieved at my not continuing my visits to little Britain[1]—yet I think I have as far as a Man can do who has Books to read to [*for* and] subjects to think upon—for that reason I have been no where else except to Wentworth place[2] so nigh at hand—moreover I have been too often in a state of health that made me think it prudent no[t] to hazard the night Air—Yet further I will confess to you I cannot enjoy Society small or numerous—I am certain that our fair friends[3] are glad I should come for the mere sake of my coming; but I am certain I bring with me a Vexation they are better without—If I can possibly at any time feel my temper coming upon me I refrain even from a promised visit. I am certain I have not a right feeling towards Women—at this moment I am striving to be just to them but I cannot—Is it because they fall so far beneath my Boyish imagination? When I was a Schoolboy I though[t] a fair Woman a pure Goddess, my mind was a soft nest in which some one of them slept though she knew it not—I have no right to expect more than their reality. I thought them etherial above Men—I find then [*for* them] perhaps equal—great by comparison is very small—Insult may be inflicted in more ways than by Word or action—one who is

1 *little Britain*: The London home of Reynolds's family and that of his sisters. Keats had evidently ceased visiting them between 26 May (see his letter to Bailey of 21, 25 May) and leaving London on 22 June. As Keats's next extant letter to Bailey is that of 10 June, there must have been a further exchange of letters between the two men (now lost) in which Keats told Bailey of his decision. As his convoluted explanation shows, Keats evidently turned against the Reynolds sisters rather earlier than is usually thought.
2 *Wentworth place*: i.e., to visit the Dilkes or Brown.
3 *our fair friends*: The Reynolds sisters.

tender of being insulted does not like to think an insult against another—I do not like to think insults in a Lady's Company—I commit a Crime with her which absence would have not known—Is it not extraordinary? When among Men I have no evil thoughts, no malice, no spleen—I feel free to speak or to be silent—I can listen and from every one I can learn—my hands are in my pockets I am free from all suspicion and comfortable. When I am among Women I have evil thoughts, malice spleen—I cannot speak or be silent—I am full of Suspicions and therefore listen to no thing—I am in a hurry to be gone—You must be charitable and put all this perversity to my being disappointed since Boyhood—Yet with such feelings I am happier alone among Crowds of men, by myself or with a friend or two—With all this trust me Bailey I have not the least idea that Men of different feelings and inclinations are more short sighted than myself—I never rejoiced more than at my Brother's Marriage and shall do so at that of any of my friends—. I must absolutely get over this—but how? The only way is to find the root of evil, and so cure it "with backward mutters of dissevering Power"[1] That is a difficult thing; for an obstinate Prejudice can seldom be produced but from a gordian complication[2] of feelings, which must take time to unravell and care to keep unravelled—I could say a good deal about this but I will leave it in hopes of better and more worthy dispositions—and also content that I am wronging no one, for after all I do think better of Womankind than to suppose they care whether Mister John Keats five feet hight likes them or not. You appeard to wish to avoid any words on this subject—don't think it a bore my dear fellow—it shall be my Amen—I should not have consented to myself these four Months tramping in the highlands but that I thought it would give me more experience, rub off more Prejudice, use [me] to more hardship, identify finer

1 *backward . . . Power*: Milton's *Comus* (1637), l. 817, part of the spell which the two brothers fail to use to counter the threat against their sister's charity by the pagan god Comus.

2 *gordian complication*: A complicated knot tied by King Gordius of Gordium, which Alexander the Great cut through with his sword, hence an intricate problem.

scenes load me with grander Mountains, and strengthen more my reach in Poetry, than would stopping at home among Books even though I should reach Homer—By this time I am comparitively a a mountaineer—I have been among wilds and Mountains too much to break out much about the[i]r Grandeur. I have fed upon Oat cake—not long enough to be very much attached to it—The first Mountains I saw, though not so large as some I have since seen, weighed very solemnly upon me. The effect is wearing away—yet I like them mainely—

(continued on Isle of Mull, 22 July, p. 213 below)

To Tom Keats

(continued)

18, 20, 21 July 1818

[Cladich, Saturday evening, 18 July] Last Evening we came round the End of Loch Fine to Inverary—the Duke of Argyle's Castle[1] is very modern magnificent and more so from the place it is in—the woods seem old enough to remember t[w]o or three changes in the Crags about them—the Lake was beautiful and there was a Band at a distance by the Castle. I must say I enjoyed t[w]o or three common tunes—but nothing could stifle the horrors of a solo on the Bag-pipe—I thought the Beast would never have done—Yet I was doomed to hear another—On ente[r]ing Inverary we saw a Play Bill—Brown was knock'd up from new shoes—so I went to the Barn alone where I saw the Stranger[2] accompanied by a Bag pipe—There they went on about 'interesting creaters' and 'human nater'—till the Curtain fell and then

1 *Inverary . . . Castle*: Inverary Castle, built by the fifth Duke of Argyll in a Palladian and neo-Gothic style between 1746 and 1789.

2 *the Stranger*: A popular translation of *Menschenhass und Reue* (1788), a sentimental drama by August von Kotzebue (1761–1819), first acted at Drury Lane in 1798. Wordsworth complained of the vogue for 'sickly German tragedies'. *Lover's Vows*, an adaptation of Kotzebue by Elizabeth Inchbald (1753–1821), is the play performed in *Mansfield Park* (1814).

Came the Bag pipe—When M[rs] Haller fainted[1] down went the Curtain and out came the Bagpipe—at the heartrending, shoe-mending reconciliation the Piper blew amain—I never read or saw this play before; not the Bag pipe, nor the wretched players themselves were little in comparison with it—thank heaven it has been scoffed at lately[2] almost to a fashion—

Of late two dainties were before me plac'd[3]
   Sweet holy pure sacred and innocent
   From the ninth sphere to me benignly sent
That Gods might know my own particular taste—
First the soft bag pipe mourn'd with zealous haste
   The Stranger next with head on bosom bent
   Sigh'd; rueful again the piteous bag-pipe went
Again the Stranger sighings fresh did waste[4]
O Bag-pipe thou didst steal my heart away
   O Stranger thou my nerves from Pipe didst charm
O Bag pipe—thou did'st reassert thy sway
   Again thou Stranger gave'st me fresh alarm—
Alas! I could not choose. Ah! my poor heart
Mum chance[5] art thou with both obliged to part.

I think we are the luckiest fellows in Christendom—Brown could not proced this morning on account of his feet and lo there is thunder and rain—
[Ford, Monday morning] July 20th For these two days past we have been so badly accommodated more particularly in coarse food that I have not been at all in cue to write. Last night poor Brown with his feet blistered and scarcely able to walk, after a trudge of 20 Miles down the Side of Loch Awe had no supper but Eggs and Oat Cake—we have lost the sight of white bread

1 *M[rs] Haller fainted*: The heroine faints at the end of Act IV when she recognizes a stranger as the husband she left three years earlier: they are reconciled in the final act.
2 *scoffed at lately*: Reynolds had reviewed the play adversely in the *Champion* (2 March 1817).
3 *Of late . . . me plac'd*: First published in 1873 (*Texts*), then in HBF (1883).
4 *sighings fresh did waste*: Keats first wrote 'sighd in discontent'.
5 *Mum chance*: 'Mumchance', tongue-tied.

entirely—Now we had eaten nothing but Eggs all day—about 10 a piece and they had become sickening—. To day we have fared rather better—but no oat Cake wanting—we had a small Chicken and even a good bottle of Port—but all together the fare is too coarse—I feel it a little—another week will break us in—I forgot to tell you that when we came through Glencroe it was early in the morning and we were pleased with the noise of Shepherds Sheep and dogs in the misty heights close above us—we saw none of them for some time, till two came in sight creeping among the Craggs like Emmets,[1] yet their voices came quite plainly to us—The Approach to Loch Awe was very solemn towards nightfall—the first glance was a streak of water deep in the Bases of large black Mountains—We had come along a complete mountain road, where if one listened there was not a sound but that of Mountain Streams We walked 20 Miles by the side of Loch Awe—eve[r]y ten steps creating a new and beautiful picture—sometimes through little wood—there are two islands on the Lake each with a beautiful ruin—one of them rich in ivy—[2]

[Kimelfort, Tuesday morning, 21 July] We are detained this morning by the rain. I will tell you exactly where we are—We are between Loch Craignish and the Sea just opposite Long Island[3]—Yesterday our walk was of this description—the near Hills were not very lofty but many of their Steeps beautifully wooded—the distant Mountains in the Hebrides very grand the Saltwater Lakes coming up between Crags and Islands fulltided and scarcely ruffled—sometimes appearing as one large Lake, sometimes as th[r]ee distinct ones in different directions—At one point we saw afar off a rocky opening into the main Sea—We have also seen an Eagle or two. They move about without the least motion of Wings when in an indolent fit—I am for the first time in a country where a foreign Language is spoken—they gabble away Gælic at a vast rate—

1 *Emmets*: Ants (an archaic or dialect word).

2 *beautiful ruin . . . ivy*: Innischonnel Castle (twelfth century) and the remains of a chapel with a walled-in graveyard on Innish Errich (Walker).

3 *Long Island*: The Isle of Luing ('long').

numbers of them speak English—There are not many Kilts in Argylshire[1]—At Fort William they say a Man is not admitted into Society without one—the Ladies there have a horror at the indecency of Breeches. I cannot give you a better idea of Highland Life than by describing the place we are in—The Inn or public is by far the best house in the immediate neighbourhood—It has a white front with tolerable windows—the table I am writing on su[r]prises me as being a nice flapped Mehogany one; at the same time the place has no watercloset nor anything like it. You may if you peep see through the floor chinks into the ground rooms. The old Grandmother of the house seems intelligent though not over clean. N.B. No snuff being to be had in the village, she made us some. The Guid Man is a rough looking hardy stout Man who I think does not speak so much English as the Guid wife who is very obliging and sensible and moreover though stockingless, has a pair of old Shoes—Last night some Whisky Men sat up clattering Gælic till I am sure one o'Clock to our great annoyance—There is a Gælic testament on the Drawers in the next room—White and blue China has crept all about here—Yesterday there passed a Donkey laden with tin-pots—opposite the Window there are hills in a Mist—a few Ash trees and a mountain stream at a little distance—They possess a few head of Cattle—If you had gone round to the back of the House just now—you would have seen more hills in a Mist—some dozen wretched black Cottages scented of peat smoke which finds i[t]s way by the door or a hole in the roof—a girl here and there barefoot There was one little thing driving Cows down a slope like a mad thing—there was another standing at the cowhouse door rather pretty fac'd all up to the ankles in dirt—

[Oban, Tuesday afternoon, 21 July] We have walk'd 15 Miles in a soaking rain to Oban opposite the Isle of Mull which is so near Staffa we had though[t] to pass to it—but the expense is 7 Guineas and those rather extorted—Staffa you see is a fashionable place and therefore every one concerned with it either in

1 *not many Kilts in Argylshire*: Highland dress had been banned after the brutal suppression of the Jacobite rebellion at the Battle of Culloden (1746).

this town or the Island are what you call up[1]—'t is like paying sixpence for an apple at the playhouse—this irritated me and Brown was not best pleased—we have therefore resolved to set northward for fort William tomorrow morning—I feel [*for* fell] upon a bit of white Bread to day like a Sparrow—it was very fine—I cannot manage the cursed Oatcake—Remember me to all and let me hear a good account of you at Inverness—I am sorry Georgy had not those Lines.[2] Good bye.

Your affectionate Brother
John——

To Benjamin Bailey

(continued)

22 July 1818

[Glen More (?), Isle of Mull, Wednesday evening, 22 July] We have come this evening with a Guide, for without was impossible, into the middle of the Isle of Mull, pursuing our cheap journey to Iona and perhaps staffa—we would not follow the common and fashionable mode from the great imposition of expense. We have come over heath and rock and river and bog to what in England would be called a horrid place—yet it belongs to a Shepherd pretty well off perhaps—The family speak not a word but gælic and we have not yet seen their faces for the smoke which after visiting every cr<a>nny, (not excepting my eyes very much incommoded for writing), finds it[s] way out at the <door.> I am more com<f>ortable than I could have imagined in such a place, and so is Brown—The People are all very kind. We lost our way a little yesterday and enquiring at a Cottage, a yound [*for* young] Woman without a word threw on her cloak and walked a Mile in a missling rain and splashy way to put us right again. I could not have had a greater pleasure in these parts than your mention of my Sister—She is

1 *up*: Well-to-do.
2 *Georgy . . . Lines*: His letter to George and Georgiana (27, 28 June), which had been sent on to Tom from Liverpool (see above, p. 168 and n).

very much prisoned from me[1]—I am affraid it will be some time before I can take her to many places I wish—I trust we shall see you ere long in Cumberland—at least I hope I shall before my visit to America more than once I intend to pass a whole year with George if I live to the completion of the three next—My sisters well-fare and the hopes of such a stay in America will make me observe your advice—I shall be prudent and more careful of my health than I have beeen—I hope you will be about paying your first visit to Town after settling when we come into Cumberland—Cumberland however will be no distance to me after my present journey—I shall spin to you [in] a minute—I begin to get rather a contempt for distances. I hope you will have a nice convenient room for a Library. Now you are so well in health do keep it up by never missing your dinner, by not reading hard and by taking proper exercise. You'll have a horse I suppose so you must make a point of sweating him. You say I must study Dante—well the only Books I have with me are those three little Volumes.[2] I read that fine passage you mention a few days ago. Your Letter followed me from Hampstead to Port Patrick and thence to Glasgow—you must think me by this time a very pretty fellow—One of the pleasantest bouts we have had was our walk to Burns's Cottage, over the Doon and past Kirk Alloway—I had determined to write a Sonnet in the Cottage. I did but lauk it was so wretched I destroyed it[3]—howev[r] in a few days afterwards I wrote some lines cousin-german[4] to the Circumstance which I will transcribe or rather cross scribe in the front of this—Reynolds's illness has made him a new Man—he will be stronger than ever—before I left London he was really getting a fat face—Brown keeps on writing volumes of adventures to Dilke—when we get in of an evening and I have perhaps taken my rest on a couple of Chairs he affronts my indolence and Luxury by pulling

1 *prisoned from me*: For Keats's complaints about the difficulties Richard Abbey put in the way of Fanny seeing her brothers, see above, pp. 97–8.

2 *Dante . . . Volumes*: For Keats's copy of Cary's translation, see above, p. 160 and n.

3 *Sonnet . . . destroyed it*: See above p. 197 and n.

4 *cousin-german*: i.e., first cousin, from Latin *germanus* ('of the same race').

out of his knapsack 1st his paper—2[ndy] his pens and last his ink—Now I would not care if he would change about a little—I say now, why not Bailey take out his pens first sometimes—But I might as well tell a hen to hold up her head before she drinks instead of afterwards—Your affectionate friend

John Keats—

There is a joy in footing slow across a silent plain[1]
Where Patriot Battle has been fought when Glory had the
gain;
There is a pleasure on the heath where Druids old have been,
Where Mantles grey have rustled by and swept the nettles
green:
There is a joy in every spot, made known by times of old,
New to the feet, although the tale a hundred times be told:
There is a deeper joy than all, more solemn in the heart,
More parching to the tongue than all, of more divine a smart,
When weary feet forget themselves upon a pleasant turf,
Upon hot sand, or flinty road, or Sea shore iron scurf,
Toward the Castle or the Cot where long ago was born
One who was great through mortal days and died of fame
unshorn.
Light Hether bells may tremble then, but they are far away;
Woodlark may sing from sandy fern,—the Sun may hear his
Lay;
Runnels may kiss the grass on shelves and shallows clear
But their low voices are not heard though come on travels
drear;
Bloodred the sun may set b[e]hind black mountain peaks;
Blue tides my sluice and drench their time in Caves and
weedy creeks;
Eagles may seem to sleep wing wide upon the Air;
Ring doves may fly convuls'd across to some high cedar'd
lair;
But the forgotten eye is still fast wedded to the ground—

1 *There . . . plain*: As promised, Keats crosses the first three pages of his letter with a fair copy of his poem. This differs from Brown's transcript of the original draft, the text followed when it was first printed in 1822 (*Texts*).

As Palmer's that with weariness mid desert shrine hath found.
At such a time the Soul's a Child, in Childhood is the brain
Forgotten is the worldly heart—alone, it beats in vain—
Aye if a Madman could have leave to pass a healthful day,
To tell his forehead's swoon and faint when first began decay,
He might make tremble many a Man whose Spirit had gone forth
To find a Bard's low Cradle place[1] about the silent north.
Scanty the hour and few the steps beyond the Bourn of Care,
Beyond the sweet and bitter world—beyond it unaware;
Scanty the hour and few the steps because a longer stay
Would bar return and make a Man forget his mortal way.
O horrible! To lose the sight of well remember'd face,
Of Brother's eyes, Of Sister's Brow, constant to every place;
Filling the Air as on we move with Portraiture intense
More warm than those heroic tints that fill a Painter's sense—
When Shapes of old come striding by and visages of old,
Locks shining black, hair scanty grey and passions manifold.
No, No that horror cannot be—for at the Cable's length
Man feels the gentle Anchor pull and gladdens in its strength—
One hour half ideot he stands by mossy waterfall,
But in the very next he reads his Soul's memorial:
He reads it on the Mountain's height where chance he may sit down
Upon rough marble diadem, that Hills eternal crown.
Yet be the Anchor e'er so fast, room is there for a prayer
That Man may never loose his Mind <on> Mountains bleak and bare;
That he may stray league after League some great Berthplace to find,
And keep his vision clear from speck, his inward sight unblind—

1 *a Bard's low Cradle place*: i.e., Where Burns was born (as Keats's comments to Bailey make clear, this poem was written in reaction to the unsatisfactory sonnet he had written in Burns's birthplace).

To Tom Keats

23, 26 July 1818[1]

[Harvard MS]

Dun an cullen[2] [Thursday morning, 23 July]

My dear Tom,

Just after my last had gone to the Post in came one of the Men with whom we endeavoured to agree about going to Staffa—he said what a pitty it was we should turn aside and not see the Curiosities. So we had a little talk and finally agreed that he should be our guide across the Isle of Mull—We set out,[3] crossed two ferries, one to the isle of Kerrara of little distance, the other from Kerrara to Mull 9 Miles across—we did it in forty minutes with a fine Breeze—The road through the Island, or rather the track is the most dreary you can think of—betwe[e]n dreary Mountains—over bog and rock and river with our Breeches tucked up and our Stockings in hand—About eight o Clock we arrived at a shepherd's Hut into w<h>ich we could scarcely get for the Smoke through a door lower than my shoulders—We found our way into a little compartment with the rafters and turf thatch blackened with smoke—the earth floor full of Hills and Dales—We had some white Bread with us, made a good Supper and slept in our Clothes in some Blankets, our Guide snored on another little bed about an Arm's length off—This morning we came about sax Miles to Breakfast by rather a better path and we are now in by comparison a Mansion—Our Guide is I think a very obliging fellow—in the way this morning he sang us two Gælic songs—one made by a Mrs Brown on her husband's being drowned the other a jacobin one on Charles Stuart.[4] For some

1 Endorsed by Tom: 'Rec^{d} August 3rd | Ans^{d} D^{o} D^{o}.' Keats subsequently copied out a large part of this letter in that to the George Keatses on 18 September 1819 (p. 420 below).

2 *Dun an cullen*: 'The house under the waterfall' (its ruin was located by Walker in 1979).

3 *We set out*: On 22 July.

4 *Charles Stuart*: Charles Edward Stuart (1720–88), The Young Pretender or Bonnie Prince Charlie, the cause of the Jacobite Rebellion of 1745.

time Brown has been enquiring out his Genealogy here—he thinks his Grandfather came from long Island[1]—he got a parcel of people about him at a Cottage door last Evening—chatted with ane who had been a Miss Brown and who I think from a likeness must have been a Relation—he jawed with the old Woman—flatterd a young one—kissed a child who was affraid of his Spectacles and finally drank a pint of Milk—They handle his Spectacles as we do a sensitive leaf—.

[Oban, Sunday] July 26th Well—we had a most wretched walk of 37 Miles across the Island of Mull and then we crossed to Iona or Icolmkill from Icolmkill we took a boat at a bargain to take us to Staffa and land us at the head of Loch Nakgal[2] whence we should only have to walk half the distance to Oban again and on a better road—All this is well pass'd and done with this singular piece of Luck that there was an intermission in the bad Weather just as we saw Staffa at which it is impossible to land but in a tolerable Calm Sea—But I will first mention Icolmkill—I know not whether you have heard much about this Island, I never did before I came nigh it. It is rich in the most interesting Antiqu[i]ties. Who would expect to find the ruins of a fine Cathedral Church, of Cloisters, Colleges, Mona[s]taries and Nunneries in so remote an Island? The Beginning of these things was in the sixth Century under the superstition of a would-be Bishop-saint who landed from Ireland and chose the spot from its Beauty—for at that time the now treeless place was covered with magnificent Woods. Columba in the Gaelic is Colm signifying Dove—Kill signifies church and I is as good as Island—so I-colm-kill means the Island of Saint Columba's Church—Now this Saint Columba became the Dominic[3] of the barbarian Christians of the north and was famed also far south—but more especially was reverenced by the Scots the Picts the Norwegians the Irish. In a course of years perhaps the Iland was considered the most holy ground of the north, and the old kings of the afore mentioned nations chose it for their burial place—We were shown a spot in the Churchyard where they say 61 kings are

1 *long Island*: The Isle of Luing ('long').
2 *Loch Nakgal*: Loch Na Keal.
3 *Dominic*: Obsolete form of 'Dominican'.

buried 48 Scotch from Fergus 2nd to Macbeth 8 Irish 4 Norwegian and 1 french[1]—they lie in rows compact—Then we were shown other matters of later date but still very ancient—many tombs of Highland Chieftains—their effigies in complete armour face upwards—black and moss covered—Abbots and Bishops of the island always of one of the chief Clans—There were plenty Macleans and Macdonnels, among these latter the famous Macdonel Lord of the Isles[2]—There have been 300 Crosses in the Island but the Presbyterains[3] destroyed all but two, one of which is a very fine one and completely covered with a shaggy coarse Moss—The old Schoolmaster an ignorant little man but reckoned very clever, showed us these things—He is a Macklean and as much above 4 foot as he is under 4 foot 3 inches—he stops at one glass of wiskey unless you press another and at the second unless you press a third. I am puzzled how to give you an Idea of Staffa. It can only be represented by a first rate drawing—One may compare the surface of the Island to a roof—this roof is supported by grand pillars of basalt standing together thick as honey combs The finest thing is Fingal's Cave—it is entirely a hollowing out of Basalt Pillars. Suppose now the Giants who rebelled against Jove had taken a whole Mass of black Columns and bound them together like bunches of matches—and then with immense Axes had made a cavern in the body of these columns—of course the roof and floor must be composed of the broken ends of the Columns—such is fingal's Cave except that the Sea has done the work of excavations and is continually dashing there—so that we walk along the sides of the cave on the pillars which are left as if for convenient Stairs—the roof is arched somewhat gothic wise and the length of

1 *61 kings . . . 1 french*: *A Description of the Curious Monuments and Antiquities in the Island of Icolmkill* ([Edinburgh], 1791) says there were forty-eight Scottish kings, four Irish and eight Norwegian, along with graves of the 'Chiefs of the Clans', but with no mention of a French king (p. 5). Keats appears to have drawn his information, not entirely accurately, from their diminutive 'Schoolmaster' guide, identified by Rollins as Allan Maclean, who was teaching in Iona from 1790 onwards (citing Lachlan Maclean, *Historical Account of Iona* (Edinburgh, 1833), pp. 88 ff.).

2 *Macdonel . . . Isles*: Donald Macdonald (d. 1420/25), 2nd Lord of the Isles.

3 *Presbyterains*: Perhaps a phonetic spelling of the Scottish pronunciation.

some of the entire side pillars is ~~80~~ /50/ feet—About the island you might seat an army of Men each on a pillar—The length of the Cave is 120 feet and from its extremity the view into the sea through the large Arch at the entrance—the colour of the colums is a sort of black with a lurking gloom of purple therin—For solemnity and grandeur it far surpasses the finest Cathedrall—At the extremity of the Cave there is a small perforation into another cave, at which the waters meeting and buffetting each other there is sometimes produced a report as of a cannon heard as far as Iona which must be 12 Miles—As we approached in the boat there was such a fine swell of the sea that the pillars appeared rising imm<ed>iately out of the crystal—But it is impossible to describe it—

Not Aladin magian[1]
Ever such a work began,
Nor the Wizard of the Dee[2]
Ever such dream could see
Not St John in Patmos isle
In the passion of his toil
When he saw the churches seven
Golden aisled built up in heaven[3]
Gazed at such a rugged wonder.
As I stood its roofing under
Lo! I saw one sleeping there
On the marble cold and bare
While the surges washed his feet
And his garments white did beat

1 *Not Aladin magian*: First published in 1836 (*Texts*). 'Magian' usually means 'Of or pertaining to the Magi', but *OED* gives the rare poetical meaning 'magical', citing Keats's *Endymion*, III, 264–5, '. . . to draw / His magian fish through hated fire and flame'.

2 *Wizard of the Dee*: Keats is remembering Milton's *Lycidas*, l. 55, 'Nor yet where Deva spreads her wizard stream': Milton asks why the tutelary deities of Wales and the River Dee had not protected Edward King from drowning in the Irish Sea. In Arthurian legend the 'Fisher King', guardian of the Holy Grail, fished in the waters of the Dee.

3 *St John in Patmos isle*: Revelation 1:4, 9, 11, 20.

Drench'd about the sombre rocks,
On his neck his well grown locks
Lifted dry above the Main
Were upon the curl again—
What is this and what art thou?
Whisper'd I and touch'd his brow.
What art thou and what is this?
Whisper'd I and strove to kiss
The Spirits hand to wake ~~him up~~ /his eyes./
Up he started in a thrice.
I am Lycidas said he
Fam'd in funeral Minstrelsey—
This was architected thus
By the great Oceanus
Here his mighty waters play
Hollow Organs all the day
Here by turns his dolphins all
Finny palmer's great and small
Come to pay devotion due—
Each a mouth of pea[r]ls must strew
~~Many a Mortal comes to see~~
~~This Cathedrall of the S~~
Many a Mortal of these days
Dares to pass our sacred ways
Dares to touch audaciously
This Cathedral of the Sea—
I have been the Pontif priest
Where the Waters never rest
Where a fledgy sea bird choir
Soars for ever—holy fire
I have hid from Mortal Man.
~~Old~~ Proteus is my Sacristan.
But the stupid eye of Mortal
Hath pass'd /beyond/ the Rocky portal
So for ever will I leave
Such a taint and soon unweave
All the magic of the place—
'Tis now free to stupid face

To cutters and fashion boats
To cravats and to Petticoats.
The great Sea shall war it down
For its fame shall not be blow<n>
At every farthing quadrille dance.
So saying with a Spirits glance
He dived—

I am sorry I am so indolent as to write such stuff as this—it cant be help'd—The western coast of Scotland is a most strange place—it is composed of rocks Mountains, mountainous and rocky Islands intersected by Lochs—you cannot go but a small distance any where from salt water in the highlands
I have a slight sore throat and think it best to stay a day or two at <O>ban. Then we shall proceed to Fort William and Inverness—Where I am anxious to be on account of a Letter from you—Brown in his Letters puts down every little circumstance I should like to do the same but I <c>onfess myself too indolent and besides next winter <ever>y thing will come up in prime order as we verge on such and such things Have you heard in any way of George? I should think by this time he must have landed—I in my carelessness never thought of knowing where a letter would find him on the other side—I think Baltimore but I am affraid of directing to the wrong place—I shall begin some chequer work[1] for him directly and it will be ripe for the post by the time I hear from you next after this—I assure you I often long for a seat and a Cup o' tea at well Walk—especially now that mountains, castles and Lakes are becoming common to me—yet I would rather summer it out for on the whole I am happier than when I have time to be glum—perhaps it may cure me—Immediately on my return I shall begin studying hard with a peep at the theatre now and then—and depend upon it I shall be very luxurious—With respect to Women I think I shall be able to conquer my passions hereafter better than I have yet done. You will help me to talk of george next winter and we will go now and then to see Fanny—Let me

1 *chequer work*: i.e., a crossed letter, which Keats apparently never wrote.

hear a good account of your health and comfort telling me truly how you do alone—

Remember me to all including M^{r} and Mrs Bentley—

Your most affectionate Brother

Joh<n>—

The two men stayed at Oban, probably from 26 to 29 July, in hopes of curing what Keats's called his 'slight sore throat', but Brown described as a 'violent cold'. They then spent five days walking to Letterfinlay, staying at Fort William and climbing Ben Nevis on the way. Keats seems to have written no letters during this period.

To Tom Keats
3, 6 August 1818

[Harvard MS]

My dear Tom, Ah mio Ben.[1] Letter Findlay August 3rd [Monday]

We have made but poor progress Lately, chiefly from bad weather for my throat is in a fair way of getting quite well, so I have had nothing of consequence to tell you till yesterday when we went up Ben Nevis, the highest Mountain in Great Britain—On that account I will never ascend another in this empire—Skiddaw is no thing to it either in height or in difficulty. It is above 4300 feet from the Sea level and Fortwilliam stands at the head of a Salt water Lake,[2] consequently we took it completely from that level. I am heartily glad it is done—it is almost like a fly crawling up a wainscoat—Imagine the task of

1 *Ah mio Ben*: Keats addresses Ben Nevis punning on the song 'Caro mio ben' ('My dear beloved'), attributed to Tommaso Giordani (*c.* 1730–1806), an Italian composer active in England and Ireland, or to the unrelated Guiseppe Giordani (1751–98). The song's title and Keats's anthropomorphizing of Ben Nevis lead to the comic dialogue in the latter part of the letter.
2 *Salt water Lake*: Loch Linnhe.

mounting 10 Saint Pauls without the convenience of Stair cases. We set out about five in the morning with a Guide in the Tartan and Cap and soon arrived at the foot of the first ascent which we immediately began upon—after much fag and tug and a rest and a glass of whiskey apiece we gained the top of the first rise and saw then a tremendous chap above us which the guide said was still far from the top—After the first Rise our way lay along a heath valley in which there was a Loch[1]—after about a Mile in this Valley we began upon the next ascent more fo[r]midable by far than the last and kept mounting with short intervals of rest untill we got above all vegetation, among nothing but loose Stones which lasted us to the very top—the Guide said we had three Miles of a stony ascent—we gained the first tolerable level after the valley to the height of what in the Valley we had thought the top and saw still above us another huge crag which still the Guide said was not the top—to that we made with an obstinate fag and having gained it there came on a Mist, so that from that part to the verry top we walked in a Mist. The whole immense head of the Mountain is composed of large loose stones—thousands of acres—Before we had got half way up we passed large patches of snow and near the top there is a chasm some hundred feet deep completely glutted with it—Talking of chasms they are the finest wonder of the whole—the[y] appear great rents in the very heart of the mountain though they are not, being at the side of it, but other huge crags arising round it give the appearance to Nevis of a shattered heart or Core in itself—These Chasms are 1500 feet in depth and are the most tremendous places I have ever seen—they turn one giddy if you choose to give way to it—We tumbled in large stones and set the echoes at work in fine style. Sometimes these chasms are tolerably clear, sometimes there is a misty cloud which seems to steam up and sometimes they are entirely smothered with clouds—After a little time the Mist cleared away but still there were large Clouds about attracted by old Ben to a certain distance so as to form as it appeard large dome curtains which kept sailing about, opening and shutting at intervals here and there and

1 *Loch*: Lochan Meall-an-t'Suidhe.

everrywhere; so that although we did not see one vast wide extent of prospect all round we saw something perhaps finer—these cloud-veils opening with a dissolving motion and showing us the mountainous region beneath as through a loop hole—these Mouldy[1] loop holes ever varrying and discovering fresh prospect east, west north and South—Then it was misty again and again it was fair—then puff came a cold breeze of wind and bared a craggy chap we had not yet seen though in close neighbourhood—Every now and then we had over head blue Sky clear and the sun pretty wa[r]m. I do not know whether I can give you an Idea of the prospect from a large Mountain top—You are on a stony plain which of course makes you forget you are on any but low ground—the horison or rather edges of this plain being above 4000 feet above the Sea hide all the Country immediately beneath you, so that the next objects you see all round next to the edges of the flat top are the Summits of Mountains of some distance off—as you move about on all side you see more or less of the near neighbour country according as the Mountain you stand upon is in different parts steep or rounded—but the most new thing of all is the sudden leap of the eye from the extremity of what appears a plain into so vast a distance On one part of the top there is a handsome pile of stones[2] done pointedly by some soldiers of artillery, I climed onto them and so got a little higher than old Ben himself. It was not so cold as I expected—yet cold enough for a glass of Wiskey now and then—There is not a more fickle thing than the top of a Mountain—what would a Lady give to change her head-dress as often and with as little trouble!—There are a good many red deer upon Ben Nevis we did not see one—the dog we had with us keep [*for* kept] a very sharp look out and really languished for a bit of a worry—I have said nothing yet of out [*for* our] getting on among the loose stones large and small sometimes on two sometimes on three, sometimes four legs—sometimes two and stick, sometimes three and stick, then four again, then two<,> then a jump<,> so that we kept on ringing changes on foot, hand, Stick, jump

1 *Mouldy*: Perhaps a slip for 'cloudy' (Rollins).
2 *a handsome pile of stones*: No longer identifiable (Walker).

boggl<e,>[1] s[t]umble, foot, hand, foot, (very gingerly) stick again, and then again a game at all fours. After all there was one Mrs Cameron of 50 years of age and the fattest woman in all inverness shire who got up this Mountain some few years ago—true she had her servants but then she had her self—She ought to have hired Sysiphus[2]—"Up the high hill he heaves a huge round—Mrs Cameron"[3] 'T is said a little conversation took place between the mountain and the Lady—After taking a glass of Wiskey as she was tolerably seated at ease she thus begun

Mrs C—[4]

Upon my Life Sir Nevis I am pique'd
That I have so far panted tugg'd and reek'd
To do an honor to your old bald pate
And now am sitting on you just to bate,
Without your paying me one compliment.
Alas 't is so with all, when our intent
Is plain, and in the eye of all Mankind
We fair one's show a preference, too blind!
You Gentleman immediatly turn ~~tale~~./tail—/
O let me then my hapless fate bewail!
Ungrateful Baldpate have I not disdaind
The pleasant Valleys—have I not mad braind
Deserrted all my Pickles and preserves
My China closet too—with wretched Nerves
To boot—say /wretched/ ingrate have I not
Le[f]t my soft cushion chair and caudle pot.
'T is true I had no corns—no! thank the fates
My Shoemaker was always Mr Bates.
And if not Mr Bates why I'm not old!
Still dumb ungrateful Nevis—still so cold!

1 *boggl<e,>*: From the verb 'to boggle', meaning 'to start with a fright, to shy as a startled horse'.

2 *Sysiphus*: King Sisyphus of Corinth, punished in Hades for his misdeeds by eternally rolling a stone uphill.

3 *Up . . . Mrs Cameron*: Compare Pope's translation of Homer's *Odyssey* XI, 736, 'Up the high hill he heaves a huge round stone.'

4 *Mrs C—*: First published in HBF (1883).

(Here the Lady took some more wiskey and was putting even more to her lips when she dashed to the Ground for the Mountain began to grumble which continued for a few Minutes before he thus began,)

Ben Nevis

What whining bit of tongue and Mouth thus dares
Distur'd my Slumber of a thousand years—
Even so long my sleep has been secure
And to be so awaked I'll not endur<e.>
Oh pain—for since the Eagle's earliest scream
I've had a dam'd confounded ugly dream
A Nightmare sure—What Madam was it ~~true~~ /you?/
It cannot be! My old eyes are not true!
Red-Crag,[1] My Spectacles! Now let me see!
Good Heavens Lady how the gemini
Did you get here? O I shall split my Sides!
I shall earthquake—

Mrs C—

Sweet Nevis do not quake, for though I love
You[r] honest Countenance all things above
Truly I should not like to be convey'd
So far into your Bosom—gentle Maid
Loves not too rough a treatment gentle sir
Pray thee be calm and do not quake nor stir
No not a Stone or I shall go in fits—

Ben Nevis

I must—I shall—I meet not such tit bits
I meet not such sweet creatures eve[r]y day
By my old night cap night and day
I must have one sweet Buss—I must and shall!
Red Crag!—What Madam can you then repent
Of all the toil and vigour you have spent
To see Ben Nevis and to touch his nose?

1 *Red-Crag*: (Keats's note) 'A domestic of Ben's/'

Red Crag I say! O I must have you close!
Red crag, there lies beneath my farthest toe
A vein of Sulphur—go dear Red Crag go—
And rub your flinty back against it—budge!
Dear Madam I must kiss you, faith I must!
I must Embrace you with my dearest gust!
Block-head,[1] d'ye hear—Blockhead I'll make her feel
There lies beneath my east legs northern heel
A cave of young earth dragons—well my boy
Go thithers quick and so complete my joy
Take you a bundle of the largest pines
And where the sun on fiercest Phosphor shines
turn to the beginning[2]
Fire them and ram them in the Dragons' nest
Then will the dragons fry and fizz their best
Until ten thousand now no bigger than
Poor Aligators poor things of one span
Will each one swell to twice ten times the size
Of northern whale—then for the tender prize—
The moment then—for then will red Crag rub
His flinty back and I shall kiss and snub[3]
And press my dainty morsel to my breast
Blockhead make haste!
O Muses weep the rest—
The Lady fainted and he thought her dead
So pulled the clouds again about his head
And went to sleep again—soon was she rous'd
By her affrigh[t]ed Servants—next day hous'd
Safe on the lowly ground she bless'd her fate
That fainting fit was not delayed too late

But what surprises me above all is how this Lady got down again—I felt it horribly—'T was the most vile descent—shook

1 *Block-head*: (Keats's note) 'another domestic of Ben's.'
2 *turn to the beginning*: An instruction to Tom to turn to the continuation in his 'crossing' on the first page of the letter.
3 *snub*: Possibly Keats's invention (i.e., nuzzle, as with a snub nose).

me all to pieces—Over leaf you will find a Sonnet I wrote on the top of Ben Nevis[1]—

[Inverness, Thursday evening, 6 August] We have just entered Inverness. I have three Letters from you and one [from] Fanny—and one from Dilke I would set about crossing this all over for you but I will first write to Fanny and Mrs Wilie then I will begin another to you[2] and not before because I think it better you should have this as soon as possible—My Sore throat is not quite well and I intend stopping here a few days

Read me a Lesson muse, and speak it loud[3]
  Upon the top of Nevis blind in Mist!
I look into the Chasms and a Shroud
  Vaprous doth hide them; just so much I wist
Mankind do know of Hell: I look o'erhead
  And there is sullen Mist; even so much
Mankind can tell of Heaven; Mist is spread
  Before the Earth beneath me—even such
Even so vague is Man's sight of himself.
  Here are the craggy Stones beneath my feet;
Thus much I know, that a poor witless elf
  I tread on them; that all my eye doth meet
    Is mist and Crag—not only on this height
    But in the World of thought and mental might—

Good bye till tomorrow

Your most affectionate Brother
John—

1 *Sonnet . . . Ben Nevis*: Brown later reported that Keats 'sat on the edge of that fearful precipice, fifteen hundred feet perpendicular from the valley below, and wrote this sonnet' ('Life of John Keats', *KC*, II, 63).
2 *I have three . . . another to you*: None of the five letters to Keats has survived, and of the three letters Keats intended to write only that to Mrs Wylie is known (see next).
3 *Read . . . loud*: First published 1822.

To Mrs Ann Wylie
6 August 1818

[Jeffrey transcript (1845)]

[Thursday evening]
Inverness 6th August 1818

My dear Madam—

It was a great regret to me that I should leave all my friends, just at the moment when I might have helped to soften away the time for them. I wanted not to leave my Brother Tom, but more especially, beleive me, I should like to have remained near you, were it but for an atom of consolation, after parting with so dear a daughter; My brother George has ever been more than a brother to me, he has been my greatest friend, & I can never forget the sacrifice you have made for his happiness. As I walk along the Mountains here, I am full of these things, & lay in wait, as it were, for the pleasure of seeing you, immediately on my return to town. I wish above all things, to say a word of Comfort to you, but I know not how. It is impossible to prove that black is white, It is impossible to make out, that sorrow is joy or joy is sorrow[1]———Tom tells me that you called on Mr Haslam with a Newspaper giving an account of a Gentleman in a Fur cap, falling over a precipice[2] in Kirkudbrightshire. If it was me, I did it in a dream, or in some magic interval between the first & second cup of tea; which is nothing extraordinary, when we hear that Mahomet, in getting out of Bed, upset a jug of water, & whilst it was falling, took a fortnight's trip as it seemed to Heaven: yet was back in time to save one drop of water being

1 *sorrow is joy or joy is sorrow*: See Byron's *Manfred* (1817), I. i. 10, 'Sorrow is knowledge', a phrase Keats quoted earlier when writing to Reynolds on 3 May (see above, p. 151).

2 *Gentleman . . . precipice*: The 'Wonderful Escape' of a man in a 'fur-cap' who fell near the Devil's Miln (i.e., Mill), Rumbling Bridge Gorge, Perth and Kinross, but fortunately landed in a 'deep pool' was reported in the *Caledonian Mercury* (2 July 1818), p. 4, col. 3. Keats moves the location of the accident to coincide with his and Brown's itinerary.

spilt.[1] As for Fur caps I do not remember one beside my own, except at Carlisle—this was a very good Fur cap, I met in the High Street, & I daresay was the unfortunate one. I daresay that the fates seeing but two Fur caps in the North, thought it too extraordinary, & so threw the Dies which of them should be drowned. The lot fell upon Jonas—I daresay his name was Jonas. All I hope is, that the gaunt Ladies said not a word about hanging, if they did, I shall one day regret that I was not half drowned in Kirkudbright.[2] Stop! let me see!—being half drowned by falling from a precipice is a very romantic affair—Why should I not take it to myself? Keep my secret & I will. How glorious to be introduced in a drawing room to a lady who reads Novels, with—"Mr So & so—Miss so & so—Miss so & so. this is Mr so & so. who fell off a precipice, & was half drowned Now I refer it to you whether I should loose so fine an opportunity of making my fortune—No romance lady could resist me—None—Being run under a Waggon; side lamed at a playhouse; Apoplectic, through Brandy; & a thousand other tolerably decent things for badness would be nothing; but being tumbled over a precipice into the sea—Oh it would make my fortune—especially if you could continue to hint, from this bulletins authority, that I was not upset on my own account, but that I dashed into the waves after Jessy of Dumblane[3]—& pulled her out by the hair—But that, Alas! she was dead or she would have made me happy with her hand—however in this you may use your own discretion—But I must leave joking & seriously aver, that I have been werry romantic indeed, among these Mountains & Lakes. I have got wet through day after day, eaten oat cake, & drank whiskey, walked up to my knees in Bog, got a sore throat, gone to see

1 *we hear . . . being spilt*: This story is told by Joseph Addison in the *Spectator*, No. 94 (18 June 1711), see Jack Stillinger, *Modern Language Notes*, 71 (1956), p. 341.

2 *hanging . . . Kirkudbright*: Proverbially, 'If you're born to be hanged you'll never be drowned.'

3 *Jessy of Dumblane*: 'Jessie the Flower o' Dunblane', a popular song by the Paisley 'Weaver Poet' Robert Tannahill (1774–1810), set to music by Robert Archibald Smith.

Icolmkill & Staffa, met with wholesome food, just here & there as it happened; went up Ben Nevis, & N.B. came down again; Sometimes when I am rather tired, I lean rather languishingly on a Rock, & long for some famous Beauty to get down from her Palfrey in passing; approach me with her—saddle bags—& give me—a dozen or two capital roast beef sandwiches—When I come into a large town, you know there is no putting ones Knapsack into ones fob; so the people stare—We have been taken for Spectacle venders, Razor sellers, Jewellers, travelling linnen drapers, Spies, Excisemen, & many things else, I have no idea of—When I asked for letters at the Post Office, Port Patrick; the man asked what Regiment? I have had a peep also at little Ireland. Tell Henry[1] I have not Camped quite on the bare Earth yet; but nearly as bad, in walking through Mull—for the Shepherds huts you can scarcely breathe in, for the smoke which they seem to endeavour to preserve for smoking on a large scale. Besides riding about 400, we have walked above 600 Miles, & may therefore reckon ourselves as set out.

I wish my dear Madam, that one of the greatest pleasures I shall have on my return, will be seeing you & that I shall ever be

Yours with the greatest Respect & sincerity

John Keats—

*Keats did not stay at Inverness for a 'few days' to cure his 'Sore throat'. Instead, Brown, believing him 'too unwell for fatigue and privation', forced him to see a doctor about the 'violent cold' he had caught in Mull. He thought Keats 'too thin and fevered to proceed on [their] journey' (*L, I, *p. 362). The two men travelled by coach to Cromarty, where Brown saw Keats off 'in the Smack for London', which cleared the port on 8 August (*Inverness Courier and General Advertiser, *13 August 1818).*

1 *Henry*: Mrs Wylie's elder son.

18 August to 1 December 1818
Well Walk

Keats landed at London Bridge on Tuesday, 18 August, after a nine-day voyage, and immediately made his way to the Dilkes' home in Wentworth Place, arriving that evening. Mrs Dilke described him as being 'as brown and shabby as you can imagine; scarcely any shoes left, his jacket all torn at the back, a fur cap, a great plaid, and his knapsack'. There Keats was shocked to learn that Tom had suffered a serious relapse. He returned to Well Walk, where Tom was dangerously ill. Keats was to remain there for just over three months looking after Tom, socializing when he was able, and beginning to write Hyperion. *When Keats met Fanny Brawne is unknown. They may have been introduced at the Dilkes in August soon after he arrived from Scotland, but the meeting possibly took place in late October or November. They certainly knew one another by December 1818 (see below, p. 268).*

To Fanny Keats
19 August 1818

[British Library MS]

Hampstead August 18th
[*for* Wednesday, 19][1]

My dear Fanny,

I am affraid you will [think] me very negligent in not having answered your Letter—I see it is dated June 12—I did not

1 Date from postmark. Keats's error.

arrive at Inverness till the 8th [*for* 6th] of this Month so I am very much concerned at your being disappointed so long a time. I did not intend to have returned to London so soon but have a bad sore throat from a cold I caught in the island of Mull: therefore I thought it best to get home as soon as possible and went on board the Smack from Cromarty—We had a nine days passage and were landed at London Bridge yesterday—I shall have a good deal to tell you about Scotland—I would begin here but I have a confounded tooth ache—Tom has not been getting better since I left London and for the last fortnight has been worse than ever—he has been getting a little better for these two or three days—I shall ask Mr Abbey to let me bring you to Hampstead. If Mr A should see this Letter tell him that he still must if he pleases forward the Post Bill to Perth as I have empowered my fellow traveller to receive it[1]—I have a few scotch pebbles for you from the Island of Icolmkill—I am affraid they are rather shabby—I did not go near the Mountain of Cairn Gorm—I do not know the Name of George's ship—the Name of the Port he has gone to is Philadelphia when[c]e he will travel to the Settlement[2] across the Country—I will tell you all about this when I see you—The Title of my last Book is 'Endymion' you shall have one soon—I would not advise you to play upon the Flageolet however I will get you one if you please—I will speak to Mr Abbey on what you say concerning school—I am sorry for your poor Canary. You shall have another volume of my first Book. My tooth Ache keeps on so that I cannot writ[e] with any pleasure—all I can say now is that you[r] Letter is a very nice one without fault and that you will hear from or see in a few days if his throat will let him,

Your affectionate Brother
John.

1 *receive it*: Abbey had already posted a draft for £30 on 8 August (Rollins).
2 *Name . . . Settlement*: George and Georgiana's ship, the *Telegraph*, had set sail for Liverpool on 7 July, landing at Philadephia fifty-one days later. It took them until October to reach Illinois (Walker, pp. 8–10). Keats did not hear from George until 12 May 1819. Only then did he learn that instead of joining Birkbeck's 'Settlement' George had gone into business with John James Audubon (see below, p. 367).

To C. W. Dilke
20, 21 September 1818

[Keats House MS]

[Well Walk, Hampstead, Sunday]

My dear Dilke,

According to the Wentworth place Bulletin you have left Brighton much improved: therefore now a few lines will be more of a pleasure than a bore. I have a few things to say to you and would fain begin upon them in this fo[u]rth line: but I have a Mind too well regulated to proceed upon any thing without due preliminary remarks—you may perhaps have observed that in the simple process of eating radishes I never begin at the root but constantly dip the little green head in the salt—that in the Game of Whist if I have an ace I constantly play it first—So how can I with any face begin without a dissertation on letter writing—Yet when I consider that a sheet of paper contains room for only three pages, and a half how can I do justice to such a pregnant subject? however as you have seen the historry of the world stamped as it were by a diminishing glass in the form of a chronological Map, so will I 'with retractile claws'[1] draw this into the form of a table[2]—whereby it will occupy merely the remainder of this first page—

Folio——— Parsons, Lawyers, Physians [*for* Physicians] out of place—Ut Eustace[3]—Thornton[4] out of practice or on their travels—

1 *with retractile claws*: Dante's *Inferno*, XVII, 101, in H. F. Cary's translation (1814).

2 *a table*: Keats's 'dissertation on letter writing' takes the 'form of a table', consisting of a list of paper sizes and types in diminishing order, accompanied by his identification of the sort of people who use each kind for their letters. (The last three sizes are invented.)

3 *Eustace*: John Chetwode Eustace's *A Tour through Italy* (1813, from 1815 *A Classical Tour through Italy and Sicily*).

4 *Thornton*: Thomas Thornton's *The Present State of Turkey* (1807).

My dear Dilke
According to the Wentworth place Bulletin you have left Brighton much improved: therefore now a few lines will be more of a pleasure than a bore. I have a few things to say to you and would fain begin upon them in this fourth line: but I have a Mind too well regulated to proceed upon any thing without due preliminary remarks – you may perhaps have observed that in the simple process of eating radishes I never begin at the root but constantly dip the little green head in the salt – That in the Game of Whist if I have an ace I constantly play it first – So how can I with any face begin without a dissertation on letter writing – Yet when I consider that a sheet of paper contains room only for three pages and a half how can I do justice to such a pregnant subject? however as you have seen the history of the world stamped as it were by a diminishing glass in the form of a chronological Map, so will I 'with retractile claws' draw this in to the form of a table – whereby it will occupy merely the remainder of this first page –

Folio – Parsons, Lawyers, Statesmen, Physicians out of place – ut – Eustace – Thornton – out of practise or on their travels –
Foolscap 1. Superfine! rich or noble poets – ut Byron. 2 common ut egomet –
Quarto – Projectors, Patentees, Presidents, Potatoe growers –
Bath Boarding schools, and suburbans in general
Gilt edge Dandies in general, male female and literary –
Octavo or tears All who make use of a lascivious seal –
Duodec. May be found for the most part on Milliners and Dressmakers Parlour tables –
Strip At the Playhouse doors, or any where –
Slip Being but a variation –
Snip So called from its size being disguised by a twist –

3. *To C. W. Dilke, 20 September 1818, p. 1, 26.6 × 19.7 cm*

Fools cap—	1 superfine! rich or noble poets—ut Byron. 2 common ut egomet[1]—
Quarto—	Projectors, Patentees, Presidents, Potatoe growers—
Bath[2]	Boarding schools, and suburbans in general
Gilt edge	Dandies in general, male female and literary—
Octavo or tears	All who make use of a lascivious seal—
Duodec—	May be found for the most part on Milliners and Dressmakers Parlour tables—
Strip	At the Playhouse doors, or any where—
Slip	Being but a variation—
Snip	So called from its size being disguised by a twist—

I suppose you will have heard that Hazlitt has on foot a prosecution against Blackwood[3]—I dined with him a few days sinc[e] at Hessey's—there was not a word said about [it], though I understand he is excessively vexed—Reynolds by what I hear is almost over happy and Rice is in town. I have not seen him nor shall I for some time as my throat has become worse after getting well, and I am determined to stop at home till I am quite well—I was going to Town tomorrow with Mrs D. but I though[t] it best, to ask her excuse this morning—I wish I could say Tom was any better. His identity presses upon me so all day that I am obliged to go out—and although I intended to have given some time to study alone I am obliged to write, and plunge into abstract images to ease myself of his countenance his voice and feebleness—so that I live now in a continual fever—it must be poisonous to life although I feel well. Imagine 'the hateful siege of contraries'[4]—if I think of fame of poetry it seems a crime to me, and yet I must do so or

1 *ut egomet*: (Latin) *ut* (such as) *egomet* (myself).

2 *Bath*: i.e., 'bath-post', a type of hot pressed letter paper embossed with a crown and 'BATH'.

3 *Hazlitt . . . Blackwood*: The same issue of *Blackwood's Magazine* (August 1818) that attacked Keats in the 'Cockney School of Poetry' had also libelled Hazlitt, who threatened to sue the publishers, leading to an out-of-court settlement.

4 *the hateful siege of contraries*: *Paradise Lost*, IX, 121–2.

suffer—I am sorry to give you pain—I am almost resolv'd to burn this—but I really have not self possession and magninimity enough to manage the thing othe[r]wise—after all it may be a nervousness proceeding from the Mercury[1]—

[Monday, 21 September] Bailey I hear is gaining his Spirits and he will be yet what I once thought impossible a cheerful Man—I think he is not quite so much spoken of in Little Brittain. I forgot to ask Mrs Dilke if she had any thing she wanted to say immediately to you—This morning look'd so unpromising that I did not think she would have gone—but I find she has on sending for some volumes of Gibbon—I was in a little funk yesterday, for I sent an unseal'd note of sham abuse, until I recollected from what I had heard Charles say, that <the ser>vant could neither read nor write—not even to her Mother as Charles observed. I have just had a Letter from Reynolds—he is going on gloriously. The following is a translation of a Line of Ronsard—

> 'Love poured her Beauty into my warm veins'[2]—

You have passed your Romance and I never gave into it or else I think this line a feast for one of your Lovers—How goes it with Brown?

Your sincere friend
John Keats—

To J. H. Reynolds
22 (?) September 1818

[Woodhouse transcript (1821?)]

[Well Walk, Hampstead, Tuesday]

My dear Reynolds,

Believe me I have rather rejoiced in your happiness than fretted at your silence. Indeed I am grieved on your account that I

1 *Mercury*: See above, p. 58 and n.
2 *Love . . . veins*: The last line of Keats's translation of a sonnet by the French poet Pierre de Ronsard (1524–85), copied into his letter to Reynolds next day.

am not at the same time happy—But I conjure you to think at Present of nothing but pleasure "Gather the rose &c"[1] Gorge the honey of life. I pity you as much that it cannot last for ever, as I do myself now drinking bitters.—Give yourself up to it—you cannot help it—and I have a Consolation in thinking so—I never was in love—Yet the voice and shape of a woman[2] has haunted me these two days—at such a time when the relief, the feverous relief of Poetry seems a much less crime—This morning Poetry has conquered—I have relapsed into those abstractions which are my only life—I feel escaped from a new strange and threatening sorrow.—And I am thankful for it—There is an awful warmth about my heart like a load of Immortality.

Poor Tom—that woman—and Poetry were ringing changes in my senses—now I am in comparison happy—I am sensible this will distress you—you must forgive me. Had I known you would have set out so soon I could have sent you the 'Pot of Basil' for I had copied it out ready.—Here is a free translation of a Sonnet of Ronsard, which I think will please you—I have the loan of his works—they have great Beauties.

Nature withheld Cassandra in the skies &c &c[3]

(here follow the 1st 12 lines of the Sonnet—Then 2 strokes are drawn for the last lines thus)

—— —— —— ——
—— —— ——

1 *Gather the rose &c*: Keats quotes either Spenser's *The Faerie Queene*, II. xii. 75, 'Gather the rose of loue, whilest yet is time', or Fairfax's translation of Tasso's *Gerusalemme Liberata*, XVI, 15, 'Gather the rose of loue, while yet thou mast.'

2 *a woman*: Jane Cox, whom Keats had met at the Reynoldses shortly after his return from Scotland. See his description of her to the George Keatses below, p. 247.

3 *Nature . . . &c &c*: Keats's translation of Ronsard (whose works Woodhouse had lent him) was not published until *1848*. Woodhouse had made separate copies of the translation.

I had not the original by me when I wrote it, and did not recollect the purport of the last lines—I should have seen Rice ere this—but I am confined by Sawrey's mandate in the house now, and have as yet only gone out in fear of the damp night—You know what an undangerous matter it is. I shall soon be quite recovered—Your offer I shall remember as though it had even now taken place in fact—I think it can not be—Tom is not up yet—I can not say he is better. I have not heard from George.

Y[r] affect[te] friend John Keats.

Lockhart's fourth attack (signed 'Z.') on Hunt and the 'Cockney School' was published in the August issue of Blackwood's Magazine *and reached the public on* 1 *(?) September* 1818. *As expected, this notorious review pilloried Keats. Putting together* Poems *(1817) and* Endymion, *the anonymous reviewer advised 'the starved apothecary' to go 'back to the shop, Mr John, back to the "plasters, pills, ointment boxes", &c.' Any hopes that the influential Tory* Quarterly Review, *longer established and with a larger circulation, might be less party political were dashed when its critical onslaught on* Endymion *appeared anonymously on 27 (?) August. Although it was written by J. W. Croker (1780–1857), Keats, like many at the time, mistakenly believed its author to be William Gifford, editor of the* Quarterly. *Keats's friends were bitterly disappointed, but he put up a brave front. His publisher James Hessey reported that he was in 'good spirits' at the dinner party he gave on 14 September and 'does not seem to care at all about Blackwood'. However, on the same occasion Keats told Woodhouse that he would 'write no more', and early in October he reportedly lay awake a 'whole night' talking to Cowden Clarke with 'sensative-bitterness'* [sic] *about the* Quarterly's *'unfair treatment'. Those around Keats were concerned about his reaction to the reviews. This is clear from his next letter to James Hessey, and from those Reynolds and Woodhouse sent him on 14 and 21 October (quoted below, pp. 242 and 260–61).*

To James Hessey
8 October 1818

[Woodhouse transcript (1821?)]

[Well Walk, Hampstead, Thursday]

My dear Hessey.

You are very good in sending me the letter from the Chronicle[1]—and I am very bad in not acknowledging such a kindness sooner.—pray forgive me—It has so chanced that I have had that paper every day—I have seen today's. I cannot but feel indebted to those Gentlemen who have taken my part—As for the rest, I begin to get a little acquainted with my own strength and weakness.—Praise or blame has but a momentary effect on the man whose love of beauty in the abstract makes him a severe critic on his own Works. My own domestic criticism has given me pain without comparison beyond what Blackwood or the Quarterly could possibly inflict. and also when I feel I am right, no external praise can give me such a glow as my own solitary reperception & ratification of what is fine. J.S. is perfectly right in regard to the slip-shod Endymion. That it is so is no fault of mine,—No!—though it may sound a little paradoxical. It is as good as I had power to make it—by myself—Had I been nervous about its being a perfect piece, & with that view asked advice, & trembled over every page, it would not have been written; for it is not in my nature to fumble—I will write independantly.—I have written independently <u>without Judgment</u>—I may write independently <u>& with judgment</u> hereafter.—The Genius of Poetry must work out its own salvation in a man: It cannot be matured by law & precept, but

1 *letter from the Chronicle*: The letter by J. S. (published in the *Morning Chronicle* the previous Saturday) defending Keats against Croker's attack in the *Quarterly Review*. Its author was probably John Scott (1783–1821), who later died in a duel resulting from his attack upon *Blackwood's Magazine*. As Keats notes, a second letter defending him (signed 'R. B.') was published by the same newspaper on 8 October.

by sensation & watchfulness in itself—That which is creative must create itself—In Endymion, I leaped headlong into the Sea, and thereby have become better acquainted with the Soundings, the quicksands, & the rocks, than if I had stayed upon the green shore, and piped a silly pipe, and took tea & comfortable advice.—I was never afraid of failure; for I would sooner fail than not be among the greatest—But I am nigh getting into a rant. So, with remembrances to Taylor & Woodhouse &c I am

Yrs very sincerely
John Keats.

The following Sunday, 11 October, J. H. Reynolds's vigorous defence of Endymion *against the 'unfeeling arrogance, and cold ignorance' of the* Quarterly*'s attack was reprinted by Hunt in the* Examiner. *Two days later Reynolds visited Keats. They discussed how Keats should react to his critics, and returned to the idea of publishing a joint volume of tales based on Boccaccio. Before Reynolds left, Keats gave him the manuscript of 'Isabella; or, The Pot of Basil' for his opinion.*

Reynolds responded next morning, Wednesday, 14 October. 'As to ["Isabella"] I am of all things anxious that you should publish it, for its completeness will be a full answer to all the ignorant malevolence of cold lying Scotchmen and stupid Englishmen . . . I am confident, Keats, that the Pot of Basil hath that simplicity and quiet pathos, which are of sure sovereignty over all hearts. I must say that it would delight me to have you prove yourself to the world, what we know you to be;—to have you annul the Quarterly Review, by the best of all answers.' He continued by saying that 'we were <to print > together— ~~but~~ /I give over all intention and/ you ought to be alone. I can never write anything now—my mind is taken the other way:—But I shall set my heart on having you, high, as you ought to be. Do you get Fame,—and I shall have it in being your affectionate and steady friend' (L, I, *pp.* 376–7).

Keats thought Reynolds's generous and selfless letter important enough to enclose it with the one he began writing that day to George and Georgiana Keats.

tears will come into your Eyes—let them—and embrace each other—thank heaven for what happiness you have and after thinking a moment or two that you suffer in common with all Mankind hold it not a sin to regain your cheerfulness—I will relieve you of one of uneasiness overleaf: I retu[r]ned I said on account of my health—I am now well from a bad sore throat which came of bog trotting in the Island of Mull—of which you shall hear by the coppies I shall make from my Scotch Letters—Your content in each other is a delight to me which I cannot express—the Moon is now shining full and brilliant—she is the same to me in Matter, what you are to me in Spirit—If you were here my dear Sister I could not pronounce the words which I can write to you from a distance: I have a tenderness for you, and an admiration which I feel to be as great and more chaste than I can have for any woman in the world. You will mention Fanny—her character is not formed; her identity does not press upon me as yours does. I hope from the bottom of my heart that I may one day feel as much for her as I do for you—I know not how it is, but I have never made any acquaintance of my own—nearly all through your medium my dear Brother—through you I know not only a Sister but a glorious human being—And now I am talking of those to whom you have made me known I cannot forbear mentioning Haslam as a most kind and obliging and constant friend—His behaviour to Tom during my absence and since my return has endeared him to me for ever—besides his anxiety about you. Tomorrow I shall call on your Mother and exchange information with her—On Tom's account I have not been able to pass so much time with her as I would otherwise have done—I have seen her but twice—on[c]e I dined with her and Charles—She was well, in good Spirits and I kept her laughing at my bad jokes—We went to tea at Mrs Millar's and in going were particularly struck with the light and shade through the Gate way at the Horse Guards. I intend to write you such Volumes that it will be impossible for me to keep any order or method in what I write: that will come first which is uppermost in my Mind, not that which is uppermost in my heart—besides I should wish to give you a picture of our Lives here whenever by a touch I can do it; even as you must see by the last sentence our walk past Whitehall all in good health and spirits—this I am certain of, because I felt so much pleasure from the simple idea of your playing a game at Cricket—At Mrs Millars I saw Henry[1] quite well—there was Miss Keasle—and the goodnatured Miss Waldegrave[2]—Mrs Millar began a long story and you know it is her Daughter's way to help her on as though her tongue were ill of the gout—Mrs M. certainly tells a Story as though she had been taught her Alphabet in Crutched Friars.[3] Dilke has been very unwell; I found him very ailing on my return—he was under Medical care for some time, and then went to the Sea Side whence he has returned well[4]—Poor little M^rs^ D— has had another gall-stone attack; she was well ere I returned—she is now at Brighton—Dilke was greatly pleased to hear from you and will write a Letter for me to enclose—He seems greatly desirous of hearing from you of the Settlement itself—I came by ship from Inverness[5] and was nine days at Sea without being sick—a little Qualm now and then put me in mind of you—however as soon as you touch the thore [*for* shore] all the horrors of sick[n]ess are soon forgotten; as was the case with a Lady on board who could not hold her head up all the way. We had not been in the Thames an hour before her tongue began to some tune; paying off as it was fit she should all old scores. I was the only Englishman on board. There was a downright Scotchman who hearing that there had been a bad crop of Potatoes in England had brought some triumphant Specimens from Scotland—these he exhibited with national pride to all the Lightermen, and

1 *Henry*: Henry Wylie (1783–1846), Georgiana's brother, lived with his aunt Mrs Amelia Millar and her daughter Mary in Henrietta Street, Covent Garden.

2 *Miss Keasle . . . Miss Waldegrave*: Mary Ann Keasle (who married Henry on 23 December 1819) and Mary Waldegrave were boarders there (Crutcher, pp. 201–2). For Keats's later remarks on Miss Keasle, see below, pp. 271, 313, 434.

3 *Crutched Friars*: An area near Tower Hill, London, named after an order of Catholic mendicant friars who carried a staff surmounted by a cross (or 'crutch').

4 *Sea Side . . . well*: He had left Brighton before 20 September.

5 *Inverness*: In fact, Cromarty, twenty miles north-east of Inverness.

Watermen from the Nore to the Bridge.[1] I fed upon beef all the way; not being able to eat the thick Porridge which the Ladies managed to manage with large awkward horn spoons into the bargain. Severn has had a narrow escape of his Life from a Typhous fever: he is now gaining strength—Reynolds has returned from a six weeks enjoyment in Devonshire, he is well and persuades me to publish my pot of Basil as an answer to the attacks made on me in Blackwood's Magazine and the Quarterly Review.[2] There have been two Letters in my defence in the Chronicle and one in the Examiner, coppied from the Alfred Exeter paper, and written by Reynolds[3]—I do not know who wrote those in the ~~Quarterly~~/ Chronicle/ —This is a mere matter of the moment—I think I shall be among the English Poets after my death.[4] Even as a Matter of present interest the attempt to crush me in the ~~Chro~~ Quarterly has only brought me more into notice and it is a common expression among book men "I wonder the Quarterly should cut its own throat."[5] It does me not the least harm in Society to make me appear little and rediculous:[6] I know when a Man is superior to me and give him all due respect—he will be the last to laugh at me and as for the rest I feel that I make an impression upon them which insures me personal respect while I am in sight whatever they may say when my back is turned—Poor Haydon's eyes will not suffer him to proceed with his picture—he has been in the Country—I have seen him but once since my return—I hurry matters together here because I do not know when the Mail sails—I shall enqu[i]re tomorrow and then shall know whether to be particular or general in my letter—you shall have

1 *the Nore to the Bridge*: i.e., from the Nore, off Sheerness, to London Bridge. 'Lighters' were flat-bottomed boats for unloading cargo from ships to land.
2 *attacks . . . Review*: On these, see above, pp. 240–41.
3 *two Letters . . . Reynolds*: On these, see above, pp. 241 n. and 242.
4 *among the English Poets after my death*: Keats is possibly referring to John Bell's series *Poets of Great Britain* (1776–82).
5 *I wonder . . . own throat*: A view shared by Richard Woodhouse (*L*, I, p. 379) and Keats's publisher James Hessey (*KC*, I, 53).
6 *rediculous*: Keats's characteristic misspelling.

at least two sheets a day[1] till it does sail whether it be three days or a fortnight—and then I will begin a fresh one for the next Month. The Miss Reynoldses are very kind to me—but they lately have displeased me much and in this way—Now I am coming the Richardson.[2] On my return, the first day I called they were in a sort of taking or bustle about a Cousin of theirs[3] who having fallen out with her Grandpapa in a serious manner, was invited by M[rs] R— to take Asylum in her house—She is an east indian[4] and ought to be her Grandfather's Heir. At the time I called M[rs] R. was in conference with her up stairs and the young Ladies were warm in her praises down stairs calling her genteel, interresting and a thousand other pretty things to which I gave no heed, not being partial to 9 days wonders—Now all is completely changed—they hate her; and from what I hear she is not without faults—of a real kind: but she has othe[r]s which are more apt to make women of inferior charms hate her. She is not a Cleopatra; but she is at least a Charmian.[5] She has a rich eastern look; she has fine eyes and fine manners. When she comes into a room she makes an impression the same as the Beauty of a Leopardess. She is too fine and conscious of her Self to repulse any Man who may address her—from habit she thinks that nothing particular.[6] I always find myself more at ease with such a woman; the picture before me always gives me a life and animation which I cannot possibly feel with any thing inferiour—I am at such times too much occupied in admiring to be awkward or on a tremble. I forget myself entirely because I live in her. You will by this time think I am in love with her;

1 *two sheets a day*: In fact, Keats completed more than two sheets at this sitting, but only one and a half thereafter.

2 *coming the Richardson*: That is, writing in the style of the epistolary novels of Samuel Richardson (1689–1761).

3 *Cousin of theirs*: Jane Cox, the daughter of Mrs Reynolds's only brother, was born in India and became her grandfather's heir following the death of her father, an employee of the East India Company.

4 *east indian*: Eurasian. *OED* B.1 cites Maria Edgeworth's *Harrington* (1817), I, vii, p. 147, 'Who is she?' 'An East Indian, I should guess, by her dark complexion.'

5 *Charmian*: Cleopatra's attendant in *Antony and Cleopatra*.

6 *particular*: Flirtatious.

so before I go any further I will tell you I am not—she kept me awake one Night[1] as a tune of Mozart's might do—I speak of the thing as a passtime and an amuzement than which I can feel none deeper than a conversation with an imperial woman the very 'yes' and 'no' of whose Lips is to me a Banquet.[2] I dont cry to take the moon home with me in my Pocket not [*for* nor] do I fret to leave her behind me. I like her and her like because one has no <u>sensations</u>—what we both are is taken for granted—You will suppose I have by this had much talk with her—no such thing—there are the Miss Reynoldses on the look out—They think I dont admire her because I did not stare at her—They call her a flirt to me—What a want of knowledge? she walks across a room in such a manner that a Man is drawn towards her with a magnetic Power. This they call flirting! they do not know things. They do not know what a Woman is. I believe tho' she has faults—the same as Charmian and Cleopatra might have had—Yet she is a fine thing speaking in a worldly way: for there are two distinct tempers of mind in which we judge of things—the worldly, theatrical and pantomimical; and the unearthly, spiritual and etherial—in the former Buonaparte, Lord Byron and this Charmian hold the first place in our Minds; in the latter John Howard,[3] Bishop Hooker rocking his child's cradle[4] and you my dear Sister are the conquering feelings. As a Man in the world I love the rich talk of a Charmian; as an eternal Being I love the thought of you. I should like her to ruin me, and I should like you to save me. Do not think my dear Brother from this that my Passions are head long or likely to be ever of any pain to you—no

1 *she kept me awake one Night*: On 22 (?) September Keats had told Reynolds that 'the voice and shape of a woman has haunted me these two days' (p. 239 above).

2 *Lips . . . Banquet*: See Benedick's description of Claudio in *Much Ado about Nothing*, II. iii. 20: 'His words are a very fantastical banquet.'

3 *John Howard*: (1726?–1790) Penal reformer.

4 *Bishop Hooker . . . cradle*: Richard Hooker (1554?–1600), Anglican theologian and author of *Laws of Ecclesiastical Politie* (1593–7). He was not a bishop: Walton's Life of Hooker (1666) records that he rocked his children's cradle.

"I am free from Men of Pleasure's cares
By dint of feelings far more deep than theirs"

This is Lord Byron,[1] and is one of the finest things he has said—I have no town talk for you, as I have not been much among people—as for Politics they are in my opinion only sleepy because they will soon be too wide awake[2]—Perhaps not—for the long and continued Peace of England itself has given us notions of personal safety which are likely to prevent the reestablishment of our national Honesty—There is of a truth nothing manly or sterling in any part of the Government. There are many Madmen In the Country, I have no doubt, who would like to be beheaded on tower Hill merely for the sake of eclat,[3] there are many Men like Hunt[4] who from a principle of taste would like to see things go on better, there are many like Sir F. Burdett[5] who like to sit at the head of political dinners—but there are none prepared to suffer in obscurity for their Country—the motives of our wo[r]st Men are interest and of our best Vanity—We have no Milton, no Algernon Sidney[6]—Governers in these days loose the title of Man in exchange for that of Diplomat and Minister—We breathe in a sort of Officinal[7] Atmosphere—All the departments of Government have strayed far from Spimpicity [*for* Simplicity] which is the greatest of Strength—there is as much difference in this respect between

1 *Lord Byron*: Not Byron but Leigh Hunt's *The Story of Rimini* (1816), III, 121–2, 'And had been kept from men of pleasure's cares / By dint of feelings still more warm than theirs.'

2 *as for Politics . . . wide awake*: In fact, despite the peace following Napoleon's defeat in 1815, the politics and economies of England and Europe were unsettled. Nevertheless, 'No less than for Keats's career as a poet, 1819 was in many ways to be an *annus mirabilis* for the radical movement' (Mee).

3 *eclat*: i.e., publicity (from the French).

4 *Hunt*: Possibly Leigh Hunt, but is more probably aimed at Henry ('Orator') Hunt (1773–1835), a flamboyant radical.

5 *Sir F. Burdett*: Sir Francis Burdett (1770–1844), MP, aristocratic radical reformer.

6 *Algernon Sidney*: (1622–83) Republican, executed for his part in the Rye House Plot, one of the heroes of Whigs and Reformers for his opposition to the Stuarts.

7 *Officinal*: 'Characteristic of a shop or shopkeeper' (*OED*).

the present Government and oliver Cromwell's, as there is between the 12 Tables of Rome and the volumes of Civil Law which were digested by Justinian.[1] A Man now entitlerd [*sic*] Chancellor has the same honour paid to him whether he be a Hog or a Lord Bacon.[2] No sensation is created by Greatness but by the number of orders a Man has at his Button holes Notwithstand[3] the part which the Liberals take in the Cause of Napoleon I cannot but think he has done more harm to the life of Liberty than any one else could have done: not that the divine right Gentlemen have done or intend to do any good—no they have taken a Lesson of him and will do all the further harm he would have done without any of the good—The worst thing he has done is, that he has taught them how to organize their monstrous armies—The Emperor Alexander it is said intends to divide his Empire as did Diocletian—creating two Czars besides himself, and continuing the supreme Monarch of the whole[4]—Should he do this and they for a series of Years keep peacable among themselves Russia may spread her conquest even to China—I think a very likely thing that China itself may fall Turkey certainly will—Meanwhile european north Russia will hold its horns against the rest of Europe, intrieguing constantly with France. Dilke, whom you know to be a Godwin perfectibil[it]y Man, pleases himself with the idea that America will be the country to take up the human intellect where england leaves off[5] —I differ there with him greatly—A

1 *oliver Cromwell's ... Justinian*: Keats compares the 'simplicity' of Cromwell's 'republican' government following the execution of Charles I in 1649 with that of Rome's Twelve Tables (*c.* 450 BC), its earliest legal code, with the complexity of the Emperor Justinian's attempt to codify a thousand years of Roman law in the *Corpus Juris Civilis* (AD 529–35).

2 *Lord Bacon*: Francis Bacon (1561–1626), philosopher, essayist and statesman.

3 *Notwithstand*: See below, p. 258 n.

4 *Emperor Alexander . . . the whole*: Alexander I (1777–1825). The *Gentleman's Magazine* (September 1818) reported that 'Russia is to be divided into three parts [. . .] while he remains supreme head of the whole' (Rollins). In 286 BC Diocletian divided the Roman Empire into two halves, the Eastern and Western.

5 *Godwin . . . leaves off*: In his *Enquiry Concerning Political Justice* (1793) William Godwin (1756–1836) propounded philosophical anarchism and

country like the united states whose greatest Men are Franklins and Washingtons will never do that—They are great Men doubtless but how are they to be compared to those our countrey men Milton and the two Sidneys—The one is a philosophical Quaker full of mean and thrifty maxims the other sold the very Charger who had taken him through all his Battles—Those American's are great but they are not sublime Man—the humanity of the United States can never reach the sublime—Birkbeck's[1] mind is too much in the American Stryle [*for* Style]—you must endeavour to infuse a little Spirit of another sort into the Settlement, always with great caution, for thereby you may do your descendents more good than you may imagine. If I had a prayer to make for any great good, next to Tom's recovery, it should be that one of your Children should be the first American Poet. I have a great mind to make a prophecy and they say prophecies work out their own fullfillment.

'Tis 'the witching time of night'[2]
Orbed is the Moon and bright
And the Stars they glisten, glisten
Seeming with bright eyes to listen
For what listen they?
For a song and for a cha[r]m
See they glisten in alarm
And the Moon is waxing warm
To hear what I shall say.

---

believed that mankind was capable of continual rational improvement. Keats knew this work and Godwin's novels. Godwin was linked with the Keats circle through Shelley (who married his daughter Mary) and Leigh Hunt. The poem *Eighteen Hundred and Eleven* (1811) by Laetitia Barbauld (1743–1825) foresees the Americas replacing Europe's cultural and economic imperialism.

1 *Birkbeck's*: Keats's comment is aimed at Birkbeck's pragmatic (and over-optimistic) *Notes on a Journey . . . to the Territory of Illinois* (1818) and his *Letters from Illinois* (1818) encouraging emigration to his Settlement. Taylor had given George a copy of the latter.

2 *'Tis . . . night*: First published 1837. *the witching time of night*: *Hamlet*, III. ii. 378.

Moon keep wide thy golden ears
Hearken Stars, and hearken Spheres
Hearken thou eternal Sky
I sing an infant's lullaby,
A pretty Lullaby!
Listen, Listen, listen, listen
Glisten, glisten, glisten, glisten
And hear my lullaby?
Though the Rushes that will make
Its cradle still are in the lake:
Though the linnen then that will be
Its swathe is on the cotton tree;
Though the wo[o]llen that will keep
It wa[r]m, is on the silly sheep;
Listen Stars light, listen, listen
Glisten, Glisten, glisten, glisten
And hear my lullaby!
Child! I see thee! Child I've found thee
Midst of the quiet all around thee!
Child I see thee! Ch[i]ld I spy thee
And thy mother sweet is nigh thee!
Child I know thee! Child no more
But a Poet <u>ever</u>more
See, See the Lyre, the Lyre
In a flame of fire
Upon the little cradle's top
Flaring, flaring, flaring.
Past the eyesight's bearing—
Awake it from its sleep
And see if it can keep
Its eyes upon the blaze.
Amaze, Amaze!
It stares, it stares, it stares
It dares what no one dares
It lifts its little hand into the flame
Unharm'd, and on the strings
Paddles a little tune and ~~signs~~ /sings/
With dumb endeavour sweetly!

Bard thou art completely!
Little Child
O' the western wild
Bard art thou completely!—
Sweetly, with dumb endeavour.—
A Poet now or never!
Litt[l]e Child
O' the western wild
A Poet now or never!

(continued 16 October, p. 254 below)

To Fanny Keats
16 October 1818

[British Library MS]

My dear Fanny, Hampstead Friday Morn

You must not condemn me for not being punctual to Thursday, for I really did not know whether it would not affect poor Tom too much to see you.[1] You know how it hurt him to part with you the last time. At all events you shall hear from me; and if Tom keeps pretty well tomorrow—I will see Mr Abbey the next day, and endeavour to settle that you shall be with us on Tuesday or Wednesday—I have good news from George—He has landed safely with our Sister—they are both in good health—their prospects are good—and they are by this time nighing to their journeys end—you shall hear the particulars soon—

Your affectionate Brother
John—

Tom's love to you.

1 *not being punctual . . . see you*: Keats had postponed Fanny's planned visit to Well Walk on 15 October.

To George and Georgiana Keats
(continued)
16, 21, 24, October 1818

[Late evening, 16 October 1818] This is friday, I know not what day of the Month—I will enquire tomorrow for it is fit you should know the time I am writing. I went to Town yesterday, and calling at M[rs] Millar's was told that your Mother would not be found at home—I met Henry[1] as I turned the corner—I had no leisure to return, so I left the letters with him—He was looking very well—Poor Tom is no better tonight—I am affraid to ask him what Message I shall send from him—And here I could go on complaining of my Misery, but I will keep myself cheerful for your Sakes. With a great deal of trouble I have succeeded in getting Fanny to Hampstead—she has been several times—M[r] Lewis[2] has been very kind to Tom all the Summer there has been scar[c]e a day passed but he has visited him, and not one day without bringing or sending some fruit of the nicest kind. He has been very assiduous in his enquiries after you—It would give the old Gentleman a great pleasure if you would send him a Sheet enclosed in the next parcel to me, after you receive this—how long will it be first—Why did I not write to Philadelphia? Really I am sorry for that neglect—I wish to go on writing ad infinitum, to you—I wish for interresting matter, and a pen as swift as the wind—But the fact is I go so little into the Crowd now that I have nothing fresh and fresh every day to speculate upon, except my own Whims and Theroies—I have been but once to Haydon's, onece to Hunt's, once to Rices, once to Hessey's I have not seen Taylor,[3] I have not been to the Theatre—Now if I had been

1 *Henry*: Henry Wylie.
2 *M[r] Lewis*: David Lewis was an older Hampstead neighbour with strong democratic beliefs (see below, p. 307).
3 *once to Haydon's . . . Taylor*: Since his return on 18 August Keats had dined at Hessey's in Fleet Street on 14 September (see above, pp. 237, 240). There is no record of his visits to Haydon, the Hunts or the Rice family.

many times to all these and was still in the habit of going I could on my return at night have each day something new to tell you of without any stop—But now I have such a dearth that when I get to the end of this sentence and to the bottom of this page I much [*for* must] wait till I can find something interesting to you before I begin another.— After all it is not much matter what it may be about; for the very words from such a distance penned by this hand will be grateful to you—even though I were to coppy out the tale of Mother Hubbard or Little Red Riding Hood—I have been over to Dilke's this evening—there with Brown we have been talking of different and indifferent Matters—of Euclid, of Metaphisics of the Bible, of Shakspeare of the horrid System and conseque[nce]s of the fagging at great Schools—I know not yet how large a parcel I can send—I mean by way of Letters—I hope there can be no objection to my dowling up[1] a qui[r]e made into a small compass—That is the manner in which I shall write. I shall send you more than Letters—I mean a tale—which I must begin on account of the activity of my Mind; of its inability to remain at rest—It must be prose and not very exciting. I must do this because in the way I am at present situated I have too many interruptions to a train of feeling to be able to w[r]ite Poetry— So I shall write this Tale,[2] and if I think it worth while get a duplicate made before I send it off to you—

This is a fresh beginning [Wednesday] the 21st October— Charles and Henry were with us on Sunday and they brought me your Letter to your Mother—we agreed to get a Packet off to you as soon as possible. I shall dine with your Mother tomorrow, when they have promised to have their Letters ready. I shall send as soon as possible without thinking of the little you may have from me in the first parcel, as I intend as I said to begin another Letter of more regular information. Here I want to communicate so largely in a little time that I am puzzled where to direct my attention. Haslam has promised to let

1 *dowling up*: 'Dowl', 'To knead or mix up bread, dough, &c. in a hurry' (Joseph Wright, *English Dialect Dictionary*).
2 *I shall write this Tale*: He is not known to have written the 'Tale'.

me know from Capper and Hazlewood.[1] For want of something better I shall proceed to give you some extracts from my Scotch Letters—Yet now I think on it why not send you the letters themselves—I have three of them at present—I beli[e]ve Haydon has two which I will get in time.[2]
[Saturday (morning?), 24 October] I dined with your Mother & Henry at Mrs Millar's on thursday[3] when they gave me their Letters Charles's I have not yet he has promised to send it. The thought of sending my scotch Letters has determined me to enclose a few more which I have received and which will give you the best cue to how I am going on better than you could otherwise know—Your Mother was well and I was sorry I could not stop later. I called on Hunt yesterday—it has always been my fate to meet Ollier there—On thursday I walked with Hazlitt as far as covent Garden: he was going to play Rackets—I think Tom has been rather better these few last days—he has been less nervous. I expect Reynolds tomorrow [Continued evening, 24 October, after returning from London] Since I wrote thus far I have met with that same Lady again,[4] whom I saw at Hastings and whom I met when we were going to the English Opera.[5] It was in a street which goes from Bedford Row to Lamb's Conduit Street—I passed her and turrned back—she seemed glad of it; glad to see me and not offended at my passing her before We walked on towards Islington where

1 *Capper and Hazlewood*: Stockbrokers of 15 Angel Court, Throgmorton Street, London, who acted as forwarding agents.

2 *Haydon . . . in time*: Haydon never returned Keats's two journal letters to Tom of 10–14 July and 3–6 August 1818, but pasted them into his journal.

3 *thursday*: 22 October.

4 *I have met . . . Lady again*: Keats had met Mrs Isabella Jones at Hastings in May or June the previous summer, where she was under the protection of a wealthy Irishman, Donal O'Callaghan. She spent the winters in London and was known to others in the Keats circle, including his publisher John Taylor. She is thought to have proposed the subject of 'The Eve of St Agnes' to Keats, and continued to take an interest him. For the possible identification of her as Mrs Isabella Jones (*fl.* 1805–43), widow of Lieutenant William Jones, who died at Trafalgar on Nelson's *Victory*, see Roe, pp. 169–72.

5 *the English Opera*: The Lyceum Theatre in the Strand: Rollins conjectures that the brothers went to the opera 'shortly before George's marriage in May 1818'.

we called on a friend of her's who keeps a Boarding School.[1] She has always been an enigma to me—she has been in a Room with you and with Reynolds and wishes we should be acquainted without any of our common acquaintance knowing it. As we went along, some times through shabby, sometimes through decent Street[s] I had my guessing at work, not knowing what it would be and prepared to meet any surprise—First it ended at this Hou<s>e at Islington: on parting from which I pressed to attend her home. She consented and then again my thoughts were at work what it might lead to, tho' now they had received a sort of genteel hint from the Boarding School. Our Walk ended in 34 Gloucester Street Queen Square—not exactly so for we went up stairs into her sitting room—a very tasty sort of place with Books, Pictures a bronze statue of Buonaparte, Music, æolian Harp; a Parrot a Linnet—A Case of choice Liquers &c &c &.

She behaved in the kindest manner—made me take home a Grouse for Tom's dinner—Asked for my address for the purpose of sending more game—As I had warmed with her before and kissed her—I though[t] it would be living backwards not to do so again—She had a better taste: she perceived how much a thing of course it was and shrunk from it—not in a prudish way but in as I say a good taste—She cont[r]ived to disappoint me in a way which made me feel more pleasure than a simple kiss could do—She said I should please her much more if I would only press her hand and go away. Whether she was in a different disposition when I saw her before—or whether I have in fancy wrong'd her I cannot tell—I expect to pass some pleasant hours with her now and then: in which I feel I shall be of service to her in matters of knowledge and taste: if I can I will—I have no libidinous thought about her—she and your George are the only women à peu près de mon age whom I would be content to know for their mind

1 *a friend of her's . . . Boarding School*: Gittings in *John Keats: The Living Year* (1954), pp. 32, 204, identifies the friend as Mrs Green at Duncan Terrace, near the Angel, Islington, the wife of Lieutenant-Colonel Thomas Green, 6th Regiment of Native Infantry, Madras Presidency. There was a Miss Green's Boarding School nearby.

and friendship alone—I shall in a short time write you as far as I know how I intend to pass my Life—I cannot think of those things now Tom is so unwell and weak. Notwithstand[1] your Happiness and your recommendation I hope I shall never marry. Though the most beautiful Creature were waiting for me at the end of a Journey or a Walk; though the carpet were of Silk, the Curtains of the morning Clouds; the chairs and Sofa stuffed with Cygnet's down; the food Manna, the Wine beyond Claret, the Window opening on Winander mere, I should not feel—or rather my Happiness would not be so fine, as [*first written as* and] my Solitude is sublime. Then instead of what I have described, there is a Sublimity to welcome me home—The roaring of the wind is my wife and the Stars through the window pane are my Children. The mighty abstract Idea I have of Beauty in all things stifles the more divided and minute domestic happiness—an amiable wife and sweet Children I contemplate as a part of that Bea<u>ty. but I must have a thousand of those beautiful particles t<o> fill up my heart. I feel more and more every day, as my imagination strengthens, that I do not live in this world alone but in a thousand worlds—No sooner am I alone than shapes of epic greatness are stationed around me,[2] and serve my Spirit the office which is equivalent to a King's body guard—then 'Tragedy, with scepter'd pall, comes sweeping by"[3] According to my state of mind I am with Achilles shouting in the Trenches[4] or with Theocritus in the Vales of Sicily. Or I throw [*first written as* through] my whole being into Triolus and repeating those lines, 'I wander, like a lost soul upon the stygian Banks staying for waftage,'[5] I melt into the air with a voluptuousness so delicate that I am

1 *Notwithstand*: *OED* cites this as a late occurrence of the obsolete form of 'Notwithstanding'.

2 *No sooner . . . around me*: Keats was working on *Hyperion* at this time, but far from being alone, he was looking after Tom in Well Walk.

3 *Tragedy . . . sweeping by*: Adapted from Milton's 'Il Penseroso', ll. 97–8.

4 *Achilles . . . Trenches*: In 1849 Benjamin Bailey remembered Keats's 'enthusiastic admiration' for Homer's Achilles, 'especially when he is described as "shouting in the trenches"' (*KC*, II, 277). Pope translated the *Iliad* XVIII, 228, as 'Thrice from the trench his dreadful voice he raised.'

5 *like a lost . . . waftage*: Troilus describing his longing for Cressida to Pandarus in *Troilus and Cressida*, III. ii. 8–9.

content to be alone—These things combined with the opinion I have of the generallity of women—who appear to me as children to whom I would rather give a Sugar Plum than my time, form a barrier against Matrimony which I rejoice in. I have written this that you might see I have my share of the highest pleasures and that though I may choose to pass my days alone I shall be no Solitary. You see therre is nothing spleenical[1] in all this. The only thing that can ever affect me personally for more than one short passing day, is any doubt about my powers for poetry—I seldom have any, and I look with hope to the nighing time when I shall have none. I am as happy as a Man can be—that is in myself I should be happy if Tom was well, and I knew you were passing pleasant days—Then I should be most enviable—with the yearning Passion I have for the beautiful, connected and made one with the ambition of my intellect. Th[i]nk of my Pleasure in Solitude, in comparison of my commerce with the world—there I am a child—there they do not know me not even my most intimate acquaintance—I give into their feelings as though I were refraining from irritating <a> little child—Some think me middling, others silly, others foolish—every one thinks he sees my weak side against my will; when in truth it is with my will—I am content to be thought all this because I have in my own breast so great a resource. This is one great reason why they like me so; because they can all show to advantage in a room, and eclipese from a certain tact one who is reckoned to be a good Poet—I hope I am not here playing tricks 'to make the angels weep':[2] I think not: for I have not the least contempt for my species; and though it may sound paradoxical: my greatest elevations of soul leave me every time more humbled—Enough of this—though in your Love for me you will not think it enough.

(continued 31 October, p. 264 below)

1 *spleenical*: *OED*'s sole 'rare' example: Keats's nonce word returns 'spleneti-cal' to its physiological roots.

2 *to make the angels weep*: Isabella to Angelo in *Measure for Measure*, II. ii. 117–22, 'man, proud man, / . . . Plays such fantastic tricks before high heaven / As makes the angels weep.'

To Fanny Keats
26 October 1818

[British Library MS]

[Monday, Well Walk, Hampstead]

My dear Fanny,

I called on Mr Abbey in the beginning of last Week:[1] when he seemed averse to letting you come again from having heard that you had been to other places besides Well Walk—I do not mean to say you did wrongly in speaking of it, for there should rightly be no objection to such things: but you know with what People we are obliged in the course of Childhood to associate; whose conduct forces us into duplicity and fa[l]shood to them. To the worst of People we should be openhearted: but it is as well as things are to be prudent in making any communication to any one, that may throw an impediment in the way of any of the little pleasures you may have. I do not recommend duplicity but prudence with such people. Perphaps I am talking too deeply for you: if you do not now, you will understand what I mean in the course of a few years. I think poor Tom is a little Better: he sends his love to you—I shall call on Mr Abbey tomorrow: when I hope to settle when to see you again. Mrs Dilke has been for some time at Brighton—she is expected home in a day or two. She will be pleased I am sure with your present. I will try for permission for you to remain here all Night should Mrs D. retu[r]n in time.[2]

Your affectionate Brother
John—

The next day Keats sat down to write a considered reply to a worried letter from Richard Woodhouse, posted a week earlier

1 *I called . . . last Week*: Probably on Monday, 19 October.

2 *I will try . . . in time*: In the event Richard Abbey continued to prevent Fanny visiting her brothers.

(L, I, pp. 378–82). Woodhouse said he had 'met with that malicious, but weak & silly article on Endymion in the last Quarterly Review' while away in the country and, on returning to London, recalled his 'late conversation' with Keats at Hessey's dinner in mid-September. 'I understood you to say, you thought there was now nothing original to be written in poetry; that its riches were already exhausted,—& all its beauties forestalled—& That you should, consequently, write no more.'

He disagreed with Keats's mistaken 'premises'—'For my part I believe most sincerely, that the wealth of poetry is unexhausted & inexhaustible . . . the true born Son of Genius, who creates for himself the world in which his own fancy ranges who culls from it fair forms of truth beauty & purity & apparels them in hues chosen by himself, should hold a different language—he need never fear that the treasury he draws on can be exhausted, nor despair of being always able to ma<ke> an original selection.' Woodhouse then testified to his passionate belief in Keats's pre-eminence in a period of 'vitiated' taste. 'I believe there has appeared one bard who "preserves his vessel" in purity independance & honor—who judges of the beautiful for himself, careless who thinks with him—who pursues his own selfappointed & selfapproved course right onward—who stoops not from his flight to win sullied breath from the multitude—and who "leans away" for highest heaven, and sings, pointing for his [illegible word]—to a standard of excellence dimly visible as yet even to himself . . . '

Woodhouse concluded, 'The world, I hope & trust, is not quite so dead dull and ungrateful as you may have apprehended—or as a few malevolent spirits may have given you reason to imagine[.] It contains, I know, many who have a warm "affection for the cause Of stedfast Genius toiling gallantly,"—many who, tho' personally unknown to you, look with the eye of hope & anticipation to your future course—but very few who in sincere wishes for your welfare, & passion for your fame, exceed, Dear Keats,

Yours most truly,
Richd Woodhouse
Temple 21st Octr 1818.'

To Richard Woodhouse
27 October 1818

[Harvard MS]

[Well Walk, Hampstead, Tuesday]

My dear Woodhouse,

Your Letter gave me a great satisfaction; more on account of its friendliness, than any relish of that matter in it which is accounted so acceptable in the 'genus irritabile'[1] The best answer I can give you is in a clerklike manner to make some observations on two principle points, which seem to point like indices into the midst of the whole pro and con, about genius, and views and atchievements[2] and ambition and cœtera. 1st As to the poetical Character itself, (I mean that sort of which, if I am any thing, I am a Member; that sort distinguished from the wordsworthian or egotistical sublime;[3] which is a thing per se and stands alone)[4] it is not itself—it has no self—it is every thing and nothing—It has no character—it enjoys light and shade; it lives in gusto,[5] be it foul or fair, high or low, rich or poor, mean or elevated—It has as much delight in conceiving an Iago as an Imogen. What shocks the virtuous philosop[h]er,

1 *genus irritabile*: 'An irritable race', Horace's description of poets (*Epistles*, II. ii. 102).

2 *atchievements*: Possibly also with the meaning, 'An escutcheon or ensign armorial, granted in memory of some achievement or distinguished feat' (*OED* 3).

3 *egotistical sublime*: Keats follows Hazlitt in setting Wordsworth's egotism against Shakespearean empathy and intensity. Here Keats rejects the Wordsworthian mode more clearly than in his letter to Reynolds on the 'Chambers' of human life (3 May 1818, pp. 152–3 above). Keats's thinking here is closely related to his idea of 'Negative Capability' (21, 27 (?) December 1817, p. 79 above).

4 *a thing . . . alone*: See *Troilus and Cressida*, I. ii. 15–16, 'he is a very man per se, / And stands alone.'

5 *lives in gusto*: Drawn from Keats's reading of Hazlitt's essay 'On Gusto', which first appeared in the *Examiner* (26 May 1816): its opening sentence reads, 'Gusto in art is power or passion defining any object.'

delights the camelion Poet. It does no harm from its relish of the dark side of things any more than from its taste for the bright one; because they both end in speculation. A Poet is the most unpoetical of any thing in existence; because he has no Identity—he is continually in for—and filling some other Body—The Sun, the Moon, the Sea and Men and Women who are creatures of impulse are poetical and have about them an unchangeable attribute—the poet has none; no identity—he is certainly the most unpoetical of all God's Creatures. If then he has no self, and if I am a Poet, where is the Wonder that I should say I would write no more? Might I not at that very instant [have] been cogitating on the Characters of Saturn and Ops?[1] It is a wretched thing to confess; but is a very fact that not one word I ever utter can be taken for granted as an opinion growing out of my identical nature—how can it, when I have no nature? When I am in a room with People if I ever am free from speculating on creations of my own brain, then not myself goes home to myself: but the identity of every one in the room begins to to [*for* so] press upon me[2] that, I am in a very little time an[ni]hilated—not only among Men; it would be the same in a Nursery of children: I know not whether I make myself wholly understood: I hope enough so to let you see that no dependence is to be placed on what I said that day.

In the second place I will speak of my views, and of the life I purpose to myself—I am ambitious of doing the world some good: if I should be spared that may be the work of maturer years—in the interval I will assay to reach as high a summit in Poetry as the nerve[3] bestowed upon me will suffer. The faint conceptions I have of Poems to come brings the blood frequently into my forehead—All I hope is that I may

1 *Saturn and Ops*: Protagonists in *Hyperion*: Saturn appears at the poem's start and he rouses Ops at II, 110–17. As Keats was writing the poem at this time, this comment may perhaps be an indication of his progress.

2 *press upon me*: Compare his remark to Dilke on 20 September about Tom's 'identity' pressing upon him and forcing him to 'write, and plunge into abstract images' (p. 237 and n above).

3 *nerve*: 'Strength, vigour, energy' (*OED* 10, *obs*.).

not lose all interest in human affairs—that the solitary indifference I feel for applause even from the finest Spirits, will not blunt any acuteness of vision I may have. I do not think it will—I feel assured I should write from the mere yearning and fondness I have for the Beautiful even if my night's labours should be burnt every morning and no eye ever shine upon them. But even now I am perhaps not speaking from myself: but from some character in whose soul I now live. I am sure however that this next sentence is from myself. I feel your anxiety, good opinion and friendliness in the highest degree, and am

Your's most sincerely
John Keats[1]

To George and Georgiana Keats

(concluded)

31 October 1818

[Saturday, 31 October] Haslam has been here this morning, and has taken all the Letter's except this sheet, which I shall send him by the Twopenny, as he will put the Parcel in the Boston post Bag by the advice of Capper and Hazlewood, who assure him of the safety and expedition that way—the Parcel will be forwarded to Warder[2] and thence to you all the same. There will not be a Philadelphia Ship for these six weeks—by that time I shall have another Letter to you. Mind you I mark this Letter A.[3] By the time you will receive this you will have I trust passed through the greatest of your fatigues. As it was with your Sea sickness I shall not hear of them till they are past. Do not set to your occupation with too great an a[n]xiety—

1 Woodhouse sent a full account of Keats's letter and his ideas on the poetical character to John Taylor shortly after receiving it (see *L*, I, pp. 388–90).

2 *Warder*: John Warder & Sons, shipping agents in Philadelphia.

3 *Letter A*: 'B' is written on the first page of Keats's journal letter of 16 December 1818–4 January 1819.

take it calmly—and let your health be the prime consideration. I hope you will have a Son, and it is one of my first wishes to have him in my Arms—which I will do please God before he cuts one double tooth. Tom is rather more easy than he has been: but is still so nervous that I can not speak to him of these Matters—indeed it is the care I have had to keep his Mind aloof from feelings too acute that has made this Letter so short a one—I did not like to write before him a Letter he knew was to reach your hands—I cannot even now ask him for any Message—his heart speaks to you—Be as happy as you can. Think of me and for my sake be cheerful. Believe me my dear Brother and sister

Your anxious and affectionate Brother

John—

This day is my Birth day—

All our friends have been anxious in their enquiries and all send their rembrances

To James Rice
24 November 1818

[Harvard MS]

My dear Rice, Well Walk—[Tuesday] Novr 24—

Your amende honorable, I must call 'un surcroit d'amitié' for I am not at all sensible of any thing but that you were unfortunately engaged and I was unfortunately in a hurry. I completely understand your feeling in this mistake, and find in it that ballance of comfort which remains after regretting your uneasiness—I have long made up my Mind to take for granted the genuine heartedness of my friends notwithstanding any temporery ambiguousness in their behaviour or their tongues; nothing of which how[ev]er I had the least scent of this morning. I say completely understand; for I am everlastingly getting my mind into such like painful trammels—and am even at this moment suffering under them in the case of a friend of ours. I will tell you—Two most unfortunate and paralel slips—it seems downright preintention. A friend says to me 'Keats I shall go and see Severn this week' 'Ah' says I 'You want him to take your Portrait' and again 'Keats' says a friend 'When will you come to town again' 'I will' says I 'let you have the Mss next Week' In both these I appeard to attribute and [*for* an] interested motive to each of my friends' questions—the first made him flush; the second made him look angry—And yet I am innocent—in both cases my Mind leapt over every interval to what I saw was per se a pleasant subject with him—You see I have no allowances to make—you see how far I am from supposing you could show me any neglect. I very much regret the long time I have been obliged to exile from you—for I have had one or two rather pleasant occasions to confer upon with you—What I have heard from George is favorable—I expect soon a Letter from the Settlement itself—

Your sincere friend
John Keats

I cannot give any good news of Tom—

Tom Keats, whose 'last days . . . were of the most distressing nature', was nursed to the end by Keats. He died at Well Walk 'quietly & without pain' at 8 a.m. on Tuesday, 1 December. Keats left the brothers' lodgings and went to Wentworth Place to give Charles Brown the news. At Keats's request Brown wrote on his behalf to Woodhouse (and no doubt other friends) informing him of Tom's death. Brown suggested that Keats should leave Well Walk and share his half of Wentworth Place, an invitation Keats swiftly accepted. Keats's note to his sister, most probably written shortly after Tom's death, prepares her for the worst.

To Fanny Keats
1 December 1818[1]

[British Library MS]

[?Well Walk]
Tuesday Morn

My dear Fanny,

Poor Tom has been so bad that I have delayed your visit hither—as it would have been so painful to you both. I cannot say he is any better this morning—he is in a very dangerous state—I have scar[c]e any hopes of him—Keep up your spirits for me my dear Fanny—repose entirely in

Your affectionate Brother
John.

1 Rollins dates this letter Monday, 30 November, even though Keats writes 'Tuesday Morn' and it is postmarked 12 a.m., Hampstead, 1 December 1819.

December 1818 to 27 June 1819
Wentworth Place

Keats moved in with Brown and threw himself into social life for the next two weeks. This began with an overnight trip on 4 December to Crawley in Sussex for the long-awaited prize fight between Jack Randall and Ned Turner, returning for Tom's burial in the family church on 7 December. In the next few days Keats saw his sister, the family of George's wife, the Dilkes, Haslam and Haydon, and went to the theatre.

On 15 December he found himself in an embarrassing situation. He appears to have given Mrs Reynolds the impression the previous day that he was free to spend Christmas Day with her and her family. Keats had, however, already accepted an earlier invitation from Mrs Brawne to spend Christmas at her home. His clumsy attempt to rectify any misunderstanding in the following letter can only have reinforced, if it did not occasion, the Reynolds family's dislike of Fanny Brawne.

To Mrs Charlotte Reynolds

15 (?) December 1818

[Princeton MS]

My dear Mrs Reynolds, Wentworth Place Tuesd—

When I left you yesterday, 't was with the conviction that you thought I had received no previous invitation for Christmas day: the truth is I had, and had accepted it under the conviction that I should be in Hampshire[1] at the time: else believe me I should not have done so, but kept in Mind my old friends. I will not speak of the proportion of pleasure I may receive at different Houses—that never enters my head—you may take for a truth that I would have given up even what I did see to be a greater pleasure, for the sake of old acquaintanceship—time is nothing—two years[2] are as long as twenty—

Yours faithfully
John Keats

To George and Georgiana Keats

16, 17, 18, 22, 29 (?), 31 December 1818, 2–4 January 1819

[Harvard MS]

[Wentworth Place, Wednesday, 16 December]

B[3] My dear Brother and Sister,

You will have been prepared, before this reaches you for th<e> worst news you could have, nay if Haslam's letter arrives in proper time, I have a consolation in thinking the first shock will be past before you receive this. The last days of poor Tom were of the most distressing nature; but his last moments were not so painful, and his very last was without a pang—I will not enter into any parsonic comments on death—yet the common observations of the commonest people on death are as true as their proverbs. I have scarce a doubt of immortality of some nature of [*for* or] other—neither had Tom. My friends have been exceedingly kind to me every one of them—Brown detained me at his House. I suppose no one could have had their time made smoother than mine has been. During poor

1 *Christmas day . . . Hampshire*: Keats seems to be saying that he planned to go with Brown to spend Christmas with the Snooks in Hampshire at Bedhampton, and therefore meant to refuse Mrs Brawne's invitation.
2 *two years*: Keats had first met Reynolds in autumn 1816.
3 *B*: Keats had 'marked' his previous letter to George and Georgiana of 14–31 October 1818 as 'A' (pp. 243 ff. above).

Tom's illness I was not able to write and since his death the task of beginning has been a hindrance to me. Within this last week I have been every where—and I will tell you as nearly as possible how all go on—With Dilke and Brown I am quite thick—with Brown indeed I am going to domesticate—that is we shall keep house together—I Shall have the front parlour and he the back one—by which I shall avoid the noise of Bentley's Children[1]—and be the better able to go on with my Studies—which ave [*for* have] been greatly interrupted lately, so that I have not the Shadow of an idea of a book in my head, and my pen seems to have grown too goutty for verse. How are you going on now? The going[s] on of the world make me dizzy—there you are with Birkbeck[2]—here I am with brown—sometimes I fancy an immense separation, and sometimes, as at present, a direct communication of spirit with you. That will be one of the grandeurs of immortality—there will be no space and consequently the only commerce between spirits will be by their intelligence of each other—when they will completely understand each other—while we in this world merely comp[r]ehend each other in different degrees—the highe<r> the degree of good so higher is our Love and friendship—I have been so little used to writing lately that I am affraid you will not smoke my meaning so I will give an extple [*for* example]—Suppose Brown or Haslam or any one whom I understand in the n[e]ther degree to what I do you, were in America, they would be so much the farth<er> from me in proportion as their identity was less impressed upon me. Now the reason why I do not feel at the present moment so far from you is that I rememb<er> your Ways and Manners and actions; I known [*for* know] you[r] manner of thinking, you[r] manner of feeling: I know what shape your joy or your sorrow w<ou>ld take, I know the manner of you[r] walking, standing, sauntering, sitting down, laugh<ing,> punning, and eve[r]y action so truly that you seem

1 *Bentley's Children*: See above, p. 56.

2 *with Birkbeck*: George and Georgiana were not in Birkbeck's Settlement now or later. In autumn 1818 they were living with the Audubons in Henderson, Kentucky, but moved to Louisville in January 1819.

near to me. You will rem<em>ber me in the same manner—and the more when I tell you that I shall read a passage of Shakspeare every Sunday at ten o Clock—you read one <a>t the same time and we shall be as near each other as blind bodies can be in the same room—I saw your Mother the day before yesterday, and intend now frequently to pass half a day with her—she sceem'd [*for* seem'd] tolerably well. I called in Henrietta Street and so was speaking with your Mother about Miss Millar—we had a chat ab<out> Heiresses—she told me I think of 7 or eight dying Swains. Charles was not at home. I think I have heard a little more talk about Miss Keasle—a<ll> I know of her is, she had a new sort of shoe on of bright leather l<i>ke our Kna<p>sacks—Miss Millar gave me one of her confounded pinches. N.B. did not like it. Mrs Dilke went with me to see Fanny last week, and Haslam went with me last Sunday—she was well—she gets a little plumper and had a little Colour. On Sunday I brought from her a present of facescreens and a work bag for Mrs D. they were r<eall>y very pretty—From walthamstow we walked to Bethnal green[1]—w[h]ere I fell so tired from my long walk that I was obliged to go to Bed at ten—Mr and Mrs <. . .> were there—Haslam has been excess<iv>ely kind—and his anxiety about you is great<. I never> meet him but we <ha>ve some chat thereon<.> He is always doing me some good turn—he gave me this thin paper for the purpose of writing to you. I have been passing an hour this morning with Mr Lewis—he wants news of you very much. Haydon was here yesterday—he amused us much by speaking of young Hopner who went with Captn Ross on a voyage of discovery to the Poles[2]—The Ship was sometimes entirely surrounded with vast mountains and crags of ice and in a few Minutes not a particle was to be seen all round the Horizon. Once they met with so

1 *Bethnal green*: Where Haslam lived with his parents.

2 *young Hopner* ... *Poles*: Lieutenant Henry Hoppner (1795–1833) was second in command of the *Alexander*, which accompanied Captain Sir John Ross's *Isabella* on the Arctic expedition that rediscovered Baffin Bay. Their return in November 1818 excited considerable interest in the newspapers. Ross's account of the expedition, *A Voyage of Discovery*, was published in April 1819 with illustrations by Hoppner.

vast a Mass that th[e]y gave themselves over for lost; their last recourse was in meeting it with the Bowsp[r]it, which they did, and split it asunder and glided through it as it parted for a great distance—one Mile ane [*for* and] more Their eyes were so fatigued with the eternal dazzle and whiteness that they lay down on their backs upon the deck to relieve their sight on the blue Sky. Hopner describes his dreadful we[a]riness at the continual day—the sun ever moving in a circle round above their heads—so pressing upon him that he could not rid himself of the sensation even in the dark Hold of the Ship—The Esquimaux are de<s>cribed as the most wretched of Beings—they float from the Summer to their winter residences and back again like white Bears on the ice floats—They seem never to have washed, and so when their features move, the red skin shows beneath the cracking peal of dirt. They had no notion of any inhabitants in the World but themselves. The sailors who had not seen a Star for some time, when they came again southwards, on the hailing of the first revision, of one all ran upon deck with feelings of the most joyful nature. Haydon's eyes will not <s>uffer him to proceed with his Picture—his Physician tells him he must remain two months more, inactive. Hunt keeps on in his old way—I am completely tired of it all—He has lately publish'd a Pocket-Book call'd the litrerary Pocket-Book—full of the most sickening stuff you can imagine.[1] Reynolds is well—he had become an edinburgh Reviewer[2]—I have not heard from Bailey Rice I have seen very little of lately—and I am very sorry for it. The Miss R's[3] are all as usual—Archer[4] above all people called on me one day—he wanted some information, by my

1 *litrerary Pocket-Book . . . imagine*: Despite these comments, Hunt's *Literary Pocket-Book* ('1818' for 1819) first published Keats's 'Four seasons fill the measure of the year' and 'To Ailsa Rock' and was a commercial success, establishing the pattern for the Victorian literary annual.

2 *edinburgh Reviewer*: i.e., writing for the *Edinburgh Review* and not *Blackwood's (Edinburgh) Magazine*.

3 *R's*: Reynoldses.

4 *Archer*: Possibly Archibald Archer, an instructor in portrait painting at the Royal Academy; or John Archer, the partner of Thomas Mower Keats, whose Cheapside hatter's business had been bankrupted (Roe, pp. 289–91).

means, from Hunt and Haydon, concerning some Man they knew. I got him what he wanted, but know none of the whys and wherefores. Poor Kirkman[1] left wentworth place one evening about ha<lf> past eight and was stopped, beaten and robbed of his Watch in Pond Street. I saw him a few days since, he had not recovered from his bruize I called on Hazlitt the day I went to Romney Street—I gave John Hunt[2] extracts from your Letters—he has taken no notice. I have seen Lamb lately—Brown and I were taken by Hunt to Novello's[3]—there we were devastated and excruciated with bad and repeated puns—Brown dont want to go again. We went the other evening to see Brutus a new Trageday by Howard Payne,[4] an American—Kean was excellent—the play was very bad—It is the first time I have been since I went with you to the Lyceum—

Mrs Brawne who took Brown's house for the Summer, still resides in Hampstead—she is a very nice woman—and her daughter senior[5] is <I t>hink beautiful and elegant, graceful, silly, fashionable and strange we <h>ave a li<ttle> tiff now and then—and she behaves a little better, or I mus<t> have sheered off—I find by a sidelong report from your Mother that I am to be invited to Miss Millar's birthday dance—Shall I dance with Miss Waldegrave? Eh! I shall be obliged to shirk a good many there—I s<hall> be the only Dandy there—and indeed I merely comply with the invitation that the party may no[t] be entirely destitute of a specimen of that Race. I shall appear in a

1 *Kirkman*: 'Probably George Buchanan Kirkman [1798–1860], stationer, a relative of George Felton Mathew' (Gittings).

2 *John Hunt*: Leigh Hunt's brother, the publisher and printer of the *Examiner*.

3 *Novello's*: Vincent Novello (1781–1861), a musician and music publisher. The musical evenings he held with his wife Mary in their family home were a fixture in Hunt's literary and musical circle.

4 *Brutus . . . Howard Payne*: *Brutus, or, The Fall of Tarquin* by John Howard Payne (1791–1852) was first performed at Drury Lane on 3 December 1818. A great success, it ran for forty-one nights.

5 *daughter senior*: The first mention of Fanny Brawne in the letters. Mrs Brawne had rented Brown's half of Wentworth Place while he and Keats were walking in Scotland, and was now living nearby with her family at Elm Cottage, Hampstead.

complete dress of purple Hat and all—with a list <of> the beauties I have conquered embroidered round my Calv<es.>

Thursday [17 December] This morning is so very fine, I should have walked over to Walthamstow if I had thought of it yesterday—What are you doing this morning? Have you a clear hard frost as we have? How do you come on with the gun? Have you shot a Buffalo? Have you met with any Pheasants? My Thoughts are very frequently in a foreign Country—I live more out of England than in it—The Mountains of Tartary are a favourite lounge, if I happen to miss the Allegany ridge, or have no whim for Savoy. There must be great pleasure in pursuing game—pointing your gun—no, it wont do—now no—rabbit it—now bang—smoke and feathers—where is it? Shall you be able to get a good pointer or so? Have you seen Mr Trimmer—He is an acquaintance of Peachey's.[1] Now I am not addressing miself to G. minor, and yet I am—for you are one—Have you some warm furs? By your next Letters I shall expect to hear exactly how you go on—smother nothing—let us have all—fair and foul all plain—Will the little bairn have made his entrance before you have this? Kiss it for me, and when it can first know a cheese from a Caterpillar show it my picture twice a Week—You will be glad to hear that Gifford's attack[2] upon me has done me service—it has got my Book among several Sets—Nor must I forget to mention once more, what I suppose Haslam has told you, the present of a £25 note I had anonymously sent me—I have many things to tell you—the best way will be to make coppies of my correspondence; and I must not forget the Sonnet I received with the Note—Last Week I received the following from Woodhouse, whom you must recollect—"My dear Keats,—I send enclosed a Letter which, when read take the trouble to return to me. The History of its reaching me is this. My Cousin, Miss Frogley of Hounslow borrowed my copy of

1 *Peachey's*: James Peachey, a schoolfellow of John and George and trainee solicitor in London, acted as a contact between George and a party of emigrants to Birkbeck's Settlement led by Charles Trimmer (Gigante, pp. 119–20).

2 *Gifford's attack*: i.e., Croker's attack in the *Quarterly* (see above, pp. 240–41).

Endymion for a specified time—Before she had time to look into it; she and my friend Mr H^y Neville of Esher, who was house Surgeon to the late Princess Charlotte, insisted upon having it to read for a day or two, and undertook to make my Cousin's peace with me on account of the extra delay—Neville told me that one of the Misses Porter (of romance Celebrity)[1] had seen it on his table, dipped into it, and expressed a wish to read it—I desired he would keep it as long, and lend it to as many, as he pleased, provided it was not allowed to slumber on any one's shelf. I learned subsequently from Miss Frogley that these Ladies had requested of Mr Neville, if he was acquainted with the Author the Pleasure of an introduction—About a week back the enclosed was transmitted by Mr Neville to my Cousin, as a species of apology for keeping her so long without the Book—And she sent it to me, knowing it would give me Pleasure—I forward it to you for somewhat the same reason, but principally because it gives me the opportunity of naming to you (which It would have been fruitless to do before) the opening there is for an introduction to a class of society, from which you may possibly derive advantage as well as gratification, if you think proper to avail yourself of it. In such case I should be very happy to further your Wishes. But do just as you please. The whole is entirely entre nous—Your's &c—R.W." Well—now this is Miss Porter's Letter to Neville—"Dear Sir, As my Mother is sending a Messenger to Esher, I cannot but make the same the bearer of my regrets for not having had the pleasure of seeing you, the morning you called at the gate—I had given orders to be denied: I was so very unwell with my still adhæsive cold; but had I known it was you I should have taken off the interdict for a few minutes, to say, how very much I am delighted with Endymion—I had just finished the Poem, and have done as you permitted lent it to Miss Fitzgerald. I regret you are not personally acquainted with the Author: for I should have been

1 *Misses Porter . . . Celebrity*: Jane Porter (1776–1850), a novelist now remembered for *The Scottish Chiefs* (1810), but her historical romance *Thaddeus of Warsaw* (1803) was immensely successful in her lifetime. Her sister Anna Maria (1780–1832) was a novelist and poet.

happy to have acknowledged to him, through the advantage of your Communication the very rare delight my Sister and myself have enjoyed this first fruits of Genius. I hope the illnatured Review will not have damaged (or damped) such true Parnassian fire—it ought not to when Life is granted &c" and so she goes on—Now I feel more obliged than flattered by this—so obliged that I will not at present give you an extravaganza of a Lady Romancer. I will be introduced to them if it be merely for the pleasure of writing to you about it—I shall certainly see a new race of People—I shall more certainly have no time for them—Hunt has asked me to meet Tom Moore some day—so you shall hear of him. The night we went to Novello's there was a complete set to of Mozart and punning—I was so completely tired of it that if I were to follow my own inclinations I should never meet any one of that set again, not even Hunt—who is certainly a pleasant fellow in the main when you are with him—but in reallity he is vain, egotistical and disgusting in matters of taste and in morals—He understands many a beautiful thing; but then, instead of giving other minds credit for the same degree of perception as he himself possesses—he begins an explanation in such a curious manner that our taste and self-love is offended continually. Hunt does one harm by making fine things petty and beautiful things hateful—Through him I am indifferent to Mozart, I care not for white Busts—and many a glorious thing when associated with him becames [*for* becomes] a nothing—This distorts one's mind—make[s] one's thoughts bizarre—perplexes one in the standard of Beauty—Martin is very much irritated against Blackwood for printing some Letters in his Magazine which were Martin's property—he always found excuses for Blackwood till he himself was injured and now he is enraged—I have been several times thinking whether or not I should send you the examiners as Birkbeck no doubt has all the good periodical Publications—I will save them at all events.—I must not forget to mention how attentive and useful M[rs] Bentley has been—I am sorry to leave her—but I must, and I hope she will not be much a looser by it—Bentley is very well—he has just brought me a cloathes' basket of Books. Brown has gone to town to day to take his Nephews who are on a visit her[e] to see the Lions—I am passing a Quiet day—which I have not done a long while—and if I do continue so—I feel I must again begin with my poetry—for if I am not in action mind or Body I am in pain—and from that I suffer greatly by going into parties where from the rules of society and a natural pride I am obliged to smother my Spirit and look like an Idiot—because I feel my impulses given way to would too much amaze them—I live under an everlasting restraint—never relieved except when I am composing—so I will write away.

Friday [18 December]. I think you knew before you left England that my next subject would be 'the fall of Hyperion" I went on a little with it last night[1]—but it will take some time to get into the vein again. I will not give you any extracts because I wish the whole to make an impression—I have however a few Poems which you will like and I will copy out on the next sheet—I shall dine with Haydon on Sunday and go over to Walthamstow on Monday if the frost hold—I think also of going into Hampshire this Christmas to Mr Snooks—they say I shall be very much amused—But I dont know[2]—I think I am in too huge a Mind for study—I must do it—I must wait at home, and let those who wish come to see me. I cannot always be (how do you spell it?) trapsing—Here I must tell you I have not been able to keep the journal or write the Tale I promised—now I shall be able to do so—I will write to Haslam this morning to know when the Packet sails and till it does I will write someth[i]ng eve[r]y day—after that my journal shall go on like clockwork—and you must not complain of its dullness—for what I wish is to write a quantity to you—knowing well that dullness itself will from me be interesting to you—You may conceive how this not having been done has weighed upon me—I shall be able to judge from your next what sort of information will be of most service or amusement to you. Perhaps as you were fond of giving me sketches of character you may like a little pic nic of scandal even across the Atlantic—But

1 *the fall of Hyperion . . . last night*: i.e, *Hyperion: A Fragment*, not Keats's later rewriting as *The Fall of Hyperion*.

2 *I think also . . . I dont know*: He did not go until January: see below, p. 298.

now I must speak particularly to you my dear Sister—for I know you love a little quizzing, better than a great bit of apple dumpling—Do you know Uncle Redall?[1] He is a little Man with an innocent, powdered, upright head; he lisps with a protruded under lip—he has two Neices each one would weigh three of him—one for height and the other for breadth—he knew Barttolozzi[2]—he gave a supper and ranged his bottles of wine all up the kitchen and cellar stairs—quite ignorant of what might be drank—it might have been a good joke to pour on the sly bottle after bottle into a washing tub and roar for more—If you were to trip him up it would discompose a Pigtail and bring his under lip nearer to his nose. He never had the good luck to loose a silk Handkerche[i]f in a Crowd and has only one topic of conversation—Bartolotzzi—Shall I give you Miss Brawn? She is about my height—with a fine style of countenance of the lengthen'd sort—she wants sentiment in every feature—she manages to make her hair look well—her nostrills are fine—though a little painful—he[r] mouth is bad and good—he[r] Profil[e] is better than her full-face which indeed is not full put [*for* but] pale and thin without showing any bone—Her shape is very graceful and so are her movements—her Arms are good her hands badish—her feet tolerable—she is not seventeen[3]—but she is ignorant—monstrous in her behaviour flying out in all directions, calling people such names—that I was forced lately to make use of the term Minx—this is I think no[t] from any innate vice but from a penchant she has for acting stylishly. I am however tired of such style and shall decline any more of it—She had a friend to visit her lately—you have known plenty such—Her face is raw as if she was standing out in a frost—her lips raw and seem always ready for a Pullet—she plays the Music without one sensation but the feel of the ivory at her fingers—she is a downright Miss without one set

1 *Uncle Redall*: Keats gives Georgiana Keats a fuller, if sanitized, account of George Reddell's party than he had given his brothers a year earlier (see above, pp. 85).

2 *Barttolozzi*: Francesco Bartolozzi (1728–1815), a famous engraver, worked in London (1764–1801).

3 *not seventeen*: She was eighteen on 9 August 1818.

off—we hated her and smoked her and baited her, and I think drove her away—Miss B— thinks her a Paragon of fashion, and says she is the only woman she would change persons with—What a Stupe—She is superio[r] as a Rose to a Dandelion—When we went to bed Brown observed as he put out the Taper what an ugly old woman that Miss Robinson would make—at which I must have groan'd aloud for I'm sure ten minutes. I have not seen the thing Kingston again—George will describe him to you—I shall insinuate some of these Creatures into a Comedy some day—and perhaps have Hunt among them—

Scene, a little Parlour—enter Hunt— Gattie[1]—Hazlitt—Mrs Novello[2]—Ollier—

Gattie) Ha! Hunt! got into your new house? Ha! Mrs Novello seen Altam and his Wife?[3] Mrs N. Yes (with a grin) its Mr Hunts is'nt it? Gattie. Hunts' no ha! Mr Olier I congratulate you upon the highest compliment I ever heard paid to the Book. Mr Haslit, I hope you are well (Hazlitt—yes Sir, no Sir—Mr Hunt (at the Music) La Biondina &c[4] Hazlitt did you ever hear this—La Biondina &c —Hazlitt—O no Sir—I never—Olier—Do Hunt give it us over again—divino—

Gattie/ divino—Hunt when does your Pocket Book[5] come out—/Hunt/ What is this abso[r]bs me quite? O we are sp[i]nning on a little, we shall floridize soon I hope—Such a thing was very much wanting—people think of nothing but money-getting—now for me I am rather inclined to the liberal side of things—<but> I am reckoned lax in my christian principles —& & & &c

(continued 22 December, p. 281 below)

1 *Gattie*: John Byng Gattie (1788–1828) worked in the Treasury and had a fine tenor voice. With his brothers he was a member of the Hunt and Novello circle. Their sister Maria was married to Edmund Ollier.

2 *Mrs Novello*: Mary (1789–1854), the wife of Vincent Novello.

3 *Altam and his Wife*: Charles Ollier's novel *Altham and his Wife: A Domestic Tale* (1818).

4 *La Biondina &c*: 'La biondina in gondoleto', a popular song by Antonio Lamberti (1757–1832).

5 See above, p. 272 and n.

After putting aside his letter to George and Georgiana on 18 December Keats wrote to Woodhouse thanking him for offering to introduce him as the author of Endymion *to the Misses Porter, but concluded, 'look here Woodhouse—I have a new leaf to turn over—I must work—I must read—I am unable to affrod* [for *afford*] *time for new acquaintances—I am scarcely able to do my duty to those I have'* (L, *I, p. 412). On 21 December he dined with Haydon.*

To B. R. Haydon
22 December 1818

[Harvard MS]

My dear Haydon, Tuesday Wentworth Place—

Upon my Soul I never felt your going out of the room at all—and believe me I never rhodomontade any where but in your Company—my general Life in Society is silence. I feel in myself all the vices of a Poet, irritability, love of effect and admiration—and influenced by such devils I may at times say more rediculous things than I am aware of—but I will put a stop to that in a manner I have long resolved upon—I will buy a gold ring and put it on my finger—and from that time a Man of superior head shall never have occasion to pity me, or one of inferior Nunskull to chuckle at me—I am certainly more for greatness in a Shade than in the open day—I am speaking as a mortal—I should say I value more the Priviledge of seeing great things in loneliness—than the fame of a Prophet—Yet here I am sinning—so I will turn to a thing I have thought on more—I mean you[r] means till your Picture be finished: not only now but for this year and a half have I thought of it. Believe me Haydon I have that sort of fire in my Heart that would sacrifice every thing I have to your service—I speak without any reserve—I know you would so for me—I open my heart to you in a few words—I will do this sooner than you shall be distressed: but let me be the last stay—ask the rich lovers of art first—I'll tell you why—I have a little money which may enable me to study and to travel three or four years[1]—I never expect to get any thing by my Books: and moreover I wish to avoid publishing—I admire Human Nature but I not like Men—I should like to compose things honourable to Man—but not fingerable over by Men. So I am anxious to exist with[out] troubling the printer's devil or drawing upon Men's and Women's admiration—in which great solitude I hope God will give me strength to rejoice Try the long purses—but do not sell your drawing or I shall consider it a breach of friendship. I am sorry I was not at home when Salmon[2] called—Do write and let me know all your present whys and wherefores—

Your's most faithfully
John Keats

To George and Georgiana Keats
(continued)
22, 29 (?), 31 December 1818, 2–4 January 1819

[Tuesday, 22 December 1818] It is some days since I wrote the last page—and what have I been about since I have no Idea—I dined at Haslam's on sunday—with Haydon yesterday and saw Fanny in the morning—she was well—Just now I took out my poem[3] to go on with it—but the thought of my writing so little to you came upon me and I could not get on—so I have began at random—and I have not a word to say—and yet my thoughts are so full of you that I can do nothing else. I shall be confined at Hampstead a few days on account of a sore throat—the first thing I do will be to visit your Mother again—The last time I saw Henry he show'd me his first engraving which I thought capital—M[r] Lewis called this morning and brought some

1 *a little money . . . four years*: Keats was presumably writing in expectation of receiving his share of Tom's estate: on Christmas Eve he asked his publisher for a loan of £30, of which £20 was 'for a friend' (*L*, I, p. 117).
2 *Salmon*: Haydon notes 'My Servant', namely, the six-foot-three Corporal John Salmon, who also served as Haydon's model.
3 *my poem*: *Hyperion*.

american Papers. I have not look'd into them—I think we ought to have heard of you before this—I am in daily expectation of Letters—Nil desperandum—M[rs] [*for* M[r]] Abbey wishes to take Fanny from School—I shall strive all I can against that—There has happened great Misfortune in the Drewe Family—old Drewe has been dead some time; and lately George Drewe expired in a fit[1]—on which account Reynolds has gone into Devonshire—He dined a few days since at Horace Twisse's with Liston[2] and Charles Kemble[3]—I see very little of him now, as I seldom go to little Britain because the Ennui always seizes me there, and John Reynolds is very dull at home—Nor have I seen Rice—How you are going on is a Mystery to me—I hope a few days will clear it up. I never know the day of the Month—

On Christmas Day Keats was with Fanny Brawne and her family at Elm Cottage, Hampstead. Fanny later described this as 'the happiest day I had ever then spent'.

[Tuesday, 29 (?) December 1818] It is very fine here to-day though I expect a Thundercloud or rather a snow cloud in less than an hour—I am at present alone at Wentworth place—Brown being at Chichester[4] and M[r] & M[rs] Dilke making a little stay in Town. I know not what I should do without a Sunshiny morning now and then—it clears up one's spirits—Dilke and I frequently have some chat about you—I have now and then some doubts but he seems to have a great confidence—I think there will soon be perceptible a chance [*for* change] in the fashionable slang literature of the day—it seems to me that Reviews have had their day—that the public have been surfeited—there will soon be some new folly to keep the Parlours in talk—What it is I care not—We have seen three literary Kings in our

1 *Drewe Family . . . a fit*: Reynolds was engaged to Eliza Drewe. Her father William had died in Exeter on 11 November, and her younger brother George died there of an 'apoplexy' on Christmas Day 1818.

2 *Liston*: John Liston (*c*. 1766–1846), a comic actor.

3 *Charles Kemble*: (1775–1854) Actor, theatre manager and Kean's rival.

4 *Brown being at Chichester*: With Charles Dilke's parents.

Time—Scott—Byron—and then the scotch nove<ls>.[1] All now appears to be dead—or I may mistake—literary Bodies may still keep up the Bustle which I do not hear—Haydon show'd me a letter he had received from Tripoli—Ritchey[2] was well and in good Spirits, among Camels, Turbans, Palm Trees and sands—You may remember I promised to send him an Endymion which I did not—howeever he has one—you have one—One is in the Wilds of america—the other is on a Camel's back in the plains of Egypt. I am looking into a Book of Dubois's[3]—he has written directions to the Players—one of them is very good. "In singing never mind the music—observe what time you please. It would be a pretty degradation indeed if you were obliged to confine your genius to the dull regularity of a fiddler—horse hair and cat's guts—no, let him keep your time and play your tune—dodge him"—I will now copy out the Letter and Sonnet I have spoken of—The outside cover was thus directed 'Messrs Taylor and Hessey (Booksellers) No 93 Fleet Street London' and it contained this 'Messrs Taylor and Hessey are requested to forward the enclosed letter by some safe mode of conveyance to the Author of Endymion, who is not known at Teignmouth: or if they have not his address, they will return the letter by post, directed as below, within a fortnight "Mr P. Fenbank P.O. Teignmouth" 9th Novr 1818—In this sheet was enclosed the following—with a superscription 'Mr John Keats Teignmouth'—Then came Sonnet to John Keats—which I would not copy for any in the world but you—who know that I scout "mild light and loveliness" or any such nonsense in myself

1 *Scott—Byron . . . scotch nove<ls>*: Keats is thinking of Scott as both poet and novelist. His authorship of the Waverley novels had been known since spring 1818.
2 *Ritchey*: Keats had met Joseph Ritchie at Haydon's 'immortal dinner' on 28 December 1818 (see above, p. 83).
3 *a Book of Dubois's*: Edward Dubois's *My Pocket Book* (2nd edn 1808).

Star of high promise!—not to this dark age
  Do thy mild light and loveliness belong;—
  For it is blind intolerant and wrong;
Dead to empyreal soarings, and the rage
Of scoffing spirits bitter war doth wage
  With all that bold integrity of song.
  Yet thy clear beam shall shine through ages strong
To ripest times a light—and heritage.
And there breathe now who dote upon thy fame,
  Whom thy wild numbers wrap beyond their being,
Who love the freedom of thy Lays—their aim
  Above the scope of a dull tribe unseeing—
And there is one whose hand will never scant
From his poor store of fruits all thou can'st want.

November, 1818. turn over

I tu[r]n'd over and found a £25-note—Now this appears to me all very proper—if I had refused it—I should have behaved in a very bragadochio dunderheaded manner—and yet the present galls me a little. and I do not know whether I shall not return it if I ever meet with the donor—after whom to no purpose I have written—I have your Min[i]ature on the Table George the great[1]—its very like—though not quite about the upper lip—I wish we had a better of you little George—I must not forget to tell you that a few days since I went with Dilke a shooting on the heath and stot [*for* shot] a Tomtit—There were as many guns abroad as Birds—I intended to have been at Chichester this Wednesday—but on account of this sore throat I wrote him (Brown) my excuse yesterday—
Thursday [31 December] (I will date when I finish—I received a Note from Haslam yesterday—asking if my letter is ready—now this is only the second sheet—notwithstanding all my promises—But you must reflect what hindrances I have had—However on sealing this I shall have nothing to prevent my

1 *Min[i]ature ... George the great*: Joseph Severn's miniature (now in Keats House) is set in a narrow wooden frame covered with cloth, which once had a hinged front cover.

proceeding in a gradual journal—which will increase in a Month to a considerable size. I will insert any little pieces I may write—though I will not give any extracts from my large poem[1] which is scarce began—I what [*for* want] to hear very much whether Poetry and literature in general has gained or lost interest with you—and what sort of writing is of the highest gust with you now. With what sensation do you read Fielding?—and do not Hogarth's pictures seems an old thing to you? Yet you are very little more removed from general association than I am—recollect that no Man can live but in one society at a time—his enjoyment in the different states of human society must depend upon the Powers of his Mind—that is you can imagine a roman triumph, or an olympic game as well as I can. We with our bodily eyes see but the fashion and Manners on one country for one age—and then we die—Now to me manners and customs long since passed whether among the Babylonians or the Bactrians are as real, or eveven [*for* even] more real than those among which I now live—My thoughts have turned lately this way—The more we know the more inadequacy we discover in the world to satisfy us—this is an old observation; but I have made up my Mind never to take any thing for granted—but even to examine the truth of the commonest proverbs—This however is true—Mrs Tighe[2] and Beattie[3] once delighted me—now I see through them and can fine nothing in them—or [only] weakness—and yet how many they still delight! Perhaps a superior being may look upon Shakspeare in the same light—is it possible? No—This same inadequacy is discovered (forgive me little George you know I don't mean to put you in the mess) in Women with few exceptions—the Dress Maker, the blue Stocking and the most charming sentimentalist differ but in a Slight degree, and are equally smokeable—But I'll go no further—I may be speaking sacrilegiously—and on my word I have thought so little that I

1 *my large poem*: *Hyperion*.
2 *Mrs Tighe*: Mary Tighe's *Psyche* (1805, etc.) influenced Keats's early poems.
3 *Beattie*: James Beattie's uncompleted *The Minstrel* (1771–4) foreshadows Wordsworth's *The Prelude*.

have not one opinion upon any thing except in matters of taste—I never can feel certain of any truth but from a clear perception of its Beauty—and I find myself very young minded even in that perceptive power—which I hope will encrease—A year ago I could not understand in the slightest degree Raphael's cartoons[1]—now I begin to read them a little—and how did I lea[r]n to do so? By seeing something done in quite an opposite spirit—I mean a picture Guido's in which all the Saints, instead of that heroic simplicity and unaffected grandeur which they inherit from Raphael, had each of them both in countenance and gesture all the canting, solemn melo dramatic mawkishness of Mackenzie's father Nicholas[2]—When I was last at Haydon's I look[ed] over a Book of Prints taken from the fresco of the Church at Milan the name of which I forget[3]—in it are comprised Specimens of the first and second age of art in Italy—I do not think I ever had a greater treat out of Shakspeare—Full of Romance and the most tender feeling—magnificence of draperies beyond any I ever saw not excepting Raphael's—But Grotesque to a curious pitch—yet still making up a fine whole—even finer to me than more accomplish'd works—as there was left so much room for Imagination. I have not heard one of this last course of Hazlitt's lecture's—They were upon 'Wit and Humour,' the english comic writers.'

Saturday Jan[y] 2nd Yesterday M[r] [and] M[rs] D and myself dined at M[rs] Brawne's—nothing particular passed. I never intend here after to spend any time with Ladies unless they are

1 *Raphael's cartoons*: Two Raphael cartoons were on loan from the Royal collection at the British Institution from 1816. Keats could also have seen engravings of them. He goes on to compare the Renaissance classicism of Raphael (1483–1520) with the (inferior) baroque paintings of Guido Reni (1575–1642).

2 *Mackenzie's father Nicholas*: Henry MacKenzie (1745–1831), the author of *The Man of Feeling* (1771), first published 'The Story of Father Nicholas' in the Edinburgh *Lounger* (16 August–9 September 1786). 'The opposition Keats makes between "grandeur" and "mawkishness" suggests he is still trying to distance his interest in the "human heart" from the effeminate associations of Mackenzie's brand of sensibility' (Mee).

3 *a Book of Prints . . . I forget*: In fact, Carlo Lasinio's *Pitture a fresco del Campo Santo di Pisa* (Florence, 1812).

handsome—you lose time to no purpose—For that reason I shall beg leave to decline going again to Redall's or Butlers or any Squad where a fine feature cannot be mustered among them all—and where all the evening's amusement consists in saying your good health' your good health, and YOUR good health—and (o I beg your pardon) your's Miss ——. and such thing[s] not even dull enough to keep one awake—with respect to amiable speaking I can read—let my eyes be fed or I'll never go out to dinner any where—Perhaps you may have heard of the dinner given to Thos Moore in Dublin, because I have the account here by me in the Philadelphia democratic paper—The most pleasant thing that accured [*for* occurred] was the speech Mr Tom made on his Farthers [*for* Father's] health being drank—I am affraid a great part of my Letters are filled up with promises and what I will do rather than any great deal written—but here I say once for all—that circumstances prevented me from keeping my promise in my last, but now I affirm that as there will be nothing to hinder me I will keep a journal for you. That I have not yet done so you would forgive me if you knew how many hours I have been repenting of my neglect—For I have no thought pervading me so constantly and frequently as that of you—my Poeem[1] cannot frequently drive it away—you will retard it much more that [*for* than] You could by taking up my time if you were in England—I never forget you except after seeing now and then some beautiful woman—but that is a fever—the thought of you both is a passion with me but for the most part a calm one—I asked Dilke for a few lines for you—he has promised them—I shall send what I have written to Haslam on Monday Morning. what I can get into another sheet tomorrow I will—there are one or two little poems you might like—I have given up snuff very nearly quite—Dilke has promised to sit with me this evening, I wish he would come this minute for I want a pinch of snuff very much just now—I have none though in my own snuff box—My sore throat is much better to day—I think I might venture on a crust—Here are the Poems—they will explain themselves—as all poeems should do with out any comment

1 *my Poeem*: *Hyperion*.

Ever let the Fancy roam,[1]
Pleasure never is at home.
At a touch sweet pleasure melteth
Like to bubbles when rain pelteth:
Then let winged fancy wander
To wards heaven still spread beyond her—
Open wide the mind's cage door
She'll dart forth and cloudward soar.
O sweet Fancy, let her loose!
Summer's joys are spoilt by use,
And the enjoying of the spring
Fades as doth its blossoming:
Autumn's red-lipp'd fruitage too
Blushing through the mist and dew
Cloys with kissing. What do then?
Sit thee in an ingle when
The sear faggot blazes bright,
Spirit of a winter night;
When the soundless earth is muffled,
And the caked snow is shuffled
From the Ploughboy's heavy shoon:
When the night doth meet the noon
In a dark conspiracy
To banish vesper from the sky.
Sit thee then and send abroad
With a Mind self overaw'd
Fancy high commission'd; send her,—
She'll have vassals to attend her—
She will bring thee, spite of frost,
Beauties that the Earth has lost;
She will bring thee all together
All delights of summer weather;
All the faery buds of May
On sp[r]ing turf or scented spray;
All the heaped Autumn's wealth
With a still, mysterious stealth;

1 *Ever let the Fancy roam*: Published with some alterations in *1820*.

She will mix these pleasures up,
Like three fit wines in a cup
And thou shalt quaff it—Thou shalt hear
Distant harvest carols clear,
Rustle of the reaped corn
Sweet Birds antheming the Morn;
And in the same moment hark
To the early April lark,
And the rooks with busy caw
Forraging for sticks and straw.
Thou shalt at one glance behold
The daisy and the marigold;
White plumed lillies and the first
Hegd<er>ow primrose that hath burst;
Shaded Hyacynth alway
Sapphire Queen of the Mid-may;—
And every leaf and every flower
Pearled with the same soft shower.
Thou shalt see the fieldmouse creep
Meagre from its celled sleep,
And the snake all winter shrank
Cast its skin on sunny bank;
Freckled nest eggs shalt thou see
Hatching in the hawthorn tree;
When the hen bird's wing doth rest
Quiet on its mossy nest—
Then the hurry and alarm
When the Beehive casts its swa[r]m—
Acorn's ripe down pattering
While the autumn breezes sing,
For the same sleek throated mouse
To store up in its winter house.
O sweet Fancy, let her loose!
Eve[r]y joy is spoilt by use,
Every pleasure, every joy—
Not a Mistress but doth cloy.
Wheere's the cheek that doth not fade
Too much gaz'd at? Where's the Maid

Whose lip mature is ever new?
Where's the eye however blue
Doth not weary? Where's the face
One would meet in every place?
Where's the voice however soft
one would hear too oft and oft?
At a touch sweet pleasure melteth
Like to bubbles when rain pelteth.
Let then winged fancy find
Thee a Mistress to thy mind.
Dulcet-eyed as Cere's[1] daughter
Ere the God of torment taught her
How to frown and how to chide:
With a waist, and with a side
White as Hebe's[2] when her Zone
Slipp'd its golden clasp, and down
Fell her kirtle to her feet,
While she held the goblet sweet,
And Jove grew languid—Mistress fair,
Thou shalt have that tressed hair
Adonis tangled all for spite;
And the mouth he would not kiss,
And the treasure he would miss,
And the hand he would not press,
And the warmth he would distress,
  O the Ravishment—the Bliss!
Fancy has her there she is—
Never fulsome, ever new,
There she steps! and tell me who
Has a Mistress to [*for* so] divine?
Be the palate ne'er so fine
She cannot sicken.
                    Break the Mess [*for* Mesh]
Of the Fancy's silken leash

1 *Cere's*: Proserpine, abducted by Pluto, 'the God of torment'.
2 *Hebe's*: Hebe, goddess and cupbearer to the gods, until she was dismissed by Jupiter for exposing herself.

Where she's tether'd to the heart—
Quickly break her prison string
And such joys as these she'll bring
Let the winged fancy roam
Pleasure never is at home.

I did not think this had been so long a Poem—I have another not so long—but as it will more conveniently be coppied on the other side I will just put down here some observations on Caleb Williams by Hazlitt—I meant to say S[t] Leon for although he has mentioned all of the Novels of Godwin very finely I do not quote them, but this only on account of its being a specimen of his usual abrupt manner, and fiery laconiscism—He says of S[t] Leon[1] 'He is a limb torn off from Society. In possession of eternal youth and beauty, he can feel no love; surrounded, tantalized and tormented with riches, he can do no good. The faces[2] of Men pass before him as in a speculum; but he is attached to them by no common tie of sympathy or suffering. He is thrown back into himself and his own thoughts. He lives in the solitude of his own breast,—without wife or child or friend or Enemy in the world. <u>His is the solitude of the Soul, not of woods, or trees or mountains</u>—but the desert of society—the waste and oblivi[on] of the heart. He is himself alone. His existence is purely intellectual, and is therefore intolerable to one who has felt the rapture of affection, or the anguish of woe..' As I am about it I might as well give you his caracter of Godwin as a Romancer "Whoever else is, it is pretty clear that the author of Caleb Williams is not the Author of waverley. Nothing can be more distinct or excellent in their several ways than these two writers. If the one owes almost every thing to external observation and traditional character, the other owes every thing to internal conception and contemplation of the possible workings of the human Mind. There is little knowledge of the world,

1 *a specimen . . . S[t] Leon*: Keats's two quotations from Hazlitt's views on William Godwin's *St Leon* (1799) and his other novels are from the *Examiner* (27 December 1818), pp. 825–6, which printed an extract from his *Lectures on the English Comic Writers*, which Keats had been unable to attend.
2 *faces*: Hazlitt has 'races'.

little variety, neither an eye for the picturesque, nor a talent for the humourous in Caleb Williams, for instance, but you can not doubt for a moment of the originality of the work and the force of the conception. The impression made upon the reader is the exact measure of the strength of the authors genius. For the effect both in Caleb Williams and S[t] Leon, is entirely made out, not by facts nor dates, by blackletter or magazine learning, by transcript nor record, but by intense and patient study of the human heart, and by an imagination projecting itself into certain situations, and capable of working up its imaginary feelings to the height of reality." This appears to me quite correct—now I will copy the other Poem—it is on the double immortality of Poets—

Bards of Passion and of Mirth[1]
Ye have left your souls on earth—
Have ye souls in heaven too
Double liv'd in regions new?
Yes—and those of heaven commune
With the s[p]heres of Sun & Moon;
With the noise of fountains wondrous,
And the parle of voices thundrous;
With the Whisper of heavens trees,
And one anothers, in soft ease
Seated on elysian Lawns,
Browsed by none but Dian's fawns;
Underneath large bluebells tented
Where the daisies are rose scented,
And the rose herself has got
Perfume that on earth is not.
Where the nightingale doth sing
Not a senseless tranced thing;
But melodious truth divine
Philosophic numbers fine;
Tales and golden histories
Of Heaven and its Mysteries.
    Thus ye live on Earth and then

1 *Bards of Passion and of Mirth*: Published with some alterations in *1820*.

On the Earth ye live again;
And the souls ye left behind you
Teach us here the way to find you,
Where your other Souls are joying
Never slumber'd, never cloying.
Here your earth born souls still speak
To mortals of the little week
They must sojourn with their cares;
Of their sorrows and delights
Of their Passions and their spites;
Of their glory and their shame—
What doth strengthen and what maim.
Thus ye teach us every day
Wisdom though fled far away.
  Bards of Passion and of Mirth
Ye have left your Souls on Earth
Ye have souls in heaven too
Double liv'd in Regions new!

These are specimens of a sort of rondeau which I think I shall become partial to—because you have one idea amplified with greater ease and more delight and freedom than in the sonnet—It is my intention to wait a few years before I publish any minor poems—and then I hope to have a volume of some worth—and which those people will realish who cannot bear the burthen of a long poem—In my journal I intend to copy the poems I write the days they are written—there is just room I see in this page to copy a little thing I wrote off to some Music as it was playing—

I had a dove and the sweet dove died,[1]
  And I have thought it died of grieving:
O what could it mourn for? it was tied
  With a silken thread of my own hands weaving.
Sweet little red-feet why did you die?
Why would you leave me—sweet dove why?

1 *I had a dove . . . died*: First published in *1848*. Possibly written for Fanny Keats.

You liv'd alone on the forest tree
Why pretty thing could you not live with me?
I kiss'd you oft, and I gave you white peas—
Why not live sweet<ly as> in the green trees—

Sunday [3 January 1819].

I have been dining with Dilke to day—He is up to his Ears in Walpole's letters Mr Manker[1] is there; I have come round to see if I can conjure up any thing for you—Kirkman came down to see me this morning—his family have been very badly off lately—He told me of a villainous trick of his Uncle William in Newgate Street who became sole Creditor to his father under pretence of serving him, and put an execution on his own Sister's goods—He went in to the family at Portsmouth; conversed with them, went out and sent in the Sherif's officer—He tells me too of abominable behaviour of Archer to Caroline Mathew[2]—Archer has lived nearly at the Mathews these two years; he has been amusing Caroline all this time—and now he has written a Letter to Mrs M— declining on pretence of inability to support a wife as he would wish, all thoughts of marriage. What is the worst is, Caroline is 27 years old—It is an abominable matter—He has called upon me twice lately—I was out both times—What can it be for—There is a letter to day in the Examiner to the Electors of westminster on Mr Hobhouse's account—In it there is a good Character of Cobbet[3]—I have not the paper by me or I would copy it—I do not think I

1 *Mr Manker*: John (?) Mancur, who acted as Brown's literary and financial agent. Probably a friend of Dilke, who was editing Horace Walpole's letters, published by John Martin's firm in four volumes as *The Private Correspondence of Horace Walpole, Earl of Orford* (1820).

2 *Archer to Caroline Mathew*: Kirkman was a relative of the Mathew sisters. Keats's verses addressed to Caroline Mathew (who was actually twenty-six) and her sister Ann were published in *Poems* (1817). They were cousins of George Felton Mathew, briefly a poetic friend of Keats. For Archer and his earlier approach to Keats, see above, pp. 272–3.

3 *Electors of westminster . . . Character of Cobbet*: The letter 'To the Electors of Westminster' in the *Examiner* (3 January 1819), pp. 2–6, supported the candidacy of John Cam Hobhouse (1786–1869), friend of Byron, and one of two reformist candidates. They split the vote in February, letting in the Whig George Lamb. William Cobbett (1762–1835), author and publisher of the

have mentioned the Discovery of an african kingdom—the account is much the same as the first accounts of Mexico—all magnificence—there is a Book being written about it[1]—I will read it and give you the cream in my next. The ramance we have heard upon it runs thus: they have window frames of gold—100,000 infantry—human sacrifices—The Gentleman who is the adventurer has his wife with him—she I am told is a beautiful little sylphid woman—her husband was to ha<v>e been sacrificed to their Gods and was led through a Chamber filled with different instruments of torture with priveledge to choose what death he would die, without their having a thought of his aversion to such a death they considering it a supreme distinction—However he was let off and became a favorite with the King, who at last openly patronised him; thoug<h> at first on account of the Jealousy of his Ministers he was wont to hold conversations with his Majesty in the dark middle of the night—All this sounds a little Bluebeardish—but I hope it is true—There is another thing I must mention of the momentous kind;—but I must mind my periods in it—Mrs Dilke has two Cats—a Mother and a Daughter—now the Mother is a tabby and the daughter a black and white like the spotted child—Now it appears ominous to me for the doors of both houses are opened frequently—so that there is a complete thorough fare for both Cats (there being no board up to the contrary) they may one and several of them come into my room ad libitum. But no—the Tabby only comes—whether from sympathy from ann the mai<d> or me I can not tell—or whether Brown has left behind him any atmospheric sp[i]rit of Maidenhood I can not tell. The Cat is not an old Maid herself—her daughter is a proof of it—I have questioned her—I have look'd at the lines of her paw—I have felt her pulse—to no purpose—Why should the old Cat come to me? I ask myself—and myself

Political Register (1802–35), originally a Conservative paper reaching a new mass readership, had embraced the cause for radical reform.

1 *a Book being written about it*: Thomas Bowdich (1791–1824) published his *Mission from Cape Coast Castle to Ashantee* (1819) the following month: Keats's 'ramance' account is a fanciful embroidery.

has not a word to answer. It may come to light some day; if it does you shall hear of it<.> Kirkman this morning promised to write few lines for you and send them to Haslam. I do not think I have any thing to say in the Business way—You will let me know what you would wish done with your property in England—What things you would wish sent out—but I am quite in the dark about what you are doing—if I do not hear soon I shall put on my Wings and be after you—I will in my next, and after I have seen your next letter—tell you my own particular idea of America. Your next letter will be the key by which I shall open your hearts and see what spaces want filling, with any particular information—Whether the affairs of Europe are more or less interesting to you—whether you would like to hear of the Theatre's—of the bear Garden—of the Boxers—the Painters—The Lecturers—the Dress—The Progress of Dandyism—The Progress of Courtship—or the fate of Mary Millar—being a full true and très particular account of Miss M's ten Suitors—How the first tried the effect of swearing; the second of stammering; the thi[r]d of whispering;—the fourth of sonnets—the fifth of spanish leather boots the sixth of flattering her body—the seventh of flattering her mind—the eighth of flattering himself—the ninth stuck to the Mother—the tenth kissed the Chambermaid and told her to tell her Mistress—But he was soon discharged his reading lead him into an error—he could not sport the Sir Lucius[1] to any advantage—And now for this time I bid you good by—I have been thing [*for* thinking] of these sheets so long that I appear in closing them to take my leave of you—but that is not it—I shall immediatly as I send this off begin my journal—when some days <I> shall write no more than 10 lines and others 10 times as much<.> Mrs Dilke is knocking at the wall for Tea is ready—I will tell you what sort of tea it is and then bid you—Good bye—

This is monday morning [4 January]—no thing particular

1 *Sir Lucius*: The Irishman Sir Lucius O'Trigger in Sheridan's *The Rivals* (1775).

happened yesterday evening, except that <just> when the tray came up M[rs] Dilke and I had a battle with celery stalks—she sends her love to you—I shall close this and send it immediately to Haslam—remaining ever

My dearest brother and sister
Your most affectionate Brother
John—

To B. R. Haydon
10 (?) January 1819

[Harvard MS]

My dear Haydon, Wentworth place [Sunday]

We are very unlucky—I should have stopped to dine with you, but I knew I should not have been able to leave you in time for my plaguy sore throat; which is getting well—

I shall have a little trouble in procuring the Money[1] and a great ordeal to go through—No trouble indeed to any one else—or ordeal either—I mean I shall have to go to town some thrice, and stand in the Bank an hour or two—to me worse than any thing in Dante—I should have less chance with the people around me than Orpheus had with the Stones—I have been writing a little now and then lately: but nothing to speak of—being discontented and as it were moulting—yet I do not think I shall ever come to the rope or the Pistol: for after a day or two's melancholy, although I smoke more and more my own insufficiency—I see by little and little more of what is to be done, and how it is to be done, should I ever be able to do it— On my Soul there should be some reward for that continual 'agonie ennuíyeuse." I was thinking of going into Hampshire for a few days. I have been delaying it longer than I

1 *procuring the Money*: Keats was attempting to raise £500 of his own money from Abbey to lend to Haydon against a bond (*L*, II, p. 40). His inability to do so led to ill-feeling on both sides.

intended—You shall see me soon; and do not be at all anxious, for this time I really will do, what I never did before in my life, business in good time, and properly—With respect to the Bond—it may be a satisfaction to you, to let me have it: but as you do love me do not let there be any mention of interest, although we are mortal men—and bind ourselves for fear of death—

Your's for ever
John Keats

On 18 or 19 January Keats finally made his journey to Hampshire, joining Brown in Chichester at the home of Charles Dilke's father. The two men left shortly afterwards to stay with the Snook family at Bedhampton, where Keats was ill much of the time. Even so, he went to the consecration of the chapel in Stansted Park. This contributed to the vivid window imagery in 'The Eve of St Agnes', whose first draft he completed before returning to Wentworth Place at the beginning of February.

To Fanny Keats

11 February 1819

[British Library MS]

My dear Fanny, Wentworth Place—
Feb^{y}—Thursday—

Your Letter to me at Bedhampton hurt me very much,—What objection can the[r]e be to your receiving a Letter from me? At Bedhampton I was unwell and did not go out of the Garden Gate but twice or thrice during the fortnight I was there—Since I came back I have been taking care of myself—I have been obliged to do so, and am now in hopes that by this care I shall get rid of a sore throat which has haunted me at intervals nearly a twelvemonth. I had always a presentiment of not being able to succeed in persuading Mr Abbey to let you remain longer at School—I am very sorry he will not consent. I recommend you to keep up all that you know and to learn more by yourself however little. The time will come when you will be more pleased with Life—look forward to that time and, though it may appear a trifle, be careful not to let the idle and retired Life you lead fix any awkward habit or behaviour on you—whether you Sit or walk—endeavour to let it be in a seemely and if possible a graceful manner. We have been very little together: but you have not the less been with me in thought—You have no one in the world besides me who would sacrifice any thing for you—I feel myself the only Protector you have. In all your little troubles think of me with the thought that there is at least one person in England who if he could would help you out of them—I live in hopes of being able to make you happy—I should not perhaps write in this manner, if it were not for the fear of not being able to see you often, or long together—I am in hopes Mr Abbey will not object any more to your receiving a letter now and then from me—How unreasonable!—I want a few more lines from you for George—there are some young Men, acquaintances of a Schoolfellow of mine, going out to Birkbeck's at the latter end of this Month—I am in expectation every day of hearing from George—I begin to fear his last letters Miscarried. I shall be in town tomorrow—if you should not be in town, I shall send this little parcel by the Walthamstow Coach. I think you will like Goldsmith.[1] Write me soon—

Your affectionate Brother
John—

Mrs Dilke has not been very well—she is gone a walk to town to day for exercise

1 *Goldsmith*: Fanny's copy of *Goldsmith's Poems and Essays* (1817), inscribed 'Fanny M. Keats from her affectionate Brother John', is at Harvard.

4. *Journal letter to George and Georgiana Keats, 14 February–5 May 1819, p. 1, 22.6 × 18.5 cm*

To George and Georgiana Keats
14, 19 February, 3 (?), 12, 13, 17, 19 March, 15, 16, 21, 30 April, 4, 5 May 1819

[Harvard MS][1]

Letter C— [Wentworth Place] sunday Morn Feby 14— My dear Brother & Sister—How is it we have not heard from you from the Settlement yet? The Letters must surely have miscarried—I am in expectation every day—Peachey wrote me a few days ago saying some more acquaintances of his were preparing to set out for Birkbeck—therefore I shall take the opportunity of sending you what I can muster in a sheet or two—I am still at Wentworth Place—indeed I have kept in doors lately, resolved if possible to rid myself of my sore throat—consequently i have not been to see your Mother since my return from Chichester—but my absence from her has been a great weight upon me—I say since my return from Chichester—I believe I told you I was going thither—I was nearly a fortnight at Mr John Snook's and a few days at old Mr Dilke's[2]—Nothing worth speaking of happened at either place—I took down some of the thin paper and wrote on it a little Poem call'd 'St Agnes Eve'—which you shall have as it is when I have finished the blank part of the rest for you—I went out twice at Chichester to old Dowager card parties—I see very little now, and very few Persons—being almost tired of Men and things—Brown and Dilke are very kind and considerate towards me—The Miss Reynoldses have been stoppi[n]g next door lately—but all very

1 The final sheet of this letter, mostly written on 4 and 5 May 1819 (pp. 366–7 below), substantially corrects Jeffrey's transcript of the part written on 4 and 5 May, mistakenly dated 3 May, the source of Rollins's text. The autograph nevertheless still lacks one sheet, the text of which is based on Jeffrey's transcript (see below, p. 312 n). The final sheet was donated to Harvard in 1995.
2 *Mr John Snook's . . . Mr Dilke's*: John Snook (1780–1863), a farmer, miller and baker, lived at the Old Mill House, Bedhampton. He was a friend of Brown's and was married to Charles Dilke's sister. Dilke's father and mother lived in Chichester.

dull—Miss Brawne and I have every now and then a chat and a tiff—Brown and Dilke are walking round their Garden hands in Pockets making observations. The Literary world I know nothing about—There is a Poem from Rogers dead born—and another satire is expected from Byron call'd Don Giovanni[1]—Yesterday I went to town for the first time for these three weeks—I met people from all parts and of all sets—Mr Towers[2]—one of the Holts—Mr Domine Williams—Mr Woodhouse Mrs Hazlitt and Son—Mrs Webb—Mrs Septimus Brown—Mr Woodhouse was looking up at a Book-window in newgate street and being short-sighted twisted his Muscles into so queer a stupe[3] that I stood by in doubt whether it was him or his brother, if he has one and turning round saw Mr[s] Hazlitt with that little Nero her son—Woodhouse on his features subsiding proved to be Woodhouse and not his Brother—I have had a little business with Mr Abbey—From time to time he has behaved to me with a little Brusquerie—this hurt me a little especially wheen I knew him to be the only Man in England who dared to say a thing to me I did not approve of without its being resented or at least noticed—so I wrote him about it and have made an alteration in my favor—I expect from this to see more of Fanny—who has been quite shut out from me. I see Cobbet has been attacking the Settlement[4]—but I cannot tell what to believe—and shall be all out at elbous till I hear from you. I am invited to Miss Millar's Birthday dance on the 19th I am nearly sure I shall no<t> be able to go—a Dance would injure my throat very much. I see very little of Reynolds. Hunt I hear is going on very badly—I mean in money Matters I shall

1 *a Poem ... dead born*: Samuel Rogers's *Human Life* (1819) was well received. *Don Giovanni*: Although *Don Juan* (Cantos I–II) was published in July 1819 anonymously and without Murray's name as publisher, its authorship was known in literary London.

2 *Mr Towers*: The husband of Charles Cowden Clarke's sister Isabella.

3 *stupe*: Here, a piece of flannel, etc., wrung out, medicated and used for fomenting a wound, etc. (OED).

4 *Cobbet ... the Settlement*: Cobbett questioned the wisdom of Birkbeck's Settlement in his *Political Register* (6 and 13 February 1819). He was not alone in doing so.

not be surprised to hear of the worst—Haydon too in consequence of his eyes is out at elbows. I live as prudently as it is possible for me to do. I have not seen Haslam lately—I have not seen Richards for this half year—Rice for three Months or C C. C. for god knows when—When I last called in Hen[r]ietta Street—M[rs] Millar was verry unwell—Miss Waldegrave as staid and self possessed as usual—Miss Millar was well—Henry was well—There are two new tragedies—one by the Apostate Man,[1] and one by Miss Jane Porter[2]—Next week I am going to stop at Taylor's for a few days when I will see them bothe and tell you what they are—M[rs] and M[r] Bentley are well and all the young Carrots. I said nothing of consequence passed at Snook's—no more than this that I like the family very much M[r] and M[rs] Snook were very kind—we used to have over a little Religion and politicts together almost every evening—and sometimes about you—He proposed writing out for me all the best part of his experience in farming to send to you if I should have an opportunity of talking to him about it I will get all I can at all events—but you may say in your answer to this what value you place upon such information. I have not seen M[r] Lewis lately for I have shrunk from going up the hill—M[r] Lewis went a few morning[s] ago to town with M[rs] Brawne they talked about me—and I heard that M[r] L Said a thing I am not at all contented with—Says he 'O, he is quite the little Poet' now this is abominable—you might as well say Buonaparte is quite the little Soldier—You see what it is to be under six foot and not a lord—There is a long fuzz to day in the examiner about a young Man who delighted a young woman with a Valentine—I think it must be Ollier's.[3] Brown and I are thinking of passing the summer at Brussels if we do we shall go

1 *the Apostate Man*: Richard Lalor Sheil (1791–1851), writer and politician, whose *The Apostate* was first performed in 1817; his *Evadne*, produced at Covent Garden on 10 February 1819, was a success despite Keats's later comments (p. 312–13 below).

2 *Miss Jane Porter*: Her tragedy *Switzerland* had a single performance at Drury Lane on 15 February.

3 *Valentine . . . Ollier's*: Charles Lamb, not Ollier, published 'Valentine's Day – (14th of February)' in the *Examiner* (14 February 1819), p. 108.

about the first of May—We i e Brown and I sit opposite one another all day authori_z_ing (N. B. an s instead of a z would give a different meaning) He is at present writing a Story of an old Woman who lived in a forest and to whom the Devil or one [of] his Aid de feus came one night very late and in disguise—The old Dame sets before him pudding after pudding—mess after mess—which he devours and moreover casts his eyes up at a side of Bacon hanging over his head and at the same times [*for* time] asks whither her Cat is a Rabbit—On going he leaves her three pips of eve's apple—and some how—she, having liv'd a virgin all her life, begins to repent of it and wishes herself beautiful enough to make all the world and even the other world fall in love with her—So it happens—she sets out from her smoaky Cottage in magnificent apparel; the first city She enters eve[r]y one falls in love with her—from the Prince to the Blacksmith. A young gentleman on his way to the church to be married leaves his unfortunate Bride and follows this nonsuch—A whole regiment of soldiers are smitten at once and follow her—A whole convent of Monks in corpus christi procession join the Soldiers—The Mayor and Corporation follow the same road—Old and young, deaf and dumb—all but the blind are smitten and form an immense concourse of people who—what Brown will do with them I know not—The devil himself falls in love with her flies away with her to a desert place—in consequence of which she lays an infinite number of Eggs—The Eggs being hatched from time to time fill the world with many nuisances such as John Knox—George Fox—Johanna Southcote—Gifford[1]—There have been within a fortnight eight failures of the highest consequence in London—Brown went a few evenings since to Davenport's[2] and on his coming in he talk'd about bad news in the City with such a face, I began

1 *Gifford*: William Gifford (in mistake for J. W. Croker) is characterized as a fanatic like the Calvinist John Knox (*c.* 1505–72); the Quaker George Fox (1624–91); and the prophet Joanna Southcott (1750–1814).

2 *Davenport's*: Burridge Davenport, a merchant in Mincing Lane, lived at 2 Church Row, Hampstead. He and his family were kind to Tom Keats in his final illness, and continued to be friendly towards Keats and later Fanny Brawne.

to think of a national Bankruptcy—I did not feel much surprised—and was rather disappointed. Carlisle, a Bookseller on the Hone principle has been issuing Pamphlets from his shop in fleet Street Called the Deist—he was conveyed to Newgate last Thursday—he intends making his own defence.[1] I was surprised to hear from Taylor the amount of Murray the Booksellers last sale—what think you of £25,000? He sold 4000 coppies of Lord Byron.[2] I am sitting opposite the Shakspeare I brought from the Isle of wight—and I never look at it but the silk tassels on it give me as much pleasure as the face of the Poet itself—except that I do not know how you are going on—In my next Packet as this is one by the way, I shall send you the Pot of Basil, St Agnes eve, and if I should have finished it a little thing call'd the 'eve of St Mark'[3] you see what fine mother Radcliff names I have—it is not my fault—I did not search for them—I have not gone on with Hyperion—for to tell the truth I have not been in great cue for writing lately—I must wait for the sp[r]ing to rouse me up a little—The only time I went out from Bedhampton was to see a Chapel consecrated—Brown I and John Snook the Boy, went in a chaise behind a leaden horse Brown drove, but the horse did not mind him—This Chapel is built by a Mr Way[4] a great Jew converter—who in that line has spent one hundred thousand Pounds—He maintains a great number of poor Jews—Of course his communion plate was stolen—he spoke to the Clerk about it—The Clerk said he was very sorry adding—'I dare shay your honour its among ush' The Chapel is built in Mr Way's park—The Consecration was—not amusing—there were numbers of carriages, and his house

1 *Carlisle . . . own defence*: For Keats's later and fuller account of Richard Carlile, see below, pp. 424–5. *Hone*: For William Hone, see above, p. 78.

2 *4000 coppies of Lord Byron*: The concluding Canto 4 of *Childe Harold's Pilgrimage* (1818).

3 *eve of St Mark*: Keats wrote 'The Eve of St Mark' on '13/17 Feby 1819' (Woodhouse, *Texts*).

4 *Mr Way*: Lewis Way (1772–1840), a lay minister and religious activist, spent much of his inherited wealth in attempting to convert Jews to Christianity. His chapel in Stansted Park was consecrated on 25 January 1819. Its Gothic windows may have influenced the imagery in 'The Eve of St Agnes', ll. 208–16.

crammed with Clergy—they sanctified the Chapel—and it being a wet day consecrated the burial ground through the vestry window. I begin to hate Parsons—they did not make me love them that day—when I saw them in their proper colours—A Parson is a Lamb in a drawing room and a lion in a Vestry—The notions of Society will not permit a Parson to give way to his temper in any shape—so he festers in himself—his features get a peculiar diabolical self sufficient iron stupid exp[r]ession—He is continually acting—His mind is against every Man and every Mans mind is against him—He is an Hippocrite to the Believer and a Coward to the unbeliever—He must be either a Knave or an Ideot—And there is no Man so much to be pitied as an ideot parson—The soldier who is cheated into an esprit du corps—by a red coat, a Band and Colours for the purpose of nothing—is not half so pitiable as the Parson who is led by the nose by the Bench of Bishops—and is smothered in absurdities—a poor necessary subaltern of the Church—

(continued 19 February 1819, p. 307 below)

To B. R. Haydon
18 (?) February 1819

[Harvard MS]

Wentworth Place—

My dear Haydon, [?Thursday, 18 February]

My throat has not suffered me yet to expose myself to the night air: however I have been to town in the day time—have had several interviews with my guardian—have written him a rather plain spoken Letter—which has had its effect; and he now seems inclined to put no stumbling block in my way: so that I see a good prospect of performing my promise What I should have lent you ere this if I could have got it, was belonging to poor Tom—and the difficulty is whether I am to inherit it before my Sister is of age; a period of six years—Should it be so I must incontinently take to Corderoy Trowsers. But I am nearly confident 't is all a Bam[1]—I shall see you soon—but do let me have a line to day or tomorrow concerning your health and spirits

Your sincere friend
John Keats

To George and Georgiana Keats

(continued)

19 February 1819

Friday Feby 18 [*for* 19]—The day before yesterday I went to Romney Street—your Mother[2] was not at home—but I have just written her that I shall see her on wednesday. I call'd on Mr Lewis this morning—he is very well—and tells me not to be uneasy about Letters the chances being so arbitrary—He is going on as usual among his favorite democrat papers—We had a chat as usual about Cobbett: and the westminster electors. Dilke has lately been verry much harrassed about the manner of educating his Son—he at length decided for a public school—and then he did not know what school—he at last has decided for Westminster; and as Charley is to be a day boy, Dilke will remove to Westminster. We lead verry quiet lives here—Dilke is at present in greek histories and antiquit[i]es—and talks of nothing but the electors of Westminster and the retreat of the ten-thousand—I never drink now above three glasses of wine—and never any spirits and water. Though by the bye the other day—Woodhouse took me to his coffee house—and ordered a Bottle of Claret—now I like Claret whenever I can have Claret I must drink it.—'t is the only palate affair that I am at all sensual in—Would it not be a good Speck to send you some vine roots—could I [*for* it] be done? I'll enquire—If you could make some wine like Claret to d[r]ink

1 *a Bam*: A hoax.
2 *your Mother*: Mrs James Wylie, Georgiana's mother, lived at 3 Romney Street, Westminster, with her son Charles.

on summer evenings in an arbour! For really 't is so fine—it fills the mouth one's mouth with a gushing freshness—then goes down cool and feverless—then you do not feel it quarrelling with your liver—no it is rather a Peace maker and lies as quiet as it did in the grape—then it is as fragrant as the Queen Bee; and the more ethereal Part of it mounts into the brain, not assaulting the cerebral apartments like a bully in a bad house looking for his trul and hurrying from door to door bouncing against the waistcoat [*for* wainscot]; but rather walks like Aladin about his own enchanted palace so gently that you do not feel his step—Other wines of a heavy and spirituous nature transform a Man to a Silenus; this makes him a Hermes—and gives a Woman the soul and imortality of Ariadne for whom Bacchus always kept a good cellar of claret—and even of that he could never persuade her to take above two cups—I said this same Claret is the only palate-passion I have I forgot game I must plead guilty to the breast of a Partridge, the back of a hare, the backbone of a grouse, the wing and side of a Pheasant and a Woodcock passim Talking of game (I wish I could make it) the Lady whom I met at Hastings and of whom I said something in my last I think,[1] has lately made me many presents of game, and enabled me to make as many—She made me take home Pheasant the other day which I gave to Mrs Dilke; on which, tomorrow, Rice, Reynolds and the Wentworthians will dine next door—The next I intend for your Mother. These moderate sheets of paper are much more pleasant to write upon than those large thin sheets which I hope you by this time have received—thought [*for* though] that cant be now I think of it—I have not said in any Letter yet a word about my affairs—in a word I am in no despair about them—my poem has not at all succeeded—in the course of a year or so I think I shall try the public again—in a selfish point of view I should suffer my pride and my contempt of public opinion to hold me silent—but for your's and fanny's sake I will pluck up a spirit, and try again—I have no doubt of success in a course of years if I persevere—but it must be patience—for the Reviews have

1 *the Lady . . . I think*: Mrs Isabella Jones (see above, pp. 256–8).

enervated and made indolent mens minds—few think for themselves—These Reviews too are getting more and more powerful and especially the Quarterly—They are like a superstition which the more it prostrates the Crowd and the longer it continues the more powerful it becomes just in proportion to their increasing weakness—I was in hopes that when people saw, as they must do now, all the trickery and iniquity of these Plagues they would scout them, but no they are like the spectators at the Westminster cock-pit—they like the battle and do not care who wins or who looses—Brown is going on this morning with the story of his old woman and the Devil—He makes but slow progress—the fact is it is a Libel on the Devil and as that person is Brown's Muse, look ye, if he libels his own Muse how can he expect to write—Either Brown or his muse must turn tale—Yesterday was Charley Dilkes birth day—Brown and I were invited to tea—During the evening noth[i]ng passed worth notice but a little conversation between Mrs Dilke and Mrs Brawne—The subject was the watchman—It was ten o'Clock and Mrs Brawne who lived during the summer in Brown's house and now lives in the Road, recognized her old Watchman's voice and said that he came as far as her now: 'indeed'; said 'Mrs D. 'does he turn the Corner?' There have been some Letters pass between me and Haslam: but I have not seen him lately—the day before yesterday—which I made a day of Business, I call'd upon him—he was out as usual—Brown has been walking up and down the room a breeding—now at this moment he is being delivered of a couplet—and I dare say will be as well as can be expected—Gracious—he has twins! I have a long Story to tell you about Bailey—I will say first the circumstances as plainly and as well as I can remember, and then I will make my comment. You know that Bailey was very much cut up about a little Jilt in the country somewhere; I thought he was in a dying state about it when at Oxford with him: little supposing as I have since heard, that he was at that very time making impatient Love to Marian Reynolds—and guess my astonishment at hearing after this that he had been trying at Miss Martin[1]—So matters have been. So Matters stood—when he got ordained and went to a Curacy near Carlisle where the family of the Gleigs reside—There his susceptible heart was conquered by Miss Gleig[2]—and thereby all his connections in town have been annulled—both male and female—I do not now remember clearly the facts—These however I know—He showed his correspondence with Marian to Gleig—return[e]d all her Letters and asked for his own—he also wrote very abrubt Letters to M[rs] Reynolds—I do know any more of the Martin affair than I have written above—No doubt his conduct has been verry bad. The great thing to be considered is—whether it is want of delicacy and principle or want of Knowledge and polite experience—And again Weakness—yes that is it—and the want of a Wife—yes that is it—and then Marian made great Bones of him, although her Mother and sister have teased her very much about it. Her conduct has been very upright throughout the whole affair—She liked Bailey as a Brother—but not as a Husband—especially as he used to woo her with the Bible and Jeremy Taylor under his arm—they walked in no grove but Jeremy Taylors—Marians obstinacy is some excuse—but his so quickly taking to miss Gleig can have no excuse—except that of a Ploughmans who wants a wife—The thing which sways me more against him than any thing else is Rice's conduct on the occasion; Rice would not make an immature resolve: he was ardent in his friendship for Bailey; he examined the whole for and against minutely; and he has abandoned Bailey entirely. All this I am not supposed by the Reynoldses to have any hint of—It will be a good Lesson to the Mother and Daughters—nothing would serve but Bailey—If you mentioned the word Tea pot—some one of them came out with an a propos about Bailey—noble fellow—fine fellow! was always in their mouths—this may teach them that the man who

1 *Miss Martin*: Perhaps the sister of John Martin (see p. 52 n).

2 *Miss Gleig*: Hamilton Gleig (b. 1793) was the sister of George Robert Gleig (1796–1888), who had been a student with Bailey at Magdalen Hall, Oxford (see above, p. 58 n). Their father George Gleig (1753–1840) was the Scottish Episcopal Bishop of Brechin.

redicules romance is the most romantic of Men—that he who abuses women and slights them—loves them the most—that he who talks of roasting a Man alive would not do it when it came to the push—and above all that they are very shallow people who take every thing literal A Man's life of any worth is a continual allegory—and very few eyes can see the Mystery of his life—a life like the scriptures, figurative—which such people can no more make out than they can the hebrew Bible. Lord Byron cuts a figure—but he is not figurative—Shakspeare led a life of Allegory; his works are the comments on it—

(continued 3 (?) March 1819, p. 312 below)

To Fanny Keats
27 February 1819

[British Library MS]

My dear Fanny, Wentworth Place Saturday Morn—

I intended to have not failed to do as you requested, and write you as you say once a fortnight. On looking to your letter I find there is no date; and not knowing how long it is since I received it I do not precisely know how great a sinner I am—I am getting quite well; and M[rs] Dilke is getting on pretty well—You must pay no attention to M[rs] Abbey's unfeeling and ignorant gabble—You can't stop an old woman's crying any more than you can a Child's—The old woman is the greatest nuisance because she is too old for the rod. Many people live opposite a Blaksmith's till they cannot hear the hammer—I have been in Town for two or three days and came back last night. I have been a little concerned at not hearing from George—I continue in daily expectation. Keep on reading and play as much on the music and the grassplot as you can. I should like to take possession of those Grasplots for a Month or so; and send M[rs] A— to Town to count coffee berries instead of currant Bunches, for I want you to teach me a few common dancing steps—and I would buy a Watch box to practise them in by myself—I think I had better always pay the postage of these Letters. I shall send you another book the first time I am in Town early enough to book it with one of the morning Walthamstow Coaches—You did not say a word about your Chilblains—Write me directly and let me know about them—Your Letter shall be answered like an echo—

Your affectionate Brother
John—

To George and Georgiana Keats

(continued)

3 (?) March 1819

[Wednesday, 3 (?) March 1819][1] On Monday we had to dinner Severn & Cawthorn[2] the Bookseller & print virtuoso; in the evening Severn went home to paint & we other three went to the play to see Sheild's new tragedy ycleped Evadné[3]—in the morning Severn & I took a turn round the Museum, There is a Sphinx there of a giant size, & most voluptuous Egyptian expression, I had not seen it before—The play was bad even in comparison with <u>1818</u> the Augustan age of the Drama, "Comme on sait" as Voltaire says.—the whole was made up of a virtuous young woman, an indignant brother, a suspecting lover, a libertine prince, a gratuitous villain, a Street in Naples, a Cypress grove, lillies & roses, virtue & vice, a bloody sword, a spangled jacket, One Lady Olivia, One Miss ONeil alias Evadné, alias Bellamira, alias—Alias—Yea & I say unto you a

1 The next three paragraphs were written on a sheet Keats accidentally omitted when posting this letter. He forwarded it to George and Georgiana with his journal letter of 17–27 September 1819. The text is preserved in Jeffrey's transcript (1845) along with Keats's covering note of 18 September (for which see below, p. 418–19). For the date see Rollins, II, pp. 67–68nn.

2 *Cawthorn*: James Cawthorn, a bookseller at 24 Cockspur Street (1808–34), published Byron's *English Bards and Scotch Reviewers* (1809).

3 *Evadné*: They saw the forty-second performance of Sheil's play on 1 March at Covent Garden.

greater than Elias—there was Abbot,[1] & talking of Abbot his name puts me in mind of a Spelling book lesson, descriptive of the whole Dramatis personae—Abbot—Abbess—Actor—Actress— The play is a fine amusement as a friend of mine once said to me—"Do what you will" says he "A poor gentleman who wants a guinea, cannot spend his two shillings better than at the playhouse— The pantomime[2] was excellent, I had seen it before & enjoyed it again— Your Mother & I had some talk about Miss K.[3]—says I will Henry have that Miss K. a lath with a boddice, she who has been fine drawn—fit for nothing but to cut up into Cribbage pins, to the tune of 15.2;[4] One who is all muslin; all feathers & bone; Once in travelling she was made use of as a lynch pin; I hope he will not have her, though it is no uncommon thing to be <u>smitten with a staff</u>; though she might be very useful as his walking stick, his fishing rod, his toothpic—his hat stick (she runs so much in his head) let him turn farmer, she would cut into hurdles; let him write poetry she would be his turnstyle; Her gown is like a flag on a pole; she would do for him if he turn freemason; I hope she will prove a flag of truce; When she sits languishing with her one foot, on a stool, & one elbow on the table, & her head inclined, she looks like the sign of the crooked billet—or the frontispeice to Cinderella or a teapaper wood cut of Mother Shipton at her studies; she is a make-believe— She is a bon a side a thin young—'Oman—But this is mere talk of a fellow creature; yet pardie I would not that Henry have her—Non volo ut eam possideat, nam, for it would be a bam, for it would be a sham— Don't think I am writing a petition to the

1 *Lady Olivia . . . Miss ONeil . . . Abbot*: Actors in Sheil's plays. Mrs John Fawcett (née Gaudry) played Lady Olivia in *Evadne*, in which Eliza O'Neill (1791–1872) took the title role, as well as that in *Bellamira*, in which William Abbot (1790–1843) acted the King of Naples.

2 *pantomime*: A performance of Charles Farley's *Harlequin Munchausen, or, The Fountain of Love* (1818) was the afterpiece on Monday, 1 March (see Rollins, II, 68n).

3 *Miss K*: Mary Ann Keasle, Henry Wylie's future wife (see p. 245 and n). (Jeffrey misread 'K.' as 'H.'

4 *15.2*: A score in cribbage.

Governors of St Lukes;[1] no, that would be in another style. May it please your worships; forasmuch as the undersigned has committed, transferred, given up, made over, consigned, and aberrated himself, to the art & mystery of poetry; for as much as he hath cut, rebuffed, affronted, huffed, & shirked, and taken stint, at all other employments, arts, mysteries, & occupations honest, middling & dishonest; for as much as he hath at sundry times, & in diverse places, told truth unto the men of this generation, & eke to the women, moreover; for as much as hath kept a pair of boots that did not fit, & doth not admire Sheild's play, Leigh Hunt, Tom Moore, Bob Southey & Mr Rogers; & does admire Wm Hazlitt: more over for as more, as he liketh half of Wordsworth, & none of Crabbe; more over-est for for as most; as he hath written this page of penmanship—he prayeth your Worships to give him a lodging—witnessed by R^d^ Abbey & Co. cum familiaribus & Consanguiniis (signed) Count de Cockaigne—

The nothing of the day is a machine called the Velocepede—It is a wheel-carriage to ride cock horse upon, sitting atride & pushing it along with the toes, a rudder wheel in hand. they will go seven miles an hour, A handsome gelding will come to eight guineas, however they will soon be cheaper, unless the army takes to them I look back upon the last month, & find nothing to write about, indeed I do not recollect one thing particular in it—It's all alike, we keep on breathing. The only amusement is a little scandal of however fine a shape, a laugh at a pun—& then after all we wonder how we could enjoy the scandal, or laugh at the pun,

I have been at different times turning in my head whether I should go to Edinburgh & study for a physician; I am afraid I should not take kindly to it, I am sure I could not take fees—& yet I should like to do so; it is not worse than writing poems, & hanging them up to be flyblown on the Reviewshambles—Every body is in his own mess— Here is the parson at Hampstead[2] quarreling with all the world, he is in the wrong

1 *St Lukes*: St Luke's Hospital for Lunatics, founded in 1750.
2 *parson at Hampstead*: Rollins identifies as Rev. Samuel White (1765–1841).

by this same token; when the black Cloth was put up in the Church for the Queen's mourning, he asked the workmen to hang it the wrong side outwards, that it might be better when taken down, it being his perquisite—Parsons will always keep up their Character, but as it is said there are some animals, the Ancients knew, which we do not; let us hope our posterity will miss the black badger with the tri-cornered hat: Who knows but some Revisor of Buffon or Pliny, may put an account of the parson in the Appendix; No one will then believe it any more than we beleive in the Phoenix. I think we may class the lawyer in the same natural history of Monsters; a green bag will hold as much as a lawn sleeve— The only difference is that the one is fustian, & the other flimsy; I am not unwilling to read Church history at present & have Milner[1] in my eye his is reckoned a very good one—

(continued 12 March 1819, p. 317 below)

To B. R. Haydon
8 March 1819

[HBF transcript (1901)][2]

Wentworth Place.
[Monday]

My dear Haydon,

You must be wondering where I am and what I am about! I am mostly at Hampstead, and about nothing; being in a sort of qui [*for* cui] bono temper, not exactly on the road to an epic

1 *Milner*: Joseph Milner's *The History of the Church of Christ*, 5 vols (1794–1809).

2 *The Complete Works of John Keats*, ed. H. B. Forman, 5 vols (Glasgow: Gowans & Gray, 1900–1901), V, pp. 14–15. The largest part of Rollins's text is from the partial transcript in Sotheby's *Catalogue of Valuable Letters and Historical Documents* (11–12 March 1898), lot 179. However, Forman's transcript of the letter's full text and postmark, most probably based on the original, is followed here: the substantive variants in L are noted below.

poem. Nor must you think I have forgotten you. No, I have about every three days been to Abbey's and to the Law[y]ers. Do let me know how you have been getting on, and in what spirits you are.

You got out gloriously in yesterday's Examiner.[1] What a set of little people we live amongst! I went the other day into an ironmonger's shop—without any change in my sensations—men and tin kettles are much the same in these days—they do not study like children at five and thirty—but they talk like men of[2] twenty. Conversation is not a search after knowledge, but an endeavour at effect.

In this respect two most opposite men, Wordsworth and Hunt, are the same. A friend of mine observed the other day that if Lord Bacon were to make any remark in a party of the present day, the conversation would stop on the sudden. I am convinced of this, and from this I have come to this[3] resolution—never to write for the sake of writing or making a poem, but from running over with any little knowledge or[4] experience which many years of reflection may perhaps give me; otherwise I will be dumb. What imagination I have I shall enjoy, and greatly, for I have experienced the satisfaction of having great conceptions without the trouble[5] of sonnetteering. I will not spoil my love of gloom by writing an Ode to Darkness!

With[6] respect to my livelihood, I will not write for it,—for I will not run[7] with that most vulgar of all crowds, the literary. Such things I ratify by looking upon myself, and trying myself at lifting mental weights, as it were. I am three and twenty, with

1 *You got . . . Examiner*: In January and February Haydon had arranged a successful private exhibition of his pupils' copies of Raphael's cartoons, which was attacked vituperatively. The *Examiner* published his pugnacious reply, which continued his feud with the Royal Academy, on 7 March 1819, pp. 157–8.
2 *of*] at *L.*
3 *this*] the *L.*
4 *or*] and *L.*
5 *trouble*] toil *L.*
6 *With*] And with *L.*
7 *run*] mix *L.*

what you are. In doing this give me leave to borrow the familiarity of your style:—for the fidelity of the picture I shall be answerable. You are a little person, but a considerable cat's paw; and so far worthy of notice. Your clandestine connection with persons high in office constantly influences your opinions, and alone gives importance to them. You are the government critic, a character nicely differing from that of a government spy—the invisible link, that connects literature with the Police." Again—"Your employers M[r] Gifford, do not pay their hirelings for nothing—for condescending to notice weak and wicked sophistry; for pointing out to contempt what excites no admiration; for cautiously selecting a few specimens of bad taste and bad grammar where nothing else is to be found "They want your invincible pertness, your mercenary malice, your impenetrable dullness, your barefaced impudence, your pragmatical self sufficiency, your hypocritical zeal, your pious frauds to stand in the gap of their Prejudices and pretensions, to fly blow and taint public opinion, to defeat independent efforts, to apply not the touch of the scorpion but the touch of the Torpedo to youthful hopes, to crawl and leave the slimy track of sophistry and lies over every work that does not 'dedicate its sweet leaves' to some Luminary of the tresury bench, or is not fostered in the hot bed of corruption—This is your office; "this is what is look'd for at your hands and this you do not baulk"—to sacrifice what little honesty and prostitute what little intellect you possess to any dirty job you are commission'd to execute. "They keep you as an ape does an apple in the corner of his jaw, first mouth'd to be at last swallow'd"—You are by appointment literary toad eater to greatness and taster to the court—You have a natural aversion to whatever differs from your own pretensions, and an acquired one for what gives offence to your superiors. Your vanity panders to your interest, and your malice truckles only to your love of Power. If your instinctive or premeditated abuse of your enviable trust were found wanting in a single instance; if you were to make a single slip in getting up your select committee of enquiry and greenbag report of the state of Letters, your occupation would be gone. You would never after obtain a squeeze of the hand from a great man, or a smile from a Punk of Quality. The great and powerful (whom you call wise and good) do not like to have the privacy of their self love startled by the obtrusive and unmanageable claims of Literature and Philosophy, except through the intervention of people like you, whom; if they have common penetration, they soon find out to be without any superiority of intellect; or if they do not whom they can despise for their meanness of soul. You "have the office opposite to saint Peter" You "keep a corner in the public mind, for foul prejudice and corrupt power to knot and gender in"; you volunteer your services to people of quality to ease scruples of mind and qualmes of conscience; you lay the flattering unction of venal prose and laurell'd verse to their souls—You persuade them that there is neither purity of morals, nor depth of understanding, except in themselves and their hangers on; and would prevent the unhallow'd names of Liberty and humanity from ever being whispered in years [*for* ears] polite! You, sir, do you not all this? I cry you mercy then: I took you for the Editor of the Quarterly Review!" This is the sort of feu de joie[1] he keeps up—there is another extract or two—one especially which I will copy tomorrow—for the candles are burnt down and I am using the wax taper—which has a long snuff on it—the fire is at its last click—I am sitting with my back to it with one foot rather askew upon the rug and the other with the heel a little elevated from the carpet—I am writing this on the Maid's tragedy which I have read since tea with Great pleasure—Besides this volume of Beaumont & Fletcher—there are on the tabl[e] two volumes of chaucer[2] and a new work of Tom Moores call'd 'Tom Cribb's memorial to Congress—nothing in it—These are trifles—but I require nothing so much of you as that you will give me a like description of yourselves, however it may be when you are writing to me—Could I see the same thing done of any great Man long since dead it would be a great delight: as to know in what position

1 *feu de joie*: A rifle salute (*OED* 2).
2 *Beaumont & Fletcher . . . chaucer*: Keats's copy of the four-volume *The Dramatic Works of Jonson, Beaumont and Fletcher* (1811) is in Keats House, and his fourteen-volume edition of Chaucer (1782) in the British Library.

Shakspeare sat when he began 'To be or not to be"—such thing[s] become interesting from distance of time or place. I hope you are both now in that sweet sleep which no two beings deserve more that [*for* than] you do—I must fancy you so—and please myself in the fancy of speaking a prayer and a blessing over you and your lives—God bless you—I whisper good night in your ears and you will dream of me—

(continued 13 March 1819, p. 322 below)

To Fanny Keats
13 March 1819

[British Library MS]

Wentworth Place
My dear Fanny, [Saturday] March 13th

I have been employed lately in writing to George,—I do not send him very short letters—but keep on day after day—There were some young Men I think I told you of who were going to the Settlement: they have changed their minds, and I am disappointed in my expectation of sending Letters by them—I went lately to the only dance I have been to these twelve months or shall go to for twelve months again—it was to our Brother in laws' cousin's[1]—She gave a dance for her Birthday and I went for the sake of Mrs Wylie—I am waiting every day to hear from George. I trust there is no harm in the silence: other people are in the same expectation as we are—On looking at your seal I cannot tell whether it is done or not with a Tassi[e][2]—it seems to me to be paste—As I went through Leicester Square lately I

1 *Brother in laws' cousin's*: Mary Millar of Henrietta Street. He told George and Georgiana the dance was on Friday, 19 February (see above, p. 302).

2 *Tassi[e]*: James Tassie (1735–99), a modeller and portrait medallionist, whose shop at 20 Leicester Square was taken over by his nephew William Tassie (1777–1860), invented a vitreous enamel suitable for seals. These carried neoclassical images with mottoes or portraits of famous people.

was going to call and buy you some, but not knowing but you might have some I would not run the chance of buying duplicates—Tell me if you have any or if you would like any—and whether you would rather have motto ones like that with which I seal this letter;[1] or head of great Men such as Shakspeare, Milton &c—or fancy pieces of Art; such as Fame, Adonis &c—those gentry you read of at the end of the English Dictionary. Tell me also if you want any particular Book; or Pencils, or drawing paper—any thing but live Stock—Though I will not now be very severe on it, remembring how fond I used to be of Goldfinches, Tomtits, Minnows, Mice, Ticklebacks, Dace, Cock salmons and all the whole tribe of the Bushes and the Brooks: but verily they are better in the Trees and the water—though I must confess even now a partiality for a handsome Globe of gold-fish—then I would have it hold 10 pails of water and be fed continually fresh through a cool pipe with another pipe to let through the floor—well ventilated they would preserve all their beautiful silver and Crimson—Then I would put it before a handsome painted window and shade it all round with myrtles and Japonicas. I should like the window to open onto the Lake of Geneva—and there I'd sit and read all day like the picture of somebody reading—The weather now and then begins to feel like spring; and therefore I have begun my walks on the heath again. Mrs Dilke is getting better than she has been as she has at length taken a Physician's advice—She ever and anon asks after you and always bids me remember her in my Letters to you—She is going to leave Hampstead for the sake of educating their Son Charles at the Westminster school.[2] We (Mr Brown and I) shall leave at the beginning of

1 *I seal this letter*: The seal is lost. For his letters to Fanny, Keats sometimes used a seal of a lyre with the motto 'Qui me negligee me désole' ('By neglect you have ruined me'), but more often used one with Shakespeare's head. As promised, Keats bought Fanny some Tassie seals, including a head of Shakespeare (see below, p. 479).

2 *Westminster school*: Attached to Westminster Abbey, the school dates from the eleventh century. Ben Jonson, John Dryden and Sir Christopher Wren were educated there. For Keats's comments on Dilke's only child, (Sir) Charles Wentworth Dilke (1810–69), art patron and MP, see below, p. 340.

may; I do not know what I shall do or where be all the next Summer. Mrs Reynolds has had a sick house; but they are all well now—You see what news I can send you I do—we all live one day like the other as well as you do—the only difference is being sick and well—with the variations of single and double knocks; and the story of a dreadful fire in the Newspapers[1]—I mentioned Mr Brown's name—yet I do not think I ever said a word about him to you—He is a friend of mine of two years standing—with whom I walked through Scotland; who has been very kind to me in many things when I most wanted his assistance and with whom I keep house till the first of M<ay—> you will know him some day.[2] The name o<f the> young Man who came with me[3] is—William Haslam—Ever,

Your affectionate Brother
John.

To George and Georgiana Keats
(continued)

13, 17, 19 March 1819

Saturday 13 March. I have written to Fanny this morning; and received a note from Haslam—I was to have dined with him tomorrow: he give[s] me a bad account of his Father, who has not been in Town for 5 weeks—and is not well enough for company—Haslam is well—and from the prosperous state of some love affair he does not mind the double tides he has to work—I have been a Walk past westend—and was going to call at Mr Monkhouse's—but I did not, not being in the humour—I know not why Poetry and I have been so distant lately I must make some advances soon or she will cut me entirely. Hazlitt

1 *story . . . Newspapers*: On 9 March the *Morning Chronicle* reported on 'Dreadful Fires' in Spitalfields (London), Edinburgh and Dublin.
2 *you will . . . some day*: Richard Abbey prevented her meeting Brown.
3 *young Man . . . with me*: Haslam accompanied Keats on his visit to Fanny on 13 December 1818 (see above, p. 271).

has this fine Passage in his Letter[.][1] Gifford, in his Review of Hazlitt's characters of Shakspeare's plays, attacks the Coriolanus critique—He says that Hazlitt has slandered Shakspeare in saying that he had a leaning to the arbit[r]ary side of the question. Hazlitt thus defends himself "My words are "Coriolanus is a storehouse of political commonplaces. The Arguments for and against aristocracy and d[e]mocracy, on the Preveleges of the few and the claims of the many, on Liberty and slavery, power and the abuse of it, peace and war, are here very ably handled, with the spirit of a poet and the acuteness of a Philosopher. Shakspeare himself seems to have had a leaning towards the arbit[r]ary side of the question, perhaps from some feeling of contempt for his own origin, and to have spared no occasion of ba[i]ting the rabble. What he says of them is very true; what he says of their betters is also very true, though he dwells less upon it." I then proceed to account for this by shewing how it is that "the cause of the people is but little calculated for a subject for Poetry; or that the language of Poetry naturally falls in with the language of power." I affi[r]m, Sir, that Poetry, that the imagination, generally speaking, delights in power, in strong excitement, as well as in truth, in good, in right, whereas pure reason and the moral sense approve only of the true and good. I proceed to show that this general love or tendency to immediate excitement or theatrical effect, no matter how produced, gives a Bias to the imagination often consistent [*for* inconsistent] with the greatest good, that in Poetry it triumphs over Principle, and bribes the passions to make a sacrifice of common humanity. You say that it does not, that there is no such original Sin in Poetry, that it makes no such sacrifice or unworthy compromise between poetical effect and the still small voice of reason—And how do you prove that there is no such principle giving a bias to the imagination, and a false colouring to poetry? Why by asking in reply to the

1 *Hazlitt . . . Letter[.]*: Keats returns to quoting from Hazlitt's 'Letter to William Gifford, Esq.' (*Works*, 9, pp. 36–7). Gifford in the *Quarterly Review* (January 1818), pp. 458–66, had wilfully misrepresented Hazlitt's views on Coriolanus in his *Characters of Shakespeare's Plays?* (1817).

instances where this principle operates, and where no other can with much modesty and simplicity—"But are these the only topics that afford delight in Poetry &c" No; but these objects do afford delight in poetry, and they afford it in proportion to their strong and often tragical effect, and not in proportion to their strong and often tragical effect,[1] and not in proportion to the good produced, or their desireableness in a moral point of view? "Do we read with more pleasure of the ravages of a beast of prey than of the Shepherds pipe upon the Mountain?" No but we do read with pleasure of the ravages of a beast of prey, and we do so on the principle I have stated, namely from the sense of power abstracted from the sense of good; and it is the same principle that makes us read with admiration and reconciles us in fact to the triumphant progress of the conquerors and mighty Hunters of mankind, who come to stope [*for* stop] the shepherd's Pipe upon the Mountains and sweep away his listening flock. Do you mean to deny that there is any thing imposing to the imagination in power, in grandeur, in outward shew, in the accumulation of individual wealth and luxury, at the expen[s]e of equal justice and the common weal? Do you deny that there is any thing in the "Pride, Pomp and Circumstance of glorious war, that makes ambition virtue'? in the eyes of admiring multitudes? Is this a new theory of the Pleasures of the imagination, which says that the pleasures of the imagination do not take rise sol[el]y in the calculations of the understanding? Is it a paradox of my creating that "one murder makes a villain millions a Hero!" or is it not true that here, as in other cases, the enormity of the evil overpowers and makes a convert of the imagination by its very magnitude? You contradict my reasoning, because you know nothing of the question, and you think that no one has a right to understand what you do not. My offence against purity in the passage alluded to, "which contains the concentrated venom of my malignity," is, that I have admitted that there are tyrants and slaves abroad in the world; and you would hush the matter up,

1 *not . . . effect*: Keats mistakenly copied this phrase out a second time, but made it a negative.

and pretend that there is no such thing in order that there may be nothing else. Farther I have explained the cause, the subtle sophistry of the human mind, that tolerates and pampers the evil in order to guard against its approaches; you would conceal the cause in order to prevent the cure, and to leave the proud flesh about the heart to harden and ossify into one impenetrabl[e] mass of selfishness and hypocrisy, that we may not "sympathise in the distresses of suffering virtue" in any case in which they come in competition with the fictitious [*for* factitious] wants and "imputed weaknesses of the great." You ask "are we gratified by the cruelties of Domitian or Nero?" No, not we—they were too petty and cowardly to strike the imagination at a distance; but the Roman senate tolerated them, addressed their perpetrators, exalted them into gods, the fathers of the people; they had pimps and scribblers of all sorts in their pay, their Senecas, &c till a turbulent rabble thinking that there were no injuries to Society greater than the endurance of unlimited and wanton oppression, put an end to the farce and abated the nuisance as well as they could. Had you and I lived in those times we should have been what we are now, I "a sour mal content," and you "a sweet courtier." The manner in which this is managed: the force and innate power with which it yeasts and works up itself—the feeling for the costume of society; is in a style of genius—He hath a demon as he himself says of Lord Byron—We are to have a party this evening—The Davenports from Church row—I dont think you know any thing of them—they have paid me a good deal of attention—I like Davenport himself—The mames [*for* names] of the rest are Miss Barnes Miss Winter with the Children—

<Marc>h 17th—Wednesday—On sunday I went to Davenports' w[h]ere I dined—and had a nap. I cannot bare a day anhilated [*for* annihilated] in that manner—there is a great difference between an easy and an uneasy indolence—An indolent day—fill'd with speculations even of an unpleasant colour—is bearable and even pleasant alone—when one's thoughts cannot find out any th[i]ng better in the world; and experience has told us that locomotion is no change: but to have nothing to do, and to be surrounded with unpleasant human identities; who press

upon one just enough to prevent one getting into a lazy position; and not enough to interest or rouse one; is a capital punishment of a capital crime: for is not giving up, through goodnature, one's time to people who have no light and shade a capital crime? Yet what can I do?—they have been very kind and attentive to me. I do not know what I did on monday—nothing—nothing—nothing—I wish this was any thing extraordinary—Yesterday I went to town: I called on Mr Abbey<;> he began again (he has don[e] it frequently salety [*for* lately] <abou>t that <hat-ma>king concern—saying he wish[es] you had hear<ken>ed to it: he wants to make me a H<at-maker>[1]—I really believe 't is all interested: for from the manner he shope [*for* spoke] withal and the card he gave me I think he is concerned in <Hat-ma>king himself. He speaks well of Fanny<'s> health—Hodgkinson[2] is married—From this I think he takes a little Latitude—Mr A was waiting very impatien[t]ly for his return to the counting house—and mean while observed how strange it was that Hodgkinson should have been not able to walk two months ago and that now that he should be married.—"I do not,' says he 'think it will do him any good: I should not be surprised if he should die of a consumption in a year or <two.> I called at Taylor's and found that he and Hilto<n> had set out to dine with me: so I followed them immediately back—I walk'd with them townwards again as far as Cambden Town and smoak'd home a Segar—This morning I have been reading the 'False one"[3] I have been up to Mrs Bentley's—shameful to say I was in bed at

1 *a H<at-maker>*: Richard Abbey's evidently serious proposal that Keats should enter the hat-making business was repeated six months later (see below, p. 422) and was a career he had earlier proposed to George. Nicholas Roe identifies the Cheapside hatter, Joseph Keats (d. January 1819), distantly related to Keats, as probably the man in whose shop Abbey had 'some concern' (Roe, pp. 4–5, 306, 344).

2 *Hodgkinson*: Cadman Hodgkinson (1793–1832), Abbey's chief clerk, became a junior partner in the business, but later set up on his own (Gigante, pp. 59–61). George Keats left Abbey's firm after falling out with him, the cause of Keats's dislike here and later (see below, pp. 374, 402–3, 423, 539). Keats, or Keats and his brothers, earlier had some kind of financial dealings with him (*L*, I, p. 248).

3 *the 'False one"*: (*c.* 1620) by Beaumont and Fletcher.

ten—I mean this morning—The Blackwood's review has committed themselves in a scandalous heresy—they have been putting up Hogg the ettrick shepherd against Burns[1]—The senseless villains. I have not seen Reynolds Rice or any of our set lately—. Reynolds is completely limed in the law: he is not only reconcil'd to it but hobbyhorses upon it—Blackwood wanted very much to see him[2]—the scotch cannot manage by themselves at all—they want imagination—and that is why they are so fond of Hogg, who has a little of it—

Friday 19th [March] Yesterday I got a black eye—the first time I took a Cr<ricket> Bat—Brown who is always one's friend in a disaster <app>lied a lee<ch to> the eyelid, and there is no infla<mm>ation this morning though the ball hit me dir<ectl>y on the sight—'t was a white ball—I am glad it was not a clout—This is the second black eye I have had since leaving school—during all my <scho>ol days I never had one at all—we must e<a>t a peck before we die—This morning I am in a sort of temper indolent and supremely careless: I long after a stanza or two of Thompson's Castle of indolence[3]—My passions are all alseep [*for* asleep] from my having slumbered till nearly eleven and weakened the animal fibre all over me to a delightful sensation about three degrees on this side of faintness—if I had teeth of pearl and the breath of lillies I should call it langour—but as I am[4] I must call it Laziness—In this state of effeminacy the fibres of the brain are relaxed in common with the rest of the body, and to such a happy degree that pleasure has no show of enticement and pain no unbearable frown. Neither Poetry, nor Ambition, nor Love have any alertness of countenance as they pass by me: they seem rather like

1 *Hogg ... Burns*: James Hogg (1770–1835), the 'Ettrick Shepherd', then known as a poet not a novelist, had been recently compared with Robert Burns in *Blackwood's Review* (February 1819) in which Hogg was involved editorially.

2 *Blackwood ... him*: In early 1819 William Blackwood attempted, unsuccessfully, to persuade Reynolds to write for his eponymous periodical.

3 *Thompson's ... indolence*: *The Castle of Indolence* (1748) by James Thomson (1700–48).

4 *as I am*: (Keats's note) 'especially as I have a black eye'.

three figures on a greek vase—a Man and two women—whom no one but myself could distinguish in their disguisement.[1] This is the only happiness; and is a rare instance of advantage in the body overpowering the Mind. I have this moment received a note from Haslam in which he expects the death of his Father who has been for some time in a state of insensibility—his mother bears up he says very well—I shall go to twon [*for* town] tommorow to see him. This is the world—thus we cannot expect to give way many hours to pleasure—Circumstances are like Clouds continually gathering and bursting—while we are laughing the seed of some trouble is put into the wide arable land of events—while we are laughing it sprouts is [*for* it] grows and suddenly bears a poison fruit which we must pluck—Even so we have leisure to reason on the misfortunes of our friends; our own touch us too nearly for words. Very few men have ever arrived at a complete disinterestedness of Mind; very few have been influenced by a pure desire of the benefit of others—in the greater part of the Benfactors ~~of~~ & to Humanity some meretricious motive has sullied their greatness—some melodramatic scenery has fa[s]cinated them—From the manner in which I feel Haslam's misfortune, I perceive how far I am from any humble standard of disinterestedness—Yet this feeling ought to be carried to its highest pitch, as there is no fear of its ever injuring society—which it would do I fear pushed to an extremity—For in wild nature the Hawk would loose his Breakfast of Robins and the Robin his of Worms The Lion must starve as well as the swallow—The greater part of Men make their way with the same instinctiveness, the same unwandering eye from their purposes, the same animal eagerness as

1 *three figures . . . disguisement*: These 'figures' are the source of Keats's 'Ode on Indolence'. Roe (pp. 307–11) believes the 'ode' to have been written now: the opium he thinks Keats would have taken for his 'black eye' induced the 'dream-vision' of the 'figures' described in his letter, which immediately inspired the poem. Keats's editors, while allowing the possibility that the 'ode' was written as early as March, have on balance placed its composition after the great 'Spring Odes' on the grounds that 'Indolence' seems to turn its back on them and because, writing on 9 June, Keats spoke of the 'abatement' of his 'love of fame' and quotes l. 54 of the 'ode' (see below, p. 372).

the Hawk—The Hawk wants a Mate, so does the Man—look at them both they set about it and procure on[e] in the same manner—They want both a nest and they both set about one in the same manner—they get their food in the same manner—The noble animal Man for his amusement smokes his pipe—the Hawk balances about the Clouds—that is the only difference of their leisures. This it is that makes the Amusement of Life—to a speculative Mind. I go among the Feilds and catch a glimpse of a stoat or a fieldmouse peeping out of the withered grass—the creature hath a purpose and its eyes are bright with it—I go amongst the buildings of a city and I see a Man hurrying along—to what? The Creature has a purpose and his eyes are bright with it. But then as Wordsworth says, "we have all one human heart"[1]— there is an ellectric fire in human nature tending to purify—so that among these human creature[s] there is continu[a]lly some birth of new heroism—The pity is that we must wonder at it: as we should at finding a pearl in rubbish—I have no doubt that thousands of people never heard of have had hearts comp[l]etely disinterested: I can remember but two—Socrates and Jesus—their Histories evince it—What I heard a little time ago, Taylor observe with respect to Socrates, may be said of Jesus—That he was so great a man that though he transmitted no writing of his own to posterity, we have his Mind and his sayings and his greatness handed to us by others. It is to be lamented that the history of the latter was written and revised by Men interested in the pious frauds of Religion. Yet through all this I see his splendour. Even here though I myself am pursueing the same instinctive course as the veriest human animal you can think of—I am however young writing at random—straining at particles of light in the midst of a great darkness—without knowing the bearing of any one assertion of any one opinion. Yet may I not in this be free from sin? May there not be superior beings amused with any graceful, though instinctive attitude my mind m[a]y fall into, as I am entertained with the alertness of a Stoat or the anxiety of a Deer? Though a quarrel in the streets is a thing to be hated, the energies

1 *we . . . heart*: 'The Old Cumberland Beggar', l. 153.

displayed in it are fine; the commonest Man shows a grace in his quarrel—By a superior being our reasoning[s] may take the same tone—though erroneous they may be fine—This is the very thing in which consists poetry; and if so it is not so fine a thing as philosophy—For the same reason that an eagle is not so fine a thing as a truth—Give me this credit—Do you not think I strive—to know myself? Give me this credit—and you will not think that on my own accou[n]t I repeat Milton's lines

> "How charming is divine Philosophy
> Not harsh and crabbed as dull fools suppose
> But musical as is Apollo's lute"[1]—

No—no for myself—feeling grateful as I do to have got into a state of mind to relish them properly—Nothing ever becomes real till it is experienced—Even a Proverb is no proverb to you till your Life has illustrated it—I am ever affraid that your anxiety for me will lead you to fear for the violence of my temperament continually smothered down: for that reason I did not intend to have sent you the following sonnet—but look over the two last pages and ask yourselves whether I have not that in me which will well bear the buffets of the world. It will be the best comment on my sonnet; it will show you that it was written with no Agony but that of ignorance; with no thirst of any thing but knowledge when pushed to the point though the first steps to it were throug[h] my human passions—they went away, and I wrote with my Mind—and perhaps I must confess a little bit of my heart—

> Why did I laugh tonight? No voice will tell:[2]
> No God, no Deamon of severe response
> Deigns to reply from heaven or from Hell.—
> Then to my human heart I turn at once—
> Heart! thou and I are here sad and alone;
> Say, wherefore did I laugh? O mortal pain!
> O Darkness! Darkness! ever must I moan

1 *How . . . lute*: Milton's *Comus*, ll. 476–8.
2 *Why . . . tell*: First published in *1848*.

To question Heaven and Hell and Heart in vain!
Why did I laugh? I know this being's lease
My fancy to its utmost blisses spreads:
Yet could I on this very midnight cease,
And the world's gaudy ensigns see in shreds.
Verse, fame and Beauty are intense indeed
But Death intenser—Deaths is Life's high mead."

I went to bed, and enjoyed an uninterrupted sleep—Sane I went to bed and sane I arose.

(continued 15 April 1819, p. 337 below)

To Joseph Severn
29 March 1819

[Harvard MS]

My dear Severn, Wentworth Place
—Monday—af^t^—

Your note gave me some pain, not on my own account, but on yours—Of course I should mev [*for* never] suffer any petty vanity of mine to hinder you in any wise; and therefore I should say, 'put the miniature in the exhibition'[1] if only myself was to be hurt. But, will it not hurt you? What good can it do to any future picture—Even a large picture is lost in that canting place—what a drop of water in the ocean is a Miniature. Those who might chance to see it for the most part if they had ever heard of either of us—and know what we were and of what years would laugh at the puff of the one and the vanity of the other I am however in these matters a very bad judge—and would advise you to act in a way that appears to yourself the

1 *put . . . exhibition*: Despite Keats's advice, Severn exhibited both his well-known miniature of Keats and his painting *Hermia and Helena* at the Royal Academy's exhibition at Somerset House in May 1819 (nos. 940 and 267 in the catalogue). Keats's comment on 'that canting place' reflects Haydon's contempt for the Royal Academy.

best for your interest. As your He[r]mia and Helena is finished send that without the prologue of a Miniature. I shall see you soon, if you do not pay me a visit sooner—there's a Bull for you.

Yours ever sincerely
John Keats—

To Fanny Keats
31 March 1819

[Keats House MS][1]

[Wentworth Place]
Wednesday—

My dear Fanny,

I shall be going to town tomorrow and will call at the Nursery on the road for those roots and seeds you want, which I will send by the Walthamstow stage. The best way, I thought, for you to lea[r]n to answer those questions, is to read over the little book,[2] which I sent from a Bookseller's in town, or you should have had a Letter with it—Tell me whether it will do: if not I will put down the answers for you—I have not yet heard from George—Perhaps if I just give you the heads of the answers it may be better—though I think you will find them all in that little book—

Ans[r] 1—It was instituted by John the Baptist when he baptised those people in the river Jordan who bel[i]eved through him in the coming of Christ—and more particularly when he baptised christ himself.

2 It corresponds to the Jewish Circumcision

1 This letter was not published until 1934.

2 *lea[r]n . . . book*: Fanny was learning her catechism. The 'little book' Keats sent was perhaps one of the many editions of Thomas Marshall's *The Catechism set forth in the Book of Common Prayer*, first published in 1679. Despite his dislike of institutionalized Christianity and parsons, Keats's answers are strikingly well informed (see Robert M. Ryan, *Keats: The Religious Sense* (Princeton: Princeton University Press, 1976), pp. 186–8).

3 The meaning is that we are confirmed members of Christ It is not administered till 14 years of age because before that age the mind [is] not judged to be sufficiently mature and capaple [*for* capable]. The act of confirmation imposes on the Christian self circumspection; as by that ceremony the Christian duties of God fathers and godmothers is annulled and put and [*for* an] end to—as you see in the catechism—"they promise and vow three things in my name"—Confirmation absolves this obligation.

4 There are two Sacraments of our Church—Baptism and the Lord's Supper. The Church of Rome has seven Sacraments. The church of Rome includes several ceremonies (I forget what they are) and the civil rite of marriage—I believe Confi[r]mation is a Sacrament with them—Extreme unction or the annointing the extremities of dying persons with holy water. The reason why we have but two Sacraments is—that it is proved from the Scriptures by the great protestant reformers—that only two are commanded by god—the rest adopted by the Church of Rome are human institutions.

5 You must here repeat your belief—and say the question is to[o] hard for you.

6 Look in Isaia for "A virgin shall conceive" &c—Look in the Psalms for "The Kings of the Earth set themselves and the Princes take counsel together" and "they parted my Garments among them &" and "My god, my god why hast thou forsaken me &c" In Jeremia "Comfort ye, comfort ye &" In Daniel The stone cut out of the mountain without hands that breaks the image in pieces is a type of the Kingdom of Christ—Look at the 2nd Chat. Isaiah—Chap 7–9—'For unto us a Child is bo[r]n"—11 Jeremiah Chap xxxi Micah Chap 5—Zechariah Chap 6 and Chap 13 verse 6. Those I have marked will be sufficient—You will remember their completion in the new testament—

7th The communion of saints is the fruition they enjoy in heaven among one another and in the Divinity of Christ—

8th It was instituded [*for* instituted] on the night of the feast of the Passover at the Last supper with the Twelve; the night Judas betrayed Christ—and you may see in the 26 Mathew—It corresponds to the "Feast of the Passover in the Jewish Ritual—

9 They expected Christ to be a temporal Prince and being disappointed, rejected him—
10 Look to the Catchism—'What is your duty towards God?
11th The Prophecy to our first parents is this—Genesis 3 Chapter—verse [15] "And I will put enmity between thee and the woman and between thy seed and her seed: it shall bruize thy head and thou shall bruize his heel—Christ the Son of David by dying on the Cross triumphed over death and the grave from which he saved mankind; and in that way did he 'bruize the Serpent's head"—

Your affectionate Parson
John—

On Saturday, 3 April the Dilke family moved out of their half of Wentworth Place and Mrs Brawne and Fanny, with her younger sister Margaret ('Tootts', b. 1809) and her brother Samuel (b. 1804), came to live next door to Brown and Keats.

To Fanny Keats

12 April 1819

[British Library MS]

My dear Fanny, Wentworth Place
[Monday]

I have been expecting a Letter from you about what the Parson said to your answers—I have thought also of writing to you often, and I am sorry to confess that my neglect of it has been but a small instance of my idleness of late—which has been growing upon me, so that it will require a great shake to get rid of it. I have written nothing, and almost read nothing—but I must turn over a new leaf—One most discouraging thing hinders me—we have no news yet from George—so that I cannot with any confidence continue the Letter I have been preparing for him. Many are in the same state with us and many have heard from the Settlement—They must be well however: and we must consider this silence as good news—I ordered some bulbous roots for you at the Gardeners, and they sent me some, but they were all in bud—and could not be sent, so I put them in our Garden There are some beautiful heaths now in bloom in Pots—either heaths or some seasonable plants I will send you instead—perhaps some that are not yet in bloom that you may see them come out—Tomorrow night I am going to a rout—a thing I am not at all in love with—Mr Dilke and his Family have left Hampstead—I shall dine with them to day in Westminster where I think I told you they were going to reside for the sake of sending their Son Charles to the Westminster School. I think I mentioned the Death of Mr Haslam's Father—Yesterday week the two Mr Wylies dined with me. I hope you have good store of double violets—I think they are the Princesses of flowers and in a shower of rain, almost as fine as barley sugar drops are to a schoolboy's tongue. I suppose this fine weather the lambs tails give a frisk or two extraordinary—when a boy would cry huzza and a Girl O my! a little Lamb frisks its tail. I have not been lately through Leicester Square—the first time I do I will remember your Seals—I have thought it best to live in Town this Summer, chiefly for the sake of books, which cannot be had with any comfort in the Country—besides my Scotch jou[r]ney gave me a doze of the Picturesque with which I ought to be contented for some time. Westminster is the place I have pitched upon—the City or any place very confined would soon turn me pale and thin—which is to be avoided. You must make up your mind to get Stout this summer—indeed I have an idea we shall both be corpu<lent> old folkes with tripple chins and stum<py> thumbs—

Your affectionate Brother
John

On Monday, 13 April 1819 Keats, who had written to Haydon explaining that he was, after all, unable to lend any money, received the painter's reply: 'My dear Keats / Why did you hold out such delusive hopes every letter on such slight foundations?—you have led me on step by step, day by day; never telling the exact circumstances; you paralized my exertion in other quarters . . . I am plunged into all my old difficulties . . . if you could not have commanded it you should have told me so at once I declare to you I scarcely know which way to turn' (L, *II, p. 53). Keats replied by return.*

To B. R. Haydon
13 April 1819

[Harvard MS]

[Wentworth Place]

My dear Haydon, Tuesday—

When I offered you assistance I thought I had it in my hand; I thought I had nothing to do, but to do. The difficulties I met with arose from the alertness and suspicion of Abbey; and especially from the affairs being still in a Law[y]er's hand—who has been drain[i]ng our Property for the last 6 years of eve[r]y charge he could make—I cannot do two things at once, and thus this affair has stopped my pursuits in every way—from the first prospect I had of difficulty. I assure you I have harrassed myself 10 times more than if I alone had been concernned in so much gain or loss. I have also ever told you the exact particulars as well as and as literally as my hopes or fear could translate them—for it was only by parcels that I found all those petty obstacles which for my own sake should not exist a moment—and yet why not—for from my own imprudence and neglect all my accounts are entirely in my Guardians Power[1]—This has taught me a Lesson. hereafter I will be more correct. I find myself possessed of much less than I thought for and now if I had all on the table all I could do would

1 *all my accounts . . . Guardians Power*: Keats's admission that at age twenty-three 'all' his 'accounts' concerning his inheritance were still in Richard Abbey's hands, and about which he relied entirely on his guardian for information, is remarkable. These opening sentences show his unquestioning trust in Abbey's honesty and underline Keats's apparently constitutional aversion to taking money matters seriously. Keats's suspicions centre on William Walton (of Walton and Gliddons, solicitors), who had been his grandmother's lawyer.

be to take from it a moderate two years subsistence and lend you the rest; but I cannot say how soon I could become possessed of it. This would be no sacrifice nor any matter worth thinking of—much less than parting as I have more than once done with little sums which might have gradually formed a library to my taste—These sums amount to gether to nearly 200, which I have but a chance of ever being repaid or paid at a very distant period. I am humble enough to put this in writing from the sense I have of your struggling situation and the great desire that you should [do] me the justice to credit the unostentatious and willing state of my nerves on all such occasions. It has not been my fault—I am doubly hurt at the slight[l]y rep[r]oachful tone of your note ~~as well as~~ and at the occasion of it,—for it must be some other disappointment; you seem'd so sure of some important help when I last saw you—now you have maimed me again; I was whole I had began reading again—when your note came I was engaged in a Book—I dread as much as a Plague the idle fever of two months more without any fruit. I will walk over the first fine day: then see what aspect your affairs have taken, and if they should continue gloomy walk into the City to Abbey and get his consent for I am persuaded that to me alone he will not concede a jot[1]

* * *[2]

To George and Georgiana Keats

(continued)

15, 16, 21, 30 April 1819

|| This is [Thursday] the 15th of April—you see what a time it is since I wrote—all that time I have been day by day expecting Letters from you—I write quite in the dark—In the hopes of a Letter daily I have deferred that I might write in the light—I was in town yesterday and at Taylors heard that young

1 *not concede a jot*: In the event Keats was able to get a small advance from Abbey, of which he lent £30 to Haydon (which was still not repaid on 17 June: see below, p. 376).
2 Signature and address cut off.

Brikbeck [*for* Birkbeck] had been in Town and was to set forward in six or seven days—so I shall dedicate that time to making up this parcel ready for him—I wish I could hear from you to make me "whole and general as the casing air"[1] A few days after the 19th of april [*for* March] I received a note from Haslam contain[i]ng the news of his father's death—The Family has all been well—Haslam has his father's situation—The Framptons[2] have behaved well to him—The day before yesterday I went to a rout at Sawrey's—it was made pleasant by Reynolds being there, and our getting into conversation with one of the most beautiful Girls I ever saw—She gave a remarkable prettiness to all those commonplaces which most women who talk must utter—I liked Mrs Sawrey very well. The Sunday before last your Brothers were to come by a long invitation—so long that for the time I forgot it when I promised Mrs Brawne to dine with her on the same day—On recollecting my engagement with your Brothers I immediately excused myself with Mrs Brawn but she would not hear of it and insisted on my bringing my friends with me. So we all dined at Mrs Brawne's. I have been to Mrs Bentley's this morning and put all the Letters two [*for* to] and from you and poor Tom and me—I have found some of the correspondence between him and that degraded Wells and Amena[3]—It is a wretched business. I do not know the rights of it—but what I do know would I am sure affect you so much that I am in two Minds whether I will tell you any thing about it—And yet I do not see why—for any thing tho' it be unpleasant, that calls to mind those we still love, has a compensation in itself for the pain it occasions—so very likely tomorrow I may set about coppying thee whole of what I have about it: with no sort of a Richardson self satisfaction—I hate it to a sickness—and I am affraid more from indolence of mind than any thing else I wonder how people exist with all their

1 *whole ... casing air*: *Macbeth*, III. iv. 23.
2 *The Framptons*: Frampton and Sons, wholesale greengrocers, Leadenhall Street, his employers.
3 *correspondence ... Amena*: For Keats's later comments on reading the letters, see below, pp. 345–6.

worries. I have not been to Westminster but once lately and that was to see Dilke in his new Lodgings—I think of living somewhere in the neighbourhood myself—Your mother was well by your Brothers' account. I shall see her perhaps tomorrow—yes I shall—We have had the Boys[1] here lately—they make a bit of a racket—I shall not be sorry when they go. I found also this morning in a note from George to you my dear sister a lock of your hair which I shall this moment put in the miniature case. A few days ago Hunt dined here and Brown invited Davenport to meet him. Davenport from a sense of weakness thought it incumbent upon him to show off—and pursuant to that never ceased talking and boaring all day, till I was completely fagged out—Brown grew melancholy—but Hunt perceiving what a complimentary tendency all this had bore it remarkably well—Brown grumbled about it for two or three days—I went with Hunt to Sir John Leicester's gallery[2] there I saw Northcote[3]—Hilton—Bewick and many more of great and Little note. Haydons picture is of very little progress this last year—He talk[s] about finishing it next year—Wordsworth is going to publish a Poem called Peter Bell—what a perverse fellow it is! Why wilt he talk about Peter Bells—I was told not to tell—but to you it will not be tellings—Reynolds hearing that said Peter Bell was coming out, took it into his head to write a skit upon it call'd Peter Bell.[4] He did it as soon as thought on it is to be published this morning, and comes out before the real Peter Bell, with this admirable motto from the "Bold stroke for a Wife' '"I am the real Simon Pure" '[5] I would be just as well to trounce Lord Byron in the same

1 *the Boys*: Brown's two nephews.

2 *Sir John Leicester's gallery*: Sir John Fleming Leicester (1762–1827), art patron, from 1818 made his collection in Hill Street, Mayfair, available to the public.

3 *Northcote*: James Northcote (1746–1831) was a painter and author.

4 *Peter Bell*: J. H. Reynolds's witty parody, published by Taylor and Hessey, appeared anonymously on 16 April, shortly after Wordsworth's *Peter Bell* (written in 1798) had been advertised and two weeks before it was published. Later in the letter Keats drafted his review of Reynolds's skit (pp. 149–50 below).

5 *Simon Pure*: The Quaker preacher in *A Bold Stroke for a Wife* (1718), a comedy by Susannah Centlivre (?1669–1723).

manner. I am still at a stand in versifying—I cannot do it yet with any pleasure—I mean however to look round at my resources and means—and see what I can do without poetry—To that end I shall live in Westminster—I have no doubt of making by some means a little to help on or I shall be left in the Lurch—with the burden of a little Pride—However I look in time—The Dilkes like their lodging in Westminster tolerably well. I cannot help thinking what a shame it is that poor Dilke should give up his comfortable house & garden for his Son, whom he will certainly ruin with too much care—The boy has nothing in his ears all day but himself and the importance of his education—Dilke has continually in his mouth "My Boy" This is what spoils princes: it may have the same effect with Commoners. Mrs Dilke has been very well lately—But what a shameful thing it is that for that obstinate Boy Dilke should stifle himself in Town Lodgings and wear out his Life by his continual apprehension of his Boys fate in Westminsterschool, with the rest of the Boys and the Masters—Eve[r]y one has some wear and tear—One would think Dilke ought to be quiet and happy—but no—this one Boy—makes his face pale, his society silent and his vigilanc<e> jealous—He would I have no doubt quarrel with any one who snubb'd his Boy—With all this he has no notion how to manage him O what a farce is our greatest cares! Yet one must be in the pother for the sake of Clothes food and Lodging. There has been a squabble between Kean and one Mr Bucke—There are faults on both sides—on Bucks the faults are positive to the Question: Keans fault is a want of genteel knowledge and high Policy—The formor writes knavishly foolish and the other silly bombast. It was about a Tragedy written by said Mr Bucke;[1] which it appears Mr Kean kick'd at—is [*for* it] was so bad—. After a little struggle of Mr Bucke's against Kean—drury Lane had the Policy to bring it one [*for* on] and Kean the impolicy not to appear in it—It was damn'd—The people in the Pit had a favou[r]ite call on the night of "Buck Buck rise up" and "Buck Buck how many horns do I hold up. Kotzebue the German

1 *Tragedy . . . Mr Bucke*: The preface to Charles Bucke's tragedy *The Italians: or, the Fatal Accusation* (1819) complained about his treatment by Kean.

Dramatist and traitor to his country was murdered lately by a young student whose name I forget—he stabbed himself immediately after crying out Germany! Germany![1] I was unfortunat<e> to miss Richards the only time I have been for many months to see him. Shall I treat you with a little extempore.

When they were come unto the Faery's Court[2]
They rang—no one at home—all gone to sport
And dance and kiss and love as faery's do
For Faries be as humans lovers true—
Amid the woods they were so lone and wild
Where even the Robin feels himself exild
And where the very brooks as if affraid
Hurry along to some less magic shade.
'No one at home'! the fretful princess cry'd
'And all for nothing such a drery ride
And all for nothing my new diamond cross
No one to see my persian feathers toss
No one to see my Ape, my Dwarf, my Fool
Or how I pace my otahaietan mule
Ape, Dwarf and Fool why stand you gaping there
Burst the door open, quick—or I declare
Ill switch you soundly and in pieces tear'.
The Dwarf began to tremble and the Ape
Star'd at the Fool, the Fool was all agape
The Princess grasp'd her switch but just in time
The dwarf with piteous face began to rhyme.
'O mighty Princess did you ne'er hear tell
What your poor servants know but too too well
Know you the three 'great crimes' in faery land
The first alas! poor Dwarf I understand
I made a whipstock of a faery's wand
The next is snoring in their company

1 *Kotzebue . . . Germany*: August von Kotzebue (1761–1819), the dramatist, was stabbed to death by a theology student, Karl Ludwig Sand, on 23 March 1819 as an enemy of the German people. The *Examiner*, which depicted Sand as a patriotic hero, followed the story from 4 April.

2 *When . . . Court*: First published 1888 (in part), 1890 (in full).

The next, the last the direst of the th[r]ee
Is making free when they are not at home
I was a Prince—a baby p[r]ince—my doom
You see, I made a whipstock of a wand
My top has henceforth slept in faery land.
He was a P[r]ince, the Fool a grown up Prince
But he has never been a king's son since
He fell a snoring at a faery Ball—
Your poor Ape was a Prince, and he poor thing
Picklock'd a faerry's boudour—now no King
But ape—so pray you highness stay awhile
'T is sooth indeed We know it to our sorrow—
Persist and you may be an ape tomorrow—
While the Dwarf spake the Princess all for spite
Peal'd the brown hazel twig to lilly white
Clench'd her small teeth, and held her lips apart
Try'd to look unconcern'd with beating heart
They saw her highness had made up her mind
A quavering[1] like thee reeds before the wind—
And they had had it, but o happy chance
The Ape for very fear began to dance
And grin'd as all his ugliness did ache—
She staid her vixen fingers for his sake
He was so very ugly: then she took
Her pocket ~~glass~~ mirror and began to look
First at herself and at him and then
She smil'd at her own beauteous face again.
Yet for all this—for all her pretty face—
She took it in her head to see the place
Women gain little from experience
Either in Lovers husbands or expence
The more the beauty, the more fortune too
Beauty before the wide world never knew
So each Fair reasons—tho' it oft miscarries.
She thought her pretty face would please the faries
'My darling Ape I wont whip you to day

1 *A quavering*: Altered from 'They quaver'd' to 'And quaver'd' to 'A quavering'.

Give me the Picklock Sirrah and go play—
They all three wept—but counsel was as vain
As crying cup biddy to drops of rain—
Yet lingeringly did the sad Ape forth draw
The Picklock from the Pocket in his Jaw.
The Princess took it and dismounting straight<t>
Trip'd in blue silver'd slippers to the gate
And touch'd the wards, the Door ~~opes~~ /full/ cou[r]teou[s]ly
Opened—she enter'd with her servants three
Again it clos'd and there was nothing seen
But the Mule grasing on the herbage green.

End of Canto xii

Canto the xiii

The Mule no sooner saw himself alone
Than he prick[ed] up his Ears—and 'said well done,
At least unhappy Prince I may be free—
No more a Princess shall side saddle me.
O king of Othaietè—tho a Mule
'Aye every inch a king'—tho—'Fortune's fool'
Well done—for by what Mr Dwarfy said
I would not give a sixpenc[e] for her head'
Even as he spake 'he trotted in high glee
To the knotty side of an old Pollard tree
And rub his sides against the mossed bark
Till his Girths burst and left him naked stark
Except his Bridle—how get rid of that
Buckled and tied with many a twist and plait
At last it struck him to pretend to sleep
And then the thievish Monkies down would creep
And filch the unpleasant trammels quite away
No sooner thought of than adown he lay
Sham'd a good snore—the Monkey-men descende[d]
And whom they thought to injure they befriended.
They hung his Bridle on a topmost bough
And of[f] he went run, trot, or any how—

———

Brown is gone to bed—and I am tired of rhyming—there is a north wind blowing playing young gooseberry with the trees—I dont care so it he[l]ps even with a side wind a Letter to me—for I cannot put faith in any reports I hear of the Settlement some are good some bad—Last Sunday I took a Walk towards highgate and in the lane that winds by the side of Lord Mansfield's park[1] I met M[r] Green our Demonstrator at Guy's[2] in conversation with Coleridge—I joined them, after enquiring by a look whether it would be agreeable—I walked with him a[t] his alderman-after dinner pace for near two miles I suppose In those two Miles he broached a thousand things—let me see if I can give you a list—Nightingales, Poetry—on Poetical Sensation—Metaphysics—Different genera and species of Dreams—Nightmare—a dream accompanied by a sense of touch—single and double touch—A dream related—First and second consciousness—the difference explained between will and Volition—so m[an]y metaphysicians from a want of smoking the second consciousness—Monsters—the Kraken—Mermaids—southey believes in them—southeys belief too much diluted—A Ghost story—Good morning—I heard his voice as he came towards me—I heard it as he moved away—I had heard it all the interval—if it may be called so. He was civil enough to ask me to call on him at Highgate Good Night!

[Friday, 16 April] It looks so much like rain I shall not go to town to day; but put it off till tomorrow—Brown this morning is writing some spenserian stanzas against M[rs] Miss Brawne and me; so I shall amuse myself with him a little: in the manner of Spenser—

> He is to weet a melancholy Carle[3]
> Thin in the waist, with bushy head of hair
> As hath the seeded thistle when in parle
> It holds the Zephyr ere it sendeth fair

1 *Lord Mansfield's park*: Millfield Lane and Kenwood House.

2 *M[r] Green . . . Guy's*: Joseph Henry Green (1791–1863), surgeon and natural philosopher, co-editor of Coleridge's literary remains, had completed his apprenticeship at St Thomas' Hospital in 1816.

3 *He . . . Carle*: First printed in *1848*.

Its light balloons into the summer air
Therto his beard had not began to bloom
No brush had touch'd his chin or razor sheer
No care had touch[ed] his cheek with mortal doom
But new he was and bright as scarf from persian loom—

Ne cared he for wine, or half and half
Ne cared he for fish or flesh or fowl
And sauces held he worthless as the chaff
He ~~scorn'd~~ /'sdeign'd/ the swine herd at the wassail bowl
Ne with lewd ribbalds sat he cheek by jowl
Ne with sly Lemans in the scorner's chair
But after water brooks this Pilgrim's soul
Panted, and all his food was woodland air
Though he would ofttimes feast on gillyflowers rare—

The slang of cities in no wise he knew
Tipping the wink to him was hethen greek
He sipp'd no olden Tom or ruin blue[1]
Or nantz[2] or cheery brandy drank full meek
By many a Damsel hoarse and rouge of cheek
Nor did he know each aged Watchman's beat—
Nor in obscured perlieus would he seek
For curled Jewesses with ankles neat
Who as they walk abroad make tinkling with their feet—

This character would ensure him a situation in the establishment of patient Griselda—The servant has come for the little Browns this morning—they have been a toothache to me which I shall enjoy the riddance of—Their little voices are like wasps stings—'Some times I am all wound with Browns.'[3] We had a claret feast some little while ago There were Dilke, Reynolds, Skinner, Mancur, John Brown, Martin, Brown and I—We all got a little tipsy—but pleasantly so—I enjoy Claret to a degree—I have been looking over the correspondence of the

1 *olden Tom . . . ruin blue*: Both names for gin.
2 *nantz*: Brandy from Nantes.
3 *Some . . . Browns*: Compare Caliban in *The Tempest*, II. ii. 12–13, 'Sometime am I / All wound with adders.'

pretended Amena and Wells[1] this evening—I see now the whole cruel deception—I think Wells must have had an accomplice in it—Amena's Letters are in a Man's language, and in a Man's hand imitating a woman's—The instigations to this diabolical scheme were vanity, and the love of intrigue. It was no thoughtless hoax—but a cruel deception on a sanguine Temperament, with every show of friendship. I do not think death too bad for the villain—The world would look upon it in a differrent light should I expose it—they would call it a frolic—so I must be wary—but I consider it my duty to be prudently revengeful. I will hang over his head like a sword by a hair. I will be opium to his vanity—if I cannot injure his interests—He is a rat and he shall have ratsbane to his vanity—I will harm him all I possibly can—I have no doubt I shall be able to do so—Let us leave him to his misery alone except when we can throw in a little more—The fifth canto of Dante pleases me more and more—it is that one in which he meets with Paulo and Francesca—I had passed many days in rather a low state of mind and in the midst of them I dreamt of being in that region of Hell. The dream was one of the most delightful enjoyments I ever had in my life—I floated about the whirling atmosphere as it is described with a beautiful figure to whose lips mine were joined at [*for* as] it seem'd for an age—and in the midst of all this cold and darkness I was warm—even flowery tree tops sprung up and we rested on them sometimes with the lightness of a cloud till the wind blew us away again—I tried a Sonnet upon it—there are fourteen lines but nothing of what I felt in it—o that I could dream it every night—

> As Hermes once took to his feathers light[2]
> When lulled Argus, baffled, swoon'd and slept
> So on a delphic reed my idle spright

1 *Amena and Wells*: Charles Jeremiah Wells (1800–1879), lawyer, minor poet and schoolfellow of Tom Keats, had sent him clumsy, fictitious love letters signed 'Amena Bellefila'. Tom took them for real. Keats broke off all relations with Wells, believing Tom's health to have been badly affected by the hoax.
2 *As Hermes . . . light*: First published (signed 'Caviare') in the *Indicator* (28 June 1820), with substantive alterations.

So play'd, so charm'd so conquer'd, so bereft
The dragon world of all its hundred eyes
And seeing it asleep so fled away:—
Not to pure Ida with its snow~~clad~~ /cold skies,/
Nor unto Tempe where Jove grieved that day,
But to that second circle of sad hell,
Where in the gust, the whirlwind and the flaw
Of Rain and hailstones lovers need not tell
Their sorrows—Pale were the sweet lips I saw
Pale were the lips I kiss'd and the fair fo[r]m
I floated with about that melancholy storm—

I want very very much a little of your wit my dear sister—a Letter or two of yours just to bandy back a pun or two across the Atlantic and send a quibble over the Floridas—Now you have by this time crumpled up your large Bonnet, what do you wear—a cap! do you put your hair in papers of a night? do you pay the Miss Birkbeck's a morning visit—have you any tea? or to [*for* do] you milk and water with them—What place of Worship do you go to—the Quakers the Moravians, the Unitarians or the Methodists—Are there any flowers in bloom you like—any beautiful heaths—Any Streets full of Corset Makers. What sort of shoes have you to fit those pretty feet of yours? Do you desire Comp^{ts} to one another? Do you ride on Horseback? What do you have for breakfast, dinner and supper? without mentioning lunch and bever and wet[1] and snack—and a bit to stay one's stomach—Do you get any spirits—now you might easily distill some whiskey—and going into the woods to set up a whiskey spop [*for* shop] for the Monkeys—Do you and the miss Birkbecks get groggy on any thing—a little so so ish so as to be obliged to be seen home with a Lantern—You may perhaps have a game at puss in the corner—Ladies are warranted to play at this game though they have not whiskers. Have you a fiddle in the Settlement—or at any rate a jew's harp—which will play in spite of ones teeth—When you have nothing else to do for a whole day I tell you how you may employ it—First get up and when you are

1 *bever and wet*: A small meal and a drink.

dress'd, as it would be pretty early, with a high wind in the woods give George a cold Pig[1] with my Complements. Then you may saunter into the nearest coffee-house and after taking a dram and a look at the chronicle—go and frighten the wild boars upon the strength—you may as well bring one home for breakfeast serving up the hoofs garnished with bristles and a grunt or two to accompany the singing of the kettle—then if George is not up give him a colder Pig always with my Compliments—When you are both set down to breakfast I advise you to eat your full share—but leave off immediately on feeling yourself inclined to any thing on the other side of the puffy—avoid that for it does not become young women—After you have eaten your breakfast—keep your eye upon dinner—it is the safest way—You should keep a Hawk's eye over your dinner and keep hovering over it till due time then pounce taking care not to break any plates—While you are hovering with your dinner in p[r]ospect you may do a thousand things—put a hedgehog into Georges hat—pour a little water into his rifle—soak his boots in a pail of water—cut his jacket round into shreds like a roman kilt or the back of my grandmothers stays—sow <u>off</u> his buttons

[Wednesday morning, 21 April][2] Yesterday I could not write a line I was so fat[i]gued for the day before, I went to town in the morning called on your Mother, and returned in time for a few friends we had to dinner. There were Taylor Woodhouse, Reynolds—we began cards at about 9 o'Clock, and the night coming on and continuing dark and rainy they could not think of returning to town—so we played at Cards till very daylight—and yesterday I was not worth a sixpence—Your mother was very well but anxious for a Letter. We had half an hours talk and no more for I was obliged to be home. M^rs and Miss Millar were well—and so was Miss Waldegrave—I have asked your Brothers here for next Sunday—When Reynolds was here on Monday—he asked me to give Hunt a hint to take notice of his Peter Bell in the Examiner—the best thing I can do is to write a little notice of

1 *a cold Pig*: Wake by splashing with cold water or pulling off the bedclothes.
2 By now Keats had abandoned *Hyperion*, because Woodhouse copied the text on 20 April (*Texts*, p. 230).

it myself which I will do here and copy it out if it should suit my Purpose[1]—Peter-Bell There have been lately advertized two Books both Peter Bell by name; what stuff the one was made of might be seen by the motto, 'I am the real Simon Pure". This false florimel[2] has hurried from the press and obtruded herself into public notice while for ought we know the real one may be still wandering about the woods and mountains. Let us hope she may soon ~~make her~~ appear~~ance~~ and make good her right to the magic girdle—The Pampleteering Archimage[3] we can perceive has rather a splenetic love than a downright hatred to real florimels—if indeed they ~~sing~~ had been so christened—or had even a pretention to play at bob cherry with Barbara Lewthwaite:[4] but ~~the rest are we~~ he has a fixed aversion to those three rhyming Graces Alice Fell,[5] Susan Gale, and Betty Foy;[6] ~~and who can wonder at it?~~ and now at lenght [*for* length] especially to Peter Bell—fit Apollo. ~~The writer of this little skit from understanding~~ It may be seen from one or two Passages ~~of~~ in this little skit, that the writer of it has felt the finer parts of Mr Wordsworth ~~Poetry~~, and perhaps expatiated with his more remote and sublimer muse; ~~who sits aloof in a cheerful sadness, and~~ This as far as it relates to Peter Bell is unlucky. The more he may love the sad embroidery of the Excursion; the more he will hate the coarse Samplers of Betty Foy and Alice Fell; and as they come from the same hand, the better will be able to imitate that which can be imitated. to wit Peter Bell—as far as can be imagined from the obstinate Name—We repeat, it is very unlucky—this real Simon Pure is in parts the very Man—there is a pernicious likeness in the scenery a 'pestilent

1 *a little notice . . . my Purpose*: Keats's review, drafted here, was published in the *Examiner* (25 April 1819), p. 270, together with extracts from Reynolds's preface and poem.
2 *false florimel*: The false Florimell of Spenser's *The Faerie Queene*, III. viii. 5–20, created as the double of Florimell, the type of chastity and virtue.
3 *Archimage*: Archimago, the enchanter in *The Faerie Queene*, I and II.
4 *Barbara Lewthwaite*: The child in Wordsworth's 'The Pet Lamb'.
5 *Alice Fell*: A girl in Wordsworth's poem of the same name in *Poems in Two Volumes* (1807).
6 *Susan Gale . . . Betty Foy*: Characters in 'The Idiot Boy': both poems were published in *Lyrical Ballads* (1798). Reynolds, like Keats, preferred Wordsworth's contemplative poems to his narratives of rural life.

humour' in the rhymes and an inveterate cadence in some of the Stanzas that must be lamented—If we are one part ~~pleased~~ /amused/ at this we are th[r]ee parts sorry that an appreciator of Wordsworth should show so much temper at this really provoking name of Peter Bell—! This will do well enough—I have coppied it and enclosed it to Hunt—You will call it a little politic—seeing I keep clear of all parties. I say something for and against both parties—and suit it to the tune of the examiner—I mean to say I do not unsuit it—and I believe I think what I say nay I am sure I do—I and my conscience are in luck to day—which is an excellent thing—The other night I went to the Play with Rice, Reynolds and Martin—we saw a new dull and half damnd opera call'd 'the heart of Mid Lothian' that was on Saturday[1]—I stopt at Taylors on sunday with Woodhouse—and passed a quiet sort of pleasant day. I have been very much pleased with the Panorama of the ships at the north Pole—with the icebergs, the Mountains, the Bears the Walrus—the seals the Penguins—and a large whale floating back above water—it is impossible to describe the place[2]—Wednesday Evening—

La belle dame sans merci—[3]

O what can ail thee knight at a[r]ms
  Alone and palely loitering?
The sedge has withered from the Lake
  And no birds sing!

O what can ail thee knight at a[r]ms
  So haggard and so woe begone?

1 *the heart . . . on Saturday*: Daniel Terry's musical drama *The Heart of Midlothian*, performed at Covent Garden on Saturday, 17 April.
2 *Panorama . . . place*: This depiction of the 'North Coast of Spitzbergen', based on the drawings of Frederick William Beechey (1796–1856), who accompanied Sir John Franklin on his unsuccessful 'Polar Expedition', had opened on Easter Monday, 12 April at Henry Aston Barker's Panorama in Leicester Square (*Morning Chronicle*, 8 April 1819).
3 *La belle . . . merci*: First published (signed 'Caviare') in the *Indicator* (10 May 1820), with substantial alterations. Stillinger, *Texts*, pp. 232, 234, dates this and the following poem 21 or 28 April.

The squirrel's granary is full
And the harvest's done.

I see ~~death's~~ /a/ lilly on thy brow
With anguish moist and fever dew,
And on thy cheeks ~~death's~~ /a/ fading rose
Fast Withereth too—

I met a Lady in the ~~Wilds~~ Meads
Full beautiful, a faery's child
Her hair was long, her foot was light
And her eyes were wild—

I made a Garland for her head,
And bracelets too, and fragrant Zone
She look'd at me as she'd did love
And made sweet moan—

I set her on my pacing steed
And nothing else saw all day long
For sidelong would she bend and sing
A faerys song—

She found me roots of relish sweet
And honey wild and ~~honey~~ /manna/ dew
And sure in language strange she said
I love thee true—

She took me to her elfin grot
And there she wept /and sigh'd full sore/[1]
And there I shut her wild wild eyes
With kisses four.

And there she lulled me asleep
And there I drean'd [*for* dream'd] Ah Woe betide!
The latest dream I ever dreamt
On the cold hill side

1 *And there . . . full sore*: This clause is written above '~~and there she sighed /full/ sore~~'.

I saw pale kings and Princes too
  Pale warriors death pale were they all
They cried La belle dame sans merci
  Thee hath in thrall.

I saw their starv'd lips in the gloam
  /~~All tremble~~/ With horrid warning /gaped/ wide ~~agape~~
And I awoke and found me here
  On the cold hill's side

And this is way [for why] I ~~wither~~ sojourn here
  Alone and palely loitering;
Though the sedge is wither'd frome the Lak[e]
  And no birds sing— — . . . .

Why four kisses—you will say—why four because I wish to restrain the headlong impetuosity of my Muse—she would have fain said 'score' without hurting the rhyme—but we must temper the Imagination as the Critics say with Judgment. I was obliged to choose an even number that both eyes might have fair play: and to speak truly I think two a piece quite sufficient—Suppose I had said seven; there would have been three and a half a piece—a very awkward affair—and well got out of on my side—

Chorus of Faries ~~three~~ 4 Fire, air, earth and water—
Salamander, Zephyr, Dusketha Breama—[1]

Sal.	Happy happy glowing fire!
Zep.	Fragrant air, delicious light!
Dusk.	Let me to my glooms retire
Bream—	I to ~~my~~ greenweed rivers bright.

Salam—

Happy, happy glowing fire
Dazzling bowers of soft retire!
Ever let my nourish'd wing
Like a bats s[t]ill wandering

1 *Salamander* ... *Breama*: First published in *1848*.

~~Ever beat~~ /Faintless fan/ your fiery spaces
Spirit sole in deadly places
In unhaunted roar and blaze
Open eyes that never daze
Let me see the myriad shapes
Of Men and Beasts and Fish and apes
Portray'd in many a fiery den,
And wrough[t] by spumy bitumen
On the deep intenser roof
Arched every way aloof
Let me breathe upon my Skies
And anger their live tapestries
Free from cold and every care
Of chilly rain and shivring air.

Zephyr.

Spright of fire—away away!
Or your very roundelay
Will sear my plumeage ~~all~~ /newly/ budded
From its quilled sheath ~~and~~ /all/ studded
with the selfsame dews that fell
On the May-grown Asphodel.
Spright of fire away away!

Breama

Sp[r]ight of fire, away away!
Zephyer blue eyed faery turn
And see my cool sedge shaded urn
Where its rests its mossy brim
Mid water mint and cresses dim
~~Where~~ /And/ the flowers ~~amid~~ /in/ sweet troubles
Lift their eyes above the bubbles
Like our Queen when she would pleaise
To sleep and Oberon will tease—
Love me blue eyed Faery true
~~For in~~ soothly I am sick for you—

Zephyr

Gentle Bre[a]ma by the first
Violet young nature nurst
I will bathe myself with thee
So you sometime follow me
To my home far far in west
~~Far beyond the~~
Far beyond the search and quest
O the golden browed sun—
Come with me oer tops of trees
To my fragrant Pallaces
Where they ever floating are
Beneath the cherish of a star
~~Who with~~ /Call'd/ Vesper—who with silver veil
Ever Hides ~~his brightness~~ his brilliance pale
Ever gently drows'd doth keep
Twilight of the Fays to sleep
Fear not that your watry hair
Will thirst in drouthy ringlets there—
Clouds of stored summer rains
That shalt taste before the stains
Of the mountain soil they take
And too unlucent for thee make
I love thee ch[r]ystal faery true
Sooth I am as sick for you

Salam—

Out ye agueish Faeries out!
~~Chillier than the water~~
Chilly Lovers what a rout,
Keep ye with your frozen breath
Colder than the mortal death—
Adder-eyed Dusketha, speak
Shall we leave these and go seek
In the Earths wide Entrails old
Couches wa[r]m as theirs is cold
O for a fiery gloom and thee

Dusketha so enchantingly
  Freck[l]e wing'd and lizard sided!

Dusketha

By thee spright I will be guided
I ~~lo~~ care not for cold or heat
Frost and Flame or sparks or sleet
To my essence are the same
But I honor more the flame—
Spright of fire I follow thee
Wheresoever it m[a]y be,
To the ~~very fire~~ torrid /spouts/ fountains
Underneath earth quaked mountains
Or at thy supreme desire
Touch the very pulse of fire
With my bare unlidded eyes

Salam—

Sweet Dusketha: Paradise!
Off ye icy spirits—fly
Frosty creatures of sky—

Dusketha

Breathe upon them fiery spright

Zephyr Bre[a]ma to each other

~~let us fly~~
~~Ah, my love, my life~~
Away Away to our delight

Salam

Go and feed on icicles ~~will we~~ /while we/
Bedded in tongued flames will be

Dusketha

Lead me to those fevrous glooms
Sp[r]ight of fire

Breana
Me to the blooms
~~Soft~~ Blue eyed Zephyr of those flowers
Far in the west w[h]ere May cloud lours
And the beams of still vesper, where winds are all wist
Are shed through the rain and the milder mist
And twilight your floating bowers—

I have been reading lately two very different books Robertson's America[1] and Voltaire's Siecle De Louis xiv[2] It is like walking arm and arm between Pizarro and the great-little Monarch. In How lementabl[e] a case do we see the great body of the people in both instances: in the first, where Men might seem to inherit quiet of Mind from unsophisticated senses; from uncontamination of civilisation; and especially from their being as it were estranged from the mutual helps of Society and its mutual injuries—and thereby more immediately under the Protection of Providence—even there they had mortal pains to bear as bad; or even worse than Ba[i]liffs, Debts and Poverties of civilised Life—The whole appears to resolve into this—that Man is originally 'a poor forked creature'[3] subject to the same mischances as the beasts of the forest, destined to hardships and disquietude of some kind or other. If he improves by degrees his bodily accomodations and comforts—at each stage, at each accent there are waiting for him a fresh set of annoyances—he is mortal and there is still a heaven with its Stars abov[e] his head. The most interesting question that can come before us is, How far by the persevering endeavours of a seldom appearing Socrates Mankind may be made happy—I can imagine such happiness carried to an extreme—but what must it end in?—Death—and who could in such a case bear with death—the whole troubles of life which are now frittered away in a series of years, would the[n] be accumulated for the last days of a being who instead of hailing its approach, would leave this

1 *Robertson's America*: William Robertson's *History of America*, 2 vols (1777, etc.).
2 *Voltaire's . . . xiv*: Keats owned a copy of *Le Siècle de Louis XIV* (1751, etc.).
3 *a poor forked creature*: *King Lear*, III. iv. 106–7.

world as Eve left Paradise—But in truth I do not at all believe in this sort of perfectibility—the nature of the world will not admit of it—the inhabitants of the world will correspond to itself—Let the fish philosophise the ice away from the Rivers in winter time and they shall be at continual play in the tepid delight of summer. Look at the Poles and at the sands of Africa, Whirlpools and volcanoes—Let men exterminate them and I will say that they may arrive at earthly Happiness—The point at which Man may arrive is as far as the paral[l]el state in inanimate nature and no further—For instance suppose a rose to have sensation, it blooms on a beautiful morning it enjoys itself—but there comes a cold wind, a hot sun—it can not escape it, it cannot destroy its annoyances—they are as native to the world as itself: no more can man be happy in spite, the world[l]y elements will prey upon his nature—The common cognomen of this world among the misguided and superstitious is 'a vale of tears' from which we are to be redeemed by a certain arbit[r]ary interposition of God and taken to Heaven—What a little circumscribe[d] straightened notion! Call the world if you Please '"The vale of Soul-making" Then you will find out the use of the world (I am speaking now in the highest terms for human nature admitting it to be immortal which I will here take for granted for the purpose of showing a thought which has struck me concerning it) I say '<u>Soul making</u>' Soul as distinguished from an Intelligence—There may be intelligences[1] or sparks of divinity in millions—but they are not Souls till they acquire identities, till each one is personally itself. I[n]telligences are atoms of perception—they know and they see and they are pure, in short they are God—how then are Souls to be made? How then are these sparks which are God to have identity given them—so as ever to possess a bliss peculiar to each ones individual existence? How, but by the medium of a world like this? This point I sincerely wish to consider because I think it a grander system of salvation than the chrystain religion—or rather it is a system of Spirit-creation—This is effected by three

1 *intelligences*: Compare Adam thanking Raphael in *Paradise Lost*, VIII, 180–1, 'How fully hast thou satisfied me, pure / Intelligence of heaven, angel serene.'

grand materials acting the one upon the other for a series of years—These three Materials are the Intelligence—the human heart (as distinguished from intelligence or Mind) and the World or Elemental space suited for the proper action of Mind and Heart on each other for the purpose of forming the Soul or Intelligence destined to possess the sense of Identity. I can scarcely express what I but dimly perceive—and yet I think I perceive it—that you may judge the more clearly I will put it in the most homely form possible—I will call the world a School instituted for the purpose of teaching little children to read—I will call the human heart the horn Book used in that School—and I will call the Child able to read, the Soul made from that school and its hornbook. Do you not see how necessary a World of Pains and troubles is to school an Intelligence and make it a soul? A Place where the heart must feel and suffer in a thousand diverse ways! Not merely is the Heart a Hornbook, It is the Minds Bible, it is the Minds experience, it is the teat from which the Mind or intelligence sucks its identity—As various as the Lives of Men are—so various become their souls, and thus does God make individual beings, Souls, Identical Souls of the sparks of his own essence—This appears to me a faint sketch of a system of Salvation which does not affront our reason and humanity—I am convinced that many difficulties which christians labour under would vanish before it—There is one wh[i]ch even now Strikes me—the Salvation of Children—In them the Spark or intelligence returns to God without any identity—it having had no time to learn of, and be altered by, the heart—or seat of the human Passions—It is pretty generally suspected that the chr[i]stian scheme has been coppied from the ancient persian and greek Philosophers. Why may they not have made this simple thing even more simple for common apprehension by introducing Mediators and Personages in the same manner as in the hethen mythology abstractions are personified—Seriously I think it probable that this System of Soul-making—may have been the Parent of all the more palpable and personal Schemes of Redemption, among the Zoroastrians the Christians and the Hindoos. For as one part of the human species must have their carved Jupiter;

so another part must have the palpable and named Mediatior and saviour, their Christ their Oromanes and their Vishnu—If what I have said should not be plain enough, as I fear it may not be, I will but [*for* put] you in the place where I began in this series of thoughts—I mean, I began by seeing how man was formed by circumstances—and what are circumstances?—but touchstones of his heart—? and what are touchstones?—but proovings of his hearrt?—and what are proovings of his heart but fortifiers or alterers of his nature? and what is his altered nature but his soul?—and what was his soul before it came into the world and had These provings and alterations and perfectionings?—An intelligence—without Identity—and how is this Identity to be made? Through the medium of the Heart? And how is the heart to become this Medium but in a world of Circumstances?—

There now I think what with Poetry and Theology you may thank your Stars that my pen is not very long winded—

Yesterday I received two Letters from your Mother and Henry which I shall send by young Birkbeck with this—

Friday—April 30—Brown has been rummaging up some of my old sins—that is to say sonnets I do not think you remember them, so I will copy them out as well as two or three lately written—I have just written one on Fame—which Brown is transcribing and he has his book and mine I must employ myself perhaps on a sonnet on the same subject—

On Fame[1]

You cannot eat your cake and have it too

Proverb.

How /fever'd/ is that ~~Man misled~~ /Man/ who cannot look
Upon his mortal days with temperate blood
Who vexes all the leaves of his Life's book
And robs his fair name of its maidenhood
It is as if the rose should pluck herself
Or the ripe plum finger its misty bloom

1 *On Fame*: Drafted here and later revised; first published in *1848*.

As if a clear Lake meddling with itself
  Should ~~fill~~ /cloud/ its pureness with a muddy gloom[1]
But the rose leaves herself upon the Briar
For winds to kiss and grateful Bees to ~~taste~~ feed
And the ripe plumb ~~still~~ /~~will~~ still/ wears its dim attire
  The undisturbed Lake has crystal space—
  Why then should Man /leasing the world for grace/[2]
~~And spoil burn our pleasures in his selfish fire—~~
Spoil his salvation by a fierce miscreed

Another on Fame[3]

Fame like a wayward girl will still be coy
  To those who woo her with too slavish knees
  But makes surrender to some thoughtless boy
And dotes the more upon a heart at ease—
She is a Gipsey will not speak to those
  Who have not learnt to be content without her
A Jilt whose ear was never whisper'd close
  Who think[s] they scandal her who talk about her—
A very Gipsey is she Nilus born,
Sister in law to jealous Potiphar.—
Ye lovesick Bards, repay her scorn for scorn.
Ye lovelorn Artists madmen that ye are,
Make your best bow to her and bid adieu
Then if she likes it she will follow you—

To Sleep[4]

O soft embalmer of the still midnight
  Shutting with careful fingers and benign
Our gloom-pleas'd eyes embowered from the light,
  Enshaded in forgetfulness divine—
O soothest sleep, if so it please the[e] close
  In midst of this thine hymn my willing eyes,

1 *gloom*: Written 'gloon'.
2 *Why then . . . for grace*: Written above '~~his own bright name deface~~'.
3 *Another on Fame*: First published in 1837, then *1848*.
4 *To Sleep*: First published in 1838, then *1848*.

Or wait the amen, ere thy poppy throws
  Around my bed it[s] dewy Charities—
Then save me or the passed day will shine
Upon my pillow breeding many woes.
Save me from curious conscience that still lords
Its strength for darkness, borrowing[1] like ~~the~~ /a/ Mole—
Turn the key deftly in the oiled wards
And seal the hushed Casket of my soul.

The following Poem—the last I have written is the first and the only one with which I have taken even moderate pains—I have for the most part dashed of[f] my lines in a hurry—This I have done leisurely—I think it reads the more richly for it and will I hope encourage me to write other thing[s] in even a more peacable and healthy spirit. You must recollect that Psyche was not embodied as a goddess before the time of Apuleius the Platonist who lived afteir the A[u]gustan age, and consequently the Goddess was never worshipped or sacrificed to with any of the ancient fervour—and perhaps never thought of in the old religion—I am more orthodox that [*for* than] to let a hethen Goddess be so neglected—

Ode to Psyche—[2]

O Goddess hear these tuneless numbers, rung
  By sweet enforcement, and remembrance dear,
And pardon that thy secrets should be sung
  Even ~~to~~ into thine own soft-chonched ear!
Surely I dreamt to day; or did I see
The winged Psyche, with awaked eyes?
I wander'd in a forest thoughtlessly,
And on the sudden, fainting with surprise,
Saw two fair Creatures couched side by side
In deepest grass beneath the whisp'ring fan
Of leaves and trembled blossoms, where there ran

1 *borrowing*: Copying error for 'burrowing'.
2 Ode to Psyche: Published with revisions in *1820*.

A Brooklet scarce espied
'Mid hush'd, cool-rooted flowers, fragrant eyed,
Blue, freckle-pink, and budded syrian[1]
They lay, calm-breathing on the bedded grass.
Their arms embraced and their pinions too;
Their lips touch'd not, but had not bid adiew,
As if disjoined by soft-handed slumber,
And ready still past kisses to outnumber,
At tender eye dawn of aurorian love.
The winged boy I knew:
But who wast thou O happy happy dove?
His Psyche true?

O lastest born, and loveliest vision far
  Of all Olympus faded Hierarchy!
Fairer than Phœbe's sapphire-region'd star,
  Or Vesper amorous glow worm of the sky;
Fairer than these though Temple thou hadst none,
  Nor Altar heap'd with flowers;
Nor virgin choir to make delicious moan
  Upon the midnight hours;
No voice, no lute, no pipe no incense sweet
  From chain-swung Censer teeming
No shrine, no grove, no Oracle, no heat
  Of pale-mouth'd Prophet dreaming!

O Bloomiest! though too late for antique vows;
  Too, too late for the fond believing Lyre,
When holy were the haunted forest boughs,
  Holy the air, the water and the fire:
Yet even in these days so far retir'd
From happy Pieties, thy lucent fans,
Fluttering among the faint Olympians,

1 *budded syrian*: Keats's publishers persuaded him to print 'budded Tyrian', an unnecessary alteration. Laura E. Campbell believes Keats refers to Syrian rue, a yellow flower, with medicinal use as a narcotic (*English Language Notes*, 33.2 (1995), pp. 53–8) or he could be referring to the Syrian (i.e., Damascus) Rose.

I see, and sing by my own eyes inspired.
O let me be thy Choir and make a moan
Upon the midnight hours;
Thy voice, thy lute, thy pipe, thy incense sweet
From swinged Censer teeming;
Thy Shrine, thy Grove, thy Oracle, thy heat
Of pale-mouth'd Prophet dreaming!
Yes I will be thy Priest and build a fane
In some untrodden region of my Mind,
Where branched thoughts new grown with pleasant pain,
Instead of pines shall murmur in the wind.
Far, far around shall those dark cluster'd trees
Fledge the wild-ridged mountains steep by steep,
And there by Zephyrs, streams and birds and bees
The moss-lain Dryads shall be ~~charmed~~ /lull'd/ to sleep.
And in the midst of this wide-quietness
A rosy Sanctuary will I dress
With the wreath'd trellis of a working brain;
With buds and bells and stars without a mane [*for* name];
With all the gardener, fancy e'er could ~~frame~~ /feign/
Who breeding flowers will never breed the same—
And there shall be for thee all soft delight
That shadowy thought can win;
A bright torch, and a casement ope at night,
To let the warm Love in—

Here endeth ye Ode to Psyche

Incipit altera Sonneta.

I have been endeavouring to discover a better sonnet stanza than we have. The legitimate does not suit the language over-well from the pouncing rhymes—the other kind appears too elegaic—and the couplet at the end of it has seldom a pleasing effect—I do not pretend to have succeeded—it will explain itself—

If by dull rhymes our English must be chaind[1]
And, like Andromeda, the Sonnet sweet,
Fetterd in spite of pained Loveliness;
Let us find out, if we must be constrain'd,
Sandals more interwoven and complete[2]
To fit the naked foot of Poesy—
Let us inspect the Lyre, and weigh the stress
Of every chord, and see what may be gain'd
By ear industrious and attention meet.
Misers of sound and syllable no less
Than Midas of his coinage, let us be
Jealous of dead leaves in the bay wreath crown
So if we may not let the Muse be free,
She will be bound with garlands of her own.

Here endeth the other Sonnet—

(continued 4 May 1819, p. 366 below)

To Fanny Keats
1 May (?) 1819

[Harvard MS]

My dear Fanny, Wentworth Place Saturday—

If it were but six o Clock in the morning I would set off to see you to day: if I should do so now I could not stop long enough for a how d'ye do—it is so long a walk through Hornsey and Tottenham—and as for Stage Coaching it besides that it is very expensive it is like going into the Boxes by way of the pit—I cannot go out on Sunday—but if on Monday it should promise as fair as to day I will put on a pair of loose easy palatable boots and me rendre chez vous—I continue increasing

1 *If by . . . be chaind*: First published in 1836, then *1848*.
2 *Sandals . . . complete*: The final leaf of this letter (given to the Harvard Keats Collection in 1995) starts with this line.

my letter to George to send it by one of Birkbeck's sons who is going out soon[1]—so if you will let me have a few more lines, they will be in time—I am glad you got on so well with Monsr le Curè—is he a nice Clergyman—a great deal depends upon a cock'd hat and powder—not gun powder, lord love us, but lady-meal, violet-smooth, dainty-scented lilly-white, feather-soft, wigsby-dressing, coat-collar-spoiling whisker-reaching, pig-tail loving, swans down-puffing, parson-sweetening powder—I shall call in passing at the tottenham nursery and see if I can find some seasonable plants for you. That is the nearest place—or by our la'kin or lady kin, that is by the virgin Mary's kindred, is there not a twig manufacturer in Walthamstow? M^r^ & Mrs Dilke are coming to dine with us to day—they will enjoy the country after Westminster—O there is nothing like fine weather, and health, and Books, and a fine country, and a contented Mind, and Diligent habit of reading and thinking, and an amulet against the ennui—and, please heaven, a little claret-wine cool out of a cellar a mile deep—with a few or a good many ratafia cakes—a rocky basin to bathe in, a strawberry bed to say your prayers to Flora in, a pad nag to go you ten miles or so; two or three sensible people to chat with; two or th[r]ee spiteful folkes to spar with; two or three odd fishes to laugh at and two or three numskuls to argue with—instead of using dumb bells on a rainy day—

Two or three Posies[2]
With two or three simples
Two or three Noses
With two or th[r]ee pimples—
Two or th[r]ee wise men
And two or three ninny's
Two or three purses
And two or three guineas
Two or three raps

1 *Birkbeck's sons . . . soon*: Richard, Morris Birkbeck's eldest son, having sorted out family matters in England, was preparing to join his family in Illinois.
2 *Two or three Posies*: First published in HBF (1883).

At two or three doors
Two or three naps
Of two or three hours—
Two or three Cats
And two or three mice
Two or th[r]ee sprats
At a very great price—
Two or three sandies
And two or three tabbies
Two or th[r]ee dandies—
And two M[rs] ——[1] mum!
Two or three Smiles
And two or three frowns
Two or th[r]ee Miles
To two or three towns
Two or three pegs
For two or three bonnets
Two or three dove's eggs
To hatch into sonnets—

Good bye I've an appoantment—can't stop pon word—good bye—now dont get up—open the door myself—go-o-o d bye—see ye Monday

J—K—

To George and Georgiana Keats

(concluded)

4, 5 May 1819

This is the 3rd of May [*for* Tuesday, 4 May][2] and every thing is in delightful forwardness, the violets are not witherd before the first peeping of the first rose—Yesterday I walk[ed] to

1 *M[rs]*——: Abbeys.

2 In his letter of 1 May (?) to Fanny Keats had promised to visit his sister on *Monday*, 3 May (p. 364): he then misdates Wednesday, 5 May 1819 as *May 4* in the next section of this letter.

Walthamstow through the fields, through Highgate, Hornsey and Tottenham—I call'd in my way on the Houghtons[1]—they were well and enquired after you—Fanny was well, but she is grown so much lately as to be thin and I do not thing [*for* think] very strong—Mrs Abbey was ill, and Miss Abby lookd not much better—Fanny is very sensible in my mind—she does not grow very pretty—We took a walk in the Garden and about the Village. She complains about Mrs Abbey's behaviour—I long to send her some Letters from you—I only want some Letters from you to make the spring in proper time—

Wednesday May 4 [*for* 5]—I went to Town this morning and calling at Taylors they told me that I must let young Birkbeck have the Packet immediately—so I shall seal it tonight and be in Town early tomorrow morning—I hope I shall see him—for the sake of his seeing you afterwards—I have been waiting for Taylor to perform his promise of inviting young B. to meet me at his House—I suppose he has had no opportunity. I have heard to day that the Packets from Illoinois had been robbed and that accounts for my not having received any Letters—Tho I have never been very uneasy about it, and have constantly kept your mother from any despondence about it. Rice and Reynolds came with me from Town and drank Tea—they both desire particularly their Remembrances. You must let me know every thing—how parcels come and go—what Papers Birkbecks has and what newspaper you want and other things. God bless you, my dear Brother & Sister. Your ever affectionate Brother

John Keats

On 12 May Keats 'at last' received a letter from George containing, 'considering all things, good news'. He must have learnt that George was not at Birkbeck's Settlement, and been told about his partnership with John James Audubon (1785–1851), which was to prove disastrous (see below, pp. 411 and 415). By the end of the month Keats, who knew that Brown would as usual be letting his half of Wentworth Place over the

1 *Houghtons*: For the Haughtons, see above, p. 119 and n.

5. *Charles Brown, pencil portrait of Keats, 1819*

summer, was thinking about how to spend his own summer and considering his future. At some time in June he and Fanny Brawne came to an 'understanding' and became unofficially engaged.

To Mary-Ann Jeffery[1]

31 May 1819

[Harvard MS]

C. Brown Esq$^{re's}$
My dear Lady, [Wednesday] Wentworth Place—Hampstead—

I was making a day or two ago a general conflagration of all old Letters and Memorandums, which had become of no interest to me—I made however, like the Barber-inquisitor in Don Quixote some reservations—among the rest your and your Sister's Letters. I assure you you had not entirely vanished from my Mind, or even become shadows in my remembrance: it only needed such a memento as your Letters to bring you back to me—Why have I not written before? Why did I not answer your Honiton Letter? I had no good news for you—every concern of ours, (ours I wish I could say) and still must say <u>ours</u>—though George is in America and I have no Brother left—Though in the midst of my troubles I had no relation except my young sister I have had excellent friends. Mr B. at whose house I now am, invited me,—I have been with him ever since. I could not make up my mind to let you know these things. Nor should I now—but see what a little interest will do—I want you to do me a Favor; which I will first ask and then tell you the reasons. Enquire in the Villages round Teignmouth if there is any Lodging commodious for its cheapness; and let me know where it is and what price. I have the choice as it were of two Poisons (yet I ought not to call this a Poison) the one is voyaging to and from

1 *Mary-Ann Jeffery*: For the identification of the Jeffery family and the two sisters Mary-Ann and Sarah Frances ('Fanny'), see Gittings, Appendix 5. (Rollins mistakenly identifies the recipient of this and the next letter as 'Sarah Jeffrey'.)

India for a few years;[1] the other is leading a fevrous life alone with Poetry—This latter will suit me best—for I cannot resolve to give up my Studies It strikes me it would not be quite so proper for you to make such inquiries—so give my love to your Mother and ask her to do it. Yes, I would rather conquer my indolence and strain my ne[r]ves at some grand Poem—than be in a dunderheaded indiaman—Pray let no one in Teignmouth know any thing of this—Fanny must by this time have altered her name—perhaps you have also—are you all alive? Give my Comp[ts] to M[rs]— your Sister. I have had good news, (tho' 'tis a queerish world in which such things are call'd good) from George—he and his wife are well—I will tell you more soon—Especially dont let the Newfoundland fisherman know it—and especially no one else—I have been always till now almost as careless of the world as a fly—my troubles were all of the Imagination—My Brother George always stood between me and any dealings with the world—Now I find I must buffet it—I must take my stand upon some vantage ground and begin to fight—I must choose between despair & Energy—I choose the latter—though the world has taken on a quakerish look with me, which I once thought was impossible—

> 'Nothing can bring back the hour
> Of splendour in the grass and glory in the flower'[2]

I once thought this a Melancholist's dream—

But why do I speak to you in this manner? No believe me I do not write for a mere selfish purpose—the manner in which I have written of myself will convince you. I do not do so to Strangers. I have not quite made up my mind—Write me on the receipt of this—and again at your Leisure; between whiles you shall hear from me again—

Your sincere friend
John Keats

1 *voyaging . . . few years*: Keats told Charles Dilke that he was thinking of 'at least two' possibilities: 'South America or Surgeon to an I[n]diaman' (*L*, II, p. 114).

2 *Nothing . . . flower*: Wordsworth's 'Ode: Intimations of Immortality', ll. 180–81.

To Mary-Ann Jeffery
9 June 1819

[Transcript, 1893][1]

Wentworth Place
[Wednesday]

My Dear young Lady,—I am exceedingly obliged by your two letters—Why did I not answer your first immediately was that I have had a little aversion to the South of Devon from the continual remembrance of my Brother Tom. On that account I do not return to my old Lodgin[g]s in Hampstead though the people of the house have become friends of mine—This however I could think nothing of, it can do no more than keep one's thoughts employed for a day or two. I like your description of Bradley very much and I dare say shall be there in the course of the summer; it would be immediately but that a friend with ill health and to whom I am greatly attached[2] call'd on me yesterday and proposed my spending a Month with him at the back of the Isle of Wight. This is just the thing at present—the morrow will take care of itself—I do not like the name of Bishop's Teigntown—I hope the road from Teignmouth to Bradley does not lie that way—Your advice about the Indiaman is a very wise advice, because it just suits me, though you are a little in the wrong concerning its destroying the energies of Mind: on the contrary it would be the finest thing in the world to strengthen them—To be thrown among people who care not for you, with whom you have no sympathies forces the Mind upon its own resourses, and leaves it free to make its speculations of the differences of human character and to class them with the calmness of a Botanist. An Indiaman is a little world. One of the great reasons that the english have produced the finest writers in the world; is, that the English world has

1 A. F. Sieveking, 'Some Unedited Letters of John Keats', *Fortnightly Review* 60 (1893), pp. 734–5.
2 *a friend . . . attached*: James Rice.

ill-treated them during their lives and foster'd them after their deaths. They have in general been trampled aside into the bye paths of life and seen the festerings of Society. They have not been treated like the Raphaels of Italy. And where is the Englishman and Poet who has given a magnifacent Entertainment at the christening of one of his Hero's Horses as Boyardo[1] did? He had a Castle in the Appenine. He was a noble Poet of Romance; not a miserable and mighty Poet of the human Heart. The middle age of Shakspeare was all c[l]ouded over; his days were not more happy than Hamlet's who is perhaps more like Shakspeare himself in his common every day Life than any other of his Characters—Ben Johnson was a common Soldier and in the Low countries, in the face of two armies, fought a single combat with a french Trooper and slew him—For all this I will not go on board an Indiaman, nor for examples sake run my head into dark alleys: I dare say my discipline is to come, and plenty of it too. I have been very idle lately, very averse to writing; both from the overpowering idea of our dead poets and from abatement of my love of fame. I hope I am a little more of a Philosopher than I was, consequently a little less of a versifying Pet-lamb.[2] I have put no more in Print or you should have had it. You will judge of my 1819 temper when I tell you that the thing I have most enjoyed this year has been writing an ode to Indolence. Why did you not make your long-haired sister put her great brown hard fist to paper and cross your Letter? Tell her when you write again that I expect chequer-work—My friend Mr Brown is sitting opposite me employed in writing a Life of David. He reads me passages as he writes them stuffing my infidel mouth as though I were a young rook—Infidel Rooks do not provender with Elisha's Ravens.[3] If he goes on as he has begun your new Church had better not

1 *Boyardo*: Matteo Maria Boiardo (1441–94), the author of *Orlando innamorato* (1487), was reputed to have ordered the church bells to be rung when he thought of a name for one of his heroes.

2 *Pet-lamb*: Compare 'Ode on Indolence', l. 54. This letter provides the basis for the normal dating of the 'ode' (but see above, p. 328 n).

3 *Infidel Rooks . . . Elisha's Ravens*: Elijah (not Elisha) was brought food by ravens (1 Kings 17:6).

proceed, for parsons will be superseeded—and of course the Clerks must follow. Give my love to your Mother with the assurance that I can never forget her anxiety for my Brother Tom. Believe also that I shall ever remember our leave-taking with you.

Ever sincerely yours'

John Keats.

To Fanny Keats
9 June 1819

[British Library MS]

My dear Fanny, Wentworth Place.
[Wednesday]

I shall be with you next monday at the farthest—I could not keep my promise of seeing you again in a week because I am in so unsett[l]ed a state of mind about what I am to do—I have given up the Idea of the Indiaman; I cannot resolve to give up my favorite studies: so I purpose to retire into the Country and set my Mind at work once more. A Friend of Mine[1] who has an ill state of health called on me yesterday and proposed to spend a little time with him at the back of the Isle of Wight where he said we might live very cheaply—I agreed to his proposal. I have taken a great dislike to Town I never go there—some one is always calling one [*for* on] me and as we have spare beds they often stop a couple of days—I have written lately to some Acquaintances in Devonshire concer[n]ing a cheap Lodging and they have been very kind in letting me know all I wanted—They have described a pleasant place which I think I shall eventually retire to. How came you on With my young Master Yorkshire Man?[2] Did not Mrs A. sport her Carriage and one? They really surprised me with super civility—how did Mrs A. manage it? How is the old tadpole gardener and little Master

1 *A Friend of Mine*: Rice.
2 *Yorkshire Man*: Presumably a young relative of the Abbeys who came from the Yorkshire borders.

next door? it is to be hop'd they will both die some of these days. Not having been to Town I have not heard whether M[r] A— purposes to retire from business. Do let me know if you have heard any thing more about it. I[f] he should not I shall be very disappointed—If any one deserves to be put to his shifts it is that Hodgkinson—As for the other[1] he would live a long time upon his fat and be none the worse for a good long lent. How came miladi to give one Lisbon wine—had she drained the Gooseberry? Truly I cannot delay making another visit—asked to take Lunch, whether I will have ale, wine take sur g ar,—objection to green—like cream—thin bread and butter—another cup—agreeable—enough sugar—little more cream—two weak 12 shillin & &c &c lord I must come again

We are just going to Dinner I must must with this to the Post—Your affectionate Brother

John—

To Fanny Keats
17 June 1819

[British Library MS]

My dear Fanny, [Thursday] Wentworth Place

Still I cannot affo[r]d to spend money by Coachire and still my throat is not well enough to warrant my walking—I went yesterday to ask M[r] Abbey for some money; but I could not on account of a Letter he showed me from my Aunt's Solicitor[2]—You do not understand the business—I trust it will not in the end be detrimental to you. I am going to try the Press onece more and to that end shall retire to live cheaply in the country and compose myself and verses as well as I can—I have very

1 *the other*: i.e., Abbey, the senior partner.

2 *my Aunt's Solicitor*: Margaret Jennings, widow of Captain John Jennings (d. 1809), brother of Keats's mother. Keats's aunt seems to have threatened action in Chancery over Tom's share of their grandfather's legacy (Gittings, *John Keats*, p. 475).

good friends ready to help me—and I am the more bound to be careful of the money they lend me—It will all be well in the course of a year I hope—I am confident of it, so do not let it trouble you at all—Mr Abbey showed me a Letter he had received from George containing the news of the birth of a Niece[1] for us—and all doing well—he said he would take it to you—so I suppose to day you will see it. I was preparing to enqu[i]re for a Situation with an Apothecary, put [*for* but] Mr Brown persuads me to try the press once more; so I will with all my industry and ability. Mr Rice a friend of mine in ill health has proposed ret[i]ring to the back of the isle of wight—which I hope will be cheap in the summer—I am sure it will in the winter. Thence you shall frequently hear from me and in the Letters I will coppy those lines I may write which will be most pleasing to you in the confidence you will show them to no one—I have not run quite aground yet I hope, having written this morning to several people to whom I have lent money, requesting repayment. I shall henceforth shake off my indolent fits, and among other reformation be more diligent in writing to you and mind you always answer me—I shall be obliged to go out of town on Saturday and shall have no money till tomorrow, so I am very sorry to think I shall not be able to come to Walthamstow—The Head Mr Seve[r]n did of me[2] is now too dear but here inclosed is a very capital Profile done by Mr Brown.[3] I will write again on Monday or Tuesday[4]—M^r and Mrs Dilke are well—

Your affectionate Brother
John—Ans^r 1<u>Thursday</u>

1 *Niece*: Georgiana Emily (1819–55).

2 *Head Mr Seve[r]n did of me*: This must refer to the miniature exhibited in May at the Royal Academy, against Keats's advice (see above, p. 331).

3 *Profile done by Mr Brown*: Brown's paper silhouette (dated 1819) is now in the Harvard Keats Collection.

4 *I will . . . Tuesday*: The next extant letter he wrote was on 1 July.

28 June to 8 October 1819
Shanklin and Winchester

*The threat of their aunt's lawsuit mentioned by Keats in his letter to Fanny on 17 June created a financial crisis for him. Unable to get any money from Abbey he was, as he told Haydon, 'driven ... into necessity' (*L, II, *p. 120). The situation was resolved by Charles Brown, who lent him 'some money for the present' and advised Keats to set about recovering the £200 and more he had lent to friends. Brown, whose comic opera* Narensky *(1814) had been a success at Drury Lane, further proposed that Keats should write a tragedy for the London stage over the summer. He would supply the plot and each man would take a half share of the profits. In the meantime, Keats should, as planned, go to the Isle of Wight with James Rice, where Brown would join Keats some weeks later.*

On Sunday, 27 June Keats travelled with Rice overnight to Portsmouth. On the way their coach was caught in a 'heavy shower': Keats's consequent cold developed into a persistent sore throat. The two men crossed to the Isle of Wight the following day and settled in lodgings at Shanklin. There Keats started writing 'Lamia', began work on the tragedy Otho the Great *and by 25 July was working on* The Fall of Hyperion: A Dream.

To Fanny Brawne
1 July 1819

[HBF transcript (1883)]

Shanklin,
Isle of Wight, Thursday.

My dearest Lady,

I am glad I had not an opportunity of sending off a Letter which I wrote for you on Tuesday night—'twas too much like one out of Ro[u]sseau's Heloise.[1] I am more reasonable this morning. The morning is the only proper time for me to write to a beautiful Girl whom I love so much: for at night, when the lonely day has closed, and the lonely, silent, unmusical Chamber is waiting to receive me as into a Sepulchre, then believe me my passion gets entirely the sway, then I would not have you see those R[h]apsodies which I once thought it impossible I should ever give way to, and which I have often laughed at in another, for fear you should [think me] either too unhappy or perhaps a little mad. I am now at a very pleasant Cottage window, looking onto a beautiful hilly country, with a glimpse of the sea; the morning is very fine. I do not know how elastic my spirit might be, what pleasure I might have in living here and breathing and wandering as a free as a stag about this beautiful Coast if the remembrance of you did not weigh so upon me. I have never known any unalloy'd Happiness for many days together: the death or sickness of some one has always spoilt my hours—and now when none such troubles oppress me, it is you must confess very hard that another sort of pain should haunt me. Ask yourself my love whether you are not very cruel to have so entrammelled me, so destroyed my freedom. Will

1 *Ro[u]sseau's Heloise*: The epistolary novel *Julie, ou la nouvelle Héloïse* (1761) by Jean-Jacques Rousseau (1712–78) was immediately translated by William Kendrick and ran into many editions. Mee cites Hazlitt's essay on Rousseau in *The Round Table*, likening him to Wordsworth: 'His interest in his own thoughts and feelings was always wound up to the highest pitch.'

you confess this in the Letter you must write immediately and do all you can to console me in it—make it rich as a draught of poppies to intoxicate me—write the softest words and kiss them that I may at least touch my lips where yours have been. For myself I know not how to express my devotion to so fair a form: I want a brighter word than bright, a fairer word than fair. I almost wish that we were butterflies and liv'd but three summer days—three such days with you I could fill with more delight than fifty common years could ever contain. But however selfish I may feel, I am sure I could never act selfishly: as I told you a day or two before I left Hampstead, I will never return to London if my Fate does not turn up Pam[1] or at least a Court-card. Though I could centre my Happiness in you, I cannot expect to engross your heart so entirely—indeed if I thought you felt as much for me as I do for you at this moment I do not think I could restrain myself from seeing you again tomorrow for the delight of one embrace. But no—I must live upon hope and Chance. In case of the worst that can happen, I shall still love you—but what hatred shall I have for another! Some lines I read the other day are continually ringing a peal in my ears:

> To see those eyes I prize above my own
> Dart favors on another—
> And those sweet lips (yielding immortal nectar)
> Be gently press'd by any but myself—
> Think, think Francesca, what a cursed thing
> It were beyond expression![2]

J.

Do write immediately. There is no post from this Place, so you must address Post Office, Newport, Isle of Wight. I know

1 *Pam*: The jack of clubs, the highest trump in Five-Card Loo.

2 *To see . . . beyond expression*: Lines from *The Duke of Milan* (1623), I, iii, by Philip Massinger (1583–1640); W. Gifford (ed.), *The Plays of Philip Massinger* (3rd edn, 1840), p. 66. The Duke to Marcelia, whose name Keats alters to Francesca (thus casting himself as Paolo; see his sonnet on Dante's Paolo and Francesca above, pp. 346–7).

before night I shall curse myself for having sent you so cold a Letter; yet it is better to do it as much as in my senses as possible. Be kind as the distance will permit to your

J. Keats.

Present my Compliments to your mother, my love to Margaret and best remembrances to your Brother—if you please so.

To Fanny Keats
6 July 1819

[British Library MS]

Shanklin
Isle of Wight
Tuesday July 6th—

My dear Fanny,

I have just received another Letter from George full of as good news as we can expect. I cannot inclose it to you as I could wish, because it contains matters of Business to which I must for a Week to come have an immediate reference. I think I told you the purpose for which I retired to this place—to try the fortune of my Pen once more, and indeed I have some confidence in my success: but in every event, believe me my dear sister, I shall be sufficiently comfortable, as, if I cannot lead that life of competence and society I should wish, I have enough knowledge of my gallipots[1] to ensure me an employment & maintenance. The Place I am in now I visited once before and a very pretty place it is were it not for the bad Weather. Our window looks over house tops and Cliffs onto the Sea, so that when the Ships sail past the Cottage chimneys you may take them for Weathercocks. We have Hill and Dale forest and Mead and plenty of Lobsters. I was on the Portsmouth Coach the

1 *gallipots*: Small containers used for ointments and medicines by apothecaries, hence a nickname for them. Keats was probably remembering Lockhart's dismissive reference to his profession in his attack on the 'Cockney School' in *Blackwood's Magazine*.

Sunday before last in that heavy shower—and I may say I went to Portsmouth by water—I got a little cold and as it always flies to my throat I am a little out of sorts that way—There were on the Coach with me some common french people, but very well behaved—there was a woman amongst them to whom the poor Men in ragged coats were more gallant than ever I saw gentleman to a Lady at a Ball—When we got down to walk up hill—one of them pick'd a rose, and on remounting gave it to the women with—'Ma'mselle—voila une bell rose!' I am so hard at work that perhaps I should not have written to you for a day or two if Georges Letter had not diverted my attention to the interests and pleasure of those I love—and ever believe that when I do not behave punctually it is from a very necessary occupation, and that my silence is no proof of my not thinking of you, or that I want more than a gentle philip to bring you[r] image with every claim before me—You have never seen mountains, or I might tell you that the hill at Steephill is I think almost of as much consequence as Mount Rydal on Lake Winander. Bonchurch[1] too is a very delightful Place—as I can see by the Cottages all romantic—covered with creepers and honeysickles with roses and eglantines peeping in at the windows. Fit abodes, for the People I guess live in them, romantic old maids fond of no<vels> or soldiers widows with a pretty jointure—or a<ny> body's widows or aunts or any things given to Poetry and a Piano forte—as far as in 'em lies—as people say. If I could play upon the Guitar I might make my fortune with an old song—and get to [*for* two] blessings at once—a Lady's heart and Rheumatism. But I am almost affraid to peep at those little windows—for a pretty window should show a pretty face, and as the world goes chances are against me. I am living with a very good fellow indeed, a Mr Rice—He is unfortunately labouring under a complaint which has for some years been a burthen to him—This is a pain to me. He has a greater tact in speaking to people of the village than I have, and in those matters is a great amusement as well [as] a good friend to me. He

1 *Bonchurch*: A seaside village between Shanklin and Ventnor. The Victorians added holiday villas to the quaint cottages seen by Keats.

bought a ham the other day for say[s] he 'Keats I don't think a Ham is a wrong thing to have in a house.' Write to me, Shanklin Isle of Wight as soon as you can; for a Letter is a great treat to me here—believeing me ever your affectionate Brother, John—

To Fanny Brawne
8 July 1819

[Historical Society of Pennsylvania MS]

[Shanklin, Thursday]
July 8th

My sweet Girl,

Your Letter gave me more delight, than any thing in the world but yourself could do; indeed I am almost astonished that any absent one should have that luxurious power over my senses which I feel. Even when I am not thinking of you I receive your influence and a tenderer nature steeling upon me. All my thoughts, my unhappiest days and nights have I find not at all cured me of my love of Beauty, but made it so intense that I am miserable that you are not with me: or rather breathe in that dull sort of patience that cannot be called Life. I never knew before, what such a love as you have made me feel, was; I did not believe in it; my Fancy was affraid of it, lest it should burn me up. But if you will fully love me, though there may be some fire, 't will not be more than we can bear when moistened and bedewed with Pleasures. You mention 'horrid people' and ask me whether it depend on them, whether I see you again—Do understand me, my love, in this—I have so much of you in my heart that I must turn Mentor when I see a chance of ha[r]m beffaling you. I would never see any thing but Pleasure in your eyes, love on your lips, and Happiness in your steps. I would wish to see you among those amusements suitable to your inclinations and spirits; so that our loves might be a delight in the midst of Pleasures agreeable enough, rather than a resource from vexations and cares—But I doubt much, in case of the worst, whether I shall be philosopher enough to follow my own Lessons:

if I saw my resolution give you a pain I could not. Why may I not speak of your Beauty, since without that I could never have lov'd you—I cannot conceive any beginning of such love as I have for you but Beauty. There may be a sort of love for which, without the least sneer at it, I have the highest respect, and can admire it in others: but it has not the richness, the bloom, the full form, the enchantment of love after my own heart. So let me speak of you[r] Beauty, though to my own endangering; if you could be so cruel to me as to try elsewhere its Power. You say you are affraid I shall think you do not love me—in saying this you make me ache the more to be near you. I am at the diligent use of my faculties here, I do not pass a day without sprawling some blank verse or tagging some rhymes; and here I must confess, that, (since I am on that subject,) I love you the more in that I believe you have liked me for my own sake and for nothing else—I have met with women whom I really think would like to be married to a Poem and to be given away by a Novel. I have seen your Comet,[1] and only wish it was a sign that poor Rice would get well whose illness makes him rather a melancholy companion: and the more so as to conquer his feelings and hide them from me, with a forc'd Pun. I kiss'd your writing over in the hope you had indulg'd me by leaving a trace of honey—What was your dream? Tell it me and I will tell you the interpretation thereof. Ever yours my love!

John Keats—

Do not accuse me of delay—we have not here an opportunity of sending letters every day—Write speedily—

1 *Comet*: A 'most magnificent Comet' was observed in London on the night of Saturday, 3 July (*Morning Post*, 5 July 1819).

To J. H. Reynolds
11 July 1819

[Woodhouse transcript (1821?)]

Extract

From a letter to the same—Dated Shanklin n[r] Ryde Isle of Wight. Sunday 12 [*for* 11] July 1819.—

My dear Reynolds,

* * * * * *

You will be glad to hear under my own hand (tho' Rice says we are like sauntering Jack & Idle Joe[1] h)ow diligent I have been, & am being. I have finished the Act,[2] and in the interval of beginning the 2[d] have proceeded pretty well with Lamia, finishing the 1st part which consists of about 400 lines. I have great hopes of success, because I make use of my Judgment more deliberately than I yet have done; but in Case of failure with the world, I shall find my content. And here (as I know you have my good at heart as much as a Brother,) I can only repeat to you what I have said to George[3]—that however I sho[d] like to enjoy what the competences of life procure, I am in no wise dashed at a different prospect. I have spent too many thoughtful days & moralized thro' too many nights for that, and fruitless wo[d] they be indeed, if they did not by degrees make me look upon the affairs of the world with a healthy deliberation. I have of late been moulting: not for fresh feathers & wings: they are gone, and in their stead I hope to have a pair of patient sublunary legs. I have altered, not from a Chrysalis into a butterfly, but the Contrary. having two little loopholes, whence I may look out into the stage of the world: and that world on our coming here I almost forgot. The first time I sat

1 *sauntering Jack & Idle Joe*: From the satire 'An Epitaph', ll. 1–2, by Matthew Prior (1664–1721): 'Interr'd beneath this Marble Stone, / Lie Saunt'ring Jack and Idle Joan' (*Poems on Several Occasions*, 1718).
2 *the Act*: Of *Otho the Great*.
3 *what I have said to George*: This letter is no longer known.

down to write, I co[d] scarcely believe in the necessity of so doing. It struck me as a great oddity—Yet the very corn which is now so beautiful, as if it had only took to ripening yesterday, is for the market: So, why sho[d] I be delicate.—

* * *

To Fanny Brawne
15 (?) July 1819

[HBF transcript (1883)]

Shanklin
Thursday Evening

My love,

I have been in so irritable a state of health these two or three last days, that I did not think I should be able to write this week. Not that I was so ill, but so much so as only to be capable of an unhealthy teasing letter. To night I am greatly recovered only to feel the languor I have felt after you touched with ardency. You say you might perhaps have made me better: you would then have made me worse: now you could quite effect a cure: What fee my sweet Physician would I not give you to do so. Do not call it folly, when I tell you I took your letter last night to bed with me. In the morning I found your name on the sealing wax obliterated. I was startled at the bad omen till I recollected it must have happened in my dreams, and they you know fall out by contraries. You must have found out by this time I am a little given to bode ill like the raven; it is my misfortune not my fault; it has proceeded from the general circumstances of my life, and rendered every event suspicious. However I will no more trouble either you or myself with sad Prophecies; though so far I am pleased at it as it has given me opportunity to love your disinterestedness towards me. I can be a raven no more; you and pleasure take possession of me at the same moment. I am afraid you have been unwell. If through me illness have touched you (but it must be with a very gentle hand) I must be selfish enough to feel a little glad at it. Will you forgive me this? I have been reading lately an oriental tale of a very beautiful color—It is of a city of melancholy men, all made so by this circumstance. Through a series of adventures one of them each by turns reach some gardens of Paradise where they meet with a most enchanting Lady; and just as they are going to embrace her, she bids them shut their eyes—they shut them—and on opening their eyes again find themselves descending to the earth in a magic basket. The remembrance of this Lady and their delights lost beyond all recovery render them melancholy ever after.[1] How I applied this to you, my dear; how I palpitated at it; how the certainty that you were in the same world with myself, and though as beautiful, not so talismanic as that Lady; how I could not bear you should be so you must believe because I swear it by yourself. I cannot say when I shall get a volume ready. I have three or four stories half done, but as I cannot write for the mere sake of the press, I am obliged to let them progress or lie still as my fancy chooses. By Christmas perhaps they may appear, but I am not yet sure they ever will. 'Twill be no matter, for Poems are as common as newspapers and I do not see why it is a greater crime in me than in another to let the verses of an half-fledged brain tumble into the reading-rooms and drawing room windows. Rice has been better lately than usual: he is not suffering from any neglect of his parents who have for some years been able to appreciate him better than they did in his first youth, and are now devoted to his comfort. Tomorrow I shall, if my health continues to improve during the night, take a look fa[r]ther about the country, and spy at the parties about here who come hunting after the picturesque like beagles. It is astonishing how they raven down scenery like children do sweetmeats. The wondrous Chine here is a very great

1 *an oriental tale . . . ever after*: A partial summary of the inset story in 'The History of the Basket' in Henry Weber's *Tales of the East* (1812), II, pp. 667–74. There the narrator is expelled from the other-worldly garden of delights when, not satisfied with the slave girls she supplies him with nightly, he seeks to consummate his love with the Lady herself.

Lion:[1] I wish I had as many guineas as there have been spy-glasses in it. I have been, I cannot tell why, in capital spirits this last hour. What reason? When I have to take my candle and retire to a lonely room, without the thought as I fall asleep, of seeing you tomorrow morning? or the next day, or the next—it takes on the appearance of impossibility and eternity—I will say a month—I will say I will see you in a month at most, though no one but yourself should see me; if it be but for an hour. I should not like to be so near you as London without being continually with you: after having once more kissed you Sweet I would rather be here alone at my task than in the bustle and hateful literary chitchat. Meantime you must write to me—as I will every week—for your letters keep me alive. My sweet Girl I cannot speak my love for you. Good night! and

Ever yours
John Keats.

To Fanny Brawne
25 July 1819

[Harvard MS]

[Shanklin]
Sunday Night

My sweet Girl,

I hope you did not blame me much for not obeying your request of a Letter on Saturday: we have had four[2] in our small room playing at cards night and morning leaving me no undisturb'd op[p]ortunity to write. Now Rice and Martin are gone I am at liberty. Brown to my sorrow confirms the account you give of your ill health. You cannot conceive how I ache to

1 *Chine . . . Lion*: Compare Keats's earlier description of the Chine on 17 April 1817 (p. 24 above).
2 *four*: i.e., Keats, Rice and Charles Brown, who had arrived to stay at Shanklin about 23 July to work on *Otho the Great*, together with their publisher acquaintance John Martin, who happened to be staying across the road with his sister (see below, p. 417).

be with you: how I would die for one hour——for what is in the world? I say you cannot conceive; it is impossible you should look with such eyes upon me as I have upon you: it cannot be—Forgive me if I wander a little this Evening, for I have been all day employ'd in a very abstr[a]ct Poem[1] and I am in deep love with you—two things which must excuse me. I have, believe me, not been an age in letting you take possession of me; the very first week I knew you I wrote myself your vassal; but burnt the Letter as the very next time I saw you I thought you manifested some dislike to me. If you should ever feel for Man at the first sight what I did for you, I am lost—Yet I should not quarrel with you, but hate myself if such a thing were to happen—only I should burst if the thing were not as fine as a Man as you are as a Woman. Perhaps I am too vehement, then fancy me on my knees, especially when I mention a part of you[r] Letter which hurt me; you say speaking of M[r] Severn 'but you must be satisfied in knowing that I admired you much more than your friend' My dear love, I cannot believe there ever was or ever could be any thing to admire in me especially as far as sight goes—I cannot be admired, I am not a thing to be admired—You are, I love you; all I can bring you is a swooning admiration of your Beauty—I hold that place among Men which snub nos'd brunette's with meeting eyebrows do among women—They are trash to me—unless I should find one among them with a fire in her heart like the one that burns in mine. You absorb me in spite of myself—you alone: for I look not forward with any pleasure to what is call'd being settled in the world; I tremble at domestic cares—yet for you I would meet them though if it would leave you the happier I would rather die than do so. I have two luxuries to brood over in my walks, your Loveliness and the hour of my death. O that I could have possession of them both in the same minute. I hate the world: it batters too much the wings of my self will, and would I could take a sweet poison from your lips to send me out of it. From no others would I take it—I am indeed astonish'd to find myself so careless of all cha[r]ms but yours—rememb[e]ring as I do

1 *a very abstr[a]ct Poem*: *The Fall of Hyperion.*

got over my darling lounging habits a little; it is with scarcely any pain I come to this dating from Shankling and Dr Dilke, The Isle of Wight is but so so &c. Rice and I passed rather a dull time of it. I hope he will not repent coming with me. He was unwell and I was not in very good health: and I am affraid we made each other worse by acting upon each others spirits. We would grow as melancholy as need be. I confess I cannot bear a sick person in a House especially alone—it weighs upon me day and night—and more so when perhaps the Case is irretrievable—Indeed I think Rice is in a dangerous state. I have had a Letter from him which speaks favourably of his health at present—Brown and I are pretty well harnessed again to our dog-cart. I mean the Tragedy which goes on sinkingly—We are thinking of introducing an Elephant but have not historical referance within reach to determine as to Otho's Menagerie. When Brown first mention'd this I took it for a Joke; however he brings such plausible reasons, and discourses so eloquently on the dramatic effect that I am giving it a serious consideration. The Art of Poetry is not sufficient for us, and if we get on in that as well as we do in painting we shall by next winter crush the reviews and the royal Academy. Indeed if Brown would take a little of my advice he could not fail to be the first pallet of his day. But odd as it may appear, he says plainly he cannot see any force in my plea for putting Skies in the back ground—and leaving indian ink out of an ash tree—The other day he was sketching Shanklin Church and as I saw how the business was going on, I challenged him to a trial of Skill—he lent me Paper and Pencil—we keep the Sketches to contend for the Prize at the Gallerry—I will not say whose I think best—but really I do not think Brown's done to the top of the Art—A word or two on the Isle of Wight—I have been no further than Steephill. If I may guess I should [say] that there is no finer part in the Island than from this Place to Steephill—I do not hesitate to say it is fine. Bonchurch is the best.[1] But I have been so many finer walks, with a back ground of lake and mountain instedd

1 *Bonchurch is the best*: Compare with his earlier description to his sister, p. 380 above.

of the sea, that I am not much touch'd with it, though I credit it for all the Surprise I should have felt if it had taken my cockney maidenhead—But I may call myself an old Stager in the picturesque, and unless it be something very large and overpowering I cannot receive any extraordinary relish. I am sorry to hear that Charles is so much oppress'd at Westminster: though I am sure it will be the finest touch stone for his Metal in the world—His troubles will grow day by day less, as his age and strength increase. The very first Battle he wins will lift him from the Tribe of Manassah.[1] I do not know how I should feel were I a Father—but I hope I should strive with all my Power not to let the present trouble me—When your Boy shall be twenty, ask him about his childish troubles and he will have no more memory of them than you have of yours—Brown tells me Mrs Dilke sets off to day for Chichester—I am glad—I was going to say she had a fine day—but there has been a great Thunder cloud muttering over Hampshire all day—I hope she is now at supper with a good Appetite—So Reynolds's Piece succeeded[2]—that is all well. Papers have with thanks been duly received. We leave this Place on the 13th and will let you know where we may be a few days after—Brown says he will write when the fit comes on him. If you will stand law expences I'll beat him back into one before his time—When I come to town I shall have a little talk with you about Brown and one Jenny Jacobs. Open daylight! he don't care. I'm affraid the[r]e will be some more feet for little stockings—*of Keats' making. (I mean the feet.)*.[3] Brown here tried at a piece of Wit but it failed him, as you see though long a brewing,—*this is a 2nd lie*—Men should never despair—you see he has tried again and succeeded to a miracle—He wants to try again, but as I have a right to an inside place in my own Letter—I take possession. Your sincere friend. John Keats—

1 *Tribe of Manassah*: For Gideon's and the tribe of Manasseh's defeat of the Midianites see Judges 6.

2 *Reynolds's Piece succeeded*: For Reynolds's farce see below, p. 420.

3 This and next italicised phrase are in Brown's handwriting.

To Fanny Brawne
5, 6 August 1819

[Maine Historical Society MS]

My dear Girl, Shanklin Thursday Night—

You say you must not have any more such Letters as the last: I'll try that you shall not by running obstinate the other way—Indeed I have not fair play—I am not idle enough for proper downright love-letters—I leave this minute a scene in our Tragedy and see you (think it not blasphemy) through the mist of Plots speeches, counterplots and counter speeches—The Lover is madder than I am—I am nothing to him—he has a figure like the Statue of Maleager[1] and double distilled fire in his heart. Thank God for my diligence! were it not for that I should be miserable. I encourage it, and strive not to think of you—but when I have succeeded in doing so all day and as far as midnight, you return as soon as this artificial excitement goes off more severely from the fever I am left in—Upon my soul I cannot say what you could like me for. I do not think myself a fright any more than I do M^r A Mr B. and M^r C—yet if I were a woman I should not like A— B. C. But enough of this—So you intend to hold me to my promise of seeing you in a short time. I shall keep it with as much sorrow as gladness: for I am not one of the Paladins of old[2] who liv'd upon water grass and smiles for years together—What though would I not give to night for the gratification of my eyes alone? This day week we shall move to Winchester; for I feel the want of a Library. Brown will leave me there to pay a visit to Mr Snook at Bedhampton: in his absence I will flit to you and back. I will stay very little while; for as I am in a train of writing now I fear to disturb it—let it have its course bad or good—in it I shall try

1 *Statue of Maleager*: Skopas's sculpture of the Greek hero Meleager, known only through copies.

2 *Paladins of old*: The Twelve Paladins or Peers were the legendary warriors of Charlemagne's court: none answers Keats's description.

my own strength and the public pulse. At Winchester I shall get your Letters more readily; and it being a cathedral City I shall have a pleasure always a great one to me when near a Cathedral, of reading them during the service up and down the Aisle—Friday Morning [6 August] Just as I had written thus far last night, Brown came down in his morning coat and nightcap, saying he had been refresh'd by a good sleep and was very hungry—I left him eating and went to bed being too tired to enter into any discussions. You would delight very greatly in the walks about here, the Cliffs, woods, hills, sands, rocks &c about here. They are however not so fine but I shall give them a hearty good bye to exchange them for my Cathedrall—Yet again I am not so tired of Scenery as to hate Switzerland—We might spend a pleasant Year at Berne or Zurich—if it should please Venus to hear my 'Beseech thee to hear us O Goddess" And if she should hear god forbid we should what people call, settle—turn into a pond, a stagnant Lethe—a vile crescent, row or buildings. Better be imprudent moveables than prudent fixtures—Open my Mouth at the Street door like the Lion's head at Venice to receive hateful cards Letters messages.[1] Go out an<d> wither at tea parties; freeze at dinners; bake at dance<s> simmer at routs. No my love, trust yourself to me and I will find you nobler amusements; fortune favouring. I fear you will not receive this till Sunday or Monday: as the irishman would write do not in the mean while hate me—I long to be off for Winchester for I begin to dislike the very door post<s h>ere—the names, the pebbles. You ask after my health, not telling me whether you are better. I am quite well. You going out is no proof that you are: how is it? Late hours will do you great harm—What fairing[2] is it? I was alone for a couple of days while Brown went gadding over the country with his ancient knapsack. Now, I like his society as wells [*for* well] as any Man's, yet regretted his return—it broke in upon me like a Thunderbolt—I had got in a

1 *Lion's head . . . messages*: In Venice the Bocca di Leone ('lion's mouth') was a receptacle for anonymous accusations of crimes, etc., to the authorities.
2 *fairing*: A complimentary gift of any kind.

dream among my Books—really luxuriating in a solitude and silence you alone should have disturb'd—

Your ever affectionate
John Keats—

On Thursday, 12 August Keats and Brown left Shanklin for Winchester, narrowly avoiding an accident while crossing from Cowes to Southampton.

To Benjamin Bailey
[last leaf only]
14 August 1819

[Harvard MS]

[Winchester, Saturday]

* * *

We removed to Winchester for the convenience of a Library and find it an exceeding pleasant Town, enriched with a beautiful Cathedrall and surrounded by a fresh-looking country. We are in tolerably good and cheap Lodgings. Within these two Months I have written 1500 Lines, most of which besides many more of prior composition you will probably see by next Winter. I have written two Tales, one from Boccacio call'd the Pot of Basil; and another call'd S[t] Agnes' Eve on a popular superstition; and a third call'd Lamia (half finished—I <hav>e a<l>so been writing parts of my Hyperion[1] and <c>ompleted 4 Acts of a Tragedy. It was the opinion of most of my friends that I should never be able to <write> a <s>cene—I will endeavour to wipe awa<y the prejudice—> I sincerely hope you will be pleased when my Labours since we last saw each other shall reach you—One of my Ambitions is to make as great a revolution in modern dramatic writing as Kean has done in

1 *Hyperion*: *The Fall of Hyperion*.

acting—another to upset the drawling of the blue stocking literary world—if in the course of a few years I do these two things I ought to die content—and my friends should drink a dozen of Claret on my Tomb—I am convinced more and more every day that (excepting the human friend Philosopher) a fine writer is the most genuine Being in the World—Shakspeare and the paradise Lost every day become greater wonders to me—I look upon fine Phrases like a Lover—I was glad to see, by a Passage in one of Brown's Letters some time ago from the north that you were in such good Spirits[1]—Since that you have been married and in congra[tu]lating you I wish you every continuance of them—Present my Respects to Mrs Bailey. This sounds oddly to me, and I dare say I do it awkwardly enough: but I suppose by this time it is nothing new to you—Brown's remembrances to you—As far as I know we shall remain at Winchester for a goodish while—

Ever your sincere friend
John Keats.

To Fanny Brawne
16 August 1819

[Harvard MS]

Winchester August 17th [*for* Monday, 16][2]

My dear Girl—what shall I say for myself? I have been here four days and not yet written you—'t is true I have had many teasing letters of business[3] to dismiss—and I have been in the Claws, like a Serpent in an Eagle's, of the last act of our Tragedy—This is no excuse; I know it; I do not presume to offer it—I have no right either to ask a speedy answer to let me know

1 *I was glad . . . good Spirits*: Keats's truncated northern walk meant he could not make his promised visit to Bailey in late summer 1818. However, Brown spent some days with Bailey on his way back from Scotland (*KC*, II, 285).
2 Date from postmark, Keats's error.
3 *letters of business*: None survives.

how lenient you are—I must remain some days in a Mist—I see you through a Mist: as I dare say you do me by this time—Believe in the first Letters I wrote you: I assure you I felt as I wrote—I could not write so now—The thousand images I have had pass through my brain—my uneasy spirits—my unguess'd fate—all sp[r]ead a veil between me and you—Remember I have had no idle leisure to brood over you—'t is well perhaps I have not—I could not have endured the throng of Jealousies that used to haunt me before I had plunged so deeply into imaginary interests. I would feign, as my sails are set, sail on without an interruption for a Brace of Months longer—I am in complete cue—in the fever; and shall in these four Months do an immense deal—This page as my eye skims over it I see is excessively unloverlike and ungallant—I cannot help it—I am no officer in yawning quarters; no Parson-romeo—My Mind is heap'd to the full; stuff'd like a cricket ball—if I strive to fill it more it would burst—I know the generallity of women would hate me for this; that I should have so unsoften'd so hard a Mind as to forget them; forget the brightest realities for the dull imaginations of my own Brain—But I conjure you to give it a fair thinking; and ask yourself whether 't is not better to explain my feelings to you, than write artificial Passion—Besides you would see through it—It would be vain to strive to deceive you—'T is harsh, harsh, I know it—My heart seems now made of iron—I could not write a proper answer to an invitation to Idalia—You are my Judge: my forehead is on the ground—You seem offended at a little simple innocent childish playfulness in my last—I did not seriously mean to say that you were endeavouring to make me keep my promise—I beg your pardon for it—'T is but just you[r] Pride should take the alarm—seriously—You say I may do as I please—I do not think with any conscience I can; my cash-recourses are for the present stopp'd; I fear for some time—I spend no money but it increases my debts—I have all my life thought very little of these matters—they seem not to belong to me—It may be a proud sentence; but, by heaven, I am as entirely above all matters of interest as the Sun is above the Earth—And though of my own money I should be careless; of my Friends I must be spare. You see how

I go on—like so many strokes of a Hammer—I cannot help it—I am impell'd, driven to it. I am not happy enough for silken Phrases, and silver sentences—I can no more use soothing words to you than if I were at this moment engaged in a charge of Cavalry—Then you will say I should not write at all—Should I not? This Winchester is a fine place; a beautiful Cathedral and many other ancient building[s] in the Environs. The little coffin of a room at Shanklin, is changed for a large room—where I can promenade at my pleasure—looks out onto a beautiful—blank side of a house—It is strange I should like it better than the view of the sea from our window at Shanklin—I began to hate the very posts there—the voice of the old Lady over the way was getting a great Plague—The Fisherman's face never altered any more than our black tea-p<ot—> the nob however was knock'd off to my little relief<.> I am g<ettin>g a great dislike of the picturesque; and can only relish it over again by seeing you enjoy it—One of the pleasantest things I have seen lately was at Cowes—The Regent in his Yatch (I think they spell it) was anchored oppoisite—a beautiful vessel—and all the Yatchs and boats on the coast, were passing and repassing it; and curcuiting and tacking about it in every direction—I never beheld any thing so, silent, light, and graceful—As we pass'd over to Southampton, there was nearly an accident—There came by a Boat well mann'd; with t[w]o naval officers at the stern—Our Bow-lines took the top of their little mast and snapped it off close by the bord—Had the mast been a little stouter they would have been upset—In so trifling an event I could not help admiring our seamen—Neither Officer nor man in the whole Boat moved a Muscle—they scar[c]ely notic'd it even with words—Forgive me for this flint-worded Letter—and believe and see that I cannot think of you without some sort of energy—though mal a propos—Even as I leave off—it seems to me that a few more moments thought of you would uncrystallize and dissolve me—I must not give way to it—but turn to my writing again—if I fail I shall die hard—O my love, your lips are growing sweet again to my fancy—I must forget them—Ever your affectionate

Keats—

*By mid-August Keats was desperately short of money. His attempts to recover loans made to his friends had met with no success, there was no hope of obtaining anything through Abbey, and Brown was short of ready money. In this dilemma, and no doubt following Brown's advice, Keats approached his publishers for a loan to support him through the summer. The two men wrote a joint letter addressed to John Taylor at his business address. This is usually printed as two separate letters, but it is clearly a single document, intended as a promissory note relying on Keats's future success, but underwritten by Brown. Taylor was so taken aback by Keats's tone that he immediately forwarded the letter to Richard Woodhouse asking for advice, apparently enclosing a draft reply in the negative. Woodhouse answered on 31 August. He reassured Taylor that Keats's 'Pride' was 'a noble pride' and 'nothing more than literary Pride', and offered £50 of his own to help tide Keats over. In addition, Woodhouse enclosed the letter Keats wrote to Reynolds on 24 August (pp. 400–401 below), the day after the joint letter sent to Taylor, as proof of his positive interpretation of the nature of Keats's proper pride (*L, *II, pp. 150–52). In response, Taylor and Hessey finally arranged to send Keats a bill for £30 on 4 September (see below, pp. 405–6).*

Keats and Charles Brown to John Taylor
23 August 1819

[Harvard MS]

My dear Taylor— Winchester Monday morn.
24 [*for* 23] Aug^st[1]

You will perceive that I do not write you till I am forced by necessity: that I am sorry for. You must forgive me for entering abrubtly on the subject, merely p[r]efixing an intreaty that you will not consider my business manner of wording and

1 Date from postmark. Keats's error.

proceeding any distrust of, or stirrup standing[1] against you; but put it to the account of a desire of order and regularity—I have been rather unfortunate lately in money concerns—from a threatened chancery suit—I was deprived at once of all recourse to my Guardian I relied a little on some of my debts being paid—which are of a tolerable amount—but I have had not one pound refunded—For these three Months Brown has advanced me money: he is not at all flush, and I am anxious to get some elsewhere—We have been together engaged (this I should wish to remain secret) in a Tragedy which I have just finish'd; and from which we hope to share moderate Profits. Being thus far connected, Brown proposed to me, to stand with me responsible for any money you may advance to me to drive through the summer—I must observe again that it is not from want of reliance on you[r] readiness to assist me that I offer a ~~Bond~~/ill/; but as a relief to myself from a too lax sensation of Life—which ought to be responsible which requires chains for its own sake—duties to fulfil with the more earnestness the less strictly they are imposed Were I completely without hope—it might be different—but am I not right to rejoice in the idea of not being Burthensome to my friends? I feel every confidence that if I choose I may be a popular writer; that I will never be; but for all that I will get a livelihood—I equally dislike the favour of the public with the love of a woman—they are both a cloying treacle to the wings of independence. I shall ever consider them (People) as debtors to me for verses, not myself to them for admiration—which I can do without. I have of late been indulging my spleen by composing a preface at them: after all resolving never to write a preface at all. 'There are so many verses', would I have said to them', give me so much means to buy pleasure with as a relief to my hours of labour—You will observe at the end of this if you put down the Letter 'How a solitarry life engenders pride and egotism!' True: I know it does but this Pride and egotism will enable me to write finer things than any thing else could—so I will indulge it—Just so much as

1 *stirrup standing*: Perhaps standing up in the stirrups to show pride (see *OED*).

I am hu[m]bled by the genius above my grasp, am I exalted and look with hate and contempt upon the literary world—A Drummer boy who holds out his hand familiarly to a field marshall—that Drummer boy with me is the good word and favour of the public—Who would wish to be among the commonplace crowd of the little-famous—who are each individually lost in a throng made up of themselfes? is this worth louting[1] or playing the hypocrite for? To beg suffrages for a seat on the benches of a myriad aristocracy in Letters? This is not wise—I am not a wise man—T is Pride—I will give you a definition of a proud Man—He is a Man who has neither vanity nor wisdom—One fill'd with hatreds cannot be vain—neither can he be wise—Pardon me for hammering instead of writing—Remember me to Woodhouse, Hessey and all in Percey street[2]—

Ever yours sincer[e]ly
John Keats

[Written by Charles Brown on the reverse of the final page's 'doublings']

Dear Sir,

Keats has told me the purport of this letter. Had it been in my power to have prevented this application to you, I would have done so. What property I have is locked up, sending me quarterly & half yearly driblets, insufficient for the support of us both. I am fully acquainted with his circumstances,—the monies owing to him amount to £230,—the Chancery Suit will not I think eventually be injurious to him,—and his perseverance in the employment of his talents,—will, in my opinion, in a short time, place him in a situation more pleasant to his feelings as far as his pocket is considered—Yet, for all this, I am aware, a man of business should have every security in his power, and Keats especially would be uncomfortable at borrowing unless he gave all in his power; besides his own name to a Bill he has none to offer but

1 *louting*: Bow to, submit to (*OED*). Keats had recently employed the verb in *Otho the Great*, III. i. 17.
2 *Percey street*: The home of the artists Peter DeWint and William Hilton.

mine, which I readily agree to, and (speaking in a business-like way) consider I possess ample security for doing so. It is therefore to be considered as a matter of right on your part to demand my name in conju[n]ction with his; and if you should be inclined to judge otherwise, still it would be painful to him not to give you a double security when he can do so, & painful to me to have it withheld when it ought to be given.

Your's sincerely Cha[s] Brown.

[Keats's postscript]

P.S. I have read what Brown has said on the other side—He agrees with me that this manner of proceeding might appear to[o] harsh, distant and indelicate with you. This however will place all in a clear light. Had I to borrow money of Brown and were in your house, I should request the use of your name in the same manner—

To J. H. Reynolds
24 August 1819

[Berg MS]

My dear Reynolds, Winchest[r] August 25[th]—
[*for* Tuesday, 24][1]

By this Post I write to Rice[2] who will tell you why we have left Shanklin; and how we like this Place—I have indeed scar[c]ely any thing else to say, leading so monotonous a life except I was to give you a history of sensations, and day-night mares. You would not find me at all unhappy in it; as all my thoughts and feelings which are of the selfish nature, home speculations every day continue to make me more Iron—I am convinced more and more day by day that fine writing is next to fine doing the top thing in the world; the Paradise Lost becomes a greater wonder—The more I know what my diligence may in time probably

1 Date from postmark. Keats's error.
2 *I write to Rice*: Letter lost.

effect; the more does my heart distend with Pride and Obstinacy—I feel it in my power to become a popular writer—I feel it in my strength to refuse the poisonous suffrage of a public—My own being which I know to be becomes of more consequence to me than the crowds of Shadows in the Shape of Man and women that inhabit a kingdom. The Soul is a world of itself and has enough to do in its own home—Those whom I know already and who have grown as it were a part of myself I could not do without: but for the rest of Mankind they are as much a dream to me as Miltons Hierarchies. I think if I had a free and healthy lasting organisation of heart and Lungs—as strong as an ox's—so as to be able [to bear] unhurt the shock of extreme thought and sensation without weariness, I could pass my Life very nearly alone though it should last eighty years. But I feel my Body too weak to support me to the height; I am obliged continually to check myself and strive to be nothing. It would be vain for me to endeavour after a more reasonable manner of writing to you: I have nothing to speak of but myself—and what can I say but what I feel? If you should have any reason to regret this state of excitement in me, I will turn the tide of your feelings in the right channel by mentioning that it is the only state for the best sort of Poetry—that is all I care for, all I live for. Forgive me for not filling up the whole sheet; Letters become so irksome to me that the next time I leave London I shall petition them all to be spar'd me. To give me credit for constancy and at the same wa[i]ve letter writing will be the highest indulgence I can think of.

Ever your affectionate friend
John Keats

To Fanny Keats
28 August 1819

[British Museum MS]

My dear Fanny, Winchester [Saturday] August 28th

You must forgive me for suffering so long a space to elapse between the dates of my letters. It is more than a fortnight since

I left Shanklin, chiefly for the purpose of being near a tolerable Libraтry, which after all is not to be found in this place—However we like it very much: it is the pleasantest Town I ever was in, and has the most reccommendations of any. There is a fine Cathedrall which to me is always a sourse of amusement; part of it built 1400 years ago; and the more modern by a magnificent Man, you may have read of in our History, called William of Wickham.[1] The whole town is beautifully wooded—From the Hill at the eastern extremity you see a prospect of Streets, and old Buildings mixed up with Trees—Then There are the most beautiful streams about I ever saw—full of Trout—There is the Foundation of St Croix about half a mile in the fields—a charity greatly abused—We have a Collegiate School, a roman catholic School; a chapel ditto and a Nunnery![2] And what improves it all is, the fashionable inhabitants are all gone to Southampton. We are qui[e]t—except a fiddle that now and then goes like a gimlet through my Ears—Our Landlady's Son not being quite a Proficient—I have still been hard at work, having completed a Tragedy I think I spoke of to you—But there I fear all my labour will be thrown away for the present, as I hear Mr Kean is going to America—For all I can guess I shall remain here till the middle of October—when Mr Brown will return to his house at Hampstead: whither I shall return with him. I some time since sent the Letter I told you I had received from George[3] to Haslam with a request to let you and Mrs Wylie see it: he sent it back to me for very insufficient reasons, without doing so; and I was so irritated by it that I would not send it travelling about by the post any more: besides the postage is very expensive. I know Mrs Wylie will think this a great neglect. I am sorry to say my temper gets the better of me—I will not send it again. Some correspondence I have had with Mr Abbey about George's affairs—and I must confess he

1 *William of Wickham*: William of Wykeham (1324–1404), Bishop of Winchester and founder of New College, Oxford, and Winchester College.

2 *St Croix . . . Nunnery*: For these sights, see the notes below on 'Keats' Walk', pp. 436–7.

3 *the Letter . . . from George*: The letter containing business matters he had 'just received' on 6 July (p. 379 above).

has behaved very kindly to me as far as the wording of his Letter went—Have you heard any further mention of his retiring from Business? I am anxious to hear wether Hodgkinson, whose name I cannot bear to write, will in any likelihood be thrown upon himself—The delightful Weather we have had for two Months is the highest gratification I could receive—no chill'd red noses—no shivering—but fair Atmosphere to think in—a clean towel mark'd with the mangle and a basin of clear Water to drench one's face with ten times a day: no need of much exercise—a Mile a day being quite sufficient—My greatest regret is that I have not been well enough to bathe though I have been two Months by the sea side and live now close to delicious bathing—Still I enjoy the Weather I adore fine Weather as the greatest blessing I can have. Give me Books, fruit, french wine and fine whether [*for* weather] and a little music out of doors, played by somebody I do not know—not pay the price of one's time for a gig—but a little chance music: and I can pass a summer very quietly without caring much about Fat Louis, fat Regent or the Duke of Wellington. Why have you not written to me? Because you were in expectation of George's Letter and so waited? Mr Brown is copying out our Tragedy of Otho the gr<eat> in a superb style—better than it deserves—there as I said is labour in vain for the present—I had hoped to give Kean another opportunity to shine.[1] What can we do now? There is not another actor of Tragedy in all London or Europe—The Covent Garden Company is execrable—Young[2] is the best among them and he is a ranting coxcombical tasteless Actor—A Disgust A Nausea—and yet the very best after Kean—What a set of barren asses are actors! I should like now to promenade you round you[r] Gardens—apple tasting—pear-tasting—plum-judging—apricot nibbling—peach sc[r]unching—Nectarine-sucking and Melon carving—I have

1 *Kean . . . to shine*: Edmund Kean (as Keats mentions earlier) was planning to go to America in autumn 1819, but he was held to his contract at Drury Lane. Keats, who greatly admired his acting, believed, like Brown, that Kean was the key to their play's commercial success.

2 *Young*: Charles Mayne Young (1777–1856) had been with the Covent Garden company since 1808, but Kean challenged his supremacy from 1814.

also a great feeling for antiquated cherries full of sugar cracks—and a white currant tree kept for company—I admire lolling on a lawn by a water-lillied pond to eat white currants and see gold fish: and go to the Fair in the Evening if I'm good—There is not hope for that—one is sure to get into some mess before evening—Have these hot days I brag of so much been well or ill for your health? Let me hear soon—

Your affectionate Brother
John—

To John Taylor
31 August 1819

[Harvard MS]

Winchester Septr 1st
[*for* Tuesday, 31 August][1]

My dear Taylor,

Brown and I have been employed for these three weeks past from time to time in writing to our different friends: a dead silence is our ownly answer: we wait morning after morning and nothing: tuesday is the day for the Examiner to arrive; this is the second tuesday which has been barren even of a news paper—Men should be in imitation of Spirits 'responsive to each others note'[2]—Instead of that I pipe and no one hath danced—We have been cursing this morning like Mandeville and Lisle[3]—With this I shall send by the same Post a third Letter to a friend of mine—who though it is of no consequence has neither answer[e]d right or left—We have been much in want of news from the Theatres having heard that Kean is going to America—but no—not a word—Why I should come on you with all these complaints, I cannot explain to myself: especially as I suspect you must be in the Country—Do answer me soon

1 Date from postmark. Keats's error.
2 *responsive . . . note*: *Paradise Lost*, IV, 683.
3 *Mandeville and Lisle*: Characters in William Godwin's *Mandeville* (1817).

for I really must know something. I must steer myself by the rudder of information—And I am in want of a Month's cash—now believe me I do not apply to you as if I thought you had a gold Mine. no. I understand these matters well enough now having become well acquainted with the disbu[r]sements every Man is tempted to make beyond his means—From this time I have resolved myself to refuse all such requests: tell me you are not flush and I shall thank you heartily—That is a duty you owe to yourself as well as to me. I have mulcted Brown to[o] much: let it be my last sin of the kind. I will try what use it will be to insist on my debts being paid.

Ever yours sincerely
John Keats—

To James Hessey
5 September 1819

[Harvard MS]

My dear Hessey, Winchester, Sunday Sep^{tr} 5th

I received this morning yours of yesterday enclosing a 30£ bank post bill.[1] I have been in fear of Winchester Jail for some time: neither Brown nor myself could get an answer from any one—This morning I hear that some unknown part of a Sum due to me and for which I had been waiting three weeks has been sent to Chichester by mistake[2]—Brown has borrow'd money of a freind of his in Hampshire—A few days ago we had but a few shillings left—and now between us we have 60£ besides what is waiting in the Chichester post office. To be a complete Midas I suppose some one will send me a pair of asses ears by the waggon—There has been such an embargo laid on

1 *30£ ... bill*: The £30 Hessey forwarded was part of the £50 Woodhouse had advanced (*KC*, I, 85–6).
2 *a Sum ... mistake*: Haslam's repayment of a loan of £30 or £40 (*L*, II, p. 154n).

our corresponde<nce> that I can sca[r]cely believe your Letter was only dated yesterday—It seems miraculous—

Ever yours sincerely
John Keats.

I am sorry to hear such a bad account of himself from Taylor—

To John Taylor
5 September 1819

[Harvard MS]

Winchester [Sunday] Sep^{tr} 5th

My dear Taylor,

This morning I received yours of the 2nd and with it a Letter from Hessey enclosing a Bank post Bill of 30£—an ample sum I assure you: more I had no thought of. You should no[t] have delay'd so long in fleet Street; leading an inactive life as you did was breathing poison: you will find the country air do more for you than you expect. But it must be proper country air; you must choose a spot. What sort of a place is Retford? You should live in a dry, gravelly, barren, elevated country open to the currents of air, and such a place is generally furnnish'd with the finest springs—The neighbourhood of a rich inclosed fulsome manured arrable Land especially in a valley and almost as bad on a flat, would be almost as bad as the smoke of fleetstreet. Such a place as this was shanklin only open to the south east and surrounded by hills in every other direction—From this south east came the damps from the sea which having no egress the air would for days together take on an unhealthy idiosyncrasy[1] altogether enervating and weakening as a city Smoke—I felt it very much—Since I have been at Winchester I have been improving in health—it is not so confined—and there is on one side of the city a dry chalky down where the air is worth six pence a pint. So if you do not get better at Retford do not

1 *idiosyncrasy*: Peculiarity of physical or physiological constitution, unexpected or adverse reaction to a drug, etc. (*OED*).

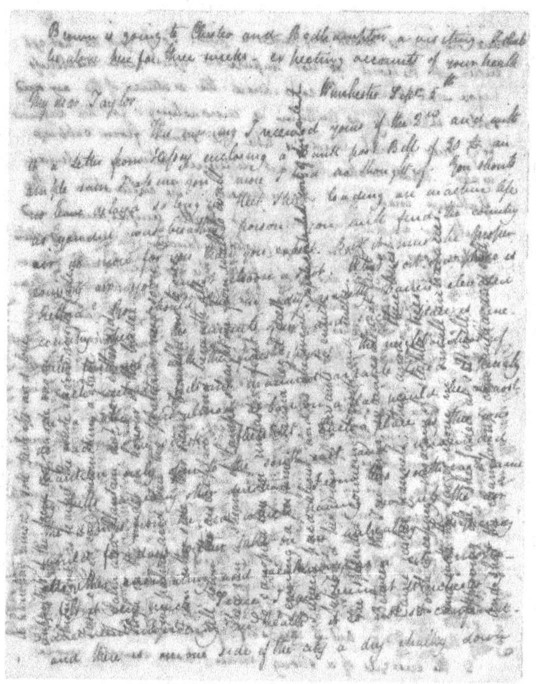

6. To John Taylor, 5 September 1819, p. 1, 24.9 × 20.4 cm. Crossed letter with draft of 'Lamia', II, 122–43

impute it to your own weakness before you have well considered the nature of the air and soil—especially as Autumn is encroaching: for the autumn fogs over a rich land is like the steam from cabbage water—What makes the great difference between valemen flatland men, and Mountaineers? The cultivation of the earth in a great measure—Our hea[l]th temperament and dispositions are taken more (notwithstanding the contradiction of the history of cain and abel) from the air we breathe than is generally imagined. See the difference between a Peasant and a Butcher. I am convinced a great cause of it is the difference of the air they breathe—The one takes his mingled with the fume of slaughter the other with the damp exhalement from the glebe—The teeming damp that comes from the plough furrow is of great effect in taming the fierceness of a strong Man more than his labour—let him be mowing furze upon a Mountain and at the days end his thoughts will run upon a withe axe[1] if he ever had handled one, let him leave the Plough and he will think qu[i]etly of his supper—Agriculture is the tamer of men; the steam from the earth is like drinking their mother's milk—It enervates their natures. This appears a great cause of the imbecillity of the Chinese. And if this sort of atmosphere is a mitigation to the energies of a strong man; how much more must it injure a weak one—unoccupied—unexerciced—For what is the cause of so many men maintaining a good state in Cities but occupation—An idle man; a man who is not sensitively alive to self interest in a city cannot continue long in good Health—This is easily explained. If you were to walk liesurely through an unwholesome path in the fens, with a little horror of them you would be sure to have your ague. But let macbeth cross the same path, with the dagger in the air leading him on, and he would never have an ague or any thing like it. You should give these things a serious consideration. Notts I believe is a flat County—You should be on the slope of one of the dry barren hills in somersetshire. I am convinced there is as harmful Air to be breath'd in the country as in Town.

1 *withe axe*: 'Axes made by grinding the edge of a suitable pebble, and fixing it in a with [i.e., withy] handle' (*OED*, 1865).

I am greatly obliged to you for your Letter. Perhaps if you had had strength and spirits enough you would have felt offended by my offering a note of hand; or rather express'd it. However, I am sure you will give me credit for not in any wise mistrusting you; or imagining you would take advantage of any power I might give you over me. No, it proceeded from my serious resolve not to be a gratuitous borrower: from a great desire to be correct in money matters; to have in my desk the Chronicles of them to refer to, and know my worldly non-estate: besides in the case of my death such documents would be but just: if merely as memorials of the friendly turns I had had done to me—Had I known of your illness I should not of written in such a fierry phrase in my first Letter[1]—I hope that shortly you will be able to bear six times as much. Brown likes the Tragedy very much: but he is not a fit judge, as I have only acted as Midwife to his plot, and of course he will be fond of his child. I do not think I can make you any extracts without spoiling the effect of the whole when you come to read it. I hope you will then not think my labour mispent. Since I finish'd it I have finish'd Lamia: and am now occupied in revising St Agnes' Eve and studying Italian. Ariosto I find as diffuse, in parts, as Spenser. I understand completely the difference between them—I will cross the letter with some lines from Lamia. Brown's kindest remembrances to you: and I am ever

your most sincere friend John Keats—

A haunting music, sole and lone[2]
Supportress of the faery roof, made moan
Throughout, as fearful the whole charm might fade.
Fresh carved cedar, mimicking a glade
Of Palm and Plantain, met, from either side,
High in the midst in honour of the bride.
Two palms, and then two plantains, and so on,

1 *my first Letter*: The joint letter with Brown of 23 August.

2 *A haunting . . . lone*: An intermediate draft of 'Lamia' II, 122–62, of which the final paragraph ('Soft went the music . . . napkin for his thumb') was discarded.

From either side, their stems branch'd one to one
All down the aisled place; and beneath all
There ran a stream of lamps straight on from wall to wall.
So canopied lay an untasted feast
Teeming a perfume. Lamia regal drest
Silverly pac'd about, and as she went
In pale contented sort of discontent
Mission'd her viewless Servants to enrich
The splendid cornicing of nook and niche.
Between the Tree stems, wainscoated at first
Came jasper pannels; then, anon, there burst
Forth creeping imagery of slighter trees
And with the larger wove in small intricacies.
Approving all, she faded at self will,
And shut the chamber up close hush'd and still,
Complete, and ready for the revels rude,
When dreadful guests would come to spoil her solitude.
  The day came soon and all the gossip rout.
O senseless Lycius! Dolt! Fool! Madman! Lout!
Why would you murder happiness like yours,
And show to common eyes these secret bowers?
  The Herd came; and each guest, with buzzy brain,
Arriving at the Portal, gaz'd amain,
And enter'd wond'ring; for they knew the Street,—
Remember'd it from childhood all complete,
Without a gap, but ne'er before had seen
That royal Porch, that high built fair demesne;
So in went one and all maz'd, curious and keen.
Save one; who look'd thereon with eye severe,
And, with calm-planted steps, walk'd in austere;
'T was Appolonius:—something to he laught;
As though some knotty problem, that had daft
His patient thought, had now begun to thaw,
And solve, and melt;—'t was just as he foresaw!
  Soft went the music, and the tables all
Sparkled beneath the viewless banneral
Of Magic; and dispos'd in double row
Seem'd edged Parterres of white bedded snow,

Adorne'd along the sides with living flowers
Conversing, laughing after sunny showers:
And, as the pleasant appetite entic'd,
Gush came the wine, and sheer the meats were slic'd.
Soft went the Music; the flat salver sang
Kiss'd by the emptied goblet,—and again it rang:
Swift bustled by the servants:—here's a health
Cries one—another—then, as if by stealth,
A Glutton drains a cup of Helicon,
Too fast down, down his throat the brief delight is gone.
"Where is that Music?" cries a Lady fair.
"Aye, where is it my dear? Up in the air"?
Another whispers 'Poo!' saith Glutton "Mum!"
Then makes his shiny mouth a napkin for his thumb.
& & &—

This is a good sample of the Story.

Brown is going to Chi[chest]er and Bedhampton a visiting—I shall be alone here for three weeks—expecting accounts of your health

Shortly after, Brown left for a three-week visit to the Snook family at Bedhampton and did not rejoin Keats in their Winchester lodgings until 1 October.

A few days after Brown's departure, Keats received an extremely disturbing letter from his brother on Friday, 10 September. George's letter, dated 24 July, brought the news that he was in desperate financial straits. The very substantial sum he had invested that spring in John James Audubon's venture to build a steamboat for the Ohio–Mississipi river traffic had been entirely lost when Audubon was declared bankrupt. Audubon, later famous as a naturalist, may well have acted dishonestly. Nevertheless, George and Georgiana were apparently on good terms with Audubon's family when George left for England in November (see below, p. 480).

Keats immediately caught the overnight coach to London, arriving at the Bell and Crown Inn, Holborn, early Saturday

morning after a twelve-hour journey. He went to see Richard Abbey and arranged to meet him after business on Monday evening to discuss George's predicament. He then took the opportunity to go, with no forewarning, to his publishers' office, 93 Fleet Street, where he asked James Hessey about the possibilities of immediate publication, but met with a refusal. Keats stayed the night there and on Sunday breakfasted with Richard Woodhouse in his rooms at the Temple. The two men had an animated conversation lasting six hours before Woodhouse took the three o'clock coach to Bristol. Keats's description of the revisions he had made to 'The Eve of St Agnes', making the poem sexually explicit, shocked the lawyer, whose report of their meeting to his publisher came close to destroying Taylor's support of Keats (see below, p. 460). After Woodhouse had left, Keats dined with George's in-laws, the Wylie family.

First thing the following morning, Monday, 13 September, Keats wrote to Fanny Brawne from Fleet Street saying he dared not come to see her in Hampstead. However, as he did not post it until late that evening (see below, p. 422 and note) his letter did not reach her until the next day and gave the impression, deliberately or not, that he had already left London.

To Fanny Brawne
13 September 1819

[Rollins transcript]

Fleet Street, Monday Morn[1]

My dear Girl,

I have been hurried to Town by a Letter from my brother George; it is not of the brightest intelligenc[e] Am I mad or not? I came by the Friday night coach—and have not yet been to Hampstead. Upon my soul it is not my fault, I cannot resolve to mix any pleasure with my days: they go one like another undistinguishable. If I were to see you to day it would destroy the

1 The letter is postmarked Lombard Street, Tuesday, 8 a.m., 14 September.

half comfortable sullenness I enjoy at present into dow[n]-right perplexities. I love you too much to venture to Hampstead, I feel it is not paying a visit, but venturing into a fire. Que feraije? as the french novel writers say in fun, and I in earnest: really what can I do? Knowing well that my life must be passed in fatigue and trouble, I have been endeavouring to wean myself from you: for to myself alone what can be much of a misery? As far as they regard myself I can despise all events: but I cannot cease to love you. This morn[i]ng I scarcely know what I am doing. I am going to Walthamstow—I shall return to Winchester tomorrow; whence you shall hear from me in a few days—I am a Coward, I cannot bear the pain of being happy: t is out of the question: I must admit no thought of it.

Yours ever affectionately
John Keats

After writing this letter Keats went to see his sister in Walthamstow. On his return to central London he attempted to see various friends, but only James Rice was 'at home', where John Martin joined them. At seven o'clock that evening he had his meeting with Abbey to discuss George's financial situation and the threatened Chancery suit. Keats's journeyings backwards and forwards across London that afternoon intersected with the huge crowds welcoming Henry Hunt on his triumphal progress through the city, leaving Islington at about 4 p.m. and arriving at the Strand by 7.30 p.m. (see below, p. 425).

Keats did not return to Winchester on Tuesday, as he had told Fanny. Instead, he spent the day in London, visited his old friend Haslam and probably spent the evening at Covent Garden Theatre, before catching the Winchester coach on Wednesday morning, 15 September. Once settled in Winchester, Keats wrote to George explaining the legal obstacles to the prompt release of capital from Tom's estate, and outlining his own parlous financial situation. He delayed completing what turned into a long letter until 27 September, in the hopes of having positive news from Richard Abbey.

To George and Georgiana Keats
17, 18, 20, 21, 24, 25, 27 September 1819

[Morgan MS]

My dear George, Winchester[17] Septr Friday—

I was closely employed in reading and composition, in this place, whither I had come from Shanklin, for the convenience of a library, when I received your last, dated July 24th. You will have seen by the short Letter I wrote from Shanklin, how matters stand beetween us and Mrs Jennings.[1] They had not at all mov'd and I knew no way of ove[r]coming the inveterate obstinacy of our affairs. On receiving your last I immediately took a place in the same night's coach for London—Mr Abbey behaved extremely well to me, appointed Monday evening at 7 to meet me and observed that he should drink tea at that hour. I gave him the inclosed note and showed him the last leaf of yours to me. He really appeared anxious about it; promised he would forward your money as quickly as possible—I think I mentioned that Walton was dead—He will apply to Mr Gliddon the partner; endeavour to get rid of Mrs Jennings's claim and be expeditious. He has received an answer from my Letter to Fry—that is something.[2] We are certainly in a very low estate: I say we, for I am in such a situation that were it not for the assistance of Brown & Taylor, I must be as badly off as a Man can be. I could not raise any sum by the promise of any Poem—no, not by the mortgage of my intellect. We must wait a little while. I really have hopes of success. I have finish'd a Tragedy which if it succeeds will enable me to sell what I may have in manuscript to a good advantage. I have pass'd my time

1 *short Letter . . . Mrs Jennings*: Keats's letter about the threatened Chancery suit is not known.

2 *Walton . . . something*: The law firm of Walton and Gliddon represented the Keats children in the Chancery suit over their inheritance. Fry, who lived in Holland, was their second trustee with Abbey: Keats needed power of attorney, which he did not receive until November (pp. 470–71 below), to act in his place with Abbey to sell Tom's stock (Gittings, *John Keats*, pp. 527–8, 548).

in reading, writing and fretting—the last I intend to give up and stick to the other two. They are the only chances of benefit to us. Your wants will be a fresh spur to me. I assure you you shall more than share what I can get, whilst I am still young—the time may come when age will make me more selfish. I have not been well treated by the world—and yet I have capitally well—I do not know a Person to whom so many purse strings would fly open as to me—if I could possibly take advantage of them—which I cannot do for none of the owners of these purses are rich—Your present situation I will not suffer myself to dwell upon—when misfortunes are so real we are glad enough to escape them, and the thought of them. I cannot help thinking Mr Audubon a dishonest man—Why did he make you believe that he was a Man of Property?[1] How is it his circumstances have altered so suddenly? In truth I do not believe you fit to deal with the world; or at least the american worrld—But good God—who can avoid these chances—You have done your best—Take matters as coolly as you can and confidently expecting help from England, act as if no help was nigh. Mine I am sure is a tolerable tragedy—it would have been a bank to me, if just as I had finish'd it I had not heard of Kean's resolution to go to America. That was the worst news I could have had. There is no actor can do the principal character besides Kean. At Covent Garden there is a great chance of its being damn'd. Were it to succeed even there it would lift me out of the mire. I mean the mire of a bad reputation which is continually rising against me. My name with the literary fashionables is vulgar—I am a weaver boy[2] to them—a Tragedy would lift me out of this mess. And mess it is as far as it regards our Pockets—But be not cast down any more than I am. I feel I can bear real ills better than imaginary ones. Whenever I find myself growing vapourish, I rouse myself, wash and put on a clean

1 *Mr Audubon . . . Property*: Audubon's dishonesty has been accepted as fact by later writers. For a measured account of the conflicting evidence, see Crutcher, pp. 69–76.

2 *a weaver boy*: Samuel Bamford (1788–1872), a working-class radical, had recently published *The Weaver Boy, or Miscellaneous Poems* (1819). 'Specimens' of *The Weaver Boy* were published in the *Examiner* (15 August).

shirt brush my hair and clothes, tie my shoestrings neatly and in fact adonize as I were going out—then all clean and comfortable I sit down to write. This I find the greatest relief—Besides I am becoming accustom'd to the privations of the pleasures of sense. In the midst of the world I live like a Hermit. I have forgot how to lay plans for enjoyment of any Pleasure. I feel I can bear any thing, any misery, even imp[r]isonment—so long as I have neither wife nor child. Perpaps you will say yours are your only comfort—they must be. I return'd to Winchester the day before yesterday and am now here alone, for Brown some days before I left, went to Bedhampton and there he will be for the next fortnight. The term of his house will be up in the middle of next month when we shall return to Hampstead. On Sunday I dined with your Mother and Henry and Charles in Henrietta Street—M[rs] and Miss Millar were in the Country—Charles had been but a few days returned from Paris. I dare say you will have letters exp[r]essing the motives of his Journey. M[rs] Wylie and Miss Waldegrave seem as qu[i]et as two Mice there alone. I did not show your last—I thought it better not. For better times will certainly come and why should they be unhappy in the main time. On Monday Morning I went to Walthamstow—Fanny look'd better than I had seen her for some time. She complains of not hearing from you appealing to me as if it was half my fault—I had been so long in retirement that London appeared a very odd place I could not make out I had so many acquaintance, and it was a whole day before I could feel among Men—I had another strange sensation there was not one house I felt any pleasure to call at. Reynolds was in the Country and saving himself I am p[r]ejudiced against all that family. Dilke and his wife and child were in the Country—Taylor was at Nottingham—I was out and every body was out. I walk'd about the Streets as in a strange land—Rice was the only one at home—I pass'd some time with him. I know him better since we have liv'd a month together in the isle of Wight. He is the most sensible, and even wise Man I know—he has a few John Bull prejudices; but they improve him. His illness is at times alarming. We are great friends, and there is no one I like to pass a day with better. Martin call'd in to bid him good bye before he set out for Dublin. If you would like to hear one of his jokes[1] here is one which at the time we laugh'd at a good deal. A Miss — with three young Ladies, one of them Martin's sister had come a gadding in the Isle of wight and took for a few days a Cottage opposite ours—we dined with them one day, and as I was saying they had fish—Miss — said she thought they tasted of the boat—No says Martin very seriously they haven't been kept long enough. I saw Haslam he is very much occupied with love and business being one of Mr Saunders executors and Lover to a young woman He show'd me her picture by Severn[2]—I think she is, though not very cunning, too cunning for him. Nothing strikes me so forcibly with a sense of the rediculous as love—A Man in love I do think cuts the sorryest figure in the world—Even when I know a poor fool to be really in pain about it, I could burst out laughing in his face—His pathetic visage becomes irrisistable. Not that I take Haslam as a pattern for Lovers—he is a very worthy man and a good friend—His love is very amusing. Somewhere in the Spectator is related an account of a Man inviting a party of stutter[e]rs and squinters to his table.[3] 'T would please me more to scrape together a party of Lovers, not to dinner—no to tea. The[re] would be no fighting as among Knights of old—

> Pensive they sit, and roll their languid eyes[4]
> Nibble their to[a]sts, and cool their tea with sighs,
> Or else forget the purpose of the night
> Forget their tea—forget their appetite.
> See with cross'd arms they sit—ah hapless crew
> The fire is going out, and no one rings
> For coals, and therefore no coals betty brings.

1 *Martin . . . jokes*: For John Martin's visit to Shanklin in July 1819, when Keats heard his joke, see above, p. 386 and n.

2 *Haslam . . . Severn*: Haslam married his first wife Mary (d. 1822) not long after on 16 October 1819.

3 *Spectator . . . table*: *Spectator*, No. 371.

4 *Pensive . . . eyes*: The only known text of this extemporary satire. Not published until 1877.

A Fly is in the milk pot—must he die
Circled by a humane society?
No no there m[r] Werter takes his spoon
Inverts it—dips the handle and lo, soon
The little struggler sav'd from perils dark
Across the teaboard draws a long wet mark.
Romeo! Arise! take Snuffers by the handle
There's a large Cauliflower in each candle.
A winding-sheet—Ah me! I must away
To no 7 just beyond the Circus gay.
'Alas' my friend! your Coat sits very well:
Where may your Taylor live'?' 'I may not tell—
'O pardon me—I'm absent now and then"
Where might my Taylor live?—I say again
I cannot tell. let me no more be teas'd—
He lives in wapping might live where he pleas'd

You see I cannot get on without writing as boys do at school a few nonsense verses—I begin them and before I have written six the whim has pass'd—if there is any th[i]ng deserving so respectable a name in them. I shall put in a bit of information any where just as it strikes me. M[r] Abbey is to write to me as soon as he can bring matters to bear, and then I am to go to Town to tell him the means of forwarding to you through Capper and Hazlewood—I wonder I did not put this before—I shall go on tomorrow—it is so fine now I must take a bit of a walk—

[18th September 1819[1]— In looking over some of my papers, I found the above specimen of my carelessness[2]—It is a

1 This paragraph in square brackets is a separate note Keats sent with this letter and was probably written later in the day: it is now known only through Jeffrey's transcript (1845) and he mistakenly dated it '1820'.

2 *above specimen of my carelessness*: Refers to a 'sheet' of Keats's journal letter of 14 February–5 May 1819, written on 3 (?) March, but accidentally omitted when making up the packet to send to America. The 'sheet' and its explanatory note are missing from the Harvard holograph. Jeffrey had access to both, but his transcript of 1845 gives Keats's explanatory note of 18 September 1819 as part of the earlier letter, where it is usually printed. For Jeffrey's text of the missing 'sheet' see above, pp. 312–15.

sheet you ought to have had long ago my letter must have appeared very unconnected, but as I number the sheets you must have discovered how the mistake happened— how many things have happened since I wrote it. How have I acted contrary to my resolves; The interval between writing this sheet, & the day I put this supplement to it, has been completely filled with the most generous & friendly actions of Brown towards me. How frequently I forget to speak of things, which I think of & feel most. T'is very singular, the idea about Buffon, above, has been taken up by Hunt in the Examiner, in some papers which he calls 'A Preter-Natural History'[1]]

Saturday [same day]—

With my inconstant disposition it is no wonder that this morning, amid all our bad times and misfortunes, I should feel so alert and well spirited. At this moment you are perhaps in a very different State of Mind. It is because my hopes are very paramount to my despair. I have been reading over part of a short poem I have composed lately call'd 'Lamia'—and I am certain there is that sort of fire in it which must take hold of people in some way—give them either pleasant or unpleasant sensation. What they want is a sensation of some sort. I wish I could pitch the key of your spirits as high as mine is—but your organ loft is beyond the reach of my voice—I admire the exact admeasurement of my niece in your Mother's letter—O the little span long elf[2]—I am not in the least judge of the proper weight and size of an infant. Never trouble yourselves about that: she is sure to be a fine woman—Let her have only delicate nails both on hands and feet and teeth as small as a May-fly's. who will live you his life on a square inch of oak-leaf. And nails she must have quite different from the market women here who plough into the butter and make a quatter [*for* quarter] pound taste of it. I intend to w[r]ite a letter to you Wifie and there I may say more on this little plump subject—I hope she's

1 *taken up . . . History*: *Examiner* (1, 8, 15 August 1819).
2 *O the . . . long elf*: *The Sad Shepherd*, II. viii. 53, by Ben Jonson (1572/3–1637).

plump—'Still harping on my daughter'[1]—This Winchester is a place tolerably well suited to me; there is a fine Cathedral, a College, a Roman-Catholic Chapel, a Methodist do, an independent do,—and there is not one loom or any thing like manufacturing beyond bread & butter in the whole City. There are a number of rich Catholic in the place. It is a respectable, ancient aristocratical place—and moreover it contains a nunnery[2]—Our set are by no means so hail fellow, well met, on literary subjects as we were wont to be. Reynolds has turn'd to the law. Bye the bye, he brought out a little piece at the Lyceum call'd <u>one, two, th[r]ee, four, by advertisement</u>.[3] It met with complete success. The meaning of this odd title is explained when I tell you the principal actor is a mimic who takes off four of our best performers in the course of the farce—Our stage is loaded with mimics. I did not see the Piece being out of Town the whole time it was in progess. Dilke is entirely swallowed up in his boy: 't is really lamentable to what a pitch he carries a sort of parental mania—I had a Letter from him at Shanklin—He went on a word or two about the isle of Wight which is a bit of hobby horse of his; but he soon deviated to his boy. 'I am sitting' says he "at the window expecting my Boy from School." I suppose I told you some where that he lives in Westminster, and his boy goes to the School there. where he gets beaten, and every bruise he has and I dare say deserves is very bitter to Dilke. The Place I am speaking of, puts me in mind of a circumsta[n]ce occured lately at Dilkes—I think it very rich and dramatic and quite illustrative of the little quiet fun that he will enjoy sometimes. First I must tell you their house is at the corner of Great Smith Street, so that some of the windows look into one Street, and the back windows into another round the corner—Dilke had some old people to dinner, I know not who—but there were two old ladies among them—Brown was

1 *Still . . . daughter*: *Hamlet*, II. ii. 187–8.

2 *respectable . . . nunnery*: Compare with his description of Winchester to Fanny Keats (p. 402 above).

3 <u>*one, two*</u> . . . <u>*advertisement*</u>: Reynolds's comic drama, whose 'odd title' Keats goes on to explain, was first acted on 17 July 1819. It ran for fifty nights and was published shortly afterwards.

there—they had known him from a Child. Brown is very pleasant with old women, and on that day, it seems, behaved himself so winningly they [*for* that] they became hand and glove together and a little complimentary. Brown was obliged to depart early. He bid them good bye and pass'd into the passage—no sooner was his back turn'd than the old women began lauding him. When Brown had reach'd the Street door and was just going, Dilke threw up the Window and call'd 'Brown! Brown! They say you look younger than ever you did!' Brown went on and had just turn'd the corner into the other street when Dilke appeared at the back window crying "Brown! Brown! By God, they say you're handsome!" You see what a many words it requires to give any identity to a thing I could have told you in half a minute. I have been reading lately Burton's Anatomy of Melancholy; and I think you will be very much amused with a page I here coppy for you.[1] I call it a Feu de joie round the batteries of Fort S[t] Hyphen-de-Phrase on the birthday of the Digamma.[2] The whole alphabet was drawn up in a Phalanx on the cover of an old Dictionary. Band playing "Amo, Amas &c" "Every Lover admires his Mistress, though she be very deformed of herself, ill-favored, wrinkled, pimpled, pale, red, yellow, tann'd, tallow-fac'd, have a swoln juglers platter face, or a thin, lean, chitty face, have clouds in her face, be crooked, dry, bald, goggle-eyed, blear-eyed or with staring eyes, she looks like a squis'd cat, hold her head still awry, heavy, dull, hollow-eyed, black or yellow about the eyes, or squint-eyed, sparrow-mouth'd, Persean-hook-nosed, have a sharp fox nose, a red nose, China flat, great nose, nare simo patuloque, a nose like a promontory, gubber-tush'd, rotten teeth, black, uneven, brown teeth, beetle brow'd, a witches beard, her breath stink all over the room, her nose drop winter and summer, with a Bavarian poke under her chin, a sharp chin, lave-eared, with a long crane's neck, which stands awry too, pendulis mammis

1 *Burton's Anatomy . . . for you*: *The Anatomy of Melancholy* (1621), III. 2. iv. 1, by Robert Burton (1577–1640).

2 *Feu de joie . . . Digamma*: A rifle salute (*OED* 2), here celebrating the birth of the Greek letter digamma.

her dugs like two double jugs, or else no dugs in the other extream, bloody-falln fingers, she have filthy, long, unpaired, nails, scabbed hands or wrists, a tan'd skin, a rotton carcass, crooked back, she stoops, is lame, splea footed, as slender in the middle as a cow in the wast, gowty legs, her ankles hang over her shooes, her feet stink, she breed lice, a meer changeling, a very monster, an aufe imperfect, her whole complexion savors, an harsh voice, incondite gesture, vile gate, a vast virago, or an ugly tit, a slug, a fat fustilugs, a trusse, a long lean rawbone, a Skeleton, a Sneaker, (si qua patent meliora puta) and to thy Judgement looks like a mard in a Lanthorn, whom thou couldst not fancy for a world, but hatest, loathest, and wouldst have spit in her face, or blow thy nose in her bosom, remedium amoris to another man, a dowdy, a Slut, a scold, a nasty rank, rammy, filthy, beastly quean, dishonest per adventure, obscene, base, beggarly, rude, foolish, untaught—peevish, Irus' daughter, Thersite's sister, Grobian's Scholler; if he love her once, he admires her for all this, he takes no notice of any such errors or imperfections of boddy or mind—" There's a dose for you—fine!! I would give my favourite leg to have written this as a speech in a Play: with what effect could Mathews[1] pop-gun it at the pit! This I think will amuse you more than so much Poetry. Of that I do not like to copy any as I am affraid it is too mal apropo for you at present—and yet I will send you some—for by the time you receive it things in England may have taken a different turn. When I left M[r] Abbey on monday evening I walk'd up Cheapside but returned to put some letters in the Post[2] and met him again at Bucklersbury: we walk'd together th[r]ough the Poultry as far as the hatter's shop he has some concern in—He spoke of it in such a way to me, I though[t] he wanted me to make an offer to assist him in it.[3] I do believe if I could be a hatter I might be one. He seems

1 *Mathews*: Charles Mathews (1776–1835), a comic actor.

2 *letters in the Post*: The 'letters' Keats posted at the General Post Office in Lombard Street probably included one to Charles Brown (see below, p. 456), as well as the one written to Fanny Brawne that morning.

3 *wanted me . . . in it*: For Abbey's earlier proposal that Keats should enter the hat-making business, see above, p. 326.

anxious about me. He began blowing up Lord Byron while I was sitting with him, however Says he the fellow says true things now & then; at which he took up a Magasine and read me some extracts from Don Juan, (Lord Byron's last flash poem) and particularly one against literary ambition.[1] I do think I must be well spoken of among sets, for Hodgkinson is more than polite, and the coffee-german[2] endeavour'd to be very close to me the other night at covent garden[3] where I went at half-price before I tumbled into bed—Every one however distant an acquaintance behaves in the most conciliating manner to me—You will see I speak of this as a matter of interest. On the next Street [*for* Sheet] I will give you a little politics. In every age there has been in England for some two or th[r]ee centuries subjects of great popular interest on the carpet: so that however great the uproar one can scarcely prophesy any material change in the government; for as loud disturbances have agitated this country many times. All civil[is]ed countries become gradually more enlighten'd and there should be a continual change for the better. Look at this Country at present and remember it when it was even though[t] impious to doubt the justice of a trial by Combat—

From that time there has been a gradual change—Three great changes have been in progress—First for the better, next for the worse, and a third time for the better once more. The first was the gradual an[ni]hilation of the tyranny of the nobles. when kings found it their interest to conciliate the common people, elevate them and be just to them. Just when baronial Power ceased and before standing armies were so dangerous, Taxes were few. Kings were lifted by the people over the head of their nobles, and those people held a rod over Kings. The change for the worse in Europe was again this. The obligation of Kings to

1 *Don Juan . . . literary ambition*: Byron's *Don Juan*, I, 218: Cantos I and II had been published anonymously in July 1819.

2 *coffee-german*: Keats's mocking name for Hodgkinson, Abbey's partner in his tea-dealing business.

3 *at covent garden*: Keats probably saw *Blue-Beard; or, Female Curiosity!* (1798) by George Colman (1762–1836), the second piece played on 14 September.

the Multitude began to be forgotten—Custom had made noblemen the humble servants of Kings—Then Kings turned to the Nobles as the adorners of the[i]r power, the slaves of it, and from the people as creatures continually endeavouring to check them. Then in every Kingdom therre was a long struggle of Kings to destroy all popular privileges. The english were the only people in europe who made a grand kick at this. They were slaves to Henry 8th but were freemen under william 3rd at the time the french were abject slaves under Lewis 14th The example of England, and the liberal writers of france and england sowed the seed of opposition to this Tyranny—and it was swelling in the ground till it burst out in the french revolution—That has had an unlucky termination. It put a stop to the rapid progress of free sentiments in England; and gave our Court hopes of turning back to the despotism of the 16 century. They have made a handle of this event in every way to undermine our freedom. They spread a horrid superstition against all inovation and improvement—The present struggle in England of the people is to destroy this superstition. What has rous'd them to do it is their distresses—Perpaps on this account the pres'ent distresses of this nation are a fortunate thing—tho so horrid in the[i]r experience. You will see I mean that the french Revolution but [*for* put] a tempor[a]ry stop to this third change, the change for the better—Now it is in progress again and I thing [*for* think] in an effectual one. This is no contest between whig and tory—but between right and wrong. There is scarcely a grain of party spirit now in England—Right and Wrong considered by each man abstractedly is the fashion. I know very little of these things. I am convinced however that apparently small causes make great alterations. There are little signs wher[e]by we many [*for* may] know how matters are going on—This makes the business about Carlisle the Bookseller[1] of

1 *Carlisle the Bookseller*: Richard Carlile (1790–1843), radical publisher, writer and freethinker, had set up shop in Fleet Street that month. His republication of Thomas Paine's *The Age of Reason* (1793) led to his arrest on 11 February and his eventual trial and imprisonment in October 1819. Keats had reported his arrest to the George Keatses in February (p. 305 above).

great moment in my mind. He has been selling deistical pamphlets, republished Tom Payne and many other works held in superstitious horror. He even has been selling for some time immense numbers of a work call[ed] 'The Deist' which comes out in weekly numbers—For this Conduct he I think has had above a dozen inditements issued against him; for which he has found Bail to the amount of many thousand Pounds—After all they are affraid to prosecute: they are affraid of his defence: it would be published in all the papers all over the Empire: they shudder at this: the Trials would light a flame they could not extinguish. Do you not think this of great import? You will hear by the papers of the proceedings at Manchester and Hunt's triumphal entry into London[1]—I[t] would take me a whole day and a quire of paper to give you any thing like detail—I will merely mention that it is calculated that 30.000 people were in the streets waiting for him—The whole distance from the Angel Islington to the Crown and anchor[2] was lined with Multitudes. As I pass'd Colnaghi's window I saw a profil[e] Portraict of Sands the destroyer of Kotzebue.[3] His very look must interest every one in his favour—I suppose they have represented him in his college dress—He seems to me like a young Abelard—A fine Mouth, cheek bones (and this is no joke) full of sentiment; a fine unvulgar nose and plump temples. On looking over some Letters I found the one I wrote intended for you from the foot of Helvellyn to Liverpool—but you had sail'd and therefore It was returned to me. It contained among other nonsense an

1 *Manchester ... London*: Henry Hunt (1773–1835), radical, chaired the reform meeting at St Peter's Fields, Manchester, on 16 August, which was broken up by the armed yeomanry, who killed fifteen people and injured hundreds more. It became known as the Peterloo Massacre, a defining event in the agitation for parliamentary reform. Hunt was arrested, but on his release went to London for the triumphal procession witnessed by Keats.
2 *Crown and anchor*: A tavern in the Strand and a known site for political meetings. Keats's '30.000' is a slip for the '300,000'-strong crowd reported by *The Times* the next day.
3 *Sands ... Kotzebue*: See above, p. 341. Colnaghi's print shop was at 23 Cockspur Street, off the Strand. Keats passed the shop on the way back from his unsuccessful attempt to call on the Dilkes in Great Smith Street (see above, p. 416).

Acrostic of my Sister's name—and a pretty long name it is. I wrote it in a great hurry which you will see. Indeed I would not copy it if I thought it would ever be seen by any but yourselves—

[copies out his acrostic 'Give me your patience Sister while I frame', written on 27 June 1818 (p. 170 above)]

I sent you in my first Packet some of my scotch Letters. I find I have kept one back which was written in the most interesting part of our Tour, and will copy parts of it in the hope you will not find it unamusing I would give now any thing for Richardson's power of making mountains of mole hills. Incipit Epistola Caledoniensa, Dunancullen—I did not know the day of the month for I find I have not dated it—Brown must have been asleep. "Just after my last had gone to the post["] (before I go any further I must premise that I would send the identical Letter insted of taking the trouble to copy it: I do not do so for fear it would spoil my notion of the neat manner in which I intent [*for* intend] to fold these thin genteel sheets—The original is written on course paper—and the soft ones would ride in the Post-bag very uneasy; perhaps there might be a quarrel—)

[copies out his letter to Tom of 23 and 26 July 1818 almost to the end of the poem 'Not Aladin magian' (pp. 217–21 above)]

I ought to make a large Q here:[1] but I had better take the opportunity of telling you I have got rid of my haunting sore throat—and conduct myself in a manner not to catch another You speak of Lord Byron and me—There is this great difference between us. He describes what he sees—I describe what I imagine—Mine is the hardest task. You see the immense difference—The Edinburgh review are affraid to touch upom [*for* upon] my Poem—They do not know what to make of it—they do not like to condemn it and they will not p[r]aise it for fear—They are as shy of it as I should be of wearing a Quaker's

1 Q *here*: To mark the end of Keats's quotation (mainly accurate) from his letter.

hat—The fact is they have no real taste—they dare not compromise their Judgements on so puzzling a Question—If on my next Publication they should praise me and so lug in Endymion—I will address [them] in a manner they will not at all relish—The Cowardliness of the Edinburgh is worse than the abuse of the Quarterly.

On Sunday, 19 September Keats walked in the autumn countryside and drafted 'To Autumn'. The same day Woodhouse began his letter to John Taylor detailing his conversation with Keats the previous Sunday, in particular the changes Keats had made to 'The Eve of St Agnes': 'There was another alteration, which I abused for "a full hour by the <u>Temple</u> clock." You know if a thing has a decent side, I generally look no further—As the Poem was orig^{y} written, <u>we</u> innocent ones (ladies & myself) might very well have supposed that Porphyro . . . went over the "Dartmoor black" . . . to be married, in right honest chaste & sober wise. But, as it is now altered, as soon as M. has confessed her love, P. winds by degrees his arm round her, presses breast to breast, and acts all the acts of a bonâ fide husband, while she fancies she is only playing the part of a Wife in a dream. This alteration is of about 3 stanzas; and tho' there are no improper expressions but all is left to inference, and tho' profanely speaking, the Interest on the reader's imagination is greatly heightened, yet I do apprehend it will render the poem unfit for ladies, & indeed scarcely to be mentioned to them among the "things that are."—He says he does not want ladies to read his poetry: that he writes for men—& that if in the former poem there was an opening for a doubt what took place, it was his fault for not writing clearly & comprehensibly—that he sh^{d} despise a man who would be such an eunuch in sentiment as to leave a ~~Girl~~ maid, with that Character about her, in such a situation: & sho^{d} despise himself to write about it &c &c &c—and all this sort of Keats-like rhodomontade' (L, II, *p. 163).*

Monday [20 September]—This day is a grand day for winchester—they elect the Mayor. It was indeed high time the place should have some sort of excitement. There was nothing going on—all asleep—Not an old Maids Sedan returning from a card party—and if any old women have got tipsy at christenings they have not exposed themselves in the Street—The first night tho' of our arrival here there was a slight uproar took place at about ten of the clock—We heard distinctly a noise patting down the high street as of a walking Cane of the good old dowager breed; and a little minute after we heard a less voice obse[r]ve 'what a noise the ferril made.'—it must be loose." Brown wanted to call the Constables, but I observed 't was only a little breeze and would soon pass over. The side-streets here are excessively maiden lady like—The door steps always fresh from the flannel. The knockers have a very staid ser[i]ous, nay almost awful qu[i]etness about them—I never saw so quiet a collection of Lions, and rams heads—The doors most part black with a little brass handle just above the key hole—so that you may easily shut yourself out of your own house—he! he! There is none of your Lady Bellaston[1] rapping and ringing here—no thundering-Jupiter footmen no opera-trebble-tattoos—but a modest lifting up of the knocker by a set of little wee old fingers that peep through the grey mittens, and a dying fall thereof—The great beauty of Poetry is, that it makes every thing every place interesting—The palatine venice and the abbotine Winchester are equally interesting—Some time since I began a Poem call'd 'the Eve of St Mark[2] quite in the spirit of Town quietude. I think it will give you the sensation of walking about an old county Town in a coolish evening. I know not whether I shall ever finish it—I will give it far as I have gone. Ut tibi placent![3]

1 *Lady Bellaston*: The promiscuous London aristocrat in Fielding's *Tom Jones* with whom the hero has an affair.

2 *the Eve of St Mark*: Written between 13 and 17 February 1819, shortly after returning from Chichester, where Keats had written 'The Eve of St Agnes'. First published in 1848.

3 Ut tibi placent: (Latin) 'May they please you.'

Upon a Sabbath day it fell;
Thrice holy was the sabbath bell
That call'd the folk to evening prayer.
The City Streets were clean and fair
Fron [*for* From] wholesome drench of April rains,
And on the western window pains
The chilly sunset faintly told
Of immaturd, green vallies cold,
Of the green, thorny, bloomless hedge,
Of Rivers new with spring tide sedge,
Of Primroses by shelterd rills,
And Dasies on the aguish hills.
Thrice holy was the sabbath bell:
The silent streets were crowded well
With staid and pious companies
Wa[r]m from their fireside oratries,
And moving with demurest air
To even song and vesper prayer.
Each arched porch and entry low
Was fill'd with patient crowd and slow,
With whispers hush, and shuffling feet
While play'd the organs loud and sweet.
The Bells had ceas'd, the Prayers begun,
And Bertha had not yet half done
A curious volume, patch'd and torn,
That all day long, from earliest morn,
Had taken captive her fair eyes
Among its golden broideries:—
Perplex'd her with a thousand things—
The Stars of heaven, and Angels wings;
Martyrs in a fiery blaze:
Azure Saints 'mid silver rays;
Aron's breastplate, and the seven
Candlesticks John saw in heaven;
The winged Lion of St Mark,
And the Covenental Arck
With its many Misteries
Cherubim and golden Mice.

Bertha was a Maiden fair,
Dwelling in the old Minster square:
From her fireside she could see
Sidelong its rich antiquity,
Far as the Bishop's garden wall,
Where Sycamores and elm trees tall
Full leav'd the forest had outstript,
By no sharp north wind ever nipt,
So sheltered by the mighty pile.
Bertha arose, and read awhile
With forehead 'gainst the window pane,—
Again she tried, and then again,
Until the dusk eve left her dark
Upon the legend of St. Mark:
From pleated lawn-frill fine and thin
She lifted up her soft warm chin
With aching neck and swimming eyes
All daz'd with saintly imageries.
All was gloom, and silent all,
Save now and then the still foot fall
Of one returning homewards late
Past the echoing minster gate.
The clamourous daws that all the day
Above tree tops and towers play,
Pair by Pair had gone to rest,
Each in their ancient belfry nest
Where asleep they fall betimes
To music of the drowsy chimes.
All was silent, all was gloom
Abroad and in the homely roon [*for* room];—
Down she sat, poor cheated soul,
And struck a swart Lamp from the coal,
Leaned forward with bright drooping hair
And slant book full against the glare.
Her shadow, in uneasy guise,
Hover'd about, a giant size,
On ceiling, beam, and old oak chair,
The Parrot's cage and pannel square,

And the warm-angled winter screne,
On which were many monsters seen,
Call'd, Doves of Siam, Lima Mice,
And legless birds of Paradise,
Macaw, and tender Av'davat,
And silken-furr'd Angora Cat.
Untir'd she read—her shadow still
Glowerd about as it would fill
The room with gastly forms and shades—
As though some ghostly Queen of Spades
Had come to mock behind her back,
And dance, and ruffle her garments black.
Untir'd she read the Legend page
Of holy Mark from youth to age,
On Land, on sea, in pagan-chains,
Rejoicing for his many pains.
Sometimes the learned Eremite
With golden star, or daggar bright,
Refer'd to pious poesies
Written in smallst crow quill size
Beneath the text and thus the rhyme
Was parcell'd out from time to time:

What follows is an imitation of the Authors in Chaucer's time—'t is more ancient than Chaucer himself and perhaps betwe[e]n him and Gower

---

——Als writeth he of swevenis
Men han beforne they waken in blis,
When that hir friends thinke hem bounde
In crimpide shroude farre under grounde:
And how a litling childe mote be
A scainte er its natavitie,
Gif that the modre (Gode her blesse)
Kepen in Solitarinesse,
And kissen devoute the holy croce.
Of Goddis love and Sathan's force
He writithe; and things many moe,

Of swiche thinges I may not show,
Bot I must tellen verilie
Somedele of Saintè Cicilie,
And chieflie what he auctoreth
Of Saintè Markis life and dethe.

I hope you will like this for all its Carelessness—I must take an opportunity here to observe that though I am writing to you I am all the while writing at your Wife—This explanation will account for my speaking sometimes hoity-toityishly. Whereas if you were alone I should sport a little more sober sadness. I am like a squinti[n]g gentleman who saying soft things to one Lady ogles another—or what is as bad in arguing with a person on his left hand appeals with his eyes to one one [*for* on] the right. His Vision is elastic he bends it to a certain object but having a patent sp[r]ing it flies off. Writing has this disadvan[ta]ge of speaking. one cannot write a wink, or a nod, or a grin, or a purse of the Lips, or a smile—O law! One can-[not] put ones pinger [*for* finger] to one's nose, or yerk ye in the ribs, or lay hold of your button in writing—but in all of the most lively and titterly parts of my Letter you must not fail to imagine me as the epic poets say—now here, now there, now with one foot pointed at the ceiling, now with another—now with my pen on my ear, now with my elbow in my mouth—O my friends you loose the action—and attitude is every thing as Fusili[1] said when he took up his leg like a Musket to shoot a Swallow just darting behind his shoulder. And yet does not the word mum! go for ones finger beside the nose—I hope it does. I have to make use of the word Mum! before I tell you Severn has got a little Baby—all his own let us hope—He told Brown he had given up painting and had tu[r]n'd modeller. I hope sincerely tis not a party concern; that no M^{r} — or xxxx is the real Pinxit and Severn the poor Sculpsit to this work of art[2]—You know he has long studied in the Life-

1 *Fusili*: Keats is punning on 'fusil'(a musket) and the painter Henry Fuseli (1741–1825).
2 *Pinxit* . . . *Sculpsit* . . . *art*: Severn's illegitimate son Henry was born on 31 August 1819. Keats plays on the artist who creates (*pinxit*) and the engraver (*sculpsit*) who merely reproduces.

Academy.[1] Haydon—yes your wife will say, 'here is a sum total account of Haydon again I wonder your Brother don't put a monthly bulleteen in the Philadelphia Papers about him—I wont hear—no—skip down to the bottom—aye and there are some more of his verses, skip (lullaby-by) them too" "No, lets go regularly through" "I wont hear a word about Haydon—bless the child, how rioty she is!—there go on there" Now pray go on here for I have a few words to say about Haydon—Before this Chancery threat had cut of[f] every legitimate supp[l]y of Cash from me I had a little at my disposal: Haydon being very much in want I lent him 30£ of it. Now in this se-saw game of Life I got nearest to the ground and this chancery business rivetted me there so that I was sitting in that uneasy position where the seat slants so abominably. I applied to him for payment[2]—he could not—that was no wonder. but goodman Delver,[3] where was the wonder then, why marry, in this, he did not seem to care much about it—and let me go without my money with almost nonchalance when he aught to have sold his drawings to supply me. I shall perhaps still be acquainted with him, but for friendship that is at an end. Brown has been my friend in this he got him to sign a Bond payable at ~~two~~ three Months—Haslam has assisted me with the return of part of the money you lent him. Hunt—'there,' says your wife, 'there's another of those dull folkes—not a syllable about my friends—well—Hunt—what about Hunt pray—you little thing see how she bites my finger—my! is not this a tooth"—Well, when you have done with the tooth, read on—Not a syllable about your friends Here are some syllables. As far as I could smoke things on the Sunday before last, thus matters stood in Henrietta street—Henry was a greater blade than ever I remember to have seen him. He had on a very nice coat, a becoming waistcoat and buff trowsers—I think his face has lost a little of the spanish-brown, but no flesh. He carv'd some beef exactly to suit my appetite, as if I had been measured

1 *Academy*: Slang for a brothel.
2 *I applied to him for payment*: See his letter to Haydon of 17 June 1819 (*L*, II, pp. 119–20).
3 *goodman Delver*: *Hamlet*, V. i. 14–15.

for it. As I stood looking out of the window with Charles after dinner, quizzing the Passengers, at which, I am sorry to say he is too apt, I observed that his young, son of a gun's whiskers had begun to curl and curl—little twists and twists; all down the sides of his face getting properly thickish on the angles of the the visage, He certainly will have a notable pair of Whiskers. "How shiny your gown is in front" says Charles "Why, dont you see 't is an apron says Henrry" Whereat I scrutiniz'd and behold your mother had a purple stuff gown on, and over it an apron of the same colour, being the same cloth that was used for the lining—and furthermore to account for the shining it was the first day of wearing. I guess'd as much of the Gown—but that is entre-nous. Charles likes england better than france. They've got a fat, smiling, fair Cook as ever you saw—she is a little lame, but that improves her. it makes her go more swimmingly. When I ask'd 'Is M[rs] Wylie within' she gave such a large, five-and-thirty-year-old smile, it made me look round upon the fo[u]rth stair—it might have been the fifth—but that's a puzzle. I shall never be able if I were to set myself a recollecting for a year, to recollect that—I think I remember two or three specks in her teeth but I really cant say exactly. Your mother said something about Miss Keasle—what that was is quite a riddle to me now—Whether she had got fatter or thinner, or broader or longer—straiter, or had taken to the zig zags—Whether she had taken to, or left off, asses Milk—that by the by she ought never to touch—how much better it would be to put her out to nurse with the Wise woman of Brentford.[1] I can say no more on so spare a subject. Miss Millar now is a different morsell if one know how to divide and subdivide, theme her out into sections and subsections—Say a little on every part of her body as it is divided in common with all her fellow creatures, in Moor's Almanac. But Alas! I have not heard a word about her. no cue to begin upon. There was indeed a buzz about her and her mother's being at old M[rs] So and So's <u>who was like to die</u>—as the jews say—but I dare say, keeping up their dialect, <u>she was</u>

1 *Wise woman of Brentford*: *The Merry Wives of Windsor*, IV. v. 23–4, which has 'Brainford'.

not like to die. I must tell you a good thing Reynolds did: 't was the best thing he ever said. You know at taking leave of a party at a door way, sometimes a Man dallies and foolishes and gets awkward, and does not know how to make off to advantage—Good bye well—good-bye—and yet he does not—go—good bye and so on—well—good bless you—You know what I mean. Now Reynolds was in this predicament and got out of it in a very witty way. He was leaving us at Hampstead. He delay'd, and we were joking at him and even said, 'be off'—at which he put the tails of his coat between his legs, and sneak'd off as nigh like a spanial as could be. He went with flying colours: this is very clever—I must, being upon the subject, tell you another good thing of him; He began, for the service it might be of to him in the law, to learn french. He had Lessons at the cheap rate of 2. 6 per fag. and observed to Brown 'Gad says he, the mans [*for* man] sells his Lessons so cheap he must have stolen 'em.' You have heard of Hook the farce writer.[1] Horace Smith said to one who ask'd him if he knew Hook "Oh yes' Hook and I are very intimate." There's a page of Wit for you—to put John Bunyan's emblems[2] out of countenance. Tuesday [morning, 21 September]—You see I keep adding a sheet daily till I send the packet off—which I shall not do for a few days as I am inclined to write a good deal: for there can be nothing so remembrancing and enchaining as a good long letter be it composed of what it may—From the time you left me, our friends say I have altered completely—am not the same person—perhaps in this letter I am for in a letter one takes up one's existence from the time we last met—I dare say you have altered also—eve[r]y man does—Our bodies every seven years are completely fresh materiald—seven years ago it was not this hand that clench'd itself against Hammond[3]—We are like the

1 *Hook the farce writer*: Theodore Edward Hook (1788–1841), writer and hoaxer.

2 *John Bunyan's emblems*: Bunyan's *Book for Boys and Girls: Or, Country Rhymes for Children* (1686) was frequently reprinted with illustrations in the eighteenth century with the title *Divine Emblems*.

3 *Hammond*: Thomas Hammond, a surgeon in Edmonton with whom Keats served his apprenticeship.

relict garments of a Saint: the same and not the same: for the careful Monks patch it and patch it: till there's not a thread of the original garment left, and still they show it for St Anthony's shirt. This is the reason why men who had been bosom friends, on being separated for any number of years, afterwards meet coldly, neither of them knowing why—The fact is they are both altered—Men who live together have a silent moulding and influencing power over each other—They interassimulate. 'T is an uneasy thought that in seven years time the same hands cannot greet each other again. All this may be obviated by a willful and dramatic exercise of our Minds towards each other. Some think I have lost that poetic ardour and fire 't is said I once had—the fact is perhaps I have: but instead of that I hope I shall substitute a more thoughtful and quiet power. I am more frequently, now, contented to read and think—but now & then, haunted with ambitious thoughts. Qui[e]ter in my pulse, improved in my digestion; exerting myself against vexing speculations—scarcely content to write the best verses for the fever they leave behind. I want to compose without this fever. I hope I one day shall. You would scarcely imagine I could live alone so comfortably "Kepen in solitarinesse" I told Anne, the servent here, the other day, to say I was not at home if any one should call. I am not certain how I should endu[r]e loneliness and bad weather together. Now the time is beautiful. I take a walk every day for an hour before dinner and this is generally my walk[1]—I go out at the back gate across one street into the Cathedral yard, which is always interesting; then I pass under the trees along a paved path, pass the beautiful front of the Cathedral, turn to the left under a stone door way—then I am on the other side of the building—which leaving behind me I pass on through two college-like squares seemingly built for the dwelling place of Deans and Prebendaries—garnished with grass and shaded with trees. Then I pass through one of the old

1 *my walk*: 'Keats' Walk', the route given by Winchester Tourist Information (www.visitwinchester.co.uk/keats-walk), follows 'only one mile of my walk' because Keats failed to describe 'the other two' miles of his one-hour daily walk (see below).

city gates and then you are in one College-Street through which I pass and at the end thereof crossing some meadows and at last a country alley of gardens I arrive, that is, my worship arrives at the foundation of Saint Cross, which is a very interesting old place, both for its gothic tower and alms-square and for the appropriation of its rich rents to a relation of the Bishop of Winchester[1]—Then I pass across St Cross meadows till you come to the most beautifully clear river—now this is only one mile of my walk I will spare you the other two till after supper when they would do you more good—You must avoid going the first mile just after dinner. I could advise you to put by all this nonsense until you are lifted out of your difficulties—but when you come to this part feel with confidence what I now feel that though there can be no stop put to troubles we are inheritors of there can and must be and [*for* an] end to immediate difficulties. Rest in the confidence that I will not omit any exertion to benefit you by some means or other. If I cannot remit you hundreds, I will tens and if not that ones. Let the next year be managed by you as well as possible—the next month I mean for I trust you will soon receive Abbey's remittance. What he can send you will not be a sufficient capital to ensure you any command in America. What he has of mine I nearly have anticipated by debts. So I would advise you not to sink it, but to live upon it in hopes of my being able to encrease it—To this end I will devote whatever I may gain for a few years to come—at which period I must begin to think of a security of my own comforts when quiet will become more pleasant to me than the World—Still I would have you doubt my success[2]—'T is at present the cast of a die with me. You say 'these things will be a great torment to me.' I shall not suffer them to be so. I shall only exert myself the more—while

1 *Saint Cross . . . Bishop of Winchester*: The Hospital of St Cross, a medieval foundation. Francis North (1772–1861), later 6th Earl of Guildford, who enjoyed the sinecure as Master of St Cross, had been appointed by his father Bishop of Winchester. The scandal was ended in 1853.

2 *I would . . . success*: Keats perhaps meant to write 'I would not have you doubt'.

the seriousness of their nature will prevent me from missing up[1] imaginary griefs. I have not had the blue devils once since I received your last—I am advised not to publish till it is seen whether the Tragedy will or will not succeed—Should it, a few mo[n]ths may see me in the way of acquiring property; should it not it will be a drawback and I shall have to perform a longer literary Pilgrimage—You will perceive that it is quite out of my interest to come to America—What could I do there? How could I employ myself? Out of the reach of Libraries. You do not mention the name of the gentleman who assists you.[2] 'T is an extraordinary thing. How could you do without that assistance? I will not trust myself with brooding over this. The following is an extract from a Letter of Reynolds to me "I am glad to hear you are getting on so well with your writings. I hope you are not neglecting the revision of your Poems for the press: from which I expect more than you do"—the first thought that struck me upon reading your last, was to mo[r]tgage a Poem to Murray: but on more consideration I made up my mind not to do so: my reputation is very low: he would perhaps not have negociated my bill of intellect or given me a very small sum. I should have bound myself down for some time. 'T is best to meet present misfortunes; not for a momentary good to sacrifice great benefits which one's own untramell'd and free industry may bring one in the end. In all this do never think of me as in any way unhappy: I shall not be so. I have a great pleasure in thinking of my responsibility to you and shall do myself the greatest luxury if I can succeed in any way so as to be of assistance to you. We shall look back upon these times—even before our eyes are at all dim—I am convinced of it. But be careful of those Americans—I could almost advise you to come whenever you have the sum of 500£ to England—Those Americans will I am affraid still fleece you—If ever you should think of

1 *missing up*: Sometimes emended to 'nursing up'. *OED* records 'miss' as a transitive verb meaning 'to call someone a Miss': Keats may have meant creating 'imaginary griefs', as might an adolescent girl.

2 *gentleman who assists you*: Possibly William Bakewell, Audubon's brother-in-law, was lending money to George who was investing in a sawmill near Louisville with his brother Tom Bakewell (Gigante, pp. 305–6).

such a thing you must bear in mind the very different state of society here—The immense difficulty of the times—The great sum required per annum to maintain yourself in any decency. In fact the whole is with Providence. I know now [*for* not] how to advise you but by advising you to advise with yourself. In your next tell me at large your thoughts, about america; what chance there is of succeeding there: for it appears to me you have as yet been somehow deceived. I cannot help thinking M[r] Audubon has deceived you. I shall not like the sight of him—I shall endeavour to avoid seeing him—You see how puzzled I am—I have no meridian to fix you to—being the Slave of what is to happen. I think I may bid you finally remain in good hopes: and not teise yourself with my changes and variations of Mind—If I say nothing decisive in any one particular part of my Letter. you may glean the truth from the whole pretty correctly—You may wonder why I had not put your affairs with Abbey in train on receiving your Letter before last, to which there will reach you a short answer[1] dated from shanklin. I did write and speak to Abbey but to no purpose. You[r] last, with the enclosed note has appealed home to him—He will not see the necessity of a thing till he is hit in the mouth. 'T will be effectual—I am sorry to mix up foolish and serious things together—but in writing so much I am obliged to do so—and I hope sincerely the tenor of your mind will maintain itself better. In the course of a few months I shall be as good an Italian Scholar as I am a french one—I am reading Ariosto at present: not manageing more than six or eight stanzas at a time. When I have done this language so as to be able to read it tolerably well—I shall set myself to get complete in latin and there my learning must stop. I do not think of venturing upon Greek. I would not go even so far if I were not persuaded of the power the knowle[d]ge of any language gives one. the fact is that I like to be acquainted with foreign languages. It is besides a nice way of filling up intervals &c Also the reading of Dante in [*for* is] well worth the while. And in latin there is a fund of curious literature of the middle ages—The Works of many great Men Aretine and Sanazarius

1 *Short answer*: No longer extant.

and Machievel—I shall never become attach'd to a foreign idiom so as to put it into my writings. The Paradise lost though so fine in itself is a corruption of our Language—it should be kept as it is unique—a curiosity. a beautiful and grand Curiosity. The most remarkable Production of the world—A northern dialect accommodating itself to greek and latin inversions and intonations. The purest english I think—or what ought to be the purest—is Chatterton's—The Language had existed long enough to be entirely uncorrupted of Chaucer's gallicisms and still the old words are used—Chatterton's language is entirely northern—I prefer the native music of it to Milton's cut by feet I have but lately stood on my guard against Milton. Life to him would be death to me. Miltonic verse cannot be written but it [*for* in] the vein of art—I wish to devote myself to another sensation—

(continued 24 September, p. 456 below)

To J. H. Reynolds
21 September 1819

[Woodhouse transcript (1821?)]

Winchester. Tuesday

My dear Reynolds,

I was very glad to hear from Woodhouse that you would meet in the Country. I hope you will pass some pleasant time together. Which I wish to make pleasanter by a brace of letters,[1] very highly to be estimated, as really I have had very bad luck with this sort of game this season. I "kepen in solitarinesse,"[2] for Brown has gone a visiting. I am surprized myself at the pleasure I live alone in. I can give you no news of the place here, or any other idea of it but what I have to this effect

1 *brace of letters*: Keats addressed this letter to Woodhouse's family home in Bath, where he knew Reynolds planned to visit him from his annual holiday in Devonshire. He began the next letter to Woodhouse later that evening.
2 *kepen in solitarinesse*: 'The Eve of St Mark', l. 106.

written to George. Yesterday I say to him was a grand day for Winchester. They elected a Mayor—It was indeed high time the place should receive some sort of excitement. There was nothing going on: all asleep: not an old maid's sedan returning from a card party: and if any old woman got tipsy at Christenings they did not expose it in the streets. The first night tho' of our arrival here, there was slight uproar took place at about 10 o'the Clock. We heard distinctly a noise patting down the high Street as of a walking cane of the good old Dowager breed; and little minute after we heard a less voice observe "What a noise the ferril made—it must be loose"—Brown wanted to call the Constables, but I observed 'twas only a little breeze, and would soon pass over.—The side streets here are excessively maiden-lady like: the door steps always fresh from the flannel. The knockers have a staid serious, nay almost awful quietness about them.—I never saw so quiet a collection of Lions' & Rams' heads—The doors most part black, with a little brass handle just above the keyhole, so that in Winchester a man may very quietly shut himself out of his own house. How beautiful the season is now—How fine the air. A temperate sharpness about it. Really, without joking, chaste weather—Dian skies—I never lik'd stubble fields so much as now—Aye better than the chilly green of the Spring. Somehow a stubble plain looks warm—in the same way that some pictures look warm—this struck me so much in my Sunday's walk that I composed upon it.[1] I hope you are better employed than in gaping after weather. I have been at different times so happy as not to know what weather it was—No I will not copy a parcel of verses. I always somehow associate Chatterton with autumn. He is the purest writer in the English Language. He has no French idiom, or particles like Chaucer—'tis genuine English Idiom in English words. I have given up Hyperion[2]—there were too many Miltonic inversions in it—Miltonic verse cannot be written but in an artful or rather artist's humour. I wish to give myself up to other sensations. English ought to be kept up. It may be

1 *I composed upon it*: 'To Autumn'.
2 *Hyperion*: *The Fall of Hyperion*.

interesting to you to pick out some lines from Hyperion and put a mark × to the false beauty proceeding from art, and one || to the true voice of feeling. Upon my soul 'twas imagination I cannot make the distinction—Every now & then there is a Miltonic intonation—But I cannot make the division properly. The fact is I must take a walk: for I am writing so long a letter to George; and have been employed at it all the morning. You will ask, have I heard from George. I am sorry to say not the best news—I hope for better—This is the reason among others that if I write to you it must be in such a scraplike way. I have no meridian to date Interests from, or measure circumstances—To night I am all in a mist; I scarcely know what's what—But you knowing my unsteady & vagarish disposition, will guess that all this turmoil will be settled by tomorrow morning. It strikes me to night that I have led a very odd sort of life for the two or three last years—Here & there—No anchor—I am glad of it.—If you can get a peep at Babbicomb before you leave the country, do.—I think it the finest place I have seen, or—is to be seen in the South.[1] There is a Cottage there I took warm water at, that made up for the tea. I have lately skirk'd [*for* shirk'd] some friends of ours, and I advise you to do the same, I mean the blue-devils—I am never at home to them. You need not fear them while you remain in Devonshire. there will be some of the family waiting for you at the Coach office—but go by another Coach.—I shall beg leave to have a third opinion in the first discussion you have with Woodhouse—just half way—between both. You know I will not give up my argument—In my walk to day I stoop'd under a rail way that lay across my path, and ask'd myself "Why I did not get over" Because, answered I, "no one wanted to force you under"—I would give a guinea to be a reasonable man—good sound sense—a says what he thinks, and does what he says man—and did not take snuff—They say men near death however mad they may have been, come to their senses—I hope I shall here in this letter—there is a decent space to be very sensible in—many a good proverb has

1 *Babbicomb . . . South*: Keats evidently visited Babbacombe in spring 1818 (see above, p. 141).

been in less—Nay I have heard of the statutes at large being chang'd into the Statutes at Small and printed for a watch paper. Your sisters by this time must have got the Devonshire ees—short ees—you know 'em—they are the prettiest ees in the Language. O how I admire the middle siz'd delicate Devonshire girls of about 15. There was one at an Inn door holding a quartern of brandy—the very thought of her kept me warm a whole stage—and a 16 miler too—"You'll pardon me for being jocular."[1]

Ever your affectionate friend
John Keats—

To Richard Woodhouse
21, 22 September 1819

[Harvard MS]

Dear Woodhouse, [Winchester] Tuesday [evening]—

If you see what I have said to Reynolds before you come to your own dose you will put it between the bars unread; provided they have begun fires in Bath—I should like a bit of fire to night—one likes a bit of fire—How glorious the Blacksmiths' shops look now—I stood to night before one till I was verry near listing for one. Yes I should like a bit of fire—at a distance about 4 feet 'not quite hob nob'—as wordsworth says[2]—The fact was I left Town on Wednesday—determined to be in a hurry—You don't eat travelling—you're wrong—beef—beef—I like the look of a sign—The Coachman's face says eat eat, eat—I never feel more contemptible than when I am sitting by a good looking coachman—One is nothing—Perhaps I eat to persuade myself I am somebody. You must be when slice after slice—but it wont do—the Coachman nibbles a bit of bread—he's favour'd—he's had a Call—a Hercules Methodist—Does

1 *You'll . . . jocular*: Master Vellum's catchphrase in Addison's comedy *The Drummer* (1715).
2 *not quite . . . says*: Wordsworth's 'The Idiot Boy', l. 289.

he live by bread alone? O that I were a Stage Manager—perhaps that's as old as 'doubling the Cape'—"How are ye old 'un? hey! why dont'e speak?' O that I had so sweet a Breast to sing as the Coachman hath! I'd give a penny for his Whistle—and bow to the Girls on the road—Bow—nonsense—'t is a nameless graceful slang action—Its effect on the women suited to it must be delightful. It touches 'em in the ribs—en passant—very off hand—very fine—Sed thongum formosa vale vale inquit Heigh ho la![1] You like Poetry better—so you shall have some I was going to give Reynolds—

Season of Mists and mellow fruitfulness,[2]
  Close bosom friend of the maturing sun;
Conspiring with him how to load and bless
  The vines with fruit that round the thatch eves run;
To bend with apples the moss'd cottage trees,
  And fill all fruit with ripeness to the core;
    To swell the gourd, and plump the hazle-shells
With a white kernel; to set budding more,
  And still more later flowers for the bees
  Untill they think wa[r]m days will never cease
    For summer has o'erbrimm'd their clammy Cells.

Who hath not seen thee oft, amid thy stores?
  Sometimes, whoever seeks abroad may find
Thee sitting careless on a granary floor,
  Thy hair soft-lifted by the winmowing wind;
Or on a half reap'd furrow sound asleep,
Dased with the fume of poppies, while thy hook
    Spares the next swath and all its twined flowers;
And sometimes like a gleaner thou dost keep

1 *Sed . . . la*: A punning replacement of 'thongum' (whip) for 'longum' in 'Et longum "formose, vale, vale," inquit, "Iolla"' ('he bade fair Iollas a long farewell') in Virgil's *Eclogues*, III. 79.

2 *Season . . . fruitfulness*: Printed in *1820* with a few variants. For a detailed account of the actual agricultural and economic conditions in the countryside surrounding Winchester, see Richard Marggraf Turley, Jane Elizabeth Archer and Howard Thomas, 'Keats, "To Autumn", and the New Men of Winchester', *Review of English Studies*, n.s. 63 (2012), pp. 797–817.

Stready thy laden head across a brook;
Or by a Cyder press, with patient look,
Thou watchest the last oozings hours by hours—

Where are the songs of spring? Aye, Where are they?
Think not of them, thou hast thy music too.
While barred clouds bloom the soft-dying day
And touch the stubble plains with rosy hue:
Then in a wailful quire the small gnats mourn
Among the river sallows, borne aloft
Or sinking as the light wind lives and dies;
And full grown Lambs loud bleat from hilly bourne:
Hedge crickets sing, and now with treble soft
The Red breast whistles from a garden Croft
And gather'd Swallows twitter in the Skies—

I will give you a few lines from Hyperion[1] on account of a word in the last line of a fine sound—

'Mortal! That thou may'st understand aright
I humanize my sayings to thine ear,
Making comparisons of earthly things;
Or thou might'st better listen to the wind
Though it blows legend-laden th[r]ough the trees.

I think you will like the following description of the Temple of Saturn—

I look'd around upon the carved sides
Of an old sanctuary, with roof august
Builded so high, it seem'd that filmed clouds
Might sail beneath, as o'er the stars of heaven.
So old the place was I remember none
The like upon the earth; what I had seen
Of grey Cathedrals, buttress'd walls, rent towers
The superanuations of sunk realms,

1 *Lines from Hyperion*: *The Fall of Hyperion* (first published 1857), II, 1–4, 6 and I, 61–86.

Or nature's rocks hard toil'd in winds and waves,
Seem'd but the failing of decrepit things
To that eternal-domed monument—
Upon the marble, at my feet, there lay
Store of strange vessels and large draperies
Which needs had been of dyed asbestus wove,
Or in that place the moth could not corrupt,
So white the linen, so, in some, distinct
Ran imageries from a sombre loom.
All in a mingled heap confused there lay
Robes, golden tongs, censer and chafing dish
Girdles, and chains and holy jewelries.
Turning from these, with awe once more I rais'd
My eyes to fathom the space every way;
The embossed roof, the silent massive range
Of Columns north and south, ending in Mist
Of nothing; then to the eastward where black gates
Were shut against the Sunrise evermore—

I see I have completely lost my direction—So I e'en make you pay double postage. I had begun a sonnet in french of Ronsard—on my word 't is verry capable of poetry—I was stop[p]ed by a circumstance not worth mentioning—I intended to call it La Platonique Chevalresque—I like the second line—

Non ne suis si audace a languire
De m'empresser au cœur vos tendres mains. &c.

Here is what I had written for a sort of induction—

Fanatics have their dreams wherewith they weave[1]
A Paradise for a Sect; the savage too
From forth the loftiest fashion of his sleep
Guesses at Heaven: pity these have not
Trac'd upon vellum, or wild indian leaf
The shadows of melodious utterance:
But bare of laurel they live, dream, and die,

1 *Fanatics . . . weave*: *The Fall of Hyperion*, I, 1–11.

For Poesy alone can tell her dreams,
With the fine spell of words alone can save
Imagination from the sable charm
And dumb enchantment—

My Poetry will never be fit for any thing it does n't cover its ground well—You see she is off her guard and does n't move a peg though Prose is coming up in an awkward style enough—Now a blow in the spondee will finish her—But let it get over this line of circumvallation[1] if it can. These are unpleasant Phrase[s.]

Now for all this you two must write me a letter apiece—for as I know you will interread one another—I am still writing to Reynolds as well as yourself—As I say to George I am writing to you but at your Wife—And dont forget to tell Reynold's of the fairy tale Undine[2]—Ask him if he has read any of the American Brown's novels[3] that Hazlitt speaks so much of—I have read one call'd Wieland—very powerful—something like Godwin—Between Schiller and Godwin—A Domestic prototype of S[c]hiller's Armenian[4]—More clever in plot and incident than Godwin—A strange american scion of the German trunk. Powerful genius—accomplish'd horrors—I shall proceed tomorrow—

(continued next day, p. 450 below)

1 This passage was added after the page was completed, written vertically round the lines of poetry at the top of the page.
2 *Undine*: George Soane's newly published *Undine: or, the Spirit of the Waters* (1818), a translation from the German of F. H. K. La Motte Fouqué (1777–1843).
3 *Brown's novels*: *Wieland: or, the Transformation: An American Tale* (1798) by Charles Brockden Brown (1771–1810) was influenced by Godwin.
4 *S[c]hiller's Armenian*: In 1800 William Render translated *The Armenian: or, the Ghostseer* by Friedrich Schiller (1759–1805).

To Charles Brown
22 September 1819

[Brown transcript (1836–40)]

[Winchester, Wednesday morning]

* * *

Now I am going to enter on the subject of self. It is quite time I should set myself doing something, and live no longer upon hopes. I have never yet exerted myself. I am getting into an idle minded, vicious way of life, almost content to live upon others. In no period of my life have I acted with any self will, but in throwing up the apothecary-profession. That I do not repent of. Look at x x x x x x x:[1] if he was not in the law he would be acquiring, by his abilities, something towards his support. My occupation is entirely literary; I will do so too. I will write, on the liberal side of the question, for whoever will pay me. I have not known yet what it is to be diligent. I purpose living in town in a cheap lodging, and endeavouring, for a beginning, to get the theatricals of some paper. When I can afford to compose deliberate poems I will. I shall be in expectation of an answer to this. Look on my side of the question. I am convinced I am right. Suppose the Tragedy should succeed,—there will be no harm done. And here I will take an opportunity of making a remark or two on our friendship, and all your good offices to me. I have a natural timidity of mind in these matters: liking better to take the feeling between us for granted, than to speak of it. But, good God! what a short while you have known me! I feel it a sort of duty thus to recapitulate, however unpleasant it may be to you. You have been living for others more than any man I know. This is a vexation to me; because it has been depriving you, in the very prime of your life, of pleasures which it was your duty to procure. As I am speaking in general terms this may appear nonsense; you perhaps will not

1 *x x x x x x x*: Reynolds.

understand it: but if you can go over, day by day, any month of the last year,—you will know what I mean. On the whole, however, this is a subject that I cannot express myself upon. I speculate upon it frequently; and, believe me, the end of my speculations is always an anxiety for your happiness. This anxiety will not be one of the least incitements to the plan I purpose pursuing. I had got into a habit of mind of looking towards you as a help in all difficulties. This very habit would be the parent of idleness and difficulties. You will see it is a duty I owe myself to break the neck of it. I do nothing for my subsistence—make no exertion. At the end of another year, you shall applaud me,—not for verses, but for conduct. If you live at Hampstead next winter——I like x x x x x x x x x x[1] and I cannot help it. On that account I had better not live there. While I have some immediate cash, I had better settle myself quietly, and fag on as others do. I shall apply to Hazlitt, who knows the market as well as any one, for something to bring in a few pounds as soon as possible. I shall not suffer my pride to hinder me. The whisper may go round; I shall not hear it. If I can get an article in the "Edinburg", I will. One must not be delicate. Nor let this disturb you longer than a moment. I look forward, with a good hope, that we shall one day be passing free, untrammelled, unanxious time together. That can never be if I continue a dead lump. x x x x x x x x x x x x x x x[2] I shall be expecting anxiously an answer from you. If it does not arrive in a few days, this will have miscarried, and I shall come straight to x x x x[3] before I go to town, which you, I am sure, will agree had better be done while I still have some ready cash. By the middle of October I shall expect you in London. We will then set at the Theatres. If you have any thing to gainsay, I shall be even as the deaf adder which stoppeth her ears.[4]

* * *

1 *x x x x x x x x x x*: Fanny Brawne.
2 *x x x x x x x x x x x x x x x*: Passage omitted.
3 *I shall . . . x x x x*: To see Brown in Bedhampton.
4 *deaf adder . . . her ears*: Psalm 58:4.

To Richard Woodhouse
(continued)

22 September 1819

[Winchester, 22 September] Wednesday—I am all in a Mess here—embowell'd in Winchester. I wrote two Letters to Brown one from said Place, and one from London, and neither of them has reach'd him—I have written him a long one this morning and am so perplex'd as to be an object of Curiosity to you quiet People. I hire myself a show waggan and trompetour. Here's the wonderful Man whose Letters wont go!—All the infernal imaginarry thunderstorms from the Post-office are beating upon me—so that 'unpoeted I write" Some curious body has detained my Letters—I am sure of it. They know not what to make of me—not an acquaintance in the Place—what can I be about? so they open my Letters—Being in a lodging house, and not so self will'd, but I am a little cowardly I dare not spout my rage against the Ceiling—Besides I should be run th[r]ough the Body by the major in the next room—I don't think his wife would attempt such a thing—Now I am going to be serious—After revolving certain circumstances in my Mind; chiefly connected with a late american letter—I have determined to take up my abode in a cheap Lodging in Town and get employment in some of our elegant Periodical Works—I will no longer live upon hopes—I shall carry my plan into execution speedily—I shall live in Westminster—from which a walk to the British Museum will be noisy and muddy—but otherwise pleasant enough—I shall enquire of Hazlitt how the figures of the market stand. O that I could [write] somthing agrest[1] rural, pleasant, fountain-vo[i]c'd—not plague you will [*for* with] unconnected nonsense—But things won't leave me <u>alone</u>. I shall be in Town as soon as either of you—I only wait for an answer from Brown: if he receives mine which is now a very moot point—I will give you a few reasons

1 *agrest*: Belonging to the open country, hence rustic (*OED* rare).

why I shall persist in not publishing The Pot of Basil—It is too smokeable—I can get it smoak'd at the Carpenters shaving chimney much more cheaply—There is too much inexperience of live [*for* life], and simplicity of knowledge in it—which might do very well after one's death—but not while one is alive. There are very few would look to the reality. I intend to use more finesse with the Public. It is possible to write fine things which cannot be laugh'd at in any way. Isabella is what I should call were I a reviewer 'A weak-sided Poem' with an amusing sober-sadness about it. Not that I do not think Reynolds and you are quite right about it—it is enough for me. But this will not do to be public—If I may say so, in my dramatic capacity I enter fully into the feeling: but in Propria Persona I should be apt to quiz it myself—There is no objection of this kind to Lamia—A good deal to St Agnes Eve—only not so glaring—Would a[s] I say I could write you something sylvestran. But I have no time to think: I am an otiosus-peroccupatus[1] Man—I th[i]nk upon crutches, like the folks in your Pump room—Have you seen old Bramble yet[2]—they say he's on his last legs—The gout did not treat the old Man well so the Physician superseded it, and put the dropsy in office, who gets very fat upon his new employment, and behaves worse than the other to the old Man—But he'll have his house about his ears soon—We shall have another fall of Siege-arms—I suppose Mrs Humphrey persists in a big-belley—poor thing she little thinks how she is spo[i]ling the corners of her mouth—and making her nose quite a piminy. Mr Humphrey I hear was giving a Lecture in the gaming-room—When some one call'd out Spousey! I hear too he has received a challenge from a gentleman who lost that evening—The fact is Mr H. is a mere nothing out of his Rod-room [*for* Bed-room].—Old Tabitha died in being bolstered up for a whist-party. They had to cut again—Chowder died long ago—Mrs H. laments that the last time they put him (i.e. to breed) he didn't take—They say he was a direct descendant of Cupid and Veney in the

1 *otiosus-peroccupatus*: Keats means 'pointlessly preoccupied'.
2 *Have . . . yet*: Keats begins a mock continuation of *Humphry Clinker* (1771) by Tobias Smollett (1721–71).

Spectator—This may be eisily known by the Parish Books—If you do not write in the course of a day or two: direct to me to Rice's—Let me know how you pass your times and how you are—

Your si<n>cere friend
John Keats—

Hav'nt heard from Taylor—

To C. W. Dilke
22 September 1819[1]

[Keats House]

My dear Dilke, Winchester Wednesday Eve—

Whatever I take too for the time I cannot l[e]ave off in a hur[r]y; letter writing is the go now; I have consumed a Quire at least. You must give me credit, now, for a free Letter when it is in real[i]ty an interested one, on two points, one requestive, the other verging to the pros and cons—As I expect they will lead me to seeing and conferring with you in a short time, I shall not enter at all upon a letter I have lately received from george of not the most comfortable intelligence: but proceed to these two points, which if you can theme out into sexions and subsexions, for my edification, you will oblige me. The first I shall begin upon, the other will follow like a tail to a Comet. I have written to Brown on the subject, and can but go over the same Ground with you in a very short time, it not being more in length than the ordinary paces between the Wickets. It concerns a resolution I have taken to acqu[i]re something by temporary writing in periodical works. You must agree with me how unwise it is to keep feeding upon hopes, which depending so much on the state of temper and imagination, appear gloomy or bright, near or afar off just as it happens—Now an act has three parts—to act, to do, and to perform—I mean I should do something for my immediate welfare—Even if I am swept away like a Spider from

1 Keats decided not to send this letter: instead he wrote a brief letter to Dilke on 1 October (p. 461 below).

a drawing room I am determined to spin—home spun any thing for sale. Yea, I will trafic. Any thing but Mortgage my Brain to Blackwood. I am determined not to lie like a dead lump. If Reynolds had not taken to the law, would he not be earning something? Why cannot I—You may say I want tact—that is easily acqui[r]ed. You may be up to the slang of a cock pit in three battles. It is fortunate I have not before this been tempted to venture on the common.[1] I should a year ago have spoken my mind on every subject with the utmost simplicity. I hope I have learnt a little better and am confident I shall be able to cheat as well as any literary Jew of the Market and shine up an article on any thing without much knowle[d]ge of the subject, aye like an orange. I would willingly have recourse to other means. I cannot; I am fit for nothing but literature. Wait for the issue of this Tragedy? No—there cannot be greater uncertainties east west, north and south than concerning dramatic composition. How many months must I wait! Had I not better begin to look about me now? If better events supersede this necessity what harm will be done? I have no trust whatever on Poetry—I dont wonder at it—the ma[r]vel it [*for* is] to me how people read so much of it. I think you will see the reasonableness of my plan. To forward it I purpose living in a cheap Lodg[i]ng in Town, that I may be in the reach of books and information, of which there is here a plentiful lack. If I can [find] any place comfitable I will settle myself and fag till I can affrad [*for* afford] to buy Pleasure—which if [I] never can afford I must go Without—Talking of Pleasure, this moment I was writing with one hand, and with the other holding to my Mouth a Nectarine—good god how fine—It went down soft pulpy, slushy, oozy—all its delicious embonpoint melted down my throat like a large beatified Strawberry. I shall certainly breed. Now I come to my request. Should you like me for a neighbour again? Come, plump it out, I wont blush. I should also be in the neighbourhood of Mrs Wylie, which I shou[l]d be glad of, though that of course does not influence me. Therefore will you look about Marsham, or rodney [*for* Romney] street for a couple of rooms for me. Rooms like

1 *to venture on the common*: i.e., prostitute my abilities.

the gallants legs in massingers time "as good as the times allow, Sir."[1] I have written to day to Reynolds, and to Woodhouse. Do you know him? He i<s> a Friend of Taylors at whom Brown has taken one of his funny odd dislikes. I'm sure he's wrong, because Woodhouse likes my Poetry—conclusive. I ask your opinion and yet I must say to you as to him, Brown that if you have any thing to say against it I shall be as obstinate & heady as a Radical. By the Examiner coming in your hand writing you must be in Town. They have put [me] into spirits. Notwithstand my aristocratic temper I cannot help being verry much pleas'd with the present public proceedings.[2] I hope sincerely I shall be able to put a Mite of help to the Liberal side of the Question before I die. If you should have left Town again (for your Holidays cannot be up yet) let me know—when this is forwarded to you—A most extraordinary mischance has befallen two Letters I wrote Brown—one from London whither I was obliged to go on business for George; the other from this place since my return. I cant make it out. I am excessively sorry for it. I shall hear from Brown and from you almost together for I have sent him a Letter to day: you must positively agree with me or by the delicate toe nails of the virgin I will not open your Letters. If they are as David says 'suspicious looking letters" I wont open them—If St John had been half as cunning he might have seen the revelations comfortably in his own room, without giving Angels the trouble of breaking open Seals.[3] Remember me to Mrs D.— and the Westmonsteranian and believe me

Ever your sincere friend
John Keats—

1 *as good . . . allow, Sir*: Massinger's *A Very Woman* (1655), III. i.; W. Gifford (ed.), *The Plays of Philip Massinger* (3rd ed., 1840), p. 450.

2 *the present public proceedings*: Keats had just received the Sunday, 19 September issue of the *Examiner* containing a report of Henry Hunt's entry to London, which he had witnessed on 13 September (p. 425 above). As Mee points out, Keats seems to distinguish here between *Radical* (irresponsible) and *Liberal* politics (his own and Hunt's).

3 *Angels . . . Seals*: A references to Sheridan's *The Rivals* (1775), IV. i., which has 'malicious-looking letter', and Revelation 5–6.

To Charles Brown
23 September 1819[1]

[Brown transcript (1836–40)]

[Winchester, Thursday]

* * *

Do not suffer me to disturb you unpleasantly: I do not mean that you should not suffer me to occupy your thoughts, but to occupy them pleasantly; for, I assure you, I am as far from being unhappy as possible. Imaginary grievances have always been more my torment than real ones. You know this well. Real ones will never have any other effect upon me than to stimulate me to get out of or avoid them. This is easily accounted for. Our imaginary woes are conjured up by our passions, and are fostered by passionate feeling; our real ones come of themselves, and are opposed by an abstract exertion of mind. Real grievances are displacers of passion. The imaginary nail a man down for a sufferer, as on a cross; the real spur him up into an agent. I wish, at one view, you could see my heart towards you. 'Tis only from a high tone of feeling that I can put that word upon paper—out of poetry. I ought to have waited for your answer to my last before I ~~send~~ /wrote/ this. I felt, however, compelled to make a rejoinder to your's. I had written to x x x x[2] on the subject of my last,—I scarcely know whether I shall send my letter now. I think he would approve of my plan; it is so evident. Nay, I am convinced, out and out, that by prosing for awhile in periodical works I may maintain myself decently.

* * *

1 Brown mistakenly thought this letter was written on the same day as his preceding letter of 22 September.

2 *I had written to x x x x*: Keats's unsent letter to Dilke, written the previous evening.

To George and Georgiana Keats

(continued)

24, 25, 27 September 1819

[Winchester, Friday, 24 September] I have been obliged to intermiten your Letter for two days (this being Friday morn) from having had to attend to other correspondence. Brown who was at Bedhampton, went thence to Chichester, and I still directing my letters [to] Bedhampton—there asore [*for* arose] a misunderstand about them—I began to suspect my Letters had been stopped from curiosity. However yesterday Brown had four Letters from me all in a Lump—and the matter is clear'd up—Brown complained very much in his Letter to me of yesterday of the great alteration the Disposition of Dilke has undergone—He thinks of nothing but 'Political Justice'[1] and his Boy—Now the first political duty a Man ought to have a Mind to is the happiness of his friends. I wrote Brown a comment on the subject,[2] wherein I explained what I thought of Dilke's Character. Which resolved itself into this conclusion. That Dilke was a Man who cannot feel he has a personal identity unless he has made up his Mind about every thing. The only means of strengthening one's intellect is to make up ones mind about nothing—to let the mind be a thoroughfare for all thoughts. Not a select party. The genus is not scarce in population. All the stubborn arguers you meet with are of the same brood—They never begin upon a subject they have not preresolved on. They want to hammer their nail into you and if you turn the point, still they think you wrong. Dilke will never come at a truth as long as he lives; because he is always trying at it. He is a Godwin-methodist. I must not forget to mention

1 *Political Justice*: William Godwin's *Political Justice* (1793), the fullest exposition of his philosophical anarchism. Keats distrusted Godwin's belief that reason alone was sufficient to perfect man and society.

2 *I wrote . . . the subject*: Probably in one of the passages omitted in Brown's transcript of the preceding letter.

that your mother show'd me the lock of hair—'t is of a very dark colour for so young a creature. When it is two feet in length I shall not stand a barley corn higher. That's not fair—one ought to go on growing as well as others—At the end of this sheet I shall stop for the present—and sent [*for* send] it off. You may expect another Letter immediately after it. As I never know the day of the mo[n]th but by chance I put here that this is the 24th September. I would wish you here to stop you ears, for I have a word or two to say to your Wife—My dear sister, In the first place I must quarrel with you for sending me such a shabby sheet of paper—though that is in some degree made up for by the beautiful impress[i]on of the seal. You should like to know what I was doing—The first of May—let me see—I cannot recollect. I have all the Examiners ready to send—They will be a great treat to you when they reach you—I shall pack them up when my Business with Abbey has come to a good conclusion and the remittance is on the road to you—I have dealt round your best wishes to our friends, like a pack of cards but being always given to cheat, myself, I have turned up ace. You see I am making game of you. I see you are not all all happy in that America. England however would not be over happy for us if you were here. Perpaps 'twould be better to be teased herre than there. I must preach patience to you both. No step hasty or injurious to you must be taken. Your observation on the moschetos gives me great pleasure T is excessively poetical and humane. You say let one large sheet be all to me: You will find more than that in diffrent parts of this packet for you. Certainly I have been caught in rains. A Catch in the rain occasioned my last sore throat—but As for red-hair'd girls upon my word I do not recollect ever having seen one—Are you quizzing me or Miss Waldegrave when you talk of promenading. As for Pun-making I wish it was as a good a trade as pin-making—there is very little business of that sort going on now. We struck for wages like the manchester wevers[1]—

1 *We struck . . . wevers*: The strike of Manchester and Lancashire handloom weavers in September and October 1818. For Keats's sympathy for Belfast's weavers, see above, pp. 188–9.

but to no purpose—so we are all out of employ—I am more lucky than some you see by having an opportunity of exporting a few—getting into a little foreign trade—which is a comfortable thing. I wish I could get change for a pun in silver currency. I would give three and a half any night to get into Drury-pit—But they wont ring at all. No more will notes will you say—but notes are differing things—though they make together a Pun mote[1]—as the term goes. If I were your Son I shouldn't mind you, though you rapt me with the Scissars—But lord! I should be out of favor sin the little un be comm'd. You have made an Uncle of me, you have, and I don't know what to make of myself. I suppose next there'll be a Nevey. You say—in may last, write directly. I have not received your Letter above 10 days. The though[t] of you[r] little girl puts me in mind of a thing I heard a Mr Lamb say. A child in a[r]ms was passing by his chair toward the mother, in the nurses a[r]ms—Lamb took hold of the long clothes saying 'Where, god bless me, "Where does it leave off?"

Saturday [25 September]. If you would prefer a joke or two to any thing else I have too [*for* two] for you fresh hatchd. just ris as the Baker's wives say by the rolls. The first I play'd off at Brown—the second I played on myself. Brown when he left me "Keats! says he "my good fellow (staggering upon his left heel, and fetching an irregular pirouette with his right) Keats says he (depressing his left eyebrow and elevating his right one ((tho by the way, at the moment, I did not know which was the right one)) Keats says he (still in the same posture but farthermore both his hands in his waistcoat pockets and jutting out his stomach) "Keats—my—g-o-ood fell o-o-o-ooh! says he (interlarding his exclamation with certain ventriloquial parentheses)—no this is all a lie—He was as sober as Judge when a judge happens to be sober; and said "Keats, if any Letters come for me—Do not forward them, but open them and give me the marrow of them in few words. At the time when I wrote my first to him no Letters had arrived—I thought I would invent one, and as I had not time to manufacture a long one I dabbed

1 *Pun-mote*: A pun on bon mot, unless Keats meant to write 'note' and pun on 'pound note'.

off as [*for* a] short one—and that was the reason of the joke succeeding beyond my expectations. Brown let his house to a Mr Benjamin a Jew. Now the water which furnishes the house is in a tank sided with a composition of lime and the lime imp[r]-egnates the water unpleasantly—Taking advantage of this circumstance I pretended that Mr Benjamin had written the following short note—"Sir. By drinking your damn'd tank water I have got the gravel—what reparation can you make to me and my family? Nathan Benjamin" By a fortunate hit, I hit upon his right hethen name—his right Pronomen. Brown in consequence it appears wrote to the surprised Mr Benjamin the following "Sir, I cannot afford you any remuneration until your gravel shall have formed into a Stone when I will cut you with Pleasure. C. Brown" This of Browns Mr Benjamin has answered insisting on an explatinon [*for* explanation] of this singular circumstance. B. says "when I read your Letter and his following I roared, and in came Mr Snook who on reading them seem'd likely to burst the hoops of his fat sides—so the Joke has told well—Now for the one I played on myself—I must first give you the scence [*for* scene] and the dramatis Personæ—There are an old M[a]jor and his youngish wife live in the next apartments to me—His bed room door opens at an angle with my sitting room door. Yesterday I was reading as demurely as a Parish Clerk when I heard a rap at the door—I got up and opened it—no one was to be seen—I listened and I heard some one in the Major's room—Not content with this I went up stairs and down look'd in the cubboards—and watch'd—At last I set myself to read again not quite so demurely—when there came a louder rap—I arose determin'd to find out who it was—I look out the Stair cases were all silent—"This must be the Major's wife said I—at all events I will see the truth" so I rapt me at the Major's door and went in to the utter surprise and confusion of the Lady who was in reality there—after a little explanation, which I can no more describe than fly, I made my retreat from her convinced of my mistake. She is to all appearance a silly body and is really surprised about it—She must have been—for I have discoverd that a little girl in the house was the Rappee—I assure you she has nearly make me sneeze.[1] If the Lady tells tits I shall put a very grave and moral face on the matter with the old Gentleman, and make his little Boy a present of a humming top—

On the same day (Saturday, 25 September) John Taylor sent Woodhouse his reactions to Keats's alterations of 'The Eve of St Agnes': 'This Folly of Keats is the most stupid piece of Folly I can conceive . . . it excites in me the Strongest Sentiments of Disapprobation—Therefore my dear Rich[d] if he will not so far concede to my Wishes as to leave the passage as it originally stood, I must be content to admire his Poems with some other Imprint' (L, *II, pp. 182–3).*

[27 September] My Dear George—This Monday morning the 27[th] I have received your last dated July 12[th] You say you have not heard from England these three months—Then my Letter from Shanklin wr[i]tten I think at the end of July cannot have reach'd you. You shall not have cause to think I neglect you. I have kept this back a little time in expectation of hearing from M[r] Abbey—You will say I might have remained in Town to be Abbey's messenger in these affairs. That I offer'd him—but he in his answer convinced me he was anxious to bring the Business to an issue—He observed that by being himself the agent in the whole, people might be more expeditious. You say you have not heard for th[r]ee mo[n]ths and yet you[r] letters have the tone of knowing how our affairs are situated by which I conjecture I acquainted you with them in a Letter previous to the Shanklin one. That I may not have done. To be certain I will here state that it is in consequence of M[rs] Jennings threatning a Chancery suit that you have been kept from the receipt of monies and myself deprived of any help from Abbey—I am glad you say you keep up your Spirits—I hope you make a true statement on that score—Still keep them up—for we are all young—I can only repeat here that you shall hear from me again immediately—Notwithstanding their bad intelligence I

1 *Rappee . . . sneeze*: Punning on rappee, 'a coarse kind of snuff'.

have experienced some pleasure in receiving so correctly two Letters from you, as it give[s] me if I may say so a distant Idea of Proximity. This last improves upon my little niece—Kiss her for me. Do not fret yourself about the delay of money on account of any immediate opportunity being lost: for in a new country whoever has money must have opportunity of employing it in many ways. The report runs now more in favor of Kean stopping in England. If he should I have confident hopes of our Tragedy—If he smokes the hotblooded character of Ludolph—and he is the only actor that can do it—He will add to his own fame, and improve my fortune—I will give you half a dozen lines of it before I part as a specimen—

> "Not as a Swordsman would I pardon crave,
> But as a Son: the bronz'd Centurion
> Long-toil'd in foreign wars, and whose high deeds
> Are shaded in a forest of tall spears,
> Known only to his troop, hath greater plea
> Of favour with my Sire than I can have—"[1]

Believe me my dear brother and Sister—

Your affectionate and anxious Brother
John Keats[2]

To C. W. Dilke
1 October 1819

[Keats House MS]

My dear Dilke, Winchester Friday Oct[r] 1st

For sundry reasons, which I will explain to you when I come to Town, I have to request you will do me a great favor as I must call it knowing how great a Bore it is. That your

1 *Not as . . . I can have*: *Otho the Great*, I. iii. 24–9.
2 *John Keats*: Keats's signature, together with words and letters on its verso, was cut from the letter at some point; it was bought back by the Morgan Library in 1941.

imagination may not have time to take too great an alarm I state immediat[e]ly that I want you to hire me a[1] couple of rooms in Westminster. Quietness and ch[e]apness are the essentials: but as I shall with Brown be returned by next Friday you cannot in that space have sufficient time to make any choice selection, and need not be very particular as I can when on the spot suit myself at leisure. Brown bids me remind you not to send the Examiners after the third. Tell M[rs] D. I am obliged to her for the late ones which I see are directed in her hand—Excuse this mere business letter for I assure you I have not a syllable at hand on any subject in the world.

Your sincere friend
John Keats—

To B. R. Haydon

3 October 1819

[Harvard MS]

My dear Haydon, Winchester Sunday Morn.

Certainly I might: but, a few Months pass away before we are aware; I have a great aversion, to letter writing which grows more and more upon me; and a greater to summon up circumstances before me of an unpleasant nature—I was not willing to trouble you with them. Could I have dated from my Palace in Milan you would have heard from me—Not even now will I mention a word of my affairs—only that "I Rab am here"[2] but shall not be here more than a Week more, as I purpose to settle in Town and work my way with the rest. I hope I shall never be so silly as to injure my health and industry for the future by speaking, writing or fretting about my non-estate. I have no quarrel, I assure you, of so weighty a nature, with the world, on my own account as I have on yours. I have done nothing—except for the amusement of a few people who refine upon

1 *hire me a*: (Keats's note) 'A Sitting Room and bed room for myself alone.'
2 *I Rab am here*: Burns's 'Second Epistle to J. Lapraik', l. 60.

their feelings till any thing in the ununderstandable way will go down with them—people predisposed for sentiment. I have no cause to complain because I am certain any thing really fine will in these days be felt. I have no doubt that if I had written Othello I should have been cheered by as good as Mob as Hunt. So would you be now if the operation of painting were as universal as that of writing—It is not: and therefore did it behove men I could mention among whom I must place Sir G. Beaumont[1] to have lifted you up above sordid cares—That this has not been done is a disgrace to the country. I know very little of Painting, yet your pictures follow me into the Country—when I am tired with reading I often think them over and as often condemn the spirit of modern Connoisseurs Upon the whole indeed you have no complaint to make being able to say what so few Men can "I have succeeded." On sitting down to write a few lines to you these are the uppermost in my mind, and however I may be beating about under the arctic while your spirit has passed the line, you may lay too a minute and consider I am earnest as far as I can see. Though at this present "I have great dispositions to write"[2] I feel every day more and more content to read. Books are becoming more interesting and valuable to me—I may say I could not live without them. If in the course of a fortnight you can procure me a ticket to the british musœum I will make a better use of it than I did in the first instance. I shall go on with patience in the confidence that if I ever do any thing worth remembring the Reviewers will no more be able to stumble-block me than the Academy could you. They have the same quarrel with you that the Scotch nobles had with Wallace—The fame they have lost through you is no joke to them. Had it not been for you Fuseli would have been not as he is major but maximus domo.[3] What the Reviewers can put a hindrance to must be—a nothing—or mediocre

1 *Sir G. Beaumont*: Sir George Beaumont (1753–1827), art patron and painter, with whom Haydon had fallen out.

2 *I have . . . to write*: *The Merry Wives of Windsor*, III. i. 20–21, 'I have great dispositions to cry.'

3 *Had it . . . maximus domo*: i.e., but for Haydon, Fuseli would have been the greatest, instead of a leading painter.

which is worse. I am sorry to say that since I saw you I have been guilty of——a practical Joke upon Brown which has had all the success of an innocent Wild fire among people—Some day in the next week you sh<a>ll hear it from me by word of Mouth—I hav<e not> seen the portentous Book which was scu<mm>er'd at you[1] just as I left town. It may be light enough to serve you as a Cork Jacket and save you for awhile the trouble of swimming. I heard the Man went raking and rummaging about like any Richardson. That and the Memoirs of Menage[2] are the first I shall be at. From Sr G— B's Lord Ms and particularly Sr John Leicesters[3] good lord deliver us—I shall expect to see your Picture plumped out like a ripe Peach—you would not be very willing to give me a slice of it—I came to this place in the hopes of meeting with a Library but was disappointed. The High Street is as quiet as a Lamb; the knockers are dieted To three raps per diem. The walks about are interresting—from the many old Buildings and arch ways—The view of the high street through the Gate of the City, in the beautiful September evening light has amused me frequently. The bad singing of the Cathedral I do not care to smoke.—being by myself I am not very coy in my taste. At St Cross there is an interresting Picture of Albert Durers—who living in such warlike times perhaps wasforcedtopaintinhisGauntlets—sowemustmakeallallowances—

I am my dear Haydon
yours ever
John Keats

Brown has a few words to say and will cross this

1 *portentous Book . . . at you*: In his *A Desultory Exposition of an Anti-British System of Incendiary Publication* (1819) William Paulet Carey (1759–1839), Irish art critic and dealer, replied to Haydon's attack on the Royal Academy. *scummered*: 'voided (ordure)' (*OED*).

2 *Memoirs of Menage*: *Menagiana* (1694), a collection of the witticisms and table talk of the French scholar Gilles Ménage (1613–92).

3 *Sr G— B's Lord Ms . . . Sr John Leicesters*: 'Lord Ms' is Henry Phipps, Earl of Mulgrave (1755–1831), who, like Sir George Beaumont, was a patron with whom Haydon had fallen out. Sir John Leicester, whose gallery Keats had visited with Hunt (p. 339 above), was advised by William Paulet Carey.

10 October 1819 to January 1820
Wentworth Place

Keats and Brown returned to Hampstead on Friday or Saturday, 8 or 9 October. Keats finally saw Fanny Brawne at Wentworth Place on Sunday, 10 October, spending the day with her, but not on their own. The next day he stayed in the lodgings which had been found for him at 25 College Street, Westminster, round the corner from Dilke and his family.

To Fanny Brawne
11 October 1819

[Harvard MS]

College Street [Monday]

My sweet Girl,

I am living to day in yesterday: I was in a complete fa[s]cination all day. I feel myself at your mercy. Write me ever so few lines and tell you [*for* me] you will never for ever be less kind to me than yesterday—You dazzled me—There is nothing in the world so bright and delicate—When Brown came out with that seemingly true story again[s]t me last night, I felt it would be death to me if you had ever believed it—though against any one else I could muster up my obstinacy—Before I knew Brown could disprove it I was for the moment miserable. When shall we pass a day alone? I have had a thousand kisses, for which with my whole soul I thank love—but if you should deny me the thousand and first—'t would put me to the proof how great a misery I could live through. If you should ever carry your threat yesterday into execution—believe me 't is not my pride, my vanity or any petty passion would torment me—really 't would hurt my heart—I could not bear it—I have seen Mrs Dilke this morning—she says she will come with me any fine day—

Ever yours
John Keats

Ah hertè mine![1]

To Fanny Brawne
13 October 1819

[Haverford College MS]

25 College Street [Wednesday].

My dearest Girl,

This moment I have set myself to copy some verses out fair. I cannot proceed with any degree of content. I must write you a line or two and see if that will assist in dismissing you from my Mind for ever so short a time. Upon my Soul I can think of nothing else—The time is passed when I had power to advise and warn you again[s]t the unpromising morning of my Life—My love has made me selfish. I cannot exist without you—I am forgetful of every thing but seeing you again—my Life seems to stop there—I see no further. You have absorb'd me. I have a sensation at the present moment as though I was dissolving—I should be exquisitely miserable without the hope of soon seeing you. I should be affraid to separate myself far from you. My sweet Fanny, will your heart never change? My love, will it? I have no limit now to my love—You[r] note came in just here—I cannot be happier away from you—'T is richer than an Argosy of Pearles. Do not threat me even in jest. I have been astonished that Men could die Martyrs for religion—I have shudder'd at it—I shudder no more. I could be martyr'd for my

1 *Ah hertè mine*: Chaucer, *Troilus and Criseyde*, V. 228–9, 'O herte myn, Criseyde, O swete fo! / O lady myn, that I love and na mo!' Troilus's words lamenting Criseyde's fateful departure to the Greek camp.

Religion—Love is my religion—I could die for that—I could die for you. My Creed is Love and you are its only tenet—You have ravish'd me away by a Power I cannot resist; and yet I could resist till I saw you; and even since I have seen you I have endeavoured often "to reason against the reasons of my Love."[1] I can do that no more—the pain would be too great—My Love is selfish. I cannot breathe without you.

Yours for ever
John Keats

Keats said he stayed in College Street for only 'two or three days', and so probably left the following day. He spent the weekend and Monday, 18 October, at Hampstead. His next letter was written from the Dilkes' house in Westminster the next morning and posted from College Street that afternoon. About this time Keats and Brown submitted their tragedy Otho the Great *to Drury Lane Theatre.*

To Fanny Brawne
19 October 1819

[Harvard MS]

Great Smith Street
Tuesday Morn

My sweet Fanny,

On awakening from my three days dream ("I cry to dream again")[2] I find one and another astonish'd at my idleness and thoughtlessness—I was miserable last night—the morning is always restorative—I must be busy, or try to be so. I have several things to speak to you of tomorrow morning. M[rs] Dilke I should think will tell you that I purpose living at Hampstead—I must impose chains upon myself—I shall be able to do

1 *to reason . . . Love*: A phrase used by Giovanni, confessing his incestuous love for and to his sister Annabella, in *'Tis Pity She's a Whore* (1633), I. iii. 78, by John Ford (1586–after 1639).

2 *I cry to dream again*: Caliban in *The Tempest*, III. ii. 138.

nothing—I sho[u]ld like to cast the die for Love or death—I have no Patience with any thing else—if you ever intend to be cruel to me as you say in jest now but perhaps may sometimes be in earnest be so now—and I will—my mind is in a tremble, I cannot tell what I am writing.

Ever my love yours
John Keats

Keats probably saw Fanny Brawne the next morning as planned, and moved back to living next door with Brown at Wentworth Place, where he remained until the following spring. He resumed work on his tragedy King Stephen, *but gave it up in November and worked on his uncompleted satire 'The Jealousies: A Faery Tale' (also known as 'The Cap and Bells: or, the Jealousies'), in the latter part of 1819. Throughout this period, Keats continued to be worried about his own and George's financial situation.*

To Fanny Keats

26 (?) October 1819

[British Library MS]

My dear Fanny, Wentworth Place [Tuesday]

My Conscience is always reproaching me for neglecting you for so long a time. I have been returned from Winchester this fortnight and as yet have not seen you. I have no excuse to offer—I should have no excuse. I shall expect to see you the next time I call on M[r] A about Georges affairs which perplex me a great deal—I should have to day gone to see if you were in Town, but as I am in an i[n]dustrious humour (which is so necessary to my livelihood for the future) I am loath to break through it though it be merely for one day, for when I am inclined I can do a great deal in a day—I am more fond of pleasure than study (many men have prefer'd the latter) but I have become resolved to know something which you will credit when I tell you I have left off animal food that my brains may never henceforth be in a greater mist than is theirs by nature—I took Lodgings in Westminster for the purpose of being in the reach of Books, but am now returned to Hampstedd being induced to it by the habit I have acquired of this room I am now in and also from the pleasure of being free from paying any petty attentions to a diminutive housekeeping. Mr Brown has been my great friend for some time—without him I should have been in, perhaps, personal distress—as I know you love me though I do not deserve it, I am sure you will take pleasure in being a friend to Mr Brown even before you know him—My Lodgings for two or three days were close in the neighbourhood of Mrs Dilke who never sees me but she enquires after you—I have had letters from George lately which do not contain, as I think I told you in my last, the best news. I have hopes for the best—I trust in a good termination to his affairs which you please god will soon hear of—It is better you should not be teased with the particulars—The whole amount of the ill news is that his mercantile speculations[1] have not had success in consequence of the general depression of trade in the whole province of Kentucky and indeed all america—I have a couple of shells for you you will call pretty—

Your affectionate Brother

John—

To Joseph Severn
10 November 1819

[Harvard MS]

Wentworth Place
Wednesday.

Dear Severn,

Either Your Joke about staying at home is a very old one or I really call'd. I dont remember doing so. I am glad to hear you

1 *mercantile speculations*: George's financial problems were exacerbated by the Panic of 1819, when frontier banks collapsed.

have finish'd the Picture[1] and am more anxious to see it than I have time to spare: for I have been so very lax, unemployed, unmeridian'd, and objectless these two months that I even grudge indulding [*for* indulging] (and that is no great indulgence considering the Lecture is not over till 9 and the lecture room seven miles from wentworth Place) myself by going to Hazlitt's Lecture[2]—If you have hours to the amount of a brace of dozens to throw away you may sleep nine of them here in your little Crib and chat the rest—When your Picture is up and in a good light I shall make a point of meeting you at the Academy if you will let me know when—If you should be at the Lecture tomorrow evening I shall see you—and congratulate you heartily—Haslam I know "is very Beadle to an amorous sigh"[3]

Your sincere friend
John Keats.

To George and Georgiana Keats
12 November 1819[4]

[Rollins transcript]

[Wentworth Place]
Friday Evening
Nov[r]

My dear George,

You must think my delay very great. I assure it is no fault of mine. Not expecting you would want money so soon I did not

1 *the Picture*: *The Cave of Despair*, submitted that month for the Royal Academy Exhibition at Somerset House.
2 *Hazlitt's Lecture*: Hazlitt's second lecture on the dramatic literature of the Elizabethan age was to be given on 12 (not 11) November at the Surrey Institution. Keats did not attend.
3 *is very . . . amorous sigh*: Berowne in *Love's Labour's Lost*, III. i. 165, which has 'humorous sigh'.
4 The Historical Society of Pennsylvania is currently unable to locate this MS. The letter, with the news that Keats had raised £100 for George, did not reach Edgartown, Mass., until 23 February 1820. By then George was already on his way back to America after his desperate trip to England.

send for the necessary power of attorney from Holland[1] before I received you[r] Letter which reached me in the middle of the summer at Shanklin. I wrote for it then immediately and received it about ten days ago. You will also be much disappointed by the smallness of the Sum remitted to Warder's: there are two reasons for it, first that the Stocks are so very low, and secondly that M[r] Abbey is unwilling to venture more till this business of M[rs] Jennings is completely at rest. M[r] Abbey promised me to day that he would do all in his power to forward it expressing his wish that by the time it was settled she would make no claim the Stocks might recover themselves so that your property should not be sold out at so horrible a disadvantage. I know not what comfort to give you under these circumstances. Our affairs are in an awkward state. You have done as much as a man can do: I am not as yet fortunate. I should, in duty, endeavour to write you a Letter with a comfortable nonchalance, but how can I do so when you are in so perplexing a situation, and I not able to help you out of it. The distance between us is so great, the Posts so uncertain. We must hope. I am aff[r]aid you are no more than myself form'd for a gainer of money. I have been daily expecting to hear from you again. Does the steam boat make any return yet?[2] Whether I shall at all be set affloat upon the world depends now upon the success of Tragedy I spoke of. We have heard nothing from Elliston who is now the Renter of Drury Lane[3] since the piece was sent in which was three weeks and more ago. The reason may be that Kean has not return'd, whose opinion Elliston will partly rely on. Brown is still very sanguine. The moment I have any certain intelligence concerning it I will let you know. I have not been to see Fanny since my return from Winchester—I have written and received a Letter from her. M[r] Abbey says she is

1 *from Holland*: i.e., from Mr Fry in Holland, allowing Keats to act with Abbey and cash in Tom's stock (see above, p. 414). At the end of this letter Keats says he had received a 'most abusive Letter' from Fry.

2 *Does the . . . any return yet*: See p. 411 above for George's disastrous investment in Audubon's riverboat venture, which had already failed.

3 *Elliston . . . Drury Lane*: Robert William Elliston (1774–1831), actor and theatre manager, had just taken over Drury Lane.

getting stouter. I call'd in Rodney [*for* Romney] Street about a fortnight since. Your Mother was quite well, and Charles was to set out for Paris on the day following. I do not call so often as I should do if I had any good news to tell—I am there in the character of a Prevaricator. I must not tell the truth. Mr Abbey shows at times a little anxiety about me he wanted me the other day to turn Bookseller. Why does he not make some such proposal to you? Yet he can not care much for I till yesterday had had no money of him for ten months and he never enquired how I liv'd: nor how I had paid my last Christmas Bills (still unpaid) though I repeatedly mentioned them to him. We are not the only toilers and sufferers in the World. Hunt was arrested the other day.[1] He soon however dated from his own house again. Hazlitt has begun another course of Lectures, on the Writers of Elizabeth's reign—I hear he quoted me in his last Lecture[2]—Our Set still continue separate as we get older, each follows with more precision the bent of his own Mind. Brown and I by living together are an exception. Rice continues to every one his friendly behaviour his illness and his wit stick by him as usual. In a note to me the other day he sent the following Pun—Tune—the Harlot's Lament—

Between the two P—x's I've lost every Lover,
But a difference I found 'twixt the great and the small:
For by the Small Pox I gott {pitted} all over
By the other I did not get {pittied} at all.

Reynolds has settled in Lodgings very near to Rice's and seems set in for the Law. Dilke and I call[ed] upon at his office the other day. We ta[l]ked about you; you being mostly my subject with him. He says you should have kept to your original design;[3] in which I differ from him entirely. I think you have done perfectly right. I have this moment received a Letter from Severn,

1 *Hunt . . . other day*: Leigh Hunt had evidently suffered one of his recurrent financial crises.
2 *his last Lecture*: In fact, Hazlitt's first lecture, given on 5 November, in which he quoted 'Sleep and Poetry', l. 127.
3 *your original design*: i.e., of going to Birkbeck's Settlement in Illinois.

whom I have not seen for some time, he tell[s] me he has finish'd a picture of Spenser's Cave of despair which is designed to contend for the Prize at the Academy and is now hung up there for Judgement[1]—He wishes me to see it. I have been endeavouring to write lately, but with little success as I require a little encouragement, as [*for* and a] little better fortun<e> to befall you and happier news from you before I can wr<i>te with an untrammell'd mind. Nothing could have in all its circumstances fallen out worse for me than the last year has done, or could be more damping to my poetical talent—I comfort myself in the idea that you are a consolation to each other. Haslam told me the last time I saw him that he was about to write to you. He is entirely taken up with his Sweet-heart—I feel very loath to write more than this Sheet—you must excuse the shortness of this Letter for the length of the last and the length of the next I hope, if any thing occurs to enspirit <me a> little. Fanny would like a Letter from you. I should <think> that Abbey from the delay of Walton's house has employed <another> Lawyer on our Business. Mrs Jennings has not instituted <an>y action against us yet, nor has she withdrawn her claim I think I told you that even if she were to lose her cause we sho[u]ld have to pay the expences of the Suit. You urg'd me to get Mr Abbey to advance you money—but that he will by no means do—for besides the risk of the law (small enough indeed) he will never be persu[a]ded but you will loose it in America. For a bit of treat in the heart of all this I had a most abusive Letter from Fry—committing you and myself to destruction without reprieve—In your next Letter make some questions regularly upon which you wish to be in<form>ed concerning our's and any other subject and I will answer <them as> amply as I can—My dear Sister God bless you and your <baby gir>l. The enquir[i]es about you are very frequent—My dear George I remain, in hopes,

Your most affectionate Brother
John Keats

1 *a picture . . . for Judgement*: On 10 December Severn's oil painting *The Cave of Despair* won the Royal Academy's gold medal for students, the first time it had been awarded for twelve years.

To Joseph Severn
15 November 1819

[Harvard MS]

My dear Severn,

Wentworth Place
Monday Morn—

I am very sorry that on Tuesday I have an appointment in the City of an undeferable nature; and Brown on the same day has some business at Guildhall. I have not been able to figure your manner of executing the Cave of despair, therefore it will be at any rate a novelty and surprise to me—I trust in the right side. I shall call upon you some morning shortly early enought to catch you before you can get out—when we will proceed to the Academy. I think you must be suited with a good painting light in your Bay window. I wish you to return the Compliment by going with me to see a Poem I have hung up for the Prize in the Lecture Room of the surry Institution.[1] I have many Rivals the most threatning are An Ode to Lord Castlereagh, and a news [*for* new] series of Hymns for the New, new Jerusalem Chapel[2]—You had best put me in your Cave of despair—

Ever yours sincerely
John Keats

1 *a Poem . . . Institution*: A joking reference to Hazlitt's quotation from Keats in his first lecture. Mee identifies the 'series of Hymns' as Joseph Proud's *Hymns and Psalms for the Use of the Lord's New Church, signified by the New Jerusalem* (5th edn., 1818).

2 *Jerusalem Chapel*: The Swedenborgian New Jerusalem Temple had been consecrated on Whit Sunday, 1819 (*Morning Chronicle*, 28 May 1819, p.1, col. 1).

To John Taylor
17 November 1819

[Morgan MS]

Wentworth Place
Wednesday,

My dear Taylor,

I have come to a determination not to publish any thing I have now ready written; but for all that to publish a Poem before long and that I hope to make a fine one. As the marvellous is the most enticing and the surest guarantee of harmonious numbers I have been endeavouring to persuade myself to untether Fancy and let her manage for herself—I and myself cannot agree about this at all. Wonders are no wonders to me. I am more at home amongst Men and women. I would rather read Chaucer than Ariosto[1]—The little dramatic skill I may as yet have however badly it might show in a Drama would I think be sufficient for a Poem—I wish to diffuse the colouring of St Agnes eve throughout a Poem in which Character and Sentiment would be the figures to such drapery—Two or three such Poems, if God should spare me, written in the course of the next six years, would be a famous gradus ad Parnassum altissimum[2]—I mean they would nerve me up to the writing of a few fine Plays—my greatest ambition—when I do feel ambitious. I am sorry to say that is very seldom. The subject we have once or twice talked of appears a promising one, The Earl of Leicester's historry. I am this morning reading Holingshed's Elisabeth,[3] You had some Books awhile ago, you promised to lend me, illustrative of my Subject. If you can lay hold of them

1 *Chaucer than Ariosto*: Setting Chaucer's realism against Ariosto's romance.
2 *gradus . . . altissimum*: The *Gradus ad Parnassum* was a schoolbook, an aid to the composition of Latin poetry.
3 *Holingshed's Elisabeth*: Keats had access either to an early edition of the *Chronicles* (1577) of Raphael Holinshed (d. ?1580) or to the six-volume edition of 1807.

or any others which may be serviceable to me I know you will encourage my low-spirited Muse by sending them—or rather by letting me know when our Errand cart Man shall call with my little Box. I will endeavour to set my self selfishly at work on this Poem that is to be—

Your sincere friend
John Keats—

To James Rice
December 1819

[Harvard MS]

Wentworth Place

My dear Rice,

As I want the coat on my back mended, I would be obliged if you will send me the one Brown left at your house, by the Bearer—During your late contest I hea[r]d regular reports of you; how that your time was entirely taken up, and you[r] health improving—I shall call in the course of a few days and see wh[e]ther your promotion has made any difference in your Behaviour to us—I suppose Reynolds has given you an account of Brown and Elliston[1]—As he has not rejected our Tragedy I shall not venture to call him directly a fool; but as he wishes to put it off till next season I cant help thinking him little better than a Knave—That it will not be acted this Season is yet uncertain—Perpaps we may give it another furbish and try it at covent Garden. 'T would do one's heart good to see Macready[2] in Ludolph. If you do not see me soon it will be from the humour of writing, which I have had for three days, continuing—I must say to the Muses what the maid says to the

1 *Brown and Elliston*: Brown had sent *Otho the Great* to Elliston at Drury Lane in late October (p. 471 above).

2 *Macready*: William Charles Macready (1793–1873), Kean's counterpart at Covent Garden: Keats earlier believed that only Kean could act the part of Ludolph. If this plan was pursued it was unsuccessful. The tragedy was not performed until the twentieth century.

Man—"take me while the fit is on me"—Would you like a true Story "There was a Man and his Wife who being to go a long journey on foot, in the course of their travels came to a River which rolled knee deep over the pebbles—In these cases the Man generally pulls off his shoes and stockings and carries the woman over on his Back. This Man did so; and his Wife being pregnant and troubled, as in such cases is very common, with strange longings, took the strangest that ever was heard of—Seeing her Husband's foot, a han[d]some on [*for* one] enough, look very clean and tempting in the clear water, on their arrival at <the> other bank she earnestly demand<ed> a bit of it; he being an affectionate fellow and fearing for the comeliness of his child gave her a bit which he cut off with his Clasp knife—Not satisfied she asked another morsel—supposing there might be twins he gave her a slice more. Not yet contented she craved another Piece. "You Wretch cries the Man, would you wish me to kill myself? take that!" Upon which he stabb'd her with the knife, cut her open and found three Children in her Belly two of them very comfortable with their mouth's shut, the third with its eyes and mouth stark staring open. "Who would have thought it" cried the Wid<ow>er, and pursued his journey—, Brown has a little rumbling in his Stomach this morning—

Ever yours sincerely
John Keats—

To Fanny Keats
20 December 1819

[British Library MS]

My dear Fanny, Wentworth Place
Monday Morn—

When I saw you last,[1] you ask'd me whether you should see me again before Christmas—You would have seen me if I had been quite well. I have not, though not unwell enough to have

1 *I saw you last*: Keats had visited her on 18 November.

prevented me—not indeed at all—but fearful le[s]t the weather should affect my throat which on exertion or cold continually threatens me—By the advice of my Doctor I have had a wa[r]m great Coat made and have ordered some thick shoes—so furnish'd I shall be with you if it holds a little fine before Christmas day—I have been very busy since I saw you especially the last Week and shall be for some time, in preparing some Poems to come out in the Sp[r]ing and also in hightening the interest of our Tragedy—Of the Tragedy I can give you but news semi-good. It is accepted at Drury Lane with a promise of coming out next season: as that will be too long a delay we have determined to get Elliston to bring it out this Season or to transfer it to Covent Garden. This Elliston will not like, as we have every motive to believe that Kean has perceived how suitable the principal Character will be for him. My hopes of success in the literary world are now better than ever—Mr Abbey, on my calling on him lately, appeared anxious that I should apply myself to something else—He mentioned Tea Brokerage. I supposed he might perhaps mean to give me the Brokerage of his concern, which might be executed with little trouble and a good profit; and therefore said I should have no objection to it especially as at the same time it occured to me that I might make over the business to George—I questioned him about it a few days after. His mind takes odd turns. When I became a Suitor he became coy. He did not seem so much inclined to serve me. He described what I should have to do in the progress of business. It will not suit me. I have given it up. I have not heard again from George which rather disappoints me, as I wish to hear before I make any fresh remittance of his property. I received a note from Mrs Dilke a few days ago inviting me to dine with her on Xmas day, which I shall do. Mr Brown and I go on in our old dog trot of Breakfast, dinner (not tea for we have left that off) supper Sleep, Confab, stirring the fire and reading. Whilst I was in the Country last summer Mrs Bentley tells me a woman in mour[n]ing call'd on me,—and talk'd something of an aunt of ours—I am so careless a fellow I did not enquire, but will particularly. On Tuesday I am going to hear some Schoolboys Speechify on breaking up day[1]—I'll lay you a pocket pi[e]ce we shall have 'My name is norval'[2] I have not yet look'd for the Letter you mention'd as it is mix'd up in a box full of papers—you must tell me, if you can recollect, the subject of it. This moment Bentley brought a Letter from George for me to deliver to Mrs Wylie—I shall see her and it before I see you. The direction was in his best hand, written with a good Pen and sealed with a Tassi[e]'s Shakspeare such as I gave you—We judge of peoples hearts by their Countenances; may we not judge of Letters in the same way? if so, the Letter does not contain unpleasant news—Good or bad spirits have an effect on the handwriting. This direction is at least unnervous and healthy. Our Sister is also well, or George would have made strange work with Ks and Ws. The little Baby is well o<r> he would have formed precious vowels and Consonants—He sent off the Letter in a hurry, or the mail bag was rather a wa[r]m birth, or he has worn out his Seal, for the Shakespeare's head is flattened a little. This is close muggy weather as they say at the Ale houses—

I am, ever, my dear Sister
Yours affectionately
John Keats—

Two days later Keats was still 'rather unwell' and warned his sister he could not 'promise certainly' to see her before Christmas. Nor had he yet seen George's letter to Mrs Wylie with the news that he was coming to England to realize his share of Tom's capital. George landed at Liverpool and was in London by Sunday, 9 January, when the two brothers dined with Georgiana's family.

1 *breaking up day*: Most likely that of Dilke's son at Westminster School.
2 *My name is norval*: The first lines of the tragedy *Douglas* (1756) by John Home (1722–1808), a favourite recitation piece (see William Enfield's *The Speaker* (1799), p. 53).

To Georgiana Keats

13, 15, 17, 28 January 1820

[University of Texas, Yale University MS][1]

My dear Sister, Thursday Jany 13th 1820—

By the time you receive this your troubles will be over—I wish you knew they were half over; I mean that George is safe in England, and in good health—To write to you by him is almost like following ones own Letter in the Mail that it may not be quite so I will leave common intelligence out of the question and write wide of him as I can—I fear I must be dull having had no goodnatured flip from fortune's finger since I saw you, and so [*for* no] side way comfort in the success of my friends—I could almost promise that if I had the means I would accompany George back to america and pay you a Visit of a few Months. I should not think much of the time or my absence from my Books, or I have no right to think, for I am very idle: but then I ought to be diligent and at least keep myself within the reach of materials for diligence. Diligence! that I do not mean to say, I should say dreaming over my Books, or rather other peoples Books. George has promised to bring you to England when the five years have elapsed, I regret very much that I shall not be able to see you before that time; and even then I must hope that your affairs will be in so prosperous a way as to induce you to stop longer. Yours is a hardish fate to be so divided from your friends and settled among a people you hate—you will find it improve—you have a heart that will take hold of your Children—Even Georges absence will make things better—his return will ban[i]sh what must be your greatest sorrow and at the same time minor ones with it. Robinson Crusoe when he saw himself in danger of perishing on the Waters

1 The first eight pages are at Texas, the last two (beginning '<u>Friday 27th</u>', p. 488 below) at Yale.

look'd back to his island as to the haven of his Happiness and on gaining it once more was more content with his Solitude. We smoke George about his little Girl, he runs the common beaten road of every father, as I dare say you do of every Mother—there is no Child like his Child—so original! original forsooth However I take you at your words; I have a lively faith that yours is the very gem of all Children—Aint I its Unkle?

On Henry's Marriage[1] there was a piece of Bride cake sent me—it miss'd its way—I suppose the Carrier or Coachman was a Conjuror and wanted it for his own private use—Last Sunday George and I dined at Millars—there were your Mother and Charles with Fool Lacon Esq[re] who sent the sly disinterested Shawl to Miss Millar with his own heathen name engraved in the Middle—Charles had a silk Handkerchief belonging to a Miss Grover with whom he pretended to be smitten and for her sake kept exhibiting and adoring the Handkerchief all the evening. Fool Lacon Esq[re] treated it with a little venturesome trembling Contumely, whereon Charles set him quietly down on the floor—from where he as quietly got up—This process was repeated at supper time, when your Mother said "If I were you M[r] Lacon I would not let him do so." Fool Lacon Esq[re] did not offer any remark. He will undoubtedly die in his bed. Your Mother did not look quite so well on Sunday—M[rs] Henry Wylie is excessively quiet before people, I hope she is always so. Yesterday we dined at Taylor's in Fleet Street—George left early after dinner to go to Deptford—He will make all square there for me—I could not go with him. I did not like the amusement—Haslam is a very good fellow indeed; he has been excessively anxious and kind to us. But is this fair? He has an innamorata at Deptford and he has been wanting me for some time past to see her.[2] This is a thing which it is impossible not to shirk. A Man is like a Magnet, he must have a repelling end—so how am I to see Haslams lady and family if I even

1 *Henry's Marriage*: Henry Wylie's marriage to Mary Ann Keasle.

2 *He has . . . see her*: Haslam had married his 'innamorata' Mary on 16 October 1819.

went; for by the time I got to greenwich I should have repell'd them to Blackheath and by the time I got to Deptford, they would be on Shooters hill, when I came to shooters Hill, they would alight at Chatham and so on till I drove them into the Sea, which I think might be inditeable—The Evening before yesterday we had a paino forte hop at Dilkes—There was very little amusement in the room but a Scotchman to hate—Some people you must have observed have a most unpleasant effect upon you when you see them speaking in profile—this Scotchman is the most accomplish'd fellow in this way I ever met with. The effect was complete—It went down like a dose of bitters and I hope will improve my digestion—At Taylor's too there was a Scotchman—not quite so bad for he was as clean as he could get himself. Not having succeeded at Drury Lane with our Tragedy, we have been making some alterations and are about to try Covent Garden—Brown has just done patching up the Copy, as it is altered—The only reliance I had on it was in Kean's acting—I am <u>not</u> affraid it will be damn'd in the Garden[1]—You said in one of your Letters that there was noth[i]ng but Haydon and Co in mine—There can be nothing of him in this for I never see him or Co—George has introduc'd to us an American of the Name of Hart—I like him in a Mod[e]rate way—He was at Mrs Dilkes party; and sitting by me, we begun talking about english and american ladies—The Miss Reynolds' and some of their friends made not a very inticing row opposite us—I bade him mark them and form his Judgement of them—I told him I hated Englishmen because they were the only Men I knew. He does not understand this—Who would be Bragadocio to Johnny Bull? Johnny's house is his Castle, and a precious dull Castle it is. What a many Bull Castles there are in So and So Crescent—I never wish myself an unvers[e]d visitor an[d] news monger but when I write to you. I should like for a day or two to have somebody's knowledge, Mr Lacon's for instance of all the different folks of a wide acquaintance to tell you about—Only let me have his knowledge of family minutiæ and I would set them in a proper light but bless me I never go

1 *damn'd in the Garden*: *Otho the Great* was refused by Covent Garden.

any where—my pen is no more gar[r]ulous than my tongue—Any third person would think I was addressing myself to a Lover of Scandal. But we know we do not love scandal but fun, and if Scandal happens to be fun that is no fault of ours. There were very pretty pickings for me in Georges Letters about the Prairie Settlement, if I had any taste to turn them to account in England.[1] I knew a friend of Miss Andrews yet I never mention'd her to him: for after I had read the letter I really did not recollect her Story. Now I have been sitting here a half hour with my invention at work to say something about your Mother or Charles or Henry but it is in vain—I know not what to say—Three nights since George went with your Mother to the play[2]—I hope she will soon see mine acted. I do not remember ever to have thank'd you for your tassels to my Shakspeare there he hangs so ably supported opposite me. I thank you now. It is a continual memento of you. If you should have a Boy do not christen him John, and persuade George not to let his partiality for me come across—'T is a bad name, and goes against a Man—If my name had been Edmund I should have been more fortunate—I was surprised to hear of the State of Saciety at Louisville, is [*for* it] seems you are just as rediculous there as we are here—threepenny parties, half penny Dances—the best thing I have heard of is your Shooting, for it seems you follow the Gun. Give my Compliments to Mrs Audubon and tell her I cannot think her either good looking or honest—Tell Mr Audubon he's a fool—and Briggs[3] that 't is well I was not Mr A—

Saturday Jany 15 It is strange that George having to stop so short a time in England I should not have seen him for nearly two days—He has been to <H>aslam's and does not encourage

1 *Georges Letters . . . England*: George's lost letters gave the lie to Birkbeck's misleading claims for his Illinois Settlement, also known as the 'English Prairie'.

2 *the play*: Shakespeare's *The Comedy of Errors* and a pantomime, *Harlequin and Don Quixote*, at Covent Garden.

3 *Briggs*: Charles Briggs, a schoolfellow of the Keats brothers, emigrated to Kentucky and later moved to New Orleans, from where he forwarded George's letters to England.

me to follow his example—He had given promise to dine with the same party tomorrow, but has sent an excuse which I am glad of as we shall have a pleasant party with us tomorrow. We expect Charles here today—This is a beautiful day; I hope you will not quarrel with it if I call it an american one. The Sun comes upon the snow and makes a prettier candy than we have on twelvth [*for* twelfth] cakes.[1] George is busy this morning in making copies of my verses—He is making now one of an Ode to the nightingale, which is like reading an account of the b[l]ack hole at Calcutta on an ice bergh. You will say this is a matter of course, I am glad it is, I mean that I should like your Brothers more, the more I know them. I should spend much more time with them if our lives were more run in paral[l]el, but we can talk but on one subject that is you—The more I know of Men the more I know how to value entire liberality in any of them. Thank God there are a great many who will sacrifice their worldly interest for a friend: I wish there were more who would sacrifice their passions. The worst of Men are those whose self interests are their passion—the next those whose passions are their self-interest. Upon the whole I dislike Mankind: whatever people on the other side of the question may advance they cannot deny that they are always surprised at hearing of a good action and never of a bad one. I am glad you have something [to] like in America, Doves—Gertrude of Wyoming and Birkbeck's book[2] should be bound up together like a Brace of Decoy Ducks—One is almost as poetical as the other. Precious miserable people at the Pra[i]rie. I have been sitting in the Sun whilest I wrote this till it became quite oppressive, this is very odd for January—The vulcan fire is the true natural heat for Winter: the Sun has nothing to do in winter but to give a 'little glooming light much like a Shade"[3]—Our irish servant[4]

1 *twelvth cakes*: Twelfth Night cakes, a forerunner of Christmas cakes.
2 *Gertrude of Wyoming . . . Birkbeck's book*: *Gertrude of Wyoming* (1809) is a popular poem by Thomas Campbell (1777–1844), depicting a pastoral world destroyed by the savagery of war. For Birkbeck's account of Illinois, see above, p. 156 n.
3 *little . . . Shade*: *The Faerie Queene*, I. i. 14.
4 *irish servant*: Abigail O'Donaghue.

has piqued me this morning by saying that her Father in Ireland was very much like my Shakspeare only he had more color than the Engraving. You will find on Georges return that I have not been neglecting your affairs. The delay was unfortunate, not faulty;—perhaps by this time you have received my three last letters[1] not one of which had reach'd [you] before George sail'd, I would give two <pe>nce to have been over the world as much as he has—I wish I had money enough to do nothing but travel about for years—Were you now in England I dare say you would be able (setting aside the pleasure you would have in seeing your mother) to suck out more amusement for Saciety than I am able to do. To me it is as dull here as Louisville could be. I am tired of the Theatres. Almost all the parties I may chance to fall into I know by heart—I know the different Styles of talk in different places: what subjects will be started how it will proceed, like an acted play, from the first to the last Act—If I go to Hunt's I run my head into many-times heard puns and music. To Haydon's worn out discourses of poetry and painting: the Miss Reynolds I am affraid to speak to for fear of some sickly reiteration of Phrase or Sentiment. When they were at the dance the other night I tried manfully to sit near and talk to them, but to not [*for* no] purpose, and if I had 't would have been to no purpose still—My question or observation must have been an old one, and the rejoinder very antique indeed. At Dilkes I fall foul of Politics. 'T is best to remain aloof from people and like their good parts without being eternally troubled with the dull processes of their every day Lives. When once a person has smok'd the vapidness of the routine of Saciety he must have either self interest or the love of some sort of distinction to keep him in good humour with it. All I can say is that standing at Charing cross and looking east west north and south I can see nothing but dullness—I hope while I am young to live retired in the Country, when I grow in years and have a right to be idle I shall enjoy cities more. If the American Ladies are worse than the English they must be very bad—You say you

1 *my three last letters*: Presumably those of 14 February–5 May, 17–27 September and 12 November 1819.

should like your Emily brought up here. You had better bring her up yourself. You know a good number of english Ladies what encomium could you give of half a dozen of them—the greater part seem to me downright American. I have known more than one Mrs Aubudon their affectation and politeness cannot transcend ours—
Look at our Cheapside Tradesmans sons and daughters—only fit to be taken off by a plague—I hope now soon to come to the time when I shall never be forc'd to walk through the City and hate as I walk—
Monday Jany 17 George had a quick rejoinder to his Letter of excuse to Haslam so we had not his company yesterday which I was sorry for as there was our old set. I know three witty people all distinct in their excellence—Rice, Reynolds and Richards. Rice is the wisest, Reynolds the playfullest, Richards the out o' the wayest. The first makes you laugh and think, the second makes you laught [*for* laugh] and not think, the third puzzles your head—I admire the first, I enjoy the second, I stare at the third—The first is Claret, the second Ginger beer, the third Crême de Bzrapqmdrag. The first is inspired by Minerva, the second by Mercury, the third by Harlequin Epigram Esqre—The first is neat in his dress, the second slovenly, the third uncomfortable—The first speaks adagio, the second al[l]egretto, the third both together—The first is swiftean, the second Tom cribean,[1] the third Shandean—and yet these three Eans are not three Eans but one Ean. Charles came on Saturday, but went early: he seems to have schemes and plans and wants to get off—He is quite right, I am glad to see him employed at his years. You remember I wrote you a Story about a woman named Alice being made young again—or some such stuff—In your next Letter tell me whether I gave it as my own or whether I gave it as a matter Brown was employed upon at the time. He read it over to George the other day, and George said he had heard it all before—So Brown suspects I have been giving You his Story as my own—I should like to set him right in it by your

1 *Tom cribean*: Thomas Moore's comic poem *Tom Crib's Memorial to Congress* (1819).

Evidence. George has not return'd from Town when he does I shall tax his memory. We had a young, long, raw, lean Scotchman with us yesterday calld Thornton—Rice for fun or for mistake would persist in calling him Stevenson—I know three people of no wit at all, each distinct in his excellence. A. B, and C. A is the soolishest [*for* foolishest], B the sulkiest, C is a negative—A makes you yawn, B makes you hate, as for C you never see him though he is six feet high. I bear the first, I forbear the second I am not certain that the third is. The first is gruel, the Second Ditch water, the third is spilt—he ought to be wip'd up   A is inspired by Jack o' the Clock—B, has been dull'd by a russian Sargeant, C— they say is not his Mothers true Child but that she bought him of the Man who cries 'young Lambs to sell." T wang dillo dee. .[1] This you must know is the Amen to nonsense. I know many places where Amen should be scratched out, rubb'd over with pou[n]ce[2] made of Momus's[3] little finger bones, and in its place 'T wang-dillo-dee,' written. This is the word I shall henceforth be tempted to write at the end of most modern Poems—Every American Book ought to have it. It would be a good distinction in Saciety. My Lords Wellington, Castlereagh and Canning and many more would do well to wear T wang-dillo-dee written on their Backs instead of wearing ribbands in their Button holes—How many people would go sideways along walls and quickset hedges to keep their T wang dillo dee out of sight, or wear large pigtails to hide it. However there would be so many that the T wang dillo dees would keep one another in Countenance—which Brown cannot do for me. I have fallen away lately. Thieves and Murderers would gain rank in the world—for would any one of them have the poorness of Spirit to condescend to a T wang dillo dee—"I have robb'd in many a dwelling house, I have kill'd many a fowl many a goose and many a Man," (would such a gentleman say) but thank heaven I was never yet a T wang dillo dee"—Some Philosophers in the Moon who spy at our Globe

1 *T wang dillo dee*: 'Twangdillo-dee' was a nonsense refrain in popular songs.
2 *pou[n]ce*: A fine powder made from cuttlefish bone, used to blot ink.
3 *Momus*: Greek god of satire and mockery.

as we do at theirs say that T wang dillo dee is written in large Letters on our Globe of Earth—They say the beginning of the T is just on the spot where London stands. London being built within the Flourish—wan reach downward and slant as far a[s] Tumbutoo in africa, the tail of the G. goes slap across the Atlantic into the Rio della Plata—the remainder of the Letters wrap round new holland and the last e terminates on land we have not yet discoverd. However I must be silent, these are dangerous times to libel a man in, much more a world.

Friday 27th [*for* 28th] I wish you would call me names. I deserve them so much. I have only written two sheets for you, to carry [*for* to be carried] by George and those I forgot to bring to town and have therefore to forward them to Liverpool <George> went this morning at 6 o Clock by the Liverpool Coach—His being on his journey to you, prevents me regreeting [*for* regretting] his short stay—I have no news of any sort to tell you. Henry is wife-bound in Cambden Town there is no getting him out. I am sorry he has not a prettier wife: indeed 't is a shame: she is not half a wife. I think I could find some of her relations in Buffon[1], or Capt Cook's voyages,[2] or the <hie>rogueglyphics in Moors almanack,[3] or upon a Chinese Clock door, the Shepherdesses on her own mantlepiece, or in a c<rue>l sampler in which she may find herself worsted, or in a dutch toy shop windown [*for* window], or one of the Daughters in the Ark, or in any picture shop window. As I intend to retire into the Country where there will be mo [*for* no] sort of news, I shall not be able to write you very long Letters—Besides I am affraid the Postage comes to too much; which till now I have not been aware of. We had a fine Packing up at *<torn, 7 or 8 missing words>* other things I saw *<torn, missing line>* People in milatay [*for* military] Bands are generally seriously occupied—none may or can

1 *Buffon*: An English translation of *L'Histoire naturelle* (1749–88) by the naturalist Georges-Louis Leclerc, Comte de Buffon (1707–88).

2 *Capt Cook's voyages*: An account of the circumnavigation of the world by James Cook (1728–79) first appeared in 1773.

3 *Moors almanac*: *Vox Stellarum* (1697) by the astrologer Francis Moore (1657–1714) has survived as *Old Moore's Almanac* and once featured an annual 'Hieroglyphick' woodcut forecasting the following year's events.

laugh at their work but the Kettle Drum Long-drum Dº Triangle, and Cymbals—Thinking you might want a Ratcatcher I put your mother's old quaker-colour'd Cat into the top of your bonnet—she's wi' kitten, so you may expect to find a whole family—I hope the family will not grow too large for its Lodging. I shall send you a close written Sheet on the first of next Month but for fear of missing the Liverpool Post I must finish here. God bless you and <your> little Girl—

Your affectionate Brother
John Keats—

28 January to September 1820
Illness, Fanny Brawne, and *Lamia, Isabella, The Eve of St Agnes, and Other Poems*

Early on Friday, 28 January Keats saw off George on his return journey to America. George reached Liverpool after a thirty-six-hour coach journey in freezing cold weather. From there he wrote to his brother and sister, apologizing to Fanny for 'not taking final leave' of her at the end of his three-week visit. He sailed for New York aboard the Courier *on 1 February.*

The following Thursday, 3 February, Keats went into town. Charles Brown recalled his return that night: 'at eleven o'clock, he came into the house in a state that looked like fierce intoxication. Such a state in him, I knew, was impossible; it therefore was the more fearful. I asked hurriedly, "What is the matter?—are you fevered?" "Yes, yes," he answered, "I was on the outside of the stage this bitter day till I was severely chilled,—but now I don't feel it. Fevered!—of course, a little."' Brown persuaded him to go to bed. 'I entered his chamber as he leapt into bed. On entering the cold sheets, before his head was on the pillow, he slightly coughed, and I heard him say,—"That is blood from my mouth." I went towards him; he was examining a single drop of blood upon the sheet. "Bring me the candle, Brown; and let me see this blood." After regarding it steadfastly, he looked up in my face, with a calmness of countenance I can never forget, and said,—"I know the colour of that blood;—it is arterial blood;—I cannot be deceived in that colour;—that drop of blood is my death-warrant;—I must die." I ran for a surgeon; my friend was bled; and at five in the morning, I left him after he had been, some time, in a quiet sleep'

('Life of Keats', KC, II, 73–4). After being bled by the surgeon, George Rodd, Keats was placed on a vegetable diet and ordered to avoid excitement, including writing. His doctors, now and later, continued to hold out hopes that he would recover.

To Fanny Brawne
4 (?) February 1820

[Facsimile (1938)][1]

[Wentworth Place, Friday]

Dearest Fanny, I shall send this the moment you return. They say I must remain confined to this room for some time. The consciousness that you love me will make a pleasant prison of the house next to yours. You must come and see me frequently: this evening, without fail—when you must not mind about my speaking in a low tone for I am ordered to do so though I <u>can</u> speak out.

Yours ever
sweetest love.—
J Keats

turn over

Perhaps your Mother is not at home and so you must wait[2] till she comes—You must see me to night and let me hear[3] you promise to come tomorrow—

Brown told me you were all out—I have been looking for the Stage the whole afternoon—Had I known this I could not have remain'd so silent all day—

1 *The Romantics 1801–1820: An Exhibition of Books and Autograph Letters from the Collection of Frank J. Hogan* (Los Angeles: Zamorano Club, 1938), p. 16.

2 *wait*: Rollins has 'watch'.

3 *hear*: Originally 'have' but overwritten.

To Fanny Keats
6 February 1820

[British Library MS]

Wentworth Place
Sunday Morning.

My dear Sister,

I should not have sent those Letters[1] without some notice if Mr Brown had not persuaded me against it on account of an illness with which I was attacked on Thursday. After that I was resolved not to write till I should be on the mending hand: thank God, I am now so. From imprudently leaving off my great coat in the thaw I caught cold which flew to my Lungs. Every remedy that has been applied has taken the desired effect, and I have nothing now to do but stay within doors for some time. If I should be confined long I shall write to Mr Abbey to ask permission for you to visit me. George has been running great chance of a similar attack,[2] but I hope the sea air will be his Physician in case of illness—the air out at sea is always more temperate than on land—George mentiond, in his Letters to us, something of Mr Abbey's regret concer[n]ing the silence kept up in his house. It is entirely the fault of his Manner—You must be careful always to wear warm cloathing not only in frost but in a Thaw—I have no news to tell you. The half built houses opposite us stand just as they were and seem dying of old age before they are brought up. The grass looks very dingy, the Celery is all gone, and there is nothing to enliven one but a few Cabbage Sta[l]ks that seem fix'd on the superannuated List. Mrs Dilke has been ill but is better. Several of my friends have been to see me. Mrs Reynolds was here this morning and the two Mr Wylies. Brown has been very alert about me, though

1 *those Letters*: Probably from George Keats.
2 *similar attack*: George, writing to Fanny from Liverpool on 30 January, to apologize for failing to see her during his trip to England, reported that he had been soaked with water while sleeping, but was well. He also mentioned Abbey's complaint that Fanny was silent during meals (*L*, II, pp. 248–9).

a little wheezy himself this weather. Every body is ill. Yesterday evening Mr Davenport, a gentleman of hampstead sent me an invitation to supper, instead of his coming to see us, having so bad a cold he could not stir out—so you [see] tis the weather and I am among a thousand. Whenever you have an inflamatory fever never mind about eating. The day on which I was getting ill I felt this fever to a great height, and therefore almost entirely abstained from food the whole day. I have no doubt experience'd a benefit from so doing—The Papers I see are full of anecdotes of the late king: how he nodded to a Coal heaver and laugh'd with a Quaker and lik'd boil'd Leg of Mutton. Old Peter Pindar[1] is just dead: what will the old king and he say to each other? Perhaps the king may confess that Peter was in the right, and Peter maintain himse<lf> to have been wrong. You shall hear from me again on tuesday.

Your affectionate Brother
John.

To Fanny Keats
8 February 1820

[British Library MS]

My dear Fanny— Wentworth Place
Tuesday morn.

I had a slight return of fever last night, which terminated favourably, and I am now tolerably well, though weak from small quantity of food to which I am obliged to confine myself: I am sure a mouse would sta[r]ve upon it.

Mrs Wylie came yesterday. I have a very pleasant room for a sick person. A Sopha bed is made up for me in the front Parlour which looks on to the grass plot as you remember Mrs Dilkes does. How much more comfortable than a dull room up stairs, where one gets tired of the pattern of the bed curtains. Besides

1 *the late king . . . Peter Pindar*: George III died on 29 January. Peter Pindar (see above, p. 111), who satirized the king, had died on 14 January.

I see all that passes—for instanc[e] now, this morning, if I had been in my own room I should not have seen the coals brought in. On sunday between the hours of twelve and one I descried a Pot boy. I conjectured it might be the one o'Clock beer—Old women with bobbins and red cloaks and unpresuming bonnets I see creeping about the heath. Gipseys after hare skins and silver spoons. Then goes by a fellow with a wooden clock under his arm that strikes a hundred and more. Then comes the old french emigrant (who has been very well to do in france) whith [*for* with] his hands joined behind on his hips, and his face full of political schemes. Then passes Mr David Lewis a very good-natured, goodlooking old gentleman whas [*for* who] has been very kind to Tom and George and me. As for those fellows the Brickmakers they are always passing to and fro. I mus'n't forget the two old maiden Ladies in well walk who have a Lap dog between them, that they are very anxious about. It is a corpulent Little Beast whom it is necessary to coax along with an ivory-tipp'd cane. Carlo our Neighbour Mrs Brawne's dog and it meet sometimes. Lappy thinks Carlo a devil of a fellow and so do his Mistresses. Well they may—he would sweep 'em all down at a run; all for the Joke of it. I shall desire him to peruse the fable of the Boys and the frogs:[1] though he prefers the tongues and the Bones.[2] You shall hear from me again the day after tomorrow

Your affectionate Brother
John Keats

1 *fable . . . frogs*: In Aesop's fable boys throwing stones at frogs are told by one of the frogs that what is fun for the boys is death for them.

2 *tongues and the Bones*: Bottom's choice of music in *A Midsummer Night's Dream*, IV. i. 26–7, which has 'tongs' rather than 'tongues'.

To Fanny Brawne
10 (?) February 1820

[Harvard MS]

[Wentworth Place, Thursday]

My dearest Girl—

If illness makes such an agreeable variety in the manner of you[r] eyes I should wish you sometimes to be ill. I wish I had read your note before you went last night that I might have assured you how far I was from suspecting any coldness: You had a just right to be a little silent to one who speaks so plainly to you. You must believe you shall, you will that I can do nothing say nothing think nothing of you but what has its spring in the Love which has so long been my pleasure and torment. On the night I was taken ill when so violent a rush of blood came to my Lungs that I felt nearly suffocated—I assure you I felt it possible I might not survive and at that moment though[t] of nothing but you—When I said to Brown 'this is unfortunate' I thought of you—'T is true that since the first two or three days other subjects have entered my head—I shall be looking forward to Health and the Spring and a regular routine of our old Walks. Your affectionate

J. K—

On the same day Keats told his sister he hoped he was 'a little more verging towards improvement. Yesterday morning being very fine, I took a walk for a quarter of an hour in the garden and was very much refresh'd by it' (L, *II, p. 255).*

To Fanny Brawne
February (?) 1820

[HBF transcript (1883)]

[Wentworth Place]

My sweet love, I shall wait patiently till tomorrow before I see you, and in the mean time, if there is any need of such a thing, assure you by your Beauty, that whenever I have at any time written on a certain unpleasant subject, it has been with your welfare impress'd upon my mind. How hurt I should have been had you ever acceded to what is, notwithstanding, very reasonable![1] How much the more do I love you from the general result! In my present state of Health I feel too much separated from you and could almost speak to you in the words of Lorenzo's Ghost to Isabella

Your Beauty grows upon me and I feel
A greater love through all my essence steal.[2]

My greatest torment since I have known you has been the fear of you being a little inclined to the Cressid; but that suspicion I dismiss utterly and remain happy in the surety of your Love, which I assure you is as much a wonder to me as a delight. Send me the words "Good night" to put under my pillow.

Dearest Fanny,
Your affectionate
J. K.

1 *How hurt . . . reasonable*: Keats had evidently proposed breaking their engagement.
2 *Your Beauty . . . steal*: 'Isabella; or, The Pot of Basil', ll. 319–20.

health and spirits. I am sorry to hear of your relapse and hypochondriac symptoms attending it. Let us hope for the best as you say. I shall follow your example in looking to the future good rather than brooding upon present ill. I have not been so worn with lengthen'd illnesses as you have therefore cannot answer you on your own ground with respect to those haunting and deformed thoughts and feelings you speak of. When I have been or supposed myself in health I have had my share of them, especially within this last year. I may say that for 6 Months before I was taken ill I had not passed a tranquil day—Either that gloom overspred me or I was suffering under some passionate feeling, or if I turn'd to versify that acerbated the poison of either sensation. The Beauties of Nature had lost their power over me. How astonishingly (here I must premise that illness as far as I can judge in so short a time has relieved my Mind of a load of deceptive thoughts and images and makes me perceive things in a truer light)—How astonishingly does the chance of leaving the world impress a sense of its natural beauties on us. Like poor Falstaff, though I do not babble, I think of green fields. I muse with the greatest affection on every flower I have known from my infancy—their shapes and coulours as are [*for* are as] new to me as if I had just created them with a superhuman fancy—It is because they are connected with the most thoughtless and happiest moments of our Lives—I have seen foreign flowers in hothouses of the most beautiful nature, but I do not care a straw for them. The simple flowers of our sp[r]ing are what I want to see again.

Brown has left the inventive and taken to the imitative art—he is doing his forte which is copying Hogarth's heads.

He has just made a purchace of the methodist meeting Picture,[1] which gave me a horrid dream a few nights ago. I hope I shall sit under the trees with you again in some such place as the isle of Wight—I do not mind a game at cards in a saw pit or wagon; but if ever you catch me on a stage coach in the winter full against the wind bring me down with a brace of

1 *methodist meeting Picture*: *Credulity, Superstition and Fanaticism* (1762), a print by William Hogarth (1697–1764), satirizes Methodism.

bullets and I promise not to 'peach'. Remberme [*for* Remember me] to Reynolds and say how much I should like to hear from him: that Brown returned immediately after he went on Sunday, and that I was vex'd at forgetting to ask him to lunch for as he went towards the gate I saw he was fatigued and hungr<y.>

I am
my dear Rice
ever most sincer[e]ly yours
John Keats

I have broken this open to let you know I was surprised at seeing it on the table this morning; thinking it had gone long ago[1]

To Fanny Brawne
February (?) 1820

[Harvard MS]

[Wentworth Place]

My dearest Girl,

According to all appearances I am to be separated from you as much as possible. How I shall be able to bear it, or whether it will not be worse than your presence now and then, I cannot tell. I must be patient, and in the mean time you must think of it as little as possible. Let me not longer detain you from going to Town—there may be no end to this emprisoning of you. Perpaps you had better not come before tomorrow evening: send me however without fail a good night

You know our situation—what hope is there if I should be recovered ever so soon—my very health with [*for* will] not suffer me to make any great exertion. I am recommended not even to read poetry much less write it. I wish I had even a little hope. I cannot say forget me—but I would mention that there

1 *I have ... long ago*: Written on 16 February, when the letter was finally posted.

are impossibilities in the world. No more of this—I am not strong enough to be weaned—take no notice of it in your good night. Happen what may I shall ever be my dearest Love

Your affectionate

J— K—

To Fanny Brawne
February (?) 1820

[Harvard MS]

[Wentworth Place]

My dearest Girl, how could it ever have been my wish to forget you? how could I have said such a thing? The utmost stretch my mind has been capable of was to endeavour to forget you for you own sake seeing what a change [*for* chance] there was of my remaining in a precarious state of health. I would have borne it as I would bear death if fate was in that humour: but I should as soon think of choosing to die as to part from you. Believe too my Love that our friends think and speak for the best, and if the best is not our best it is not their fault, When I am better I will speak with you at large on these subjects, if there is any occasion—I think there is none. I am rather nervous to day perhaps from being a little recovered and suffering my mind to take little excursions beyond the doors and windows. I take it for a good sign, but as it must not be encouraged you had better delay seeing me till tomorrow. Do not take the trouble of writing much: merely send me my goodnight. Remember me to your Mother and Margaret. Your affectionate

J— K—

To Fanny Brawne
February (?) 1820

[Yale MS]

[Wentworth Place]

My dearest Fanny,

Then all we have to do is be patient.[1] Whatever violence I may sometimes do myself by hinting at what would appear to any one but ourselves a matter of necessity, I do not think I could bear any approach of a thought of losing you. I slept well last night, but cannot say that I improve very fast. I shall expect you tomorrow, for it is certainly better that I should see you seldom. Let me have your good night. Your affectionate

J— K—

*On 19 February Keats told Fanny Keats that he was 'Being confined almost entirely to vegetable food', but that his doctor assured him 'there are no dangerous Symptoms about me and that quietness of mind and fine weather will restore me' (*L, *II, p. 261).*

To Fanny Brawne
February (?) 1820

[Harvard MS]

[Wentworth Place]

My dearest Fanny,

I read your note in bed last night and that might be the reason of my sleeping so much better. I th[i]nk Mr Brown is right in supposing you may stop too long with me, so very nervous

1 *Then ... patient*: Keats had suggested that they should break off their engagement, but Fanny had refused.

as I am. Send me every evening a written Good night. If you come for a few minutes about six it may be the best time. Should you ever fancy me too low-spirited I must warn you to ascbribe it to the medicine I am at present taking which is of a nerve-shaking nature—I shall impute any depression I may experience to this cause. I have been writing with a vile old pen the whole week, which is excessively ungallant. The fault is in the Quill: I have mended it and still it is very much inclin'd to make blind es. However these last lines are in a much better style of penmanship thof [*for* though] a little disfigured by the smear of black currant jelly; which has made a little mark on one of the Pages of Brown's Ben Jonson, the very best book he has. I have lick'd it but it remains very purpl~~ue~~—I did not know whether to say purple or blue, so in the mixture of the thought wrote purplue which may be an excellent name for a colour made up of those two, and would suit well to start next spring. Be very careful of open doors and windows and going without your duffle grey—God bless you Love!—

J. Keats—

P.S. I am sitting in the back room—Remember me to your Mother—

To Fanny Brawne
February (?) 1820

[HBF transcript (1883)]

[Wentworth Place]

My dear Fanny,

Do not let your mother suppose that you hurt me by writing at night. For some reason or other your last night's note was not so treasureable as former ones. I would fain that you call me <u>Love</u> still. To see you happy and in high spirits is a great consolation to me—still let me believe that you are not half so happy as my restoration would make you. I am nervous, I own, and may think myself worse than I really am; if so you must indulge me, and pamper with that sort of tenderness you have manifested towards me in different Letters. My sweet creature when I look back upon the pains and torments I have suffer'd for you from the day I left you to go to the isle of Wight; the extasies in which I have pass'd some days and the miseries in their turn, I wonder the more at the Beauty which has kept up the spell so fervently. When I send this round I shall be in the front parlour watching to see you show yourself for a minute in the garden. How illness stands as a barrier betwixt me and you! Even if I was well——I must make myself as good a Philosopher as possible. Now I have had opportunities of passing nights anxious and awake I have found other thoughts intrude upon me. "If I should die," said I to myself, "I have left no immortal work behind me—nothing to make my friends proud of my memory—but I have lov'd the principle of Beauty in all things, and if I had had time I would have made myself remember'd." Thoughts like these came very feebly whilst I was in health and every pulse beat for you—now you divide with this (may I say it?) "last infirmity of noble minds"[1] all my reflection.

God bless you, Love—
J. Keats—

To Fanny Brawne
February (?) 1820

[Princeton MS]

[Wentworth Place]

My dearest Girl,

You spoke of having been unwell in your last note: have you recovered? That Note has been a great delight to me. I am stronger than I was: the Doctors say there is very little the matter with me. but I cannot believe them till the weight and tightness of my Chest is mitigated. I will not indulge or pain myself by complaining of my long separation from you. God

1 *last infirmity of noble minds*: Milton's *Lycidas*, l. 71.

alone knows whether I am destined to taste of happiness with you: at all events I myself know thus much, that I consider it no mean Happiness to have lov'd you thus far—if it is to be no further I shall not be unthankful—if I am to recover, the day of my recovery shall see me by your side from which nothing shall separate me. If well you are the only medicine that can keep me so. Perpahs [*for* perhaps] aye surely I am writing in too depress'd a state of mind—ask your Mother to come and see me; she will bring you a better account than mine.

Every your affectionat

John Keats—

To Fanny Brawne
24 (?) February 1820

[Lilly Library MS]

[Wentworth Place, Thursday]

My dearest Girl,

In deed I will not deceive you with respect to my Health. This is the fact as far as I know. I have been confined three weeks and am not yet well—this proves that there is something wrong about me which my constitution will either conquer or give way to—Let us hope for the best. Do you hear the Th[r]ush singing over the field? I think it is a sign of mild weather—so much the better for me. Like all Sinners now I am ill I philosophise aye out of my attachment to [e]very thing, Trees, flowers, Thrushes Sp[r]ing, Summer, Claret &c &c aye every thing but you— —my Sister would be glad of my company a little longer. That Thrush is a fine fellow I hope he was fortunate in his choice this year—Do not send any more of my Books home. I have great pleasure in the thought of you looking on them.

Ever yours

my sweet Fanny

J. K—

On 24 February Keats wrote to his sister, 'I am sorry to hear you have been so unwell: now you are better keep so . . . I am much the same as when I wrote last. When I am well enough to return to my old diet I shall get stronger. If my recovery should be delay'd long I will ask Mr Abbey to let you visit me—Keep up your Spirits as well as you can' (L, *II, pp.* 265–6).

To Fanny Brawne
27 February 1820[1]

[Princeton MS]

[Wentworth Place, Sunday]

My dearest Fanny,

I had a better night last night than I have had since my attack, and this morning I am the same as when you saw me. I have been turning over two volumes of Letters written between Ro[u]sseau and two Ladies[2] in the perplexed strain of mingled finesse and sentiment in which the Ladies and gentlemen of those days were so clever, and which is still prevalent among Ladies of this Country who live in a state of re[a]soning romance. The Likeness however only extends to the mannerism not to the dexterity. What would Rousseau have said at seeing our little correspondence! What would his Ladies have said! I don't care much—I would sooner have Shakspeare's opinion about the matter. The common gossiping of washerwomen must be less disgusting than the continual and eternal fence and attack of Rousseau and these sublime Petticoats. One calls herself Clara and her friend Julia two of Rousseau's Heroines—they all the same time christen poor Jean Jacques St Preux—who is

1 Date based on next letter, which records that Barry Cornwall gave him a copy of his 'Dramatic Scenes yesterday'.

2 *Letters . . . Ladies*: *Correspondance originale et inédite de J. J. Rousseau avec Mme Latour de Franqueville et M. de Peyrou*, 2 vols (Paris, 1803), in which, as Keats later notes, Rousseau is addressed as St Preux, the protagonist of his novel *Julie, ou la nouvelle Héloïse* (1761), a copy of which Keats possessed.

the pure cavalier of his famous novel. Thank God I am born in England with our own great Men before my eyes—Thank god that you are fair and can love me without being Letter-written and sentimentaliz'd into it—Mr Barry Cornwall has sent me another Book, his first, with a polite note—I must do what I can to make him sensible of the esteem I have for his kindness If this north east would take a turn it would be so much the better for me. Good bye, my love, my dear love, my beauty—

love me for ever—

J— K—

To J. H. Reynolds
28 February 1820

[Texas MS]

[Wentworth Place, Monday]

My dear Reynolds,

I have been improving since you saw me: my nights are better which is I think a very encouraging thing. You mention your cold in rather too slighting a manner—if you travel outside have some flannel aga[i]nst the wind—which I pope [*for* hope] will not keep on at this rate when you are in the Packet boat. Should it rain do not stop upon deck though the Passengers should vomit themselves inside out. Keep under Hatches from all sort of wet. I am pretty well provided with Books at present, when you return I may give you a commission or two—Mr B. C. has sent me not only his Sicilian Story but yesterday his Dramatic Scenes[1]—this is very polite and I shall do what I can to make him sensible I think so. I confess they tease me—they are composed of Amiability, the Seasons, the Leaves,

1 *Mr B. C. . . . Dramatic Scenes*: Barry Cornwall (the pseudonym of Brian Waller Procter (1787–1874)) sent Keats his *Dramatic Scenes* (1819) and *A Sicilian Story* (1820). The latter had been advertised on 13 December 1819 and reviewed in the *Examiner* on 2 January 1820. For Hunt's failure to deliver the former book, see Keats's letter to Dilke of 4 March. In late July Cornwall sent Keats a copy of his *Marcian Colonna: An Italian Tale* (1820).

the Moon &c. upon which he rings (according to Hunt's expression) triple bob majors.[1] However that is nothing—I think he likes poetry for its own sake, not his. I hope I shall soon bee well enough to proceed with my fa[i]ries[2] and set you about the notes on Sundays and Stray-days. If I had been well enough I should have liked to cross the water with you. Brown wishes you a pleasant voyage—Have fish for dinner at the sea ports, and don't forget a bottle of Claret. You will not meet with so much to hate at Brussels as at Paris. Remember me to all my friends. If I were well enough I would paraphrase an ode of Horace's for you, on your embarking in the seventy years ago style—the Packet will bear a comparison with a roman galley at any rate.

Ever yours affectionately
J. Keats

To Fanny Brawne
28 (?) February 1820

[Facsimile (1912)][3]

[Wentworth Place, Monday]

My dearest Girl,

I continue much the same as usual, I think a little better. My Spirits are better also, and consequently I am more resign'd to my confinement. I dare not think of you much or write much to you—Remember me to all.

Ever your affectionate
John Keats—

1 *triple bob majors*: Properly, a treble bob major, a peal rung upon eight bells.
2 *my fa[i]ries*: Keats's unfinished satire 'The Jealousies: A Faery Tale' (also known as 'The Cap and Bells'), which was to be published under the feigned authorship of 'Lucy Vaughan Lloyd' and to which Reynolds was to have added mock-serious notes.
3 Thomas J. Barratt, *The Annals of Hampstead* (London, 1912), II, p. 162.

To Fanny Brawne

29 (?) February 1820

[Harvard MS]

[Wentworth Place, Tuesday]

My dear Fanny,

I think you had better not make any long stay with me when Mr Brown is at home—whe[ne]ver he goes out you may bring your work.[1] You will have a pleasant walk to day. I shall see you pass. I shall follow you with my eyes over the Heath. Will you come towards evening instead of before dinner—when you are gone, 't is past—if you do not come till the evening I have something to look forward to all day. Come round to my window for a moment when you have read this. Thank your Mother, for the preserves, for me. The raspberry will be too sweet not having any acid; therefore as you are so good a girl I shall make you a present of it. Good bye

My sweet Love!
J. Keats

1 *I think you . . . bring your work*: This injunction has been variously interpreted as being caused by Brown's supposed dislike of Fanny (Gittings, *John Keats*, pp. 558–9), by Keats's fear that Fanny would flirt with Brown (Roe, pp. 362–3) or because Keats had been told to avoid any excitement for medical reasons (Rollins, II, p. 269 n, citing Brown's earlier advice above, pp. 501–2). Keats's motives were undoubtedly mixed, but there is no reason to think Brown disliked Fanny.

To Fanny Brawne
1 March (?) 1820

[Keats House MS]

[Wentworth Place, Wednesday]

My dearest Fanny,

The power of your benediction is of not so weak a nature as to pass from the ring[1] in four-and twenty hours—it is like a sacred Chalice once consecrated and ever consecrate. I shall kiss your name and mine where your Lips have been—Lips! why should a poor prisoner as I am talk about such things. Thank God, though I hold them the dearest pleasures in the universe, I have a consolation independent of them in the certainty of your affection. I could write a song in style of Tom Moore's Pathetic about Memory[2] if that would be any relief to me—No. it would not. I will be as obstinate as a Robin, I will not sing in a cage—Health is my expected heaven and you are the Houri[3]—this word I believe is both singular and plural—if only plural, never mind—you are a thousand of them.

Ever yours affectionately
my dearest—

J. K.

1 *the ring*: A seal ring of agate or carnelian, a gift from Fanny Brawne with their names engraved on it; Keats was wearing it when he moved to stay with the Hunts (p. 537 below).

2 *Tom Moore's . . . Memory*: Thomas Moore wrote a number of melancholy lyrics.

3 *Houri*: One of the virgins in the Muslim paradise promised to believers; a voluptuously beautiful woman.

My dearest Fanny,

The power of your benediction is of not so weak a nature as to pass from the ring in four and twenty hours – it is like a sacred Chalice once consecrated and ever consecrate. I shall kiss your name and mine where your Lips have been – Lips! why should a poor prisoner as I am talk about such things. Thank God, though I hold them the dearest pleasures in the universe, I have a consolation independent of them in the certainty of your

7. To Fanny Brawne, 1 March (?) 1820, p. 1, 18.7 × 11.2 cm

To C. W. Dilke
4 March 1820

[Keats House MS]

[Wentworth Place, Saturday]

My dear Dilke,

Since I saw you I have been gradually, too gradually perhaps, improving; and though under an interdict with respect to animal food living upon pseudo victuals, Brown says I have pick'd up a little flesh lately. If I can keep off inflammation for the next six weeks I trust I shall do very well. You certainly should have been at Martin's dinner for making an index is surely as dull work as engraving.[1] Have you heard that the Bookseller is going to tie himself to the manger eat or not as he pleases? He says Rice shall have his foot on the fender notwithstanding. Reynolds is going to sail the salt seas. Brown has been mightily progressing with his Hogarth.[2] A damn'd melancholy picture it is, and during the first week of my illness it gave me a psalm singing nightmare, that made me almost faint away in my sleep. I know I am better, for I can bear the Picture. I have experienced a specimen of great politeness from M[r] Barry Cornwall. He has sent me his books. Some time ago he had given his first publish'd book to Hunt for me; Hunt forgot to give it and Barry Cornwall thinking I had received it must have though[t] me [a] very neglectful fellow.[3] Notwithstan[din]g he sent me his second book and on my explaining that I had not received his first he sent me that also—I am sorry to see by M[rs] D's note that she has been so unwell with the spasms. Does she

1 *an index . . . engraving*: Dilke was completing the index of the four-volume *Private Correspondence of Horace Walpole, Earl of Orford* (1820), undertaken for John Martin's firm (see above, p. 52), which had organized a dinner for its engravers.

2 *Brown . . . Hogarth*: See above p. 498 for Brown's purchase of Hogarth's engraving.

3 *Barry Cornwall . . . fellow*: See above, p. 506.

continue the Medicines that benefited her so much? I am affraid not. Remember me to her and say I shall not expect her at Hampstead next week unless the Weather changes for the warmer. It is better to run no chance of a supernumery cold in March. As for you you must come. You must improve in your penmanship; your writing is like the speaking of a child of three years old, very understandable to its father but to no one else. The worst is it looks well—no that is not the worst—the worst is, it is worse than Bailey's. Bailey's looks legible and may perchance be read; your's looks very legible and may perchance not be read—I would endeavour to give you a facsimile of your word Thistlewood[1] if I were not minded on the instant that Lord chesterfield has done some such thing to his Son. Now I would not bathe in the same River with lord C. though I had the upper hand of the stream. I am grieved that in writing and speaking it is necessary to make use of the same particles as he did.[2] Cobbet[3] is expected to come in. O that I had two double plumpers for him.[4] The ministry are not so inimical to him but ~~they~~ /it/ would like to put him out of Coventry. Casting my eye on the other side I see a long word written in a most vile manner, unbecoming a Critic. You must recollect I have served no apprenticeship to old plays.[5] If the only copies of the greek and Latin Authors had been made by you, Bailey and Haydon they Were as good as lost. It has been said that the Character of a Man may be known by his hand writing—if the Character of the age may be known by the average goodness of said, what a

1 *Thistlewood*: Arthur Thistlewood (1770–1820) had just been arrested for his suspected part in the Cato Street Conspiracy.

2 *Lord chesterfield . . . he did*: Keats evidently shared Samuel Johnson's view of Chesterfield's *Letters to his Son* (1774) as teaching 'the morals of a whore and manners of a gentleman dancing-master'.

3 *Cobbet*: William Cobbett returned from America in November 1819 and stood in the Coventry election of 12 March 1820. Despite the hopes of Keats and the *Examiner*, he was narrowly defeated.

4 *double plumpers for him*: A 'plumper' is 'A vote cast at an election for a single candidate when the voter has the right to vote for two or more' (*OED*).

5 *old plays*: Dilke had edited the six-volume *Old English Plays, being a Selection from the Early Dramatic Writers* (1814–16), published by John Martin.

slovenly age we live in. Look at Queen Elizabeth's Latin exercises and blush. Look at Milton's hand—I cant say a word for shakespeare—

Your sincere friend
John Keats

To Fanny Brawne
March (?) 1820

[Facsimile (1891)][1]

[Wentworth Place]

My dearest Love,

You must not stop so long in the cold—I have been suspecting that window to be open—You[r] Note half-cured me —When I want some more oranges I will tell you—these are just a propos—I am kept from food so feel rather weak—othe[r]wise very well—Pray do not stop so long up stairs—it makes me uneasy—come every now and then and stop half a minute—Remember me to your Mother

Your ever affectionate
J— Keats—

*On Monday evening, 6 March, Keats was 'taken . . . with violent palpitations of the heart', and on Wednesday Brown told Taylor that he would be 'unable to prepare his Poems for the Press for a long time'. But two days later on 10 March he reported 'Keats is so well as to be out of danger . . . there is no pulmonary affection, no organic defect whatever,—the disease is on his mind' (*L, *II, pp. 273–5).*

1 *The Archivist and Autograph Review*, IV (April 1891), between pp. 14–15.

To Fanny Brawne
March (?) 1820

[HBF transcript (1883)]

[Wentworth Place]

Sweetest Fanny,

You fear, sometimes, I do not love you as much as you wish? My dear Girl I love you ever and ever and without reserve. The more I have known you the more have I lov'd. In every way—even my jealousies have been agonies of Love, in the hottest fit I ever had I would have died for you. I have vex'd you too much. But for Love! Can I help it? You are always new. The last of your kisses was ever the sweetest; the last smile the brightest; the last movement the gracefullest. When you pass'd my window home yesterday, I was fill'd with as much admiration as if I had then seen you for the first time. You uttered a half complaint once that I only lov'd your Beauty. Have I nothing else then to love in you but that? Do not I see a heart naturally furnish'd with wings imprison itself with me? No ill prospect has been able to turn your thoughts a moment from me. This perhaps should be as much a subject of sorrow as joy—but I will not talk of that. Even if you did not love me I could not help an entire devotion to you: how much more deeply then must I feel for you knowing you love me. My Mind has been the most discontented and restless one that ever was put into a body too small for it. I never felt my Mind repose upon anything with complete and undistracted enjoyment—upon no person but you. When you are in the room my thoughts never fly out of window: you always concentrate my whole senses. The anxiety shown about our Loves in your last note is an immense pleasure to me: however you must not suffer such speculations to molest you any more: nor will I any more believe you have the least pique against me. Brown is gone out—but here is Mrs. Wylie—when she is gone I shall be awake for you.—Remembrances to your Mother.

Your affectionate

J. Keats.

Writing on 13 (?) March Charles Brown told Taylor 'Keats has been slowly recovering', had been revising 'Lamia' and wanted 'The Eve of St Agnes' to be the first poem in his new volume (L, II, p. 276). By 14 March Keats had recovered sufficiently to dine with Taylor in Fleet Street on 14 March.

To Fanny Brawne
March (?) 1820

[HBF transcript (1883)]

[Wentworth Place]

My dearest Fanny, whe[ne]ver you know me to be alone, come, no matter what day. Why will you go out this weather? I shall not fatigue myself with writing too much I promise you. Brown says I am getting stouter. I rest well and from last night do not remember any thing horrid in my dream, which is a capital symptom, for any organic derangement always occasions a Phantasmagoria. It will be a nice idle amusement to hunt after a motto for my Book which I will have if lucky enough to hit upon a fit one—not intending to write a preface.[1] I fear I am too late with my note—you are gone out—you will be as cold as a topsail in a north latitude—I advise you to furl yourself and come in a doors.

Good bye Love,
J. K.

1 *a motto . . . a preface*: There is no motto in Keats's final volume. He disowned the preface added by Taylor or Woodhouse.

To Fanny Brawne
March (?) 1820

[Harvard MS]

[Wentworth Place]

My dearest Fanny, I slept well last night and am no worse this morning for it. Day by day if I am not deceived I get a more unrestrain'd use of my Chest. The nearer a racer gets to the Goal the more his anxiety becomes so I lingering upon the borders of health feel my impatience increase. Perhaps on your account I have imagined my illness more serious than it is: how horrid was the chance of slipping into the ground instead of into your arms—the difference is amazing Love—Death must come at last; Man must die, as Shallow says;[1] but before that is my fate I feign would try what more pleasures than you have given so sweet a creature as you can give. Let me have another op[p]ortunity of years before me and I will not die without being remember'd. Take care of yourself dear that we may both be well in the Summer. I do not at all fatigue myself with writing, having merely to put a line or two here and there, a Task which would worry a stout state of the body and mind, but which just suits me as I can do no more.

Your affectionate
J. K—

To Fanny Brawne
March (?) 1820

[HBF transcript (1883)]

[Wentworth Place]

My dearest Fanny,

Though I shall see you in so short a time I cannot forbear sending you a few lines. You say I did not give you yesterday a

1 *Death . . . Shallow says*: Justice Shallow in 2 *Henry IV*, III. ii. 35–6.

minute account of my health. To-day I have left off the Medicine which I took to keep the pulse down and I find I can do very well without it, which is a very favourable sign, as it shows there is no inflammation remaining. You think I may be wearied at night you say: it is my best time; I am at my best about eight o'Clock. I received a Note from Mr. Proctor today. He says he cannot pay me a visit this weather as he is fearful of an inflammation in the Chest. What a horrid climate this is? or what careless inhabitants it has? You are one of them. My dear girl do not make a joke of it: do not expose yourself to the cold. There's the Thrush again—I can't afford it—he'll run me up a pretty Bill for Music—besides he ought to know I deal at Clementi's.[1] How can you bear so long an imprisonment at Hampstead? I shall always remember it with all the gusto that a monopolizing carle should. I could build an Altar to you for it.

Your affectionate

J. K.

To Fanny Brawne
March (?) 1820

[HBF transcript (1883)]

[Wentworth Place]

Dear Girl,

Yesterday you must have thought me worse than I really was. I assure you there was nothing but regret at being obliged to forego an embrace which has so many times been the highest gust of my Life. I would not care for health without it. Sam would not come in—I wanted merely to ask him how you were this morning. When one is not quite well we turn for relief to those we love: this is no weakness of spirit in me: you know

1 *Clementi's*: Italian composer Muzio Clementi (1752–1832) settled in England and turned to music publishing and manufacturing pianos; he gained the English rights to Beethoven's compositions.

when in health I thought of nothing but you; when I shall again be so it will be the same. Brown has been mentioning to me that some hint from Sam, last night, occasions him some uneasiness. He whispered something to you concerning Brown and old Mr. Dilke which had the complexion of being something derogatory to the former. It was connected with an anxiety about Mr. D. Sr's death and an anxiety to set out for Chichester.[1] These sort of hints point out their own solution: one cannot pretend to a delicate ignorance on the subject: you understand the whole matter. If any one, my sweet Love, has misrepresented, to you, to your Mother or Sam, any circumstances which are at all likely, at a tenth remove, to create suspicions among people who from their own interested notions slander others, pray tell me: for I feel the least attaint on the disinterested character of Brown very deeply. Perhaps Reynolds or some other of my friends may come towards evening, therefore you may choose whether you will come to see me early today before or after dinner as you may think fit. Remember me to your Mother and tell her to drag you to me if you show the least reluctance—

* * *[2]

To Fanny Keats
20 March 1820

[British Library MS]

[Wentworth Place, Monday]

My dear Fanny,

According to your desire I write to day. It must be but a few lines for I have been attack'd several times with a palpitation at

1 *Brown and old Mr Dilke . . . Chichester*: Gittings believes that Brown's anxiety to go to Chichester to see old Mr Dilke, who had been ill, was interpreted by the Brawne family as stemming from Brown's eye 'for the main chance', which had, not unnaturally, upset him (*John Keats*, pp. 563–4).

2 HBF notes 'the signature (and perhaps something with it)' was missing.

the heart and the Doctor says I must not make the slightest exertion. I am much the same to day as I have been for a week past. They say 't is nothing but debility and will entirely cease on my recovery of my strength, which is the object of my present diet.[1] As the Docter will not suffer me to write I shall ask Mr Brown to let you hear news of me for the future if I should not get stronger soon. I hope I shall be well enough to co<me> and see your flowers in bloom—

Ever your most
affectionate Brother
John—

To Fanny Brawne
March (?) 1820

[HBF transcript (1883)]

[Wentworth Place]

My dearest Girl,

As, from the last part of my note you must see how gratified I have been by your remaining at home, you might perhaps conceive that I was equally bias'd the other way by your going to Town, I cannot be easy tonight without telling you you would be wrong to suppose so. Though I am pleased with the one, I am not displeased with the other. How do I dare to write in this manner about my pleasures and displeasures? I will tho' whilst I am an invalid, in spite of you. Good night, Love!

J. K.

1 *my present diet*: Keats had been taken off his vegetable diet. His physician Dr Robert Bree (1758–1839), an authority on asthmatic diseases, believed the origin of Keats's illness was not a 'pulmonary affection' but was primarily psychosomatic and best treated by a regimen of 'tender animal food and light wine'.

To Fanny Brawne
March (?) 1820

[Princeton MS]

[Wentworth Place]

My dearest Girl,

In consequence of our company I suppose I shall not see you before tomorrow. I am much better to day—indeed all I have to complain of is want of strength and a little tightness in the Chest. I envied Sam's walk with you to day; which I will not do again as I may get very tired of envying. I imagine you now sitting in your new black dress which I like so much and if I were a little less selfish and more enthousiastic I should run round and surprise you with a knock at the door. I fear I am too prudent for a dying kind of Lover. Yet, there is a great difference between going off in warm blood like Romeo, and making one's exit like a frog in a frost—I had nothing particular to say to day, but not intending that there shall be any interruption to our correspondence (which at some future time I propose offering to Murray) I write something! God bless you my sweet Love! Illness is a long lane but I see you at the end of it, and shall mend my pace as well as possible

J— K

To Mrs Ann Wylie
24 (?) March 1820

[Harvard MS]

Wentworth Place
Friday. Morn.

My dear Mrs Wylie,

I have been very negligent in not letting you hear from me for so long a time considering the anxiety I know you feel for me. Charles has been here this morning and will tell you that I am better. Just as he came in I was sitting down to write to you, and I shall not let his visit supersede these few lines. Charles enquired whether I had heard from George. It is impossible to guess whether he has landed yet, and if he has, it will take at least a month for any communication to reach us. I hope you keep your spirits a great height above the freezing point, and live in expectation of good news next summer. Louisville is not such a Monstrous distance: if Georgiana liv'd at york it would be just as far off. You see George will make nothing of the journey here and back. His absence will have been perhaps a fortunate event for Georgiana, for the pleasure of his return will be so great that it will wipe away the consciousness of many troubles felt before very deeply. She will see him return'd from us and be convinced that the separation is not so very formidable although the Atlantic is between. If George succeeds it will be better certainly that they should stop in America: if not why not return? It is better in ill luck to have at least the comfort of ones friends than to be shipwreck'd among American's. But I have good hopes as far as I can judge from what I have heard from George. He should by this time be taught Alertness and Carefulness—If they should stop in America for five or six years let us hope they may have about three Children: then the eldest will be getting old enough to be society. The very crying will keep their ears employed, and their spirits from being melancholy. Mrs Millar I hear continues confined to her Chamber[1]—if she would take my advice I should recommender [*for* recommend her] to keep it till the middle of april and then go to some Sea-town in Devonshire which is sheltered from the east wind—which blows down the channel very briskly even in april. Give my Compliments to Miss Millar and Miss Waldegra<ve.>

* * *[2]

1 *Mrs Millar . . . Chamber*: She was seriously ill: George had learnt of her death before 18 June (*L*, II, p. 296).
2 The end of the letter is cut off.

To Fanny Keats
12 April 1820

[British Library MS]

Wentworth Place
[Wednesday] 12 April—

My dear Fanny—

Excuse these shabby scraps of paper I send you—and also from endeavouring to give you any consolation just at present for though my health is tolerably well I am too nervous to enter into any discussion in which my heart is concerned. Wait patiently and take care of your health being especially carefull to keep yourself from low spirits which are great enemies to health. You are young and have only need of a little patience. I am not yet able to bear the fatigue of coming to Walthamstow though I have been to Town once or twice. I have thought of taking a change of air. You shall hear from me immediately on my moving any where. I will ask Mrs Dilke to pay you a visit if the weather holds fine, the first time I see her. The Dog is being attended to like a Prince.

Your affectionate Brother
John

To Fanny Brawne
April (?) 1820[1]

[Rollins transcript]

[Wentworth Place]

My dear Fanny,

I am much better this morning than I was a week ago: indeed I improve a little every day. I rely upon taking a walk with you

1 *April (?) 1820* : Gittings, pp. 367, 403, dates March (?) 1820.

upon the first of may: in the mean time undergoing a babylonish captivity I shall not be jew enough to hang up my parp [*for* harp] upon a willow,[1] but rather endeavour to clear up my arrears in versifying and with returning health begin upon something new: pursuant to which resolution it will be necessary to have my or rather Taylor's manuscript,[2] which you, if you please, will send by my Messenger either to day or tomorrow. Is M^r D[ilke] with you today? You appear'd very much fatigued last night: you must look a little brighter this morning. I shall not suffer my little girl ever to be obscured like glass breath'd upon but always bright as it is her nature to. Feeding upon sham victuals and sitting by the fire will completely annul me. I have no need of an enchanted wax figure to duplicate me for I am melting in my proper person before the fire. If you meet with any thing better (worse) than common in your Magazines let me see it. Good bye my

sweetest Girl
J— K—

To Fanny Keats
21 April 1820

[British Library MS]

[Wentworth Place]

My dear Fanny,

I have been slowly improving since I wrote last. The Doctor assures me that there is nothing the matter with me except nervous irritability and a general weakness of the whole system which has proceeded from my anxiety of mind of late years and the too great excitement of poetry—Mr Brown is going to Scotland by the Smack, and I am advised for change of exercise and air to accompany him and give myself the chance of benefit from a Voyage. Mr H. Wylie call'd on me yesterday with a letter

1 *to hang . . . a willow*: Psalm 137:2.
2 *Taylor's manuscript*: Of the *Lamia* volume.

from George to his mother: George is safe on the other side of the water, perpaps by this time arrived at his home. I wish you were coming to town that I might see you; if you should be coming write to me, as it is quite a trouble to get by the coaches to Walthamstow. Should you not come to Town I must see you before I sail, at Walthamstow. They tell me I must study lines and tangents and squares and circles to put a little Ballast into my mind. We shall be going in a fortnight and therefore you will see me within that space. I expected sooner, but I have not been able to wenture to walk across the Country. Now the fine Weather is come you will not fine [*for* find] your time so irksome. You must be sensible how much I regret not being able to alleviate the unpleasantness of your situation, but trust my dear Fanny that better times are in wait for you.

Your affectionate Brother
John—

To Fanny Keats
4 May 1820

[British Library MS]

Wentworth Place
Thursday—

My dear Fanny,

I went for the first time into the City the day before yesterday, for before I was very disinclined to encounter the Scuffle, more from nervousness than real illness; which notwithstanding I should not have suffered to conquer me if I had not made up my mind not to go to Scotland, but to remove to Kentish Town till M[r] Brown returns. Kentish Town is a Mile nearer to you than Hampstead—I have been getting gradually better but am not so well as to trust myself to the casualties of rain and sleeping out which I am liable to in visiting you. M[r] Brown goes on Saturday and by that time I shall have settled in my new Lodging when I will certainly venture to you. You will forgive me I hope when I confess that I endeavour to think of you as little as possible and to let George dwell upon my mind but slightly. The reason being that I am affraid to ruminate on any thing which has the shade of difficulty or melancholy in it, as that sort of cogitation is so pernicious to health, and it is only by health that I can be enabled to alleviate your situation in future. For some time you must do what you can of yourself for relief, and bear your mind up with the consciousness that your situation cannot last for ever, and that for the present you may console yourself against the reproaches of Mrs Abbey. Whatever obligations you may have had to her ~~or her Husband~~ you have none now as she has reproach'd you. I do not know what property you have, but I will enquire into it: be sure however that beyond the obligations that a Lodger may have to a Landlord you have none to Mr Abbey—Let the surety of this make you laugh at Mrs A's foolish tattle. Mrs Dilke's Brother has got your Dog—She is now [*for* not] very well—still liable to Illness. I will get her to come and see you if I can make up my mind on the propriety of introducing a Strang[er] into Abbey's House. Be careful to let no fretting injure you[r] health as I have suffered it—health is the greatest of blessings—with heal<th> and hope we should be content to live, and so you will find as you grow older—I am

my dear Fanny
your affectionate Brother
John—

Between 4 and 7 May Keats moved into new lodgings at 2 Wesleyan Place, Kentish Town, and saw off Brown on his Scottish trip, going with him on the smack as far as Gravesend. He stayed in his new lodgings for seven weeks, initially nursing his health and receiving visitors, including Mrs Brawne, who carried his letters to Fanny back to Wentworth Place. He corrected the proofs of Lamia, Isabella, The Eve of St Agnes, and Other Poems, *and from mid-June he occasionally went into town.*

not think of any thing but me. Do not live as if I was not existing—Do not forget me—But have I any right to say you forget me? Perhaps you think of me all day. Have I any right to wish you to be unhappy for me? You would forgive me for wishing it, if you knew the extreme passion I have that you should love me—and for you to love me as I do you, you must think of no one but me, much less write that sentence. Yesterday and this morning I have been haunted with a sweet vision—I have seen you the whole time in your shepherdess dress. How my senses have ached at it! How my heart has been devoted to it! How my eyes have been full of Tears at it! I[n]deed I think a real Love is enough to occupy the widest heart—Your going to Town alone, when I heard of it was a shock to me—yet I expected it—promise me you will not for some time, till I get better. Promise me this and fill the paper full of the most endearing mames [*for* names]. If you cannot do so with good will, do my Love tell me—say what you think—confess if your heart is too much fasten'd on the world. Perhaps then I may see you at a greater distance, I may not be able to appropriate you so closely to myself. Were you to loose a favorite bird from the cage, how would your eyes ache after it as long as it was in sight; when out of sight you would recover a little. Perphaps if you would, if so it is, confess to me how many things are necessary to you besides me, I might be happier, by being less tantaliz'd. Well may you exclaim, how selfish, how cruel, not to let me enjoy my youth! to wish me to be unhappy! You must be so if you love me—upon my Soul I can be contented with nothing else. If you could really what is call'd enjoy yourself at a Party—if you can smile in peoples faces, and wish them to admire you now, you never have nor ever will love me—I see life in nothing but the cerrtainty of your Love—convince me of it my sweetest. If I am not somehow convinc'd I shall die of agony. If we love we must not live as other men and women do—I cannot brook the wolfsbane of fashion and foppery and tattle. You must be mine to die upon the rack if I want you. I do not pretend to say I have more feeling than my fellows—but I wish you seriously to look over my letters kind and unkind and consider whether the Person who wrote them can be able separation from you gives me agonies which are scarcely to be talked of. When your mother comes I shall be very sudden and expert in asking her whether you have been to Mrs. Dilke's, for she might say no to make me easy. I am literally worn to death, which seems my only recourse. I cannot forget what has pass'd. What? nothing with a man of the world, but to me deathful. I will get rid of this as much as possible. When you were in the habit of flirting with Brown you would have left off, could your own heart have felt one half of one pang mine did. Brown is a good sort of Man—he did not know he was doing me to death by inches. I feel the effect of every one of those hours in my side now; and for that cause, though he has done me many services, though I know his love and friendship for me, though at this moment I should be without pence were it not for his assistance, I will never see or speak to him until we are both old men, if we are to be. I <u>will</u> resent my heart having been made a football. You will call this madness. I have heard you say that it was not unpleasant to wait a few years—you have amusements—your mind is away—you have not brooded over one idea as I have, and how should you? You are to me an object intensely desireable—the air I breathe in a room empty of you is unhealthy. I am not the same to you—no—you can wait—you have a thousand activities—you can be happy without me. Any party, any thing to fill up the day has been enough. How have you pass'd this month? Who have you smil'd with? All this may seem savage in me. You do not feel as I do—you do not know what it is to love—one day you may—your time is not come. Ask yourself how many unhappy hours Keats has caused you in Loneliness. For myself I have been a Martyr the whole time, and for this reason I speak; the confession is forc'd from by the torture. I appeal to you by the blood of that Christ you believe in: Do not write to me if you have done anything this month which it would have pained me to have seen. You may have altered—if you have not—if you still behave in dancing rooms and other societies as I have seen you—I do not want to live—if you have done so I wish this coming night may be my last. I cannot live without you, and not only you but <u>chaste you; virtuous you</u>. The Sun rises and sets, the day passes, and you follow the bent of your inclination to a certain extent—you have no conception of the quantity of miserable feeling that passes through me in a day.—Be serious! Love is not a plaything—and again do not write unless you can do it with a crystal conscience. I would sooner die for want of you than——

Yours for ever

J. Keats.

To Fanny Brawne
June (?) 1820

[Harvard MS]

[2 Wesleyan Place]

My dearest Fanny,

My head is puzzled this morning, and I scarce know what I shall say though I am full of a hundred things. 'T is certain I would rather be writing to you this morning, notwithstanding the alloy of grief in such an occupation, than enjoy any other pleasure, with health to boot, unconnected with you. Upon my soul I have loved you to the extreme. I wish you could know the Tenderness with which I continually brood over your different aspects of countenance, action and dress. I see you come down in the morning: I see you meet me at the Window—I see every thing over again eternally that I ever have seen. If I get on the pleasant clue[1] I live in a sort of happy misery, if on the unpleasant 'tis miserable misery. You complain of my illtreating you in word thought and deed—I am sorry,—at times I feel bitterly sorry that I ever made you unhappy—my excuse is that those words have been wrung from me by the sha[r]pness of my feelings. At all events and in any case I have been wrong; could I believe that I did it without any cause, I should be the most sincere of Penitents. I could give way to my repentant feelings now, I could recant all my suspicions, I could mingle with you heart and Soul though absent, were it not for some

1 *clue*: i.e., a thread of thought (fig. from 'clue', a ball of thread).

part of your Letters. Do you suppose it possible I could ever leave you? You know what I think of myself and what of you. You know that I should feel how much it was my loss and how little yours—My friends laugh at you! I know some of them[1]—when I know them all I shall never think of them again as friends or even acquaintance. My friends have behaved well to me in every instance but one, and there they have b[e]come tattlers, and inquisitors into my conduct: spying upon a secret I would rather die than share it with any body's confidence. For this I cannot wish them well, I care not to see any of them again. If I am the Theme, I will not be the Friend of idle Gossips. Good gods what a shame it is our Loves should be so put into the microscope of a Coterie. Their laughs should not affect you (I may perhaps give you reasons some day for these laughs, for I suspect a few people to hate me well enough, for reasons I know of, who have pretended a great friendship for me) when in competition with one, who if he never should see you again would make you the saint of his memorry—These Laughers, who do not like you, who envy you for your Beauty, who would have God-bless'd-me from you for ever: who were plying me with disencouragements with respect to you eternally. People are revengeful—do not mind them—do nothing but love me—if I knew that for certain life and health will in such event be a heaven, and death itself will be less painful. I long to believe in immortality I shall never be ab<le> to bid you an entire farewell. If I am destined to be happy with you here—how short is the longest Life—I wish to believe in immortality—I wish to live with you for ever. Do not let my name ever pass between you and those laughers, if I have no other merit than the great Love for you, that were sufficient to keep me sacred and unmentioned in such society. If I have been cruel and injust I swear my love has ever been greater than my cruelty which last[s] but a minute whereas my Love come what will shall last for ever If concessions to me has hurt your Pride, god knows I have had little pride in my heart when thinking of you. Your

1 *My friends . . . them*: This was certainly true of the Reynolds sisters among others.

name never passes my Lips—do not let mine pass yours—Those People do not like me. After ~~writing~~ realing [*for* reading] my Letter you even then wish to see me. I am strong enough to walk over—but I dare not. I shall feel so much pain in parting with you again. My dearest love, I am affraid to see you, I am strong but not strong enough to see you. Will my arm be ever round you again. And if so shall I be obliged to leave you again. My sweet Love! I am happy whilst I believe your first Letter. Let me but be certain that you are mine heart and soul, and I could die more happily than I could otherwise live. If you think me cruel—if you think I have sleighted you—do muse it over again and see into my heart—My Love to you is "true as truth's simplicity and simpler than the infancy of truth"[1] as I think I once said before How could I slight you? How threaten to leave you? not in the spirit of a Threat to you—no—but in the spirit of Wretchedness in myself. My fairest, my delicious, my angel Fanny! do not believe me such a vulgar fellow. I will be as patient in illness and as believing in Love as I am able—

Yours for ever my dearest
John Keats—

To John Taylor
11 (?) June 1820

[Harvard MS]

[2 Wesleyan Place, Sunday]

My dear Taylor,

In reading over the proof of St Agnes' Eve since I left Fleet Street I was struck with what appears to me an alteration in the 7th Stanza very much for the worse: the passage I mean stands thus

"her maiden eyes incline
Still on the floor, while many a sweeping train
Pass by—"

1 *true as . . . of truth*: *Troilus and Cressida*, III. ii. 165–6.

Twas originally written

> "her maiden eyes divine
> Fix'd on the floor saw many a sweeping train
> Pass by—"

My meaning is quite destroyed in the alteration. I do not use train for concourse of passers by but for ~~Skits~~ Skirts sweeping along the floor—In the first Stanza my copy reads—2nd line

> "bitter chill it was"

to avoid the echo cold in the next line.

ever yours sincerely
John Keats

To Charles Brown
c. 16 June 1820[1]

[Brown transcript (1836–40)]

[2 Wesleyan Place, Friday]

My dear Brown,

I have only been to x x x's once since you left, when x x x x[2] could not find your letters. Now this is bad of me. I should, in this instance, conquer the great aversion to breaking up my regular habits, which grows upon me more and more. True I have an excuse in the weather, which drives one from shelter to shelter in any little excursion. I have not heard from George. My book[3] is coming out with very low hopes, though not spirits on my part. This shall be my last trial; not succeeding, I shall try what I can do in the Apothecary line. When you hear from

1 Keats's account of the exhibition in Pall Mall, coupled with his mention of the adverse weather, which was unsettled from 12–16 June, gives a more precise date than Rollins's 'about 21 June'.

2 *x x x's . . . x x x x*: Possibly the Dilkes, but Gittings thinks the Brawnes and Abigail O'Donaghue (Brown's housekeeper and mistress) are intended.

3 *My book*: (Brown's note) 'Lamia, Isabella, The eve of Saint Agnes, and other poems.'

or see x x x x x x[1] it is probable you will hear some complaints against me, which this notice is not intended to forestall. The fact is I did behave badly; but it is to be attributed to my health, spirits, and the disadvantageous ground I stand on in society. I would go and accommodate matters, if I were not too weary of the world. I know that they are more happy and comfortable than I am; therefore why should I trouble myself about it? I foresee I shall know very few people in the course of a year or two. Men get such different habits, that they become as oil and vinegar to one another. Thus far I have a consciousness of having been pretty dull and heavy, both in subject and phrase; I might add, enigmatical. I am in the wrong, and the world is in the right, I have no doubt. Fact is, I have had so many kindnesses done me by so many people, that I am cheveaux-de-frised with benefits, which I must jump over or break down. I met x x x[2] in town a few days ago, who invited me to supper to meet Wordsworth, Southey, Lamb, Haydon, and some more; I was too careful of my health to risk being out at night. Talking of that, I continue to improve slowly, but, I think, surely. All the talk at present x x x x x x x x There is a famous exhibition in Pall Mall[3] of the old english portraits by Vandyck and Holbein, Sir Peter Lely and the great Sir Godfrey. Pleasant countenances predominate; so I will mention two or three unpleasant ones. There is James the first,—whose appearance would disgrace a "Society for the suppression of women;" so very squalid, and subdued to nothing he looks. Then, there is old Lord Burleigh, the high priest of economy, the political save-all, who has the appearance of a Pharisee just rebuffed by a gospel bon-mot. Then, there is George the second, very like an unintellectual Voltaire, troubled with the gout and a bad temper. Then, there is young Devereux, the favourite, with every appearance of as slang a boxer as any in the court;

1 *x x x x x x*: Rollins suggests the newly married Bailey; Gittings suggests the Dilkes.

2 *x x x*: Probably Thomas Monkhouse.

3 *exhibition in Pall Mall*: The exhibition at the British Institution, Pall Mall, opened on 15 June.

his face is cast in the mould of blackguardism with jockey-plaster. x x x x x I shall soon begin upon Lucy Vaughan Lloyd.[1] I do not begin composition yet, being willing, in case of a relapse, to have nothing to reproach myself with. I hope the weather will give you the slip; let it show itself, and steal out of your company.[2] x x x x x x When I have sent off this, I shall write another to some place about fifty miles in advance of you.

Good morning to you.
Your's ever sincerely,
John Keats.

Maria Gisborne (1770–1837), a friend of Shelley and Godwin, reported that Keats 'burst a blood vessel' in the night of 22 June 'and in order to be well attended, he had been removed [on 23 June] from his lodgings in the neighbourhood to Mr. Hunt's.'

To Fanny Keats
23 June 1820

[British Library MS]

[13 Mortimer Terrace]
Friday Morn—

My dear Fanny,

I had intended to delay seeing you till a Book which I am now publishing was out, expecting that to be the end of this Week[3] when I would have brought it to Walthamstow: on receiving your Letter of course I set myself to come to town,

1 Lucy Vaughan Lloyd: i.e., 'The Jealousies' (see above, p. 468).
2 *show itself . . . company*: *Much Ado about Nothing*, III. iii. 53–55.
3 *a Book . . . this Week*: Taylor and Hessey advertised *Lamia, Isabella, The Eve of St Agnes, and Other Poems* as 'just published' in the *Morning Chronicle* the following Monday, 26 June, and again on Friday, 30 June.

but was not able for just as I was setting out yesterday morning a slight spitting of blood came on which returned rather more copiously at night. I have slept well and they tell me there is nothing material to fear. I will send my Book soon with a Letter which I have had from George who is with his family quite well.

Your affectionate Brother
John—

To Fanny Brawne
25 (?) June 1820[1]

[Harvard MS]

[13 Mortimer Terrace, Sunday]

My dearest Girl,

I endeavour to make myself as patient as possible. Hunt amuses me very kindly—besides I have your ring on my finger[2] and your flowers on the table. I shall not expect to see you yet because it would be so much pain to part with you again. When the Books you want came [*for* come] you shall have them. I am very well this afternoon. My dearest[3]

* * *

On 30 June Keats received advance copies of Lamia, Isabella, The Eve of St Agnes, and Other Poems. *It was published about this time.*

1 Rollins dates 'June (?) 1820', but as he notes 'the tone suggests a very recent removal', making 24 or 25 June 'a plausible guess'.
2 *your ring . . . finger*: See above, p. 509.
3 Signature cut away.

To Fanny Brawne
4 July (?) 1820

[Harvard MS]

[13 Mortimer Terrace]
Tuesday Af^{tn}

My dearest Fanny,

For this Week past I have been employed in marking the most beaututiful [*for* beautiful] passages in Spenser, intending it for you, and comforting myself in being somehow occupied to give you however small a pleasure. It has lightened my time very much. I am much better. God bless you.

Your affectionate
J. Keats

To Fanny Keats
5 July 1820

[British Library MS]

Mortimer Terrace
Wednesday

My dear Fanny,

I have had no return of the spitting of blood, and for two or three days have been getting a little stronger. I have no hopes of an entire reestablishment of my health under some months of patience. My Physician[1] tells me I must contrive to pass the Winter in Italy. This is all very unfortunate for us—we have no recourse but patience, which I am now practicing better than ever I thought it possible for me. I have this moment received a Letter from Mr Brown, dated Dunvegan Castle, Island of Skye.

1 *My Physician*: Dr George Darling (1779/80–1862) was the physician and friend of artists, among them Haydon. His opinion was supported by Dr William Lambe (1765–1847), physician and vegetarian.

He is very well in health and Spirits. My new publication has been out for some days and I have directed a Copy to be bound for you, which you will receive shortly.[1] No one can regret M[r] Hodgkinson's ill fortune: I must own illness has not made such a Saint of me as to prevent my rejoicing at his reverse. Keep yourself in as good hopes as possible; in case my illness should continue an unreasonable time many of my friends would I trust for my Sake do all in their power to console and amuse you, at the least word from me—You may depend upon it that in case my strength returns I will do all in my power to extricate you from the Abbies. Be above all things careful of your health which is the corner stone of all pleasure.

Your affectionate Brother
John—

To Fanny Keats
22 July 1820

[British Library MS]

[13 Mortimer Terrace, Saturday]

My dear Fanny,

I have been gaining Strength for some days: it would be well if I could at the same time say I [am] gaining hopes of a speedy recovery. My constitution has suffered very much for two or three years past, so as to be scar[c]ely able to make head against illness, which the natural activity and impatience of my Mind renders more dangerous—It will at all events be a very tedious affair, and you must expect to hear very little alteration of any sort in me for some time You ought to have received a copy of my Book ten days ago I shall send another message to the Booksellers. One of the M[r] Wylies will be here to day or to morrow when I will ask him to send you George's Letter. Writing the smallest note is so anoying to me that I have waited till I shall see him. M[r] Hunt does every thing in his power to make

1 *a Copy . . . shortly*: Fanny's copy, with no inscription, is at Harvard.

the time pass as agreeably with me as possible. I read the greatest part of the day, and generally take two half hour walks a day up and down the terrace which is very much pester'd with cries, ballad singers, and street music. We have been so unfortunate for so long a time, every event has been of so depressing a nature that I must persuade myself to think some change will take place in the aspect of our affairs. I shall be upon the look out for a trump card—

Your affectionate
Brother. John—

To Fanny Brawne
August (?) 1820

[Berg MS]

[13 Mortimer Terrace]

I do not write this till the last, that no eye may catch it.[1]

My dearest Girl,
I wish you could invent some means to make me happy at all without you. Every hour I am more and more concentrated in you; every thing else tastes like chaff in my Mouth. I feel it almost impossible to go to Italy—the fact is, I cannot leave you, and shall never taste one minute's content until it pleases chance to let me live with you for good. But I will not go on at this rate. A person in health as you are can have no conception of the horrors that nerves and a temper like mine go through. What Island do your friends propose retiring to? I should be happy to go with you there alone, but in company I should object to it; the backbitings and jealousies of new colonists

1 *I do not . . . catch it*: As HBF reports, Keats wrote the letter and then added this sentence and the words 'My dearest Girl', which is in darker ink. 'Obviously written in Hunt's crowded house where privacy was impossible, it appears to be the last letter to Fanny Brawne yet found, probably the last ever written' (Rollins).

who have nothing else to amuse them selves, is unbearable. M[r] Dilke came to see me yesterday, and gave me a very great deal more pain than pleasure. I shall never be able any more to endure to [*for* the] society of those who used to meet at Elm Cottage and Wentworth Place. The last two years taste like brass upon my Palate. If I cannot live with you I will live alone. I do not think my health will improve much while I am separated from you. For all this I am averse to seeing you—I cannot bear flashes of light and return into my glooms again. I am not so unhappy now as I should be if I had seen you yesterday. To be happy with you seems such an impossibility! it requires a luckier Star than mine! it will never be. I enclose a passage from one of your Letters which I want you to alter a little[1]—I want (if you will have it so) the matter express'd less coldly to me. If my health would bear it, I could write a Poem which I have in my head, which would be a consolation for people in such a situation as mine. I would show some one in Love as I am, with a person living in such Liberty as you do. Shakspeare always sums up matters in the most sovereign manner. Hamlet's heart was full of such Misery as mine is when he said to Ophelia "Go to a Nunnery, go, go!"[2] Indeed I should like to give up the matter at once—I should like to die. I am sickened at the brute world which you are smiling with. I hate men and women more. I see nothing but thorns for the future—wherever I may be next winter in Italy or nowhere Brown will be living near you with his indecencies[3]—I see no prospect of any rest. Suppose me in Rome—well, I should there see you as in a magic glass going to and from town at all hours,———I wish I could infuse a little confidence in human nature into my heart. I cannot muster any—the world is too brutal for me—I am glad there is such a thing as the grave—I am sure I shall never have any rest till I get there At any rate I will indulge myself by never seeing any more Dilke or Brown or any of their Friends. I wish

1 *I enclose . . . alter a little*: There are no signs of any enclosure.

2 *Go . . . go*: *Hamlet*, III. i. 121, 129–30.

3 *his indecencies*: Brown's son Carlino, by his Irish housekeeper Abigail O'Donaghue, had been born on 16 July 1820, while he was in Scotland.

I was either in your a[r]ms full of faith or that a Thunder bolt would strike me.

God bless you—J. K—

On Saturday, 12 August a note from Fanny Brawne, which had been delivered the previous Thursday, was finally given to Keats by Hunt's son Thornton. Its seal had been accidentally broken: Keats was so upset by this mischance that he 'wept for several hours' and, despite Hunt's entreaties, left Mortimer Terrace precipitately. That evening Keats was taken in by Mrs Brawne at Wentworth Place. He stayed there for a month, nursed by her and by Fanny Brawne until he left for Italy.

To Fanny Keats
13 August 1820

[British Library MS]

Wentworth Place [Sunday]

My dear Fanny,

'T is a long time since I received your last. An accident of an unpleasant nature occured at Mr Hunt's and prevented me from answering you, that is to say made me nervous. That you may not suppose it worse I will mention that some one of Mr Hunt's household opened a Letter of mine—upon which I immediately left Mortimer Terrace, with the intention of taking to Mrs Bentley's again; fortunately I am not in so lone a situation, but am staying a short time with Mrs Brawne who lives in the House which was Mrs Dilke's. I am excessively nervous: a person I am not quite used to entering the room half choaks me—'T is not yet Consumption I believe, but it would be were I to remain in this climate all the Winter: so I am thinking of either voyageing or travelling to Italy. Yesterday I received an invitation from Mr Shelley, a Gentleman residing at Pisa, to spend the Winter with him: if I go I must be away in a Month or even less. I am glad you like the Poems, you must hope with me th<at> time and health with pro<duce> you some more.

This is the first morning I have been able to sit to the paper and have many Letters to write if I can manage them. God bless you my dear Sister.

Your affectionate Brother
John—

To John Taylor
13 August 1820

[Morgan MS]

Wentworth Place
Sat^{y} [*for* Sunday] Morn.[1]

My dear Taylor,

My Chest is in so nervous a State, that any thing extra such as speaking to an unaccostomed Person or writing a Note half suffocates me. This Journey to Italy wakes me at daylight every morning and haunts me horribly. I shall endeavour to go though it be with the sensation of marching up against a Battery. The first spep [*for* step] towards it is to know the expense of a Journey and a years residence: which if you will ascertain for me and let me know early you will greatly serve me. I have more to say but must desist for every line I write encreases the tightness of the Chest, and I have many more to do. I am convinced that this sort of thing does not continue for nothing—If you can come with any of our friends do.

Your sincere friend
John Keats—

1 Date from postmark. Keats's error.

To Leigh Hunt

13 (?) August 1820

[Berg MS]

(An Amyntas)[1]

Wentworth Place [Sunday]

My dear Hunt,

You will be glad to hear I am going to delay a little time at M[rs] Brawnes. I hope to see you whenever you can get time for I feel really attach'd to you for your many sympathies with me, and patience at my lunes.[2] Will you send by the Bearess Lucy Vaughn Lloyd:[3] My best rem[cs] to M[rs] Hunt—

Your affectionate frien<d>
John Keats

Written in the morning: Hunt replied by return, promising to visit Keats that afternoon '& most probably every day . . . I need not say how you gratify me by the impulse which led you to write a particular sentence in your letter, for you must by now have seen by this time how much I am attached to yourself' (L, II, p. 317).

1 *An Amyntas*: Keats self-mockingly takes on the role of the lovesick protagonist in Hunt's very recently published *Amyntas, a Tale of the Woods; from the Italian of Torquato Tasso* (1820), which Hunt had dedicated to Keats, comparing him with Tasso.

2 *lunes*: In *The Winter's Tale*, II. ii. 30, Leonte's jealousy is described as 'lunes': Keats is apologizing for his irrational behaviour at Hunt's house.

3 *the Bearess Lucy Vaughn Lloyd*: The note was probably delivered by Fanny Brawne ('the Bearess'). In his haste Keats had evidently left behind the MS of 'The Jealousies' by 'Lucy Vaughan Lloyd' (see above, p. 468).

To John Taylor
14 August 1820

[Morgan MS]

Wentworth Place [Monday]

My dear Taylor—

I do not think I mentioned any thing of a Passage to Leghorn by Sea. Will you join that to your enquiries, and, if you can, give a peep at the Birth [*for* Berth], if the Vessel is in our river?

Your sincere friend
John Keats
over

P.S. Some how a Copy of Chapman's Homer, lent to me by Haydon, has disappeared from my Lodgings[1]—it has quite flown I am affraid, and Haydon urges the return of it so that I must get one at Longman's and send it to Lisson grove—or you must—or as I have given you a job on the River—ask Mistessey.[2] I had written a Note to this effect to Hessey some time since but crumpled it up in hopes that the Book might come to Light. This morning Haydon has sent another messen<ger.> The Copy was in good condition, with the head[3]—Damn all thieves! Tell Woodhouse I have not lost his Blackwood

[Endorsement by Taylor:]

Inclosed in this Letter I receved a Testamentary Paper in John Keats's Handwriting without Date on which I have indorsed a Memorandum to this Effect for the purpose of identifying it, & for better Security it is here unto annexed

John Taylor

22 Sep 1820

1 *my Lodgings*: Keats is referring to his lodgings in 2 Wesleyan Place, not the Brawnes' or Hunt's house.
2 *Mistessey*: Mr Hessey.
3 *with the head*: The frontispiece of *The Whole Works of Homer* (1616) is an engraved portrait of Chapman. Taylor was able to purchase a replacement for Haydon (*L*, II, pp. 320, 326 n).

[The Testament]

My Chest of Books divide among my friends—

In the case of my death this scrap of Paper may be serviceable in your possession.

All my estate real and personal consists in the hopes of the sale of books publish'd or unpublish'd. Now I wish Brown and you to be the first paid Creditors—the rest is in nubibus—but in case it should shower pay my Taylor the few pounds I owe him.

[Endorsed by Taylor:]

NB On the 14th August or the 15th 1820 I received this paper which is in John Keats's Handwriting inclosed in the annexed Letter which came by the 3dy Post 22 Sept 1820

John Taylor

To Charles Brown
14 August 1820

[Brown transcript (1836–40)]

[Wentworth Place, Monday]

My dear Brown,

You may not have heard from x x x x or x x x x, or in any way, that a spitting of blood, and all its weakening consequences, has prevented me from writing for so long a time. I have matter now for a very long letter, but not news; so I must cut every thing short. I shall make some confession, which you will be the only person, for many reasons, I shall trust with. A winter in England would, I have not a doubt, kill me; so I have resolved to go to Italy, either by sea or land. Not that I have any great hopes of that,—for, I think, there is a core of disease in me not easy to pull out. x x x x x x x x x x x x x x x x x[1] If I should die x x x x x I shall

1 *x x x x x x x x x x x x x x x x x*: (Brown's note) 'The omitted passage contained the secret. He went to Italy in pursuance of his physician's urgent advice.' The 'secret' was 'No doubt of his engagement to Fanny Brawne' (Rollins). However, Gittings thinks that Keats may refer 'to some more secret physical or medical cause' (*John Keats*, p. 589).

be obliged to set off in less than a month. Do not, my dear Brown, tease yourself about me. You must fill up your time as well as you can, and as happily. You must think of my faults[1] as lightly as you can. When I have health I will bring up the long arrears of letters I owe you. x x x x x x My book has had a good success among literary people, and, I believe, has a moderate sale.[2] I have seen very few people we know. x x x has visited me more than any one. I would go to x x x x x and make some inquiries after you, if I could with any bearable sensation; but a person I am not quite used to causes an oppression on my chest. Last week I received a letter from Shelley, at Pisa, of a very kind nature, asking me to pass the winter with him. Hunt has behaved very kindly to me. You shall hear from me again shortly.

Your affectionate friend,
John Keats.

To P. B. Shelley
16 August 1820[3]

[Bodleian Library MS]

Hampstead [Wednesday] August 16th

My dear Shelley,

I am very much gratified that you, in a foreign country, and with a mind almost over occupied, should write to me in the strain of the Letter beside me. If I do not take advantage of your invitation it will be prevented by a circumstance I have

1 *my faults*: (Brown's note) 'Sixteen years have not changed my opinion. I thought then, and I think now, he had no fault. On the faulty side he was scarcely human.'

2 *a good success . . . moderate sale*: Keats is repeating what he had heard from his publisher. On the same day (14 August) John Taylor told John Clare, 'We have some Trouble to get through 500 Copies of [Keats's] Work, though it is highly spoken of in the periodical Works' (Edmund Blunden, *Keats's Publisher: A Memoir of John Taylor (1781–1864)* (London : Jonathan Cape, 1936), pp. 111–12). By that time half the reviews were out, most of which were positive.

3 This very carefully written out letter looks like a fair copy.

very much at heart to prophesy[1]—There is no doubt that an english winter would put an end to me, and do so in a lingering hateful manner, therefore I must either voyage or journey to Italy as a soldier marches up to a battery. My nerves at present are the worst part of me, yet they feel soothed when I think that come what extreme may, I shall not be destined to remain in one spot long enough to take a hatred of any four particular bed-posts. I am glad you take any pleasure in my poor Poem;[2]—which I would willingly take the trouble to unwrite, if possible, did I care so much as I have done about Reputation. I received a copy of the Cenci,[3] as from yourself from Hunt. There is only one part of it I am judge of; the Poetry, and dramatic effect, which by many spirits now a days is considered the mammon. A modern work it is said must have a purpose, which may be the God—<u>an artist</u> must serve Mammon[4]—he must have "self concentration" selfishness perhaps. You I am sure will forgive me for sincerely remarking that you might curb your magnanimity and be more of an artist, and 'load every rift' of your subject with ore.[5] The thought of such discipline must fall like cold chains upon you, who perhaps never sat with your wings furl'd for six Months together. And is not this extraordina[r]y talk for the writer of Endymion? whose mind was like a pack of scattered cards—I am pick'd up and sorted to a pip. My Imagination is a Monastry and I am its Monk—you must explain my metap[cs][6] to yourself. I am in expectation of Prometheus

1 *a circumstance . . . prophesy*: 'That is, presumably by his death' (Rollins).
2 *you take . . . poor Poem*: In his letter of 27 July Shelley had written 'I have lately read your Endymion again & ever with a new sense of the treasures of poetry it contains, though treasures poured forth with indistinct profusion—This, people in general will not endure, & that is the cause of the comparatively few copies which have been sold.—I feel persuaded that you are capable of the greatest things, so but you will' (*L*, II, p. 311).
3 *the Cenci*: Shelley had asked his publishers to send Keats a copy of *The Cenci: A Tragedy in Five Acts* (1819) through Hunt. Fanny Brawne owned Keats's (now lost) marked-up copy.
4 *God . . . Mammon*: Matthew 6:24, Luke 16:13.
5 *load every rift . . . ore*: *The Faerie Queene*, II. vii. 28, line 5, 'with rich metal loaded every rifte'.
6 *metap[cs]*: Metaphysics (not an abbreviation for 'metaphor').

every day. Could I have my own wish for its interest effected you would have it still in manuscript—or be but now putting an end to the second act. I remember you advising me not to publish my first-blights, on Hampstead heath—I am returning advice upon your hands. Most of the Poems in the volume I send you have been written above two years,[1] and would never have been publish'd but from a hope of gain; so you see I am inclined enough to take your advice now. I must exp[r]-ess once more my deep sense of your kindness, adding my sincere thanks and respects for Mrs Shelley.[2] In the hope of soon seeing you <I> remain

most sincerely <yours,>

John Keats—

To Charles Brown

August (?) 1820

[Brown transcript (1836–40)]

[Wentworth Place]

My dear Brown,

x x x x x x x[3] I ought to be off at the end of this week, as the cold winds blow begin to blow towards evening;—but I will wait till I have your answer to this. I am to be introduced, before I set out, to a Dr Clarke,[4] a physician settled at Rome, who promises to befriend me in every way at Rome. The sale of

1 *above two years*: An exaggeration.

2 *I must . . . Mrs Shelley*: C. C. Clarke reported that Keats's said 'his sole motive' for turning down the invitation was that he could not be 'a free agent, even within such a circle as Shelley's' (*Recollections*, p. 151).

3 *x x x x x x x*: (Brown's note) 'The commencement is a continuation of the secret in his former letter, ending with a request that I would accompany him to Italy.' Brown later explained his refusal to do so: 'I contented myself with preparing to follow him very early in the spring, and not return, should he prefer to live there.' (In the event, Brown moved to Italy in summer 1822 and lived there for twelve years before emigrating to New Zealand.)

4 *Dr Clarke*: Dr (later Sir) James Clark (1788–1870), who moved to Rome in 1819, found Keats rooms at the Piazza di Spagna 26, opposite his own house. He later returned to London and became Queen Victoria's physician.

my book is very slow, though it has been very highly rated. One of the causes, I understand from different quarters, of the unpopularity of this new book, and the others also, is the offence the ladies take at me. On thinking that matter over, I am certain that I have said nothing in a spirit to displease any woman I would care to please: but still there is a tendency to class women in my books with roses and sweetmeats—they never see themselves dominant.[1] If ever I come to publish "Lucy Vaughan Lloyd", there will be some delicate picking for squeamish stomachs. I will say no more, but, waiting in anxiety for your answer, doff my hat, and make a purse as long as I can.

Your affectionate friend,
John Keats.

To Fanny Keats
23 August 1820

[British Library MS]

Wentworth Place
Wednesday Morning

My dear Fanny,

It will give me great Pleasure to see you here, if you can contrive it; though I confess I should have written instead of calling upon you before I set off on my journey, from the wish of avoiding unpleasant partings. Meantime I will just notice some parts of your Letter. The Seal-breaking business is over blown—I think no more of it. A few days ago I wrote to Mr Brown, asking him to befriend me with his company to Rome. His answer is not yet come, and I do not know when it will, not being certain how far he may be from the Post Office to which my communication is addressed. Let us hope he will go with me. George certainly ought to have written to you: his troubles, anxieties and fatigues are not quite a sufficient excuse. In the course of time you will be sure to find that this neglect, is not

1 *women . . . dominant*: (Brown's note rejects this criticism of Keats's poetry).

forgetfulness. I am sorry to hear you have been so ill and in such low spirits. Now you are better, keep so. Do not suffer Your Mind to dwell on unpleasant reflections—that sort of thing has been the destruction of my health—Nothing is so bad as want of health—it makes one envy Scavengers and Cinder-sifters. There are enough real distresses and evils in wait for every one to try the most vigorous health. Not that I would say yours are not real—but they are such as to tempt you to employ your imagination on them, rather than endeavour to dismiss them entirely. Do not diet your mind with grief, it destroys the constitution; but let your chief care be of your health, and with that you will meet with your share of Pleasure in the world—do not doubt it. If I return well from Italy I will turn over a new leaf for you. I have been improving lately, and have very good hopes of 'turning a Neuk"[1] and cheating the Consumption. I am not well enough to write to George myself—Mr Haslam will do it for me, to whom I shall write to day, desiring him to mention as gently as possible your complaint—I am my dear Fanny

Your affectionate Brother
John.

*Later that day Keats wrote to Haslam to say 'if I can manage it I certainly intend going speedily to Rome' and asking him to write giving the news to George in America, mentioning that 'Fanny complains sadly of not hearing from him.' He also asked Haslam to write to Mrs Wylie and her family in London on his behalf, and mentioned that he had written to Richard Abbey 'for some Money which he promised to lend me in case George did not remit part of the loan from me'. Keats was to be disappointed. Abbey replied on the very day Keats wrote to Haslam, saying, 'It is . . . not in my power to lend you any thing' (*L, II, pp. 330–31*).*

A week later, on Wednesday, 30 August, Taylor heard that Keats had suffered another haemorrhage and was 'in a very dangerous state' (L, I, p. 60). The next letter, written twelve days later, was dictated by Keats to Fanny Brawne. It is in her hand, including the signature.

1 *turning a Neuk*: i.e., 'turned a corner' (Burns's 'To Miss Ferrier', l. 15).

To Fanny Keats

11 September 1820[1]

[Rollins transcript]

[Wentworth Place]
Monday Morn[g]

My dear Fanny,

In the hope of entirely re-establishing my health I shall leave England for Italy this week and, of course I shall not be able to see you before my departure. It is not illness that prevents me from writing but as I am recommended to avoid every sort of fatigue I have accepted the assistance of a friend,[2] who I have desired to write to you when I am gone and to communicate any intelligence she may hear of me. I am as well as I can expect and feel very impatient to get on board as the sea air is expected to be of great benefit to me. My present intention is to stay some time at Naples and then to proceed to Rome where I shall find several friends or at least several acquaintances. At any rate it will be a relief to quit this cold; wet, uncertain climate. I am not very fond of living in cities but there will be too much to amuse me, as soon as I am well enough to go out, to make me feel dull. I have received your parcel and intend to take it with me. You shall hear from me as often as possible, if I feel too tired to write myself I shall have some friend to do it for me; I have not yet heard from George nor can I expect to receive any letters from him before I leave

Your affectionate brot<her>
John—

1 When Fanny Keats finally allowed HBF to publish her brother's letters in 1883 she kept back this, Keats's last letter to her, together with his 'confirmation' letter of 31 March 1819. She held onto them until her death in 1890. They were first published in 1934.

2 *a friend*: Fanny Brawne.

As yet no travelling companion for Keats had been found. The following day Haslam asked Joseph Severn to undertake this demanding task. Fortunately he agreed, and Taylor booked 'a second passage <u>*for*</u> *Keats' Friend Severn'. Haslam stayed overnight at Wentworth Place, and reported 'Keats seems comfortable & well at ease.' The next day, Wednesday, 13 September, Fanny Brawne pencilled 'Mr Keats left Hampstead' in the copy of the* Literary Pocket Book *he had given her. That night Keats stayed with Taylor in Fleet Street while waiting for his passage to Italy on the* Maria Crowther, *then 'lying off the Tower'* (L, *II, pp. 333–4). Taylor, with help from others, had arranged for £150 to be available to Keats through a Rome banking firm. In return Keats assigned his copyrights in* Poems *(1817),* Endymion *and the* Lamia *volume to Taylor and Hessey's firm for £200 on 16 September. The next morning, Sunday, 17 September, Keats boarded the* Maria Crowther *at London Dock and was seen off by Taylor, Haslam and Woodhouse, who accompanied him and Severn as far as Gravesend.*

18 September 1820 to 23 February 1821 The *Maria Crowther* and Italy

Keats set sail the next day, but the ship ran into severe storms off Brighton and after ten days of discomfort had only managed to get as far as Portsmouth, where they landed on 28 September. Keats and Severn were able to spend the day and night with Keats's and Brown's friends the Snooks at Bedhampton, before setting sail once more, but still into contrary winds. While with the Snooks Keats learnt that Brown, who cut short his Scottish holiday to see Keats off to Italy but had not reached London in time, was visiting Dilke's parents in nearby Chichester.

To Charles Brown
30 September 1820

[Harvard MS]

Saturday Sept[r] 28 [*for* 30][1]
Maria Crowther
off Yarmouth isle
of wight—

My dear Brown,

The time has not yet come for a pleasant Letter from me. I have delayed writing to you from time to time because I felt how impossible it was to enliven you with one heartening hope of my recovery; this morning in bed the matter struck me in a

1 Keats's error.

different manner; I thought I would write "while I was in some liking"[1] or I might become too ill to write at all and then if the desire to have written should become strong it would be a great affliction to me. I have many more Letters to write and I bless my stars that I have begun, for time seems to press,—this may be my best opportunity. We are in a calm and I am easy enough this morning. If my spirits seem too low you may in some degree impute it to our having been at sea a fortmight [*for* fortnight] without making any way. I was very disappointed at not meeting you at bedhamption [*for* Bedhampton], and am very provoked at the thought of you being at Chichester to day. I should have delighted in setting off for London for the sensation merely—for what should I do there? I could not leave my lungs or stomach or other worse things behind me. I wish to write on subjects that will not agitate me much—there is one I must mention and have done with it. Even if my body would recover of itself, this would prevent it—The very thing which I want to live most for will be a great occasion of my death. I cannot help it. Who can help it? Were I in health it would make me ill, and how can I bear it in my state? I dare say you will be able to guess on what subject I am harping—you know what was my greatest pain during the first part of my illness at your house. I wish for death every day and night to deliver me from these pains, and then I wish death away, for death would destroy even those pains which are better than nothing. Land and Sea, weakness and decline are great seperators, but death is the great divorcer for ever. When the pang of this thought has passed through my mind, I may say the bitterness of death is passed. I often wish for you that you might flatter me with the best. I think without my mentioning it for my sake you would be a friend to Miss Brawne when I am dead. You think she has many faults—but, for my sake, think she has not one— —if there is any thing you can do for her by word or deed I know you will do it. I am in a state at present in which woman merely as woman can have no more power over me than stocks and stones, and yet the difference of my sensations with respect

1 *while . . . liking*: Falstaff in *1 Henry IV*, III. iii. 7.

To Mrs Frances Brawne
24 (?) October 1820

[Keats House MS]

Oct[r] 24[1] Naples Harbour—
care Giovanni

My dear M[rs] Brawne,

A few words will tell you what sort of a Passage we had, and what situation we are in, and few they must be on account of the Quarantine, our Letters being liable to be opened for the purpose of fumigation at the Health Office.[2] We have to remain in the vessel ten days and are, at present shut in a tier of ships. The sea air has been beneficial to me about to as great an extent as squally weather and bad accommodations and provisions has done harm—So I am about as I was—Give my Love to Fanny and tell her, if I were well there is enough in this Port of Naples to fill a quire of Paper—but it looks like a dream—every man who can row his boat and walk and talk seems a different being from myself—I do not feel in the world—It has been unfortunate for me that one of the Passengers is a young Lady in a Consumption—her imprudence has vexed me very much—the knowledge of her complaint—the flushings in her face, all her bad symptoms have preyed upon me—they would have done so had I been in good health. Severn now is a very good fellow but his nerves are too strong to be hurt by other peoples illnesses—I remember poor Rice wore me in the same way in the isle of wight—I shall feel a load off me when the Lady vanishes out of my sight. It is impossible to describe exactly in what state of health I am—at this moment I am suffering from indigestion very much, which makes such stuff of

1 Probably a mistake for Sunday, 22 October. The *Maria Crowther* entered the Bay of Naples on 21 October and Severn's letter to Haslam, to which Keats refers, is dated 22 October.

2 *fumigation . . . Office*: Their ship was quarantined for ten days because of an outbreak of typhus in London. Keats's letter is discoloured.

like as anything – O what a misery it is to have an intellect in splints! – My Love again to Fanny – tell Tootts I wish I could pitch her a basket of grapes – and tell Sam the fellows catch here with a line a little fish much like an anchovy, pull them up fast

Mrs Brawne
Wentworth Place
Hampstead Middx
England

F P O
NO.11
1820

Remember me to Mr and Mrs Dilke – mention to Brown that I wrote him a letter at Portsmouth which I did not send and am in doubt if he ever will see it.

my dear Mrs Brawne
yours sincerely and affectionate
John Keats –

Good bye Fanny! god bless you

8. *To Mrs Brawne, 24 (?) October 1820, p. 4, 26.6 × 20.2 cm. Keats's last words to Fanny Brawne, 'Good bye Fanny! god bless you'*

this Letter. I would always wish you to think me a little worse than I really am; not being of a sanguine disposition I am likely to succeed. If I do not recover your regret will be softened if I do your pleasure will be doubled—I dare not fix my Mind upon Fanny, I have not dared to think of her. The only comfort I have had that way has been in thinking for hours together of having the knife she gave me put in a silver-case—the hair in a Locket—and the Pocket Book in a gold net—Show her this. I dare say no more—Yet <you> must not believe I am so ill as this Letter may look for if ever there was a person born without the faculty of hoping I am he. Severn is writing to Haslam, and I have just asked him to request Haslam to send you his account of my health. O what an account I could give you of the Bay of Naples if I could once more feel myself a Citizen of this world—I feel a Spirit in my Brain would lay it forth pleasantly—O what a misery it is to have an intellect in splints! My Love again to Fanny—tell Tootts[1] I wish I could pitch her a basket of grapes—and tell Sam the fellows catch here with a line a little fish much like an anchovy, pull them up fast Remember me to Mrs and Mr Dilke—mention to Brown that I wrote him a letter at Port[s]mouth which I did not send and am in doubt if he will ever see it.

my dear Mrs Brawne
yours sincerely and affectionate
John Keats—

Good bye Fanny! god bless you[2]

1 *Tootts*: Nickname for Margaret, Fanny's younger sister aged eleven. Sam(uel), her brother, was sixteen.

2 *Good bye . . . bless you*: Crammed in at the very bottom of the letter in smaller writing.

To Charles Brown
1,2 November 1820

[Brown transcript (1836–40)]

Naples. Wednesday first in November.

My dear Brown,

Yesterday we were let out of Quarantine, during which my health suffered more from bad air and a stifled cabin than it had done the whole voyage. The fresh air revived me a little, and I hope I am well enough this morning to write to you a short calm letter;—if that can be called one, in which I am afraid to speak of what I would the fainest dwell upon. As I have gone thus far into it, I must go on a little;—perhaps it may relieve the load of WRETCHEDNESS which presses upon me. The persuasion that I shall see her no more will kill me. I cannot q——[1] My dear Brown, I should have had her when I was in health, and I should have remained well. I can bear to die—I cannot bear to leave her. Oh, God! God! God! Every thing I have in my trunks that reminds me of her goes through me like a spear. The silk lining she put in my travelling cap scalds my head. My imagination is horribly vivid about her—I see her—I hear her. There is nothing in the world of sufficient interest to divert me from her a moment. This was the case when I was in England; I cannot recollect, without shuddering, the time that I was prisoner at Hunt's, and used to keep my eyes fixed on Hampstead all day. Then there was a good hope of seeing her again—Now!—O that I could be buried near where she lives! I am afraid to write to her—to receive a letter from her—to see her hand writing would break my heart—even to hear of her any how, to see her name written would be more than I can bear. My dear Brown, what am I to do? Where

1 *I cannot q——* : (Brown's note) 'He could not go on with this sentence, nor even write the word "quit",—as I suppose. The word WRETCHEDNESS above he himself wrote in large characters.' Mee glosses 'q——' as 'probably "quiff"', a slang word for the sexual act.

can I look for consolation or ease? If I had any chance of recovery, this passion would kill me. Indeed through the whole of my illness, both at your house and at Kentish Town, this fever has never ceased wearing me out. When you write to me, which you will do immediately, write to Rome (poste restante)—if she is well and happy, put a mark thus +,—if—Remember me to all. I will endeavour to bear my miseries patiently. A person in my state of health should not have such miseries to bear. Write a short note to my sister, saying you have heard from me. Severn is very well. If I were in better health I should urge your coming to Rome. I fear there is no one can give me any comfort. Is there any news of George? O, that something fortunate had ever happened to me or my brothers!—then I might hope,—but despair is forced upon me as a habit. My dear Brown, for my sake, be her advocate for ever. I cannot say a word about Naples; I do not feel at all concerned in the thousand novelties around me. I am afraid to write to her. I should like her to know that I do not forget her. Oh, Brown, I have coals of fire in my breast. It surprised me that the human heart is capable of containing and bearing so much misery. Was I born for this end? God bless her, and her mother, and my sister, and George, and his wife, and you, and all!

Your ever affectionate friend,
John Keats.

Thursday. I was a day too early for the courier. He sets out now. I have been more calm to-day, though in a half dread of not continuing so. I said nothing of my health; I know nothing of it; you will hear Severn's account from x x x x x x.[1] I must leave off. You bring my thoughts too near to ——

God bless you!

Keats and Severn left Naples a week later and reached Rome on 15 November after a slow and uncomfortable journey in a hired carriage. The two men moved into the lodgings in the Piazza di Spagna secured by Dr James Clark, who lived

1 *x x x x x x*: Haslam.

opposite. Clark's initial diagnosis was that the 'chief part of [Keats's] disease . . . seems seated in his Stomach' with 'some suspicion of disease of the heart and it may be of the lungs', caused by 'mental exertions and application' (L, II, p. 358).

To Charles Brown
30 November 1820

[Brown transcript (1836–40)]

Rome. [Thursday] 30 November 1820

My dear Brown,

'Tis the most difficult thing in the world to me to write a letter. My stomach continues so bad, that I feel worse on opening any book,—yet I am much better than I was in Quarantine. Then I am afraid to encounter the proing and conning of any thing interesting to me in England. I have an habitual feeling of my real life having past, and that I am leading a posthumous existence. God knows how it would have been—but it appears to me—however, I will not speak of that subject. I must have been at Bedhampton nearly at the time you were writing to me from Chichester—how unfortunate—and to pass on the river too! There was my star predominant![1] I cannot answer any thing in your letter, which followed me from Naples to Rome, because I am afraid to look it over again. I am so weak (in mind) that I cannot bear the sight of any hand writing of a friend I love so much as I do you. Yet I ride the little horse,[2]—and, at my worst, even in Quarantine, summoned up more puns, in a sort of desperation, in one week than in any year of my life. There is one thought enough to kill me—I have been well, healthy, alert &c, walking with her—and now—the

1 *how unfortunate . . . star predominant*: Keats refers to Brown's failed attempt to see him off from the Thames, and echoes Leontes in the *Winter's Tale*, I. ii. 201–202, 'It is a bawdy planet, that will strike / Where 'tis predominant.'

2 *I ride . . . horse*: On Dr Clark's advice Keats went riding, often in company with Lieutenant Isaac Elton, also suffering from consumption.

knowledge of contrast, feeling for light and shade, all that information (primitive sense) necessary for a poem are great enemies to the recovery of the stomach. There, you rogue, I put you to the torture,—but you must bring your philosophy to bear—as I do mine, really—or how should I be able to live? Dr Clarke is very attentive to me; he says, there is very little the matter with my lungs, but my stomach, he says, is very bad. I am well disappointed in hearing good news from George,—for it runs in my head we shall all die young. I have not written to x x x x x[1] yet, which he must think very neglectful; being anxious to send him a good account of my health, I have delayed it from week to week. If I recover, I will do all in my power to correct the mistakes made during sickness; and if I should not, all my faults will be forgiven. I shall write to x x x[2] to-morrow, or next day. I will write to x x x x x[3] in the middle of next week. Severn is very well, though he leads so dull a life with me. Remember me to all friends, and tell x x x x[4] I should not have left London without taking leave of him, but from being so low in body and mind. Write to George as soon as you receive this, and tell him how I am, as far as you can guess;—and also a note to my sister—who walks about my imagination like a ghost—she is so like Tom. I can scarcely bid you good bye even in a letter. I always made an awkward bow.

God bless you!

John Keats.

This, the last letter Keats is known to have written, was received by Brown three weeks later on 21 December. By that time Keats had suffered a serious relapse on 9 and 10 December, vomiting blood. His condition continued to deteriorate and on 24 December his Italian landlady informed the police that Keats was dying of consumption. For the next two months he was nursed by Severn, whose letters to Brown, Haslam and

1 *x x x x x*: Haslam (Rollins guesses the omitted names).
2 *x x x*: Dilke (Rollins).
3 *x x x x x*: Woodhouse (Rollins).
4 *x x x x*: Reynolds (Rollins).

9. Joseph Severn, pen and ink sketch of Keats on his deathbed, with a partial list of their books, Rome 1821

Chronology of Keats's Life

1795 31 October, born at Swan and Hoop Livery Stables, Moorfields, London, the son of Thomas and Frances Keats.

1797 28 February, birth of George Keats.

1799 18 November, birth of Tom Keats.

1800 28 November, birth of Edward Keats (died 1802).

1802 Keats's grandfather John Jennings retires with his wife to Enfield, leaving the Livery Stables to be run by Thomas Keats.

1803 Becomes a boarder at John Clarke's Enfield Academy with his brother George. Tom joins them later.
3 June, birth of Fanny (Frances Mary) Keats.

1804 16 April, Thomas Keats dies after a riding accident.
27 June, Frances Keats marries William Rawlings. The children live with their grandparents in Enfield.

1805 8 March, John Jennings, grandfather, dies leaving a substantial fortune.

1806 Alice Jennings, their grandmother, moves to Edmonton with the children. Frances Keats leaves Rawlings, and does not rejoin her children until 1809.

1810 March, Frances Keats dies.
Mid-summer, Keats leaves Enfield Academy. In July Alice Jennings appoints Richard Abbey and John Sandell as the children's guardians.

1811 Keats is apprenticed to Thomas Hammond, surgeon and apothecary in Edmonton.

1814 Writes first extant poems.
December, grandmother dies.

1815 1 October, registers at Guy's Hospital as a student.

1816 3 March, entered as dresser to the surgeons at Guy's.
5 May, 'O Solitude', first published poem, signed J. K., published in Leigh Hunt's *Examiner*.

25 July, passes examination at Apothecaries' Hall, eligible to practice.
August–September, holiday in Margate with Tom Keats.
October, working as dresser at Guy's, meets Hunt, B. R. Haydon and J. H. Reynolds.
31 October, Keats's twenty-first birthday.
November, the Keats brothers move into 76 Cheapside.
1 December, Hunt publishes 'On First Looking into Chapman's Homer' in his article on 'Young Poets' in the *Examiner*. In this month Keats completes and decides to publish first volume.

1817 10 March, *Poems* published by C. and J. Ollier (who had advertised its forthcoming publication in the *Morning Chronicle*, 3 and 7 March). In March the brothers move to 1 Well Walk, Hampstead, and Keats meets C. W. Dilke, Charles Brown and Benjamin Bailey through Reynolds. Keats also meets John Taylor and his partner J. A. Hessey, who became his publishers.
14 April–August, leaves London for the Isle of Wight, Margate, Canterbury, and Hastings, before returning to Hampstead. Drafts *Endymion*, Book I and II.
September, stays with Bailey in Oxford, where he works on Book III.
October, returns to Hampstead, ill, and takes mercury.
28 November, first draft of *Endymion* completed at Burford Bridge.
December, meets William Wordsworth, attends Haydon's 'immortal dinner'. His brothers go to Teignmouth for Tom's health.

1818 January–February, revises *Endymion*, goes to the theatre and attends Hazlitt's lectures.
March–April, looks after Tom in Teignmouth, and writes 'Isabella; or, The Pot of Basil'.
early May, *Endymion* published, and Keats returns to London with Tom.
28 May, George marries Georgiana Wylie and plans to emigrate to America.
23 June, Keats says goodbye to George and his wife in Liverpool.
25 June–8 August, Keats's and Brown's Northern walking tour. Illness forces Keats to return early.
August–December, returns to Hampstead, nurses Tom, meets Fanny Brawne, and begins *Hyperion*. His *Poems* and

Endymion are savagely reviewed in *Blackwood's Magazine* and the *Quarterly Review*.
1 December, Tom Keats dies. Keats is invited by Brown to live with him at Wentworth Place.

1819 *c.* 18–31 (?) January, visits Chichester and Bedhampton, and drafts 'The Eve of St Agnes'.
February, back at Wentworth Place Keats suffers from a 'sore throat'. Writes 'The Eve of St Mark'.
21 April, drafts 'La Belle Dame sans Merci' in his letter to George and Georgiana Keats, and drafts 'Ode to Psyche' before 30 April.
May, writes 'Ode on a Grecian Urn', 'Ode to a Nightingale' and 'Ode on Melancholy'.
15 June, is 'much in want of Money'.
27 June, leaves London with James Rice, and stays in Shanklin. Begins to write 'Lamia' and work on *Otho the Great*.
July, continues work on 'Lamia' and *Otho the Great*. Brown arrives around 23 July. Works on *The Fall of Hyperion*. 'Ode to a Nightingale' published in *Annals of the Fine Arts*.
12 August, Keats and Brown leave Shanklin and take lodgings in Winchester, where Keats continues writing.
c. 7 September, Brown leaves Keats at their Winchester lodgings.
10–15 September, Keats rushes to London, where he sees Richard Abbey, his publishers, Richard Woodhouse, and his sister, but not Fanny Brawne. On 13 September watches Henry Hunt's triumphal entry to London. Returns to Winchester.
19 September, writes 'Ode to Autumn'.
21–22 September, has given up *The Fall of Hyperion*. Decides to write for the periodicals and live in Westminster.
October, Brown returns to Winchester, and *c.* 8 October they return to London. Keats lives briefly at 25 College Street, Westminster, before returning to lodge with Brown in Wentworth Place.
November–December, gives up *King Stephen*, begins the unfinished 'Cap and Bells; or, The Jealousies'.
20 December, *Otho the Great* accepted by Drury Lane.

1820 9 January, dines with George Keats, newly arrived in London.
28 January, George leaves for Liverpool on his way back to America.
January, 'Ode on a Grecian Urn' published in *Annals of the Fine Arts*.

3 February, that night Keats suffers a severe haemorrhage and is confined to the house by his doctors. Keats offers to break off his engagement to Fanny Brawne.
March, has several attacks of heart palpitations while revising his second volume, *Lamia, Isabella, The Eve of St Agnes, and Other Poems*.
27 April, by this time his publishers have the manuscripts for the *Lamia* volume.
4–7 May, moves to 2 Wesleyan Place, Kentish Town, close to Hunt.
10 May, 'La Belle Dame' published in Hunt's *Indicator*.
c. 11 June, correcting proofs of the *Lamia* volume.
22 June, has a severe haemorrhage, and goes to live at Hunt's home, 13 Mortimer Terrace.
30 June, receives advance copies of the *Lamia* volume, which is published soon after.
5 July, his physician has told him 'to pass the Winter in Italy.'
19 July, the *Lamia* volume praised by Lamb, followed by mixed reviews in August and September. Hunt publishes a positive account in the *Indicator* (2, 9 August).
12 August, leaves Hunt's house and is taken in at Wentworth Place by Mrs Brawne, where he stays until 12 September, nursed by her and by Fanny.
16 August, declines P. B. Shelley's invitation to stay with him in Italy.
16 September, assigns his copyrights to Taylor and Hessey.
17 September, boards the *Maria Crowther* for Italy with Joseph Severn as his companion.
21 October, arrives at Naples after a distressing voyage, and held in quarantine for ten days.
15 November, reaches Rome after a slow journey by carriage, and lodges in the Piazza di Spagna.
30 November, writes last known letter to Charles Brown.

1821 23 February, dies in the arms of Severn at 11 p.m.

Keats's Correspondents

Brief biographies of Keats's correspondents are provided below. Many of these are sufficiently well known to earn a place in the *Oxford Dictionary of National Biography* (*ODNB*), which should be consulted for fuller accounts.

Abbey, Richard (1765–1837) Guardian of the three Keats children. The children's grandmother Mrs John Jennings appointed Abbey, wholesale tea merchant, St Pancras Lane, and John Sandell, merchant, as their trustees in 1810, after their mother's death. Sandell died prematurely and was succeeded by a Mr Fry, who went to Holland. Abbey was left as sole trustee and the children's channel to any proceedings in Chancery concerning their inheritance until they came of age. From 1814 Fanny Keats was based with Abbey's family at his house, Pindars, Walthamstow. Only one note by Keats to Abbey is now extant (not included here), but Keats's recurrent negotiations with him over money matters and access to his sister were fraught.

Bailey, Benjamin (1791–1853) Future clergyman and author, and a friend of Reynolds since 1814. When Keats met him in spring 1817 Bailey was an undergraduate at Magdalen Hall, Oxford, and courting Reynolds's sister Marianne. Keats stayed with him in Oxford in September 1817, drafting *Endymion*. Bailey, who had aspirations as a poet, encouraged him to read Milton and Dante. The following summer Bailey published a defence of *Endymion* and was appointed to a curacy near Carlisle. Keats had thought him 'One of the noblest men alive', but his belief in Bailey's uprightness was undercut early in 1819 when Bailey suddenly became engaged to his bishop's daughter Hamilton Gleig. Bailey's career in the Church took him to England, France and Ceylon, where he became archdeacon.

Brawne, Fanny (Frances) (1800–65) Keats first met Fanny Brawne through the Dilkes, either in August 1818, immediately after returning from Scotland, or in late October or early November that year. Keats lived next door to her in April and June 1819, when her mother rented Dilke's half of Wentworth Place, and again from mid-October 1819 to May 1820 after he returned from the Isle of Wight and Winchester. They probably became privately engaged in June 1819, though Fanny later described Christmas Day 1818 as the happiest day of her life, and Keats told her 'the very first week I knew you I wrote myself your vassal'. Despite her liveliness and animation, some of Keats's friends, like the Reynolds and Dilke families, strongly disapproved of her relationship with Keats. However, Mrs Brawne gave their engagement her blessing, despite Keats's poor prospects, and took the desperately sick Keats into her house from August to early September 1820. There she and Fanny nursed him until he left for Italy. Fanny's letters to Keats's sister, Fanny, like her later comments on Keats himself, are those of an emotionally intelligent and strong-minded woman. In 1833 she married Louis Lindo(n), with whom she had three children. Until 1859 the family lived mainly on the Continent, before returning to London. (*ODNB*)

Brawne, Frances Ricketts (Mrs Samuel) (1778?–1829) Fanny Brawne's mother, a widow, had two younger children, Samuel (1804–28) and Margaret (1809–87), nicknamed 'Toots'. She rented Brown's half of Wentworth Place in summer 1818, while Keats and Brown were on their northern walk, and from around April 1819 rented the other half from Dilke. She and her family lived there until 1829, when she died after her dress accidentally caught fire.

Brown, Charles Armitage (1787–1842) After a brief career as a merchant in Russia, an inheritance of more than £10,000 enabled Brown to live modestly as a literary man. His comic opera *Narensky; or, The Road to Yaroslaf* (1814) brought him £300 and free admission to the Drury Lane Theatre. With Dilke, an old school friend, he bought half of Wentworth Place in 1815, which he rented out in the summers. Although he stood in for Reynolds as dramatic critic of the *Champion* in summer 1816, he seems to have met Keats when he was visiting the Dilkes the following year. He was a staunch friend of Keats, inviting him to live with him after Tom's death. In addition to travelling together through Scotland in 1818 the two men completed their tragedy *Otho the Great* the following year in hopes of a commercial success. Brown's affair with his housekeeper Abigail O'Donoghue in autumn 1819 must have been evident to Keats, since their illegitimate son Charles ('Carlino') was born on 10 July 1820. After Keats's death, Brown, convinced that George had deprived his brother of a rightful part of his inheritance, fell out with Dilke, who sided with George. Brown emigrated to New Zealand in 1841, but died the following year. (*ODNB*)

Clarke, Charles Cowden (1787–1877) Author, lecturer and writer on Shakespeare. Clarke, the headmaster's son and assistant teacher at Enfield Academy, encouraged Keats's interest in poetry and music. He introduced Keats to Leigh Hunt in autumn 1816. The next year Clarke joined his parents, who had retired to Ramsgate, and thereafter saw Keats only rarely. He did not return to London until December 1820, when he became part of Hunt's literary, artistic and musical set. His *Recollections of Writers* was published posthumously by his wife and is the main source of our knowledge of the young Keats. (*ODNB*)

Dilke, Charles Wentworth (1789–1864) Dilke, a civil servant in the Admiralty's pay office, married his wife Maria in about 1808, with whom he had a son, Charles (1810–69). An enthusiast of Renaissance drama (an interest shared with Keats), Dilke had published a six-volume edition of *Old English Plays* (1814–15) and was editing Walpole's letters when he met Keats. In 1816 Dilke moved into the newly built Wentworth Place, Hampstead, two semi-detached houses, jointly owned with Charles Brown. Dilke was a firm and trusted friend, even though Keats found his belief in Godwinian perfectibility unsympathetic. In April 1819 Dilke moved to Westminster. The Dilkes' disapproval of Fanny Brawne led to a distancing of their friendship, but after Keats died Dilke was instrumental in sorting out the family's financial affairs, and he ensured that Fanny Keats received her inheritance. From 1818 Dilke began contributing articles to the periodicals, and was involved in Taylor and Hessey's *London Magazine* (1821–5). He was later editor and proprietor of the *Athenaeum* (1830–46). At his death he was a distinguished man of letters. (*ODNB*)

Haslam, William (1795/8?–1851) Haslam apparently attended Enfield Academy and was introduced to Keats by his brother George (*L*, I, p. 392). A solicitor, Haslam succeeded to his father's position as lawyer to William Frampton and Sons, wholesale grocers, 34 Leadenhall Street, London, in 1819. He was intimate with Keats while he was at Guy's Hospital and probably introduced him to Severn. Haslam was a good friend who gave practical help to Keats and to his brothers. He helped pay for Keats's final trip to Italy and persuaded Severn to travel with him. Only three of Keats's letters to him are now known (all are short and none is reproduced here).

Haydon, Benjamin Robert (1786–1846) Historical painter and diarist. Self-willed, pugnacious, improvident and desperately ambitious, Haydon came to London in 1804 determined to make his name as a history painter. The success of his painting of *Dentatus* in 1809 was marred when the Royal Academy hung it disadvantageously, the start of a lifelong feud. When Keats met him at Hunt's in autumn 1816 Haydon was riding high. He had campaigned successfully for the nation's purchase of the Elgin Marbles and was engaged on a huge painting, *Christ's Entry into Jerusalem*, not completed until 1820. Convinced of his own destiny, Haydon encouraged Keats's to think of himself in the same way. However, as early as January 1818 Keats was disillusioned by the quarrels between Haydon, Hunt and Reynolds. The two men fell out over Keats's inability to give Haydon the generous financial aid he had unwisely promised, and the painter's failure to repay a loan. Haydon's later career was marred by his delusions of grandeur and ever-deepening money problems. He committed suicide in 1846. (*ODNB*)

Hessey, James Augustus (1785–1870) Keats's publisher, in partnership with John Taylor (see below).

Hunt, (James Henry) Leigh (1784–1859) A prolific poet and literary critic, Hunt edited the liberal journal the *Examiner*. He was imprisoned in 1813 for libelling the Prince Regent. Keats admired Hunt's politics and poetry long before meeting him. Hunt published Keats's first poems and immediately introduced the new poet to his extensive literary and artistic circle. Keats's association with Hunt's 'Cockney School' ensured that his poetry was attacked by the Tory periodicals. From early on Keats needed to distance himself from the older writer, and criticized Hunt's vanity and posturing. Keats may also have resented the closeness of Hunt's relationship with Shelley in 1817 and 1818. Nevertheless, their friendship continued, as did Hunt's admiration of Keats's poetry and his generosity towards him. After Keats's sudden haemorrhage on 22 June 1820 Hunt immediately took him into his home in Mortimer Terrace. (*ODNB*)

Jeffery, Mary-Ann (1798–1850) **and Sarah** (1799–?) Gittings discovered that their name was Jeffery not Jeffrey and that there were only two sisters, not three. They were the daughters of the Teignmouth family with whom George and his sick brother Tom lodged at the seaside resort in early 1818. Keats took over from George at the beginning of March, and the two brothers returned to Hampstead two months later. The sisters had a bantering relationship with the brothers and were fond of Tom. It is sometimes thought that Mary-Ann was in love with Keats, but his letters indicate that theirs was no more than a strong friendship. She published annual verse and a volume, *Poems* (1830), influenced by Keats, under her married name Mrs I. S. Prowse.

Keats, Fanny (Frances Mary) (1803–89) The brothers' young sister, lived with the family of her guardian Richard Abbey from 1814, and boarded at the Walthamstow school of the Misses Tuckey until 1818. Abbey consistently made it difficult for her to see her brothers, though Keats persisted in writing to and visiting her. In 1824 she received her inheritance and two years later married the Spanish novelist Valentin Llanos.

Keats, George (1797–1841) Keats's brother attended Enfield Academy and worked for a time in the counting house of Richard Abbey's firm. In autumn 1816 he moved into lodgings with his brothers in Cheapside. He left Abbey's firm after a quarrel either at this time or shortly after and briefly tried his hand at business but with no success. Thereafter he lived with his brothers with no employment and no profession. In spring 1818, as soon as he came of age, George realized his substantial inheritance, married Georgiana Wylie and emigrated to America, intending to invest in George Birkbeck's Illinois Settlement the 'English Priairie'. Instead he settled in Kentucky, where he lost most of his capital through an ill-advised business venture with John James Audubon. The future naturalist at best misled both himself and George or at worst conned the young Englishman. George was forced to return to England in 1820 for his share of Tom's estate. Keats came to believe that George had put his own needs first and left him in financial distress. George later moved to Louisville, where he became a respected businessman and citizen.

Keats, Georgiana Augusta Wylie (Mrs George) (?1798 –1879) Keats's sister-in-law, the daughter, probably illegitimate,[1] of an army officer.

1 Crutcher, p. 52.

She married George Keats on 28 May 1818 and travelled with him to America, where she had eight children. After George's death she married John Jeffrey, who in 1845 transcribed some of the Keats manuscripts in her possession for R. M. Milnes's *Life, Letters, and Literary Remains*. Keats liked her and respected her independence.

Keats, Tom (1799–1818) Keats's younger brother attended Enfield Academy and worked for a time in Abbey's business. The symptoms of consumption declared themselves early. He stayed with Keats in Kent in summer 1816 and lived with his brothers in their London lodgings that autumn. In 1817 he visited France with George, and in spring 1818 went to Teignmouth, where first George and then John cared for him. He died in Hampstead on 1 December, nursed by Keats.

Reynolds, Charlotte Cox (Mrs George) (1761–1848) J. H. Reynolds's mother. Her husband George was writing master at Christ's Hospital and the family lived in Little Britain, London. Their five children included for girls, Jane (1791–1846), who became the wife of the poet Thomas Hood, Marianne (1797–1874), who was conted and the jilted by Benjamin Bailey, much to Keats's outrage, Eliza (1799–c.1870) and Charlotte (1802–84).

Reynolds, John Hamilton (1794–1852) Poet and journalist who turned to the law. From late 1815 to 1817 he was on the staff of the *Champion*, to which he contributed reviews and articles. Before meeting Keats in autumn 1816 Reynolds had already published three volumes of poetry. He promptly introduced Keats to his circle of friends. Keats's liking for the Reynolds sisters had turned to displeasure by late 1818 and became active dislike when they disapproved of Fanny Brawne. In November 1817 Reynolds, who needed the financial security to marry, took articles with the solicitor Francis Fladgate. He nevertheless continued to write. His farce *One, Two, Three, Four, Five; by Advertisement*, and *Peter Bell*, a parody of Wordsworth, were both successes in 1819. He published a final volume of poems in 1821, but despite his early success his affairs turned for the worse and he was declared bankrupt in 1838, dying a dissatisfied man in 1852. (*ODNB*)

Rice, James (1792–1832) Keats met Rice, an attorney in his father's firm, through Reynolds. The two men spent a month together in the Isle of Wight in early summer 1819. Rice persuaded Reynolds to take up law and the two men became partners, later helping Fanny Keats resolve the problems over her inheritance. Keats thought him 'the most sensible, and even wise Man I know', but very few letters to him are known. Rice was among those who contributed to the fund supporting Keats's journey to Italy.

Severn, Joseph (1793–1879) Painter, portraitist of Keats and later consul at Rome. Severn broke away from his apprenticeship as an engraver and from 1813 took evening classes at the Royal Academy. Keats was introduced to him while at Guy's Hospital. Severn painted miniatures of all three brothers, exhibiting that of Keats at the Academy's exhibition in May 1819. Although Severn and Keats met occasionally from 1816 to 1820 through their mutual interest in art, the young painter belonged to Keats's outer circle of friends. On 12 September 1820 Haslam asked him to act as Keats's companion on his journey to Rome. They embarked only five days later. Severn's motives in agreeing may have been mixed, but, with no previous experience, he nursed the dying Keats through his last distressing days. Severn's letters provide the fullest account of Keats's protracted suffering and death. He spent the rest of his long life, much of it in Italy, as an artist, and faithfully preserved Keats's memory. Severn is buried beside Keats in the Protestant Cemetery, Rome. (*ODNB*)

Taylor, John (1781–1864) Keats's publisher set up in business with James Hessey in 1806 at 93 Fleet Street, London. Under Taylor's initiative the firm subsequently diversified into literature. They published Reynolds's *The Naiad* in summer 1816. Through him they met Keats, whose *Poems* (1817) they took over from the Ollier brothers. Despite the critical attacks on *Endymion* and its poor sales, Taylor, supported by Woodhouse, remained convinced of Keats's genius and gave him moral and financial help, raising the funds for his journey to Rome. Taylor and Hessey's bookshop in Fleet Street was a meeting place for writers and artists, where Keats frequently dined and on occasions stayed overnight. From 1821 to 1825 Taylor and Hessey were proprietors of the *London Magazine*, years notable for its publication of essays by Lamb, Hazlitt and De Quincey, as well as articles by Dilke and Reynolds. Taylor was himself an active author. Early in 1821 he advertised, but never wrote, a 'Memoir and Remains of John Keats'. (*ODNB*)

Woodhouse, Richard (1788–1834) Educated at Eton and a lawyer, Woodhouse acted as legal and literary adviser to Taylor and Hessey's firm. He was early convinced of Keats's genius and not only looked after Keats's interests with his publishers but gave practical help with his financial difficulties. Woodhouse was an intelligent reader of Keats's poetry and has claims to be regarded as his first editor. His very considerable collection of Keats's manuscripts and Keatsiana, which he began as early as 1818, has been an invaluable resource for all subsequent scholars.

Wylie, Ann Amelia Griffin (Mrs James) (1761–1835) Georgiana Keats's mother, a widow, lived at 3 Romney Street, Westminster, with her younger son Charles Wylie. Her other son Henry Robert lived with his aunt Mrs Amelia Millar and cousin Mary in Henrietta Street, Covent Garden. After George's marriage Keats kept up his relationship with the Wylie family.

Acknowledgements

As always, I am indebted to the wise advice and support of Hermione Lee. I am grateful to Nicholas Roe for his generous exchange of ideas and information in the course of preparing this selection, and for the encouragement of others, notably Jenny Uglow. For raising, and helping to resolve, the question of Keats's movements in London on 13 September 1819 I am grateful to Kenneth Page, Nicholas Roe and Richard Marggraf Turley. At Penguin Books I am grateful to Alexis Kirschbaum for suggesting and commissioning this edition, to Jessica Harrison for her shrewd editing, to Anna Hervé for her careful eye on the production process and to Sarah Hulbert for her work on the revises. I am particularly indebted to Ian Pindar's exemplary copy-editing. Librarians, institutions and individuals owning manuscripts of Keats's letters have been uniformly helpful and I am grateful for the patience and help of John Anderie and Ann Upton (Haverford College); John Bidwell (Morgan Library, New York); Dr Bruce Barker-Benfield, Clive Hurst, Sarah Wheale (The Bodleian Libraries); Roy Davids (collector); Howard Doble, David Luck and Jeremy Smith (London, Metropolitan Archives); Zach Downey (Lilly Library); Thomas L. Edsall (19th Century Rare Book & Photograph Shop, Stevenson, Maryland); Arcadia Falcone (Harry Ransom Center, University of Texas); Rebecca Filner (Berg Collection, New York Public Library); Elizabeth Frengel and Mary Ellen Budney (Beinecke Library, Yale University); Sara S. Hodson (Huntington Library); Hillary S. Kativa, David Haugaard and Christopher Damiani (The Historical Society of Pennsylvania); Tracy Lamaestra (Maine Historical Society); Leslie Morris and Susan Halpert (Keats Collection, Harvard University); Kenneth Page (Keats House); Christopher Sheppard (Brotherton Library, University of Leeds); and Gabriel Swift (Princeton University Library).

Permissions

TEXTS

Beinecke Rare Book & Manuscript Library, Yale University, Georgiana Keats, 13–28 January 1820 (last two pages, Gen. Mss. 825), February (?) 1820 ('Then all we have to do . . . ', Gen. Mss. 825).

[Berg] The Henry W. and Albert A. Berg Collection of English and American Literature, The New York Public Library, Astor, Lenox and Tilden Foundations, 31 October 1816, 24 August 1819, August (?) 1820 ('I wish you could invent . . . '), 13 (?) August 1820.

The Bodleian Libraries, University of Oxford, 16 August 1820 (Abinger c. 66, ff. 72–3).

British Library, 10 May 1817 (Ashley Ms. 4869), 10 September 1817 (Add. Ms. 34019, ff. 1–2), 23 January 1818 (Add. Ms. 37538A), 10–14 July 1818 (Add. Ms. 45510), 19 August 1818 (Add. Ms. 34019, ff. 3–4), 26 October 1818 (*ditto*, ff. 11–12), 11 February 1819 (*ditto*, ff. 21–2), 27 February 1819 (*ditto*, ff. 23–4), 13 March 1819 (*ditto*, ff. 25–6), 12 April 1819 (*ditto*, ff. 29–30), 9 June 1819 (Fanny Keats, *ditto*, ff. 35–6), 17 June 1819 (*ditto*, ff. 39–40), 6 July 1819 (*ditto*, ff. 41–2), 28 August 1819 (*ditto*, ff. 43–4), 26 (?) October 1819 (*ditto*, ff. 45–6), 20 December 1819 (*ditto*, ff. 49–50), 6 February 1820 (*ditto*, ff. 53–4), 8 February 1820 (Ashley Ms. 4870), 14 February 1820 (*ditto*, ff. 57–8), 20 March 1820 (*ditto*, ff. 63–4), 1 April 1820 (*ditto*, ff. 65–6), 12 April 1820 (*ditto*, ff. 69–70), 21 April 1820 (*ditto*, ff. 71–2), 4 May 1820 (*ditto*, ff. 73–4), 23 June 1820 (*ditto*, ff. 75–6), 5 July 1820 (*ditto*, ff. 77–8), 22 July 1820 (*ditto*, ff. 79–80), 13 August 1820 (*ditto*, ff. 81–2), 23 August 1820 (*ditto*, ff. 83–4).

Harry Ransom Center, University of Texas at Austin, 15–28 January 1820 (first 8 pages), 28 February 1820 (Reynolds).

Harvard University, Keats Collection, Houghton Library (reference numbers to 'Keats MS'), *1816* late October (2.4), 20 November (1.3), 17 December (1.5).

1817 9 March (3.3, p. 49), 17 March (3.3, p. 42), 17, 18 April (3.3, p. 43), 10, 11 May (1.7), 16 May (1.8), 10 June (1.9), 4 September (1.10), 4 (?) September (3.2, f. 29^{r}), 21 September (3.3, p. 46), 28 September (1.12), 8 October (1.13), 28–30 October (1.14), 3 November (1.15), 22 November (Bailey, 1.16), 22 November (Reynolds, 3.3, p. 50), 21, 27 (?) December (3.9, f. 5^{r}).

1818 10 January (1.18), 13–19 January (3.9, f. 2^{v}), 23 January (1.20), 23–24 January (3.9, f. 3^{v}), 31 January (3.3., p. 53), 3 February (3.3, pp. 28, 55), 14 (?) February (3.9, f. 5^{v}), 21 February (1.22), 13 March (1.23), 14 March (3.3, p. 56), 24 March (1.25), 25 March (3.3, p. 74), 8 April (1.26), 9 April (3.3, p. 58), 17 April (1.27), 27 April (3.3, p. 62), 3 May (3.3, p. 64), 21, 25 May (1.28), 10 June (1.30), 27, 28 June (1.32), 29 June–2 July (3.9, f. 6^{r}), 3–9 July (1.33), 11, 13 July (3.3, p. 71), 18, 22 July (1.34), 23–26 July (1. 35), 3, 6 August (1.36), 6 August (3.9, f. 12^{r}), 22 (?) September (3.3, p. 18), 8 October (3.3, p. 13), 14 October (from Reynolds, extracts, 4.14.1), 14–31 October (1.39), 21 October (from Woodhouse, extracts, 4.20.1), 27 October (1.38), 24 November (1.40), 22 December (1.43), 16 December–4 January 1819 (1.45).

1819 10 (?) January (1.47), 14 February–5 May (1.53 and 3.9, ff. 22^{v}–3^{v}, seq. 48–50), 18 (?) February (1.49), 29 March (1.50), 13 April (1.51), 1 May (?) (1.52), 31 May (1.54), 11 July (3.3, p. 30), 14 August (1.58), 16 August (1.59), 24 August (1.60), 31 August (1.61), 5 September (Hessey, 1.62), 5 September (Taylor, 1.63), 17–27 September (note 18 September 3.9, ff. 23^{v}–24^{r}, seq. 50–51), 21 September (3.3, p. 33), 21, 22 September (1.64), 22 September (Brown, 4.3.27, f. 17), 23 September (4.3.27, f. 25), 3 October (1.65), 11 October (1.66), 19 October (1.67), 15 November (1.69), December (1.70).

1820 10 (?) February (1.71), February (?) ('According to all . . .', 1.72), February (?) ('how could it ever . . .', 1.73), 14 February (1.74), February (?) ('I read your note . . .', 1,75), 29 (?) February (1.76), March (?) ('I slept well . . .', 1.77), 24 (?) March (1.78), 15 May (4.3.27, f. 25), June (?) (1.79), 11 (?) June (1.80), about 21 June (4.3.27, f. 25), June (?) ('I endeavour . . .', 1.81), 4 July (?) (1.82), 14 August (Brown, 4.3.27, f. 27), August (4.3.27, f. 28), 30 September (1.87), 1 November (4.3.27, f. 32), 30 November (4.3.27, f. 30).

Haverford College, 13 October 1819.

Huntington Library, San Marino, September 1816 (HM11903).

Keats House (City of London, Keats House, Hampstead), 17–21 July 1818 (K/MS/02/003), 20, 21 September 1818 (K/MS/02/004), 31

March 1819 (K/MS/02/007), 31 July 1819 (K/MS/02/009), 22 September 1819 (Dilke, K/MS/02/010), 1 October 1819 (K/MS/02/011), 1 March (?) 1820 (K/MS/02/222), 4 March 1820 (K/MS/02/012), May (?) 1820 (K/MS/02/013), 24 (?) October 1820 (K/MS/02/014).

Lilly Library, Indiana University, Bloomington, Indiana, Courtesy of, 24 (?) February 1820.

Maine Historical Society, 5, 6 August 1819 (Fogg Collection 420, Box 9 (Copies), Kane to Lockhart, Vol. 30, 1819, Keats).

Morgan Library, New York, 30 January 1818 (MA 213.1), 27 February 1818 (MA 208), 24 April 1818 (MA 791), 2–5 July 1818 (MA 975), 17–27 September 1819 (MA 212), 17 November 1819 (MA210.2), 13 August 1820 (MA 218.2), 14 August 1820 (MA 214.2).

Princeton University Library, Robert H. Taylor Collection, Manuscripts Division, Department of Rare Books and Special Collections, 15 April 1817 (Box 10/20), 15 (?) December 1818 (Box 10/21), 19 February 1818 (Box 10/22), February (?) 1820 ('You spoke of . . . ', Box 10/24), 27 (?) February 1820 (Box 10/24), March (?) 1820 ('In consequence of . . . ', Box 10/24).

Private New York Collection, 30 January 1818.

The Historical Society of Pennsylvania, 9 September 1816 (Dreer Collection, #175, Box 230/43), 8 July 1819 (Simon Gratz Collection, #175, Case 11/1).

Rollins transcript, 13 September 1819, 12 November 1819, April (?) 1820 ('I am much better . . . '), 11 September 1820, reprinted by permission of the publisher of the *Letters of John Keats 1814–1821*, ed. Hyder E. Rollins, II, pp. 160, 228–31, 286, 332, Cambridge Mass.: Harvard University Press, Copyright © by the President and Fellows of Harvard College.

ILLUSTRATIONS

The map of 'Keats's Northern Walk' is from Carol Kyros Walker, *Walking North with Keats* (New Haven and London: Yale University Press, 1992). The reproductions of Keats's letters to Tom Keats (detail), C. W. Dilke, Fanny Brawne and Mrs Brawne are published by permission of City of London, Keats House, Hampstead (K/MS/02/003, 004, 222, and 014). Those to George and Georgiana Keats (MS Keats 1.53. Houghton Library, Harvard University. Gift of Arthur Houghton, 1970) and to John Taylor (MS Keats 1.63. Houghton

Library, Harvard University. Bequest of Amy Lowell, 1925) by permission of Harvard University. Charles Brown's pencil portrait of Keats from 1819 is reproduced with permission from the National Portrait Gallery, London (NPG 1963). Joseph Severn's sketch of Keats on his deathbed is published with the permission of Harvard University (Keats Collection, Houghton Library, bMS. Eng.1460).

Index

Names in **bold** refer to correspondents, page numbers in **bold** refer to letters, page numbers in *italic* refer to headnotes.